Advances in Communication Research to Reduce Childhood Obesity

Jerome D. Williams • Keryn E. Pasch
Chiquita A. Collins
Editors

Advances in Communication Research to Reduce Childhood Obesity

Springer

Editors
Jerome D. Williams
Department of Management and Global Business
Rutgers Business School-Newark and New Brunswick
Newark, NJ, USA

Keryn E. Pasch
Department of Kinesiology and Health Education
University of Texas at Austin
Austin, TX, USA

Chiquita A. Collins
School of Medicine
Johns Hopkins University
Baltimore, MD, USA

ISBN 978-1-4614-5510-3 ISBN 978-1-4614-5511-0 (eBook)
DOI 10.1007/978-1-4614-5511-0
Springer New York Heidelberg Dordrecht London

Library of Congress Control Number: 2012953470

Printed on acid-free paper

Springer is part of Springer Science+Business Media (www.springer.com)

Foreword

Childhood overweight and obesity have reached epidemic proportions in the United States. Today, more than 23 million children and adolescents—nearly one in three young people—are either obese or overweight, putting them at higher risk for serious and lifelong health problems. These youth are experiencing weight-related chronic diseases once seen only in adults, and may become the first generation in US history to live sicker and die younger than their parents. The projected burden for our healthcare system is enormous: the cost of adult obesity is estimated to be as high as $147 billion each year, including $14 billion annually for medical care alone. The prevalence and health and economic tolls of obesity are highest among African-American and Latino children and families, and those living in economically disadvantaged communities, or in short, those with fewest opportunities and resources for healthy eating and active play.

A complex array of factors contributes to the cause of youth overweight and obesity, which reflects a surplus of energy (calories) consumed over energy expended. After all, eating and physical motion are two fundamental human activities, influenced by where and how we live, what opportunities exist, and the barriers that limit or block healthier behaviors.

In 2006, the Robert Wood Johnson Foundation committed to the ambitious goal of reversing the childhood obesity epidemic by 2015. Our strategic approach is to identify the important modifiable policy and environmental drivers of childhood obesity and to discover and spread effective strategies for reducing or eliminating them, particularly to benefit children, families, and communities at greatest risk. Our work has included policy research, evaluation, action, advocacy, and communications, and it has become clear to us that communications and marketing permeate almost every aspect of those "modifiable drivers." From increasing awareness of the threat childhood obesity poses to our nation's health to promulgating promising approaches for change, we recognize that communication is an essential element to inform, appeal, influence, and affect children, families, communities, and policy makers.

To seize the power of communication to speed or hamper our progress in halting this epidemic, we eagerly joined The Center for Urban Entrepreneurship & Economic Development in the Rutgers Business School-Newark and New Brunswick in convening a 2011 meeting of leading scholars in communication and media research focused on childhood obesity prevention. Organized by the authors of this volume, the conference helped spur this compendium of work addressing key communications research findings, issues and intervention strategies.

Each of the chapters in this volume reflect that "communication" is fundamental to how we function as individuals, influencers, and as a society. More than 50 authors describe how communications profoundly shape our nation's activity and dietary practices in ways that are often challenging to track and evaluate. This volume cuts across many kinds of communications (e.g., in-school and outdoor advertising), explores innovations (such as digital marketing), discusses important legal, ethical and policy issues, and brings to bear the results of international research that can help share our domestic strategies.

We believe that a wide array of readers, including researchers, practitioners, and policy makers will benefit from this broad and deep investigation that helps disentangle how and why communication affects childhood obesity.

Princeton, NJ, USA

Dwayne C. Proctor
C. Tracy Orleans

Biographical Sketches of Contributors to Volume

Book Editors

Jerome D. Williams is the Prudential Chair in Business and Research Director of the Center for Urban Entrepreneurship and Economic Development, in the Department of Management and Global Business, Rutgers Business School-Newark and New Brunswick. His current research interests cover a number of areas in the consumer marketing domain, with an emphasis on multicultural marketing. He has conducted research on marketing communications and promotion strategies targeting multicultural market segments and consumer behavior of multicultural market segments related to public health communication issues. He was a member of the Institute of Medicine Committee on Food Marketing and Diets of Children and Youth that authored the report *Food Marketing to Children and Youth: Threat or Opportunity?*

Keryn E. Pasch is an Assistant Professor in the Department of Kinesiology and Health Education at the University of Texas, Austin. She received her Ph.D. in Epidemiology with a minor in Interpersonal Relationships Research from Division of Epidemiology and Community Health at the University of Minnesota and her Master's in Public Health in Health Behavior and Health Education from the School of Public Health at the University of North Carolina at Chapel Hill. Dr. Pasch was also a National Cancer Institute Postdoctoral Fellow in Cancer Prevention and Control in the Michael and Susan Dell Center for Healthy Living at the Austin Regional Campus of the University of Texas School of Public Health. Dr. Pasch's research program focuses on the influence of food and beverage advertising and alcohol advertising on youth risk behaviors as well as the factors that may alter the influence of advertising on behavior. Currently, she has an NIH-funded grant to document and describe outdoor food and beverage advertising around schools. Her research also focuses on how risk behaviors, including sleep, substance use, and obesity-related behaviors, may co-occur among youth as well as on developing preventive interventions to address these behaviors. Dr. Pasch is also the Chair of the Early Career Preventionist Network of the Society for Prevention Research.

Chiquita A. Collins is the Associate Dean and Interim Director of the Office of Diversity and Cultural Competence and Assistant Professor in the Department of Medicine at Johns Hopkins University School of Medicine. She has served as the Health Equity Research Director at Altarum Institute, a nonprofit health systems research and consulting organization serving government and private-sector clients, as well as a consultant with the Office for the Elimination of Health Disparities for the Texas Department of Health and Human Services. Her research interests focus on the trends and determinants of socioeconomic and racial differences in health. After completing her doctorate at the University of Michigan, she was a Robert Wood Johnson Foundation Scholar in Health Policy Research at the School of Public Health, University of California, Berkeley. Her article with David R. Williams, "US Socioeconomic and Racial Differences in Health: Patterns and Explanations," received the distinction as one of the most cited in the *Annual Review of Sociology* during a 10-year span. Her published work was used to help inform the making of the award-winning PBS documentary, *Unnatural Causes: Is Inequality Making Us Sick?*

Foreword

Dwayne C. Proctor, Ph.D., Senior Program Officer at the Robert Wood Johnson Foundation, directs national programs and strategies towards the Foundation's highest health priority—reversing the rising trend of childhood obesity in America. His professional background in public health includes designing, implementing, and evaluating health communication projects and interventions for preventing youth interpersonal violence, the spread of HIV/AIDS in West Africa, and underage drinking in high-risk populations. Prior to joining the Foundation in 2002, Dr. Proctor was assistant professor at the University of Connecticut School of Medicine, where he taught health communications and marketing approaches engaging multiethnic populations to public health, medical, and dental students. Proctor currently serves as trustee for the NAACP and advisor to the Institute for International Public Policy and is a standing member of the External Advisory Board for the University of Connecticut Center for Health Communication & Marketing and the Atlanta Falcons Youth Foundation Advisory Network. He has also held a variety of positions on the Steering Committee for the Academy for Educational Development's Innovations in Social Marketing Conferences, the Boards of Directors of the Corporation for Independent Living in Hartford, CT, and the Association of Black Foundation Executives.

C. Tracy Orleans is the Senior Scientist and first Distinguished Fellow of the Robert Wood Johnson Foundation (RWJF); she has led or co-led the Foundation's public policy- and healthcare system-based grant-making in the areas of tobacco control, physical activity promotion, childhood obesity prevention, and chronic disease management. She has developed and/or leads or co-leads numerous RWJF national research to reverse the rise in childhood obesity, including Active Living

Research, Healthy Eating Research, Bridging the Gap, the Food Marketing Work Group, and the National Collaborative for Childhood Obesity Research. A clinical health psychologist Dr. Orleans has authored or coauthored more than 230 publications, served on numerous journal editorial boards, national scientific panels, and advisory groups (e.g., Institute of Medicine, National Commission on Prevention Priorities, U.S. Preventive Services Task Force, Community Preventive Services Task Force), and as president of the Society of Behavioral Medicine. She is an elected member of the Academy of Behavioral Medicine Research and a recipient of the John Slade Tobacco Research Policy Award of the Society for Research on Nicotine & Tobacco, the Distinguished Scientist Award of the Society of Behavioral Medicine, the American Psychological Association's Meritorious Research Service Commendation, and the US Department of Health and Human Services Secretary's 2010 Innovator's Award (a group award).

Chapter Authors

Rebecca Adeigbe is a Program Coordinator at the University of Texas Health Science Center in San Antonio where she coordinates the *Salud America!* Research Network to Prevent Obesity Among Latino Children and the *Exito! Latino Cancer Research Leadership Training* program at the Institute for Health Promotion Research. Her primary research interest is in physical activity promotion to reduce chronic disease and cancer risk among underserved and minority populations. Ms. Adeigbe received her B.S. in Kinesiology and M.S. in Health and Kinesiology from the University of Texas at San Antonio.

Monika Arora, PhD, MSc, is Senior Director of HRIDAY and an Adjunct Assistant Professor at PHFI. Trained in public health and preventive cardiology, her research interests focus on positively influencing adolescent behaviors for the prevention of chronic diseases.

Eric Batch, MPP, is the Vice President of Advocacy for the Western States Affiliate of the American Heart Association. In his role with the Heart Association, Eric is responsible for managing the Advocacy/Government Relations Department for the Western States of Alaska, Arizona, California, Hawaii, Idaho, Montana, Nevada, Oregon, Utah, and Washington. Prior to joining the American Heart Association, Eric worked as a Senior Consultant with Deloitte Consulting, providing strategic guidance to private and public sector clients in change management and training. Eric has public policy experience at all three levels of government having worked in the Office of Management and Budget in Washington, DC, as a consultant to the CA Governor's office, and on campaigns at the state and local level. Eric earned a Master of Public Policy degree from the University of Southern California.

Frank J. Chaloupka, PhD, is a Professor of Economics at the University of Illinois at Chicago. Dr. Chaloupka's research focuses on the economic analysis of substance use and abuse, and emphasizes the role of prices and substance control policies in affecting the demands for tobacco, alcohol, and illicit drugs, as well as outcomes related to substance use and abuse.

Sara E. Champlin is a doctoral student in the Department of Kinesiology and Health Education at the University of Texas at Austin. She earned her MA in Advertising from UT-Austin and her BA in Psychology from Trinity University. She is interested in the relationship between health behavior and the consumption of different media forms, especially the impact of new media on adolescent and young adult behavior.

Jeff Chester is the executive director of the Center for Digital Democracy (CDD), a Washington, D.C., nonprofit. CDD's mission is to foster democratic expression and consumer protection in the digital media era. His book, *Digital Destiny: New Media and the Future of Democracy*, provides an in-depth examination on the threats to the public interest from both old and new media consolidation. As a former investigative reporter and filmmaker, Chester has been engaged in public interest policy advocacy for more than three decades. In the 1980s, he helped direct the successful campaign to establish the Independent Television Service (ITVS) for public TV. In the 1990s, he cofounded the Center for Media Education, spearheading an effort that led to passage of the 1998 Children's Online Privacy Protection Act (COPPA) and rules requiring children's educational programming for broadcasting. In 1996, Newsweek magazine named Jeff Chester one of the Internet's 50 most influential people. He was named a Stern Foundation "Public Interest Pioneer" in 2001. Jeff played a key role in organizing the grassroots opposition to the FCC's proposed media ownership rules in 2003. Under his leadership, CDD has pressed the FTC and other policy makers to address how new digital marketing practices threaten privacy and consumer welfare. He has been an author of a series of reports exposing threats from online marketing, including practices involving finance, health, and children. He was named the 2011 "Domestic Privacy Champion" by the Electronic Privacy Information Center.

Mary J. Christoph is a first-year PhD/MPH student in the I-TOPP (Illinois Transdisciplinary Obesity Prevention Program) at the University of Illinois at Urbana-Champaign. She graduated as a Public Service Scholar with a B.S. in Biology from the University of North Carolina at Chapel Hill (UNC) in 2009. She is especially interested in the coalescence of obesity and host–microbe interactions, and obesity prevention in low-income populations and developing nations. As an undergraduate she received the Fred Morrison and Robert C. Byrd Honors Scholarships.

Brian Cole, Dr.P.H., is program manager and lead analyst for the Health Impact Assessment Group at the UCLA School of Public Health, conducting and providing technical assistance on HIAs on a wide range of public policies and projects, including Living Wage Ordinances, urban redevelopment, school programs, and transportation projects. Overlapping this work in HIA, Dr. Cole is also engaged in research on the environmental determinants of physical activity in school, workplace, and community settings. He teaches courses in school-based health education and community organization for public health promotion. He earned his Doctor of Public Health degree from the UCLA School of Public Health and Bachelor degrees in Environmental Science and Biology from Washington State University.

Joanne Delk is a Measurement Coordinator for the Central Texas CATCH Middle School Project at the Michael and Susan Dell Center for Healthy Living at the University of Texas-School of Public Health, Austin Regional Campus. She earned a Master of Science in Nutrition from the University of Minnesota. Her research interests include obesity prevention, adolescent nutrition, and taste perception.

Lori Dorfman is the director of the Berkeley Studies Media Group. She earned her doctorate in 1994 from the University of California, Berkeley, School of Public Health, where she studied how television news frames health issues. Her recent research examines how local television news and newspapers portray youth and violence, and family violence. Dorfman conducts training for grassroots organizations and public health leaders, consults for government agencies and community programs across the USA and internationally, publishes articles on public health and mass communication, and teaches a course for master's students on mass communication and public health at UC Berkeley's School of Public Health. She coauthored the major texts on media advocacy: *Public Health and Media Advocacy: Power for Prevention* and *News for a Change: An Advocates' Guide to Working with the Media*. She edited *Reporting on Violence: A Handbook for Journalists*, which encourages journalists to include a public health perspective in violence reporting.

Minette (Meme) Drumwright is an associate professor in the Department of Advertising and Public Relations in the College of Communication at the University of Texas at Austin. Since 2002, she has been faculty chair of the Bridging Disciplines Program in Ethics and Leadership. She serves on the Steering Committee for the RGK Center for Philanthropic and Community Service and teaches in its Graduate Portfolio Program in Nonprofit Studies. Her research is in the areas of ethics in advertising and public relations, corporate social responsibility, and communication for nonprofit organizations. She teaches courses in ethics and law in advertising and public relations, leadership and ethics, and branding and integrated communication for nonprofit organizations. Her articles and cases have been published in a variety of books and journals, including *Journal of Marketing, Journal of Advertising, Journal of Public Policy and Marketing*, and *California Management Review*. She previously was on the Marketing faculty of the Harvard Business School, and she has a Ph.D. in business administration from the University of North Carolina at Chapel Hill.

Barbara H. Fiese is a clinical and developmental psychologist whose research focuses on family factors that promote health and wellbeing in children. She holds the Pampered Chef, Ltd., Endowed Chair in Family Resiliency and is Professor and Director of the Family Resiliency Center at the University of Illinois at Urbana-Champaign. She is considered one of the national experts in the role that shared family mealtimes may play in promoting health during early childhood and the elementary school years.

Janet E. Fulton is an epidemiologist and team leader in the Division of Nutrition, Physical Activity, and Obesity at the U.S. Centers for Disease Control and Prevention in Atlanta, Georgia. Prior to her appointment in 1998 she held teaching positions in the Department of Epidemiology at the University of Texas-Houston and in the Department of Kinesiology at Texas Woman's University. She was also a Research Associate at the Center for Epidemiologic Research at The Center for Heath Promotion and Research Development at the University of Texas-Houston. Dr. Fulton has published articles on topics such as assessing physical activity and attitudes in children, the levels of physical activity among elementary and middle school children during their physical education classes, weight loss and weight gain prevention among youth, and the association between physical activity and changes in cardiovascular disease risk factors. She was the Science Coordinator and a member of the Writing Group for the Physical Activity Guidelines for Americans and served as a technical consultant to the World Health Organization for the Global Recommendations on Physical Activity for Health. She is the 2010 recipient of the American Heart Association, Steven N. Blair Award for Excellence in Physical Activity Research. Her research interests include the epidemiology of physical activity and chronic diseases; the measurement and quantification of physical activity; and population-based promotion of physical activity. She earned her Ph.D. in 1996 in Epidemiology at the University of Texas-Houston, School of Public Health.

Kipling Gallion is an Assistant Professor of Medicine, School of Medicine, and Deputy Director of the Institute for Health Promotion Research at the University of Texas Health Science Center at San Antonio, TX. Since 1982, Mr. Gallion has participated in a wide range of applied health communication activities in Texas and across the nation as grant writer, media producer, trainer, evaluator, consultant and project director and principal investigator. He has published in a variety of books and journals and received state and national recognition for his work in health promotion research.

Jaya Ginter was born and raised in Europe as her parents worked for the Department of Defense American Schools. She attended the College of St. Benedict/St. John's University earning a degree in dietetics. Jaya received her master's degree from the University of Minnesota School of Public Health in Nutrition. While at the University of MN, Jaya worked on a variety of research projects pertaining to youth and obesity. Currently she is working as a clinical dietitian and aspires to help create a healthier world.

Harold Goldstein, DrPH, is the Executive Director of the California Center for Public Health Advocacy, which he founded in 1999. CCPHA is a nationally recognized leader in advocating for public policies to address the social, economic, and community conditions that are thought to contribute to the obesity epidemic. CCPHA has led statewide campaigns resulting in enactment of state laws getting soda and junk food out of schools, getting first-ever funding for school physical education, and establishing the nation's first state menu labeling law. Harold has a

Bachelor's degree in physiology from UC Berkeley and both Master's and Doctoral degrees in public health from UCLA.

Samantha Graff is the Research Director at ChangeLab Solutions, and she leads the organization's health and media policy work. Samantha oversees R&D by scholars from leading institutions across the country and has published peer-reviewed articles on a range of legal issues regarding tobacco control and obesity prevention. She also serves on the steering committee of the national Food Marketing Workgroup and frequently presents at national conferences on the First Amendment and other topics affecting policy efforts to address harmful commercial marketing practices. Prior to joining ChangeLab Solutions, she worked as a fellow with the William and Flora Hewlett Foundation; an associate at Wilson, Sonsini, Goodrich & Rosati; and a federal law clerk for Chief Judge Marilyn Hall Patel of the Northern District of California. She is a graduate of Harvard University and Yale Law School.

Sonya A. Grier is an Associate Professor of Marketing at the Kogod School of Business at American University. Dr. Grier conducts interdisciplinary research on topics related to target marketing, race in the marketplace, the social and health impact of commercial marketing, and social marketing. Her current research investigates the relationship between marketing activities and consumer health, with a focus on obesity prevention for African Americans. Prior to joining American University, she was a Robert Wood Johnson Foundation Health and Society Scholar at the University of Pennsylvania, and also spent 2 years as an in-house consultant at the Federal Trade Commission. Dr. Grier received her PhD in Marketing, with a minor in Social Psychology, from Northwestern University in 1996, and also has an MBA from the J.L. Kellogg Graduate School of Management at Northwestern University, with an emphasis on marketing, nonprofit management, and international business. Her undergraduate degree is also from Northwestern University.

Diana S. Grigsby-Toussaint is an Assistant Professor in the Department of Kinesiology and Community Health and the Division of Nutritional Sciences at the University of Illinois at Urbana-Champaign. As a social epidemiologist, her research attempts to elucidate how and why socio-environmental factors influence health. A major focus of her research involves exploring environmental factors that influence dietary and physical activity behaviors that may increase obesity risk, particularly among children and racial/ethnic minority groups. Her work has been funded by the Robert Wood Johnson Foundation, the USDA, and the Illinois Council for Food and Agriculture Research.

Jennifer L. Harris is the Director of Marketing Initiatives at the Rudd Center for Food Policy & Obesity at Yale University. She is responsible for identifying and coordinating research initiatives to understand and communicate the extent and impact of children's exposure to food advertising. Dr. Harris received her BA in Political Science from Northwestern University, her MBA in Marketing from The Wharton School at the University of Pennsylvania, and her PhD in Social Psychology from Yale University. She worked for 18 years as a Vice President in marketing at

American Express and ran a marketing consulting firm specializing in marketing strategy and new product and market development.

Kristen Harrison is Professor of Communication Studies at the University of Michigan and Director of the Media Psychology group at the Institute for Social Research. Her research focuses on media and marketing effects on cognitions, behaviors, and emotions related to food, bodies, eating, and nutrition among children and adolescents. Her work has been funded by the William T. Grant Foundation, the Illinois Council for Food and Agriculture Research, the Illinois Department of Human Services, and the USDA.

Paul Harrison is the Macromarketing Research Cluster Leader at the Centre for Sustainable and Responsible Organisations, and chair of the Consumer Behaviour and Advertising Program at Deakin University, Melbourne, Australia. Dr Harrison's research is in the field of consumer behavior in the context of consumerism, material culture, and the broader effect of marketing on the exploitation of humans, animals, and the environment. His work has been published in a range of media, including the *Journal of Product and Brand Management, Public Health Nutrition, Consumption, Markets and Culture, SCN News, Marketing Science* the *Journal of Nonprofit and Voluntary Sector Marketing*, as well as newspapers and magazines. Dr. Harrison also makes films that seek to bring his research to broader audiences, and he blogs about consumer behavior and other issues at his website, http://www.tribalinsight.com. Prior to becoming an academic, Paul was an opera singer, a petrol pump attendant, CEO of an international dance company, a McDonalds "Crew Member", and a customs officer.

Marian Huhman is an Assistant Professor in the Department of Communication at the University of Illinois Urbana-Champaign (UIUC). She came to UIUC in 2009 after 8 years at the Centers for Disease Control and Prevention (CDC) as a researcher and evaluator of health campaigns, in particular, the VERB campaign. She has published over 20 papers about the VERB campaign. At UIUC, Dr. Huhman teaches and conducts research and evaluation of social marketing and media campaigns and teaches a course on interpersonal contexts of health communication.

Michaela Jackson brings 10 years of professional experience in a variety of marketing and communications roles to her doctoral research program. These included positions with BP Australia, the Commonwealth Public Service, the Victorian Department of Education and Early Childhood Development, and the Department of Primary Industries. Michaela was also recruited to the Department of Human Services as part of the crisis communications team during both the H1N1 Influenza 09 (Human Swine Flu) outbreak and the Victorian Bushfire crisis. In 1998 Michaela completed a Bachelor of Business (Communications/Advertising) at the Queensland University of Technology, Brisbane. In 2008 Michaela completed the Bachelor of Professional Communications (Honors) (Professional Communications) program at RMIT University, Melbourne, where she was awarded the Vice Chancellors List Award, presented to the top two percent of graduating students. Michaela's Honors thesis examined the extent to which Australian commercial television news is comprised of publicity material. Michaela brings a keen interest in marketing communications, health, and broader social issues to her work. Dr. Paul Harrison, Professor Boyd Swinburn and Associate Professor Mark Lawrence supervise Michaela at Deakin University's Melbourne Burwood campus.

Johanna Javadizadeh worked at the Rudd Center for Food Policy and Obesity at Yale University as a Research Associate. She was responsible for examining the impact of emerging food marketing initiatives (i.e., social and digital media) on children and adolescents. Johanna earned an AB degree at Harvard and an MBA in marketing and strategy from the University of California Los Angeles, where she also completed a cross-disciplinary certificate in sustainability. Johanna spent nearly 5 years at Google, where she performed a number of roles in the fields of consumer and product marketing.

Sara Kamal, PhD, University of Texas at Austin, is an Assistant Professor of Marketing Communications at the American University in Dubai, UAE. Her research interests include the economic effects of advertising, social media, and advertising in emerging markets. Kamal's research has appeared in the International Journal of Advertising, Journal of Interactive Advertising, *International Journal of Advertising, Journal of Interactive Advertising, International Journal of Internet Marketing and Advertising* (forthcoming), as well as *Computer-Mediated Communication across Cultures: International Interactions in Online Environments, Handbook of Research in International Advertising: Special Issue on Emerging Markets and Advances in Advertising Research.*

Kyung Ok Kacy Kim is a doctoral candidate in the Department of Advertising and Public Relations at the University of Texas at Austin. She earned her BA in Economics from Chung-Ang University, Korea, an MA in Economics from SungKyungKwan University, Korea, and an MA in Advertising from the University of Texas at Austin. Her training in economics concentrated on strategic information transmission under asymmetric information in terms of Game Theory as well as marketing metrics. She intends to capitalize on her quantitative and analytical skills by conducting research in the field of advertising and marketing. Her research interests are the economic aspects of advertising, effectiveness/efficiency models, and social media.

Vivica Kraak, MS, RD, is a research fellow and a PhD candidate at Deakin University's Population Health Strategic Research Centre, School of Health and Social Development, located in Melbourne, Australia. Over the past 20 years, her professional work has focused on preventive health and wellness especially obesity prevention for children and adolescents; promoting healthy lifestyles and healthy food and eating environments; and participatory approaches to build community food security. Her current research focuses on the accountability of public–private partnerships to address global public health nutrition priorities, and corporate food and beverage marketing practices that influence young people's diet and health. Vivica received her B.S. in nutritional sciences from Cornell University and completed a coordinated M.S. in nutrition and dietetic internship at Case Western Reserve University and the University Hospitals of Cleveland.

Karen Kramer is currently a legal consultant for ChangeLab Solutions (formerly Public Health Law and Policy) in Oakland, California. Prior to her consulting work, Karen served for 20 years as the senior staff attorney for United States District Court Chief Judge Emeritus Thelton E. Henderson in San Francisco. Karen was responsible for researching and advising Judge Henderson on a wide range of legal issues arising under federal, state, and local laws, as well as drafting legal opinions and reports. She was also responsible for overseeing complex institutional reform cases and implementing court administrative projects. Karen has also worked as a staff attorney for the Ninth Circuit Court of Appeals and a litigation associate. Karen is a graduate of the University of California Hastings College of the Law and the University of California at Berkeley.

Mariah Lafleur is a Senior Associate at Samuels & Associates, a public health research and evaluation firm in Oakland that improves health by informing environmental and policy change. Her expertise encompasses chronic disease prevention in Latino populations, improving physical education and physical activity for children, and working with diverse and low-income populations. Ms. Lafleur has been involved in a variety of projects to provide healthier environments in low-income communities including Healthy Eating Active Communities (HEAC) and California Central Valley Regional Obesity Prevention (CCROPP) with The California Endowment projects with The Robert Wood Johnson Foundation's Active Living Research, Healthy Eating Research, and Salud America! initiatives that promote healthy eating and physical activity in schools and communities. Previously, Ms. Lafleur worked at Children's Hospital Oakland Research Institute to reduce obesity in low-income East Bay children and with La Clinica de La Raza to improve the nutritional status of Latinos living with HIV/AIDS. As a Peace Corps volunteer in Haiti and the Dominican Republic, she implemented projects to alleviate malnutrition and improve food security and sanitation in resource-poor rural communities. She holds an MPH from the UC Berkeley School of Public Health with an emphasis on Nutrition and is fluent in Spanish and Haitian Creole.

Vikki C. Lassiter is the Director of the African American Collaborative Obesity Research Network, a national network based at the University of Pennsylvania Perelman School of Medicine. Ms. Lassiter has centered her life's work on addressing health disparities in communities of color. She has over 17 years of diversified experience in designing and conducting community-partnered research, strategic planning, project management, and business development. Ms. Lassiter has successfully directed numerous national, state, and local professional education and multi-site research initiatives. Ms. Lassiter received her BS in Psychology from the Pennsylvania State University and her MS in Organizational Dynamics from the University of Pennsylvania.

Lara A. Latimer is a Doctoral Candidate in Health Education in the Department of Kinesiology and Health Education in the College of Education at the University of

Texas at Austin. She received her MA in Health Education from The University of Texas at Austin and her BS in Exercise and Sport Science form Texas Tech University. Her dissertation will examine in-school food and beverage promotion and its association with students' food and beverage choices and body mass index. Previous work as a Research Assistant includes aiding in the design and implementation of a weight-loss intervention with postpartum women of lower income, and the examination of elementary students' school lunch opinions and choices. Other interests include nutrition-related behaviors in relation to obesity treatment and prevention in children and adolescents.

Sarah M. Lee, PhD, is the team leader for the Research Application and Evaluation Team in the School Health Branch, Division of Population Health at the Centers for Disease Control and Prevention. She provides scientific expertise and leadership on numerous documents, resources, surveillance studies, and CDC-funded programs related to youth physical activity and obesity prevention.

Benjamin J. Li is a PhD student at Wee Kim Wee School of Communication and Information in Nanyang Technological University. His research interests include the impact of new media on adolescents and youth, and the use of digital interventions in health communication. Benjamin has worked with several health agencies, including the Singapore Ministry of Health and the Health Promotion Board, and has received research grants from agencies such as the Singapore Children's Society and the National Youth Council. He is currently involved in the development and testing of digital health interventions in various hospitals and schools in Singapore. Benjamin's work has been published in the *Journal of Adolescence.*

May O. Lwin is an Associate Professor and Associate Chair at Wee Kim Wee School of Communication and Information in Nanyang Technological University. She specializes in research in health, social, and sensory communication, and has received numerous grants and led major research projects in these areas. In the area of nutrition and physical activity, she is involved in the designing and testing intervention programs utilizing digital technology targeting a wide range of populations. She has published in leading international journals such as the *Journal of Communication, Journal of Consumer Research, Journal of Health Communication, Health Communication, Journal of Advertising*, and *Journal of Advertising Research.*

William J. McCarthy, PhD, is a Professor of Public Health and Professor of Psychology at UCLA. His current research interests include multilevel interventions to make home and neighborhood environments more supportive of eating more fruits and vegetables and engaging in recommended levels of daily physical activity. He has devoted most of his 30-year career to reducing health disparities in low-income communities, especially Latino immigrant communities. For his involvement in community-level health advocacy efforts to reduce cancer risks, the American Cancer Society awarded him their 1994 Capitol Dome award.

Jose Medina, MPH, is a Graduate Assistant with the Michael & Susan Dell Center for Healthy Living. Mr. Medina directs the evaluation of multiple intervention programs that focus on child, adolescent, and community health. He is currently pursuing a doctoral degree, with a particular focus on obesity prevention, health promotion, and chronic diseases.

Kathryn C. Montgomery is a Professor in the School of Communication at American University and Director of a new PhD program focused on the intersections of media, technology, and democracy. During the 1990s, as President and Co-Founder of the nonprofit Center for Media Education, she spearheaded the campaign that led to passage of the Children's Online Privacy Protection Act (COPPA). She is currently coprincipal investigator on a project funded by the Robert Wood Johnson Foundation studying digital marketing practices and adolescents. Some of her current research on digital food marketing can be found at digitalads.org. In addition to numerous articles and reports, Montgomery has written two books: *Target: Prime Time – Advocacy Groups and the Struggle over Entertainment Television* (Oxford University Press, 1989); and *Generation Digital: Politics, Commerce, and Childhood in the Age of the Internet* (MIT Press, 2007). She holds a Ph.D. in Film and Television Studies from the University of California, Los Angeles.

Elizabeth S. Moore is an Associate Professor and Notre Dame Chair in Marketing, University of Notre Dame. Her research interests center on marketing to children, intergenerational family studies and marketing in society. She produced a Kaiser Family Foundation Report investigating online food marketing to children, and has provided expert testimony on this topic to the Institute of Medicine, Federal Trade Commission, and Centers for Disease Control and Prevention. Her research has been recognized with "Best Article" Awards from the *Journal of Consumer Research* and the *Journal of Public Policy & Marketing*. She serves on multiple editorial boards and is an Associate Editor of the *Journal of Public Policy & Marketing*. Professor Moore graduated from Mount Holyoke College and earned her PhD. from the University of Florida.

Gaurang Nazar, MBBS, MSc, is a Research Manager with HRIDAY. Trained in clinical medicine and public health, he has played a supportive role in multiple qualitative and quantitative research studies focused on adolescent lifestyle change towards healthy behaviors in India.

Michelle R. Nelson is an associate professor of advertising at the University of Illinois at Urbana-Champaign. Nelson's research, professional experience, and teaching focus on digital and international advertising. She examines the development of advertising literacy in children and the role that literacy plays in persuasion. Nelson has published more than 40 book chapters and articles. She is the Associate Editor for the *International Journal of Advertising* and serves on the editorial boards of the *Journal of Advertising* and *Journal of Interactive Advertising*.

Carrie D. Patnode, Ph.D., is a Research Associate with the Kaiser Permanente Center for Health Research in Portland, OR. She received her Ph.D. in Behavioral Epidemiology from the Division of Epidemiology and Community Health at the

University of Minnesota and her Master's in Public Health in Behavioral Science and Health Education from the Rollins School of Public Health at Emory Universit y. Dr. Patnode worked as a Health Communication Specialist with the National Center for Chronic Disease Prevention and Health Promotion at the Centers for Disease Control and Prevention from 2001 to 2006. Currently, she conducts systematic and comparative effectiveness reviews on behalf of the U.S. Preventive Services Task Force and the Agency for Healthcare Research and Quality.

George Perlov is a marketing and communications consultant based in New York City who helps nonprofit, government, and corporate clients improve their impact in addressing a host of social, environmental, and health-related issues through strategic planning, research, and evaluation. He was previously Executive Vice President for Research and Innovation at the Advertising Council, the largest producer of public service communications campaigns in the USA. In this position he was responsible for advising the planning and research process for the Council's campaigns, monitoring, and measuring of donated media, evaluating campaign effectiveness, proprietary research the Council conducts on public service directors and social issues, international issues, as well as special strategic initiatives. He is a graduate of Oberlin College and has a Master's of Public Administration degree from Columbia University. More about his consulting practice is available at http://www.perlov.net.

Cheryl L. Perry, Ph.D., is Professor and Regional Dean with the Michael & Susan Dell Center for Healthy Living. Dr. Perry has been conducting intervention-related research specific to promoting health among children and adolescents for over 30 years now. Her studies have been conducted in the USA, India, and other countries around the world.

Tamara Piety is the Associate Dean of Faculty Development and Professor of Law at the University of Tulsa College of Law. She has published extensively on issues of commercial and corporate speech, including a book, *Brandishing the First Amendment: Commercial Expression in America* from the University of Michigan Press. She is a graduate of the University of Miami School of Law and the Harvard Law School and was a Teaching Fellow at Stanford Law School prior to joining the University of Tulsa faculty.

Natalie S. Poulos is a doctoral student in Health Education in the Department of Kinesiology and Health Education in the College of Education at the University of Texas at Austin. She received her BS in Nutritional Sciences and MS in Health Education from the University of Texas at Austin where she also completed the Coordinated Program in Dietetics to become a Registered Dietitian. Her research interests include behavioral health and community nutrition.

Lisa M. Powell is a Professor in the division of Health Policy Administration in the School of Public Health and Associate Director of the Health Policy Center in the Institute for Health Research and Policy at the University of Illinois at Chicago. Dr. Powell has extensive experience as an applied microeconomist in the empirical analysis of the effects of public policy on a series of behavioral outcomes. Much of Dr. Powell's current research is on assessing the importance of economic and environmental factors (such as food prices, sugar sweetened beverage taxes; access to food stores, eating places, and facilities for physical activity; and television food advertising exposure) on food consumption and physical activity behaviors and as determinants of body mass index and the prevalence of obesity, including related disparities. Dr. Powell's research also examines school-level food and fitness policies and the association of school meal participation and children's weight status. In other health-related work, Dr. Powell's research has examined the importance of peer and parental influences on teen smoking, while other studies have highlighted the role of prices and public policies with regard to alcohol use among college students and educational and violence related outcomes. Dr. Powell is an Associate Editor of BMC Public Health and serves on a number of national and international advisory committees.

Julie Ralston Aoki is a Staff Attorney at the Public Health Law Center at William Mitchell College of Law in St. Paul, Minnesota. Julie has extensive experience working in the areas of public policy development and consumer protection, beginning with her years at the Minnesota Attorney General's Office where she served in the Consumer Protection and Antitrust Divisions. As a staff attorney at the Public Health Law Center, she provides legal technical assistance to local governments, public health officials, and public health advocacy groups on a range of topics, including cross-cutting legal issues such as preemption, the First Amendment, and antitrust laws, as well as about legal strategies and policies designed to promote tobacco control and healthy eating, with a focus on marketing and sales practices. She also has taught Public Health Law and legal writing and advocacy as an adjunct professor at William Mitchell. She has a J.D. from the University of Iowa College of Law and a B.A. from Yale College.

Amelie G. Ramirez, DrPH, is an internationally recognized cancer and chronic disease health disparities researcher and spokesperson, is a professor of epidemiology and biostatistics at The University of Texas Health Science Center at San Antonio, where she is also the founding director of the Institute for Health Promotion Research, which researches health disparities among minorities. Over the past 30 years, Dr. Ramirez has directed many research programs focused on human and organizational communication to reduce chronic disease and cancer health disparities affecting Latinos, including cancer risk factors, clinical trial recruitment, tobacco prevention, obesity prevention, and more. Ramirez received a B.S. from The University of Houston and M.P.H. and Dr.P.H. degrees from The University of Texas Health Science Center at Houston School of Public Health. Read her blog at http://www.saludtoday.com/blog.

K. Srinath Reddy, MD, MS, is the President of PHFI. Trained in both cardiology and epidemiology, he is regarded as a global leader in preventive cardiology and a thought leader in global public health. He is committed to chronic disease prevention in developing countries.

Lindsay M. Rodrigues, MSc, is a Research Assistant with the Michael & Susan Dell Center for Healthy Living. As a public health nutritionist by training, Lindsay assists with grant development and intervention studies focused on child and adolescent health and behavior. She is currently pursuing studies to become a dietitian, with a particular interest in healthy eating interventions and sustainable diets for youth and families in low- and middle-income countries.

Vishnudas Sarda is a Biostatistician at the Rudd Center for Food Policy & Obesity at Yale University. He works with the marketing team to manage and analyze data focused on food marketing to children. Vishnu earned his MPH in Biostatistics from the University of North Texas Health Science Center, where he also served as a Data Manager and Data Analyst in an NIH-funded cancer study. He also holds a Bachelor in Medicine and Bachelor in Surgery (MBBS) degree from India where he served as a physician in the Pediatrics department.

Rebecca M. Schermbeck, MS, MPH, RD, is a Visiting Research Specialist in the Institute of Health Research and Policy at the University of Illinois at Chicago. Ms. Schermbeck received her MS in Nutrition and MPH from Saint Louis University. Her research interests include child and adolescent health, obesity prevention, nutrition, and physical activity.

Liz Schwarte, MPH, is a Partner in Ad Lucem Consulting, providing public health strategic planning, initiative design, philanthropic advising and program evaluation to foundations, public health departments, other governmental institutions, and community-based organizations. In her previous position as Senior Associate and Managing Director at Samuels & Associates, Liz managed a variety of projects focused on improving the health of communities including the Central California Regional Obesity Prevention Program (CCROPP) evaluation funded by The California Endowment and the Salud Tiene Sabor program evaluation funded by The Robert Wood Johnson Foundation's Salud America! Initiative. Her areas of expertise include public health leadership and practice, community engagement, and obesity and chronic disease prevention. Liz holds an MPH in Maternal and Child Health from the University of North Carolina School of Public Health.

Matthew Sharp is the Senior Advocate for California Food Policy Advocates' Los Angeles Office. California Food Policy Advocates is a statewide nonprofit organization whose mission is to improve the health and well being of low-income Californians by increasing their access to nutritious and affordable food. Since 1997, Matthew has led CFPA's advocacy throughout Los Angeles County to expand access to and increase participation and quality in the federal nutrition safety net, such as Food Stamps, Child Care Food Program, and School Breakfast. By providing technical assistance on program policies and sponsoring legislation to meet community needs, CFPA mobilizes partners across California to reduce hunger and obesity. Matt has provided testimony to two congressional committee hearings, 12 state assembly and senate committee hearings, and dozens of city council, school board, and county board hearings.

Anthony C. Signorelli, as the Vice President Campaign Director at the Advertising Council, leads the strategic development, creation, and evaluation of numerous multimedia advertising and cause marketing campaigns, including initiatives for the U.S. Department of Health and Human Services, Office of the First Lady, Feeding America, U.S. Olympic Committee, and American Heart Association. His work includes AME and ADDY award winning communications programs, as well as collaboration with global brands such as Disney, PepsiCo, and Kraft. Mr. Signorelli received his Masters in Business Administration from Fordham's Graduate School of Business in 2005 and currently serves as an adjunct professor within the Communications & Media Studies Department at Fordham University. He has been a featured speaker on panels and at major conferences on behalf of the Centers for Diseases Control, Novartis Pharmaceuticals, Grocery Manufacturers of America, and Children's Advertising Review Unit. Anthony lives in Verona, New Jersey, with his wife Gina and enjoys spending his free time with friends and family, which include his four sisters and six nieces and nephews.

Andrew E. Springer, DrPH, is an Assistant Professor of Health Promotion and Behavioral Sciences at the Michael & Susan Dell Center for Healthy Living at the University of Texas School of Public Health-Austin Regional Campus. Dr. Springer's research interests center on the promotion of child and adolescent health in the U.S. and Latin America and has included the evaluation of the CATCH coordinated school health program in elementary and middle schools; testing of low-cost strategies to promote elementary school children's physical activity during the school day; and assessment of risk and protective factors for adolescent health in El Salvador.

Mary Story, PhD, RD, is a Professor in the Division of Epidemiology and Community Health, and Senior Associate Dean of Academic and Student Affairs in the School of Public Health, University of Minnesota, and an Adjunct Professor in the Department of Pediatrics School of Medicine. She is the Director of the national program office for the Robert Wood Johnson Foundation Healthy Eating Research program that supports research on environmental and policy strategies to promote healthy eating among children to prevent childhood obesity. Dr. Story's PhD is in nutrition science, and her interests are in the area of child and adolescent nutrition, and childhood obesity prevention. Dr. Story has conducted numerous school- and community-based obesity prevention studies and has been a principal investigator on several NIH grants. Much of her intervention research has been with American Indian youth and their families on reservations. She has numerous publications on child nutrition and obesity prevention. Dr. Story was a member of the Institute of Medicine Committees on Food Marketing and the Diets of Children and Youth; Nutrition Standards for Foods in Schools; Childhood Obesity Prevention Actions for Local Governments; Examination of Front-of-Package Nutrition Rating Systems and Symbols and is currently on the IOM Standing Committee for Childhood Obesity Prevention, and the IOM Food and Nutrition Board. She was elected to the Institute of Medicine in 2010. She has received numerous awards for her research and work in the field of child and adolescent nutrition.

Melissa H. Stigler, PhD, MPH, is an Assistant Professor with the Michael & Susan Dell Center for Healthy Living. A behavioral epidemiologist by training, Dr. Stigler's research portfolio focuses on child and adolescent health promotion. From the last decade, she has been involved in large-scale intervention studies to promote healthy lifestyles among adolescents in India.

Glen Szczypka observes media for the Health Media Collaboratory at the Institute for Health Research and Policy at the University of Illinois at Chicago. He has extensive experience monitoring both traditional and digital media. Mr. Szczypka has integrated both television ratings and social media metadata into datasets for the analyses of exposures to health-related advertising, including antitobacco, antidrug, and antiobesity campaigns. He has also mobilized these data to study tobacco corporate PR, Direct to Consumer pharmaceutical advertising, and food industry marketing campaigns. He has worked with the Centers for Disease Control's (CDC) Office on Smoking and Health to create exposure indices for state-sponsored antitobacco advertising which were published in the agency's Tobacco Control State Highlights Report.

Elizabeth A. Vandewater, PhD, is an Associate Professor with the Michael & Susan Dell Center for Healthy Living at the University of Texas School of Public Health. Dr. Vandewater's research focuses on the impact of media and technology on children's health behaviors and health outcomes, with a special emphasis on childhood obesity and other chronic diseases.

Cayley E. Velazquez is a Postdoctoral Research Fellow in the Food, Nutrition, and Health Program, Faculty of Land and Food Systems at the University of British Columbia. She received her PhD in Health Education with a minor in Applied Statistical Modeling from the University of Texas at Austin, her MS in Health Education and Administration from Saint Joseph's University and her BS in Nutrition and Dietetics from the University of New Mexico. Cayley is also a Registered Dietitian. To date, Dr. Velazquez's research has explored the influence of food and beverage advertising on the food preferences and choices of youth, with a specific focus on the importance of attention to advertising components. Her current work aims to understand how school food environment factors, including food and beverage advertising, influence the dietary practices of youth.

Jane D. Wargo is Program Director of the Presidential Youth Fitness Program where she manages the activities of the five founding program partners. Prior to taking on this role, she was a Program analyst at the President's Council on Fitness, Sports, and Nutrition, a position she held for 9 years. A native Hoosier, Jane has a MA in wellness management from Ball State University and a BA in English from Butler University.

Ellen Wartella, PhD, is the Al-Thani Professor of Communication, Professor of Psychology and Professor of Human Development and Social Policy at Northwestern University. She studies the role of media in children's development and has a special interest in food marketing and childhood obesity. She was a member of IOM

Committee on Food Marketing and the Diets of Children and Youth (2006); she chaired the IOM study of Front of Package Nutrition Rating Symbols and Systems (2011) and is a member of the IOM committee on Advancing Progress on Obesity Prevention (2012).

Megan Weinberg is a Research Associate at the Rudd Center for Food Policy & Obesity at Yale University where she studies the breadth and impact of food marketing to children. Megan earned a BA and an MA in Psychology from Marist College and has conducted health psychology research at Yale University since 2000. On the marketing team at Rudd, she has conducted content analyses of food advertisements in various media including television, YouTube, and internet banner advertising. She has written about trends in food marketing to children and exposure to messages in TV advertisements.

Gary B. Wilcox is the John A. Beck Centennial Professor in Communication in the Department of Advertising and Public Relations, The University of Texas at Austin. His current research interests cover a number of areas in advertising, with emphasis on the impact of advertising on the economy and society. Most recently his research has focused on quantitative metrics of social media as a marketing tool. Dr. Wilcox served as Chair of the department from 1990 to 1998 and has served as the Director of Graduate Programs since 1998. In 2006, he was the recipient of the Outstanding Graduate Adviser Award from UT Austin.

Toni (Antronette) Yancey is a Professor in Department of Health Services and Co-Director, UCLA Kaiser Permanente Center for Health Equity in the School of Public Health, with research interest in chronic disease prevention and health promotion policy intervention. She serves on the Board of Directors, among others, of the Partnership for a Healthier America, supporting First Lady Obama's Let's Move campaign. Her second book, *Instant Recess: Building a Fit Nation 10 Minutes at a Time*, has just been released.

Acknowledgements

This volume grew out of a 2011 conference of leading scholars in communication and media research focused on childhood obesity prevention. The primary sponsor of this conference was the Robert Wood Johnson Foundation (RWJF); in addition we received support from The Center for Urban Entrepreneurship & Economic Development (CUEED) in the Rutgers Business School—Newark and New Brunswick (RBS). We are deeply indebted to these two organizations. Without their support, we would not have been able to take this first step that led to the publication of this volume.

We especially wish to thank C. Tracy Orleans, Senior Scientist at RWJF, for her understanding of the vision we had for this volume and having the faith in us to tackle this important topic. Her encouragement and support in our journey, from the initial proposal for the conference to the final publication of the book, always helped to buoy our spirits and stay the course as we grappled with all the typical challenges in producing such a volume. We also are grateful to her for contributing to the foreword, along with Dwayne Proctor, RWJF Director, Childhood Obesity Programs and Senior Program Officer. Also, we thank Vanessa Farrell of RWJF for all of her effort and support in assisting us with the facility and other arrangements for a successful conference.

At the conference, there were 19 papers presented (see photo of some of the presenters). In addition to these papers, we invited other authors to prepare 5 additional chapters that we felt would significantly add to the value of this work, thus resulting in the 24 chapters comprising this book. While we as Co-Chairs of the conference took on the task of organizing and editing this volume, the real credit for the success of this outcome goes to all the individual authors with whom we had the privilege of working. We wish to thank all the authors (see author bios) for making the conference a success and for sticking with us as we moved this book project toward publication. We especially thank the authors who were punctual in submitting their chapters to meet the publisher's deadlines, and to those who were less punctual, including us as co-editors. However, in all cases, the quality of the submitted chapters was outstanding, and we sincerely wish to thank all the authors for their contributions. We cannot thank all of our authors enough for their patience and always positive attitude throughout the process. In terms of navigating through the production process, we are especially grateful for the careful shepherding of Khristine Queja, Springer Editor, Public Health. Without her guidance and patience, we would have had a much more difficult time in bringing this volume to fruition.

There are many others at Springer and our respective institutions, Rutgers, The State University of New Jersey, and The University of Texas at Austin (UT), who supported us along the way, and without their services, this project would have been a much more difficult and elongated effort. However, we particularly would like to express appreciation to two individuals who were in the trenches and laboring side by side with us to make the conference and book a success. Jasmine Cordero, CUEED Administrator in RBS, and Sara Champlin, UT PhD student, served as our meeting planners and conference facilitators. Without their diligence, attention to all the day-to-day details of organizing and running a conference, and constant interaction with the presenters before and after the conference, we never would have gotten over that first hurdle of this conference and book project. Also, Sara served as research assistant to us as editors and the point person in maintaining contact with all the authors throughout the production process, in addition to finding time to co-author two of the chapters in the book. We are extremely grateful to these two individuals, and we wish to acknowledge their efforts in supporting us. They certainly deserve special recognition.

The editors would also like to express the following personal notes of thanks and acknowledgments

Jerome is especially thankful for the loving support of his wife, Lillian, of 44 years, who was a beacon of light and encouragement and provided the moral, emotional, and spiritual compass in his life to keep him focused, especially during times when he needed to be uplifted. He also thanks all of his children, Denean, Derek, Daniel, Dante, and Dachia, and their spouses and children, for always willingly accepting the family sacrifices that sometimes had to be made to accommodate his working on this book. Jerome deeply appreciates all the support from his mother-in-law, Florence B. Harrison, as she always provided encouragement for his academic achievements and endeavors, going all the way back to his days as an undergraduate student at the University of Pennsylvania in the 1960s. Finally, Jerome dedicates this book in memory of three people who were instrumental in touching and shaping his life: his parents, Jerome J. and Gloria E. Williams, and his father-in-law, Charles R. Harrison.

Keryn would like to thank her family for all of their support and guidance throughout the years. In particularly she would like to thank her father Erwin Pasch for always making sure she achieved her potential. She would also like to thank her uncle, Marvin Pasch, for being her first academic influence, her aunt Judy for igniting her love of teaching, and her cousin Lauri Pasch for bringing her to a college classroom at age 11. Keryn would also like to thank her cousins, Dana, Jason, Staci, and Ryan, and her aunt Marge Naegele for continually supporting her decisions even when they thought she was crazy. She would also like to give a big thank you to her friends and colleagues, especially Stacey Moe, Mary Hearst, Melissa Laska, and Alexandra Loukas, who have supported her and always reminded her she could do it even when she thought there was no way she could. Keryn would also like to thank her students who provide her with constant motivation and renewed energy. Finally, Keryn dedicates this book to the memory of three important women in her life, her mother, Bernice Pasch, her grandmother, Dorothy Lampert, and her grandmother, Evelyn Fleming.

Chiquita is particularly indebted to her husband, Chip, for his unyielding patience and encouragement, who has been a constant anchor in her career and family life, while always reminding her to "stop and smell the roses" along this journey. For understanding her long nights on the computer, she also thanks her sons, Ronald III and Ryan, whose love and support are always given so unconditionally. Lastly, Chiquita dedicates this book to individuals who are diligently working on behalf of others, from grassroots community groups to policy makers, to increase access and opportunity with the goal of enhancing the quality of life for all.

Jerome D. Williams
Keryn E. Pasch
Chiquita A. Collins

Contents

Part I
Overview, The IOM Report, and Integrated Marketing Communications

Chapter 1
Introduction: Childhood Obesity: Media, Advertising, Community, and Advocacy

Chiquita A. Collins, Sara E. Champlin, Keryn E. Pasch, and Jerome D. Williams

Childhood obesity is a global public health problem. The prevalence of childhood obesity has reached epidemic proportions in the USA and in other nations around the world, including both developing and developed countries, particularly in regions where the adoption of Westernized food consumption and sedentary lifestyles are evident (World Health Organization (WHO), 2010). About 155 million children worldwide are classified as either overweight or obese (Hossain, Kawar, & El Nahas, 2007). According to the Centers for Disease Control and Prevention (CDC), the proportion of children (ages 2–11) and adolescents (ages 12–17) in the USA who are obese has increased threefold or more during the past three decades (Ogden & Carroll, 2010). Nearly one-third (32%) of children and adolescents over 2 years of age are either overweight or obese, where approximately 17% (or 12.5 million) of those are obese (Ogden, Carroll, Kit, et al., 2012). The obesity epidemic is nondiscriminating; it affects both boys and girls, across all states and socioeconomic lines and among all racial and ethnic groups, yet in disproportionate ways (Kumanyika & Grier, 2006; Ogden, Lamb, Carroll, et al., 2010; Singh, Kogan, & van Dyck, 2010; Wang & Zhang, 2006). Four out of 10 African-American and Mexican-American girls between the ages of 12 and 19 are considered overweight

C.A. Collins (✉)
Office of Diversity and Cultural Competence, School of Medicine, Johns Hopkins University, 1620 McElderry Street, Reed Hall, Suite 420, Baltimore, MD 21205, USA
e-mail: ccolli49@jhmi.edu

S.E. Champlin • K.E. Pasch
Department of Kinesiology and Health Education, University of Texas, 1 University Station, D 3700, Austin, TX 78712, USA
e-mail: sara.champlin@gmail.com; kpasch@austin.utexas.edu

J.D. Williams
Department of Management and Global Business, Rutgers Business School-Newark and New Brunswick, 1 Washington Park Room 1040, Newark, NJ 07102, USA
e-mail: jeromew@business.rutgers.edu

J.D. Williams et al. (eds.), *Advances in Communication Research to Reduce Childhood Obesity*, DOI 10.1007/978-1-4614-5511-0_1,

or obese (Ogden et al., 2012). Obesity prevalence is exacerbated among youth (ages 2–17) residing in economically distressed urban neighborhoods, in remote, isolated areas such as American-Indian reservations, and in areas of the Deep South and Appalachia, which includes the states of Mississippi, Georgia, Kentucky, and Louisiana, where concentrated poverty exists (Ogden, Lamb, et al., 2010; Singh et al., 2010; Story, Evans, Fabsitz, et al., 1999).

Obesity among children and adolescents imposes a debilitating economic strain on America's health care delivery system. In the USA alone, the annual cost of managing childhood obesity and obesity-related chronic diseases almost doubled, from $126.9 million in 2001 to $237.6 million in 2005 (Trasande, Liu, Fryer, et al., 2009). Moreover, food advertising and marketing are also costly but generate large revenues for food conglomerates and restaurant chains by recognizing the tremendous purchasing power of young consumers and their families. In 2006, the latest year for which data are available, US food, beverage, and restaurant companies spent $1.6 billion to market youth-oriented products to children and adolescents, of which more than $1 billion were spent on food advertising to America's teens and $870 million on children under 12 years of age (FTC, 2008). Despite the considerable attention the epidemic has received, there remains many legal, methodological, and theoretical challenges confronting contemporary researchers who are interested in media effects on child development and health as well as creating interventions to minimize the health risks associated with childhood obesity.

Advances in Communication Research to Reduce Childhood Obesity is the first of its kind to date to comprehensively address some of the unanswered questions in the field, which critically delves into the importance of the use of new media technology (e.g., digital marketing, social media, and online applications) that may encourage food preferences and consumption patterns that potentially can lead to obesity. This volume represents a plethora of perspectives that challenge us to think outside the box about factors that are linked to unhealthy food and beverage consumption and obesity among young people. It creates a fresh platform for thinking about this richly dynamic phenomenon: it draws on new cutting-edge research, attends to global, legal, political, sociocultural, and other issues, and includes a special section on potential solutions to the pending crisis of childhood obesity.

The crux of this volume is to illuminate the role of media and its influences on childhood obesity, yet address legislative mandates, local initiatives, and corporate accountability efforts that may hinder or promote progress in reversing these alarming health trends. Several chapters provide discussions on how social environments in which young people spend most of their time—where they live, learn, and play—are major contextual influences that may impede or enhance a child's health trajectory. Each chapter discusses further directions in research, policy, and intervention that hold promise for reducing the prevalence of childhood obesity. In this broadly interdisciplinary book, experts from the fields of media studies, economics, health education, public health, and law come together to offer the first wide-ranging look at novel and innovative approaches aimed at improving children's health.

The proliferation of processed and unnatural food products, new media technology, and food marketing and advertising targeted to children is of concern to policy makers, industry, practitioners, and parents. Despite an unsuccessful effort to pass legislation in 2004 that would have authorized the Federal Trade Commission (FTC) to restrict food advertising to children, many used this time as an opportunity to spearhead their efforts by generating congressional reports, research articles, and other influential documents to illustrate the linkages between food advertising and obesity (e.g., McGinnis, Gootman, & Kraak, 2006). In 2005, the Institute of Medicine (IOM) of the National Academies underscored the need to address obesity impacting children and adolescents with a deeper understanding of the ubiquitous role the food industry plays in marketing and advertising calorie-dense foods and beverages, which cannot be overlooked as factors associated with the rise in obesity (McGinnis et al., 2006). A year later, in 2006, in response to the FTC and IOM call to action that industry do more to address advertising and childhood obesity, the Council of Better Business Bureaus (CBBB) launched the Children's Food and Beverage Advertising Initiative (CFBAI), which complements the existing National Advertising Review Council's Children's Advertising Review Unit (CARU), two self-regulatory programs to increase corporate social responsibility in the marketplace (CBBB, 2006; NARC, 2009). The CBBB is expected to provide direction, transparency, and accountability of participating companies in CFBAI who "pledged" to be more responsible for child-targeted advertising by improving basic nutrition standards for the food products they market and advertise which will potentially encourage healthier dietary choices. Participating corporations include many of the nation's largest food and beverage manufacturing companies, such as Kraft Foods, The Coca-Cola Company, General Mills, and McDonald's (CBBB, 2009; see also Chap. 6).

A third industry group, the *Sensible Food Policy Coalition*, was formed in response to the Obama Administration's Interagency Working Group (IWG)[1] with the intent of derailing the nutritional guidelines proposed by IWG which states that the food industry market food products to children which satisfy certain nutrition principles by 2016 (WHTF, 2010). Industry self-regulation is often encouraged by the FTC more so than government intervention largely because its ability to react more quickly and efficiently to consumer-related issues as well as reducing or eliminating the need for litigation against the food industry, which can be costly, time consuming, and counterproductive (Roller, Voorhees, & Lunkenheimer, 2006). Many advocate that government regulation is necessary to protect the consumer, while others oppose mandated industry practices since it would impede commercial speech.

[1] The IWG reflects a coordinated effort among four federal agencies: FTC, CDC, US Department of Agriculture, and the Food and Drug Administration to create a set of guidelines for industry to adopt in their efforts to improve nutritious foods marketed to children and teens (White House Task Force on Childhood Obesity (WHTF), 2010).

Childhood Obesity Defined

According to the World Health Organization, obesity is a disease and is defined as the condition of excess body fat to the extent to which health is impaired (WHO, 2000). Childhood obesity is determined by using an algorithm to calculate a Body Mass Index (BMI)[2] which measures body weight relative to height and is considered a valid indicator for estimating body fat.[3] The Centers for Disease Control and Prevention (CDC) and the American Pediatric Association (APA) recommend BMI measurements for children and adolescents between the ages of 2 and 19 which are age and gender specific to assess growth patterns. BMI is routinely calculated and plotted on the CDC 2000 BMI charts by health care professionals during annual well-child visits and physical exams to detect any abnormalities in weight status (Kuczmarski, Ogden, Guo, et al., 2002).[4] Children and adolescents are identified as "obese" if they are at or above the 95th percentile for their age and sex, and if they fall between the 85th and 94th percentiles are considered "overweight" (Ogden et al., 2012). National estimates based on data collected in the 1999–2010 National Health and Nutrition Survey (NHANES)[5] demonstrate that the prevalence of overweight (BMI ≥ 85th percentile) and obesity (BMI ≥ 95th percentile) among children and adolescents (aged 2–19) was 31.8% and 16.9%, respectively (Ogden et al., 2012). Non-Hispanic white children and adolescents had the lowest prevalence compared with their non-Hispanic Black and Mexican-American counterparts. African-American and Hispanic children and adolescents are more likely to be obese (39.1% each), compared to non-Hispanic whites (27.9%) (Ogden et al., 2012). Among 12- through 19-year-old boys, Mexican-Americans had the highest combined prevalence of overweight and obesity (46.0%). For girls in the same age group, non-Hispanic African-Americans had the highest prevalence of obesity compared to non-Hispanic whites (45.1% vs. 27.6%) (Ogden et al., 2012). With the exception of Hispanics, which consist of persons of any race, NHANES is limited regarding analyzing other ethnic and cultural groups due to insufficient sample size.

---

[2] BMI is derived by dividing weight in kilograms by height in meters squared (BMI = weight [kg]/height [m^2]), rounded to one decimal place.

[3] There are other body fat assessments, such as skinfold thickness measured at the abdomen, thigh, and chest areas, and girth measurements (hip and waist), yet BMI indices are customarily obtained prior to or in conjunction with other assessments (Dietz & Bellizzi, 1999).

[4] It is important to note that despite its low measurement error and good reliability and validity, BMI may not be a sensitive measure of body fatness in children who are particularly short, tall, or muscular. Hence two individuals can have the same amount of body fat yet have very different BMIs (Sardinha, Going, Teixeira, et al., 1999). There may also be racial differences in the relationship between the true proportion of body fat and BMI (Freedman, Wang, Thornton, et al., 2008).

[5] NHANES is a series of cross-sectional, nationally representative examination surveys conducted by the National Center for Health Statistics since the 1970s with the most recent survey conducted in 2009–2010. Data on weight and height were collected through direct physical examination in a mobile examination center (CDC, 2012).

Research on adults report that obesity prevalence is high among certain Asian Pacific Islanders and Native American groups, notably Samoans and Pima Indians, which underscore the need to examine overweight and obesity prevalence rates among children and adolescents of various ethnic subgroups (Kumanyika & Grier, 2006). To date, there are relatively few representative studies that have analyzed obesity among Native American and Asian and Pacific Islander children and adolescents (e.g., Story, Stevens, Himes, et al., 2003; Gordon-Larsen, Adair, & Popkin, 2003). Most of these, however, indicate that American-Indian youth tend to have higher obesity rates when compared to the national average (Story et al., 1999), while Asians tend to have relatively low rates of overweight when compared to other racial/ethnic groups (Kumanyika & Grier, 2006). There are also growing concerns of the pervasiveness of obesity among children and adolescents outside the USA Two chapters in this volume address this widespread trend in various Asian countries (see Chaps. 12 and 23).

The underlying causes for racial/ethnic disparities in childhood obesity are complex, yet efforts aimed at increasing our understanding of the contributing factors that importantly affect the racial patterning of the distribution of disease are essential. More research is needed to systematically delineate the multidimensional social concomitants of race and examine mediating factors and pathways through which demographic factors are associated with health and interact with each other (Williams & Collins, 1996; Williams, Mohammed, Leavell, et al., 2010). The diversity that exists within and across racial/ethnic populations requires further investigation since the prevalence of childhood obesity might substantially differ within certain subgroups, particularly in light of studies that have shown variations in obesity prevalence among adults.

The association between socioeconomic status (SES) and health outcomes has been observed for many years and documented in many countries (Krieger, Williams, & Moss, 1997). Unlike most Western European countries, SES is not systematically collected in national health studies in the the USA (Isaacs & Schroeder, 2004). SES has been found to be inversely related to higher BMI in adults, particularly among women (Hanson & Chen, 2007) but the evidence for children is inconsistent and remains less clear (da Veiga, da Cunha, & Sichieri, 2004). Most indicators of SES, such as education and income, are significantly patterned by race, with SES having a robust association with health (Williams & Collins, 1996). To date, only a handful of studies have examined the role of SES and obesity prevalence (e.g., Gordon-Larsen et al., 2003). A CDC report based on NHANES data show that low-income children are at greater risk of obesity when compared to children in nonpoor households (Ogden, Lamb, et al., 2010). One out of 7 low-income, preschool-age children is obese (CDC, 2011). Where you live is also a determinant of health. Features of neighborhoods or community-level factors are associated with the intersection of both racial and social dynamics. Evidence shows that ethnic minorities often bear the burden of high rates of obesity due to a disproportionate share residing in communities that are considered "toxic" environments (Ebbeling, Pawlak, & Ludwig, 2002).

Why Are Children Becoming Obese?

Experts agree that poor diet and physical inactivity are major contributing factors with regard to the rise in childhood obesity prevalence, yet the determinants of obesity are multifactorial and cannot be characterized as the result of merely behavioral factors. There are social, ecological, and environmental influences that have contributed to the increase in the accessibility and availability of food products that are less than optimal, which is partly the result of marketing tactics that promote certain foods and beverages to America's youngest members. Much of the debate about what societal changes have occurred parallel to increased obesity among children and adolescents reflect some of the following:

- *Increased consumption of convenience foods*: An increased consumption and availability of low-cost, palatable, energy-dense poor nutrient foods and beverages that are high in saturated and *trans* fat, sodium, and sugars and low in vitamins; a shift in more meals eaten outside the home; proliferation of fast-food restaurants; larger food portions or "super-size" portions served both inside and outside the home.
- *Increase of food marketing aimed at children*: Food advertising exclusively to children and their families by fast-food restaurants and other types of restaurants is an increasing trend; companies market unhealthy foods to America's youth on television programs, radio, the Internet, through product placement in movies and video games, in schools that sell "junk" food and soda (i.e., calorie-dense, nutrient-poor foods), as well as on product packages.
- *Increased access to unhealthy foods in schools:* Foods and beverages that are available for purchase in schools through à la carte school stores or cafés and vending machines, commonly referred as "competitive foods" which are sold outside of the USDA federally approved breakfast and lunch meals and are typically high in fat, sugar, and sodium.
- *Reduced physical activity*: Physical education programs and recess have been substantially scaled back or eliminated altogether which has led to a decrease in physical activity in schools across the country. Disinvestment of recreational resources, such as parks and sports facilities, as well as concerns of safety may also prevent children and youth to engage in physical activity within their residential communities.
- *Increasing use of technology*: The amount of time spent watching television, playing video games, and using personal computers have been linked to the rising prevalence of childhood obesity as a result of becoming more sedentary.
- *Food Deserts*: More than 23.5 million Americans live in food deserts – communities with no access to fresh and nutritious food –where the closest supermarket or large grocery store is more than a mile away (USDA, 2009). Residents living in underserved neighborhoods or in remote, isolated rural areas are more inclined to have limited access to full-scale supermarkets that offer a variety of affordable, healthier food options, such as fresh produce and lean meats. Most residents typically rely on convenience stores, gas station quick marts, and other retail outlets that sell food products at higher prices and tend to be less nutritious.

The root causes of obesity among children and adolescents are quite complex. There are many explanations but the challenge lies on generating effective solutions to reduce this epidemic. Evidence suggests that a child's social milieu and interpersonal communication, such as peer groups, families, teachers, and doctors and dietitians influence the choices that children make with regard to satiety and dietary habits, all of which takes place in various contexts of their social and physical environments (i.e., child care centers, schools, community). Consequentially, these interactions can increase exposure and access to either healthy or unhealthy food choices. The impact of the media on childhood obesity has gained traction in a growing body of scientific research and has mitigated individual choices and actions. Some of these investigations have been methodically diverse and have had mixed findings. Use of new technologies and increased media consumption are important contributors to less than optimal diets and other obesity-related risk factors attributing to the rising rates of obesity among young Americans.

Changes in food manufacturing and processing, dietary habits, inactive and sedentary lifestyles, residential environments and school settings, industry tactics in advertising and marketing of food products to children, as well as family history and genetic susceptibility have been identified, yet how these factors interact among each other are not fully understood.

Consequences of Childhood Obesity

Obesity has deleterious short-term and long-term consequences that may, in turn, diminish the quality of life. A body of evidence suggests that childhood obesity can be accompanied by other risk factors, such as chronic illnesses and diseases that may also carry over into adulthood and lead to premature deaths (Serdula, Ivery, Coates, et al., 1993; Dietz, 1998; Olshansky, Passaro, Hershow, et al., 2005). Until recently, children and adolescents are now being diagnosed with type 2 diabetes mellitus, elevated cholesterol, hypertension, and other comorbidities associated with obesity that were previously thought of as diseases of adults. Perhaps the most salient of these is type 2 diabetes mellitus, which now accounts for 45% of all new cases (WHO, 2008). In addition to adverse physical health consequences, obese children are also at risk of developing psychosocial problems, such as low self-esteem, depression, and social stigmatization (American Academy of Pediatrics, 2003). The consequences of obesity are further exacerbated as the result of living in communities that are more likely to have fewer opportunities to purchase affordable, healthy food choices, and less likely to have access to adequate social amenities and recreational resources to engage in physical activity. While obesity levels seem to have leveled off in recent years, projections indicate that if the epidemic continues it could potentially double among children and teens by 2030 (Ogden, Carroll, Curtin, Lamb, et al., 2010; Wang, Beydoun, Liang, et al., 2008).

Organization of This Volume

This edited volume is comprised of 24 chapters which are divided into seven sections. Part I provides key issues on childhood obesity and an update on the progress made by private-sector (food companies) and public-sector stakeholders (i.e., government, school district boards, local school policies) since the 2006 Institute of Medicine (IOM) food marketing congressional report, which reflects a comprehensive analysis of 123 peer reviewed articles addressing links between food and beverage marketing practices on food preferences, consumption behavior, diet and health among American children and adolescents (McGinnis et al., 2006). The preponderance of evidence supported these links and hence an expert committee provided ten recommendations for a multisectoral, integrated effort to promote healthier diets and reduce the risk of childhood obesity. The IOM report concluded that its data establish a "need and an opportunity [to] … turn food and beverage marketing forces toward better diets for American children and youth." To what extent has any wide-ranging progress been made regarding implementing these recommendations since the IOM food marketing report was issued? Has there been much success in legislation enacted or initiatives generated by public and private stakeholders to achieve IOM's recommendations?

In Chap. 2, Ellen Wartella and her colleagues summarize the significance of the IOM report and provide guidance on whether or not industry and government have adopted any effective initiatives in countering the increase in childhood obesity. In Chap. 3, Paul Harrison and Michaela Jackson introduce the concept of integrated marketing communications or IMC, which is widely used by food and beverage companies to market suboptimal food products that predispose children to higher risk of obesity and obesity-related health problems. The use of IMC practices to entice young people to purchase and consume certain products in the marketplace has garnered much attention in the USA and abroad. Emerging forms of marketing, such as viral marketing and product placements, are become increasingly popular especially with the increased use of the Internet and video games, along with other emerging technology such as social media (i.e., Facebook, YouTube, Twitter) among young people.

In Part II, investigators probe the regulatory efforts by the federal government and private companies concerning advertising and marketing tactics used by the food industry targeting young people and document legal and ethical issues concerning these practices. The ongoing debate of whether advertising is the real culprit in making our kids fat, which is an intriguing one, especially among those who claim that ultimately, it is the parents' responsibility regarding making decisions about what is purchased and consumed by a minor. Should companies not produce food that is attractive or appealing to the palate or taste perceptions among young people? The truth is children *are* consumers of goods and products that reflect their needs and desires, similar to that of any other demographic group. The food industry spends billions of dollars on child-oriented advertising. Large-scale food advertising has a long history of incorporating various methods of persuasion to sell products and promote brands to consumers. Minette (Meme) Drumwright and Jerome D. Williams introduce a provocative approach by exploring the role of ethics and other codes of conduct in food advertising through the perspective of three domains—industry, public health, and academia. Disentangling what is right, what is wrong, and any gray area in between in food advertising practices aimed at children is a complex proposition. Either one side of the argument or the other is evoked concerning whether child-oriented food advertising is ethical or not. Critics tend to either side against industry stating that it increases consumption of unhealthy products, while proponents argue that advertising is an important aspect of the economic system. In light of these ethical concerns, Samantha Graff and Tamara Piety elucidate the legal obstacles faced by regulators vis-à-vis commercial advertising directed toward children in the context of constitutional law, the First Amendment, and how this commercial speech doctrine has little relevance to the various tactics employed by advertising to encourage the purchase of unhealthy foods by children and their families.

The FTC regulates food advertising under its statutory authority to prohibit "deceptive or unfair" industry practices, yet some legal scholars and public health advocates argue that ads targeting children are inherently unethical and should be banned altogether or at the very least, more stringent restrictions should be imposed (FTC 2008). In 2011, the FTC released a set of guidelines to persuade the food industry in changing the way in which foods are advertised and marketed to children of all ages (less than 18 years of age) which complements the industry-led effort of CFBAI (FTC, 2011). In Chap. 6, Julie Ralston Aoki and Elizabeth Moore discuss the coordinated effort initiated by CARU and CFBAI and make the case whether or not modifications are merited to strengthen existing guidelines set forth by these two self-regulatory entities. Furthermore, corporate self-regulation of foods marketed toward children is not without its share of critics. Reports issued by the food industry document early successes in their compliance to nutritional standards; however, objectivity and scientific rigor is questionable given the nature of self-reporting, which are mainly qualitative and routinely biased, hence the need to critically evaluate from an impartial perspective. In the final chapter of Part II, Jennifer Harris and colleagues document the pros and cons of corporate self-regulation and propose methodological techniques to evaluate whether CFBAI has been or can be effective.

In Part III, we continue this discussion, grappling with ancillary issues of CFBAI self-regulatory pledges. To further illustrate whether CFBAI has lived up to its promise, Chap. 8 presents the first-to-date comprehensive examination which analyzes television advertisements aired before and after the implementation of CFBAI to show if there has been any improvement in children's total exposure to food-related advertising, particularly as it relates to the nutritional content of food and beverage products—saturated fat, sugar, sodium, and fiber content. As Lisa Powell and her colleagues note, children's exposure to unhealthy food advertisements had reduced, while fast-food ads actually increased during this time period, suggesting that despite these positive changes, fast-food ads tend to diminish any overall significant benefit in promoting healthy food products.

Food marketers use an array of effective tactics aimed at young consumers and their families with the goal of establishing brand loyalty or "the situation in which a consumer generally buys the same manufacturer originated product or service repeatedly over time rather than buying from multiple suppliers within the category" and their future purchasing behavior (AMA, 2012). In Chap. 9, Gary Wilcox and colleagues provide an extensive review of target advertising and its role in the marketplace, how it compares to the tobacco and alcohol market, and its effects on children's consumer behaviors.

Part III also explores the rapidly changing food advertising landscape and the need to incorporate more novel, cutting-edge research to capture all of the nuances that are essential to obtain a deeper meaning of understanding about the decision-making process among young consumers. Today, digital marketing techniques are routinely used by fast food, snack food, and soft drink companies aimed at children and teens. In the following chapter, Kathryn Montgomery and her colleagues present a conceptual framework that illustrates how digital marketing differs from more conventional forms of marketing and critique several promotional campaigns used routinely by food companies aimed primarily at teens. In Chap. 11, Keryn Pasch and her co-authors demonstrate a multimethod approach, including eye-tracking technology combined with qualitative interviews (focus group and personal narratives) and quantitative surveys, to obtain a better understanding of how youth perceive and process food and beverage advertising. This chapter describes the utility of eye-tracking technology, which makes it possible for health researchers to measure a participant's eye movement to objectively assess the components of food and beverage advertisements that appeal to youth.

Part IV shines a spotlight on food advertising and its increased influence on children and adolescents outside of the USA and how it is permeated throughout a young person's life, particularly in the context of place and space or geospatial environments, such as schools and neighborhoods. We begin Part IV with an intriguing chapter by Melissa Stigler and colleagues, who document how the infusion of conventional forms of advertising and traditional Asian Indian culture is used to promote westernized, nutrient-poor and calorie-dense foods which have led to a drastic shift in India's nutritional landscape.

Undoubtedly, the school environment can have a significant impact on food preferences and dietary behavior of school-age children and teens. According to a recent report by the Robert Wood Johnson Foundation, elementary schools across the nation commonly serve meals that do not meet current dietary guidelines, offering students high-fat food selections and sugar-laden beverages and other nonnutritious foods (Turner, Chaloupka, Chriqui, et al., 2010). To compound this even further, students spend a large portion of their time in school on a daily basis therefore they are exposed to an unique form of advertising, in-school marketing, which is evident through vending machines, school stores, à la carte food items as well as other mediums, such as school-related sporting events and fundraising activities. In this vein, Lara Latimer and colleagues provide a comprehensive review of in-school food marketing and report findings from a pilot study of middle-school students in Central Texas regarding exposure to food and beverage advertisements and promotion in the context of their school environments. Of particular concern, is whether on-site advertising within the halls of school buildings and on the school premises or grounds can lead to unhealthy food choices and poor dietary habits. A subsequent chapter examines whether the influence of external ads, commercial signage located in close proximity to schools, is another contributing factor. Keryn Pasch and Natalie Poulos shed light on this by systematically employing an environmental approach to assess the presence of outdoor food and beverage signage near and around school properties in Central Texas, while Diana Grigsby-Toussaint and her co-authors explore food advertising in local retail food outlets and its potential impact on childhood obesity, particularly as it relates to food and beverage marketing techniques found in African-American neighborhoods. The authors demonstrate how tie-in campaigns and the use of animated characters lure children into making unhealthy food choices.

In Part V, we continue this discussion on how the interlocking dynamics of race, ethnicity, social class, or culture play a central role in the effects of community-level food environments on individual dietary behavior. Recent reports from the *Robert Wood Johnson Foundation Commission to Build a Healthier America* show that where you live may subject a person to deleterious health consequences, particularly individuals of socially vulnerable populations which include low-SES persons and certain racial/ethnic minorities (RWJF, 2008). The presence of convenience or corner stores that sell inadequate healthy food options (i.e., fresh fruit and vegetables), along with limited or deteriorating infrastructure within a community are contributing factors to ill health, as well as the insidious forms of marketing and advertising that are employed to target ethnic minority youth. Target marketing to communities of color is problematic and seen as a form of discrimination particularly when it promotes unhealthy food and beverages, perpetuates stereotypes, and exploits cultural identities that have contributed to higher rates of obesity prevalence among Latino and African-American youth compared to their white peers (Berkeley Media Studies Group, 2010).

In the first chapter in Part V, we begin with Sonya Grier and Vikki Lassiter, who provide a historical timeline of African-Americans as consumers, explore the cultural and social underpinnings of targeting African-American consumers, and discuss how advertising companies have capitalized and profited from tapping into cultural nuances that resonate with African-American youth who tend to be trendsetters and responsive to such ads. The authors also illustrate that African-Americans are not monolithic but quite diverse in their perspectives on advertising. The importance of understanding the cultural context of communities is emphasized in order to develop health-promoting activities to counter the ubiquitous nature of "multicultural marketing." In the following two chapters, the authors complement this section by documenting the changing ethnic landscape in the USA with Latino youth comprising a sizable portion of the consumer market, as noted by Amelie G. Ramirez, Kipling Gallion, and Rebecca Adeigbe, while Karen Kramer and her colleagues indicate how the industry's egregious "predatory marketing" of junk foods to ethnic minority children and adolescents is a social justice issue as well as an economic one. Chapter 18 explores from a legal perspective whether federal civil rights or state consumer rights laws provide a potential basis for challenging target marketing of junk food to ethnic minority youth. The authors also stress the critical need for communities to become "agents of change" by increasing awareness among its residents, challenging target marketing of unhealthy foods, and mobilizing their efforts with other stakeholders to impact public policy in creating healthier food environments.

Engaging in physical activity on a daily basis is the cornerstone of health and well-being. Studies show that children who engage in active lifestyles are less likely to be overweight or obese. The set of papers in Part VI addresses media campaigns as mechanisms to increase physical activity. Evidence has shown that social marketing campaigns, such antismoking programs, can be quite effective in preventing or reducing risky behaviors among young people. Social marketing is commonly referred to the application of commercial marketing principles (i.e., the 4 "Ps" of place, price, product, and promotion) to benefit society and the intended targeted audience rather than industry per se. Toni Yancey and her colleagues chronicle social marketing physical activity campaigns from the mid-1950s to the present. The authors also discuss Instant Recess®, an innovative intervention to reduce sedentariness among school-age children, which was created by the first author and has received national recognition. It integrates brief physical activity breaks of 10-minute intervals into public school curriculum and after-school settings. Marian Huhman, one of the lead evaluators of CDC's *VERB: It's What You Do!* a social marketing campaign to increase and maintain physical activity among tweens (children aged 9–13), along with her co-author Carrie Patnode discuss the success of this effort as well as offer insight and guidance on methods by which a local community can tailor the national campaign in Chap. 20.

In a subsequent chapter, the authors take an insider perspective to recount the development and implementation of the first ever comprehensive national physical activity standards for all Americans, with specific recommendations earmarked for target age groups (i.e., children and adolescents aged 6–17). Jane Wargo, Janet Fulton, and Sarah Lee argue that despite an impressive marketing strategy used to launch *2008 Physical Activity Guidelines for Americans*, the primary target audience (health professionals and policy makers) has limited knowledge about these guidelines and hence, efforts to foster physical activity among our nation's youth have been severely truncated.

The book concludes with Part VII, which focuses on "real-time" solutions to reversing the trend in increasing rates of childhood obesity from the perspective of community, government, and industry. *Healthy People 2020*, a decennial publication produced by the US Department of Health and Human Services, is a national agenda on health promotion and disease prevention with specific objectives for America to meet within a ten-year period. With regard to reducing childhood obesity, among the target goals is to (1) reduce childhood obesity and prevent excessive weight gain among youth by 10%; (2) increase the proportion of adolescents who engage in vigorous or moderate physical activity; (3) increase the number of schools that offer healthier selections among competitive foods (food and beverages sold outside of the federal school lunch and breakfast programs); and (4) increase the proportion of adolescents who view television 2 hrs or less on a school day from 79%

to 87% with the expectation that kids will engage in more physical activities (USDHHS, 2010). Achieving the goals proposed in *Healthy People 2020* depends on the social capital of communities and the ability to foster viable options to engage in health-promoting activities.

Community-based approaches or grass-roots advocacy are viewed as promising approaches to reduce obesity prevalence, whether alone or in combination of other approaches. William McCarthy and his colleagues provide a brief overview of various successful efforts in the state of California in Chap. 22 that have been adopted to create healthier environments as the result of mobilizing constituents and influencing local officials to leverage resources to implement viable solutions either through legislative processes or other policy avenues. In a subsequent chapter, May Lwin, Benjamin Li, and Jerome D. Williams investigate how "exergames," a new type of video gaming that involves physical movements to replicate "real-life" activities (e.g., various sports), can be a viable alternative to traditional physical fitness activities and serve as an effective solution to reduce the incidence of childhood obesity in Singapore, Thailand, and Indonesia.

In our final chapter, Ad Council Campaign Director Anthony Signorelli and his co-author George Perlov offer us insight on the Ad Council's *Coalition for Healthy Children*, a joint initiative between major health organizations and food companies to integrate "healthy messaging" in food marketing campaigns with a key emphasis on three central foci: (1) to encourage children and families to opt for healthier choices; (2) reduce portion size; and (3) engage in physical activity. The authors document the rigorous testing process that was employed to verify the metrics used to assess whether the messaging clearly communicated its intended messages and if it was responsive to the target audience, youth and parents. This chapter denotes illustrative examples of several of the ways the industry incorporated health messages in their marketing and communications programs which have shown to be quite effective.

Combating childhood obesity is an ambitious undertaking. Yet as the contributors of this volume demonstrate, addressing obesity among children and adolescents requires an understanding not only of the behavioral factors (overconsumption of calories, sedentary lifestyles) that impact excessive weight gain and health complications associated with it but also of the role industry plays in influencing eating and physical activity behaviors, attitudes, culture, and personal choices. Recognizing the enormity of the obesity problem among young people cannot be fixed with a silver bullet solution is the first step. Involving all levels of government, food and beverage companies, researchers and public health advocates, as well as communities, parents, and other stakeholders, to move beyond pointing the finger of blame is critical for any success in creating viable solutions. Both private and public sectors must work in tandem using a multisectoral approach to highlight their unique strengths and avoid the pitfalls of working in silos which can easily thwart well-intentioned efforts. The key is to devise effective initiatives and policy interventions to slow down and reverse any further increases in childhood obesity by creating healthier food environments, changing the way in which food is directly marketed to children, and investing in community infrastructure to facilitate physical activity which are essential to prevent obesity from occurring in the first place.

References

American Academy of Pediatrics. (2003). Prevention of pediatric overweight and obesity. *Pediatrics, 112*(2), 424–430.

American Marketing Association [AMA]. (2012). *Definition of brand loyalty*. http://www.marketingpower.com/_layouts/Dictionary.aspx?dLetter=B.

Berkeley Media Studies Group. (2010). *Target marketing soda & fast food: Problems with business as usual*. http://www.bmsg.org/pdfs/bmsg_cche_target_marketing_brief.pdf. Accessed 3 Mar 2012.

Council of Better Business Bureaus [CBBB]. (2006). New food, beverage initiative to focus kids' ads on healthy choices; revised guidelines strengthen CARU's guidance to food advertisers [news release]. http://www.bbb.org/us/article/new-food-beverage-initiative-to-focus-kids-ads-on-healthy-choices-revised-guidelines-strengthen-carus-guidance-to-food-advertisers-672. Accessed 9 Feb 2012.

Council of Better Business Bureaus [CBBB]. (2009). The children's food and beverage advertising initiative in action: a report on compliance and implementation during 2008. Arlington, VA: Council of Better Business Bureaus. http://www.bbb.org/us/storage/0/Shared%20Documents/finalbbbs.pdf. Accessed 9 Feb 9 2012.

Center for Disease Control and Prevention. (2012). *National Health and Nutrition Examination Survey*. http://www.cdc.gov/nchs/nhanes.htm. Accessed 3 Feb 2012.

Centers for Disease Control and Prevention. (2011). *Obesity among low-income preschool children*. http://www.cdc.gov/obesity/downloads/PedNSSFactSheet.pdf. Accessed 9 Feb 2012.

da Veiga, G. V., da Cunha, A. S., & Sichieri, R. (2004). Trends in overweight among adolescents living in the poorest and regions of Brazil. *American Journal of Public Health, 94*, 1544–1548.

Dietz, W. (1998). Health consequences of obesity in youth: childhood predictors of adult disease. *Pediatrics, 101*, 518–525.

Dietz, W. H., & Bellizzi, M. C. (1999). Introduction: the use of body mass index to assess obesity in children. *The American Journal of Clinical Nutrition, 70*(suppl), 123S–125S.

Ebbeling, C. B., Pawlak, D. B., & Ludwig, D. S. (2002). Childhood obesity: public-health crisis, common sense cure. *Lancet, 360*, 473–482.

Federal Trade Commission [FTC]. (2008). *Marketing food to children and adolescents: A review of industry expenditures, activities, and self-regulation*. http://www.ftc.gov/os/2008/07/P064504foodmktingreport.pdf. Accessed 24 Jan 2012.

Federal Trade Commission [FTC]. (2011). Food for thought: Interagency working group proposal on food marketing to children. http://ftc.gov/os/2011/04/110428foodmarketfactsheet.pdf. Accessed 24 Jan 2012.

Freedman, D. S., Wang, J., Thornton, J. C., Mei, Z., Pierson, Jr, R. N., Dietz, W. H., & Horlick, M. (2008). Racial/ethnic differences in body fatness among children and adolescents. *Obesity, 16*(5), 1105–1111.

Gordon-Larsen, P., Adair, S., & Popkin, B. M. (2003). The relationship of ethnicity, socioeconomic factors, and overweight in U.S. adolescents. *Obesity Research, 11*(1), 121–29 (erratum in *Obesity Research*11, no. 4 [2003]: 597).

Hanson, M. D., & Chen, E. (2007). Socioeconomic status: race, and body mass index: The mediating role of physical activity and sedentary behaviors during adolescence. *Journal of Pediatric Psychology, 32*(3), 250–259.

Hossain, P., Kawar, B., & El Nahas, M. (2007). Obesity and diabetes in the developing world – A growing challenge. *The New England Journal of Medicine, 356*, 213–215.

Isaacs, S. L., & Schroeder, S. A. (2004). Class—The ignored determinant of the nation's health. *The New England Journal of Medicine, 351*, 1137–1142.

Krieger, N., Williams, D., & Moss, N. (1997). Measuring social class in US public health research: concepts, methodologies, and guidelines. *Annual Review of Public Health, 18*, 341–378.

Kuczmarski, R. J., Ogden, C. L., Guo, S. S., Grummer-Strawn, L. M., Flegal, K. M., Wei, R., Curtin, L. R., Roche, A. F., & Johnson, C. L. (2002). 2000 CDC growth charts for the United States: methods and development. National Center for Health Statistics. *Vital Health Statistics 11*(246).

Kumanyika, S., & Grier, S. (2006). Targeting interventions for ethnic minority and low-income populations. *Future Child, 16*(1), 187–207.

McGinnis, J. M., Gootman, J. A., Kraak, VI. (Eds). (2006). *Food marketing to children and youth: Threat or opportunity?* Washington DC: The National Academies Press. http://www.nap.edu/catalog.php?record_id=11514.

National Advertising Review Council [NARC]. (2009). *The advertising industry's process of voluntary self-regulation.* http://www.nadreview.org/09_Procedures.pdf. Accessed 9 Feb 2012.

Ogden, C. L., & Carroll, M. D. (2010). *Prevalence of obesity among children and adolescents: United States, trends 1963–1965 through 2007–2008.* National Center for Health Statistics. http://www.cdc.gov/nchs/data/hestat/obesity_child_07_08/obesity_child_07_08.pdf. Accessed 9 Feb 2012.

Ogden, C. L., Lamb, M. M., Carroll, M. D., & Flegal, K. M. (2010). *Obesity and socioeconomic status in children and adolescents: United States, 2005-2008.* NCHS Data Brief no. 51 Hyattsville, MD: National Center for Health Statistics. http://www.cdc.gov/nchs/data/databriefs/db51.pdf. Accessed 9 Feb 2012.

Ogden, C. L., Carroll, M. D., Curtin, L. R., Lamb, M. M., & Flegal, K. M. (2010). Prevalence of high body mass index in U.S. children and adolescents 2007–2008. *Journal of the American Medical Association, 303*(3), 242–249.

Ogden, C. L., Carroll, M. D., Kit, B. K., & Flegal, K. M. (2012). Prevalence of obesity and trends in body mass index among US children and adolescents, 1999–2010. *Journal of the American Medical Association, 307*(5), 483–490.

Olshansky, S. J., Passaro, D. J., Hershow, R. C., Layden, J., Carnes, B. A., Brody, J., Hayflick, L., Butler, R. N., Allison, D. B., & Ludwig, D. S. (2005). A potential decline in life expectancy in the United States in the 21st century. *The New England Journal of Medicine, 352*(11), 1138–1145.

Robert Wood Johnson Foundation Commission to Build a Healthier America [RWJF]. (2008). *America's health starts with healthy children: How do states compare?* http://www.rwjf.org/files/research/commissionchildrenshealthchartbook.pdf. Accessed 3 Mar 2012.

Roller, S. T., Voorhees, T. J., & Lukenheimer, A. K. (2006). Obesity, food marketing, and consumer litigation: Threat or opportunity? *Food and Drug Law Journal, 61*, 419–444.

Sardinha, L. B., Going, S. B., Teixeira, P. J., & Lohman, T. G., (1999). Receiver operating characteristic analysis of body mass index, triceps skinfold thickness, and arm girth for obesity screening in children and adolescents. *The American Journal of Clinical Nutrition, 70*, 1090–1095.

Serdula, M. K., Ivery, D., Coates, R. J., Freedman, D. S., Williamson, D. F., & Byers, T. (1993). Do obese children become obese adults? A review of the literature. *Preventive Medicine, 22*(2), 167–177.

Singh, G. K., Kogan, M. D., & van Dyck, P. C. (2010). Changes in state-specific childhood obesity and overweight prevalence in the United States from 2003 to 2007. *Archives of Pediatrics & Adolescent Medicine, 164*(7), 598–607.

Story, M., Evans, M., Fabsitz, R. R., Clay, T.E., Rock, B. H., & Broussard, B. (1999). The epidemic of obesity in American Indian communities and the need for childhood obesity-prevention programs. *American Journal of Clinical Nutrition, 69*(4), 747S–754S.

Story, M., Stevens, J., Himes, J., Stone, E., Rock, B. H., Ethelbah, B., & Davis, S. (2003). Obesity in American-Indian children: Prevalence, consequences, and prevention. *Preventive Medicine, 37*, S3–S12.

Trasande, L., Liu, Y., Fryer, G., & Weitzman, M. (2009). Effects of childhood obesity on hospital care and costs, 1999–2005. *Health Affairs, 28*(3/4), w751–w760.

Turner, L., Chaloupka, F. J., Chriqui, J. F., & Sandoval, A. (2010). *School policies and practices to improve health and prevent obesity: National elementary school survey results: School years 2006–07 and 2007–08* (vol. 1). Chicago, IL: Bridging the Gap Program, Health Policy Center, Institute for Health Research and Policy, University of Illinois at Chicago. http://www.bridgingthegapresearch.org. Accessed 7 Feb 2012.

U.S. Department of Agriculture [USDA]. (2009). *Access to affordable and nutritious food: measuring and understanding food deserts and their consequences*. http://www.ers.usda.gov/Publications/AP/AP036/AP036.pdf. Accessed 2 Feb 2012.

U.S. Department of Health and Human Services [USDHHS]. (2010). *Healthy people 2020*. Office of Disease Prevention and Health Promotion. Washington, DC. http://healthypeople.gov/2020/topicsobjectives2020/pdfs/HP2020objectives.pdf. Accessed 24 Jan 2012.

Wang, Y., & Zhang, Q. (2006). Are American children and adolescents of low socioeconomic status at increased risk of obesity? Changes in the association between overweight and family income between 1971 and 2002. *American Journal of Clinical Nutrition, 84*, 707–716.

Wang, Y., Beydoun, M. A., Liang, L., Caballero, B., & Kumanyika, S. K. (2008). Will all Americans become overweight or obese? Estimating the progression and cost of the US obesity epidemic. *Obesity, 16*(10), 2323–2330.

White House Task Force on Childhood Obesity [WHTF]. (2010). *Solving the problem of childhood obesity within a generation: White House task force on childhood obesity report to the president*. http://www.letsmove.gov/sites/letsmove.gov/files/TaskForce_on_Childhood_Obesity_May2010_FullReport.pdf. Accessed 4 Apr 2012.

Williams, D. R., & Collins, C. (1996). US socioeconomic and racial differences in health: Patterns and explanations. *Annual Review of Sociology, 21*, 349–386.

Williams, D. R., Mohammed, S. A., Leavell, J., & Collins, C. (2010). Race, socioeconomic status, and health: Complexities, ongoing challenges, and research opportunities. *Annals of the New York Academy of Sciences, 1186*, 69–101.

World Health Organization [WHO]. (2000). *Obesity: Preventing and managing the global epidemic: Report of a WHO consultation*. Geneva, Switzerland: World Health Organization (Technical report series no. 894).

World Health Organization [WHO]. (2008). *Preventing chronic diseases: A vital investment*. http://www.who.int/chp/chronic_disease_report/part2_ch1/en/index.html. Accessed 3 Apr 2012.

World Health Organization [WHO]. (2010). *Childhood overweight and obesity on the rise*. http://www.who.int/dietphysicalactivity/childhood/en/index.html. Accessed 1 Feb 2012.

Chapter 2
Progress on Public Policy: The Aftermath of the 2005 Institute of Medicine Report on Food Marketing and the Diets of Children and Youth

Ellen Wartella, Vivica Kraak, Mary Story, Jaya Ginter, and Elizabeth A. Vandewater

Introduction

An alarming percentage of American children and youth age 2–17 are either obese (17%) or at risk of becoming obese (32%) (IOM, 2005). Childhood obesity affects children at all ages, ethnicities, and gender; moreover, obesity rates have tripled over the past thirty years across all age groups and increased fivefold for 6- to 11-year-old children in the past 50 years. In 2005, the Institute of Medicine (IOM) released a study report on childhood obesity which acknowledged that there are many factors that have contributed to childhood obesity: changes in the built environment that promote sedentary lifestyles, school food service policies, and the rise of sales of "competitive foods" such as candy and parent family's practices of eating out and inattention to physical activity. One factor which is acknowledged in that report but was examined further in a subsequent IOM study is the role of food marketing in influencing children's diets (IOM, 2005).

This chapter draws from a report to the Robert Wood Johnson Foundation, "Assessing progress for Marketing Healthful Diets to American Children and Adolescents to Inform a National Obesity Prevention Strategy in the US" by Vivica Kraak, Mary Story, Ellen Wartella and Jaya Gintner, July 2010.

E. Wartella (✉)
Northwestern University,
1818 Hinman Avenue, Evanston, IL 60208, USA
e-mail: ewartella@gmail.com

V. Kraak • M. Story
Deakin University, Pigdons Road, Waurn Ponds, VIC 3216, Australia

J. Ginter
University of Minnesota, Minneapolis, MN, USA

E.A. Vandewater
University of Texas School of Public Health,
1200 Herman Pressler, Houston, TX 77030, USA

J.D. Williams et al. (eds.), *Advances in Communication Research to Reduce Childhood Obesity*, DOI 10.1007/978-1-4614-5511-0_2,

Food Marketing to Children and Youth: Threat or Opportunity?, (IOM, 2006) assessed the nature and extent of changes in the marketing and media landscape and how these changes had affected the diets and health of American children and adolescents. This foundational report represented the most comprehensive review of the influence of food marketing on children since the 1970s "kidvid" debates about the role of television advertising in influencing children's dental and physical health (Beales, 2004). During the mid to late 1970s, the Federal Trade Commission (FTC) conducted a review of television advertising's effect on children and initiated a rule-making process to elicit public input about the need to regulate or ban television advertising targeting young children. Specifically, during these "kidvid" hearings and commentaries, views clashed among commercial, consumer advocacy, and political interest groups that sought to influence the rulemaking process. The FTC concluded that children too young to understand the persuasive intent of advertising (i.e., that advertisers are trying to sell them a product) are an unfair target of advertising since they have difficulty scrutinizing the advertiser's message. In 1981 Congress objected to the Federal Trade Commission's attempt to ban television advertising to young children and removed the FTC's authority to regulate advertising based on the fairness doctrine. This had a twofold effect: to stop the kidvid investigation at the time and to remove oversight of marketing practices to children over the ensuing 25 years (Beales). Not until the 2006 IOM report on Food Marketing had there been systematic attention to the changing landscape of marketing to children and the likely impact of that marketing on children's health and wellness.

In this chapter, we will review the conclusions of the 2006 Food Marketing report and examine responses to the report's conclusions including current and future policy activities regarding food marketing to children.

The 2006 Report on Food Marketing and the Diets of Children and Youth

In 2004 Congress asked the Centers for Disease Control (CDC) to investigate the role that food marketing plays in influencing children's diets. The CDC then went to the IOM to convene a study committee with the specific task to "review the evidence for food and beverage marketing practices that influence the diet of children and adolescents and recommend strategies to promote a healthful diet." (IOM, 2006). This study was a joint project of the Food and Nutrition Board of the Institute of Medicine and the Board on Children Youth and Families of the National Research Council of the National Academy of Sciences. They convened a panel of 16 experts in marketing, children and television, nutrition, public health, law, and industry. The committee met over 18 months and published its report in April 2006.

The IOM report examines first, the nature of marketing practices and expenditures to children and youth. The committee estimated that $10 billion is spent on marketing all food and beverage to children and adolescents (a number that was disputed at the time) via a variety of marketing venues such as schools, grocery stores, malls, theaters, sporting events; through many media vehicles such as television, radio, print media, internet, mobile devices; and through a variety of school-based practices such as direct advertising in the schools and cafeterias and via logos on school uniforms and athletic gear. In short, marketing to children and youth is ubiquitous.

Furthermore, marketing to children and adolescents is complex because it involves diverse stakeholders with different motivations and priorities, and encompasses a broad set of integrated strategies and activities, often called integrated marketing communications. Integrated marketing uses the marketing mix of product, price, promotion, and place and a range of communication channels to provide clarity, consistency, and maximum communication impact. The marketing mix includes: *product* (i.e., quality, quantity, packaging, labeling, health claims); *price* (i.e., competitive positioning, vending and procurement, contracts and agreements, taxes and subsidies); *promotion* (i.e., how a company communicates with customers to inform, persuade, or influence purchase decisions; promotion encompasses public relations, advertising, target marketing, sales and trade promotion, integrated branding strategy); and *place* (i.e., venues and settings used to reach consumers including retail stores and schools), including the media platforms and marketing vehicles used to influence brand preferences, purchasing habits, and consumption behaviors (i.e., print, broadcast, digital, mobile devices, and Internet-based social networking sites). Advertising is traditionally defined as a form of promotion used to raise consumer awareness about branded food and beverage products or messages by an identified sponsor using paid media. Food companies usually spend about 20% of their total marketing budgets on advertising, 25% on consumer or sales promotion, and 55% on trade promotions (IOM, 2006)

In addition, the 2006 IOM report examined the adequacy of children's diets and summarized changes in those diets over the previous 30 years. The committee found that most children and adolescents have inadequate intakes both of nutrient-dense food groups (i.e., fruits and vegetables, whole grains, low-fat dairy, meat, eggs, and beans) and shortfall nutrients (i.e., potassium, fiber, calcium) recommended by the Dietary Guidelines for Americans (USHHS & USDA, 2005) and the American Heart Association (Giddings et al., 2006). The trends also showed a general increase in consumption of calories, carbohydrates, sweetened beverage, and away from home foods. Children and adolescents also were consuming higher than recommended amounts of sugars, sodium, and total and saturated fats. In short, the committee found that the dietary practices of children and youth were not consistent with recommended dietary patterns and were putting children and youth's health at risk.

The 2006 Literature Review

Importantly, the committee conducted a systematic review of 123 published studies examining the impact of TV advertising on children's food preferences, food choices, diets, and adiposity (fatness). The committee found few studies of other marketing practices and therefore focused solely on television advertising. The committee found strong effects of television advertising on food and beverage preferences, purchase requests, and short-term food and beverage consumption for 2- to 11-year olds; moderate evidence of effects on food and beverage beliefs and the usual dietary intake of 2- to 5-year olds; and insufficient evidence on a causal relationship from TV advertising to adiposity, especially for teens. While statistically, there is evidence that exposure to TV advertising is associated with adiposity in children 2 to 11 and teens 12–18, the data are primarily correlational. Therefore, the committee concluded there was insufficient evidence of a causal relationship between TV advertising and adiposity.

Major Conclusions of the 2006 IOM Report

The committee came to five major conclusions (1) food and beverage marketing influences the diets and health of children and adolescents; (2) current marketing practices are out of balance with healthful diets and create an environment that puts their health at risk; (3) companies and marketers have underutilized their potential to apply their resources and creativity to market healthful diets to young people; (4) achieving healthful diets will require sustained, multisectoral, and integrated efforts and industry leadership; and (5) public policy lacked support or authority to address emerging marketing practices that influenced young people's diets.

The IOM report suggested that marketing forces can be used to promote healthful diets for children and adolescents. Improving the marketing and media landscape must be integrated across a range of settings, sectors, and stakeholder strategies to achieve the common goal of marketing healthful diets. The report offered ten recommendations for all stakeholders to market healthful diets through integrated strategies addressing food and beverage product formulation and promotion; marketing practice standards; media and entertainment company initiatives; parents, caregivers, and families; schools; government; public and private research capacity; and monitoring and reporting on national progress.

During the IOM committee's data collection phase and deliberations, several companies had provided input to inform the report recommendations. When the IOM report was released, anticipatory actions and positive changes were already underway by specific companies and industry stakeholders to reformulate and improve the nutrient profiles of foods, beverages, and meals; provide clearer nutrition labeling and information to consumers to help them balance their calorie intake with energy expenditure; strengthen industry self-regulatory pledges to enhance the advertising standards relevant to children under 12 years; and invest in marketing communications to promote healthy lifestyles. More has occurred since the release of the 2006 report. This chapter examines the available evidence between December 2005 and January 2011 to assess progress made on these recommendations.

Method of Assessing Progress on the 2006 IOM Recommendations

A coherent assessment of progress on the recommendations of the 2006 IOM Food Marketing report involved acquiring diverse sources of evidence relevant to the specific research and policy questions. We used the principles of the LEAD Framework (locate, evaluate, assemble, decisions) to inform policy and programmatic decisions and actions of diverse stakeholders and sectors to market healthful diets to young people. The LEAD principles were developed for decision makers to use a systems perspective to identify the type of evidence required to answer specific public health questions when evidence is limited but actions must be taken. The LEAD approach was developed by an IOM expert committee in 2011 (Kumanyika, & Parker, Si, 2010); we selected this approach because it was appropriate to the research task to use all available evidence to assess policy activities.

We reviewed electronic databases and other resources to locate relevant peer-reviewed articles, industry and government reports, Congressional hearings, government Websites and media releases, including MEDLINE, Science Direct, LexisNexis, Library of Congress, Business Source Premier, and Mergent. We also conducted an Internet search to supplement these sources with industry and government reports, and relevant nonprofit, foundation and academic institution studies and reports. We selected and categorized 117 pieces of evidence including 47 published reports or articles and 70 media stories and assigned an evaluation of the progress toward the recommendations. We applied five qualitative research criteria to guide the selection and interpretation of resources included in the analysis (1) the importance and relevance of the available evidence; (2) clarity, coherence, and quality of the research design; (3) our professional judgment about stakeholder or sector compliance with specific strategies or actions with attention to research bias; (4) our analysis of the context within which actions were taken; and (5) our assessment of the established credibility of the action as indicated by seeking diverse stakeholder perspectives and verifying evidence. Overall judgment of progress was assessed as no progress, limited progress, moderate progress, or extensive progress.

Assessing Progress on the 2006 Recommendations

The 2006 Food Marketing Report made ten recommendations for various stakeholders to improve the promotion of healthy diets to children and youth and their families. Recommendations 1 through 5 charged food and beverage companies, the restaurant sector, food retailers, industry trade associations, entertainment companies, and the media to use their creativity, resources, and full range of marketing practices to promote and support healthful diets for children and adolescents. Recommendation 6 charged the federal government, in partnership with the private sector, to develop a long-term, multifaceted and financially sustained social marketing program targeting parents, caregivers, and children. Recommendation 7 directed state, district, and local educational authorities to promote healthful diets for children and adolescents in the school environment. Recommendations 8 through 10 charged the federal, state, and local government to use all available public policy tools and direct the nation's research capacity to promote healthful diets for young people, and for the HHS Secretary to designate a responsible agency to monitor and report on progress for all actions within two years of the IOM report release. Progress made by each of the various stakeholders is assessed separately.

Progress Made by Food and Beverage Companies

The committee recommended that food and beverage companies should use creativity, resources, and marketing practices to promote and support more healthful diets and meals for children and youth.

The food and beverage companies have achieved moderate progress in meeting the recommendation. There is evidence that the industry has reformulated and expanded its healthier food options, reduced TV advertising for unhealthy foods and beverages, developed front of pack (FOP) labeling, and developed partnerships to promote more healthful diets.

The most direct and immediate response by the food and beverage companies was to establish a self-regulatory initiative around food marketing to children. In Fall 2006, ten food and beverage companies under the auspices of the Council of Better Business Bureaus established the Children's Food and Beverage Advertising Initiative (CFBAI), an industry self-regulatory entity (CFBAI Website, n.d.). CFBAI now has 17 members including two fast-food restaurants (McDonalds and Burger King) representing well over two-thirds of all food and beverage companies advertising to children. These companies agreed to voluntarily shift their child-directed advertising toward healthier foods. Three CFBAI monitoring reports were released at 6, 12, and 24 months (CFBAI Website, n.d.) that documented high compliance with company pledges for child-directed advertising. Several food and beverage companies promote healthy lifestyles through public–private partnerships with industry coalitions, such as the Healthy Weight Commitment Foundation and the Partnership for a Healthier America. Despite these positive actions, the evaluation of progress found that product reformulations thus far showed only incremental changes to meet healthier nutrient profiles, that there are still unhealthy foods being marketed to children and youth; and that the proliferation of various front of package labeling systems offers different criteria and different symbols for products which can confuse consumers.

Progress Made by the Restaurant Industry

The committee recommended that restaurants should establish and enforce the highest standards for the marketing of foods, beverages, and meals to children and youth. The restaurant industry has been slow to respond to this recommendation and demonstrate only limited progress.

In 2010, the Yale University Rudd Center released a study examining children's and adolescents' meal choices at 12 leading Quick Serve Restaurant chains. The study documented that only 12 children's meal combinations met established nutrition criteria for preschoolers; only 15 meals met nutrition criteria for older children; meals purchased by adolescents provided an average of 800–1,100 calories/meal, representing half of their recommended daily calories; and meals sold to young people rarely offered healthy side dishes as the default choice. Moreover, they found that most of the meals had excessive amounts of sugar, fat, and sodium (Yale University Rudd Center, 2011).

Only Subway and Walt Disney restaurants have designated healthy default choices (i.e., fruits, nonstarchy vegetables, and low-fat or fat-free milk) as the preferred side dishes and beverages, respectively, accompanying children's meals instead of high-calorie, low-nutrient options (i.e., French fries and sugar sweetened beverages). McDonald's and Burger King are the only two restaurants participating in the Children's Food and Beverage Advertising Initiative. Several other leading quick serve restaurants, including YUM! Brands (the parent company for KFC, Taco Bell, and Pizza Hut) and Subway, have not joined the Children's Food and Beverage Advertising Initiative.

Progress Made by the Industry Trade Associations

The 2006 IOM committee report recommended that industry trade associations assume leadership in harnessing industry creativity, resources, and marketing on behalf of healthful diets for children and youth. Only limited progress has been achieved so far. For instance, no trade associations belong to the Children's Food and Beverage Advertising Initiative and no trade associations have made position papers or policies publicly available to support marketing a healthful diet to children and youth.

The most significant activity on the part of industry trade associations was the announcement in December 2010 that the Grocery Manufacturers Association (GMA) (n.d.); in conjunction with the Food Marketing Institute was developing its own Front of Pack Nutrition Labeling System in conjunction with a $50 million advertising campaign. At first called Nutrition Keys, but in September 2011 changed to "Facts Up Front," this system is intended to place nutrition information about calories, saturated fat, sodium, and total sugar on the front of all food packages in the USA (GMA

Website). This system is expected to be rolled out by early 2012. The intent of this proposal is to provide more easily accessible nutritional information to consumers, especially, families as a guide to more healthful diets. However, the Grocery Manufacturers Association developed this program without input from the Food and Drug Administration or Department of Agriculture and it preempted a congressionally requested report on front of pack nutrition labeling conducted by the IOM that was released in October 2011 (IOM, 2011). Importantly, as discussed below, the Facts up Front proposal differs markedly from the IOM recommendations on front of pack nutrition labeling symbols and systems (IOM).

Progress Made by Self-Regulatory Agencies Such as the Children's Advertising Review Unit

The committee recommended that marketing practice standards should be evaluated and that the industry work through the Children's Advertising Review Unit to revise, expand, apply, enforce, and evaluate explicit industry self-regulatory guidelines beyond traditional TV advertising, use licensed characters only to promote foods and beverages that support healthful diets, and cooperate with the FTC to evaluate and enforce the expanded guidelines. Moderate progress has been achieved here.

Under the auspices of the Council of Better Business Bureaus (but separate from their Children's Advertising Review unit), a group of ten food and beverage companies created the Children's Food and Beverage Advertising Initiative within a year of the release of IOM 2006 report. By 2011, this self-regulatory body has 17 member companies and the initial pledges have been considerably advanced. In August 2011, CFBAI released new marketing commitments (CFBAI Website, n.d.). Four companies have now committed to NO advertising to children under 12: Cadbury, Coca Cola, Hershey, and Mars; Nestle USA no longer advertises its Wonka brand to children under 12. All have pledged not to use licensed characters on foods that do not meet their "healthy foods" commitment. Thirteen companies pledged to advertise only foods that meet Dietary Guidelines for Americans and Food and Drug Administration standards of "healthy." Typically, these are foods that meet the "35,10,35" standard of no more than 35% of calories from fat, less than 10% calories from saturated fat, and no more than 35% of calories from sugars or no more than 35% by weight. These companies are Burger King, Campbell Soup, ConAgra Foods, the Dannon Company, General Mills, Kellogg, Kraft Foods Global, McDonalds, Nestle USA, PEPSICO, Post Foods, Sara Lee, and Unilever. Moreover, CFBAI members have considerably expanded the media platforms covered by these pledges to include: all advertising directed to children under 12 on TV, radio, print, the Internet (including third-party Websites and company-owned Websites), advertising on video and computer games rated EC, those child directed, cell phone or PDA marketing to children (CFBAI Website, n.d.). This is a considerable advance in regulatory marketing standards expanding self-regulation to more companies, more marketing venues, and with the development of a common set of nutritional standards.

There is still room for improvement. Unfortunately, these new standards do not include marketing to adolescents. Further, they only include measured media spending (representing media categories that companies use to promote products systematically tracked by media research companies) and do not apply to unmeasured media spending (representing sales promotions, coupons, and Internet-based marketing that are not systematically tracked). Consequently, there are still marketing venues and practices not covered by the CFBAI pledges just as there is not 100% compliance to self-regulation by all food and beverage companies or trade associations. The CFBAI can and should continue to evolve its recommendations to cover more marketing practices and to expand its membership.

Progress Made by Media and Entertainment Companies

The committee recommended that the media and entertainment industry should direct its extensive power to promote healthful foods and beverages for children and youth, including incorporating foods, beverages, and story lines that promote healthful diets and by serving as accurate interpreters and reporters on findings, claims, and practices related to the diets of children and youth. Evidence would suggest that the media and entertainment industry made limited progress during the period reviewed.

The Center for Science in the Public Interest evaluated food marketing policies among media companies in 2010 (Wootan, Batada, Balekes, 2010). Their report showed that only one quarter of entertainment companies had a clear policy on food marketing to children. Where policies do exist they address the use of third-party licensed characters. The Center for Science in the Public Interest was not impressed by the policies and deemed them weak in specifying nutritional standards for products marketed through broadcast, print, and digital media and product placements in children's shows. Only Walt Disney and Sesame Workshop reported limiting child-directed marketing to products meeting specific nutrition standards. The Cartoon Network developed policies for licensed characters but lacked policies for other promotional activities. Nickelodeon neither had nutrition standards nor a clear policy about food marketing to children despite earlier public commitments to implement policies (Wootan et al., 2010).

One evaluation found that the percentage of advertisements for high-calorie and low-nutrient foods aired by entertainment companies decreased only slightly between 2005 and 2009 (before and after the CFBAI was implemented) from about nine in ten (88%) to eight in ten (79%) food advertisements. No children's entertainment companies currently participate in the CFBAI.

It may be that there has been an increase in story lines on scripted television shows which promote healthy eating practices. This is difficult to assess. Similarly, research on news stories promoting healthy eating has not been assessed. The committee recommended that government at all levels should use the full range if public policy levers to foster the development and promotion of healthful diets for children and youth. They suggested such actions as improving the nutritional aspects of school meals, using the Federal Trade Commission and Federal Communications Commission to legislate healthful food marketing in broadcasting and cable television and developing a long-term social marketing campaign to help parents, caregivers, and families (especially of children under four years old) in promoting healthful diets. Government response to these recommendations has been mixed, at best making some limited progress. For instance, the government has not developed a social marketing campaign. However, First Lady Michelle Obama's *Let's Move!* Campaign signed an agreement between the Partnership for a Healthier America and the Healthy Weight Commitment Foundation, pledging $40 million and $20 million dollars, respectively, to support obesity prevention (The White House Office of the First Lady, 2010a). The federal government released Healthy Commitment 2020 (Department of Health and Human Services, 2010) that included three social marketing objectives but excluded any reference to promoting a healthful diet to children and adolescents. Government was charged with using incentives to reward companies to promote healthier foods and beverages; using all policy tools (i.e., subsidies, taxes, legislation, and regulation) to increase fruit and vegetable availability and access; and empowering USDA to develop and test new strategies to promote healthier meals through the federal school meals programs. Not much progress has been made yet on these recommendations. Congress did establish and Interagency Working Group (2009) to recommend nutritional standards for foods marketed to children in December 2009. The four agencies are the Center for Disease Control, Food and Drug Administration, Federal Trade Commission, and USDA. The Interagency Working Group released its draft recommendations in April 2011 and during summer 2011 received comments from industry and the public. The Interagency Working Group was specifically charged with developing a set of principles to guide industry efforts to improve the nutritional profile of foods marketed to children aged 2–17. These are voluntary standards with a five-year phase in. The interim report recommended that by 2016 foods most heavily marketed to children (breakfast cereals, snack foods, candy, dairy products, baked goods, carbonated beverages, fruit juice and noncarbonated beverages, prepared foods and meals, frozen and chilled desserts, and restaurant foods) should meet two basic nutritional principles. First, foods marketed to children should provide a meaningful contribution to a healthful diet with contributions from at least one of the following: fruit, vegetable, whole grain, fat free or low fat milk, fish, extra lean meat or poultry, eggs, nuts and seeds, and beans. Second, foods should minimize nutrients with negative impact on health. Foods marketed should not contain more than 1 gram or less per RACC or less of calories of saturated fat; 0 gram per RACC of trans fat, no more than 13 grams of added sugars per serving, and no more than 210 mg per serving of sodium. Two important points should be noted about the draft report: it expands nutritional marketing standards to foods and beverages marketed to youth beyond age 12 which is the upper limit of self-regulatory actions by CARU and CFBAI; while the draft report does not specify the specific marketing venues, it could go beyond the traditional media such as print, TV, and radio to include the internet and mobile marketing for cell phones and other devices. During

Congressional hearings in the Fall 2011, the industry argued strenuously against the interim recommendations; the Interagency Working Group has not yet released the final standards as of the end of 2011.

Educational leaders, school districts, and local schools made moderate progress to create healthier eating environments for students. The IOM report charged stakeholders with developing and implementing nutrition standards for competitive foods and beverages sold or served in schools, and adopting model school wellness policies (SWP) and practices to expand the availability of foods and beverages that support a healthful diet. The IOM report on Healthy People 2020 (IOM, 2011) included objectives to increase healthy foods and beverages at schools and the number of states implementing nutrition standards for preschoolers in child-care settings increased. Despite these efforts, the Center for Science in the Public Interest (2010) found widespread availability of unhealthy competitive foods especially for older students; and in-school marketing of high-calorie, nutrient-poor foods used for classroom celebrations and school fundraisers. Most importantly in December 2010, the Healthy Hunger Free Kids Act, 2010; The White House Office of the Press Secretary, 2010; The White House (n.d.) was signed into law. This legislation is expected to improve nutrition in schools by establishing nutrition standards for competitive school foods, implement new food safety guidelines, and support public private partnerships to reduce obesity. In January 2011, USDA released a proposed rule to update the nutritional standards of meals served through the national school meals program. This suggests that movement on this recommendation is advancing now with moderate success.

Progress Made in Research and Monitoring

The 2006 IOM report made two final recommendations to encourage new policies regarding healthy eating. It recommended new research on the newer marketing techniques (especially digital media directed at youth) and their impact on children's diets and it recommended that the Secretary of Health and Human Services monitor the response to these recommendations.

There has been some progress on the research front. The major funder of research on obesity since the IOM report was released has been the Robert Wood Johnson Foundation. It supports five national programs and projects: Healthy Eating Research, Rudd Center for Food Policy and Obesity, Bridging the Gap, National Policy and Legal Analysis Network to Prevent Childhood Obesity, and African American Collaborative Obesity Research Network. In 2009, the National Collaborative on Childhood Obesity Research (NCCOR) was formed with NIH, CDC, USDA, and RWJF representatives to prioritize future research and identify best practices for community-based obesity prevention and control (NCCOR Website, n.d.).

Several government agencies have recently announced research activities. NIH supported obesity-prevention research in several areas in 2010, and it released a draft obesity research strategic plan that recommended studying the effects of broadcast and digital media marketing on decision making, energy intake, and physical activity, and testing child- and parent-friendly technologies to support behavior changes. In early 2011, USDA and the National Institute of Food and Agriculture announced that $8.6 million dollars would be available for childhood obesity research (U.S. Department of Agriculture Office of Communications Office of Communications, 2011). Finally, there has been no movement in monitoring the response to these recommendations, and by 2011 the Secretary of Health and Human Services had not yet designated a responsible agency to formally monitor and report on progress on all of the recommendations of the 2006 IOM report.

Other Policy-Related Activities

While the 2006 IOM report's recommendations have led to at least limited advancement of actions to promote healthier food options for children and to limit more unhealthy foods, there have been other policy activities which are advancing. Most importantly, there has been renewed interest in developing mechanisms to inform American consumers and especially families about the nutritional profile of packaged foods. In 2009 Congress asked the Centers for Disease Control to conduct a study to examine the use of symbols on food packages which summarize key nutritional aspects and characteristics of food products. Congress expressed concern about the proliferation of nutritional claims and symbols used on the front of food packaging and on grocery shelves that had developed in the past several years and the possibility that they may be confusing to consumers. CDC went to the Institute of Medicine for a study committee on Front of Pack Nutrition Labeling and Symbol Systems (IOM, 2011).

The IOM convened an ad hoc committee to "review systems being used by manufacturers, supermarkets, health organizations and governments in the US and abroad and the overall merits of front-label nutrition icons, the advantages and disadvantages of various approaches and the potential benefits of a single standardized front label food guidance system regulated by the FDA." (IOM, 2011). The Front of Pack Nutrient Symbols and Systems committee released its report in October 2011. It made two major recommendations. First, it recommended that the Food and Drug Administration and the Department of Agriculture "should develop, test and implement a single, standard Front of Pack system to appear on all products." The system should be one simple standard symbol, displaying calories and from 0 to 3 points for meeting acceptable levels of saturated and trans fats, sodium, and added sugars. This symbol should be in a consistent location on all packages for all grocery products. It should be consistent with the Nutrition Facts Panel on the back of the package and it should be nonproprietary and transparent. Second, the committee recommended that introduction of the Front of Pack Symbol System should include an ongoing awareness and promotion campaign that monitors and evaluates the impact of the Front of Pack Symbol System. The IOM committees report is now with the FDA and USDA for review and implementation.

Two other policy-related reports will provide insight into food marketing practices. The Federal Trade Commission is expected to release its report on expenditures on food marketing by 44 leading food and beverages companies in early 2012, and this is a follow up on the FTC's 2009 report. Finally, another IOM study committee convened to determine what recommendations of previous IOM reports should be engaged to advance progress on obesity prevention; the Advancing Progress on Obesity Prevention study report from the Institute of Medicine is expected in spring 2012.

Conclusion

The 2006 IOM report on Food Marketing and the Diets of Children and Youth has indeed been a foundational document which both established evidence on the role of food marketing in influencing children's food preferences, food choices and diets, and which led to recommendations which have been advanced with variable progress over the past six years. While some recommendations have not been advanced at all—such as the call for a national public information campaign about healthy foods and good nutrition—there has been at least limited progress on most of the other recommendations. Importantly, most of this progress has occurred in the past two years and with the prospect of other reports and studies appearing in the next two years, food marketing practices are likely to undergo changes. As a nation, we appear to be inching closer to increasingly marketing healthy foods to children and families and reducing the marketing of unhealthy foods. Since the health of our children is at stake, food marketing practices need to change as quickly as possible.

References

Beales, J. H., III. (2004). Advertising to kids and the FTC: A regulatory retrospective that advises the present. *George Mason Law Review, 12*, 873–895.

Children's Food and Beverage Advertising Initiative (CFBAI) (n.d.). Children's Food and Beverage Advertising Initiative. Retrieved from http://www.bbb.org/us/children-food-beverage-advertising-initiative/.

Giddings, S. S., Dennison, B. A., Birch, L. L., Daniels, S. R., Gillman, M. W., Lichenstein, A. H., et al. (2006). American Heart Association dietary recommendations for children and adolescents: A guide for practioners. *Pediatrics, 117*, 544–559.

Grocery Manufactures of America (GMA) (n.d.). GMA website. Retrieved from http://www.gmaonline.org/.

Healthy Hunger Free Kids Act of 2010, Public Law 111–296 (S 3307) December 13, 2010.

Interagency Working Group. (2009). Tentative proposed nutrition standards. Washington, DC, December 15.

Institute of Medicine (IOM). (2006). *Food marketing to children and youth: Threat or opportunity?* Washington, DC: The National Academies Press.

Institute of Medicine (IOM). (2005). *Preventing childhood obesity: Health in the balance*. Washington, DC: The National Academies Press.

Institute of Medicine (IOM). (2011). *Front of pack nutrition rating systems and symbols: Promoting healthier choices*. Washington, DC: National Academies Press.

Kumanyika, S. K., Parker, L., & Sim, L. J. (Eds.). (2010). *Bridging the evidence gap in obesity prevention: A framework to inform decision making*. Washington, DC: The National Academies Press.

National Collaborative on Childhood Obesity Research. (NCCOR) (n.d.). National Collaborative on Childhood Obesity Research. Retrieved from National Collaborative on Childhood Obesity Research

The White House. (n.d.). The White House website. Retrieved from http://www.whitehouse.gov/.

The White House office of the Press Secretary. (2010). President Obama signs healthy, hunger-free kids act of 2010 into law. [press release]. Retrieved from http://www.whitehouse.gov/the-press-office/2010/12/13/president-obama-signs-healthy-hunger-free-kids-act-2010-law.

The White House Office of the First Lady. (2010a). *First Lady Michelle Obama launches Let's Move: Americas' move to raise a healthier generation of kids* [press release]. Retrieved from http://www.whitehouse.gov/the-press-office/first-lady-michelle-obama-launches-lets-move-americas-move-raise-a-healthier-genera.

U.S. Department of Agriculture Office of Communications. (2011). USDA unveils critical upgrades to nutritional standards for school meals. Retrieved from http://www.usda.gov/wps/portal/usda/usdahome?contentidonly=true&contentid=2011/01/0010.xml.

U.S. Department of Health and Human Services Office of Disease Prevention and Healthy Priorities. (2010). Healthy People 2020. Publication NO. B0132, Retrieved from http://www.healthypeople.gov/2020/TopicsObjectives2020/pdfs/HP2020_brochure_with_LHI_508.pdf.

US Department of Health and Human Services (USHHS), & Department of Agriculture (USDA). (2005). *Dietary Guidelines for Americans, 2005*. Washington, DC: US Government Printing Office.

Wootan, M. G., Batada, A., & Balekes, O. (2010). *Food marketing report card: An analysis of food and entertainment company policies to self regulate food and beverage marketing to children*. Washington, DC: Center for Science in the Public Interest.

Yale University Rudd Center. (2011). *Trends in food advertising to young people: 2010 update*. New Haven, CT: Harris, J. L. & Sarda, V.

Chapter 3
Integrated Marketing Communications and Power Imbalance: The Strategic Nature of Marketing to Children and Adolescents by Food and Beverage Companies

Paul Harrison and Michaela Jackson

Context and Introduction

This chapter seeks to complement others in this book by highlighting the public health concerns associated with the use of the relatively new business practice of Integrated Marketing Communications (IMC) to promote energy-dense, nutrient-poor foods and beverages to children and adolescents, and the power imbalances inherent in this situation. Seeking to encourage international awareness and relevance of this issue we have attempted to take a global approach, while still recognizing the Australian context in which both authors work. To this end, we include three case studies of branded food products that target children as a means of demonstrating the reach and complexity of IMC in a contemporary marketplace.

Before we address this topic specifically, it is first important to briefly explore the broader social context in which both IMC and childhood obesity are situated.

Childhood Obesity and Marketing: The Social Context

During the past 40 years, global rates of overweight and obesity have risen dramatically (Withrow and Alter, 2011). In 2010 more than 155 million children worldwide were overweight (more than one in ten) and of these approximately 30–45 million were obese, or between two and three per cent of the world's 5–17-year-old children (Polmark, 2010, p. 3).

P. Harrison (✉) • M. Jackson
Deakin University,
Pigdons Road, Waurn Ponds, VIC 3216, Australia
e-mail: paul.harrison.deakin@me.com

J.D. Williams et al. (eds.), *Advances in Communication Research to Reduce Childhood Obesity*, DOI 10.1007/978-1-4614-5511-0_3,

In exploring causes for the childhood obesity epidemic, researchers have turned their focus to environmental factors. Attention has been given to sociocultural and economic changes that occurred during the 1980s and 1990s, coinciding with the pronounced increase in childhood obesity during this period (Anderson and Butcher, 2006). Highlighting the role of 'obesogenic' environments in the obesity epidemic is significant as it positions obesity as a consequence of our social environment, rather than an individual, medical problem (Swinburn 2009; Economos et al., 2001, p. S41). This has consequences for the way obesity is managed and prevented. Reframing childhood obesity as a social issue also places greater pressure on governments, industry, and policy makers to address the underlying factors that contribute to the obesity epidemic (Schwartz and Puhl, 2003; Economos et al., 2001, p. S41). Some, such as Wadden et al. (2002, p. 512) display elements of critical theory in their assertion that the root cause of the problem lies in "powerful social and cultural forces that promote an energy-rich diet and a sedentary lifestyle."

To be effective, marketing needs to engage with, and situate itself appropriately within, the broader social context (Groom and Biernatzki, 2008, p. 7). During the past 10 years, public health and related research has consistently and repeatedly pointed to parallels between changes in marketing and increases in childhood overweight and obesity rates during the past 40 years (e.g., Harris et al., 2009; Hastings et al., 2006; McGinnis et al., 2006; Mehta et al., 2010).

Coincidence or Consequence? Parallels Between Childhood Obesity and Marketing

The Institute of Medicine's systematic review of literature *Food marketing to children and youth: threat or opportunity?* establishes that there is a relationship between adiposity, diets and diet-related health, and marketing (McGinnis et al., 2006, p. 378). The World Health Organization similarly drew upon this report, and a review conducted by Hastings et al. to declare "a robust evidence base to support the fact that exposure to the commercial promotion of energy-dense, micronutrient poor foods and beverages adversely affects children's diets" (World Health Organization, 2006, p. 26). They highlight evidence of significant amounts of food and beverage promotion targeting children – children's awareness and engagement with this promotion – with the majority of this promotion being for unhealthy foods and beverages. The report argues that such promotion influences children's awareness, attitudes, behavior, and consumption (World Health Organization, 2006, p. 13). Within an Australian context Metha et al. (2010) similarly determined that the types of foods marketed towards children were primarily unhealthy, and that such marketing was perceived to have an influence on children's preference for branded and unhealthy foods.

Marketing to children as a subspecialty emerged in the business context in the 1980s (Mehta et al., 2010) and since this time there has been significant growth in products, especially food products, which specifically target this audience. Marketers can potentially benefit not only by promoting products specifically designed to appeal to children, and their parents and caregivers but also in establishing the foundations of longer term brand relationships (Asquith, 2009).

Changes have also occurred to the nature of messages and creative appeals that marketers use in reaching target consumers. During the late 1950s and early 1960s, marketing appeals targeting children underwent a shift from focusing on product attributes towards increased use of symbolism, classic archetypes, and appeals to cultural values (Schor & Ford, 2007, p. 15). For example, Schor and Ford (2007) highlight the increased role of 'cool' in marketing a variety of products and services to children and adolescents. In this way, marketing food products to children – and the growth of this subcategory as a whole – relies less on the nutritive or functional qualities of food, and more on the symbols and signs that create and reflect meaning in a child's world (Schor & Ford, 2007).

Indeed, children are recognized as a significant consumer force—whether making their own consumer decisions or through influencing those of their caregivers or family members (McGinnis, Gootman, & Kraak, 2006, p. 5). While using such appeals is effective in reaching children and establishing brand relationships, it also plays a broader role in engendering children and adolescents' role as independent consumers and legitimate members of a consumer society (Schor and Ford, 2007, p. 10; Cook, 2000).

Concerns and Responses

Rising concerns about the childhood obesity epidemic has led to regulatory and voluntary responses in many countries, and policy development by international organizations such as the World Health Organization (McGinnis et al., 2006, p. 362). In particular, there has been mounting pressure to regulate unhealthy food marketing to children (Hawkes, 2007, p. 1962). Among both public health and marketing literatures there is evidence that these industries are feeling threatened by the prospect of statutory regulation, taxation, fines, and restrictions regarding food marketing to children (Wansink & Huckabee, 2005, p. 1; Grimm, 2004, p. 44; Lewin, Lindstrom, & Nestle, 2006, p. 343). The food industry, and to a lesser extent the marketing industry, have attempted to defend their actions by suggesting calls for action within the sector that do not necessarily reduce their capacity to generate profits (Grimm, 2004; Wansink & Huckabee, p. 11). Wansink and Huckabee, for example, emphasize the importance of a laissez-faire approach favoring market-driven strategies that stimulate consumer desire for healthier food options (Wansink & Huckabee, p. 12).

In addition, food companies have sponsored research and worked to reformulate existing products to increase their health benefits; examples include the removal of trans-fats, reductions in sugar and salt, increased use of whole grains, and fortification of products with vitamins and minerals (Brownell & Warner, 2009, p. 283).

These initiatives form part of a broader repositioning of food and beverage companies and the industry as a whole. Public health professionals such as Brownell and Warner are critical of the way industry has framed their responses to childhood obesity issue, drawing similarities between the food and beverage industry and the prior actions of other threatened industries, most pointedly the tobacco industry (Sharma, Teret, & Brownell, 2010, p. 240; Brownell & Warner, 2009).

Self-regulation has emerged as a common response to this issue. Yet the majority of resulting self-regulation measures only target advertising (Hawkes, 2007, p. 1962). Advertising has historically been a dominant and influential technique in marketing, but in the face of media and audience fragmentation, technological advancements (especially the proliferation of digital technologies), and more sophisticated measurement and evaluation techniques, advertising is now one of an ever-increasing number of promotional techniques used by companies to reach their targeted audience segments. McGinnis, Gootman, and Kraak (2006, p. xiv), highlight that virtually all of the published scientific research has "focused on advertising—and television advertising in particular" but also caution that "advertising does not exist or operate in isolation from other aspects of marketing activities" (McGinnis et al., 2006, p. 21). Packaging, sales promotion, use of cartoon characters, and celebrity endorsement have also all attracted varying levels of attention from public health advocates (Hawkes, 2009; Hawkes, 2010).

The public health literature reviewed for this chapter reveals strong dissatisfaction with the current situation. Brownell and Warner (2009) and Nestle and Jacobson (2000) emphasize what they believe to be an irreconcilable situation for the food industry: profit generation rests on the increased sale of food, and similarly foods which generate the most profit for the food industry are not those that provide the healthiest options for consumers.

Method

In developing this chapter, we have synthesized information from academic databases, published reports, and professional literature. In our search, we have included databases such as Ebscohost Research Databases, Academic OneFile, Academic Search Complete, APA Full Text, Business Source Complete, Expanded Academic ASAP, Factiva, and Google Scholar. Within these databases search terms (and combinations of these terms), such as childhood obesity, marketing to children, unhealthy food marketing, Integrated Marketing Communication, and IMC, were used to identify relevant materials. Professional literature such as Stanmark Child Exposure to Food Marketing News, The International Association for the Study of Obesity Newsletter, the Rudd Center Health Digest, Croakey Health Blog, mUmbrella, and brandchannel were also consulted for items relevant to the research question as were published reports and documents from organizations such as the World Health Organization (WHO), Which?, Flinders University, Choice, the Polmark Project,

Stanmark, Consumers International, the International Association for the Study of Obesity (IASO), and the Organization for Economic Cooperation and Development (OECD).

Information search and review was conducted between November 2010 and July 2011. Publication dates, quality of publishing source, and frequency of citation (where available) were considered in reviewing sources in addition to the primary criteria of relevance of content to the research question.

We acknowledge the limitations inherent to a narrative literature review, such as subjectivity and potential for bias in selecting and reviewing sources and the lack of guaranteed breadth of coverage of available literature.

The Evolution and Growth of Integrated Marketing Communication

What Is IMC?

In broad terms, marketing's evolution can be charted through four distinct phases, corresponding to broader socioeconomic eras, viz., production orientation, product orientation, sales orientation, to marketing orientation (Lancaster & Massingham, 2011). Earlier phases are associated with the broader socioeconomic concept of modernity, characterized by mass production and consumption, dominant ideologies, order and progress (Van Raaij, 1993, p. 544; Christensen, Torp, & Firat, 2005). Marketing was typified by a focus on the product and its characteristics, and a reliance on relatively few mass media channels to deliver marketing messages to broadly segmented audiences. Marketing functions were clearly segmented, conceptualized, and implemented.

By contrast, postmodernity (which by its very nature defies definition) can be broadly characterized as a rejection of modernity, resulting from post-war economic and social transformation in the West (Ross, 1988) in (Firat & Venkatesh, 1993, p. 227). In contrast to modernity's mass production, centralization, and sense of dominant style, postmodernity is characterized by qualities such as plurality, eclecticism and inclusion, pastiche, and decentralization (Van Raaij, 1993, p. 543).

The concept of Integrated Marketing Communication (IMC) emerged as a result of a shift towards consumer-focused marketing during the 1970s and 1980s (Groom & Biernatzki, 2008). Despite generating significant discussion among marketing academics and practitioners, less than a decade ago IMC was regarded as being in its conceptual infancy, lacking an established academic or professional definition, and with its theoretical underpinnings still in development (Kitchen, Brignell, Tao, & Jones, 2004, p. 23).

Several attempts have been made to define IMC, with results varying in complexity (see definitions provided by Kitchen & Schultz, 2009; Keller, 2001; Duncan

& Caywood, 1996; Shimp & Shimp 1997; Smith et al. 1999). The definition of IMC adopted by the American Association of Advertising Agencies, and consequently one of the most frequently cited by academic and marketing industry professionals in the decade following its development, was devised by Duncan and Caywood in 1996 (Kliatchko, 2005, p. 14). This definition states that IMC is

"a concept of marketing communications planning that recognizes the added value of a comprehensive plan that evaluates the strategic roles of a variety of communication disciplines—general advertising, direct response, sales promotion, and public relations—and combines these disciplines to provide clarity, consistency, and maximum communication impact" (Duncan & Caywood 1996 in Kliatchko, 2005, p. 14).

Shimp and Shimp alternatively chose to identify five distinguishing features of IMC: 'start with the customer or prospect; use any form of relevant contact or touch point; speak with a single voice; build relationships; affect behavior,' (Shimp & Shimp, 1997, p. 20).

Shultz and Kitchen proposed four stages of marketing communications integration within an organization. The first and most rudimentary stage of IMC focus simply on coordinating different tactical elements of promotional campaigns (Schultz & Kitchen, 2000). Stage two involves gathering extensive information about markets, but not necessarily using that information in a sophisticated way for targeting. The third stage, "applying information technology," relates to the application of information technology to more effectively analyze and manage information, then using this information to target and communicate with audience segments (Schultz & Kitchen, 2000, p. 26). The final and most sophisticated stage is "financial and strategic integration" in which IMC is evaluated on an ongoing basis in terms of its return on investment (Schultz & Kitchen, 2000, p. 26).

Echoing ideas of postmodernity, some authors argue against a single definition of IMC claiming that the concept itself is not static, but has evolved since the term was coined (Fill, 2001; Kliatchko, 2005, p. 21; Schultz & Patti, 2009, p. 76). Kitchen, Kim, and Schultz (2008) proposed that IMC should be perceived more accurately as a three-dimensional model, as opposed to uniform definition. Christensen, Torp, and Firat (2005) extend the idea of plurality to warn of the risks associated with applying modern structures and restrictions to postmodern concepts and contexts (Christensen et al., 2005).

Acknowledging the concepts of flexibility, fluidity, and polyphony, we prefer to describe IMC based on its characteristics, and on descriptions provided by Shimp and Shimp (1997) and Schulz and Kitchen (2000), thereby at least recognizing the potential for movement, discussion, and change as to what comprises this concept.

IMC as Marketing Modus Operandi

Despite its theoretical challenges, IMC has been embraced by commercial marketing practitioners. IMC represents a paradigmatic shift in the way marketers view marketing communications (Gould, 2004). In the context of marketing communications, IMC has been declared "*the* major communications development in the last decade of the 20th Century" (Kitchen, Brignell, Tao, et al., 2004) p. 20.

IMC proponents argue that shifting from individual, autonomously managed marketing communications strategies (such as advertising or sales promotions) to an IMC approach means individual communications tactics no longer stand alone, but become part of a broader, synergistic communications whole designed around the consumer. In applying IMC, marketers must select the best combination of different tactics to achieve maximum effect (Keller, 2001, p. 819). IMC thus encourages broader consideration of the opportunities afforded by different marketing communications disciplines in a systematic way. Having a broader, and ever-growing, range of tactics and possible combinations at their professional disposal also enables marketers to more effectively reach audience members—combining the unique advantages of different communications mediums to achieve different objectives.

IMC has become increasingly recognized as effective, especially in the face of reduced marketing budgets, the decreasing effectiveness of traditional tactics such as television advertising, media proliferation, and changing consumer preferences (Kitchen, Brignell, Tao, et al., 2004, p. 20). In a study of senior advertising executives, respondents reported that IMC improved the effectiveness of creative ideas, offered increased consistency of communication, greater communications impact, and offered overall improved return on client investment (Kitchen, 2005, p. 74).

Earlier this century critics raised concerns that IMC was little more than a management fad (Cornelissen, 2001; Cornelissen & Lock, 2000; Kitchen, Brignell, Tao, et al., 2004). However, its supporters have countered these attacks by referring to the concept's popularity and longevity (Kitchen et al., 2008). Indeed, IMC's evolution into branding and management applications seems to offer arguments that the technique is here to stay (Kitchen, Brignell, Tao, et al., 2004). More broadly, IMC's expansion and influence is illustrated by the degree to which marketing and culture are becoming increasingly intertwined (Taylor, 2009).

IMC as Strategic Business Approach

IMC takes an 'outside in' approach by placing the customer at the core of business functions; its point of difference is that it is grounded in communications (Christensen et al., 2005). Relationships with the customer are key (Kitchen, Brignell, Tao, et al., 2004).

Early in the twenty-first century IMC was recognized as having moved beyond a communication process to being associated with management and brands (Kitchen, Brignell, Tao, et al., 2004). Effective marketing communication is no longer built on the assumption that a loyal and receptive mass audience will accept company-sponsored messages. Instead, companies recognize the need to deeply understand consumer and stakeholder decision making, and through the use of IMC, craft integrated messages that position products and brands appropriately within the minds of consumers (Proctor & Kitchen, 2002). Underlying brand values and attributes should likewise be reflected across all levels, channels, and behavior within an organization to further ensure consistency.

In the context of tobacco marketing, Dewhirst and Davis analyzed the extent to which Canadian company Imperial Tobacco Limited applied a sophisticated IMC approach to successfully build brand equity and shareholder value in the face of legal and political challenges (Dewhirst & Davis, 2005, p. 81). In the 30-year period to 2000, the firm grew its market share to 30% (Dewhirst & Davis, 2005). Further, in this case the authors found that "the legal and political environment facing the firm further facilitated ITL's adoption of an IMC mindset and structure." (Dewhirst & Davis, 2005, p. 81). Although only a handful of organizations apply IMC to the most sophisticated levels (Schultz & Kitchen, 2000, p. 26), this example demonstrates the power of IMC in not only establishing brands, but its potential as a sophisticated business strategy.

IMC: Associated Ethical Challenges and Power Imbalance

Potentially Problematic Aspects of IMC

Despite its widespread use, exploration of the ethical issues or considerations associated with IMC remain limited (Kliatchko, 2009). This is not to say that ethical issues associated with traditional forms of marketing do not apply to IMC—as part of the broader marketing discipline, IMC is subject to many of the existing ethical concerns surrounding marketing. By reviewing consumer behavior, marketing, public health, and ethics literature, the following aspects of IMC, as used to promote energy-dense, nutrient-poor foods and beverages to children and adolescents, have been identified as problematic (e.g., Nairn & Fine, 2008; Grimm, 2004; Harris, Brownell, & Bargh, 2009; Kliatchko, 2009; Powell, Dodd, & Langlands, 2010; Preston, 2004; Schor & Ford, 2007; Stanley, 2007). The first two are characteristics of marketing more broadly, while the last three have been drawn from marketing, consumer behavior, ethics, and sociology literature:

- Challenges caregiver authority
- Exploits cognitive development and processing
- Engages with target customer using multiple communication channels (Shimp & Shimp, 1997).
- Engages target consumers in co-creation
- Leverages subtlety, whereby tactics are increasingly being integrated into traditionally non-promotional opportunities.

In addition, we argue that the power disparity between individuals and industry is an underlying theme of all marketing activities, and incorporate this element in our overall model, and discuss it later in this chapter. As outlined in Fig. 3.1, taken

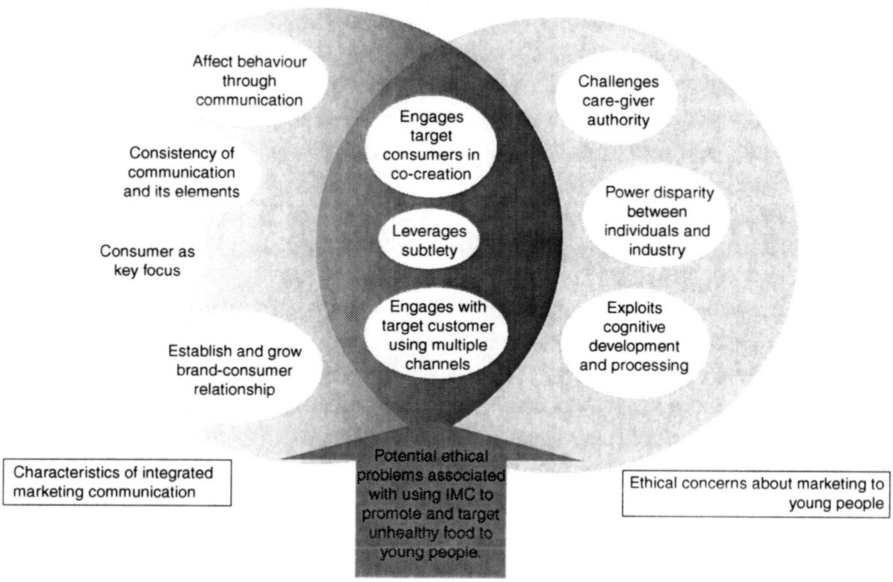

Fig. 3.1 Ethical risks associated with the use of IMC to promote unhealthy food to young people

together these characteristics represent ethical challenges unique to IMC as it is used to promote energy-dense, nutrient-poor foods and beverages to children and adolescents. The ethical implications of these characteristics are discussed below.

IMC Challenges Caregiver Authority

Parents and caregivers hold responsibility for the wellbeing of their children. We argue that this aspect of parents' role is undermined by marketing activities that seek to challenge caregiver authority; one form of which has been termed by mainstream media as "pester power." Pester power refers to children actively influencing their parents purchasing decisions and can include techniques such as nagging, as well as appeals using logic and emotion (Powell et al., 2010). Research reveals that children as young as 3 years of age successfully use pester power, and by age eight children have learned which techniques produce the best results (Powell et al.).

Using appeals such as fun, entertainment, and happiness enables marketers to build a desire amongst children and adolescents for products their parents may view as not the best choice in the long term. By targeting children and adolescents, who themselves have more limited purchasing power than their parents, marketers in essence are using children to overcome parental, and in many cases purchaser, resistance to their products. It can also be argued that marketers are taking advantage of the emotional connection between young people and their parents, and the effectiveness of word-of-mouth message delivery used by children and adolescents to present persuasive messages to their parents.

IMC Exploits Cognitive Development and Processing

Several studies have examined the cognitive abilities of children and adolescents at different ages and stages of development (for example, see Nairn & Fine, 2008; Wadden et al., 2002; Kliatchko, 2005; Hawkes, 2007). Although there is debate in this field, Piaget's theory of cognitive development and information processing models have provided popular foundations for researchers to examine when children are able to distinguish marketing and advertising content, and when they can recognize advertising's persuasive intent (Livingstone & Helsper, 2006, p. 562; Harris et al., 2009).

According to McGinnis, Gootman, and Kraak (2006), children start to develop a basic ability to recognize the persuasive intent of television advertising at around 7 or 8 years of age, but additional time and maturity is needed for children to consistently apply this skill. Young children are not fully able to view circumstances from a perspective other than their own—hence they cannot understand a marketer's perspective in promoting different products or brands (John, 1999). So while a child as young as two may be able to recognize logos (Harris et al., 2009, p. 229), they may not understand meaning behind them or the intent with which they are used.

Criticisms have been made of an age-based approach however, and of public policy that is based on a "magic age" at which children can understand advertising and thereby become better able to manage its persuasive influence (Nairn & Fine, 2008, p. 183). Some researchers argue that the notion of rational cognition and the capacity of young people to reflect upon the influence of advertising should be revised in light of our understanding of dual processing models. Fine and Harrison (2007), for example, point out that advertising targeted at children (and also that which is not) will influence children's implicit attitudes towards advertised products, and consumption, in general. From an ethical perspective, marketers and public policy makers need not only to consider whether marketing exploits children and adolescents' cognitive development but also whether it seeks to bypass these cognitive processes once they have developed (Nairn & Fine).

IMC Engages Target Consumers in Co-creation

Drawing on aspects of Marxist theory, co-creation refers to a management technique whereby marketers rely on the active participation of now allegedly "empowered, entrepreneurial, and liberated" consumers, encouraging a form of political power associated with the emergence and exploitation of creative and valuable labor (Zwick, Bonsu, & Darmody, 2008, p. 164). By positioning the consumer as being in charge, co-creation recognizes consumers' competence and consequently puts them to work. Co-creation is valuable not just in that it offers labor costs savings, but encourages deep brand engagement among both brand advocates and resisters, and enables marketers to sell value-added products at a premium (Zwick et al.).

Within the context of using IMC to market unhealthy food to children and adolescents the ethical risks of co-creation are magnified for two reasons:

1. The issue of unpaid labor becomes increasingly problematic when the creative work is performed by children and adolescents.
2. The product category children and adolescents are engaging with is a product that is implicated with the current childhood obesity epidemic.

Marketers may argue that co-creation is voluntary, therefore nullifying arguments regarding exploitation of labor. However, the voluntary nature of co-creation still stands at odds with the profit-seeking motives of the organization's that employ this technique (Zwick et al., 2008).

IMC Leverages Subtlety and Increasingly Integrates Marketing into Traditionally Non-promotional Contexts

Consumer cynicism to traditional forms of advertising and overt marketing has increased (Zwick et al., 2008; Harris & Whalen, 2006), while advertising has also been criticized for encouraging unnecessary purchases, use of harmful products, and increasing prices (Harris et al., 2006). To maintain the interest and favor of an increasingly jaded audience, marketers have developed a multitude of marketing tactics and channels that blur the once clear lines between editorial and advertising, information and entertainment (Zwick et al.). So, while marketers seek to minimize drawbacks associated with traditional advertising, consumers of all ages may be less likely to identify and be reflective when they are being marketed to, in turn making them potentially more receptive (at an implicit, rather than explicit level) to marketing messages. In a 2004 survey of marketing professionals, Grimm found that 91% believed their colleagues were "marketing to kids 'in ways they don't even notice'" (Grimm, 2004, p. 15).

Subtle messages are often designed to work on affective or implied associations, bypassing rational modes of thinking that as discussed earlier is not even fully developed among young children (Nairn & Fine, 2008; Fine and Harrison 2007). Yet research also shows that once a relationship between a brand and consumer is established, consumers who are exposed to stimulus about that brand, automatically retrieve relevant associations and information stored in their memory (Harris et al., 2009), providing a shortcut to previous brand or product experiences.

In this way, there is a gap between what consumers think they are seeing and may believe is noncommercial content, and what in fact is being delivered as marketing to a largely unknowing, and therefore more receptive audience. This point is compounded by the previously discussed argument that children are not as capable cognitively at distinguishing advertising from noncommercial content, and enhanced by the ethical risks highlighted in the next section, where we consider the volume and diversity of marketing messages.

IMC Engages with Target Customer Using Multiple Communication Channels

IMC encourages the use of multiple channels to reach target audience members. This approach makes logical sense; to close the gaps between communication "moments" essentially increases the chance of your target audience seeing your message. However, media fragmentation, and the rate at which new and potential promotional channels are being developed have resulted in media exposure overdrive (Nairn & Fine, 2008). Promotional messages are so prolific in our society that they have become a form of "social wallpaper" (Preston, 2004, p. 365).

It could also be argued that the volume of marketing for energy-dense, nutrient-poor foods and beverages continually primes children and adolescents for unhealthy food consumption of varying forms. The adverse outcome of this 'perpetual priming' is that individuals are less likely to rationally consider their choices, because this requires processing capacity and energy (Strack, Werth, & Deutsch, 2006). Therefore, the ability to maintain willpower is likely to be reduced when individuals experience ego depletion and become fatigued or stressed (Fine and Harrison, 2007). Exposure to large numbers of promotional messages contributes on some level to mental fatigue, thereby increasing our susceptibility to impulse purchasing (Strack et al.). To complete the equation, unhealthy food items are frequently placed in physical locations favorable to impulse purchase, such as supermarket checkouts, vending machines at train stations, and counters at gas stations.

Finally, as we become ever more culturally conditioned to the frequency of such messages there stops being 'a lot' of marketing material; it just becomes the norm. The number of channels being used to deliver marketing messages and resulting constant exposure to promotional messages for unhealthy food both reflects and helps to reinforce the power and legitimacy that unhealthy food marketing has come to occupy within our society.

Power Disparity as an Underlying Theme in the Ethics of IMC

The concepts of power as a concept are often referred to, yet less seldom defined. As stated by Allan, "social scientists understand that power makes the human world go around, but they have a devil of time defining it or determine where it exists" (Allan, 2006, p. 223). Accounting in part for this dilemma is the simultaneous universality and diversity of forms that characterize power.

According to Kotler (1986), marketing is increasingly becoming associated with the management of power. Within a marketing context power is manifest in both 'upstream' and 'downstream' circumstances. Upstream refers to the macro-level conditions or circumstances leading to the marketing activities of an organization, while downstream refers to the development, implementation, and evaluation of consumer-directed marketing activities. Working to influence the 'upstream' environment—a concept that Kotler refers to as *megamarketing*—are five foundations of power that marketers can influence, viz., coercion, rewards, information and expertise, prestige, and legitimacy (Kotler, p. 121).

The food and beverage industry is a well-established and powerful institution within contemporary western culture. The industry involves thousands of companies and stakeholders and millions of products, and because of its size and complexity, it is difficult to establish precisely the size and worth of this sector (Brownell & Warner, 2009, p. 263). In 2006, the World Bank estimated the worth of global food and agriculture industry at $4.8 trillion. In 2007, Euromonitor International estimated the packaged food industry alone to be worth an approximately $1.6 trillion (Murray, 2007, p. 4).

The food industry is highly diversified and fragmented but also organized and politically powerful (Brownell & Warner, 2009). Food—what, when, and how we eat—is also a key element of culture and commerce. The cultural meanings attached to food are communicated through a system of culturally interpreted signs and symbols. Marketers occupy a powerful position as cultural 'brokers', as they help contribute sociocultural meaning to goods beyond their functional purpose (Zukin & Maguire, 2004; McCracken, 1986). Within the context of marketing to children this role of marketers becomes troublesome when appeals such as cool, fun, or popularity are associated with functionally innutritious products (Hastings, McDermott, Angus, Stead, & Thomson, 2006).

The current socioeconomic climate is also associated with ideas of neo-liberalism and individualism, and consumer culture, the latter of which critics claim has entered our mindset and influenced our self-conceptualizations and identity (Knuttila, 2005). Marketing has been implicated as promoting consumption, hedonistic behavior, and undermining ethical values (Lee, Pant, & Ali, 2010).

Influential in this capacity is the mass media, which plays a critical role in delivering messages that positions food and its role within our society (Economos et al., 2001). Marketers therefore play an influential role in not only shaping the symbolic content of food through food marketing, but as buyers of media space, ensure these messages are communicated throughout society. Producing and delivering these messages requires significant resources, as the marketing budgets of food and beverage corporations attest.

Consumers not only purchase the products being advertised but also "consume" the marketing material and embedded cultural messages. Conflict theory, which claims that society is characterized by conflict and that the capitalist class who holds economic power is in a position to dominate and exploit others to maintain its position (Knuttila, 2005, p. 240), helps to frame issues around power disparity in this context. Ethical queries around power are raised when resources available to marketers and consumers are compared. Marketers have at their disposal significant budgets, staff, and technology to collect, manage, and apply this information. By comparison individuals must rely on their own initiative, the work of concerned advocacy groups and limited, and often summative, information that is publicly available through annual reporting and shareholder obligations. While individual, or even groups of, consumers can produce and deliver their own messages, a process made easier through technological advances of the last 30 years, the resources available to them are likely to pale in comparison to their corporate counterparts.

As highlighted by Preston, commercial entities are keen to keep such customer information tightly held, for both political and competitive reasons (Preston, 2004). In this way it appears that the extensive information marketers have about their consumers (Preston, 2004; Cook, 2000). their preferences, tastes, values, lifestyles, spending habits, and a range of other demographic and psychographic information far outweighs that which is available and able to be processed by individual consumers.

The issue of power disparity can also be extended to the legitimate position of the food and beverage industry in our society. From a Weberian perspective, legitimacy theory helps to explain why people consistently and voluntarily submit to authority (Humphreys, 2010a, p. 4). Legitimacy moves beyond obedience to support or acceptance by those under authority (Humphreys, 2010a, p. 3). Mechanisms used by organizations to gain legitimacy within a society can be explicit, such as offering rewards or incentives, or implicit, such as positioning products or brands within everyday cultural contexts (Humphreys, 2010b, p. 492). In exploring how organizations establish legitimacy within the casino industry, Humphreys explains legitimacy as a process in which the social world is shaped by collective stakeholders (Humphreys, 2010a). Through this process organizations facilitate social acceptance. Within the context of this discussion, legitimacy helps to explain the situation in which society permits the marketing of unhealthy food to children and adolescents and why children and adolescents, who without even representation from government, are in a relatively powerless position to oppose.

From a legal perspective, the USA offers protection for both corporate and commercial speech at differing levels under the First Amendment. Historically, corporate speech was offered full protection under the Constitution so long as it dealt with issues of public interest and importance, whereas commercial speech that sought to 'promote commercial transactions' was entitled only to limited protections (Fitzpatrick, 2005, p. 95). Commercial speech was regulated by the Federal Trade Commission and under state laws. More recently, protections offered to commercial speech seem to be expanding, as evidenced by cases such as Nike v Kasky. In light of these changes, public health advocates have remarked that regulators appear defensive in the face of aggressive attacks on First Amendment protections (Piety, 2010, p. 17). Samantha Graff and Tamara Piety discuss the role of the First Amendment in more detail in chapter 5 of this book.

Elsewhere, such as the UK and Australia countries have moved to recognize the concept of 'fairness' in consumer legislation, particularly in relation to the notion of power between two parties entering into contractual agreements. *The Australian Competition and Consumer Act* (Australian Government, 2010), a cooperative reform of the Australian Government and the States and Territories, through the Ministerial Council on Consumer Affairs and legislated in January 2011, specifically bans contracts with "unfair" terms. This, in effect, means that a consumer can argue an unequal balance of power between him or herself and a corporation, may lead to an unfair relationship. Similarly, consumer legislation in the UK protects consumers against unfair standard terms in contracts that they may make with traders. The UK Government (1999) protect consumers from terms that reduce their statutory or common law rights to impose unfair burdens on consumers. Although both these legislative terms refer to contracts, it is arguable that the notion of fairness in exchange between consumers and their purchasing behavior is somewhat translatable to the overwhelming influence of IMC in the food marketing context.

Despite the broader power dynamics and resulting imbalances discussed above there are examples that demonstrate consumer backlash to unethical or unfair practices of marketers. The possible effects of these ethical implications for marketers are highlighted when examples involving consumer backlash of any one of these elements are explored—Nike with regard to exploitation of labor (Proctor and Kitchen, 2002), the tobacco industry when the product itself is associated with public health risks, growing consumer resistance and mistrust of traditional advertising (Stanley, 2007), and in Australia examples such as the "Cash for Comment" affair that highlights consumer anger at undisclosed promotion in the guise of editorial comment.

However, the efforts of consumer advocates such as these, while admirable, again pale when compared to the combined elements that form a significant power imbalance between children and adolescents and the organizations that market unhealthy food to them. Society is structured in such a way to have legitimized this power imbalance, and through marketers' role as cultural interpreters, to ensure products such as energy-dense, nutrient-poor foods and beverages come to occupy a place within popular culture. IMC benefits marketers through increased effectiveness and efficiency, yet it is clear that its integration extends to the possible magnification of ethical risks that under traditional marketing models may not have come into as close contact with each other. In the next section of this chapter, we examine three cases that demonstrate a significant and often misunderstood strategic approach to IMC. Through examination of IMC in practice, we highlight how prolific and complex the IMC approach to communication is in relation to consumer exposure to multiple, integrated connections to branded products.

IMC in Practice

The following three case studies demonstrate the use of highly integrated marketing communications towards the target segment of children and young adults.

Cadbury Freddo Frog

Cadbury Australia's Freddo Frog chocolate was invented in 1930 as a part of then MacRoberston Chocolates children's range (Cadbury Australia, 2010) and has since become one of Australia's most popular children's chocolates (Superbrands Australia 2010). Freddo has attracted children for more than 80 years as an adventurous, fun, loveable character. Importantly for Cadbury, Freddo provides a method of recognition early in a child's cognitive development, long before they can recognize the word "Cadbury."

Fig. 3.2 Freddo Frog Packaging

The cartoon frog character and red color of the Freddo logo is likely to attract attention, encourage favorable brand associations, and enhance memory of the advertised benefit claims (Neeley and Schumann, 2004; Childers and Jass, 2002). Spokes-characters have also been shown to act as visual cues to represent a brand's attributes and result in more favorable brand attitudes (Garretson and Buton, 2005). Freddo is portrayed as likeable, active, sporty, and adventurous (Figs. 3.2 and 3.3).

Freddo Frog's packaging is well integrated with the overall strategy of the brand (Fig. 3.3). The Freddo product has been adapted to suit a variety of different occasions—such as a Christmas-themed Freddo dressed in red with a Santa's hat (Fig. 3.3). Cadbury has also expanded the original Freddo product range, including:

- A 3D Freddo with one of four surprise candies inside
- Freddo birthday cakes
- Button decorations
- Party share packs
- Christmas stockings
- Share packs (Fig. 3.4).

Cadbury uses point-of-purchase displays to communicate with consumers. These displays make it even easier for the child to recognize the product and are often found at pram or child heights (Fig. 3.5).

Fig. 3.3 variations on Freddo Frog packaging

Fig. 3.4 Product extension

Fig. 3.5 Point of purchase display

Fig. 3.6 Themes of fun, fantasy and adventure

Advertising to children and the use of entertainment as a marketing appeal has been subject to increased scrutiny in light of rising rates of childhood obesity. In Australia, 16 major food and beverage companies have voluntarily committed to the Australian Food and Grocery Council's Responsible Children's Marketing Initiative. Cadbury is one of the companies who have committed to not advertise unhealthy products to children less than 12 years of age (see http://www.afgc.org.au/cmsDocuments/Cadburypercent20CAP.pdf). Despite this commitment, Cadbury has received much criticism for its recent 'Adventures of Freddo' marketing campaign.

The campaign, which ran for five weeks to coincide with Freddo's 80th birthday, encouraged children to go online to interact with Freddo and help him solve puzzles and play games. Themes of fun, fantasy, and adventure were central to the campaign (Fig. 3.6). The television commercial is presented as a movie preview, showing highlights of the 'Adventures of Freddo' and encouraging registration at http://www.freddo.com.au. On the website the child can design their own character, who then joins the adventure with Freddo (Fig. 3.7). This blurring of the fantastical virtual world and reality, what Kathryn Montgomery in this book refers to as immersive and engaging media, is enhanced when the campaign also invites the child to complete real world challenges offline.

In this IMC campaign, Cadbury employed a number of strategies to attract the target audience, including the use of cartoon characters, music, film, interactive educational games, competition, puzzles, and free downloadable activities. The Freddo website (Fig. 3.8) features 17 games, 10 puzzles, and 24 activities. Cadbury also encouraged repeat visits to the website by releasing the first ten episodes of the game over the first ten days of the school holidays. The games and puzzles, as well

Fig. 3.7 Children can design their own character and interact virtually with Freddo

Fig. 3.8 Games, puzzles and activities featured on the Freddo website

as the take-home and online activities, represent connections between the child and the Freddo brand (Fig. 3.9). The "Adventures of Freddo" campaign encourages children to immerse themselves in the Freddo brand with interactive games and puzzles, videos, and printout offline activities.

Cadbury maintains that the campaign was not targeted at children, and is responsible marketing, because it does not show any unhealthy products, such as chocolate, in its advertising, even though the brand itself is repeatedly referred to. Cadbury also presents itself as a responsible marketer by requiring parental permission via email to use the website, by providing administrative time controls to the register, and by stating its aims are not pernicious, as it seeks "to educate and entertain children using a modern version of the cheeky, loveable frog that we have all grown up with" (http://www.freddo.com).

Commitments such as the Responsible Children's Marketing Initiative have been criticized for promoting a company whilst ignoring the actual strategies used by the company to target children (Jones et al. 2007). In their defence, Cadbury's preteens category manager Kate Watson said, "We don't actively market to children aged 12 and under. We're marketing to parents. Parents are the gatekeepers. Kids can't go on the website without parents registering the kids" (Sinclair, 2009).

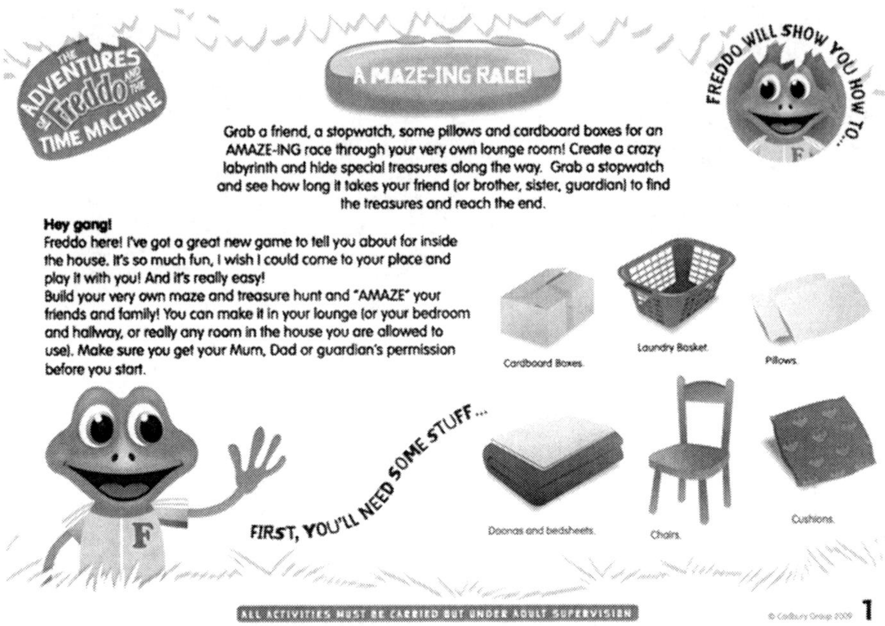

Fig. 3.9 An activity from the Freddo website

Fig. 3.10 Jodie Henry, the face of Cadbury Schweppes at the Games, with Freddo Frog and Karak at Luna Park, 2006 Commonwealth Games, Melbourne

Fig. 3.11 Freddo's affiliation with Orana Wildlife Park in New Zealand

Fig. 3.12 Example of a Freddo "showbag" and contents

Sponsorships, affiliations, and celebrity endorsements are other key strategies used by Cadbury. Cadbury aims to be associated with an active, sporty, energetic lifestyle through its sporting sponsorship (Fig. 3.10). It also wishes to be perceived as charitable, educational, and fun through its various other sponsorships and fund-raising activities. As part of the 'Adventures of Freddo' campaign, branded outdoor activities were run at aquatic centers in states throughout Australia. Similarly, in New Zealand, Freddo has been affiliated with Auckland Zoo and Orana Wildlife Park (Fig. 3.11). This sponsorship allows Cadbury to reach many children and create a lasting brand impression through fun activities and learning.

Cadbury Freddo Frog merchandise is also made available to children through various events. Cadbury showbags are available throughout the year at fairs and 'shows' in many locations throughout Australia. The Freddo showbags generally include about a dozen of different flavored Freddo chocolates plus branded items like a Freddo keychain, a Freddo tumbler, or a Freddo bag (Fig. 3.12).

Fig. 3.13 Examples of Cadbury Fundraiser boxes

Fig. 3.14 Freddo fundraising promotion

A central method Cadbury uses to enhance familiarity between its target audience and the Freddo Frog is its fundraisers (Fig. 3.13). Cadbury's fundraisers see the chocolate brought into the home, and often the child has a role selling the chocolates. Indeed, the child is made a part of the selling process, in order to fundraise for a group or club they have a recreational interest in such as a childcare centre, sporting club, or a scout group. Cadbury is prominent in the confectionary fundraising market raising millions of dollars each year, as seen in the self-promotion from the Cadbury website in Fig. 3.14.

Fig. 3.15 McDonald's logo

McDonalds Corporation

Since the opening of its first restaurant in California in 1940, McDonald's has grown to become the most iconic brand of modern times. The logo, a yellow "M" (referred to as the 'golden arches') on a red background, is recognizable across cultures and borders (Fig. 3.15). The logo has attained a level of familiarity that much of McDonald's signage is able to be presented without the company name, or in some instances, without the red background (Fig. 3.16).

McDonald's has been criticized substantially for advertising to children, which resulted in the corporation implementing a self-imposed ban on directly advertising unhealthy food to children in 2007, and redirecting marketing budgets to advertise and promote healthier options (Lee, 2008). It has since incorporated pasta zoo (recalled due to bad sales), seared chicken wrap, fruit fizz drink (with 65% fruit juice), fruit juices, and apple slices into poster that shows a glass of fruit fizz, a fruit bag, and a seared chicken mini snack wrap in a Happy Meal, which includes a toy. Given the increasing objections to advertising to children, McDonald's now aims to target 'mums', inviting a panel of mothers to visit supplier's facilities, the restaurant kitchens, and other sites to learn about its food quality.

Fig. 3.16 Variation of McDonalds logo without red background or company name

McDonald's began introducing healthier options to their menu, beginning with the grilled McChicken burger, in 1998 (Fisher, 1998). However, it is arguable that the changes introduced, such as fruit juices, salads, and cooking oil low in trans fats, and the introduction of the Heart Foundation tick, were a calculated response to attacks through litigations and books such as Fast Food Nation and movies such as "Supersize me" and "Food Inc.," rather than any authentic attempt to change consumer behavior or preferences (The Associated Press, 2007 http://www.msnbc.msn.com/id/20895437/; Sugarman & Sandman, 2006; Munger, 2004).

At McDonald's restaurants, the Happy Meal, also known as the children's meal, is prominently displayed. The Happy Meal is always accompanied by a toy. McDonald's has aligned itself with various organizations and appealing brands, such as Disney cartoon characters and most notably various Hollywood studios, to develop toys for inclusion to promote the Happy Meal product. The majority of the successful cross promotions have been for children's movies such as Shrek, Ice Age, Night at the Museum, and Fantastic Mr. Fox. The toy included in the Happy Meal is used in the IMC program as a tangible connection, along with the take home puzzles, quizzes, and activity books, that the child makes to the McDonald's brand.

Fig. 3.17 The layout of restaurants enables parents to have a quiet snack while their children play safely in the Playland

McDonald's Playlands form an important part of a child's social life, providing a recreation area outside of school to meet friends and have a good time (Powell et al., 2005). The layout of restaurants enables parents to have a quiet snack while their children have a separate area to play (Fig. 3.17). It is also a safe environment for parents and children to socialize, especially in low-income areas where playgrounds are not safe, or situations where responsible monitoring is difficult. Playlands foster a sense of enjoyment and fun among children, affection towards the parents who bring them there, and resulting feelings of good parenting (Schlosser 2002).

McDonalds use spokes-characters such as Ronald McDonald (Fig. 3.18), Hamburglar, and Mayor McCheese, which through the use of bright colors and fun themes, activities, and storylines help children to recognize the McDonald's brand. McDonald's also use easy-to-remember taglines and jingles to further help children differentiate between competitors.

McDonald's integrates the internet into its marketing structure to create enduring relationships with the consumer. The McDonald's website features information on the menu, currently sponsored events, and links to the Ronald McDonald House charity (Fig. 3.19). The US market also has access to Ronald.com (Fig. 3.20), which is targeted to younger children and features games that help them develop motor, memory, and observation skills. HappyMeal.com.au (Fig. 3.21) features interactive games and will take you to McWorld, an entire website dedicated to the entertainment of children. The site features games, puzzles, arts and crafts instructions, wallpaper, screensavers, printable coloring sheets, icons, and a parent information

Fig. 3.18 McDonald's spokes-character, Ronald McDonald

Fig. 3.19 http://www.mcdonalds.com.au

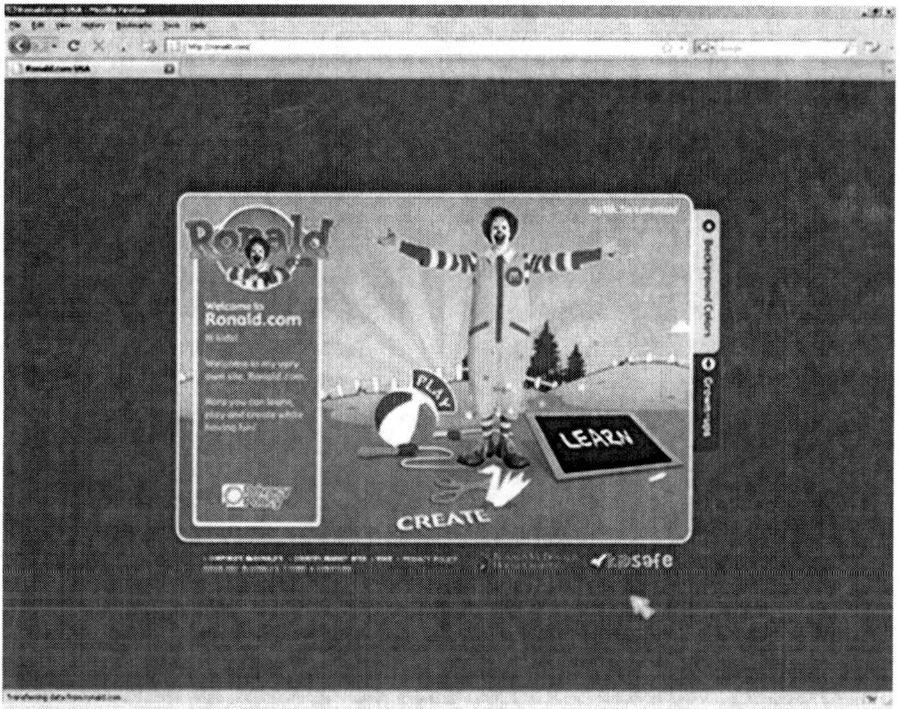

Fig. 3.20 http://www.ronald.com

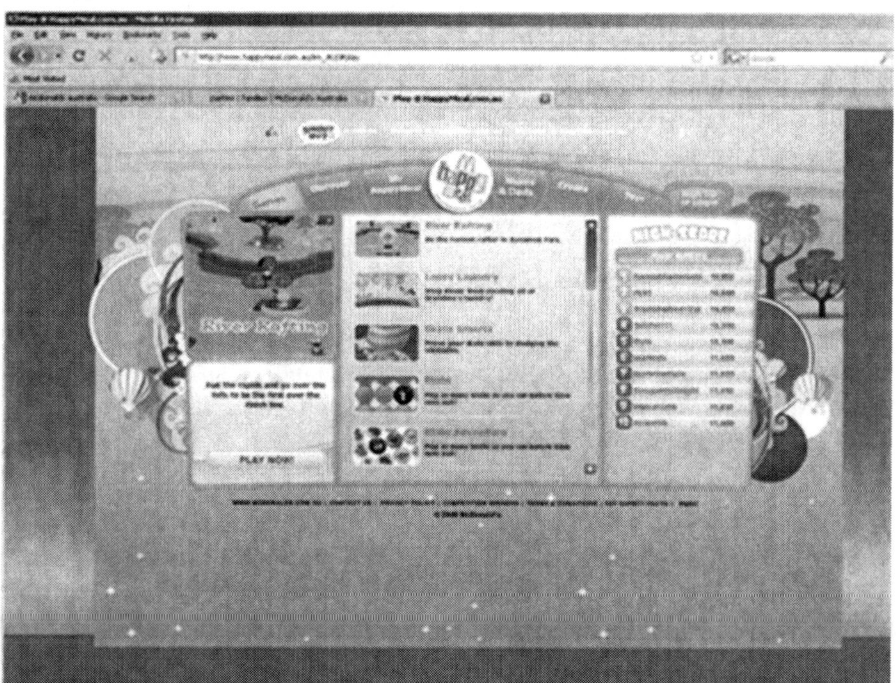

Fig. 3.21 http://www.happymeal.com

Fig. 3.22 McDonald's logo as part of sponsored community teams and events

section. HappyMeal.com has a selection of 20 games, all catering to different personality types and skills. The availability of a parental information section on the sites also creates a perception of openness and thus gains the trust of the parent.

Marketers aim to change brand attitudes via the use of product placement—the planned placement of branded products in movies or television programs. McDonald's has used product placements in various movies aimed at children and tweens, such as Richie Rich in a 1994 campaign, and Josie and the Pussycats in a 2001 campaign. On the small screen, McDonald's McCafe has featured on the Australian morning show "Sunrise" on Channel 7 as a supplier of its coffee and food. In 2005 MTV and McDonald's launched a music partnership, MTV Advance Warning, which aims to strengthen connections with young adult audience and features both the McDonald's and MTV logos.

Exposing children to the brand in strategic locations like hospitals, schools, and sporting events facilitates memory of the brand and strengthens the association of positive attributes, ensuring continuous brand recall and thus translating into increased sales.

Sponsorship of sporting events creates the association of youthfulness and an image of an active lifestyle. In Australia, McDonalds is an active sponsor of Little Athletics, whose members are in the 4–15-year-old range. In Victoria, it partners Basketball Victoria and sponsors many of Basketball Victoria's Junior Development Programs, involving 32,000 children across 480 schools. McDonald's sponsors Skill Fun and Play, a school-based program involving 9,500 children, along with McDonald's Super Mini Series for 10 years and under players, and McDonald's Champion School for secondary schoolers (Fig. 3.22). McDonald's has been a sponsor of the National Junior Classic tournament for the past 3 years; the Golden Arches are a distinctive part of the logos used by all programs. McDonalds support of a range of community charities and events increases trust in the brand and makes it easier for parents to choose McDonald's fast food over and above other competitors (Fig. 3.23).

Ronald McDonald House Charities (RMHC) has been operating successfully since 1986 with the aim of helping sick children and their families. Apart from providing accommodation and facilities, RMHC also includes National Learning programs (so that children can maintain schooling), grants for families, and the

Fig. 3.23 Billboard demonstrating support for community charity

Fig. 3.24 Ronald McDonald House Charities logo

Charlie Bell scholarships. McDonald's conducts regular events, including the "McHappy Day" where a dollar from every Happy Meal goes towards the charity but also has a RMHC charity box into which restaurant and drive-through patrons can donate coins. RMHC is allowed the use of the golden arches in its posters and advertising as well. In this case, Ronald McDonald is an interactive interpretation of the McDonald's logo, and his association with health care based charities for children is aimed to imply positive health aspects of the McDonald's restaurants (Fig. 3.24).

Fig. 3.25 Kellogg's Logo

Ronald McDonald House Charities and McDonald's restaurants located in children's hospitals create positive associations between the restaurant and the health and well-being of children. A study conducted in the US found that fast-food restaurants are common in hospitals that sponsor pediatric residency programs (Sahud et al. 2006). They also found that "a McDonald's restaurant in a children's hospital was associated with significantly increased purchase of McDonald's food by outpatients' belief that the McDonald's Corporation supported the hospital financially" (Sahud et al., 2293). This study also revealed a higher rating in the perceived healthiness of McDonald's food by survey participants.

McDonald's marketing to children is well integrated, involving the physical attributes of the restaurant, locations of restaurants, print media and signage that popularizes the logo, sophisticated and entertaining online content, product placement, event sponsorships, and even employment opportunities.

Kellogg's Nutri-Grain

Kellogg's is the leader of Australia's ready-to-eat breakfast cereal market (Superbrands, 2001). One of these products, Nutri-Grain, has become Kellogg's Australia's best-selling cereal brand, covering 11% of the ready-to-eat category (Superbrands). Studying the promotion for Kellogg's Nutri-Grain reveals a sophisticated level of integration among the brand's marketing-communication elements.

The Kellogg's logo combines the color red with a stylized version of the company's founders' signature (Fig. 3.25). These elements are likely to gain attention and encourage a certain level of trust and familiarity among consumers. The Kellogg's logo is used on all its products and in its communications for instant brand recognition.

Nutri-Grain is positioned as an energy food for power, strength, and performance (Jones et al. 2007) and primarily targets teenage boys, largely through the use of sports themes (B and T, 2003a). The Nutri-Grain package helps create this association using its no-frills, solid, big and bold front paired with blacks, browns, and reds (Fig. 3.26). Red draws attention to the three key ingredients of "CORN OATS WHEAT." The cereal pictured visually explodes off the packaging in an effort to represent the cereal's energy-giving qualities. Health benefits often form part of Nutri-Grains promotion. Nutri-Grain taglines, including "Iron man food," "helps fuel growing boys," and "You only get out what you put in," aim to create an association between working hard physically to achieve a challenging feat and eating the cereal to provide you with energy to do so.

Fig. 3.26 Nutri-grain packaging

A 1984 television commercial (TVC) showed Iron Man, Grant Kenny, running and kayaking. In the next scene he is eating Nutri-Grain and says, "tastes great." Another TVC in the same year, also with Grant Kenny, emphasized the "five vitamins and iron" and protein contained in Nutri-Grain, again branding it as "Iron Man food." A 2003 TVC "On Your Own" aimed at the teen market transported the "Iron Man food" into a futuristic hybrid football match (Fig. 3.27). Recently, Iron Man, Ky Hurst, has appeared in a TVC that showed him lifting weights, doing push-ups, shoveling coal, kayaking, running to the top of a mountain and eating Nutri-Grain. The tagline, "You only get out what you put in," is used in this TVC.

Nutri-Grain marketing also targets parents, specifically mothers. The cereal's advertising sends a strong message that part of being a good mother means providing sons with a high-energy breakfast that will help them grow into healthy, strong men. A 2009 TVC addresses mothers and informs them that "Nutri-Grain has what it take to help build your son into an Iron man."

The Nutri-Grain 2008–2009 campaign showed how the cereal can make boys into Iron Men and included advertisements run via print, radio, and online before the launch of two TVCs. The campaign focused on the mother–son relationship and the role of the mother in her son's growth and development (B & T, 2008). The ads are

Fig. 3.27 Nutri-Grain as the "Iron Man food" for football in the "On Your Own" TVC

shot from the mother's perspective and emphasize Nutri-Grain's nutritional credentials. One TVC begins showing a mother encouraging her young son as he runs to his swimming class and takes off on his journey to become an Iron Man (Fig. 3.28).

In 2008, Kellogg's announced that it would sell a branded television series about soccer-playing youngsters to Foxtel Pay TV (Lee, 2008). 'Football Superstar' follows the competition of 50 young Australians vying for a contract with Sydney Football Club's youth team and other prizes, including starring in a Nutri-Grain

Fig. 3.28 Nutri-Grain TVC showing the mothers role in the Iron Man journey

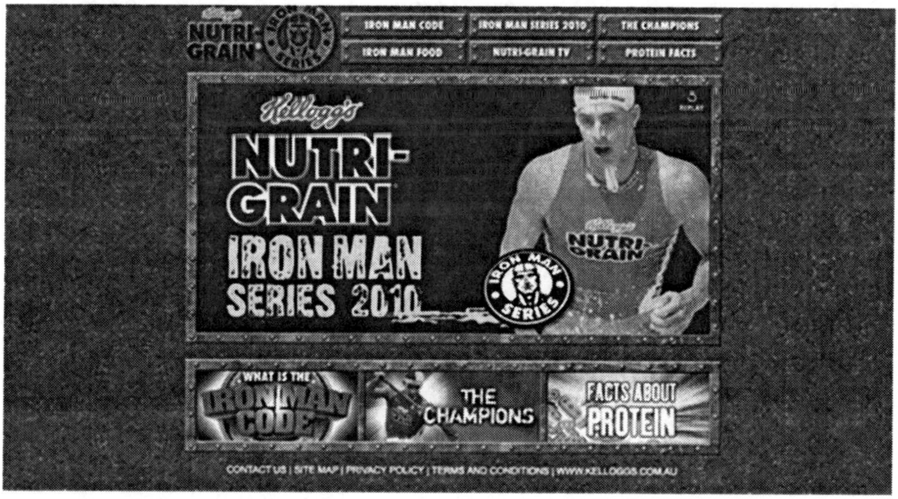

Fig. 3.29 Nutri-Grain website homepage

commercial. Nutri-Grain was provided for contestants to eat during the series, and logos were visible on training gear and on signage around the events (Sinclair, 2008). An implication of creating strong associations between the Nutri-Grain cereal and success in sport is that boys may perceive Nutri-Grain as essential in their day-to-day diet.

The Nutri-Grain website also uses browns and blacks to represent masculinity and strength. The website almost entirely focuses on Iron Men and the Kellogg's Nutri-Grain Iron Man series. On the homepage the viewer is greeted with images of Iron Men competing in the Iron Man series set to "epic-style" music (Fig. 3.29). Profiles of the Iron Men and Women are available for viewing and other information about the series is provided via links such as "the rounds," "round-by-round results," "the winners," and "behind the scenes." Links to the Iron Man Series website (http://www.ironmanseries.com.au) provide additional content about the event. Other prominent links encourage the viewer to access the "Iron Man code," to meet "the

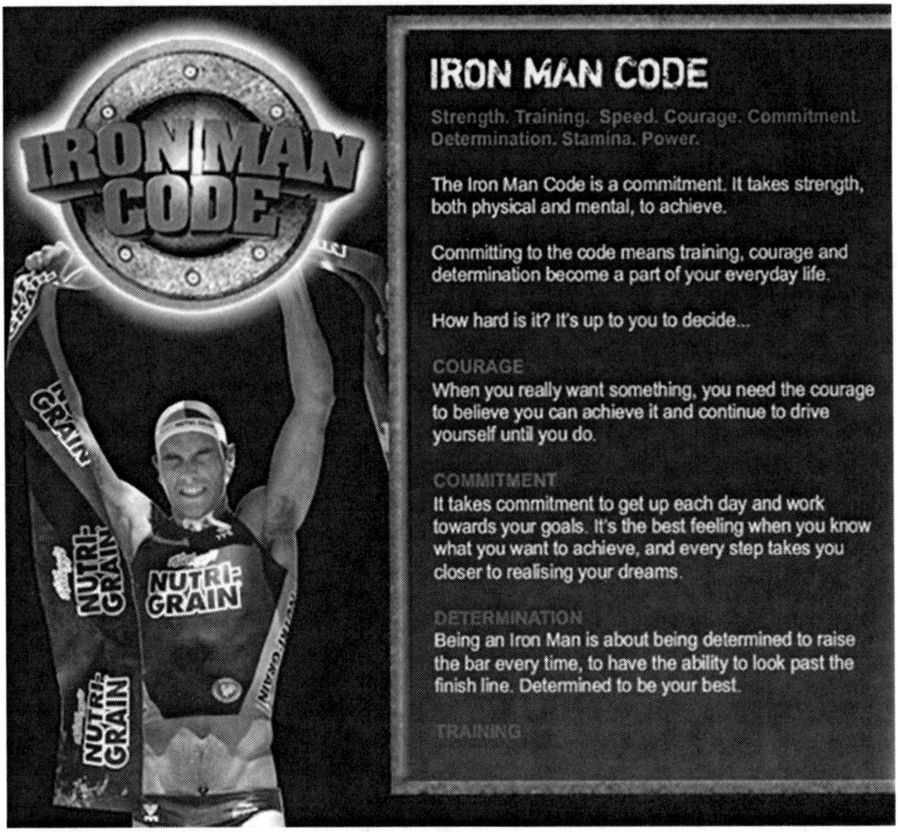

Fig. 3.30 A section of the Iron Man code found on the Nutri-Grain website

champions," and to "facts about protein" (Figs. 3.30 and 3.31). The Nutri-Grain website taps into boys dreams of achievement and glory and puts into use several interactive marketing techniques (Story and French 2004).

The sporting theme associated with Nutri-Grain extends to product promotions, which have included the chance to design team jumpers for their local football team, along with opportunities to win an X-box, music downloads, an MP3 player, and mini-speakers.

Iron men and women also act as a form of celebrity endorsement (Fig. 3.32), in which positive attitudes toward the athletes transfer to the brand. Kellogg's integrates these associations across its marketing communications to enhance brand liking amongst its target markets and serve as a risk-relief heuristic (Roselius, 1971).

Nutri-Grain is rated equally with Billabong as the brand most Australians associate with being a sports sponsor; 30% of Australians recognize the cereal as a sport sponsor (Marketing Magazine, 2009). Kellogg's Nutri-Grain sponsors, and has

Fig. 3.31 Nutri-Grain website links to Iron Men profiles

naming rights for, the Iron Man series (Figs. 3.33 and 3.34). Kellogg's is a major sponsor of Surf Life Saving Australia, as well as the Kellogg's National Leadership Camp and surf education programs. Kellogg's Nutri-Grain has also previously sponsored and had naming rights for the AFL's interactive tipping competition, the Dream Team and has sponsored the branded televisions series "Football Superstar" as discussed previously.

Kellogg's has voluntarily committed to cease advertising unhealthy products to children aged less than 12 years as part of the Australian Food and Grocery Council's Responsible Children's Marketing Initiative (RCMI) (B and T, 2009; see *http://www.afgc.org.au/cmsDocuments/Kellogg%20CAP.pdf*). It is clear that Kellogg's

Fig. 3.32 The 2009 Nutri-Grain Iron Man Series

Fig. 3.33 Iron man series logo

wishes to position itself a responsible food company playing a role in the battle against childhood obesity (Lee, 2007). Despite this, Kellogg's continues to receive criticism for their marketing to children and teenagers (Jones et al., 2007). Kellogg's was voted the winner of the 2009 Shame Award for Smoke and Mirrors by consumer group, The Parents Jury. Particularly emphasized by the group were the TV and radio advertisements that encouraged parents to buy Nutri-Grain for their "growing boys" which they say is misleading in terms of its nutritional benefits.

Fig. 3.34 Iron Men and Iron Women

Policy Implications

The Response to Date

Literature discussed in previous sections of this chapter highlights just a small selection of the significant research and inquiry that has been invested into the issues of marketing to children, childhood obesity and food marketing. However, it appears that understandings of marketing within a public health context are at times inconsistent with those proposed by marketers. Despite encouragement from the World Health Organization to adopt broad understandings of marketing that are consistent with industry definitions (*Marketing of Food and Non-Alcoholic Beverages to Children*, 2006), we found a tendency within public health documents to interpret marketing more narrowly, and often focus exclusively on the promotional aspects of the concept.

In 2004, Hawkes noted that an estimated 62 countries surveyed as part of her investigation into the global regulatory environment on marketing to children on behalf of the WHO had some form of regulation on television advertising that targeted children (Hawkes, 2007, p. iii.) In this report she also noted that the food marketing environment was rapidly evolving and that subsequent regulations were characterized by significant gaps (Hawkes, 2007, p. 57).

The risk associated with public health professionals incorrectly defining or understanding concepts such as marketing, promotion and advertising, or fixating on a single marketing tactic or channel, is that it will lead to misinterpretation and possible weakening of policy and public health responses to the childhood obesity epidemic. Despite significant research and investigation into the topic of marketing to children, IMC has only received limited acknowledgement in public health literature and discussions. This is of great concern considering IMC represents the *modus operandi* among marketers. By not recognizing the significance of IMC, and its associated ethical challenges as it relates to the issue of food marketing and the rise in childhood obesity, the public health community risks making a major oversight.

In addition to adopting an IMC approach, industry has also acted more promptly than government in delivering their response to this issue. In 2011 Kraak, Story, and Wartella completed a 5-year evaluation of progress made by different stakeholder groups in achieving the IOM recommendations as published 5 years earlier in the report *Food Marketing to Children and Youth: Threat or Opportunity* (Kraak, Story, Wartella, & Ginter, 2011, p. 3). Their evaluation found that while no one stakeholder group had made "extensive progress" toward achieving the recommendations, food and beverage companies, schools, and groups tasked with improving standards of marketing to children all demonstrated some progress (Kraak et al., p. 4). The report also concluded that government made no progress against relevant recommendations of a national social marketing campaign or nominating a single organization to centrally monitor progress.

However, as the case studies in this chapter demonstrate, the self-regulatory actions of food and beverage manufacturers and marketers still enable significant opportunities for companies to promote energy-dense, nutrient-poor foods and beverages to young people outside of traditional channels. By defining the maximum age of a child as younger than 18 years (as per the United Nations Convention on the Rights of the Child) (*Marketing of Food and Non-Alcoholic Beverages to Children*, 2006), limiting marketing behavior only to programs or media where children constitute the primary audience or limiting only advertising (*The responsible children's marketing initiative*, 2009, p. 4), marketers to still able to use a wide range of promotional techniques to deliver their desired message to their target audience, while still abiding by self-regulatory measures.

Realizing the Synergy of IMC

IMC is about synergy; about the whole being greater than the sum of the parts. Marketers who apply IMC realize this and use it to their commercial advantage. The above discussion represents the interplay of marketing characteristics, socio-cultural conditions, and ethical challenges that are associated with the use of IMC to promote energy-dense, nutrient-poor foods and beverages to children and adolescents. It seeks to illustrate that these factors do not operate in isolation, but build upon one other in a complex and dynamic way.

Marketing and public health are two very different disciplines that are connected by the global obesity epidemic. Outwardly they may be seen as opposing forces—one discipline is focused on alleviating the current problem, the other contributing to it. To make true progress, we need to look beyond the confines of our own disciplines and learn from different, if unfamiliar, paradigms. This is no small request. Yet as global responses to chronic disease remain inadequate even in the face of growing epidemiological and economic evidence (Yach, Hawkes, Gould, & Hofman, 2004, p. 2616), it is clear that new approaches are needed to help address this problem.

Public health professionals and policy makers need to understand more deeply the complex interplay of factors surrounding IMC as it is used to promote energy-dense, nutrient-poor foods and beverages to children and adolescents. There is acknowledgement that the response to date has not been sufficient in addressing this issue (Nestle & Jacobson, 2000). As stated by Harris, Brownell, and Bargh, "a fundamental question remains as to how to protect young people against the unhealthy influence of food marketing." (Harris et al., 2009, p. 216).

Rather than taking a reductionist approach that seeks to analyze the individual components of this situation, we argue that a more holistic and dynamic approach is recommended. IMC represents a paradigm shift away from traditional conceptualizations of marketing. Similarly, its response requires a similar paradigm shift to traditional public health responses. The first step in this shift is recognizing and understanding IMC, the broader environmental factors and dynamics that support it, and its implications in the issue of promoting energy-dense, nutrient-poor foods and beverages to young people.

Conclusion

The public health community has thoroughly analyzed and documented concerns regarding the involvement of food marketing in the childhood obesity epidemic. Significant resources have been invested investigating this issue and consequently a sizable body of literature is available to explain the impact of advertising and marketing on opinion, consumer behavior, and preference, how marketing affects and is interpreted by children, the amount of marketing material children are exposed to, and the responses of the food and beverage industry to these concerns.

However, in the same period that this research has been conduced, marketing as a concept has not remained static, but itself has undergone a transformation. From its beginnings as a modern concept, characterized by individual channels and techniques that were managed, implemented, and delivered relatively independently, marketing has been impacted and indeed shaped the transition toward postmodernity, in which marketing itself plays a central role (Firat & Venkatesh, 1993, p. 229).

Researchers have turned their focus to environmental factors to help explore causes for the childhood obesity epidemic. In doing so, public health professionals and researchers need to recognize that marketing is no longer dominated by the same approach that it was as little as 25 years ago. Since this time IMC, grounded in concepts of postmodernity, has become the dominant marketing paradigm. Despite theoretical challenges, IMC has been embraced by commercial marketing practitioners and represents both a powerful way of promoting brands and as a broader business strategy.

IMC used to promote energy-dense, nutrient-poor foods and beverages presents ethical implications which derive from the concept itself, inherited ethical challenges associated with marketing more broadly, and broader sociocultural conditions which support marketing and maintain a power structure within society. IMC benefits marketers through increased effectiveness and efficiency, yet it also magnifies the possible ethical risks that underlie more traditional marketing models and their social foundations.

IMC represents a paradigm shift to traditional marketing. Similarly, its response requires a similar paradigm shift to traditional public health responses. Such an approach may be difficult and unfamiliar, is likely to be associated with its own risks, and may not be met with success. Failing to recognize this transition to an IMC paradigm, however, poses a significant threat to efforts aimed at managing the risks associated with marketing of energy-dense, nutrient-poor foods and beverages to children and adolescents. Rather than providing expedient solutions, implications, or recommendations, this chapter seeks to provide a preliminary attempt to "catch" the shape of an overlooked research and public policy issue. The first step, an awareness of IMC, and an understanding of its implications among public health professionals, is both achievable and will better position advocates to address this issue now and in the future.

Acknowledgments The authors wish to acknowledge the Centre for Sustainable and Responsible Organizations at Deakin University, Australia, for funding to assist with the development of this book chapter, and center members Kathryn Chalmers and Shwetha D'Souza for the assistance with the case studies. The authors also wish to acknowledge the Flinders University (Australia) Children and Food Marketing research project for assisting with funding to conduct the case studies contained within this chapter.

References

Allan, K. (2006). *The social lens: An invitation to social and sociological theory*. Thousand Oaks, CA: Pine Forge Press.

Anderson, P. M., & Butcher, K. F. (2006). Childhood obesity: trends and potential causes. *Future of Children, 16*(1), 19–45.

Asquith, K. (2009). A critical analysis of the children's food and beverage advertising self-regulatory initiatives. *Democratic Communiqué, 23*(2), 41–60.

Australian Government (2010), Competition and Consumer Act, Act No. 51 of 1974 as amended, taking into account amendments up to Acts Interpretation Amendment Act 2011, Canberra.

B and T. (2003a). Nutri-Grain talks to teens. 14 February 2003. Retrieved January 24, from http://www.bandt.com.au/articles/B6/0C013EB6.asp.

B and T. (2008). Breaking Campaign: Nutri-Grain turns boys into iron men. 19 December 2008. Retrieved January 24, from http://www.bandt.com.au/articles/C4/0C05C6C4.asp.

B and T. (2009). Food companies sign up to ad code. 16 June 2009. Retrieved January 27, from http://www.bandt.com.au/articles/9E/0C061A9E.asp.

Brownell, K. D., & Warner, K. E. (2009). The perils of ignoring history: big tobacco played dirty and millions died. How similar is big food? *Milbank Quarterly, 87*(1), 259–294.

Cadbury Australia. (2010). Cadbury. Retrieved January 7, 2010, from http://www.cadbury.com.au/.

Childers, T., & Jass, J. (2002). All dressed up with something to say: Effects of typeface semantic associations on brand perceptions and consumer memory. *Journal of Consumer Psychology, 12*(2), 93–106.

Christensen, L., Torp, S., & Firat, A. F. (2005). Integrated marketing communication and postmodernity: An odd couple? *Corporate Communications: An International Journal, 10*(2), 156–167.

Cook, D. T. (2000). The Other "Child Study": Figuring Children as Consumers in Market Research, 1910s-1990s. The Sociological Quarterly, 41(3), 487–507.

Cornelissen, J. P. (2001). Integrated marketing communications and the language of marketing development. *International Journal of Advertising, 20*(4), 483–498.

Cornelissen, J. P., & Lock, A. R. (2000). Theoretical concept or management fashion? Examining the significance of IMC. *Journal of Advertising Research, 40*(5), 7–16.

Dewhirst, T., & Davis, B. (2005). Brand strategy and integrated marketing communication (IMC). *Journal of Advertising, 34*(4), 81–92.

Duncan, T., & Caywood, C. (1996). The concept, process, and evolution of integrated marketing communication. In E. Thorson & J. Moore (Eds.), *Integrated communication: Synergy of persuasive voices* (pp. 13–34). Mahwah, NJ: Lawrence Erlbaum and Associates.

Economos, C., Brownson, R., DeAngelis, M., Foerster, S., Foreman, C., Gregson, J., et al. (2001). What lessons have been learned from other attempts to guide social change? *Nutrition Reviews, 59*(3), S40–S56.

Fill, C. (2001). Essentially a matter of consistency: Integrated marketing communications. *The Marketing Review, 1*(4), 409–425.

Fine, C., & Harrison, P. (2007). *Who is responsible for the protection of children? Implicit and explicit interpretations of marketing messages, in ANZMAC 2007: 3Rs, reputation responsibility relevance, University of Otago, School of Business* (pp. 2437–2437). Dunedin, N.Z.: Dept. of Marketing.

Firat, A. F., & Venkatesh, A. (1993). Postmodernity: The age of marketing. *International Journal of Research in Marketing, 10*(3), 227–249.

Fisher, S., (1998). 'Chains chew the fat', Herald Sun, Herald and Weekly Times Limited, November 1998. Accessed 10 Nov 2009.

Fitzpatrick, K. R. (2005). The legal challenge of integrated marketing communication (IMC). *Journal of Advertising, 34*(4), 93–102.

Garretson, J. A., & Buton, S. (2005). The role of spokes-characters as advertisement and package cues in integrated marketing communications. *The Journal of Marketing, 69*, 118–132.

Gautier, A. (2003). Advertising: Cyberchild Virtual worlds. Real dollars. Real kids. *Marketing Magazine* (Aukland). Accessed 2 Dec 2009.

Gould, S. J. (2004). IMC as theory and as a poststructural set of practices and discourses: a continuously evolving paradigm shift. (Integrated marketing communications). *Journal of Advertising Research, 44*(1), 66(65).

Grimm, M. (2004). Is marketing to kids ethical? *Brandweek, 45*(14), 44–48.

Groom, S. A., & Biernatzki, W. E. (2008). Integrated marketing communication: Anticipating the 'age of engage'. In *Communication research trends* (Vol. 27, pp. 3–19). Centre for the Study of Communication and Culture.

Harris, J. L., Brownell, K. D., & Bargh, J. A. (2009). The food marketing defense model: Integrating psychological research to protect youth and inform public policy. *Social Issues and Policy Review, 3*(1), 211–271.

Harris, T. L., Whalen, P. T., & Communications, R. (2006). The marketer's guide to public relations in the 21st century. South-Western Educational Publishing.

Hastings, G., McDermott, L., Angus, K., Stead, M., & Thomson, S. (2006). *The extent, nature and effects of food promotion to children: A review of the evidence*. Geneva: World Health Organisation.

Hawkes, C. (2007). Regulating and litigating in the public interest: Regulating food marketing to young people worldwide: trends and policy drivers. *American Journal of Public Health, 97*(11), 1962–1973.

Hawkes, C. (2009). Sales promotions and food consumption. *Nutrition Reviews, 67*(6), 333–342.

Hawkes, C. (2010). Food packaging: The medium is the message. *Public Health Nutrition, 13*(2), 297–299.

Humphreys, A. (2010a). Megamarketing: The creation of markets as a social process. *The Journal of Marketing, 74*(2), 1–19.

Humphreys, A. (2010b). Semiotic structure and the legitimation of consumption practices: The Case of Casino Gambling. *The Journal of Consumer Research, 37*(3), 490–510.

Jay. J., (2003) 'McDisney: Case study for the integrated media studies approach', HT-500: Growing up in a Media World, Harvard Graduate School of Education. Accessed 7 Dec 2009 http://www.jasonjay.com/papers/mcdisney.htm

John, D. (1999). Consumer socialization of children: A retrospective look at twenty-five years of research. *The Journal of Consumer Research, 26*, 183–213.

Jones, S., Phillipson, L., McVie, D., Reid, A., Lynch, M., Fabrianesi, B., et al. (2007). Food marketing to children in Australia, Cancer Council Australia, Sydney.

Keller, K. L. (2001). Mastering the marketing communications mix: Micro and macro perspectives on integrated marketing communication programs. *Journal of Marketing Management, 17*(7/8), 819–847.

Kitchen, P. J. (2005). New paradigm – IMC – under fire. *Competitiveness Review, 15(1)*, 72(9).

Kitchen, P. J., & Schultz, D. E. (2000). A response to "theoretical concept or management fashion?". *Journal of Advertising Research, 40(5)*, 17–21.

Kitchen, P. J., & Schultz, D. E. (2009). IMC: New horizon/false dawn for a marketplace in turmoil? *Journal of Marketing Communications, 15(2)*, 197-204.

Kitchen, P. J., Brignell, J., Tao, L., & Jones, G. S. (2004). The emergence of IMC: A theoretical perspective. *Journal of Advertising Research, 44(1)*, 19–30.

Kitchen, P. J., Kim, I., & Schultz, D. E. (2008). Integrated marketing communications: Practice leads theory. *Journal of Advertising Research, 48*(4), 531–546.

Kliatchko, J. (2005). Towards a new definition of Integrated Marketing Communications (IMC). *International Journal of Advertising, 24*(1), 7–34.

Kliatchko, J. G. (2009). The primacy of the consumer in IMC: Espousing a personalist view and ethical implications. *Journal of Marketing Communications, 15*(2/3), 157–177.

Knuttila, M. (2005). *Introducing sociology: A critical approach* (3rd ed.). Don Mills, ON: Oxford University Press.

Kotler, P. (1986). Megamarketing. *Harvard Business Review, 64*(2), 117–124.

Kraak, V. I., Story, M., Wartella, E. A., & Ginter, J. (2011). Industry progress to market a healthful diet to American children and adolescents. *American Journal of Preventive Medicine, 41*(3), 322–333.

Lancaster, G., & Massingham, L. (2011). *Essentials of marketing management*. London: Routledge.

Lee, J. (2007). Kellogg tries hard to shake unhealthy image. The Sydney Morning Herald. Retrieved January 26, 2010, from http://www.smh.com.au/news/business/kelloggtries-hard-to-shake-unhealthy-image/2007/11/07/1194329317433.html.

Lee, J. (2008). TV football series to kick Nutri-Grain along. The Sydney Morning Herald. Retrieved January 23, 2010, from http://www.smh.com.au/business/tv-footballseries-to-kick-nutrigrain-along-20080424-28ak.html.

Lee, M., Pant, A., & Ali, A. (2010). Does the individualist consume more? The interplay of ethics and beliefs that governs consumerism across cultures. *Journal of Business Ethics, 93*(4), 567–581.

Lewin, A., Lindstrom, L., & Nestle, M. (2006). Food industry promises to address childhood obesity: Preliminary evaluation. *Journal of Public Health Policy, 27*(4), 327–348.

Livingstone, S., & Helsper, E. J. (2006). Does advertising literacy mediate the effects of advertising on children? A Critical Examination of two linked research literatures in relation to obesity and food choice. *The Journal of Communication, 56*(3), 560–584.

Marketing Magazine. (2009). Nutri-Grain, Emirates lead sports sponsor list. 30 June 2009. Retrieved January 23, 2010, from http://www.marketingmag.com.au/news/view/nutri-grain-emirates-lead-sportssponsor-list-1374

McCracken, G. (1986). Culture and consumption: A theoretical account of the structure and movement of the cultural meaning of consumer goods. *Journal of consumer research, v13*(n1), p71(14).

McGinnis, J., Gootman, J., & Kraak, V. (Eds.). (2006). *Food marketing to children and youth: Threat or opportunity?* Washington, DC: National Academies Press.

Mehta, K., Coveney, J., Ward, P., & Handsley, E. (2010). *Children and food marketing research project: final report to South Australia Health*: Flinders University.

Munger, L. J. (2004). Comment: Is Ronald McDonald the next Joe Camel? Regulating fast food advertisements targeting children in light of the American overweight and obesity epidemic. *Connecticut Public Interest Law Journal.*

Murray, S. (2007). The World's Biggest Industry. Forbes.com. Retrieved 26 August 2011, from http://www.forbes.com/2007/11/11/growth-agriculture-business-forbeslife-food07-cx_sm_1113bigfood.html .

Nairn, A., & Fine, C. (2008). Who's messing with my mind? *International Journal of Advertising, 27*(3), 447–470.

Neeley, S. M., & Schumann, D. W. (2004). Using animated spokes-characters in advertising to young children: Does increasing attention to advertising necessarily lead to product preference? *Journal of Advertising, 33*(3), 7–23.

Nestle, M., & Jacobson, M. F. (2000). Halting the obesity epidemic: A public health policy approach. *Public Health Reports, 115*(1), 12–24.

Piety, T. R. (2010). Citizens United and the Threat to the Regulatory State. University of Michigan First Impressions.

Powell, E. C., Ambardekar, E. J., & Sheehan, K. M. (2005). Poor neighborhoods: Safe playgrounds. *Journal of Urban Health: Bulletin of the New York Academy of Medicine., 82*(3), 403–410.

Powell, S., Dodd, C., & Langlands, S. (2010). Child food promotion to the 'under 8's' in the UK. Academy of Marketing Conference.

Preston, C. (2004). Children's advertising: The ethics of economic socialisation. *International Journal of Consumer Studies, 28*(4), 364–370.

Proctor, T., & Kitchen, P. (2002). Communication in postmodern integrated marketing. *Corporate Communications: An International Journal, 7*(3), 144–154.

Robinson, T. N., Borzekowski, D. L., Matheson, D. M., & Kraemer, H. C. (2007). Effects of fast food branding on young children's taste preferences. *Archive of Pediatric Adolescent Medicine, 161*(8), 1792–797.

Roselius, T. (1971, January). Consumer ranking of risk reduction methods. *Journal of Marketing, 35*, 56–61.

Roth, M. (1995). Effects of global market conditions on brand image customization and brand performance. *Journal of Advertising, 24*(4), 55–75.

Russell, C. A. (2002). Investigating the effectiveness of product placements in television shows: The role of modality and plot connection congruence on brand memory and attitude. *The Journal of Consumer Research, 29*, 306–318.

Sahud, H. B., Binns, H. J., Meadow, W. L., & Tanz, R. R. (2006). Marketing fast food: Impact of fast food restaurants in children's hospitals. *Pediatrics, 118*(6), 2290–2297.

Schlosser, E. (2002). *Fast food nation: The dark side of the all-American meal.* New York: Perennial.

Schor, J. B., & Ford, M. (2007). From tastes great to cool: Children's food marketing and the rise of the symbolic. *The Journal of Law, Medicine & Ethics, 35*(1), 10–21.

Schultz, D. E., & Patti, C. H. (2009). The evolution of IMC: IMC in a customer-driven marketplace. *Journal of Marketing Communications, 15*(2/3), 75–84.

Schultz, D. E., & Kitchen, P. J. (2000). *Communicating globally: An integrated marketing approach.* Basingstoke: NTC Business Books, Chicago and Macmillan Business..

Sharma, L. L., Teret, S. P., & Brownell, K. D. (2010). The food industry and self regulation: Standards to promote success and to avoid public health failures. *American Journal of Public Health, 100*(2), 240–246.

Shimp, T. A., & Shimp, T. A. (1997). *Advertising, promotion & supplemental aspects of integrated marketing communications*. Dryden Press.

Sinclair, L. (2008). Hunt on for cereal thriller. The Australian. 24th April 2004. Retrieved January 23, 2010, (Factiva).

Sinclair, L. (2009). Chockie frog has ad critics hopping mad. The Australian. June 22nd. Retrieved January 11, from http://www.theaustralian.com.au/business/media/chockie-frog-has-ad-critic-shopping-mad/story-e6frg996-1225738875688122573887568859.

Smith, P. R., Pulford, A., & Berry, C. (1999). *Strategic Marketing Communications: New Ways to Build and Integrate Communications*: Kogan Page.

Stanley, T. L. (2007). Babes in brandland: As marketers grasp ever more frantically for market share, targeting kids 8-and-under is much more common–But is it any more ethical? *Brandweek, 48*(37), 28–32.

Story, M., & French, S. (2004). Food advertising and marketing directed at children and adolescents in the US. *International Journal of Behavioral Nutrition and Physical Activity, 1*, 3.

Strack, F., Werth, L., & Deutsch, R. (2006). Reflective and impulsive determinants of consumer behavior. *Journal of Consumer Psychology (Lawrence Erlbaum Associates), 16*(3), 205–216.

Sugarman, S. D., & Sandman, N. (2006). Fighting childhood obesity through performance-based regulation of the food industry. *Duke Law Journal, 56*(6), 1403–1490.

Superbrands Australia. (2001). Kellogg's Australia. Retrieved January 24, from http://www.superbrands-brands.com/volIII/frameset.html.

Superbrands Australia. (2010). Cadbury Australia. Retrieved January 15, from http://www.superbrands-brands.com/volII/brand_cadbury.htm.

Schwartz, M. B., & Puhl, R. (2003). *Childhood obesity: a societal problem to solve. Obesity Reviews*, 4(1), 57–71.

Swinburn, B. (2009). Obesity prevention in children and adolescents. *Child and Adolescent Psychiatric Clinics of North America, 18*(1), 209–223.

Taylor, T. D. (2009). Advertising and the conquest of culture. *Social Semiotics, 19*(4), 405–425.

The Polmark Project - Final Project Report - Executive Report. (2010). London: International Association for the Study of Obesity.

The responsible children's marketing initiative. (2009). Australian Food and Grocery Council.

UK Government (1999) Unfair Terms in Consumer Contracts Regulations 1999, No. 2083.

Van Raaij, W. F. (1993). Postmodern consumption. *Journal of Economic Psychology, 14*(3), 541–563.

Wadden, T. A., Foster, G. D., & Brownell, K. D. (2002). Obesity: responding to the global epidemic. *Journal of Consulting and Clinical Psychology, 70*(3), 510–525.

Wansink, B., & Huckabee, M. (2005). De-marketing obesity. *California Management Review, 47*(4), 6–18.

Withrow, D., & Alter, D. A. (2011). The economic burden of obesity worldwide: a systematic review of the direct costs of obesity. Obesity Reviews, 12(2), 131–141.

World Health Organization. (2006). Marketing of Food and Non-Alcoholic Beverages to Children. (2006). Geneva: World Health Organization.

Yach, D., Hawkes, C., Gould, C. L., & Hofman, K. J. (2004). The global burden of chronic diseases: Overcoming impediments to prevention and control. *JAMA: The Journal of the American Medical Association, 291*(21), 2616–2622.

Zukin, S., & Maguire, J. (2004). Consumers and consumption. *Annual Review of Sociology, 30*, 173–197.

Zwick, D., Bonsu, S. K., & Darmody, A. (2008). Putting consumers to work. *Journal of Consumer Culture, 8*(2), 163–196.

Part II
Legal, Ethical, and Policy Implications of Advertising

Chapter 4
The Role of Ethics in Food and Beverage Marketing to Children

Minette (Meme) Drumwright and Jerome D. Williams

Few doubt that childhood obesity is a serious threat to our nation's health; however, there is a huge debate over who is responsible and what should be done. One aspect of the debate involves significant disagreement over food and beverage marketing and advertising targeting children (Research, 2011, Williams, 2005). What does ethical and responsible food and beverage marketing to children look like? Depending on where one goes to find the answer, either to food and beverage companies (and the supporting marketing communications industry), or to the public health community, the answer may vary dramatically. To some extent, the degree to which certain marketing tactics are considered unethical may be in the eye of the beholder. What might be considered good business practice by some marketers might be considered bad ethics by the public health community. In this chapter, we will attempt to highlight the intricacies of these complicated issues by examining perceptions of different groups of the ethics of marketing food and beverage products to children. As such, the purpose of the chapter is not to establish or identify "right" or "wrong" practices, or "ethical" or "unethical" behavior. Our focus will be on stepping back as academic marketing communications researchers and applying our lenses to elucidate more fully the complexities of this often heated debate over issues of the ethics of food and beverage marketing to children. In doing so, we will first review and examine the self-regulatory efforts of the food and beverage industry during the past few years. We will then report the findings of two studies that we conducted. The first study uses in-depth interviews to investigate the perspectives of the various parties engaged in the debate regarding ethics and food and beverage marketing—the

M. (Meme) Drumwright (✉)
University of Texas at Austin,
300 W. Dean Keeton (A1200), Austin, TX 78712, USA
e-mail: minette.drumwright@austin.utexas.edu

J.D. Williams, Ph.D.
Department of Management and Global Business, Rutgers Business School-Newark and New Brunswick, 1 Washington Park Room 1040, Newark, NJ 07102, USA
e-mail: jeromew@business.rutgers.edu

J.D. Williams et al. (eds.), *Advances in Communication Research to Reduce Childhood Obesity*, DOI 10.1007/978-1-4614-5511-0_4,

industry, the public health community, and the academic community. The second study is an analysis of websites of marketing communication associations regarding content related to targeting children generally and specific issues related to childhood obesity or children's health. We conclude with a discussion of our findings.

Self-Regulatory Efforts of the Food and Beverage Industry

During the past few years, the increased criticism and scrutiny related to the obesity crisis have prompted the food and beverage industry to become actively engaged in attempts at self-regulation to encourage more responsible and ethical practices. Many companies already have committed to various pledges through a variety of initiatives, including the Children's Food and Beverage Advertising Initiative, the International Council of Beverage Association Guidelines on Marketing to Children, the International Food and Beverage Alliance Global Policy on Marketing and Advertising to Children, the EU Pledge, the Canadian Children's Food and Beverage Advertising Initiative, and the Brazil Public Commitment on Food and Beverage Advertising to Children, to name a few.[1]

Based on a recent study examining various pledges, Hawkes and Harris (2011) noted that between 2005 and 2009, the food and beverage industry developed 13 pledges on marketing to children involving 52 companies. Two of the pledges were global, two were regional, and nine applied to specific countries. Three pledges were specific to the soft drink and fast-food industries, and the remainder of the pledges were food industry wide. Ten of the pledges required companies to publish individual commitments; a total of 82 such commitments were published, many of which extended beyond the minimum standards set by the pledge initiatives. All pledges included definitions of children and child-targeted media, as well as the communication channels and marketing techniques. Companies also were permitted to set criteria for foods that were exempt from any restrictions. While noting that there were many similarities between the pledges and individual company commitments, Hawkes and Harris observed that there were also many differences. Although conceding that the development of pledges on food and beverage marketing to children in such a short span of time is impressive, the researchers observed that limitations and inconsistencies in the pledges and commitments suggest that the food industry has a long way to go if its pledges are to reduce comprehensively the exposure and power of marketing to children.

Perhaps the most notable example of a pledge is the Better Business Bureau's Children's Food and Beverage Advertising Initiative (CFBAI), which began in

[1] For more information on these and other pledges, see an international database of pledges on food marketing to children (http://www.yaleruddcenter.org/marketingpledges/) made available by the Rudd Center for Food Policy and Obesity at Yale University.

2006.[2] Through CFBAI, 17 major food companies have taken voluntary pledges to be more responsible in their marketing and advertising to children. The participating companies represent more than 85% of all packaged foods and include industry leaders such as Kellogg Co., General Mills Inc., Coca-Cola Co., McDonald's USA, and Burger King (Lochhead, 2011). The companies have publicly committed to advertising only "better for you" products to children under 12. They also have made commitments to ratchet down the salt, sugar, saturated fats, and calories in their children's products. The pledges have evolved over the years, and the industry notes that the updated pledges include marketing on mobile devices and other forms of new media (Richtel, 2011).

On the other side of the coin, the public health community and nutrition experts contend that the voluntary pledges are fraught with loopholes, and that "better for you products" is a relative term that allows companies to keep marketing unhealthy options to children (see Chap. 6 for a more in-depth discussion of CFBAI and whether or not modifications are merited to strengthen existing guidelines). Despite CFBAI and other industry pledges, many public health advocates feel that there still is tremendous room for these companies to strengthen their self-regulatory programs, especially in areas such as in-school marketing. According to some advocates, these pledges seem to allow more types of marketing than they limit.

In assessing CFBAI, Schwartz and Ustjanauskas (2012) observed that the industry has made moderate progress in both the number of companies that participate and the strength of the pledges to limit marketing of unhealthy foods to children under 12 years old. They noted that the original strategy of allowing each company to define its own criteria for "better for you" products will be replaced by 2014 with a uniform set of nutrition criteria. They also noted that CFBAI members have strengthened the criteria used to define "child-directed marketing" so that it includes traditional, digital, and social media, as well as product placement in movies primarily directed to children under 12. However, despite these positive developments, Schwartz and Ustjanauskas observed that there are still serious and significant limitations to CFBAI standards. For example, they pointed out that definitions of child-directed advertising do not include marketing outlets such as product packaging and point-of-sale promotions, and the pledges do not cover general-audience advertising on family shows watched by large numbers of children. Also, they noted that although child-directed websites are included, they are defined so narrowly that even Happymeal.com would not be covered. Furthermore, they pointed out that the largest numbers of child visitors are found on general audience websites (e.g., Domino's and Pizza Hut's main websites; MyCokeRewards.com), which are not covered by CFBAI pledges. Finally, they asserted that while CFBAI covers some aspects of marketing in elementary schools, major components of marketing that occur in school settings are exempt, including food and beverage displays, charitable fundraising activities, and public service messaging sponsored by food companies. Schwartz and Ustjanauskas (p. 86) concluded, "In

[2] For more information, see http://www.bbb.org/us/childrens-food-and-beverage-advertising-initiative/.

sum, the CFBAI has moved the needle, but it isn't enough." They offer a ray of hope by suggesting that stronger standards in 2014 may make a difference, but future research will have to bear that out.

The federal Interagency Working Group (IWG) on Food Marketing to Children is another promising way through which more can be done regarding industry pledges and self-regulation (Research, 2011). Created by the 2009 Omnibus Appropriations Act (Pub.L. 111–8), IWG is a collaborative effort of four federal agencies: the Federal Trade Commission (FTC), the Centers for Disease Control and Prevention, the Food and Drug Administration, and the US Department of Agriculture. However, so far this "promising way" is not being fulfilled. Although Congress directed the IWG to develop voluntary nutrition standards for foods and beverages marketed to children and adolescents ages 17 and younger, these standards have been met with significant industry opposition because they are stronger than those of CFBAI (Schwartz & Ustjanauskas, 2012).

Schwartz and Ustjanauskas (2012) noted three significant ways in which the IWG recommendations have been sterner than CFBAI pledges, and as such, have met industry opposition. First, the original IWG recommendations encouraged the food industry to consider children aged 12–17. CFBAI responded quite negatively to any suggestion that marketing to children 12 or older should be on the table for discussion. Second, the IWG defined "marketing" and "child-directed" more comprehensively than CFBAI. For example, "marketing" included packaging and in-store marketing, and "youth-targeted media" was defined more broadly by IWG. CFBAI argued that the IWG marketing definitions were difficult to measure, not practical for application purposes, and so broad that they encroached upon philanthropic efforts and marketing activities directed at families and adults. Third, the IWG nutrition recommendations were stronger than those of CFBAI; they required the presence of "food groups to encourage" and allowed only small amounts of sodium, saturated fat, and sugar. CFBAI argued that the IWG guidelines were too complex and difficult to apply and would threaten the palatability of products. Based on the most recent information at the writing of this chapter, Schwartz and Ustjanauskas noted that in October 2011, the FTC agreed that the focus should be on children under 12, apparently abandoning efforts to protect children in middle school and early high school. The FTC also indicated greater agreement with CFBAI definitions of marketing and "better for you" products.

It is against this background of attempts at self-regulation that we conducted our studies.

Study 1

Study 1 is based on in-depth interviews with participants in the debate on ethics and self-regulation of food and beverage marketing. The interviews were designed to solicit their observations and advice regarding ethics in food and beverage marketing.

Methods

In-depth interviews are a particularly useful approach when the research objective is to understand perceptions, beliefs, and values, especially when the researcher cannot be sure what is motivating the actors (Corbin & Strauss, 2008; McCracken, 1988; Miles & Michael Huberman, 1994). We interviewed 19 experts from various groups involved in the debates: seven informants representing the industry (food/beverage and marketing/advertising), seven informants representing the public health and nonprofit community, and five academics whose research has informed the debate. Some of the informants were identified through their participation in conferences, consortiums, and symposiums related to food and beverage marketing and public health. Others were identified through experts and press coverage.

The interview protocol consisted of a broad set of questions that permitted informants to determine which issues to focus on (see the interview protocol in Appendix A). All informants were assured of anonymity and confidentiality in an effort to reduce biases. Eighteen of the interviews were conducted by phone, and one was conducted in person. Sixteen of the interviews were audio recorded and transcribed to produce verbatim transcripts. Three informants declined the request to record the interviews, so the interviewer's notes were used in lieu of verbatim transcripts. The interview data were analyzed using standard qualitative methods (e.g., Corbin & Strauss, 2008).

Findings

Below we report the findings of our in-depth interviews as themes. Unless otherwise noted, the themes were characteristic of many of the interviews. One theme set the framework for many of our other themes:

Theme 1

There was extreme polarization between the two sides—food and beverage marketers and public health advocates—to the point that there did not appear to be much common ground.

We were not prepared for the intensity of the feelings that we encountered. A nutrition scientist on the company side described the rancor surrounding the debate and expressed a profound sense of discouragement that was common to both sides:

> I think that there is so much hyperbole going on in the advocacy groups...There are those who...say that the sky is falling in, the world is going to end, the industry is unethical. It's all this screaming going on—on both sides...I have never been so depressed about the state of affairs as I am right now because there are really serious health issues out there...but I don't see how they are ever going to solve this issue with the rhetoric that is going on out there. It just really disheartens me; it really does.

A public health advocate expressed an extreme lack of confidence in the potential of self-regulation:

> Self regulation can't work. If that is the thesis here, I don't want to waste my time [talking with you]. Self regulation can't work…Looking at self regulation is a cop out.

A nutrition scientist on the public health or advocacy side said, "Some people are crazed on one side; and some people are crazed on the other…Nobody likes to be scolded, and there is a lot of scolding going on." A former fast-food company CEO said, "There are nutrition Nazis and crazy people out there." A nonprofit CEO said, "We need to focus on how to fix things instead of throwing rocks at each other… We've got intense warfare going on…and the process is getting high jacked by extremists." What seemed to determine one's view of the situation was not whether or not she was a nutrition scientist or a marketer, but whether or not she worked for a company or a nonprofit group.

Theme 2

Like politicians of all stripes quoting Lincoln, both groups evoked the First Amendment, but they had very different views of the First Amendment and commercial speech.

Although both sides brought up the First Amendment and used it to bolster their arguments, First Amendment scholars suggest that this debate has little to do with the First Amendment. Nevertheless, debates about the meaning of the First Amendment stoked the emotions and the sense of the rightness of the respective sides.

The industry informants argued that commercial speech deserves protection in and of itself, and as such, their commercial speech should not be regulated. Period.

Public health advocates asserted that commercial speech deserves protection in as much as it provides consumers information to make rational decisions. As one public health advocate said:

> The reason that we protect commercial speech is to make sure that consumers have good product information, and none of this [debate about food marketing] has anything to do with that. [Food marketing] is bypassing any rational approach to information and going straight for an emotional response, and when you are talking about kids, it's particularly egregious.

Theme 3

Related to the general polarization and animosity are very different views of rights and responsibilities, especially with respect to marketing to children.

The company side presumed that food companies have a right to market to children as long as they do so within the letter of the law. If it is legal, it is ethical. When asked about ethical issues, one company nutrition scientist said:

> Companies are making claims within the letter of the law—"i's" dotted and "t's" crossed—and they are still being screamed at by the advocates…Companies that are working 100% within the regulations are still being sued.

Public health advocates have a very different view of ethics in food marketing. They assert that even if food marketers have the right to market unhealthy foods to children, it is not the right thing to do. As a member of the public health community said:

> Given the childhood obesity epidemic, there are real ethical problems with industry pushing mainly salty, fatty, sugary foods at kids in this context...In my mind, it's almost fact that any advertising to children under 12 is inherently deceptive...It's unethical to market to young children. Period. Specifically to advertise junk food to young children.

Preston's (1994, p. 128) statement about advertisers seems to describe many company respondents: for advertisers who believe that the law is sufficient, "ethics never really starts." Public health advocates see a number of ethical problems that company representatives do not see. For example, public health advocates see ethical problems in messages that are technically in compliance legally but that are not serving the public interest. As one advocate said:

> There are misleading messages that don't necessarily rise to the level of the FTC or FDA in that they are not out and out lies, but the companies are peddling stuff that doesn't do what they say it will...like they are advertising whole grains, and they are not in trouble with the FDA, but that doesn't mean that there is a lot of whole grains in it, and this is particularly bad when it comes to children ... or they are technically in compliance with the requirement for TV ads to children that must put the product in the context of a healthy meal, but they do so in the last half second. They are technically in compliance, but that is not in the public interest.

Public health advocates also have problems with techniques that companies are using in the digital environment. As a public health advocate said:

> Companies are using techniques to market to children, new digital techniques where they are very strategically taking advantage of children and teenagers' emotional vulnerabilities to communicate with them at an emotional level and bypass any rational analysis of product information and cueing them to want to consume these products. There is a real unfairness there.

The public health community particularly has problems with peer-to-peer marketing initiatives in which kids market to kids and with what they refer to as "immersive environments." One such immersive environment is the Doritos Asylum 626 game,[3] which brings teens into the game using their webcams and prompts them to bring their Facebook friends in as well. Again, however, most of our respondents from companies viewed the question of ethics in terms of whether or not a company and its marketing were complying with the law and regulations.

Theme 4

There was a serious and contentious debate about adolescents.

While there certainly was disagreement over marketing and advertising to children, the disagreement over adolescents was even more pronounced and acrimonious. Company representatives viewed the ethical issues related to marketing to adolescents as very dissimilar to those of marketing to children and much more akin to, if not the same as, those related to adults. As one company representative said:

[3] See Goodby, Silverstein & Partners' explanation of Doritos Asylum 626 for an award show: http://www.myawardshows.com/2010/OneShowEntertainment/asylum626.

> To try to treat adolescents like children is ridiculous when you have pregnant mothers, people who can drive cars and sign up for the military. To try to treat them like children is insulting.

Public health advocates see adolescents as vulnerable in special ways just as children are. As one academic who studies advertising to children said:

> The old model is that it is only children under 12 that we need to worry about, which is rooted in children's understanding of persuasive intent. I don't think that persuasive intent is the standard anymore. I think that the new model governing regulation or practices has to include adolescents, who are also at risk in terms of the kinds of techniques that are reaching them …and their abilities to control their impulses…I think that given the rise in obesity and the fact that adolescents are engaged in risky behavior …that we need to have higher ethical standards where adolescents are concerned.

Public health advocates argue that two types of factors make adolescents vulnerable. One type is related to the adolescents themselves—their susceptibility to peer pressure, their difficulty controlling their impulses, and their inclination toward risky behavior. The other type is related to the context of adolescents in the marketplace—that adolescents have more money to spend than children and that they do not typically have parents as gatekeepers to the degree that children do. These two types of factors converge to exacerbate potential problems of adolescents. A public health advocate said, "The law is out of touch with reality…It is behind the times… It doesn't reflect reality."

Theme 5

The opposing sides have very different views of parental responsibility.

Given the disagreements about children and adolescents, it is not surprising that the two groups have different views of parental responsibility. Industry representatives view parents as the ultimate gatekeepers, as the people who should say "no" to children's desires for unhealthy food; all of their parents did say no. They claim that the public health advocates want the government to be a "nanny state," which they view as highly inappropriate. One public health advocate responded, however, by saying:

> We already have a nanny state, and the nanny is the corporations…Their default options are junk food and fast food, and they barrage children with advertising.

Theme 6

There is a twofold battle over evidence. It involves (1) science and nutrition and (2) marketing and advertising.

Some industry representatives see public health research as advocacy research rather than scientific research. As one industry scientist said:

> The public health community, their philosophy is that they don't really care what the evidence is. If they think that it is the right thing to do, it almost becomes like a religious belief. We have to do it because we don't think that it will do any harm and it has the potential to do a lot of good. I'm sitting here as a scientist saying, "Where is the proof that any of this is going to work?" …I think that they are as irresponsible as marketers who make sleazy claims.

She went on to say:

> The field of nutrition epidemiology has been disastrous for the field of nutrition science … They are using smoke and mirrors to come up with whatever they want to support. Talking with a lot of my colleagues, the statistics are so complicated, it's hard to critically evaluate that stuff. It just keeps going on and on and on.

There is debate about the evidence related to nutrition science and nutrition epidemiology, but there is also a debate about the evidence related to marketing and advertising guidelines. Regarding the Interagency Working Group guidelines, a company representative said: "There is not a whit of evidence that what they are recommending will work." A former CEO of a food company said, "I don't know of anybody who has gotten fat from watching a commercial."

From the public health side, an academic referenced evidence of a causal chain: TV advertising affects children's food preferences, which affects their eating patterns:

> When you look at the 2006 IOM [Institute of Medicine] Food Marketing Report, there is really good evidence that there is a causal chain that has been developed. TV advertising does affect children's food preferences, purchase requests, food choices, and at least in 2–12 year olds, their eating patterns. If that is the case, if you change the kinds of foods that you are marketing to children, it will have an effect.

Evidence can be a difficult issue, as a public health advocate explained:

> There is evidence. The question is, "Is it enough evidence?" And there is never as much evidence as we would like. But with soda taxes, as an example, there is plenty of evidence to show that sodas are contributing to obesity through higher caloric intakes and that people should cut back on sodas… I think that there is lots of evidence to point to [soda taxes] as a promising policy approach. There is never definitive evidence to show that it will absolutely work as a public health strategy until you do it. Even with menu labeling, there have been a lot of academic studies that show that nutrition information in restaurant settings helps, but until you have a nationwide policy in place, and consumers become accustomed to using the information, and companies start to reformulate products, you don't really know what the public health effect really is.

She went on to observe that an Institutional Review Board, an independent ethics committee that reviews research proposals, would probably never approve the types of experiments that would be needed—e.g., randomly assigning children to healthy vs. unhealthy food marketing environments.

Theme 7

Both sides see the causes of the obesity crisis as multifactorial, but they place very different weights on the importance of changing company behavior.

An industry representative explained a prevalent perspective among company informants that the public health side simplistically places too much weight on the influence of companies and too little weight on other factors:

> The obesity issue is extremely complex. Because it is so complex, the advocates try to look for what they consider an easy target, and I think that they view clamping down on industry as an easy target. It's easy to make the industry look evil… What are they doing about physical education in schools? What are they doing about safe neighborhoods so that kids

> can go out and play? Those are the tough things to do. What are they doing about single parent homes where you don't have time to prepare the kind of meals that Harriett Nelson did? Those are the really serious issues in this culture that are contributing to the problems that we have. But who do they pick on? The food industry…I wish that they would put as much passion into advocating changes in other areas of society.

A public health advocate expressed a prevalent perspective among the public health community that the culture and the environment, upon which companies have a powerful influence, must be changed:

> We must change social norms …We harken back to tobacco, but changing norms is much more complicated in the food context because one Oreo won't kill you. The causes of obesity are multifactorial. Education will only go so far. We are surrounded by a community in which the default options are junk food and fast food, so we have got to tackle changing the environment.

Theme 8

The two groups have very different perspectives in terms of solutions.

Company representatives emphasize the importance of consumer self-control, self-discipline, and personal choice supplemented by information and education in addressing the obesity crisis. In contrast, the public health and academic communities emphasize the importance of changing the environment and providing healthy default options. As one academic said, "Information is just not going to do it. People know what foods are unhealthy, and they still eat them. It's going to take something more, like calorie taxes."

Central to this debate is the question, "Will self regulation work?" Some public health advocates believe that the only solution is external regulation, such as the informant who felt that he would be wasting his time talking with us about self-regulation because it will not work. Another public health advocate held a similar, if less dogmatic, position:

> One thing that I have a hard time wrapping my head around is what would it mean to be an ethical corporation because there is not a legal infrastructure for corporations to take into account the obesity epidemic when they are developing their various products. On the one hand, we say it is an ethical problem, but I am not sure that there is a solution that lies in ethics when we are talking about artificial entities created to make a profit.

Another public health advocate had a very different perspective and saw motivating companies to be ethical as a key part of the overall solution:

> It's interesting because the way I came to our position on food marketing to kids was in part through ethical considerations. We were thinking about various approaches to legislation … and I was concerned about the timeline for legislation…and a colleague said to me, "What about appealing to the companies because it's the right thing to do?" …and we've used that as the key rationale for our public policy approach.

When asked about self-regulation as a potential solution, a former marketer said, "Regulation is not in the DNA of companies. We're much better off appealing to them with the business case—that they can be successful and ethical."

Theme 9

Neither side sees academic participants in the debate in a positive light or as a viable and productive part of the discourse.

We conclude with a theme that was sobering to us as academics. It deals with the manner in which academics are seen by both sides. Companies generally see academics as being on the public health side. As one company representative explained:

> The academic community is out of touch with reality. They don't have a clue as to what it is like to have to survive in business. I think that they are as much a part of the problem as the public health community by having their university public relations departments sending out press releases for every little study that they do. They want publicity. It's very competitive for them getting grant money. They are going to do the kinds of studies that will give them sensational headlines and the attention that they want. I see an awful lot of that going on.

However, academics are not necessarily seen favorably by the public health community either. A public health advocate explained that some academics are perceived as having sold out to the industry and others are unwilling to engage in public policy debates:

> You have academics all the time that take money from industry...and that research is used to support industry positions that do not have the public health in mind...Frankly, there are very few academics who are willing to spend some time doing public policy work. So there's another ethical issue. Academics are doing research rather that getting involved in the broad public policy debates. Many academics don't really see themselves as public intellectuals, and that's what they should be.

Many of the scholars involved in food marketing research appear to be public health scholars rather than business or communication scholars. As this chapter highlights, many of the questions call for academic research—not by public health scholars but by marketing and advertising scholars. We question if marketing and advertising scholars are engaged in the debate to the degree that they should be.

Study 2

Because marketing communication industry associations influence norms related to ethics and corporate responsibility, we examined the websites of these organizations with respect to content related to two topics (1) targeting children generally and (2) specific issues related to childhood obesity or children's health.

Methods

We examined the websites of 22 marketing, advertising, and public relations industry associations, including the American Association of Advertising Agencies, the American Advertising Federation, the American Marketing

Association, the American Academy of Advertising, the Marketing Research Association, the Advertising Research Foundation, the Internet and Mobile Marketing Association, and the Public Relations Society of America. For the complete list, see Appendix B. We recognize that websites change frequently, and for that reason, we report our findings at the time of our study without identifying specific associations.

Findings

On the websites, we found very little content related to advertising or marketing communication directed to children and even less on specific issues related to childhood obesity or children's health. Only eight of the 22 websites mentioned children at all, and even fewer, five websites, acknowledged that there is a difference between advertising to children and advertising to adults. With very few exceptions, statements regarding marketing to children typically appeared in a code of conduct and were general and vague, such as stating an obligation to recognize "a special commitment" to children or taking into account the "maturity of the audience to which the message is directed." An example of a notable exception was an association that took a stand against the inclusion of children under the age of 13 in any kind of word of mouth marketing program.

Mentions of specific issues related to childhood obesity or childhood health were even rarer than general mentions of children on the websites—two websites. One association stated that it supports the Children's Food and Beverage Advertising Initiative (CFBAI), and advertising to improve physical education and activity among children. Another described CFBAI, but it did not take a stance.

Even when associations take a stance on marketing and advertising to children or on childhood obesity or children's health, there typically is not an enforcement mechanism. Only a very few of the associations have processes in place to enforce their stances, principles, or codes. Even those with enforcement bodies and processes can only "admonish, suspend, or expel" a wayward practitioner or company from membership. One website explained that it had a process in place for enforcing its code for many years, but it had abandoned attempts at enforcement. It stated that the results of the efforts to enforce its code in relation to the time and resources required failed to provide a valuable return on investment for the association, its members, or the broader profession.

Discussion

We are neither nutrition scientists nor public health scholars, so we cannot comment on the debates related to evidence regarding nutrition science or nutrition epidemiology. We are, however, marketing and advertising scholars, so we may be able to provide another way to think about some of those issues. We suggest that there are some incentives for food and beverage businesses to rethink and reframe their rights and responsibilities. For example, the politics surrounding food and beverage marketing could become similar to the politics that surrounded tobacco. If that were to happen, it would be a disaster for the food and beverage industry on many fronts. The appropriateness of the analogy is beside the point. In such a case, there would be little middle ground. Moreover, external regulation would happen. Government regulation would not be the preferred course for the food and beverage industry. There are lessons that food and beverage companies should learn from the uncooperative, obstructive, and unyielding manner in which the tobacco companies reacted to criticism and scrutiny. Even if a "worst-case scenario" did not happen, finding common ground and room for effective self-regulation would certainly be advantageous for the food and beverage industry.

We also suggest that the public health community may have incentives to rethink its role and interactions with industry. Despite the desire for government regulation of the food and beverage industry, it may or may not happen; and if it happens, it may or may not solve the problems related to childhood obesity. Often venues for government regulation are toothless, yielding the worst of both worlds. Despite a near catastrophic collapse of the economy, little has been done to regulate financial markets, and even when laws exist, enforcement has been lax. The same can be said for issues involving the environment. As such, the public health community may have incentives to work more collaboratively with business to improve self-regulatory efforts as a second-best strategy.

Our in-depth interviews highlighted the polarization and rancor that exist between the food and beverage industry and the public health community. The question remains regarding whether companies can be counted on to self-regulate, but if they can, the polarization and rancor do not encourage listening, mutual understanding, or collaborative problem solving. In an attempt to foster increased understanding, we identify and elaborate on the factors that underpin these dramatic differences in perspectives and point to some ways to push forward toward solutions.

From the industry perspective, food and beverage marketers are following the basic marketing process that they and their predecessors have been trained to follow. This process is referred to as "STP" (Segmenting, Targeting, and Positioning). The initial component, "segmentation," is "the process of subdividing a market into distinct subsets of customers that behave in the same way or have similar needs. Each subset may conceivably be chosen as a market target to be reached with a distinct marketing strategy" (American Marketing Association, 2008). The STP formula is widely considered the essence of strategic marketing.[4] As such, the food and beverage industry has long viewed children as an attractive market segment, often targeting them from an early age with intense and specialized food marketing and advertising efforts. Targeting children, however, is not unique to the food and beverage industry. Marketers hope that preferences for specific brands established in

[4] For elaboration on the STP formula, see Kotler and Keller's (2006) *Marketing Management* textbook, which is widely recognized as one of the most authoritative textbooks on marketing.

childhood will carry over into adulthood. In fact, a recent academic marketing study concluded that marketers should target children before they even turn five years old in order to build lifetime brand recognition (Harris, 2009). A host of specialized market research firms focus on children, not to mention internal, proprietary research conducted by the companies themselves. One external research firm, Kidsindustries (http://www.kidsindustries.com), includes the following on its website: "We create communications that cut through the digital clutter to connect with parents and children." Another firm Smartypants (http://www.asksmartypants.com) conducts an annual online survey of brand "likeability" by children and mothers regarding a wide variety of brands. It results in the "Top 100 Kids' Most Loved Brands" list (see Chap. 9 that analyzes data from this firm.) To the industry, targeting children effectively is the lifeblood of current and future success. Moreover, as expressed by our informants, marketers believe that it is their right to do so.

In contrast to the industry, public health advocates and researchers take a dim view of aggressive marketing and advertising efforts that target children and adolescents as attractive market segments with intense and specialized marketing and advertising efforts (Story & French, 2004). They reject the claim that parents can shield their children from these efforts or control the behavior of their children in response to them. When the marketing and advertising tactics revolve around food and blur the line between advertising and entertainment, they are a source of intensifying concern for the public health community (Richtel, 2011). In this age of digital marketing, the public health community is particularly concerned that children can be targeted without the knowledge of parents by marketing and advertising that is "flying under the radar" (Harris, Suzanne, Brouwer, & Siegel, 2009). As pointed out by Montgomery et al. (Chap. 10), digital food marketing is advancing rapidly and is poised to reach a crucial tipping point in the very near future as expenditures for Internet and mobile advertising continue to rise. As one example, major brands have significantly increased their spending for online display advertising, exhibiting double-digit and in some cases triple-digit growth (Montgomery, Grier, Chester, & Dorfman, 2011). At the forefront of research and innovation in the interactive marketing arena, major food and beverage companies are investing heavily in global research and development strategies. They are working with dozens of ad agencies, marketing firms, and high-tech specialists to design campaigns that take advantage of young people's engagement with social networks, interactive games, mobile phones, online videos, and virtual worlds. Public health advocates focus on the great power that corporations wield in influencing the environment in which consumers, especially children, make choices about food. Corporations determine what types of food and beverage products are available, and they choose the marketing strategies and messages that permeate the world in which consumers make their choices. Public health advocates would tend to agree with Mick (2007) who argued that the influence of business in contemporary life is so omnipresent and powerful that it even surpasses the historical role of religion and government. To the public health community, there is an extreme power imbalance between the industry, the environment it creates, and its vulnerable target, children. As such, they emphasize the rights of children to grow and develop in healthy environments rather than the rights of marketers to target children. Kumanyika (2011) pointed to a key question at the center of the debate: should the rights of children be elevated to a level that supersedes potentially conflicting rights claimed by food marketers to identify children as a market segment that they have a right to pursue? Kumanyika also noted that the public health community has a formidable challenge in standing up to the industry, given its power, and that having rights may be less important than having the power to exercise one's rights.

Given the polarization of views, it seems difficult to find any common ground or a strategy to move forward toward a solution. Corporate social responsibility (CSR) is one approach that has the potential to suggest some new ways of thinking about the issues in a manner that is palatable or perhaps even attractive to businesses. A sophisticated and nuanced understanding of CSR is essential to arriving at new insights. During the past few years, the concept of business' responsibility has evolved from an economic model, to a legal model, to a social model, and now to a stakeholder model, which embodies a richer and more sophisticated understanding of CSR (Carroll & Buchholtz, 2009). A stakeholder model focuses not just on shareholders and maximizing their returns but also on a host of other parties that are affected by the firm—e.g., internal parties such as employees and external parties such as local communities, policy makers, activist groups, the public health community, etc. Underlying this transformation is a different and broader focus on performance and results—a new calculus of the bottom line or a multiple bottom line. The multiple bottom line approach argues that firms should be concerned not only with the traditional, economic/financial bottom line but also with a social bottom line that focuses on stakeholder relationships, an environmental bottom line that assesses the business's impact on the natural environment, and a cultural bottom line that assesses a firm's influence on the culture or cultures within which it operates (Drumwright, 2007). If food and beverage companies were to calculate overtly not just their financial bottom line, but their social, environmental, and especially their cultural bottom line, which would include their impact on the overall environment and culture in which children make food choices, they would be likely to view their responsibilities differently.

A more sophisticated understanding of CSR must be accompanied by a more sophisticated and nuanced understanding of the application of marketing concepts. Smith, Drumwright, and Gentile (2010) cautioned corporations about adhering too closely to the more traditional marketing constructs, which actually may hinder the adoption of a CSR orientation. They argued that marketers have learned too well the lessons of Levitt's (1960) classic "marketing myopia"—a distortion of strategic vision in which marketers fail to focus on the customer. They asserted that marketers have focused on the customer to the exclusion of other stakeholders, and they argued that this focus has resulted in a new form of marketing myopia, which also causes distortions in strategic vision and can lead to business failure. This "new marketing myopia" stems from three related phenomena: (1) a single-minded focus on the customer to the exclusion of other stakeholders, (2) an overly narrow definition of the customer and his or her needs, and (3) a failure to recognize the changed societal context of business that necessitates addressing multiple stakeholders. Ferrell, Gonzalez-Padron, Hult, and Maignan (2010) also cautioned firms about adhering too closely to a traditional marketing focus. They made a distinction between the concepts of market orientation and stakeholder orientation, noting that the market orientation construct focuses on customers and competitors and only indirectly on other stakeholder groups. In contrast, the stakeholder orientation construct does not designate any stakeholder group as more important than another, and the prioritization of stakeholders may change depending on the issue. Relatedly, Hult, Mena, Ferrell, and Ferrell (2011) pointed out that stakeholder theory deals with the nature of the relationships between the firm and its *various* stakeholders. Hence, they suggested that the unit of analysis is the firm along with its *network* of stakeholders, observing that marketers typically have not adopted this unit of analysis and seem to only look at the firm and one stakeholder at a time. Therefore, since marketing has not adopted a holistic stakeholder perspective, the public health community may view this as an opportunity to continue forming coalitions with other stakeholder groups, such as public policymakers and local community groups (Kramer et al., Chap. 18), putting further pressure on the food and beverage industry to adhere to responsible, ethical standards in marketing to children.

If there is a silver lining in the dark cloud of concerns over the conduct of the food and beverage industry, it is that more and more firms appear to be moving toward a greater CSR orientation. Another study conducted by the authors revealed a "pull" effect on competitors in joining the Children's Food and Beverage Advertising Initiative (CFBAI) and taking pledges (Williams & Drumwright, 2012). For example, McDonald's joined CFBAI in 2006, followed by the direct competitor, Burger King, in 2007. After Coca Cola joined CFBAI in 2006, the direct competitor, Pepsi, joined the initiative in 2007. It is encouraging that an analysis of companies that had taken either the CFBIA pledge or the Healthy Weight Commitment pledge revealed that those companies scored higher on a variety of CSR indicators than their competitors that had not taken pledges. Thus, firms with higher CSR orientations tended to join the pledge programs. An analysis of the annual revenues of pledge companies and nonpledge companies revealed that joining a pledge initiative did not appear to have a negative impact on revenues.

Study 2, which involved examining the websites of marketing, advertising, and marketing communication associations, highlighted the fact that neither children generally nor childhood obesity/health is on the agendas of these industry associations to the degree that it could or should be. Few of the industry associations' websites engage either topic in ways that are not general and vague. Because industry associations influence groups of organizations on issues related to ethics, they could be quite influential in changing norms and encouraging ethical practices related to food and beverage marketing to children. We are encouraged by the recent formation of the Institute for Advertising Ethics,[5] which is a partnership

[5] For more information, see http://www.aaf.org/default.asp?id=1236.

of the American Advertising Federation (AAF) and the Reynolds Journalism Institute of the University of Missouri School of Journalism. Its purpose is to inspire advertising, public relations, and marketing communication professionals to practice the highest personal ethics in the creation and dissemination of commercial information to consumers. It does address topics such as the blurring of advertising and entertainment and the vulnerability of children in behavioral targeting.

Pledge initiatives, such as CFBAI, operate at the level of organizations and groups of organizations, and as such, we view them as particularly critical.[6] We, along with others, acknowledge that the CFBAI pledges are less than perfect, but we also note that they have improved since they were begun in 2006. We are encouraged by the plans for increased consistency related to nutrition criteria that will be implemented across pledges by 2014. We hope that CFBAI companies will lead the industry in bold and compelling ways.

Academics have an important role to play by engaging with topics with public policy implications, such as food and beverage marketing and advertising, and providing independent, sophisticated, and credible research. As one of our informants noted, academics often are not willing to engage in broad, public policy debates. Also, many of the academics involved in the debates are public health academics, yet many of the research questions pertain to marketing and advertising. The participation, engagement, and collaboration of an interdisciplinary set of researchers, drawing from both marketing/advertising and public health and related disciplines, could play an important role in identifying solutions and understanding the most effective ways to implement them.

The transformation of food and beverage marketing is ongoing and poses serious threats to the health and well-being of young people, both children and adolescents. The old standards and solutions are inadequate. Addressing the transformation requires both new thinking and new comprehensive agendas. Success depends upon the collaborative and whole hearted engagement of the food and beverage industry, the public health community, and academics. To draw on a cliché, both sides need to be attuned to the problem of winning battles but losing the war.

Acknowledgements The authors wish to thank ChangeLab Solutions, NPLAN for their support in conducting the research for this chapter. We also wish to thank H.W. Perry, Jr., for his insightful comments on early drafts that helped significantly to shape the final version of this paper.

[6] The level of organizations and groups of organizations has been referred to as the "meso" level (House, Rousseau, & Thomas-Hunt, 1995; Drumwright, 2007). Drumwright argued that the meso level, which has been neglected in advertising ethics, is particularly important. Norms set at the meso level have a strong influence on the moral sensitivity and behavior of individual advertising practitioners. Moreover, solutions to some macro level ethical problems to which advertising contributes require the collaborative efforts of organizations or groups of organizations.

Appendix A, Interview Protocol

1. Every industry faces ethical issues in general and also ethical issues specific to the industry. What do you see as issues that could pose ethical issues in food marketing?
    - What role do you think that food marketing plays in the obesity crisis?
2. How should we think about targeting children in this context?
    - How should we think about the age of the child?
    - Are the ethical issues related to adolescents more like those related to adults or more like those related to children?
    - There has been a debate in the media about Ronald McDonald as the spokesperson for McDonald's? How should we think about issues like this?
    - There has been debate about giving away toys with fast food. How should we think about this issue?
3. How should we think about mass media?
    - Some people worry about what they refer to as the unintended consequences related to mass media advertising? How should we think about these issues?
4. How should we think about ethical issues related to food advertising in schools?
    - Are there different issues for elementary schools vs. middle schools vs. high schools?
5. How should we think ethical issues related to food marketing and electronic media?
    - Privacy?
    - Social media?
6. How does one go about changing the culture of unhealthy snacking *vis a vis* the obesity epidemic?

Consumers

- Marketers always value consumer choice. Is there ever a point when consumer choice gets outweighed by broader issues?
- How does one retrain the American consumer, who likes salty, fatty, sugary snacks?

Food Companies

- What role should the food companies play? What could keep food companies from addressing the obesity crisis as they should?
- Should food companies be cast as moral pariahs like the tobacco companies were?

Public Health Community

- What role should the public health community play? What could keep the public health community from addressing the obesity crisis as it should?

Academic Community

- What role should academics play? What could keep academics from addressing the obesity crisis as they should?

7. What would make the self-regulatory efforts of the food industry more effective?

    - What do you see as the strengths and weaknesses of self-regulation?
    - What could be done to keep politics from derailing this effort

Appendix B, Industry Associations

Marketing

- *American Marketing Association* (http://www.marketingpower.com/Pages/default.aspx)
- *Direct Marketing Association* (http://www.the-dma.org/index.php)
- *Business Marketing Association* (http://www.marketing.org)
- *Promotion Marketing Association* (http://www.pmalink.org/)
- *eMarketing Association* (http://www.emarketingassociation.com/)
- *Mobile Marketing Association* (http://mmaglobal.com/main)
- *Word of Mouth Marketing Association* (http://womma.org/main/)
- *Internet Marketing Association* (http://www.imanetwork.org/)
- *International Internet Marketing Association* (http://www.iimaonline.org/)
- *The Web Marketing Association* (http://www.webmarketingassociation.org/)

Advertising

- *American Association of Advertising Agencies* (http://www2.aaaa.org/Portal/Pages/default.aspx)
- *International Advertising Association* (http://www.iaaglobal.org/)
- *American Advertising Federation* (http://www.aaf.org/)
- *Retail Advertising and Marketing Association* (http://www.rama-nrf.org/)
- *Outdoor Advertising Association of America* (http://www.oaaa.org/)
- *Association of Hispanic Advertising Agencies* (http://www.ahaa.org/index.htm)
- *Indoor Billboard Advertising Association* (http://www.indooradvertising.org/)
- *Asian American Advertising Federation* (http://www.3af.org/)
- *Interactive Advertising Bureau* (http://www.iab.net/)

Public Relations

- *Public Relations Society of America* (http://www.prsa.org/)
- *International Public Relations Associations* (http://www.ipra.org/)
- *Institute for Public Relations* (http://www.instituteforpr.org/)

References

American Marketing Association (2008). *Market segmentation*. http://www.marketingpower.com/_layouts/Dictionary.aspx?dLetter=M#market+segmentation

Carroll, A. B., & Buchholtz, A. K. (2009). *Business and society: Ethics and stakeholder management* (7th ed.). Mason, OH: South-Western Cengage Learning.

Cobin, J. M., & Strauss, A. (2008). *Basics of qualitative research: Techniques and procedures for developing grounded theory* (3rd ed.). Los Angeles, CA: Sage Publications, Inc.

Drumwright, M. E. (2007). Advertising ethics: A multi-level theory approach. In G. Tellis & T. Ambler (Eds.), *The Sage handbook of advertising*. Los Angeles, CA: Sage Publication, Inc.

Ferrell, O. C., Tracy Gonzalez-Padron, G., Hult, T. M., & Maignan, I. (2010). From market orientation to stakeholder orientation. *Journal of Public Policy and Marketing, 29*(1), 93–96.

Food Marketing Workgroup. (2011). *The genesis of the food marketing workgroup: Where we've been & where we're going*. Berkeley, CA: Center for Science in the Public Interest and Berkeley Media Studies Group (BMSG).

Harris, M. (2009, October 23). Targeting tots could build lifelong brand recognition: Study. *Montreal Gazette*. http://www.commercialexploitation.org/news/2009/10/targetingtots.html

Harris, D., Suzanne, Y., Brouwer, C., Siegel, J. (2009, November 1). *Vigilant parents say they are often unaware of marketing techniques that draw teens, kids: Advertising industry says regulations effective, but watchdog groups disagree*. http://abcnews.go.com/WN/w_ParentingResource/vigilant-parents-unaware-marketing-techniques-draw-teens-kids/Story?id=8969255&page=1

Hawkes, C., & Harris, J. L. (2011). An analysis of the content of food industry pledges on marketing to children. *Public Health Nutrition*. doi:10.1017/S1368980011000607.

House, R., Rousseau, D. M., & Thomas-Hunt, M. (1995). The meso paradigm: A framework for the integration of micro and macro organizational behavior. *Research in Organizational Behavior, 17*, 71–114.

Hult, G. T. M., Mena, J. A., Ferrell, O. C., & Ferrell, L. (2011). Stakeholder marketing: a definition and conceptual framework. *AMS Review, 1*(1), 44–65.

Kotler, P., & Keller, K. L. (2006). *Marketing management* (12th ed.). Upper Saddle River, NJ: Prentice Hall.

Kumanyika, S. K. (2011). A question of competing rights, priorities, and principles: A postscript to the Robert Wood Johnson Foundation symposium on the ethics of childhood obesity policy. *Preventing Chronic Disease: Public Health Research, Practice, and Policy, 8*(5), A97.

Levitt, T. (1960). Marketing myopia. *Harvard Business Review, 38*, 57–66.

Lochhead, C. (2011, December 12). Food giants fight proposed nutrition guidelines. *San Francisco Chronicle*. http://www.sfgate.com/cgi-bin/article.cgi?f=/c/a/2011/12/11/MNRV1MAK70.DTL&ao=all

McCracken, G. D. (1988). *The long interview*. Newbury Park, CA: Sage.

Mick, D. G. (2007). The end(s) of marketing and the neglect of moral responsibility by the American Marketing Association. *Journal of Public Policy and Marketing, 26*(2), 289–292.

Miles, M. S., & Michael Huberman, A. (1994). *Qualitative data analysis*. Thousand Oaks, CA: Sage Publications.

Montgomery, K., Grier, S., Chester, J., Dorfman, L. (2011). *Food marketing in the digital age: A conceptual framework and agenda for research.* Research report from Robert Wood Johnson Foundation's Healthy Eating Research Program (Grant #65063).

Preston, I. (1994). *The tangled web they weave.* Madison, WI: The University of Wisconsin Press.

Research, H. E. (2011). *Food and beverage marketing to children and adolescents: An environment at odds with good health, a research synthesis, A National Program of the Robert Wood Johnson Foundation.* Minneapolis, MN: Healthy Eating Research.

Richtel, M. (2011, April 20). In online games, a path to young consumers. *The New York Times.* http://www.nytimes.com/2011/04/21/business/21marketing.html?pagewanted=all

Schwartz, M. B., & Ustjanauskas, A. (2012). Food marketing to youth: Current threats and opportunities (Editorial). *Childhood Obesity, 8*(2). doi:chi.2012.0082.schw.

Smith, C., Drumwright, M. E., & Gentile, M. (2010). The new marketing myopia. *Journal of Public Policy and Marketing, 29*(Spring), 4–11.

Story, M., & French, S. (2004). Review: Food advertising and marketing directed at children and adolescents in the US. *International Journal of Behavioral Nutrition and Physical Activity, 1*(3). http://www.ijbnpa.org/content/1/1/3.

Williams, J. (2005). Product proliferation analysis for new food and beverage products targeted to children 1994–2004. *University of Texas at Austin working paper.*

Williams, J., & Drumwright, M. E. (2012). *Ethics in food and beverage marketing to children: NPLAN report.* Oakland, CA: ChangeLab Solutions, NPLAN.

Chapter 5
The New First Amendment and Its Implications for Combating Obesity Through Regulation of Advertising

Samantha Graff and Tamara Piety

Introduction

For at least three generations, Americans have taken for granted that the government may pass laws governing food and product safety, truth in advertising, lending, and other important features of modern life. Today, however, policies that would have seemed unremarkable in the past are facing constitutional challenges. This development is the result of a campaign by large corporations to muster the First Amendment as a defense against governmental intervention in commercial activity.

The courts have been the major battleground in this campaign, and in recent years, industry groups have won major litigation victories that have upended settled expectations about the ability of government to regulate in the public interest. In just 2010 and 2011, the Supreme Court advanced the free speech rights of corporations by striking down a federal law barring independent corporate expenditures on electioneering communications[1]; Vermont's prohibition on the sale of doctors' prescription histories to drug companies for direct marketing purposes[2]; and California's ban on the sale of violent video games to minors.[3]

Industry groups also invoke the First Amendment to dissuade policymakers from pursuing measures to promote public health and welfare. Obesity prevention advocates are finding that any policy proposal relating to junk food advertising—even

[1] Citizens United v. Fed. Election Comm'n, 130 S. Ct. 876 (2010).

[2] Sorrell v. IMS Health, Inc., 131 S. Ct. 2653 (2011).

[3] Brown v. Entm't Merch. Ass'n, 131 S. Ct. 2729 (2011).

T. Piety (✉)
University of Tulsa College of Law, 3120 E. 4th Place, OK 74104, Tulsa, USA
e-mail: tamara-piety@utulsa.edu

S. Graff
ChangeLab Solutions, NPLAN, 2201 Broadway, Suite 502, CA 94612, Oakland, USA
e-mail: sgraff@changelabsolutions.org

J.D. Williams et al. (eds.), *Advances in Communication Research to Reduce Childhood Obesity*, DOI 10.1007/978-1-4614-5511-0_5,

government *recommendations* on the nutritional profile of foods that are appropriate to market to children[4]—will be met with aggressive objections that corporations' expressive rights are under siege.[5]

Many might be surprised to learn that the First Amendment has *any* relevance to marketing—and it did not for the first 200 years of the country's history. In the mid-1970s, however, the Supreme Court announced that the First Amendment limits what government can do about advertising, thus creating what has become known as the "commercial speech doctrine."[6] The doctrine began its life with the professed goals of advancing consumers' interest in receiving truthful information and the general public's interest in information flowing freely in the marketplace. Over time, the doctrine has morphed into a protective shield not only for the recipients of advertising but also, especially recently, for commercial "speakers."

In this chapter, we explore the evolution and contours of the commercial speech doctrine, emphasizing how recent developments in the US Supreme Court may present significant First Amendment obstacles to addressing childhood obesity through government restrictions on marketing. We begin with a brief overview of the American system of constitutional law, focusing on how judicial interpretation works and why the pronouncements of the Supreme Court of the USA have such a profound impact on the ability of government to regulate in the public interest. Next, we describe the evolution of the commercial speech doctrine and the mechanics of how courts evaluate the constitutionality of laws regulating commercial speech. We then explore how recent Supreme Court decisions have reshaped various elements of the commercial speech doctrine, making it increasingly difficult for government to enact policy initiatives aimed at protecting children and public health. The chapter closes by highlighting policy ideas and strategic considerations for policymakers seeking to navigate constitutional rocks and shoals on the way to a healthier food environment.

The Constitutional Context

Before we consider the First Amendment it is useful to review how constitutional law works in the USA. The word "law" can actually mean several things: a federal or state constitutional provision; a statute passed by a legislature; a local ordinance; a regulation promulgated by an executive agency; a court's interpretation of any of the above; or "common law" originating from courts that supplements the other

---

[4] Federal Trade Commission (2011). *Interagency Working Group on food marketed to children: Preliminary proposed nutrition principles to guide industry self-regulatory efforts*. http://www.ftc.gov/os/2011/04/110428foodmarketproposedguide.pdf.

[5] *See* In re Interagency Working Group on Food Marketed to Children. Comments of Viacom, Inc., FTC Project No. P094513 (Jul. 14, 2011). Available at http://www.ftc.gov/os/comments/foodmarketedchildren/07884-80045.pdf; Redish, M. H. (2011). *Childhood obesity, advertising, and the first amendment, GMAonline.org* (Jun. 8, 2011). Available at http://www.gmaonline.org/file-manager/Health_Nutrition/childhood_advertising__firstamendment.pdf.

[6] Virginia State Bd. of Pharmacy v. Virginia Citizens Consumer Council, Inc., 425 U.S. 748 (1976).

sources of law. Yet not all law is equal. Federal law overrides conflicting state and local law, and state law overrides conflicting local law. At the federal level, the Constitution trumps statutes, which trump regulations, all of which, if clearly applicable, may trump prior case law. The same tiers apply at the state level.

The Supreme Court is the final arbiter of questions of federal law, particularly constitutional law. This means that the Supreme Court's interpretation of the Constitution can invalidate efforts from the legislative and executive branches to address social problems such as obesity.

Let us take as an example the constitutional provision with which we are concerned. The First Amendment to the US Constitution provides that "Congress shall make no law . . . abridging the freedom of speech."[7] Merely reading the text of what is known as "the Free Speech Clause" provides little insight into how it might apply to, say, McDonalds' right to advertise Happy Meals on Nickelodeon. To answer that question one must look to case law *interpreting* the First Amendment—particularly the decisions of the US Supreme Court.

Most Supreme Court decisions are not unanimous,[8] and they don't need to be. When a majority agrees on a holding, that opinion is considered the decision of the Court. Often one or more of the nine Justices will write a concurrence (agreeing with the outcome but not with the majority's analysis) or a dissent (disagreeing with the outcome and the majority's analysis).

In theory, the Supreme Court is bound by "precedent," that is, its own past decisions. The fact that a type of problem has been resolved a certain way in the past is generally viewed as a basis for continuing to do so. Because it might undermine the legitimacy of the Court if it seemed as if the decisions of the Court veered this way and that too often, or that they rested on merely political grounds, the Court rarely *explicitly* overrules precedent. When it does, the Court will generally provide a rationale for doing so[9]—either referring to evolving social and political norms, or noting that recent errant cases deviated from an earlier valid precedent. More commonly, the Court will only *implicitly* overrule precedent, articulating a new rule while suggesting that the decision flows from earlier cases.[10]

The US political system relies on law, especially constitutional law, to provide continuity and predictability. We need the law to clearly delineate the boundaries between legal and illegal conduct and to give us a shared, stable link to our civic history. At the same time, the law must adapt to new challenges as they arise—challenges stemming from technological developments, changes in social customs, scientific discoveries, and the like. Courts generally resolve the tension between the goals of stability and flexibility by incorporating changing realities slowly. In this

---

[7] US Const. amend. I.

[8] Epstein, L., Landes, W. M., Posner, R. A. *Unanimous decisions in the Supreme Court* (rev. Jun. 19, 2011), http://epstein.usc.edu/research/unanDec isions.pdf.

[9] *See*, e.g., Citizens United v. Fed. Election Com'n, 130 S. Ct. 876 (2010) (overruling precedent set in Austin v. Mich. Chamber of Commerce, 494 U.S. 652 (1990)).

[10] *See* Schauer, F. (2008). Has precedent ever really mattered in the Supreme Court? *Ga. St. U. L. Rev., 24*, 381.

sense, the law is inherently conservative—not necessarily politically, but rather in the dictionary definition of "tending or disposed to maintain existing views" and "marked by moderation or caution."[11] There are times, though, when the Court (and thus the law) will make a more abrupt move that significantly changes the landscape of the past. Something like this happened in the 1970s with respect to the law's treatment of commercial advertising.

Emergence of the Commercial Speech Doctrine

The First Amendment was included in the Bill of Rights to ensure the freedom of speech from excessive government intervention. The Free Speech Clause is commonly understood to protect individuals against unreasonable interference by the government in their artistic, political, and other expressive interests.[12] First Amendment protection for advertising, however, is a relatively new idea. From the adoption of the Bill of Rights through the first half of the 20th century, advertising regulations were constitutionally indistinguishable from basic regulations of business activities. There was no First Amendment protection for advertising at all.[13] Commercial advertising was thought to be at best somewhat informative and at worst a fraudulent force aimed at misleading consumers and inflating prices.[14] But courts' views evolved in the mid-twentieth century, perhaps due to a combination of changing public perceptions and a growing body of scholarly work about the value of advertising.[15]

Whatever the reason, in the early 1970s the Supreme Court began to look differently at advertising and in 1976 flatly held that advertising—which the Court now deemed "commercial speech"—was protected by the First Amendment. The case that heralded this change, *Virginia State Board of Pharmacy v. Virginia Citizens Consumer Council*, was brought by a consumer group opposing a Virginia law that

[11] *Conservative – Definition and More from the Free Merriam-Webster Dictionary*, Merriam-Webster Online, http://www.merriam-webster.com/dictionary/conservative (last visited Jan. 31, 2012).

[12] *Cf.* Barry, B. (2007). Speechless: The Erosion of Free Expression in the American Workplace (explaining that private actors such as employers are free to restrict speech they find disagreeable).

[13] *See* Valentine v. Christensen, 316 U.S. 52 (1942), *abrogated by* Virginia State Bd. of Pharmacy v. Virginia Citizens Consumer Council, 425 U.S. 748 (1976).

[14] *See* Calfee, J. E. (1997). Fear of persuasion: A new perspective on advertising and regulation 5 (the common view was that advertising was wasteful, "distorted consumer information and preferences and was a tool for creating or buttressing monopoly power."). *See also* Posner, R. A. (1969). *The Federal Trade Commission*, 37; Chi, U. (1969). *L. Rev.* 47–89; Posner, R. A. Regulation of advertising by the FTC (American Enterprise Institute 1973).

[15] *See*, e.g., Coase, R. H. (1974). The market for goods and the market for ideas. *American Economic Review, 64*, 384; Redish, M. H. (1971). The first amendment in the marketplace: Commercial speech and the values of free expression. *George Washington Law Review, 39*, 429; Calfee, *supra* note 14; Posner, *supra* note 14.

prohibited pharmacies from engaging in price advertising.[16] The state defended the law on the grounds that price advertising was likely to result in price wars which would, in turn, lead pharmacies to cut corners, thus endangering patient well-being and safety. The plaintiffs, a consumer group, countered that price was a critical piece of information, particularly to those with low incomes, and that it was inappropriate for the state to "protect" people from this critical piece of information for their own good. The Supreme Court agreed, rejecting what it called the law's "highly paternalistic approach"[17] of shielding people from the truth and instead adopting a new constitutional standard for commercial speech.

From then on, the Court announced in *Virginia Pharmacy*, truthful commercial advertising would have some degree of First Amendment protection. The Court found that advertising merited a certain amount of protection under the First Amendment because it helps consumers make well-informed purchasing decisions. [18] In the Court's view, the free flow of commercial information benefits not only individual consumers but also society at large:

> So long as we preserve a predominantly free enterprise economy, the allocation of our resources in large measure will be made through numerous private economic decisions. It is a matter of public interest that those decisions, in the aggregate, be intelligent and well informed. To this end, the free flow of commercial information is indispensable.[19]

Virginia Pharmacy marked the Supreme Court's announcement of what is known today as the "commercial speech doctrine." A few years later, in the *Central Hudson* case of 1980,[20] the Court codified the doctrine into a four-prong test for courts to use when considering whether a governmental regulation of commercial speech restriction is valid under the First Amendment.

The *Central Hudson* test begins with a threshold question that is unusual in the First Amendment context: Is the speech false, or actually or inherently misleading, or about an illegal subject matter? If so, it is not entitled to First Amendment protection at all. An advertisement gets no First Amendment protection if it claims "this pill guarantees you'll lose five pounds per week" when in fact the pill does not work. Outside the commercial speech context, the Court has generally avoided imposing a truth test for First Amendment protection, finding that protecting some false speech is necessary to maintain overall freedom of expression.[21]

The Court has justified the lack of protection for false and misleading *commercial* speech on the grounds that speakers hoping to make a profit from selling something should be capable of backing up their claims about their products and services.[22]

---

[16] Virginia State Bd. of Pharmacy v. Virginia Citizens Consumer Council, Inc., 425 U.S. 748 (1976).

[17] *Id.* at 770.

[18] *Id.* at 763.

[19] *Id.* at 765.

[20] Central Hudson Gas & Elec. Corp. v. Pub. Serv. Comm'n of N.Y., 447 U.S. 557, 566 (1980).

[21] *See*, e.g., N.Y. Times Co. v. Sullivan, 376 U.S. 254 (1964) (protecting false speech made regarding a public figure on matter of public concern so long as it was not made knowingly or recklessly).

[22] Virginia State Bd. of Pharmacy, 425 U.S. at 777 (Stewart, J., concurring).

Table 5.1 Levels of Review

Level of Review	Applies to Regulations of:	Likelihood of Regulation Surviving a Court Challenge:
Strict scrutiny test	"Core" speech about art, politics, and other ideas	Very low
Intermediate scrutiny test *Central Hudson*)	Truthful, nonmisleading advertising, and other commercial speech	In between
Rational basis test	Commercial practices and products	Very high
Full deference to government	Advertising about illegal activity, false or inherently misleading advertising	Almost always upheld once the court finds the advertising to be unprotected

Moreover, because they have an economic motive, commercial speakers will likely continue to advertise to whatever degree is permissible and are unlikely to be unduly "chilled" by appropriate regulation which requires that their claims be truthful and not misleading.[23]

In the commercial context, then, the First Amendment extends protection only to truthful, nonmisleading commercial speech about a legal activity. The first prong of the *Central Hudson* test holds that commercial speech that is false, or which is actually or inherently misleading, is not entitled to any First Amendment protection and the government is free to ban it outright.

The remaining prongs of the *Central Hudson* test require that:

1. The law limiting commercial speech address a "substantial" state interest;
2. The law "directly advance" that substantial state interest; and
3. The law not limit speech more than necessary to accomplish its purpose.[24]

In legal parlance the *Central Hudson* test entails a form of "intermediate scrutiny." It gives the government more leeway to restrict advertising than the "strict scrutiny" test that applies to governmental attempts to regulate political or artistic speech. Strict scrutiny has been described as "strict in theory, but fatal in fact"[25] because it almost always results in the invalidation of a regulation. At the same time, intermediate scrutiny gives the government less room than the "rational basis" test applicable to most business regulations.[26] Rational basis review usually results in upholding the law in question because it grants a great deal of deference to the legislature. The chart above sets forth the various possibilities (Table 5.1).

At first the intermediate-level *Central Hudson* test fell somewhere close to the middle of the continuum. However, over time, the Supreme Court's application of

[23] *Id.*

[24] Central Hudson, 447 U.S. at 566.

[25] Gunther, G. (1972). Foreword: in search of evolving doctrine on a changing court: A model for a newer equal protection. *Harvard Law Review, 1*, 8 (1972).

[26] *See* United States v. Carolene Products Co., 304 U.S. 144, 153 (1938).

Central Hudson has crept closer to strict scrutiny in practice if not in name,[27] making it harder for the government to enact commercial speech regulations that can stand up in court.[28] And along the way, the doctrine has become increasingly speaker-centric, recognizing not only *listeners'* interests in the information conveyed in advertising but also commercial *speakers'* interests in conveying the information.

Because the level of judicial review tends to predict the outcome of a First Amendment case, consumer advocates and corporations naturally vie over how to define the categories of speech that are subject to each level of review. The two sides have differing visions of where the boundaries fall between the different categories. Both sides agree, however, that defining what makes speech "commercial" and thus subject to an intermediate standard of review is critical.

The Supreme Court has not clearly articulated how commercial speech differs from core speech. A sensible approach would be to define any speech by a commercial entity as "commercial speech."[29] But the Court has clearly rejected this approach in its most recent decisions.[30] Some industry commentators and even some Justices have advocated eliminating the distinction between core speech and commercial, making it all subject to strict scrutiny.[31]

In terms of the boundary between commercial speech and other business practices, industry generally would like to place as many commercial activities and products as possible under the rubric of commercial speech—particularly given that the new, stricter interpretation of the *Central Hudson* test offers significant protection from government interference. So, for instance, industry has argued that free tobacco samples,[32] the toy in a fast-food restaurant children's meal,[33] and a database of doctors' prescription records[34] all constitute commercial "speech," even though an average observer might think that each instance involved a noncommunicative product. In its 2011 opinion in *Sorrell v. IMS Health Inc.*, the Supreme Court observed that there is "a strong argument" to be made that a database of doctors' prescription records is protected commercial speech.[35] That suggestion does not bode well for the view that samples, toys, and databases are products subject to routine sales practice regulations.

---

[27] Vladeck, D. C. (2004). *Lessons from a story untold:* Nike v. Kasky *Reconsidered. Case Western Reserve Law Review, 1049*, 1059.

[28] *See* Lorillard Tobacco Co. v. Reilly, 533 U.S. 525, 571 (2001); Thompson v. W. States Med. Ctr., 535 U.S. 357, 377 (2002); Sorrell, 131 S. Ct. at 2673 (2011).

[29] Piety, T. R. (2006). Free advertising: The case for public relations as commercial speech. *Lewis and Clark Law Review, 10*, 367–413. *See also* Piety, T. R. (2012). Brandishing the first amendment: Commercial expression in America. University of Michigan Press.

[30] Citizens United (2010). 130 S. Ct. at 898–99.

[31] *See.* e.g., Thomas, J. (concurring). Lorillard Tobacco, 533 U.S. at 572.

[32] Ky, W. D. (2010). Commonwealth Brands, Inc. v. United States, 678 F. Supp. 2d 512.

[33] McDonald's Happy Meal Toy Lawsuit Review, http://mbaindc.blogspot.com (last visited Jan. 31, 2012).

[34] Sorrell v. IMS Health, Inc., 131 S. Ct. 2653 (2011).

[35] Id. at 2667.

Another disputed boundary surrounds the category of unprotected commercial speech—advertising that is false, actually or inherently misleading, or about illegal activity. As described above, government is free to ban this category of speech outright without having to meet the final three prongs of the *Central Hudson* test. The category is smaller than it might seem at first. Although a lot of advertising is hyperbolic, impressionistic, and designed to appeal to emotion instead of logic, the law over the past hundred years or so has developed a fairly limited class of ads that it deems actually false or actually misleading.[36]

The *Central Hudson* test is a classic example of how interpretation matters deeply in constitutional law. Since the inception of the commercial speech doctrine, consumer advocates and corporations have wrangled over the definitions, contours, and boundaries of the doctrine. Over the last couple of decades, industry has won most of those fights. Although the law in this area is still in flux, the current Supreme Court appears inclined to continue expanding the First Amendment as a safe haven for industry from government restrictions on advertising and other marketing activities. However, since the Court has not yet applied the commercial speech doctrine to a restriction on solely youth-targeted advertising,[37] there may yet be room for well-tailored regulations of junk food advertising and marketing to children.

Challenges Posed by the Commercial Speech Doctrine for Public Health

Until such time as the Supreme Court reconsiders or clarifies the commercial speech doctrine, the obesity prevention movement will have to shape proposals for reform with an eye to the challenges posed by existing law. Here, we explore the four prongs of the *Central Hudson* test, identifying nuances that have arisen in recent Supreme Court decisions that may affect policy initiatives to safeguard children and public health. We follow with a discussion of why the Court's decision in *Sorrell v. IMS Health, Inc.* raises serious questions about the continuing viability of the *Central Hudson* test.

Prong One: Unprotected Commercial Speech

Under the First Amendment, certain categories of speech—such as making false promises in an advertisement, yelling obscenities on the radio, or crying fire in a crowded theater—are unprotected because they are of extremely low social value or

[36] Piety, T. R. (2007) Market failure in the marketplace of ideas: Commercial speech and the problem that won't go away. *Loyola of Los Angeles Law Review, 41*, 181.

[37] *Cf.* Lorillard Tobacco Co. v. Reilly, 533 U.S. 525 (2001) (ruling that Massachusetts' tobacco advertising restrictions, though ostensibly directed at advertising received by children, in fact prohibited a great deal of speech intended for adults).

trigger immediate, serious danger.[38] For decades, public health and child advocates have argued that advertising to children ought to be categorized as unprotected speech because it carries serious risks of being misunderstood by children, may shape lifetime preferences for dangerous products, may undermine parental authority, or may interfere with healthy development.[39] Congress, however, has not enacted regulations based on these arguments. The reasons are political, not constitutional. For example, the FTC's attempt in the late 1970s to propose stricter regulation of advertising to children engendered a firestorm of lobbying opposition from industry (including, it should be noted, the tobacco industry), which ultimately led Congress to curtail the FTC's authority.[40]

The food, advertising, and entertainment industries predictably object to the notion that advertising to children should be considered unprotected speech, and they are now drawing fodder from a 2011 Supreme Court case. *Brown v. Entertainment Merchants Association*[41] involved a California law prohibiting the sale or rental of violent video games to minors. The law applied to games involving killing, maiming, dismembering, or sexually assaulting an image of a human being in a manner that a reasonable person would find appeals to a deviant or morbid interest of minors. The Supreme Court rejected California's argument that violent video games should be considered unprotected speech when directed at children. The Court refused to add a "wholly new category" to the list of categories that have been unprotected by "longstanding tradition."[42] *Brown* almost surely forecloses the possibility of establishing a new category of unprotected speech called, say, "harmful advertising to children."

Crucially, however, *Brown* did not upend existing categories of unprotected speech, including inherently deceptive advertising. If advertising directed at children can be shown to be inherently deceptive—and it can—then regulations targeting only that advertising should be constitutionally defensible.

An extensive body of scientific research amassed over three decades and backed by the American Academy of Pediatrics[43] and the American Psychological Association[44] compels the conclusion that advertising directed to children under twelve is inherently misleading. The evidence shows that a child's full comprehension of advertising requires three levels of understanding: the child must be able to distinguish media content from commercial advertising; the child must be able to recognize the selling intent of advertising messages; and the child must be able to recognize that the selling intent

[38] *See* Schenck v. United States, 249 U.S. 47, 52 (1919).

[39] *See*, e.g., Westen, T. (2006). Government regulation of food marketing to children: The Federal Trade Commission and the Kid-Vid Controversy. *Loyola of Los Angeles Law Review, 39*, 79.

[40] *Id.* at 83–84.

[41] Brown v. Entm't Merchs. Ass'n, 131 S. Ct. 2729 (2011).

[42] *Id.* at 2736.

[43] Committee on Communications (2006). Policy statement: Children, adolescents and advertising. *Pediatrics, 118*(6), 2563.

[44] Kunkel, D., et al. (2004). Report of the APA task force on advertising and children (American Psychological Association 2004). Available at http://www.apa.org/pi/families/resources/advertising-children.pdf.

leads to inherent bias in advertising.[45] Children generally do not master all three levels of understanding until eleven to twelve years of age because, even if they can identify an advertisement and its selling intent, they cannot apply the appropriate skepticism to the advertisement because they do not grasp exaggeration and embellishment in marketing messages.[46] The research suggests that *there is no plausible way to advertise to a young child in a nonmisleading way* and thus that the government should be able to restrict all advertising to young children—or, if it chooses, a subset of advertising to children that is deemed particularly harmful—without raising First Amendment concerns.[47]

As for adolescents, as some of the other contributions to this book discuss, a burgeoning field of scientific study is exposing their vulnerability to certain digital marketing techniques that are heavily employed by food companies. Neurological studies reveal that adolescents are significantly more vulnerable than adults to advertising messages because the part of the brain that directs impulse control, risk taking, and maturity of judgment does not fully develop until adulthood.[48] Furthermore, the proliferation of interactive and immersive marketing to teens is specifically designed to trigger subconscious, emotional reactions—bypassing rational consideration of product information.[49] These psychological tactics are particularly powerful when used to elicit positive associations with hard-to-resist, obesogenic food products.[50] To the extent these tactics can be shown to be actually or inherently misleading, the government should be free to regulate them under the first prong of the *Central Hudson* test.[51]

In summary, the first prong of the *Central Hudson* test—whether speech is truthful and not misleading—is unexplored territory as it pertains to junk food advertising to young people. Those concerned about junk food advertising may want to focus on bringing to light the degree to which such advertising is inherently or actually misleading and thus unprotected by the First Amendment from government interference. This is a worthwhile pursuit. For if an advertising regulation is subject to the remainder of the *Central Hudson* test—if the speech it regulates is, for example,

---

[45] Kunkel, D. (2010). Commentary: Mismeasurement of children's understanding of the persuasive intent of advertising. *Journal of Children and Media*, *4*(1), 109.

[46] Mills, C. M., & Keil, F. C. (2005). The development of cynicism. *Psychological Science, 16*, 385.

[47] Graff, S., Kunkel, D., Mermin, S. (2012). Government can regulate food advertising to children because cognitive research shows it is inherently misleading. *Health Affairs, 31*(2), 392–398.

[48] Pechmann, C., Levine, L., Loughlin, S., Leslie, F. (2005). Impulsive and self-conscious: Adolescents' vulnerability to advertising and promotion. *Journal of Public Policy and Marketing, 24*(2), 202; *see also* Harris, J. L., Brownell, K. D., Bargh, J. A. (2009). The food marketing defense model: Integrating psychological research to protect youth and inform public policy. *Social Issues and Policy Review, 3*(1), 211.

[49] Pradeep, A. K. (2010). The buying brain: Secrets of selling to the subconscious. *Mind.* John Wiley & Sons; Binet, L., Field, P. (2009). Empirical generalizations about advertising campaign success. *Journal of Advertising Research, 49*(2), 130

[50] Harris, Brownwell & Bargh, *supra* note 49.

[51] Harris, J., & Graff, S. (2012). Protecting young people from junk food advertising: Implications of psychological research for first amendment law. *American Journal Public Health, 102*(2), 214.

only "potentially misleading"—the chances of passing constitutional muster are significantly reduced.

Prong Two: Substantial Government Interest

Prong two of the *Central Hudson* test has not typically presented serious difficulties for policymakers. Supreme Court precedent establishes a relatively low hurdle for the government to clear in order to establish that there is an important governmental interest.[52] In commercial speech cases, industry litigants have often offered only tepid opposition to the government's claim of a substantial interest in the asserted goal for a particular regulation. More often they concede that the government has substantial reasons for enacting the challenged regulation—preferring to battle it out on prongs three and four of the *Central Hudson* test.

However, the prong two inquiry is not without teeth. In the 1995 case of *Rubins v. Coors Brewing Company* and again in the 2011 case of *Sorrell v. IMS Health, Inc.*, for example, the Supreme Court struck down consumer protection laws because it doubted the validity or coherence of the government's stated interests. These cases are significant for our purposes because the Court, in other opinions, has expressed serious doubts about some of the types of government interests that might motivate a restriction on junk food advertising to children.

On the one hand, the Supreme Court has traditionally affirmed the government's interest in regulating to protect the health, safety, and welfare of the public[53]—particularly of children.[55] Reducing childhood obesity is obviously a substantial governmental interest. Indeed, despite his hostility to the idea of regulating advertising to protect children and public health, Justice Thomas himself noted a decade ago that obesity was the second "largest contributor to mortality rates"[55] and was a problem that was "rapidly growing worse."[56] Nothing has changed in that respect since 2001. As the other chapters in this book illustrate so forcefully, obesity in the USA among children is a problem of epidemic proportions.

On the other hand, the Court has shown increasing skepticism toward what it deems "paternalistic" regulations designed to "keep people in the dark for what the government perceives to be their own good."[57] In the 2011 *Brown* case, the entertainment software industry successfully persuaded the Court to bring its anti-paternalistic sensibilities to bear on a law designed to safeguard children from violent

[52] *See* e.g., Thomas, J. (concurring). Lorillard Tobacco, 533 U.S. at 587.

[53] Rubin v. Coors Brewing Co., 514 U.S. 476 (1995).

[54] Lorillard Tobacco, 533 U.S. 525; Ginsberg v. State of New York, 390 U.S. 629 (1968); Prince v. Massachusetts, 321 U.S. 158 (1944).

[55] Lorillard Tobacco, 533 U.S. at 587 (citations omitted).

[56] *Id.*

[57] 44 Liquormart v. Rhode Island, 517 U.S. 484, 503, 510 (1996).

video games. California attempted to defend the law on the grounds that violent video games were like pornography in that there was a special state interest in restricting the dissemination of this material to children. The Court rejected that argument and distinguished its past decisions upholding laws shielding children from obscene materials, observing that those earlier decisions did not grant the government "a free-floating power to restrict the ideas to which children may be exposed."[58] The Court also looked askance at government's substituting its own judgment for that of parents: "While some of the legislation's effect may indeed be in support of what some parents of the restricted children actually want, its entire effect is only in support of what the State thinks parents *ought* to want."[59]

The Court's analysis in *Brown* technically should not inform a situation involving a junk food advertising regulation because the speech at issue in *Brown* was "artistic" and therefore subject to the highest level of First Amendment protection. But food marketers began invoking *Brown* in their own defense within days after the decision came down.[60] The marketers' arguments decry paternalism—conveniently ignoring the obvious distinction that any regulation aimed at protecting *children* is, appropriately and by definition, "paternalistic."

(*Brown's* shift in focus to parents is familiar to obesity prevention advocates. When confronted with evidence that children are not rational consumers, food and beverage companies recast the debate in terms of parental choice and claim that no matter what advertisers say to children, parents are the gatekeepers. This argument suggests that the industry is investing nearly $2 billion each year marketing to children in order to drum up demand among a group of consumers who have absolutely no role to play in purchasing decisions).

As documented in other chapters of this book, evidence about the seriousness of the governmental interests in reducing junk food marketing to children is abundant and compelling. That said, under prong three, the government must be able to show that the proposed regulation will do something to actually fix the given problem. Therefore, drafters of any legislation regulating commercial speech would be well advised to assess applicable studies and other data when deciding how to frame their interests in testimony and legislative findings. The closer the stated purposes of the law dovetail with the evidence mustered in its support, the better chance the government has of convincing a court that the law has a significant impact on the identified problem.

Prong Three: Evidence of Causation

Assuming a commercial speech regulation survives the first two prongs of the *Central Hudson* test, prong three requires the government to establish that its regulation has a direct

[58] Brown v. Entm't Merchs., 131 S. Ct. at 2736.

[59] *Id.*at 2741.

[60] *See* In re Interagency Working Group, *supra* note 5, at 9.

impact on the problem it is trying to address. The Supreme Court has indicated that the government will be in a stronger position if it is able to muster convincing scientific evidence establishing this causal relationship.[61] Like tobacco companies before them, food and beverage corporations take every opportunity to cast doubt on the impact of junk food marketing on childhood obesity (and therefore the impact of any future restrictions on such marketing), claiming that their marketing affects only brand preferences. Their rhetoric focuses on direct causality and they correctly assert that scientific studies have been unable to show a one-to-one causal relationship between food marketing and the overall diets and weight status of children.[62] Nevertheless, marketing is clearly an important factor in the creation of an overall environment in which deeply unhealthy food preferences are formed—most likely for life.

In 2005, the Institute of Medicine (IOM) released a systematic review of decades of applicable peer-reviewed studies and determined that food marketing to children is out of balance with a healthful diet, contributing to an environment that puts child health at risk.[63] Researchers speak of the evidence in terms of risk factors, not direct causality, because the consensus is that no one factor single-handedly causes high obesity rates.[64] Risk factors are identified when there is a convergence of empirical data from laboratory experiments and correlational data from the real world.[65] If a court requires government, under the third prong of *Central Hudson*, to show that junk food marketing to youth directly and unequivocally "causes" obesity, the government will likely be unable to meet the mark. On the other hand, if a court requires only that government establish that exposure to junk food marketing is a significant risk factor in predicting obesity, then the government may well succeed.

The challenge, then, is convincing a court to take a "risk factors" approach to assessing a regulation for purposes of prong three of *Central Hudson*. That may be a difficult task—especially in light of the Supreme Court's approach to the evidence in the 2011 *Brown* decision. California's main justification for banning the sale of violent video games to minors was that such games increase the likelihood that children will be violent. The majority opinion focuses on the question of causality, finding that the studies offered by California were not compelling:

> These studies have been rejected by every court to consider them, and with good reason: They do not prove that violent video games *cause* minors to act *aggressively* (which would at least be a beginning). Instead, "[n]early all of the research is based on correlation, not evidence of causation, and most of the studies suffer from significant, admitted flaws in methodology."[66]

---

[61] Lorillard Tobacco, 533 U.S. at 556–61, Edenfield v. Fane, 507 U.S. 761, 771 (1993).

[62] In re Interagency Working Group, *supra* note 5, at 24, n.42.

[63] Michael McGinnis, J. (2006). Food marketing to children and youth: Threat or opportunity? Institute of Medicine 2006.

[64] *See*, e.g., Mokdad, A. H., et al. (2003). Prevalence of obesity, diabetes, and obesity-related health risk factors. *Journal of American Medical Association*, 289(1), 76.

[65] *See*, e.g., Christopher, J. L., Murray, Lopez, A. D. (1997). Global mortality, disability, and the contribution of risk factors: Global burden of disease. *Lancet, 349*, 1436.

[66] Brown v. Entm't Merchs., 131 S. Ct. at 2739 (first emphasis added; second in the original) (quoting Video Software Dealers Ass'n v. Schwarzenegger, 556 F.3d 950, 964 (9th Cir. 2009).

The Court seized on ambiguities in the evidence to conclude that there was no consensus at all in the relevant scientific community. In doing so, it disregarded the conclusion of leading academics who had asserted that most researchers in the field had indeed arrived at a consensus that "the effect of media violence on aggressive and violent behavior was real, causal, and significant."[67]

In a dissent, Justice Breyer took a less demanding view of the amount of evidence that would be necessary to conclude that a causal relationship existed between violent videos and violent behavior in children. He surveyed the literature—from longitudinal studies to laboratory experiments, from neuroscientific studies to meta-analyses—and determined that the weight of the evidence supported the conclusion that violent video games are harmful to minors.[68] He found it particularly noteworthy that several eminent professional associations (including the American Academy of Pediatrics, the American Academy of Child & Adolescent Psychiatry, and the American Psychological Association) had released a joint statement that the research pointed "overwhelmingly" to the conclusion that there was a connection between such entertainment and aggression.[69] Justice Breyer acknowledged, "I, like most judges, lack the social science expertise to say definitively who is right."[70] Therefore, he wrote that his inclination was to defer to the judgment of knowledgeable professional organizations along with the legislative findings of the State of California.

Given the majority's exacting treatment of the evidence in *Brown*, it may be challenging to establish a proposed regulation's effectiveness under prong three of *Central Hudson* even though *Central Hudson* is an intermediate rather than strict scrutiny standard. *Brown* teaches that the more comprehensive and conclusive the studies supporting the intervention, the better.

Prong Four: Tailoring

The challenge grows greater still with the fourth and final prong of the *Central Hudson* test, the requirement that the government's means of achieving its interest "fit" its ends. Under prong four, the government cannot limit commercial speech more than necessary to accomplish its stated purpose.[71]

As the Supreme Court toughened up the *Central Hudson* test over the years, an apparent conflict between prongs three and four emerged. For example, in the 2001 case of *Lorillard v. Reilly*, Massachusetts passed a law prohibiting outdoor tobacco

---

[67] Anderson, C. A., et al. (2003). The influence of media violence on youth. *Psychological Science, 4*(3), 81, 82.

[68] Brown v. Entm't Merchs., 131 S. Ct. at 2761 (Breyer, J., dissenting); *see also id.* at 2771–78 (appendices to the dissent collecting literature on the topic of psychological harm resulting from playing violent video games).

[69] *Id.* at 2769.

[70] *Id.*

[71] Lorillard Tobacco, 533 U.S. at 563.

advertisements within a 1,000 foot radius of a school or playground.[72] The Supreme Court reviewed evidence linking tobacco advertising to youth consumption and found that the regulation passed prong three. The Court nevertheless struck the law down under prong four, finding that it limited more speech than was necessary to advance the government's stated interest. The Court felt it could not uphold a law which would have the effect of a near-complete ban on the communication of truthful information about tobacco products to adults in some, largely urban, geographical areas: "[T]he governmental interest in protecting children from harmful materials . . . does not justify an unnecessarily broad suppression of speech addressed to adults."[73]

The outcome in *Lorillard* exemplifies the paradox facing governments seeking to protect children from commercial speech that is potentially harmful to them. In order to satisfy prong three of the *Central Hudson* test, the proposed regulation must be broad enough to have a measurable impact on the desired audience—in this case, children. However, prong four requires that the regulation not be overly broad in its impact on adults.

Threading the needle between prongs three and four promises to be difficult for policymakers attempting to craft a restriction on junk food advertising to young people that will survive the full *Central Hudson* test. To increase the chance that a particular initiative will "directly advance" the government's goal of reducing childhood obesity, the regulation might be drafted to have the greatest possible reach—for instance, by banning all advertising for high-calorie, low-nutrient food. This type of full-scale ban would be more likely to have a demonstrable impact on childhood obesity rates. But, under the current interpretation of *Central Hudson*, it would almost certainly also run afoul of prong four because it would prohibit more speech than is "necessary" to address the goal. To avoid problems under prong four, an alternative regulation might forbid junk food advertising only during children's television programming. But opponents could then point to prong three of *Central Hudson*, questioning how this regulation would make any difference to children's obesity rates given myriad other sources of children's exposure to such advertising.[74]

Prong four is the obstacle on which most commercial speech regulations have foundered.

Speakers' Interests May Trump All

Although *Central Hudson* nominally remains the standard of review for commercial speech cases, the 2011 Supreme Court decision in *Sorrell v. IMS Health* raised new questions about the future of the commercial speech doctrine. The Court in *Sorrell* struck down a Vermont statute forbidding pharmacies from selling physicians' prescription

[72] *Id.* at 535–36.

[73] *Id.* at 564.

[74] *See*, e.g., Westen, *supra* note 40, at 85.

records to drug manufacturers for the purpose of marketing drugs to individual physicians. Simply put, the law prohibited sales reps from using a doctor's prescription history without the doctor's consent to tailor a pitch to that doctor. But the law did not restrict other uses of the records by, for example, academic researchers or health insurers.

The Court held that because the law barred only one type of speech—marketing—by one type of speaker—one with a marketing interest—it discriminated on the basis of content and viewpoint and therefore violated the First Amendment. The Court's concern about "discriminating" against "disfavored" speakers had been central to cases involving core political and artistic speech, but unknown in previous commercial speech cases. This rhetoric turns the original rationale for the commercial speech doctrine upside down. It moves from the focus in *Virginia Pharmacy* on *consumers'* interest in access to information, to *speakers'* interest in having free range to target whomever with whatever messages. *Sorrell* represents a culmination of what one First Amendment expert has called a "paradigm shift" from "consumer-protection rationales to speaker-protection rationales."[75]

Although the Court in *Sorrell* ultimately applied the *Central Hudson* test, it continued a decade-long trend sliding commercial speech closer to political and ideological speech for purposes of First Amendment protection. Walking through the four prongs of the *Central Hudson* test, the Court confusingly used the term "heightened scrutiny" in place of "intermediate scrutiny" to describe the standard of review.[76] The use of "heightened scrutiny" to encompass both "strict" and "intermediate" scrutiny could be read to blur the line between the two standards, signifying a novel standard that is more stringent than intermediate scrutiny. Or it could simply be a shorthand way of stating "whichever standard applies."

What remains to be seen is how lower courts will interpret *Sorrell*. It may well be that courts will gravitate to the familiar *Central Hudson* test and continue to apply it in its traditional form. But it is equally conceivable that courts will latch onto *Sorrell's* antidiscrimination approach and heightened-scrutiny catchphrase to eliminate any remaining distinction between intermediate and strict scrutiny in the commercial speech context. The most likely outcome, unless or until the Supreme Court speaks again, is a combination of both.

Conclusion: The Implications for Restrictions on Food Marketing to Children

These developments—the increasingly stringent level of scrutiny applied to commercial speech regulations; the broadening definition of "speech" in the marketing context; the rising distaste for government paternalism; the exacting demand

[75] Smolla, R. D. (2004). Free the Fortune 500! The Debate over Corporate Speech and the First Amendment. *54 Case Western Reserve Law Review*, 1277, 1292.

[76] *Id.*

for direct, causal evidence; the challenge of designing regulations that will directly advance a government goal without being overbroad; and the growing strength of corporate speech rights—suggest that opportunities may have narrowed for legislative efforts to protect children from the onslaught of junk food marketing. But policymakers do have strategies at their disposal that as of now are constitutionally promising.

One is to concentrate on the deceptive aspect of marketing to children. Inherently misleading advertising continues to be unprotected, so it is worth focusing on the argument that all advertising to children, and many techniques targeted at adolescents, can be regulated without raising First Amendment problems.

Also, the First Amendment clearly affords no protection to non-speech-related commercial activities. It is probably safe to say that corporate free speech rights are not implicated by most sales and use taxes, land use laws, government-imposed nutrition standards, or other basic regulations of products and operations. Policymakers should not be dissuaded from addressing food marketing just because companies may now threaten to challenge almost any public health legislation as a violation of their "expressive rights."

In addition, there are niches of First Amendment precedent outside the commercial speech doctrine that may provide cover to certain types of marketing-related policies—such as those limiting food and beverage marketing in schools; restricting *all* advertisements in a particular area, regardless of what they are advertising; mandating factual disclosures or warnings; or providing for government health-related messages.

Public health and child advocates should expect that many efforts to regulate junk food marketing will encounter First Amendment challenges. It is important to be wary of drawing lawsuits that generate bad precedent—that is, decisions that could hamper future policy efforts to address the childhood obesity epidemic. On the other hand, the epidemic is of such pressing urgency that it may be worthwhile testing the limits of the law to clarify, and hopefully expand, the available policy tools for improving the food marketing environment. It is, after all, entirely appropriate to be "paternalistic" in furtherance of children's welfare. And the potential negative consequences of attempting to act must be weighed against those of standing by and allowing corporate "speech" interests to trump the health and well-being of our nation's children.

Chapter 6
Self-regulation as a Tool for Promoting Healthier Children's Diets: Can CARU and the CFBAI Do More?

Julie Ralston Aoki and Elizabeth S. Moore*

Introduction

Food and beverage marketing is but one component in a multifaceted solution to the childhood obesity crisis.[1] It is an important factor, however, and has been under intense scrutiny in recent years. This is an area that poses significant regulatory challenges arising from our legal, political, and cultural frameworks, which protect some advertising as a form of speech and allow companies considerable latitude to produce and sell products. The potentials of industry self-regulation are thus of great interest, with the Federal Trade Commission (FTC) urging manufacturers to draw on their "tremendous marketing power and creative know-how" to encourage children to consume nutritious foods (Vladeck, 2011). The Institute of Medicine (IOM) has also recommended that industry, together with government, scientific, public health, and consumer groups, "establish and enforce the highest standards" for marketing products to children and youth (McGinnis, Gootman, & Kraak, 2006, p. 12).

In this chapter, we examine the structure and function of the Children's Advertising Review Unit (CARU) and the Children's Food and Beverage Advertising

---

*This research was funded by a grant from the Robert Wood Johnson Foundation's Healthy Eating Research Program.

[1] We use "food marketing" to refer to "food and beverage marketing" hereafter.

J. Ralston Aoki, J.D. (✉)
Public Health Law Center,
875 Summit Avenue, St. Paul, MN 55105, USA
e-mail: julie.ralstonaoki@wmitchell.edu

E.S. Moore, Ph.D.
University of Notre Dame, 396 Mendoza College of Business,
Notre Dame, IN 46556, USA
e-mail: emoore@nd.edu

J.D. Williams et al. (eds.), *Advances in Communication Research to Reduce Childhood Obesity*, DOI 10.1007/978-1-4614-5511-0_6,

Initiative (CFBAI)—the two primary self-regulatory programs that impact children's food marketing practices in the USA. It has been well-established that self-regulation can enjoy some benefits over government regulation (see e.g., Sharma, Teret, & Brownell, 2010). For example, neither CARU nor the CFBAI is constrained by First Amendment concerns. Well-designed self-regulatory programs can also "conserve government resources and [be] less adversarial, more flexible, and timelier" (Sharma et al., p. 242). Such programs also face challenges however—as Boddewyn (1989) has noted, "self-regulatory bodies do have to work from the inside rather than sit in judgment" of their members (p. 24). Nonetheless, the reality is that US sociopolitical dynamics have not been conducive to government regulation in this area (see, e.g., Montopoli, 2011; Washington Post, 1978). Thus, the effectiveness of these self-regulatory programs in improving children's diets has significant public health implications.

Although much has been written about CARU and the CFBAI, little attention has focused on the interplay between them. Although they are structured differently (CARU functions like an administrative agency, with a set of standards ("Guidelines") that it enforces according to procedural rules ("Procedures"), and the CFBAI is a pledge program), they share several important characteristics. Both are industry-created programs established by the Council of Better Business Bureaus (CBBB) and the National Advertising Review Council (NARC).[2] They both focus on marketing practices targeted at young children (under age 12), and address specific nutritional concerns about food marketing, albeit to different degrees. They also delineate the set of marketing practices to which their programs will apply.

To understand how these programs complement one another, we first need to understand how they operate individually. We studied how CARU's case process works, and its capacity for addressing food marketing practices. This is significant because if the CFBAI participants' contractual commitments expire or the program is disbanded, CARU would remain in place. For the CFBAI, our goal was to assess the quality of the pledge firms' marketing commitments.[3] In particular, we were interested in learning how the capacity for children's continuing exposure to advertising and marketing is affected by CFBAI provisions. We also looked to other model food marketing standards for underlying principles from which the programs might effectively draw.

As we studied the two programs, we noted areas of convergence as well as discrepancies in their functioning, and became interested in understanding more about the ways these two programs can reinforce or undermine each other. We believe that looking at how these programs work in tandem—or fail to do so—provides a fuller

---

[2] NARC is an alliance between the CBBB and the three major advertising associations (the Association of National Advertisers, the American Association of Advertising Agencies, and the American Advertising Federation).

[3] In this chapter, we do not evaluate the quality of the nutritional standards that have been set. See, for example, CSPI (Center for Science in the Public Interest [CSPI] 2009) for such an analysis.

understanding of the efficacy of self-regulatory efforts and reveals practical suggestions for how to strengthen them.

Research Method

Multiple methods were used to examine the origins, evolution, and performance of the two programs. Our dataset drew on a number of secondary sources including: (1) CARU's Guidelines from 1975, 1991, 1997, 2000, 2003, 2006, and 2009; (2) CARU Activity Reports (published in the NAD/CARU Case Reports)[4]; (3) CARU food-related case decisions (1975–2011); (4) CFBAI pledge documents (from inception through the summer of 2011); (5) CBBB compliance reports (2008, 2009, 2010a, 2011a); (6) international pledge program documents; (7) model food marketing codes [e.g., World Health Organization (WHO, 2010), Center for Science in the Public Interest (CSPI, 2005), International Obesity Task Force (International Obesity Task Force [IOTF] and Consumers International, 2008)]; and (8) brand portfolios of CFBAI participants, obtained from company websites.

CARU's case decisions for all food products and companies were analyzed from 1975 (when the first identifiable CARU case was issued) through June 2011. Throughout its existence, CARU has issued two types of cases, formal and informal. Formal cases are available through NARC's online database (http://www.narc-partners.org), NAD/CARU Case Reports, and a NARC CD-ROM (through 1998).[5] The formal cases were analyzed using a modified court opinion analysis method known as "case briefing" (see, e.g., Schmedemann & Kunz, 2007). Information from the cases was categorized and then synthesized to determine how CARU interprets and applies its guidelines, as well as to assess trends over time.[6]

A content analysis of the CFBAI documents was also conducted. Each participant's marketing commitment was compared to commitments made in international pledge programs and to other model food marketing codes. The marketing activities covered (and excluded) by the CFBAI were also examined. Part of this analysis focused on the brand portfolios offered by the participating firms. These analyses were supplemented by a review of external compliance reports (e.g., Center for Science in the Public Interest [CSPI], 2009, 2010; Harris et al., 2009; Harris, Schwartz, & Brownell, 2010a).

---

[4] Despite repeated written requests for assistance made directly to NAD and CARU and national searches of library holdings, we were not able to obtain four CARU Activity Reports issued in 1999 or early 2000.

[5] Informal cases are reported only in CARU Activity Reports and are not as readily available to the public. We believe we may be missing at most six food and beverage-related informal cases from the late 1990s, based on case numbers reported in NARC (2004). If so, the missing cases would likely have been included in the CARU Activity Reports we were unable to acquire. See footnote 4. NARC (2004) did not explain its methodology, so we could not do a true comparison between our numbers and NARC's numbers.

[6] The informal cases provided too little information to fully brief, and thus were less useful.

Historical Overview: The Self-regulation of Children's Food Advertising

The potential for a more coordinated interplay between CARU and the CFBAI becomes clearer when their mutual origins and evolutionary paths are traced. The historical roots and trajectories of the two programs are quite different, yet there are underlying commonalities. Both programs were established at points in time when the impacts of food marketing on children's health were under scrutiny, and government entities were showing interest in acting to address concerns raised by advocates and public health officials. The two programs' close ties are evidenced by the fact that the CFBAI's launch was announced in a CBBB (2006) press release that also described significant revisions to CARU's Guidelines.

In the Beginning—CARU

CARU's mission is to "promote responsible children's advertising," and to set "high standards" that "take into account the special vulnerabilities of children" (CARU, 2009, p. 3). Concerns about deceptive or unfair advertising to children played a key role in CARU's creation. During the 1970s, consumer advocacy groups filed multiple petitions asking the Federal Communications Commission (FCC) and the FTC to restrict advertising to children, and food advertising in particular (FTC, 1981). The FTC held hearings (see, e.g., Howard & Hulbert, 1973), proposed a prohibition on the use of premiums and related marketing practices,[7] and brought cases related to child-targeted marketing.[8]

It was in this context that the NARC created the National Advertising Division (NAD)[9] in 1972 and CARU 2 years later. Broad consumer protection concerns were expressed in the Guidelines' initial version, which were developed "to help ensure that advertising directed to children is *truthful*, *accurate*, and *fair* to children's perceptions" (Children's Review Unit, 1975, p. 1). Concern about food marketing and its impact on children's health was also a key factor in CARU's formation. The early Guidelines included food-related provisions that are much the same as those currently in use (Children's Review Unit, 1975).

---

[7] Advertising of Children's Premiums on Television, Proposed Guide, 39 Fed. Reg. 25,505 (July 11, 1974).

[8] See, e.g., *In re Mattel, Inc.*, 79F.T.C. 667 (1971) and its companion consent order against the advertising agency, *In re Carson-Roberts, Inc.*, 79F.T.C. 674 (1971) (both orders were later modified by 104F.T.C. 555 (1984)); and *ITT Continental Bakery Co. v. FTC*, 532 F.2d 207 (2d Cir. 1976) (modifying and enforcing FTC's 1973 order).

[9] NAD monitors marketing directed at children and adults ages 12 and over, using the same procedures as CARU (see NARC, 2011).

The decade of heightened focus on child-targeted marketing in the 1970s culminated with the FTC's attempted rulemaking now known as "Kid Vid." The specific impetuses for Kid Vid were petitions filed by consumer advocacy groups focused primarily on the advertising of sugary food products aimed at children and associated concerns about dental caries. In response, the FTC opened a rulemaking to consider whether it should promulgate regulations that would: (1) ban all TV advertising targeted at young children (i.e., under 8 years); (2) ban TV advertising of sugared foods directed to older children (ages 8–12); or (3) require that TV advertising of sugared food products directed to older children also include advertiser-funded nutritional or health disclosures (FTC, 1978). Three years later, criticism of the Kid Vid proceeding, combined with opposition to FTC efforts to address fraud in other industries, led to the passage of the FTC Improvements Act of 1980[10] (Pridgen, 2011). This law suspended the proceeding and removed the FTC's authority to regulate unfair practices in children's advertising, prohibited the agency from using funds to engage in rulemaking to address unfair advertising acts or practices for three years, and imposed new requirements and limitations on all future FTC rulemaking procedures, including those aimed at deceptive practices.[11] After the Act passed, the FTC staff recommended that the Kid Vid proceeding be terminated (FTC). Then, in 1982, the National Association of Broadcasters (NAB) and its TV advertising guidelines were dissolved after a federal court found some of the guidelines violated antitrust laws.[12] These developments left CARU as the only self-regulatory program focused on child-targeted marketing.

These events, combined with the emergence of the First Amendment's commercial speech doctrine, created lasting legal and political hurdles to government regulation of children's advertising and marketing (see Chap. 5 Graff and Piety). Some efforts were subsequently made to regulate, primarily by medium, such as the Children's Television Act of 1990[13] and the Children's Online Privacy Protection Act of 1998.[14] Among the most recent are attempts to address food marketing at a local level (e.g., premiums with children's restaurant meals).[15] However, in the current landscape, CARU and the CFBAI seem to be the key, if not only, practical mechanisms for addressing the full range of children's food marketing techniques.

---

[10] Pub. L. 96–252.

[11] Key provisions were codified at 15 U.S.C. § 57a.

[12] *United States v. National Association of Broadcasters*, 536F. Supp. 149 (D.D.C. 1982).

[13] Pub. L. No. 101–437, 104 Stat. 996 (codified at 47 U.S.C. §§ 303a–303b, 393a, 394, 397) (2011).

[14] Pub.L. 105–277, Div. C, Title XIII, 112 Stat. 2681–728 (codified at 15 U.S.C. §§ 6501–6506 (2011).

[15] At least two jurisdictions have passed laws promoting the use of toy giveaways with children's restaurant meals that meet minimum nutritional requirements [*see,* e.g., San Francisco City Ordinance No. 290–10 (Nov. 2, 2010)].

CARU's Challenge and the Rise of the CFBAI

Just as CARU was launched during a time when marketing to children (and specifically, food marketing) was under intense scrutiny, the 2006 launch of CFBAI occurred against a backdrop of increasing concern about childhood obesity and the impacts of food marketing. The FTC in particular stepped up its activity, holding hearings about marketing self-regulation in 2005, 2007, and 2009. In 2004, Congress directed the FTC to report on industry expenditures for food marketing aimed at children, which it did in 2008 (see FTC, 2008).

During the 2005 FTC hearing, the president of the Grocery Manufacturers Association (GMA) recommended that CARU's resources and enforcement capacity be strengthened, and the CARU process be made more transparent (Molpus, 2005). The GMA also called for revisions to CARU's Guidelines to better address the use of product placement, licensed characters, and "advergaming" (integration of advertising into online games). In February 2006, CARU initiated a review of its Guidelines, in consultation with industry. In October of that year, the process fractured due to disagreements between consumer packaged goods and fast-food companies—with the former reportedly being willing to accept more stringent restrictions than the latter (Edwards, 2006). Then, in November 2006, a substantial revision to CARU's Guidelines and the launch of the CFBAI were announced simultaneously.

Evolution in the CARU Guidelines

The Guidelines have been revised several times over the years to address concerns about new types of marketing and to clarify CARU's scope of authority.[16] To understand the significance of the 2006 revisions, it is useful to know a little about the Guidelines' underlying structure. The Guidelines set forth core principles which apply to all child-targeted marketing, regardless of product or medium, and also list specific provisions.[17] At least two of the core principles are relevant to obesity. The fifth principle states that products "inappropriate for children" should not be advertised directly to them, and the seventh urges marketers to capitalize on advertising's potential to promote positive behavior in children, including physical activity (CARU, 2009).

Since 1996, CARU has distinguished between its "general" Guidelines and those addressing the online collection of personal data from children (under age 13). Our study focused primarily on the general Guidelines, which are divided into topical

[16] For example, in 2000, references to point of sale and packaging were added to the description of CARU's scope of authority in its Guidelines (CARU, 2000).

[17] The 1975 Guidelines listed five core principles (Children's Review Unit, 1975); the current version has eight (CARU, 2009).

categories: deception; product presentation and claims; material disclosures and disclaimers; endorsements; blurring of advertising and editorial/program content; premiums, kids' clubs, sweepstakes, and contests; online sales; sales pressure; and unsafe and inappropriate advertising (CARU, 2009). Several of these categories contain provisions that are linked to food marketing concerns (discussed below).

The November 2006 revisions to the Guidelines signaled some key developments. First, they elaborated on the scope of CARU's authority, defining "national advertising"[18] and for the first time, adding criteria for what constitutes "primarily directed to children." Second, this revision brought back a reference to "fair" advertising (the reference in the 1975 version of the Guidelines had disappeared). Further, a new section pertaining to "deception" was added, which reflects consumer protection law principles. Provisions addressing the blurring of advertising and editorial content as well as advergaming were also added, as recommended by the GMA. Finally, this revision explicitly reflected concerns about childhood obesity and the impacts of food marketing. The language of food-related provisions relating to overconsumption and disparagement of healthy foods was expanded,[19] and the reference to physical activity was added to the core principles. Despite the fact that it had been publicly reported that minimum nutritional standards and restrictions on the use of promotions in food marketing were being considered, these were not part of the revision (Edwards, 2006).

Launch and Evolution of the CFBAI

Although CARU applies to all firms that market products to young children, the CFBAI is a pledge program that only binds companies that join it through a contract with the CBBB. Ten major food manufacturers were the founding participants in 2006.[20] Media companies and marketing agencies, also key contributors to the advertising delivery process, currently stand outside the program.

Similar to CARU, the CFBAI is organized around core principles. A key CFBAI principle states that participating companies commit to advertising that furthers the goal of promoting healthy dietary choices and lifestyles to children under 12. At the CFBAI's inception, member firms pledged that at least half of their advertising primarily directed to young children would be for messages promoting healthier dietary choices, better-for-you products, or healthy lifestyles. This applied to child-targeted placements in measured media including television, radio, print, Internet (third party websites), as well as company-owned websites, paid product placements, in-school

[18] This definition was previously only in the NAD/CARU Procedures.

[19] In 2009, a footnote was added explaining how a "nutritionally balanced meal" should be depicted (see Fig. 6.2).

[20] These were Cadbury Schweppes USA, Campbell Soup Company, The Coca Cola Company, General Mills, Inc., The Hershey Company; Kellogg Company, Kraft Foods, Inc., McDonald's, Pepsico, Inc., and Unilever.

advertising, and the use of licensed characters. Each participant prepared its own pledge, explaining how it would comply with the core principles and describing its commitment and implementation schedule.[21] Participating firms chose their own standards for defining child-targeted advertising and developed company-specific nutrition criteria (though it was required that these be consistent with established scientific and/or government standards such as the US Department of Agriculture's (USDA) dietary guidelines, or the Food and Drug Administration's (FDA) standards for health claims). The program became operational in July of 2007, though implementation dates varied across firms.

The CFBAI has evolved in significant ways. As of September 2011, there were seventeen participants who together account for 79% of the food advertising that appears during children's programming[22] (CBBB, 2010a). In 2010, the program shifted its marketing requirements so that 100% of the advertising targeted at children would be for healthy dietary choices or "better-for-you" products, and the "healthy lifestyle" option was removed (CBBB, 2009). The media to which the CFBAI applied was also expanded to include video and interactive games, DVDs (G-rated movies), mobile media (cell phones, PDAs), and word-of-mouth ads, as well as celebrity and movie tie-ins. Though not required, there has been some harmonization across firms in defining the child audience (e.g., at 35% in measured media) (CBBB, 2010a).

As noted above, these developments occurred in a context of significant public and regulatory attention focused on the nutritional profile of products marketed to children, including improved nutrition standards for school foods.[23] In addition, in 2009, Congress created the Interagency Working Group for Food Marketed to Children (IWG) made up of representatives from the Centers for Disease Control and Prevention, the FDA, the FTC, and the USDA. Congress directed the IWG to study and develop recommended standards for food marketing "when such marketing targets children who are 17 years old or younger or when such food represents a significant component" of children's diets.[24] The IWG issued tentative voluntary nutritional principles in late 2009, followed by a more detailed proposal published for public comment in April 2011 (IWG, 2011). These principles would apply to a wide range of marketing activities, targeted both at children under 12 and adolescents. Industry opposition to the proposal has been fierce (see, e.g., Bachman, 2011; Bartz, 2011), including from the CFBAI (e.g., Hernandez & Kolish, 2011; Kolish, 2011a). On the last day of the comment period in July 2011, the CFBAI announced that firm-specific nutrition criteria would be replaced by uniform product category standards by the end of 2013 (CBBB, 2011b).

[21] Company pledges can be accessed at: http://www.bbb.org/us/children-food-beverage-advertising-initiative/

[22] Burger King Corp., ConAgra Foods, Inc., The Dannon Company, Mars, Inc., Post Foods, Inc., Sara Lee, and Nestlé USA have joined the CFBAI.

[23] See Nutrition Standards for National School Lunch and School Breakfast Programs, 76 Fed. Reg. 2,494 (proposed Jan. 13, 2011) (to be codified 7 C.F.R. pts. 210, 220). Available at http://federalregister.gov/a/2011-485.

[24] 2009 Omnibus Appropriations Act (HR 1105).

How well the CFBAI and CARU work in achieving the goals of promoting healthy eating habits and minimizing consumption of nutrient-poor foods has important implications for the future. This has been underscored in the battle over the IWG's proposed principles. In his testimony to Congress in October 2011, the Director of the FTC's Bureau of Consumer Protection suggested that the IWG guidelines would be revised in a fashion that is largely consistent with existing self-regulatory initiatives (Vladeck, 2011).

Comparison of CARU and the CFBAI

When looked at in tandem, the differences between CARU and the CFBAI become more a matter of degree than kind. The CFBAI Director has described the difference as follows: "CARU and CFBAI are complementary programs. While CFBAI focuses on *what* foods are advertised to children, CARU focuses on *how* products, including foods, are advertised to children" (Kolish, 2011b, note 7). While this description is largely accurate, our study indicates that the distinction is not as clear as it may first appear. For example, as noted above, concern about food marketing was a driving force for CARU's creation, as well as for the CFBAI. So, both programs address nutritional concerns. Additionally, CARU does address the *types* of products that can be marketed to children (e.g., disallowing products that are unsafe or inappropriate) (CARU, 2009). Both programs also prescribe *how* advertisers may market products. It is this area that is perhaps the most illuminating, given inconsistencies between the programs.

CARU's Role in Monitoring Food Marketing Practices

Food marketing comprises a significant percentage of the advertising aimed at children (e.g., Holt, Ippolito, Desrochers, & Kelley, 2007; Powell, Szczypka, & Chaloupka, 2007), and food companies have readily adopted new technologies to try to reach this audience [see e.g., Montgomery (Chap. 10)]. Thus, we would expect that food marketing would represent a significant percentage of the advertising monitored by CARU.

According to its website (http://www.caru.org), CARU currently has a staff of six attorneys. It has an annual budget of $650,000 (based on 2005 reports) and receives 90% of its funding from children's advertisers (Mayer, 2005).[25] CARU's staff examines roughly 1,000 advertisements per month on television, radio, print,

[25] Companies' membership fees depend on how much they spend on children's advertising, ranging from $3,500 for firms that spend less than $1 million per year, to $75,000 for companies that spend more than $50 million annually (Ellison, 2005).

and the internet. Ads are reviewed for claims that need substantiation or for lack of compliance with one or more of the Guidelines. Firms may also file challenges to competitors' ads (though they rarely do), and CARU accepts complaints from consumers.[26] The NAD/CARU Procedures (2011) (adopted in 1990) prescribe how CARU enforces its Guidelines.[27] The Procedures require CARU to issue "case decisions" documenting its findings, which must include information similar to what court opinions contain—the identity of the advertiser; the person or entity complaining about the advertisement ("challenger"); summaries of the advertiser's and challenger's positions, and CARU's decision and reasoning, among other categories. Although CARU's decisions are not binding, if a party refuses to comply, CARU may refer the ad to the FTC where it will be given priority (Peeler, 2009). Either party may appeal CARU's decisions to the National Advertising Review Board (NARB).

CARU's cases apply the Guidelines to specific conduct (or ads), as well as advise industries about the Guidelines' scope and meaning. These functions are analogous to that of judicial opinions, which both apply and interpret laws. CARU's staff has conceded that their enforcement tools (publicity or referral to governmental entities) are weak (Lascoutx, 2002). One criticism of CARU (and its affiliate programs) has been that neither the public nor advertisers, particularly advertising agencies, are aware of their existence (Crain, 2009; Mayer, 2005).

From its inception through June 2011, CARU issued 883 formal and 887 informal cases, for a total of 1,770. Of these, 296 cases (17%) were related to food products or companies (150 formal, 146 informal). The vast majority of these food cases have involved challenges to CARU's general Guidelines ($n=241$), as opposed to online privacy ($n=40$). Challenges under both types of Guidelines were brought in 15 "combination cases." As shown in Fig. 6.1, CARU's focus on food ads, reflected as a percentage of all case activity, fluctuates over time, tending to increase when regulatory attention is focused on children's food advertising (see also Armstrong, 1984). Food ads made up the largest percentage (28.3%) of cases during the late 1970s, dropped significantly in the 1980s to 7–8%, and then increased again in the early 2000s to approximately 20%, as childhood obesity began to capture the public's attention (see e.g., Nestle, 2000). Beginning in 2004, CARU noted in ten formal cases that it was scrutinizing food ads as part of the food and advertising industries' assessment of what they could do to help with the childhood obesity problem.[28] Thus, similar to formal regulatory bodies, CARU seems to use discretion to allocate resources toward issues of current social concern. However, its food caseload dropped noticeably after the CFBAI was launched (Hoy, Childers, & Morrison, 2012).

[26] Over 90% of CARU's cases are initiated by its staff (Mayer, 2005). Most NAD cases result from competitors challenging each other's advertising (NARC, 2004).

[27] *Kellogg Co.*, Case No. 5165 (CARU April 23, 2010), p. 5.

[28] See, e.g., *Proctor & Gamble Co.*, Case No.4161 (CARU March 25, 2004) (Pringles); and *General Mills*, Case No. 4412 (CARU Nov. 11, 2005) (Reese's Puffs).

	Food & Beverage Formal Cases	All Formal Cases	Food & Beverage Informal and Expedited Cases	All Informal & Expedited Cases	Food & Beverage Cases as % of All Cases
1975-1979	28	99	--	--	28.3%
1980-84	5	64	--	--	7.8
1985-89	7	96	--	--	7.3
1990-94	6	28	22	248	10.1
1995-99	1	22	22[1]	196[2]	10.6
2000-2004	35	185	95	433	21
2005-2009	55	317	7	10	19
2010-June 2011	13	72	--	--	18
Totals	150	883	146	887	16.7

Source: www.narcpartners.org; NAD/CARU Case Reports; NARC CD-ROM.
[1] NARC (2004) previously reported that CARU issued 50 informal food and beverage cases in the 1990s.
[2] Number is likely to be slightly low due to gap in CARU Activity Reports.

Fig. 6.1 CARU case activity (1975–2011)

In reviewing CARU's case activity, we found that approximately one-fourth of its food cases ($n=72$; 58 formal; 14 informal) involved claims or depictions related to nutrition or health. Figure 6.2 summarizes the Guidelines that specifically address nutrition-related issues, lists the number of formal cases pertinent to each, and provides examples of how CARU has applied these Guidelines over the years. The first two Guidelines in the figure reflect consumer protection law principles, with cases tending to focus on the potential for children to be confused or misled about a product's nutritional content, qualities or benefits in ways that would be detrimental to their health. The remaining Guidelines address broader concerns related to nutrition and health (such as overconsumption, helping children to choose healthier options when they are available, and avoiding eating snack foods as a meal). As illustrated by the case summaries in the figure, CARU also takes a consumer protection approach in assessing these types of ads—that is, it reviews the ad's net nutritional message (not just isolated components); from the perspective of a reasonable child; and focuses on the message conveyed, not the advertiser's intended meaning (Carter, 2009; Sheldon, 2001).[29]

In an analysis of CARU's food cases issued from 2000 to 2010, Hoy et al., (2012) organized nutrition concerns raised in these cases into two general categories: (1) advertising should not imply that a food is healthier than it is (via comparative or general nutritional claims, such as fruit content); (2) advertisements should promote

[29] See e.g., *Williams v. Gerber Products Co.*, 552 F.3d 934 (9th Cir. 2008); *FTC v. Freecom Commc'ns, Inc.*, 401F.3d 1192 (10th Cir. 2005); and *Ackerman* et al. *v. Coca-Cola Co.*, No. 09–0395, slip. op. (E.D.N.Y. July 21, 2010) 2010 WL 2925955.

Current Guideline (source: "Product, Presentation & Claims" section, CARU, 2009)	# of formal cases (n= 58)[1]	Case Examples
1. "Copy, sound and visual presentations should not mislead children about product or performance characteristics . . . ." including "nutritional benefits."	12	Great A& P Tea Co., Case # 4531 (7/25/06) [fruit snacks]: CARU questioned whether packaging, which stated "FRUIT SNACKS" and "Made with Real Fruit Juice," conveyed that products contain mostly fruit juice and are nutritionally equivalent to eating fruit. Package featured Fisher-Price action figures and a maze. CARU concluded: (1) packaging was child-directed advertising; (2) phrase "Made with Real Fruit Juice" coupled with "100% Daily Value Vitamin C" could lead child to believe that product contained 100% fruit juice; (3) advertiser may not have intended to convey this message, but this is not controlling. CARU recommended advertiser stop using "Made with Real Fruit Juice" or clearly disclose % of real fruit juice (advertiser declined to provide %). Advertiser agreed to change name to "Fruit Flavored Snacks" and to modify ad in accord with CARU's decision.
2. Advertising should not mislead children about the benefits of using the product, which "may include, but are not limited to, acquisition of strength, . . . growth, . . . and intelligence."	4	Proctor & Gamble Co., Case # 4040 (4/30/03) [Sunny Delight]: CARU found that TV ad incorrectly conveyed to children that drinking Sunny D would make them strong and that it contained large amounts of fruit, through statements and images. CARU based its conclusions on the following: (1) ad focused on the word "power" not "taste"; (2) visuals showing a bottle breaking out of a concrete block, and large fresh fruit pieces; (3) beverages must be 100% fruit or vegetable juice to be called "juice" without further qualification per federal regulations. CARU asked advertiser to include a voiceover disclosing specific juice content (5%). The advertiser also agreed to change the ad's opening line, and to take CARU's concerns into consideration for future ads.
7. Product amounts featured "should not be excessive or more than would be reasonable to . . . consume . . . in the situation depicted." E.g., if an ad suggests that food is being or will be eaten, the amount should not exceed the labeled serving size or an otherwise appropriate single serving size.	9	ConAgra Foods, Case # 4711 (8/16/07) [Chef Boyardee beef ravioli]: CARU found that TV ad showing a boy/monster at night chugging a can of ravioli containing two servings could encourage children to overeat. CARU noted attention on childhood obesity, which made it "very concerned with whether serving sizes depicted in food ad[s] are excessive." ConAgra submitted parts of a consumer perception study, but these did not address children's understanding of what was eaten. So CARU used its expertise to determine what message children would take away. It concluded that overconsumption was conveyed due to several factors, including: (1) the monster's ferocious hunger; (2) the night setting; (3) the chugging; combined with (4) the copy, "Only the rich meaty sauce of CHEF BOYARDEE can tame the beast in you." CARU understood ConAgra intended to be humorous, but an advertiser is responsible for all reasonable interpretations of claims, not just intended ones. CARU also found ConAgra's attempted modifications insufficient. CARU concluded: "Given the sensitivities of the current climate, such a depiction of bestial hunger and careless over-consumption violates CARU's Guidelines." ConAgra agreed to stop running the ad.
8. Food advertising "should encourage responsible use of the product with a view toward healthy development of the child.[2] For example, advertising of food products should not discourage or disparage healthy lifestyle choices or the consumption of fruits or vegetables, or other foods recommended for increased consumption" according to federal dietary guidelines as relevant for children under 12.	16	Burger King Corp., Case # 4298 (3/9/05) [Kids Meals]: CARU was concerned that Kids Meal TV and web ads would mislead children about what options are available because they showed almost exclusively a double cheeseburger, fries, and a Coke. CARU found it a violation to show only higher-calorie, higher-fat options when there are healthier ones.[3] Though CARU's goal is to make children aware of options and not to prohibit the advertising of any options, it encouraged BK to show alternatives. Adding a disclaimer to TV ad that "Other fun Kids Meal options available" was sufficient. BK agreed to change future ads to provide clearer idea of options, and to highlight lower-calorie ones if applicable. It also agreed to modify the Kids section's first webpage to clearly convey all food options offered, and to show CARU the proposed changes before final release. Kellogg Co., # 4453 (2/14/06) [Apple Jacks]: CARU was concerned that TV, print, and web ad campaign conveyed message that apples taste bad and product's sweetness comes from cinnamon, not sugar. After a lengthy review of Kellogg's arguments, including a focus group study it provided, CARU concluded that children could reasonably take away the message that apples are bad for them, do not taste good, should be avoided as a breakfast food, and that cinnamon alone made the cereal sweet. CARU recommended Kellogg stop running the ads, and refrain from running them again. Kellogg modified ads to clarify messages about the "taste descriptor" ("sweet cinnamon"). It stated that "future ads will emphasize that 'Apple Jacks' cereal does not taste like apples while maintaining the core 'taste of sweet cinnamon' messaging . . ." and that it would prominently have apples in its "complete breakfast" disclosure. It disagreed with CARU, but agreed to stop running the ads and to not run them again.
9 Food ads should depict the product's "appropriate role . . . within the framework of the eating occasion depicted." Ads showing meal times should show food "within the framework of a nutritionally balanced meal." A footnote adds that meals should have at least 3 of 5 food groups, and preferably foods recommended for increased consumption by federal dietary guidelines. Food also should be presented in reasonable portion sizes and be appropriate for children for the meal setting featured.	10	General Mills, Case # 4412 (11/11/05) [Reese's Puffs]: CARU was concerned that TV ad might encourage excessive consumption because it depicted food in oversized or exaggerated amounts, which could misinform children about accurate serving sizes, and suggested that children in the ad were going to eat the cereal out of the box. CARU also found that the ad was not clear about whether the cereal was being used as a snack or as breakfast. Finally, CARU had concerns that the use of the "Reese's" logo, separate from the "Reese's Puffs" logo, as well as the "Reese's for breakfast!" tag would leave children familiar with the Reese's Peanut Butter Cups candy with the net impression of "candy for breakfast!" CARU was pleased by General Mills' response, which was to say ad was no longer running, with "no current plans" to run again; that it would remind its advertising agencies of the importance of depicting accurate serving sizes in cereal ad campaigns, and would "bear CARU's thoughts in mind" about clear presentations of product as breakfast cereal and not as snack food for future Reese's Puffs ads. Quaker Oats Co., Case # 997 (3/15/76) [Cap'n Crunch cereal]: CARU questioned TV ad because it emphasized a premium, and whether it properly depicted the role of the product within the framework of a balanced diet. The advertiser disagreed with CARU's "contentions" but advised the matter was "academic" since it had routinely discontinued ad as part of its marketing plans, and did not intend to re-run it.
Additionally, this provision states that snack foods should be depicted as snacks and not meals.	3	Kraft Foods Global, Case # 5204 (8/5/10) [macaroni and cheese]: TV ad showed child eating a bowl of product and nothing else. CARU noted that due to focus on childhood obesity, CARU is "particularly concerned" about nutrition-related claims and works to ensure that advertisers depict nutritionally balanced meals and that snacks are depicted as snacks, not as meal substitutes. CARU ultimately determined that the ad was acceptable and that the "eating occasion" depicted was a snack rather than a meal. CARU relied on several details of the ad for this determination, such as that the girl was seated by herself, a backpack was placed on a nearby counter (indicating that she had just returned from school), and the lighting indicated it was afternoon, not evening.

[1]Many cases referred to more than one of these guidelines; some did not refer to any of them but referred to guidelines pertaining to comparative claims, substantiation or deception. Fourteen of the nutrition-related cases did not quote or cite to specific guidelines.

[2]**Prior to the 2006 revision, this guideline included the phrase "*and development of good nutritional practices*" here (CARU 2004) (emphasis added).**

[3]CARU found this also violated the Guideline that "[w]hat is included and excluded in the initial purchase should be clearly established".

Fig. 6.2 Illustrative examples of CARU's food-related Guidelines and formal case activity

healthy eating choices (such as avoiding suggestions of excessive consumption, failing to show healthier options available for selection (e.g., milk in addition to soda), or showing snack foods eaten as a meal). We noted that together, these categories reflect the fundamental motivations for CARU's existence. The first

	Company (*CFBAI firms in italics*)	Formal cases	Informal cases	Total
1	*Kellogg Co.*[1]	16	17	33
2	*General Mills, Inc.*	14	14	28
3	*Kraft Foods Global, Inc.*[2]	11	15	25
4	*McDonald's USA*	7	7	14
	Burger King Corp.	7	5	12
5	Quaker (acquired by Pepsi in 2001)	5	6	11
6	*Mars, Inc.*[3]	3	6	9
	Procter & Gamble	4	4	8
7	*Cadbury Adams USA, LLC*[4]	3	5	8
	Nestle USA	4	3	7
8	*Campbell Soup Co.*	2	5	7
	PepsiCo[5]	2	5	7
9	*ConAgra Foods, Inc.*	3	3	6
	Dannon Co.	3	3	6
10	Chuck E. Cheese	4	1	5
	Coca-Cola Co.[6]	3	2	5
	Totals	91	101	191

[1]Kellogg acquired Keebler in late 2000, so includes Keebler cases occurring after 2000.

[2]General Foods, which originally owned Post cereals, was merged with Kraft in 1990 when both companies were owned by Philip Morris Cos. Kraft also acquired Capri Sun in 1991. So Kraft cases include one 1992 Capri Sun case and one informal and two formal Post cases. Kraft, which has since been diverged from Philip Morris (n/k/a Altria), sold Post Cereals to Ralcorp, which sale was completed in 2008.

[3]Mars has owned Masterfoods since 1967. So, Mars cases include Masterfoods cases.

[4]According to its 2007 CFBAI pledge, Cadbury Adams was a subsidiary of Cadbury Schweppes PLC; Cadbury Schweppes PLC spun off Dr. Pepper/Snapple Group (DPS) (which also markets 7 Up) in May 2008. So Cadbury cases include Dr. Pepper/7 Up and Snapple cases from prior to 2007.

[5]Pepsi acquired Quaker in 2001, so one 2005 formal Quaker case was attributed to Pepsi. Pepsi has also owned Frito-Lay since 1965, so Pepsi cases include cases involving Frito-Lay ads.

[6]Coca-Cola has owned Minute Maid since 1960. So, Coca-Cola cases include Minute Maid cases.

Fig. 6.3 Food and beverage firms with largest number of CARU challenges

encompasses consumer protection law concerns about ads conveying misleading or deceptive impressions to children. The second centers on concerns about food marketing's impact on children's health, particularly the encouragement of healthy vs. unhealthy choices—which are also precisely the public health concerns that the CFBAI was created to address.

Many of the CFBAI companies have long histories of marketing to young children, and their products account for almost 80% of all food ads aimed at this age group (CBBB, 2010a). So, one area of particular interest in our analysis was the representation of CFBAI companies in CARU cases. Figure 6.3 lists the food and beverage companies that have been involved in five or more cases during CARU's history. Thirteen of the 17 CFBAI companies appear on this list, which might be expected in part given their considerable presence in the marketplace. Simply because CARU challenges an ad does not mean that it violated the Guidelines. For example, of the 16 formal cases involving ads for Kellogg's products (the CFBAI firm with the greatest number of challenges), CARU found violations in just nine of them. In three cases it determined that the ad complied with its Guidelines; and in four cases, it either made no clear finding or administratively closed the case.[30] The listing in Fig. 6.3 suggests, however, that the CFBAI membership spans many of the key food manufacturers. It may also point to firms that should participate in the CFBAI but do not, and/or indicate that some CFBAI companies may be better than others at complying with CARU's Guidelines.

Overall, the nature of CARU's case activity indicates that it has an important role in monitoring children's food marketing, and in encouraging advertising that promotes healthy dietary choices. Moreover, these cases, and a comparison of CARU's Guidelines with the CFBAI pledge commitments, show that CARU can play a part in driving further development of the CFBAI standards in two key areas: (1) defining the child audience, and (2) demarcating what constitutes "advertising."

Defining Child-Targeted Media

The CARU Guidelines apply to national advertising primarily directed to children under 12. CARU considers four factors when determining whether an ad or marketing practice is "primarily directed" at young children and no single factor is controlling. For example, the first criterion assesses whether the media vehicle in which an ad appears was intended for young children, based on its subject matter, format, audience demographics, and other ads that appear in it.[31] Thus, the projected demographic is a key factor. For example, in a 2006 informal case CARU noted that it considered a program airing before 9:00 PM with a 35% audience share (ages 2–11) to be "children's programming."[32] It has also emphasized that audience share is but one factor, stating that "CARU does not rely on any specific percentage of audience

[30] One case was a "compliance" case, involving an ad that Kellogg previously agreed to modify pursuant to a CARU case, but failed to do so. See NARC, (2011), Sect. 4.1. Also, one Kellogg case involved multiple concerns, and CARU found compliance with one Guideline but noncompliance with another.

[31] Two of the factors are geared more towards TV, referring to whether an ad was aired during or adjacent to a show generally considered children's programming or that satisfies broadcaster's Children's Television Act obligations. The fourth factor relates to whether the advertiser intended to direct the ad primarily to children under 12 (CARU, 2009).

[32] In re *Welch Foods Inc.*, CARU Activity Report (NAD Case Report, Vol. 36, No. 5) (May/June 2006).

demographic to determine if an advertisement is directed to children."[33] Other factors that CARU has considered include:

- Whether the ad features child actors or depictions of children.[34]
- Whether the ad includes cartoon characters, premiums, or other features appealing to children.[35]
- Whether the product is likely to be inherently appealing to children, such as cookies.[36]
- The fact that characters featured in the ad are "widely licensed" and toys and playsets with these characters are sold around the country.[37]
- Whether the advertiser markets other products to children.[38]

So, rather than relying solely on a percentage, CARU reserves the ability to make contextual assessments in determining whether an ad is targeted at children, even in measured media. This flexibility is a positive feature of CARU's process which allows it to address a range of marketing channels and tools.

In defining what is "primarily directed" at children, the CFBAI framework permits even more flexibility, but one key differentiator is that each company may set its own criteria within the bounds of the pledge framework.[39] This has led to significant variation across firms, particularly in the program's early years. For example, in measured media, "child-directed" audience share ranged from 18% to 50% across firms (CBBB, 2008; CSPI, 2010). Although there continues to be some variation, most firms agree that a 35% share (as of 2010) constitutes children's programming or media.

Other Views on Child-Targeted Media

Comparison with other model food marketing codes around the world is also instructive. On this point, our analysis centered on codes that as a set reflect diverse stakeholder groups and those that could be influential either in the USA or

[33] *Ubisoft Holdings, Inc.*, Case No. 5247 (CARU Nov. 18, 2010), p. 4 (concluding that program with ages 2–11 audience share ranging from 29 to 40% was children's programming).

[34] See, e.g., *Tyson Foods, Inc.*, Case No. 5172 (CARU May 4, 2010); *Assoc. Biscuits of Amer.*, Case No. 1515 (CARU, Mar. 15, 1979).

[35] See *Kellogg Co.*, Case No. 5165 (CARU April 23, 2010); *Great Atlantic & Pacific Tea Co.*, Case No. 4531 (CARU July 25, 2006).

[36] E.g., *Assoc. Biscuits of Amer.*, Case No. 1515 (CARU, Mar. 15, 1979).

[37] See *Ubisoft Holdings, Inc.*, Case No. 5247 (CARU Nov. 18, 2010).

[38] See *CEC [Chuck E. Cheese] Entertainment*, Case No. 5210 (CARU August 27, 2010).

[39] The pledge framework requires that participants use the following factors: "the overall impression of the advertising, the target demographic based on the company's media plan, actions taken to restrict child access, such as age screening, and the audience definition for measured media" (CBBB, 2010b, p. 3).

abroad. International groups such as the WHO (2010) and the IOTF (2008) tend to take a tougher stance on what constitutes a child audience, relative to CARU or the CFBAI. In the USA, CSPI (2005) argues that ads shown in media for which children comprise 15% or more of the audience should be considered targeted at children. The IWG (2011) would set a 30% standard for children and 20% for adolescents.

Audience share is but one type of criterion, however. Both the WHO (2010) and the IOTF (2008) advocate for standards that focus on the total number of children who see or hear the advertising. This distinction is significant because children's actual exposure to advertising occurs not only during children's programming but also during programs aimed at more general audiences. For example, close to one-third of the TV ads children see appear during prime time shows (after 8:00 PM), which means that children are exposed to many more ads than those explicitly targeted at them (Holt et al., 2007). CARU acknowledged this fact in a 1979 case involving a TV ad for cookies which aired outside of traditional child programming hours.[40] It ultimately determined that the ad was acceptable, but noted that large numbers of children watch TV during much of the day and night.[41]

Both CARU and the CFBAI focus on children under 12. In contrast, the public health community, consumer advocates, and Congress have argued for the inclusion of adolescents (≤ age 17). In 2007, the UK's Office of Communication (which is similar to the FCC in the USA) enacted regulations that prohibit the advertising of foods that are high in saturated fats, trans-fatty acids, sugars, or salt to youth under age 16. This increased emphasis on adolescents is consistent with a growing body of developmental research in neuroscience, psychology, and marketing suggesting that teens may be particularly vulnerable to marketing messages for unhealthy foods (e.g., Pechmann, Levine, Loughlin, & Leslie, 2005). Expanding self-regulatory provisions to include adolescents in the USA, however, would require significant revisions to CARU and the CFBAI due to the broader set of marketing activities aimed at this group, and would likely encounter significant industry resistance as demonstrated by the reaction to the IWG proposal.[42]

In sum, with respect to the threshold definition of what is "primarily directed" to children, this discussion highlights subtle yet important differences between the CARU and CFBAI approaches. Assuming that the CFBAI firms are also expected to comply with CARU, it is puzzling that the CFBAI did not adhere more closely to CARU's benchmarks for child-targeted media from the outset. Particularly with regard to the 35% composition standard, putting aside whether this is the "best" standard, it is surprising that the CFBAI took 4 years to arrive at a position that CARU publicly declared a few months before the CFBAI launched.

---

[40] It challenged the ad based on safety concerns because it showed children sawing through a box of cookies.

[41] *Assoc. Biscuits of Amer.*, Case No. 1515 (CARU, Mar. 15, 1979).

[42] See Chap. 8 by Powell et al. for rates of adolescent exposure to food advertising in the US.

"Marketing" Versus "Advertising"—A Key Distinction

Perhaps the most significant difference between the CFBAI and CARU, however, relates to how the CFBAI defines "advertising." CFBAI's parameters for "advertising" exclude aspects of marketing that CARU includes. In doing so, the CFBAI has positioned itself to potentially undermine CARU's authority over these forms.

In essence, marketing is the discipline responsible for creating, promoting, and delivering goods and services to businesses and consumers (e.g., Kotler & Keller, 2011). A classic conceptual framework captures this set of responsibilities within the "4 P's" of marketing–product, place, price, and promotion. Advertising is embedded within the promotion component. It is an important element strategically, but is only one part of a much broader and complex set of activities designed to stimulate and manage demand. It is also the most visible component of marketing, and some have suggested, the most amenable to a regulatory (or self-regulatory) approach (Swinburn et al., 2008).

That the primary focus of both CARU and the CFBAI is advertising is apparent (beginning with their names). Yet, the two programs take different approaches in defining what types of marketing activities are covered. CARU defines advertising as "any paid commercial message, in any medium (including labeling), if: (a) it has the purpose of inducing a sale or other commercial transaction or persuading the audience of the value or usefulness of a company, product, or service; (b) it is disseminated nationally or to a substantial portion of the [US]..." and the advertiser controls the content (CARU, 2009, p. 5). The scope of what is "advertising" is further fleshed out by CARU's Guidelines, which refer to specific activities (e.g., celebrity endorsements, cyber space sponsorships) and by its cases.

In contrast, the CFBAI sets forth specific media and marketing activities to either include or exclude, as the case may be. Figure 6.4 provides an overview of CARU's and CFBAI's coverage. It is organized by the categories adopted in the FTC's (2008) report to Congress and has also been used as the basis for the IWG's (2011) recommendations.[43] As is evident from the figure, both CARU and the CFBAI cover an array of communication activities which together represent a substantial majority of advertising expenditures.[44] A clear strength of these programs is their coverage of media that have traditionally been used to target children (e.g., TV, print) as well as newer forms of digital media (e.g., third party websites, company-owned sites, mobile, video games) that are increasingly being used to reach young audiences

[43] Industry has criticized this scheme. We have drawn on it here because of its continuing role in the debate about self-regulation.

[44] The FTC (2008) report was based on data collected in 2006 from 44 food companies (including restaurants) that are primary marketers to youth (ages 2–17). It is likely that there have been some changes in how marketing resources are being allocated since publication of this report given continuing developments in media. (The FTC is expected to issue an updated report in 2012.) Consideration should also be given to the fact that advertising expenditures reflect both relative emphasis within a marketing plan as well as differential costs of media.

Marketing Medium or Practice (FTC 2008)	**Covered by CARU?**[1]	**Covered by CFBAI?**	**% of Marketing Expenditures**	
			<12	**12-17**
Television advertising	yes	yes	52.6	46.0
Radio advertising	yes	yes	0.5	5.0
Print advertising	yes	yes	1.5	2.9
Company-sponsored internet sites	yes	yes	2.1	1.1
Other internet advertising (3rd party websites)	yes	yes	2.4	1.8
Other digital advertising (PCs, mobile, other)	yes	yes	0.1	0.0
Product placements (TV, radio, movie, music, video, electronic game, etc.)	yes?	yes	0.1	0.2
Celebrity endorsements	yes	yes	0.1	0.3
In-school marketing	yes	partial[2]	8.4	4.6
Movie theater/DVDs/video game advertising	yes	partial	0.6	0.2
Licensed characters, toy co-branding, cross-promotions	yes	partial	5.2	0.8
Word-of-mouth/viral marketing	?	partial	0.1	0.2
Packaging and labeling	yes	no	6.7	2.3
In-store advertising (POS displays, promotions)	yes	no	5.5	8.9
Premiums (via contests, sweepstakes, coupons, etc.)	yes	no	6.6	2.5
Event sponsorships (entertainment)	?	no	3.5	2.5
Sport sponsorships	yes[3]	no	1.1	4.2
Cause-related marketing (philanthropy)	yes[4]	no	1.6	0.5
Other	?	?	1.5	1.9

[1]CARU applies to advertising which is national or covers a substantial portion of the U.S. (CARU, 2009).
[2]In-school marketing is covered by the CFBAI but there are multiple exclusions. It does not apply to displays of food and beverage products offered for sale, fundraising activities, charitable donations, public service messages and items provided to school administrators for their personal use (CFBAI, 2011).
[3]See *Spalding Sports Worldwide*, Case No. 4171 (CARU April 4, 2004) (Arena Football League football).
[4]See *Fleetwood Toys, Inc.*, Case No. 2715 (CARU July 1, 1989) (Children for Children dolls).

Fig. 6.4 Marketing spending and coverage in self-regulatory programs

(Moore & Rideout, 2007), including those disparately impacted by obesity (see Chap. 17 by Ramirez and Gallion).

However, the CFBAI allows its members to exclude some marketing activities (e.g., sponsorships, premiums, packaging) that are included in the model standards outlined by the IOTF (2008), CSPI (2005), and the IWG (2011). This means that the public health community, consumer advocates, and government regulators take a broader view of marketing to children than the CFBAI food companies do. What is potentially more problematic, however, is that the CFBAI allows its members to exempt some marketing strategies and media which both CARU and marketing research have identified as being particularly effective with children.

In-store Marketing and Beyond

The CFBAI explicitly allows its members to exclude packaging, point-of-sale (e.g., displays, promotions), and the use of company-owned characters.[45] Implicit exclusions include sales promotions (e.g., premiums, sweepstakes, contests), sponsorships of sports-related activities or other events, and general brand building. These types of activities are key components in "integrated marketing communications" (IMC) campaigns which use an array of marketing tools to reach their target audiences. Brand messages that appear in multiple media are more easily recalled and more persuasive (Naik & Raman, 2003). The FTC's (2008) study showed that integrated campaigns are now the norm in food marketing to children and teens (see Chap. 3 by Harrison and Jackson).

In-store marketing, in particular, has become an increasingly important component of marketing plans. According to GMA & Deloitte Consulting (2007), the grocery store is a "critical and highly attractive touch point to reach and influence consumers" (p. 3) and is considered by many to be a brand's most important marketing opportunity (see e.g., Nelson & Ellison, 2005; Underhill, 2008). This is consistent with industry data indicating that 70% of all purchase decisions are made in the store (POPAI, cited in O'Dell, 2009). The vast majority (95%) of major grocery manufacturers (which includes the CFBAI companies) are engaged in "shopper marketing," of which in-store activities are a key part (GMA, 2011). The growth in spending on "shopper marketing" is expected to outpace all other marketing tools in coming years (GMA, 2010). At the same time, expenditures in traditional media are forecasted to decline. In-store displays, sales promotions, and packaging are viewed by many marketing practitioners as among the most effective means of reinforcing brands and impacting purchase.

One argument for excluding these marketing activities from the CFBAI seems to be that they are not aimed at children, but are meant to signal to parents which products might have "child appeal" (Hernandez & Kolish, 2011). CARU's inclusion of these activities in its definition of advertising indicates, however, that marketers do direct them at children. And children are indeed being exposed to, and influenced by these marketing tools. Packaging, point-of-sale, and promotions are among the most salient marketing techniques to children (Landon & Gritschneder, 2011, see Chap. 15 by Grigsby-Toussaint et al.). Even very young children can recognize brand logos on packages (Valkenburg & Buijzen, 2005) and recall brand names that

[45] As of November 2011, Burger King is the only CFBAI participant to include some packaging and point-of-sale restrictions in its pledge.

they have seen advertised on television (Macklin, 1996). Packaging influences young children's taste preferences as well. Products presented in attractive packaging are judged to taste better than the same foods in plain wrappers (Robinson, Borzekowski, Matheson, & Kramer, 2007). For overweight children this may be more problematic, given preliminary evidence suggesting that they tend to eat more when foods are presented in a branded package (Forman, Halford, Summe, MacDougall, & Keller, 2009).

Parents recognize the power of packaging in influencing their children's product preferences and in promoting purchase requests (e.g., Ogba & Johnson, 2010). Surveys of children and teens indicate that some 70% report that they "sometimes" accompany a parent or other family member when grocery shopping (Mintel, 2008). A key reason they offer for doing so is the opportunity to influence food choices—78% say that they sometimes help choose the foods that are purchased; 18% indicate that they always do. Point-of-purchase advertising has also been shown to influence children's independent purchases (Rexha, Mizerski, & Mizerski, 2010).

Finally, it is notable that the prevalence of youth-oriented sales promotions (e.g., premiums, sweepstakes, tie-ins with licensed properties) depicted on food packages has increased since the CFBAI was launched, with few apparent differences between CFBAI participants and other manufacturers (Harris, Schwartz, & Brownell, 2010b). Sales promotions are generally much more effective at inducing immediate sales than a television commercial, which is likely to do more to build brand awareness, image, and preference (e.g., Belch & Belch, 2012).

By allowing member firms to exclude sales promotions, packaging, and point-of-sale displays from the scope of covered marketing activities, the CFBAI allows them to define "advertising" more narrowly than what both CARU and industry practice would suggest. The CARU Guidelines identify these channels as among those that raise special concerns when used with young children, and it has issued a number of cases involving these practices. For example, it has issued 13 cases involving food packaging (all formal); 30 food cases involving premiums (20 formal, 10 informal); and 63 food cases involving the use of contests, sweepstakes, and similar promotions (22 formal, 41 informal). Thus, over a third of its total food-related caseload to date ($n = 296$) involves marketing activities that the CFBAI has excluded from the pledge framework.

The CFBAI's exclusion of these activities raises concerns about its capacity to undermine CARU. This potentiality is demonstrated in a 2010 case, where CARU challenged Kellogg's Pop-Tarts packaging and website advertising on the basis that it could mislead children about the product's fruit content.[46] Kellogg responded by asserting that CARU should close the case because it is a CFBAI participant, and (1) packaging is not "primarily" child-directed advertising under the CFBAI, and (2) it does not advertise Pop-Tarts to children because it pledged not to do so. Kellogg appeared to be using its CFBAI participation to attack CARU's jurisdiction over packaging and as a shield against CARU's inquiry in general.

[46] *Kellogg Co.*, Case No. 5165 (CARU April 23, 2010).

CARU found, however, that the advertising was child directed because the packaging had cartoon characters and a cut-out premium. CARU also noted that the Pop-Tarts website had a "Kids" section which featured the characters. It concluded that the implied fruit content claim was potentially misleading to children, and should not be made in child-directed advertising in any media, including packaging. Kellogg disagreed, stating that "[u]nder no circumstances can product packaging be deemed to be advertising directed *primarily* to children under 12."[47] But it noted that it had discontinued the packaging anyway, and that it "respect[s] the self-regulatory process and will take CARU's decision into consideration in future advertising."[48]

This was the first—and so far only—CARU case where the advertiser's CFBAI participation was raised as an issue. For example, CARU recently found a Burger King ad did not comply with its guideline that ads with premiums should focus on the product, not the premium. [49] Unlike Kellogg, Burger King did not claim that the CFBAI's exclusion of premiums immunized it from CARU scrutiny. Nonetheless, to the extent that the CFBAI is viewed as a model, it would be problematic if it were to undermine CARU's assessments of what types of marketing practices are of special concern when used with young children.

Building Strong Brands

Beyond these specific exclusions, there is a larger marketing issue to consider. Advertising is not necessarily the most powerful element in the marketing mix. Often, the "product" strategy (product development, branding) and "place" (distribution channels) components of the "4 Ps" are the strongest bases for building sustainable competitive advantages. Assortment decisions, including the development of new items, reformulations, and determining the scope of product lines, are all central to product strategy. The CFBAI firms have been actively improving the nutritional profile of items they promote to children. Since the CFBAI's inception, they have either reformulated or created more than 100 products (CBBB, 2010a). This seems to be in the companies' best interests as well. According to a Hudson Institute report (2011), food companies with a higher percentage of sales in the "better-for-you" category perform better financially.

[47] *Kellogg Co.*, Case No. 5165 (CARU April 23, 2010), p. 3. In contrast, Unilever's pledge expressly acknowledges that it directs labeling and certain in-store materials to children ages 6 to 11. See Unilever pledge, available at http://www.bbb.org/us/storage/0/Shared%20Documents/Unilever%20restated%20pledge%205-25-10.pdf.

[48] *Kellogg Co.*, Case No. 5165 (CARU April 23, 2010), p. 7. The case did not address the website advertising. The most recent CFBAI compliance report mentions that "after discussion with CFBAI staff," Kellogg decided to remove the "Kids" section of the Pop-Tarts' website "in the near future" (CBBB, 2010a, p. 22). The CBBB report did not mention the CARU case.

[49] *Burger King*, Case No. 5332 (CARU April 20, 2011).

The building and maintenance of a firm's brands are also critical to product strategy. Branding has been described as the art and cornerstone of marketing (Kotler & Keller, 2011) and its value to firms is well documented (see e.g., Keller, 2008). Scholarly research further suggests that brand equity is a key issue in reaching children. Brand preferences are formed in early childhood (Bahn, 1986). Children recognize brands by ages 3–4; by age 7–8, they can name multiple brands in many product categories, use brand names as key source of product information, and often make requests by brand name (John, 1999).

Under the CFBAI, firms retain significant freedom to promote their brands without reference to specific food items. For example, McDonalds can advertise its master brand to children using its name, characters, symbols, and other brand identity elements. Features such as Ronald McDonald, Playplace, happymeal.com, and Happy Meal toys can help create positive feelings that become linked to the McDonald's brand and its product offerings. The CFBAI's willingness to allow general branding (or product line advertising) conflicts with some other food marketing policies noted earlier. For example, the IOTF (2008) recommends that there should be no marketing to children of energy-dense, nutrient-poor foods and brands associated with them.

Although the CFBAI seems to discourage the use of "equity" or product line advertising (CBBB, 2008), it does not explicitly address this issue in its pledge requirements. When discussed, equity advertising is defined as the use of logos for brand or product lines that include both SKUs that meet and do not meet a participant's nutrition criteria. Company-owned characters and brand names are explicitly exempted (CBBB, 2009). This definition appears rather narrow and leads to confusing situations where, for example, the phrase "Goldfish Central" on pfgoldfish.com is not considered advertising for all Goldfish varieties by the CFBAI. This potential for ambiguity raises the question of whether general branding (e.g., brand names, characters, slogans, branded environments) might directly or indirectly increase children's brand preferences for a product line that also includes less healthy alternatives.

There is reason to think this may be the case. Within a company's portfolio, brands play different roles. For example, a driver role reflects the degree to which a brand guides purchasing choices and shapes the usage experience (Aaker, 2004). Typically, a master brand has the dominant driver role, although sub-brands, descriptors, and endorsers may also contribute.[50] For the CFBAI brands, situations where the master brand plays a major role in building preference and choice seem likely. For example, for a branded product line like Kraft's Lunchables, we would anticipate that it is the "Lunchables" name that drives consumer purchase rather than any specific SKU or variety. Although a particular meal combination (e.g., Fun Pack Chicken Dunks—Breaded Chicken Nuggets with 100% Fruit Juice) may be eligible for promotion under the CFBAI, the question is whether other less healthy options

[50] A master or parent brand is the primary indicator of a product offering and usually visually dominant.

Product category	Brand	Total # of branded options*	Branded options listed in pledge	Additional branded options not listed in pledge		% branded options that do not meet nutritional requirements
				Meet nutritional criteria	Do not meet nutritional criteria	
*Breakfast Cereal (10%)***						
	Froot Loops (Kellogg)	3	2	0	1	33%
	Cinnamon Toast Crunch (General Mills)	2	1	0	1	50%
Prepared Foods & Meals (49%)						
	Lunchables (Kraft)	40	12	1	27	67%
	Kids Cuisine (ConAgra)	16	15	0	1	6%
	Chef Boyardee Canned Pasta (ConAgra)	29	9	0	20	69%
Snack Foods (43%)						
	Goldfish Crackers (Campbell)	32	16	12	4	13%
	Cheese Nips (Kraft)	3	1	0	2	67%
	Skippy Peanut Butter (Unilever)	9	8	0	1	11%
Dairy Products (29%)						
	Nesquik (Nestle)	16	4	1	11	69%
	Danimals (Dannon)	14	14	0	0	0%

*Total number of options (flavors or varieties) available within pledge brands. Does not include each size offered. May also include brand extensions into new categories (e.g., from cereal into cereal bars).
**To be read: 10% of branded offerings within the breakfast cereal category (includes all CFBAI participating firms) do not meet company specific nutrition criteria.

Fig. 6.5 Illustrative examples: portfolio analysis of pledge brands

also benefit because the "Lunchables" name is reinforced when children see ads for the brand in child-targeted media. There is also potential for confusion at the point-of-sale, both among parents and children, when only some alternatives (e.g. flavors or varieties) within a brand are covered by pledge provisions.

To gain some initial insight into this issue, we analyzed the brand portfolios of pledge firms. Our investigation focused on brands that the CFBAI companies have included in their pledges (as of the summer of 2011). All other brands that a firm manufactures or sells but that are not directly promoted to children were excluded. Our essential question was to what extent does a product line where one option qualifies to be marketed to children contain other branded items that do not meet the nutritional criteria that a firm has established for itself?

Figure 6.5 provides some illustrative findings.[51] To aid interpretation, we first offer a brief example. In the listing under breakfast cereals, we note that Froot Loops cereal is offered in three flavor varieties (see column 3). Two of these (Froot Loops and Froot Loops with Reduced Sugar) are listed in Kellogg's pledge (column 4). The third branded option (Froot Loops with Marshmallows) is not (column 6). So, one of

[51] The list of product categories is based on that used in the FTC (2008) report. Not all categories are reported here.

three branded alternatives (33%) does not meet the nutritional criteria the company has established for itself.[52] In the breakfast cereal category as a whole (across participant firms), only 10% of the pledge brand offerings do not meet self-imposed nutritional requirements. So, in this case, the vast majority do meet these standards.

However, there is substantial variation both within and across product categories. For instance, although only a small proportion of cereals do not meet company nutrition criteria, for dairy products the percentage rises to 29%; in snack foods to 43%; and in prepared foods and meals, 49% of the pledge brand offerings exceed self-imposed limits. This means that in these latter two categories, close to half of the branded offerings that consumers see in the store are for varieties that fail to meet the firm's nutritional criteria. Yet, the master or family brand may be advertised to children. For example, ConAgra offers 29 varieties of Chef Boyardee canned pasta, yet only 9 of these are either included in the pledge or could be. The Chef Boyardee master brand can be advertised to children via these 9 options, but there may be as many as 20 additional branded varieties or SKUs (69%) in the store that do not meet the healthier standards. Variation is also evident across brands in the same product category. In the cases shown here, we see that only 1 of 16 (6%) of Kids Cuisine meals, another ConAgra product, do not meet the firm's nutritional standards. Lunchables, a Kraft brand, stands at 67%. These kinds of disparities are not unique to this category, as evidenced by the snack food and dairy brands also listed in Fig. 6.5. Across all categories (not shown here), from 0% to some 80% of the SKUs for pledge brands fail to meet the firms' self-imposed nutrition limits. This means that although a child may see an ad for a healthier option, a large proportion of the options available in the store may be for similarly branded items that do not meet pledge standards.

The potential for confusion at the point-of-sale is clear, and may be exacerbated in the future as consumers come to rely on child-targeted advertising as a signal that the product being promoted is nutritionally sound. Moreover, because portfolios may include options with a range of nutritional profiles, brand messages may create confusion for parents and children about which products are "better for you." Our analysis here only begins to address how the communication opportunities afforded by general branding shape the marketing environment in which children learn and are persuaded. Future research is needed to determine what impact "authorized" brand messages have on children's preferences and purchase requests for other items in a brand family.

Monitoring, Enforcement, and Evaluation

A key issue in the analyses of these programs concerns the monitoring and enforcement mechanisms that have been put in place. Both the WHO (2010) and the IOTF (2008) argue that monitoring and enforcement should be done by neutral and

[52] There may be branded options that meet pledge nutrition standards but the company has chosen not to list or advertise them to children (column 5). No such varieties exist for Froot Loops.

independent parties and that the evaluation process should be transparent. This is currently not the case under the CFBAI. Although the CBBB publishes regular progress reports (CBBB, 2008, 2009, 2010a, 2011a), neither the data it collects from participants nor its own studies are available for independent review. The CFBAI also has not established a clear process for handling external complaints. CARU does better in that its review process results in published cases that explain its reasoning and outline the advertisers' positions. It has also improved its transparency over time (e.g., when it largely did away with informal cases in 2004). However, in 2009, CARU stopped reporting the name of the advertising agency in its cases despite the fact that NAD/CARU Procedures require this information.[53] This failure to follow its own requirements is puzzling and has the effect of reducing advertising agencies' accountability. Further, although CARU occasionally opens a case in response to a consumer complaint, there is no mechanism for public explanation when it declines to do so. More generally, some advocates have questioned CARU's ability to be independent when it is funded by the advertisers it is assigned to monitor (e.g., Kelly, 2005).

At a more basic level, however, there is a distinct disconnect in how these programs are evaluated by various parties. For example, CARU's sponsoring organizations claim a success or compliance rate of 95% or higher (NARC, 2004 at 95%; Lascoutx, 2005 at 97%).[54] The CBBB also reports excellent compliance records for CFBAI members (CBBB, 2008, 2009, 2010a, 2011a). The CFBAI director recently reported to a Congressional committee that it has "changed not only what products are advertised to kids, but the expectations about what should or should not be advertised to kids" (Kolish, 2011b, p. 14).

However, other studies paint a different picture. For example, Hoy et al., (2012) found that only about one-third or fewer of CARU's food cases between 2000 and 2010 were resolved in the advertiser's favor (i.e., no modification or discontinuance asked for or offered). Armstrong (1984), who looked at the first 5 years of CARU's activities, reported that only about 25% of challenged ads were found to be acceptable as-is. Similarly, we found that about 18% ($n=27$) of CARU's formal food cases from 1975 to June 2011 were resolved in the advertiser's favor. Thus, multiple independent researchers looking at CARU's activities across various periods of time all report similar results.

Fried (2006) also challenged CARU's claim of 97% effectiveness, concluding that "advertisers that have repeatedly violated its guidelines are . . . praised by CARU in press releases for participating in the self-regulatory process," as long as they agree to consider CARU's concerns in the future (p. 137). Our systematic examination of all CARU's food cases supports this conclusion. As noted above, many advertisers have been involved in multiple challenges through the years. Thus, we looked to see

---

[53] See NAD/CARU Procedures, § 2.1 (C) (2011). NAD also stopped reporting this information around the same time.

[54] See also Kunkel and Gantz (1993) (finding that 96% of TV commercials assessed complied with CARU Guidelines).

among the formal cases involving firms with multiple past challenges, how many times CARU referred to prior cases involving the same advertiser and the same type of conduct. We found a few examples where CARU cited a previous case involving the same advertiser for the same type of conduct.[55] In one case, CARU's decision referred to a prior case involving a different advertiser, but similar concerns.[56]

We also found several examples, however, where CARU clearly could have referred to prior cases involving the advertiser and the same type of problem, but did not.[57] For example, in the mid-2000s, CARU pursued three cases related to potentially misleading fruit content claims (among other concerns) in Sunny Delight ads. Figure 6.2 includes a summary of the first case in 2003, involving Proctor & Gamble (P&G).[58] Then in 2004, shortly after P&G spun off the brand to create Sunny Delight Beverages Co., CARU opened an informal case with the new company focused on the same concern.[59] Then in 2007, it brought a formal case, again involving problematic claims about Sunny D's fruit content.[60] CARU did not refer to any of the prior cases, despite the fact that it found in all three that the ads did not comply with its Guidelines. Fried (2006) noted additional examples involving Kraft and Wrigley.

A similar disconnect occurs with evaluations of the CFBAI. For example, in contrast to reports that CFBAI ads directed to children "usually are for or include nutrient dense foods that also meet reasonable limits on calories, fats, sugars and sodium" (CBBB, 2010a, p. 12), Powell et al. (Chap. 8) report that 88% of CFBAI company ads seen by children in 2009 were for foods high in saturated fat, sugar, and sodium. Kunkel, Gantz, McKinley, and Wright (2009) report similar results for CFBAI ads during children's TV programming. Further, young children's exposure to fast-food advertising has increased substantially between 2003 and 2009, including ads aired

[55] *See, e.g., Kellogg Co.*, Case No. 5165 (CARU April 23, 2010) (citing *Kellogg Co.*, Case No. 4515 (CARU June 7, 2006)) (fruit content claims on packaging); *Kellogg Co.*, Case No. 4416 (CARU Nov. 22, 2005) (referring to *Kellogg Co.*, Case No. 4337 (CARU May 27, 2005)) (fruit content claims on packaging); *Kraft Foods Inc.*, Case No. 4410 (CARU Nov. 18, 2005) (referring to *Kraft Foods Global, Inc.* Case No. 4353 (CARU June 29, 2005) (focusing on premium over product); and *Kraft Foods*, Case No. 4404 (CARU Oct. 28, 2005) (referring to *Kraft Foods*, Case No. 4319 (CARU April 26, 2005) (contest/sweepstakes disclosures).

[56] *Int. Dairy Foods Ass'n*, Case No. 4177 (CARU May 3, 2004) (referring to *Dairy Management, Inc*, Case No. 4042 (CARU Apr. 22, 2003) (relating to concerns about behavior depicted in ad).

[57] E.g., *Dannon Co.*, Case No. 4842 (CARU May 6, 2008) could have referred to *Dannon Co.*, Case No. 4737 (CARU Oct. 5, 2007) and *Dannon Co.*, Case No. 4568 (CARU Sept. 28, 2006) (regarding adequacy of material disclosures); *General Mills Inc.*, Case No. 4708 (CARU Aug. 9, 2007) could have referred to *General Mills*, Case No. 4412 (CARU Nov. 11, 2005) (suggestions of overconsumption); *Kellogg Co.*, Case No. 4540 (CARU Aug. 8, 2006) could have referred to *Kellogg Co.*, Case No. 4397 (CARU Sept. 27, 2005) (focusing on premium over product); and *McDonald's Corp.*, Case No. 5078 (CARU Aug. 28, 2009) could have referred to *McDonald's USA*, Case No. 4590 (CARU Oct. 25, 2006) (focusing on premium over product).

[58] *Proctor & Gamble Co.*, Case No. 4040 (CARU April 30, 2003).

[59] In re: *Sunny Delight Beverages*, CARU Activity Report (NAD Case Report, Vol. 34, No. 9, at 616) (Oct./Nov. 2004).

[60] *Sunny Delight Beverages Co.*, Case No. 4761 (CARU Nov. 27, 2007).

by CFBAI firms (Powell, Schermbeck, Szczypka, Chaloupka, & Braunschweig, 2011). Other studies document the poor nutritional content of fast-food products (Harris et al., 2010a) and cereal (Harris et al., 2009) marketed to children, post-CFBAI implementation.

As these examples illustrate, industry, social scientists, and advocates seem to apply different evaluative benchmarks. The CBBB/NARC evaluation processes do not address the underlying question of what outcomes should be sought and therefore measured. For example, CARU is not wrong to consider it "compliance" or "success" when companies agree to stop running problematic ads, and/or state they will take CARU's concerns into consideration for the future in situations where ads have run their flight. Those agreements are important. However, this is neither the only conception of "compliance," nor arguably the most meaningful. According to Boddewyn (1989, p. 23) compliance is achieved when practitioners "improve and internalize higher advertising standards." In this view, CARU would hold advertisers accountable not just for the specific ad under consideration but also for internalizing the values and norms represented in the CARU Guidelines *across all of their marketing efforts.*

The CFBAI could take a similar approach. Basic marketing principles indicate that advertising exposure alone is not a sufficient criterion for a campaign's success. Marketing communication programs are commonly evaluated on a number of dimensions ranging from exposure (reach), to recall, belief and attitude change, and ultimately to product choice (see e.g., Belch & Belch, 2012). It is neither sufficient nor credible for a major consumer packaged goods company or advertising agency to evaluate campaigns solely based on exposure or reach. So, in this case, if the goal is to promote healthier dietary choices, then the appropriate question is whether the program does *in fact* lead to healthier choices being made. At this juncture, we do not know the answer, and the monitoring system is not configured to allow such a determination.

Conclusions and Recommendations

Kraak et al., (2011) report that the food and beverage firms are the only industry sector to have made "moderate" progress toward fulfilling the IOM's 2006 recommendations. However, they also identified areas for improvement (Kraak et al., 2011). By focusing on the common roots and missions of CARU and the CFBAI, our study illuminates where the programs have taken inconsistent positions that may undermine self-regulatory and public health goals. It also points to specific ways that the programs could improve their processes—both individually and in tandem—to accelerate progress.

The CFBAI focuses exclusively on food advertisers and requires them to apply specific nutritional standards. As a result, the CFBAI has a greater ability than CARU to drive product reformulation and has done so. Nonetheless, CARU continues to have a meaningful role in addressing food marketing issues—indeed, the CBBB (2011a) notes that it reviews the results of CARU's monitoring activities as part of its CFBAI compliance review. CARU provides important guidance on the definition of "child directed," including what media should be covered, and which marketing techniques are more likely to raise concerns. Additionally, in at least one recent case (involving Pop-Tarts packaging), it identified a key gap in the CFBAI's coverage. This case showed that the utility of the CFBAI's nutritional standards can be limited by the narrower scope of activities to which they are applied. By defining child-targeted marketing in a more circumscribed fashion, the CFBAI operates inconsistently not only with general marketing principles but also with CARU. By allowing these exclusions and by declining to draw on CARU's precedent, the CFBAI creates an opportunity for some marketers to cast doubt on CARU's authority. Viewed in this way, the CFBAI could potentially reverse progress that CARU has made in helping firms to avoid problems in their advertising. Other reports have issued important recommendations, such as that all food and beverage companies, as well as media companies, should join the CFBAI (e.g., CSPI, 2010). Our investigation leads us to some further recommendations for improving these programs both individually and in tandem.

- The CFBAI should draw on CARU's experience and the model standards discussed above, and include packaging, point-of-sale, and the other marketing activities in the pledge program.
- Clear guidelines for "equity advertising" should be included in the pledge framework. For example, the CFBAI could require that a sizeable majority of SKUs for a pledge brand meet promised nutritional standards before the family brand can be marketed to children.
- CFBAI members should be expected to consistently comply with CARU and be able to demonstrate that they have internalized CARU's standards. For example, the CFBAI might institute a point or demerit system that could be used to rate the CFBAI companies' performances, across time and across companies, for inclusion in annual compliance reports.
- CARU could consider failure to comply with a CFBAI pledge as a lack of compliance with its Guidelines. It might also incorporate the CFBAI's nutrition criteria so that any product (regardless of CFBAI membership) that does not meet them would be considered inappropriate for children, much as CARU has done with PG-13 movies, vitamins, etc.
- CFBAI participants should develop metrics (KPIs) that track the extent to which they are shifting consumer preference and demand to healthier options as a result of pledge implementation and disclose this information to stakeholders.
- Both programs could take steps to improve the transparency of their operations and monitoring. For CARU, perhaps the most important step is to assess its overall success rate based on measures (publicly disclosed) that indicate to what degree companies adhere to the Guidelines across time and marketing campaigns. For the CFBAI, enabling public scrutiny of its operations, from contracts between the CBBB and the firms, to the companies' compliance reports, would be an advance.

The public debate about food marketing to children has been highly polarized, frequently marked by acrimony, cynicism, and distrust (see Chap. 4 Williams and

Drumwright). Yet, there are at least two key points of agreement between stakeholders: (1) that obesity is compromising children's health and must be reduced; and (2) industry self-regulation is a crucial driver of US children's food marketing practices. Under current circumstances, there is no time for smugness, nor a place for zealotry in this debate. But there is need for zeal. All stakeholders—including the food and beverage industry, with its vast creative power, resources, and influence—should be working to maximize the potentials of CARU and the CFBAI in promoting healthy food environments for children. Anything less would truly be a shame.

Acknowledgements The authors would like to thank Ellen Jantsch, Adam Pabarcus, Katie Sykes, Chelsie Thuecks, Dee Tian, Kelly Timko and Kristine Weir for their research assistance. We also would like to thank the staff at the library for the Minnesota Attorney General's Office. Finally, the authors would also like to thank the members of the Advisory Committee for the research project: Prentiss Cox, Dr. Jean Kinsey, Jennifer Pomeranz, Dr. David Walsh, and Dr. Jerome Williams.

References

Aaker, D. A. (2004). *Brand portfolio strategy*. New York, NY: Free Press.

Armstrong, G. M. (1984). An evaluation of the Children's Advertising Review Unit. *Journal of Public Policy & Marketing, 3*, 38–55.

Bachman, K. (2011). Advertisers hope house bill will squash new food guidelines. *Adweek* (July 6). http://www.adweek.com/news/advertising-branding/advertisers-hope-house-bill-will-squash-new-food-guidelines-133200. Accessed 12 Nov 2011.

Bahn, K. D. (1986). How and when do brand preferences first form? A cognitive developmental investigation. *Journal of Consumer Research, 13*(3), 382–393.

Bartz, D. (2011). US food lobby fighting hard to defend kid ads. *Reuters*. http://www.reuters.com/article/2011/11/07/us-advertising-children-idUSTRE7A66OA20111107. Accessed 21 Nov 2011.

Belch, G. E., & Belch, M. A. (2012). *Advertising and promotion–An integrated marketing communications perspective* (9th ed.). New York, NY: McGraw-Hill/Irwin.

Boddewyn, J. J. (1989). Advertising self-regulation: True purpose and limits. *Journal of Advertising, 18*(2), 19–27.

Carter, C. (2009). *Consumer protection in the States: A 50-state report on unfair and deceptive acts and practices statutes*. Nat'l Consumer Law Ctr. Inc. http://www.consumerlaw.org/issues/udap/content/UDAP_Report_Feb09.pdf. Accessed 4 Dec 2011.

Center for Science in the Public Interest [CSPI]. (2005). *Guidelines for responsible food marketing to children*. Washington, DC. http://www.cspinet.org/marketingguidelines.pdf. Accessed 30 Nov 2011.

Center for Science in the Public Interest [CSPI]. (2009). *Better-for-who? Revisiting company promises on food marketing to children*. http://cspinet.org/new/pdf/pledgereport.pdf. Accessed on 26 Nov 2011.

Children's Advertising Review Unit [CARU]. (2009). *Self-regulatory program for children's advertising* (9th ed.). New York, NY: Council of Better Business Bureaus.

Center for Science in the Public Interest [CSPI]. (2010). *Report card on food marketing policies*. http://cspinet.org/new/pdf/marketingreportcard.pdf. Accessed on 23 Nov 2011.

Children's Advertising Review Unit [CARU]. (2000). *Self-regulatory program for children's advertising* (6th ed.). New York, NY: Council of Better Business Bureaus.

Children's Review Unit (1975). *Children's advertising guidelines*. New York, NY: National Advertising Division, Council of Better Business Bureaus [reprinted in Adler, R. et al. (1977).

Research on the effects of television advertising on children: A review of the literature and recommendations for future research. Washington, DC: National Science Foundation, pp. 201–206].

Council of Better Business Bureaus [CBBB]. (2006). *New food, beverage initiative to focus kids' ads on healthy choices; revised guidelines strengthen CARU's guidance to food advertisers*. Press release, November 14. http://www.bbb.org/us/article/new-food-beverage-initiative-to-focus-kids-ads-on-healthy-choices-revised-guidelines-strengthen-carus-guidance-to-food-advertisers-672. Accessed 5 Dec 2011.

Council of Better Business Bureaus [CBBB]. (2008). *Changing the landscape of food and beverage advertising: The Children's Food and Beverage Advertising Initiative in action*. Arlington, VA: Council of Better Business Bureaus.

Council of Better Business Bureaus [CBBB]. (2009). *The Children's Food and Beverage Advertising Initiative in action: A report on compliance and implementation during 2008*. Arlington, VA: Council of Better Business Bureaus.

Council of Better Business Bureaus [CBBB]. (2010a). *The Children's Food and Beverage Advertising Initiative in action: A report on compliance and implementation during 2009*. Arlington, VA: Council of Better Business Bureaus.

Council of Better Business Bureaus [CBBB]. (2010b). *The Children's Food and Beverage Advertising Initiative program and core principles statement* (3rd ed.). Arlington, VA: Council of Better Business Bureaus.

Council of Better Business Bureaus [CBBB]. (2011a). *The Children's Food and Beverage Advertising Initiative in action: A report on compliance and implementation during 2010 and a five year retrospective: 2006–2011*. Arlington, VA: Council of Better Business Bureaus.

Council of Better Business Bureaus [CBBB]. (2011b). *Council of Better Business Bureaus announces groundbreaking agreement on child-directed food advertising*. Press release, July 14. http://www.bbb.org/us/article/Council-of-Better-Business-Bureaus-Announces-Groundbreaking-Agreement-on-Ch-28325. Accessed 28 Nov 2011.

Crain, R. (2009). Self-regulation shouldn't be advertising's best-kept secret. *Advertising Age, 80*(7), 11.

Edwards, J. (2006). Review of kids ad rules getting messy. *Brandweek, 47*(38), page number not available.

Ellison, S. (2005). Food makers propose tougher guidelines for children's ads. *Wall Street Journal-Eastern Edition, 246* (July 13), B1, B4.

Federal Trade Commission [FTC]. (1978). *FTC staff report on television advertising to children* Washington, DC: Federal Trade Commission.

Federal Trade Commission [FTC]. (1981). *In re Children's Advertising, 43 Fed. Reg. 17,967, FTC final staff report and recommendation*.

Federal Trade Commission [FTC]. (2008). *Marketing food to children and adolescents – a review of industry expenditures, activities and self-regulation*. Report to Congress. Washington, DC: Federal Trade Commission.

Forman, J., Halford, J. C. G., Summe, H., MacDougall, M., & Keller, K. L. (2009). Food branding influences ad libitum differently depending on weight status. *Appetite, 53*(1), 76–83.

Fried, E. (2006). Assessing effectiveness of self-regulation: A case study of the Children's Advertising Review Unit. *Loyola of Los Angeles Law Review, 39*(1), 93–137.

Grocery Manufacturers Association [GMA]. (2010). *Shopper Marketing 4.0–Building scalable playbooks that drive results*. Report. http://www.gmaonline.org/downloads/research-and-reports/Shopper_Marketing_4.0.pdf. Accessed 30 Nov 2011.

Grocery Manufacturers Association [GMA]. (2011). *Shopper Marketing 5.0–Creating value with shopper solutions*. Report. http://www.gmaonline.org/file-manager/Collaborating_with_Retailers/GMA_Shopper_Marketing_5.0.pdfccess.0.pdf. Accessed 29 Nov 2011.

Grocery Manufacturers Association [GMA] and Deloitte Consulting (2007). *Shopper marketing: Capturing a shopper's mind, heart and wallet*. Report. http://www.rw3.com/ufiles/file/Article4.pdf. Accessed 30 Nov 2011.

Harris, J. L., Schwartz, M. B., Brownell, K. D. et al. (2009). Cereal F.A.C.T.S.: Evaluating the nutrition quality and marketing of children's cereals. New Haven, CT: Yale University, Rudd Center for Food Policy and Obesity. http://www.cerealfacts.org/media/Cereal_FACTS_Report.pdf. Accessed 21 Nov 2011.

Harris, J. L., Schwartz, M. B., & Brownell, K. D. (2010a). Fast food F.A.C.T.S.: Evaluating fast food nutrition and marketing to youth. New Haven, CT: Yale University, Rudd Center for Food Policy and Obesity. http://fastfoodmarketing.org/media/FastFoodFACTS_Report.pdf. Accessed 4 Dec 2011.

Harris, J. L., Schwartz, M. B., & Brownell, K. D. (2010b). Marketing of foods to children and adolescents licensed characters and other promotions on packaged foods in the supermarket. *Public Health Nutrition, 13*(3), 409–417.

Hernandez, M., & Kolish, E.D. (2011). *CFBAI comment to the IWG*. http://www.bbb.org/us/storage/0/Shared%20Documents/CFBAI%20IWG%20Comment%207-14-2011.pdf. Accessed 28 Nov 2011.

Holt, D. J., Ippolito, P. M., Desrochers, D. M., & Kelley, C.R. (2007). *Children's exposure to TV advertising in 1977 and 2004, information for the obesity debate*. FTC, Bureau of Economics Staff Report.

Howard, J. A., & Hulbert, J. (1973). *Advertising and the public interest. A staff report to the Federal Trade Commission*. New York, NY: FTC, Bureau of Consumer Protection.

Hoy, M. G., Childers, C. C., & Morrison, M. (2012). The evolution of self-regulation in food advertising: An analysis of CARU cases from 2000–2010. *International Journal of Advertising, 31*(2), 257–290.

Hudson Institute. (2011). Better-for-you foods – It's just good business. http://www.hudson.org/files/documents/BFY%20Foods%20Executive%20Summary.pdf. Accessed 31 Oct 2011.

Interagency Working Group [IWG]. (2011). *Interagency Working Group on food marketed to children–preliminary proposed nutrition principles to guide self-regulatory efforts, request for comments*. http://www.ftc.gov/os/2011/04/110428foodmarketproposedguide.pdf. Accessed 31 Oct 2011.

International Obesity Task Force [IOTF] and Consumers International. (2008). *Recommendations for an international code on marketing of foods and non-alcoholic beverages to children*. London. http://www.iaso.org/site_media/uploads/ConsumersInternationalMarketingCode.pdf. Accessed 30 Nov 2011.

John, D. R. (1999). Consumer socialization of children: A retrospective look at twenty-five years of research. *Journal of Consumer Research, 26*(3), 183–213.

Keller, K. L. (2008). *Strategic brand management: Building, measuring and managing brand equity* (3rd ed.). Upper Saddle River, NJ: Pearson Prentice Hall.

Kelly, B. (2005). To quell obesity, who should regulate food marketing to children? *Globalization and Health*. doi:10.1186/1744-8603-1-9.

Kolish, E.D. (2011a). *Remarks before the Washington Legal Foundation*. http://www.bbb.org/us/storage/0/Shared%20Documents/WLF.pdf. Accessed 21 Nov 2011.

Kolish, E. D. (2011b). Summary of prepared statement of Elaine D. Kolish, Vice President and Director, Children's Food and Beverage Advertising Initiative, BBB, before the Subcommittee on Commerce, Manufacturing, and Trade, and the Subcommittee on Health of the House Energy and Commerce Committee. Food marketing: Can "voluntary" government restrictions improve children's health? (October 12).

Kotler, P., & Keller, K. L. (2011). *Marketing management* (14th ed.). Upper Saddle River, NJ: Pearson.

Kraak, V. I., Story, M., Wartella, E. A., & Ginter, J. (2011). Industry progress to market a healthful diet to American children and adolescents. *American Journal of Preventive Medicine, 41*(3), 322–333.

Kunkel, D., & Gantz, W. (1993). Assessing compliance with industry self-regulation of television advertising to children. *Journal of Applied Communication Research, 21*(2), 148–162.

Kunkel, D., Gantz, W., McKinley, C., & Wright, P. (2009). *The impact of industry self-regulation on the nutritional quality of foods advertised on television to children*. Oakland, CA: Children Now.

Landon, J., & Gritschneder, Y. (2011). *An analysis of the regulatory and voluntary landscape concerning the marketing and promotion of food and drink to children*. London: National Heart Forum.

Lascoutx, E. (2002). Children's Advertising Review Unit. *St. John's Journal of Legal Commentary, 16*(3), 649–653.

Lascoutx, E. (2005). Remarks at the Joint Workshop of the Fed. Trade Commission and the Dept. of Health & Human Services, *Perspectives on Marketing, Self-Regulation, and Childhood Obesity* (July 15). http://www.ftc.gov/bcp/workshops/foodmarketingtokids/transcript_050715.pdf.

Macklin, M. C. (1996). Preschoolers' learning of brand names from visual cues. *Journal of Consumer Research, 23*(3), 304–319.

Mayer, C. (2005). Minding Nemo: Pitches to kids feed debate about a watchdog. *Washington Post* (February 27, 2005) F01. http://www.washingtonpost.com/wp-dyn/articles/A55226-2005Feb26.html. Accessed on 28 Nov 2011.

McGinnis, J. M., Gootman, J., & Kraak, V. I. (2006). *Food marketing to children and youth: threat or opportunity?* Institute of Medicine, Washington, DC: The National Academies Press.

Mintel Oxygen (2008). *Kids' and teens' eating habits – US*. Report (September).

Molpus, M. (2005). *Written submission to the FTC and Dept. of Health and Human Services by the president and CEO of the Grocery Manufacturers Association, on behalf of Campbell Soup Co., General Mills, Inc.; The Hershey Co.; Kellogg Co.; Kraft Foods, Inc.; Nestle USA; PepsiCo, Inc.; Sara Lee Corp.; Unilever U.S., Inc.*

Montopoli, B. (2011). GOP decries nanny state push on junk food ads. CBS News, CBSNews.com, (July 7, 2011) http://www.cbsnews.com/8301-503544_162-20077584-503544.html. Accessed 11 Nov 2011.

Moore, E. S., & Rideout, V. J. (2007). The online marketing of food to children: Is it just fun and games? *Journal of Public Policy & Marketing, 26*(2), 202–220.

Naik, P. A., & Raman, K. (2003). Understanding the impact of synergy in multimedia communications. *Journal of Marketing Research, 40*(4), 375–388.

National Advertising Review Council [NARC]. (2004). *Guidance for food advertising self-regulation*. White Paper.

National Advertising Review Council [NARC]. (2011). *The advertising industry's process of voluntary self-regulation*. (Aug. 8 revision). http://www.narcpartners.org/reports/2011_Procedures.pdf. Accessed 13 Oct 2011.

Nelson, E., Ellison, S. (2005). Shelf promotion: in a shift, marketers beef up ad spending inside stores – funky displays and lighting, TV spots in Wal-Mart; unsettling Madison Avenue – fake doorknobs pitch diapers. *The Wall Street Journal* (September 21), A1.

Nestle, M. (2000). Halting the obesity epidemic. *Public Health Reports, 115*(1), 12–24.

O'Dell, P. (2009). Shopping trip. *Promo Magazine* (December 1). http://promomagazine.com/retail/marketing_shopping_trip/. Accessed 30 Nov 2011.

Ogba, I. E., & Johnson, R. (2010). How packaging affects the product preferences of children and the buyer behaviour of their parents in the food industry. *Young Consumers, 11*(1), 77–89.

Pechmann, C., Levine, L., Loughlin, S., & Leslie, F. (2005). Impulsive and self-conscious: adolescents' vulnerability to advertising and promotion. *Journal of Public Policy & Marketing, 24*(2), 202–21.

Peeler, L. (2009), *Advertising and consumer protection: Hearing before the Senate Committee on Commerce, Science and Transportation, Subcommittee on Consumer Protection, Product Safety, and Insurance* (July 22). Senate Hearing 111–484. Washington, DC: US Government Printing Office.

Powell, L. M., Schermbeck, R. M., Szczypka, G., Chaloupka, F. J., & Braunschweig, C. L. (2011). Trends in the nutritional content of television food advertisements seen by children in the United States. *Archives of Pediatrics & Adolescent Medicine*. doi:10.1001/archpediatrics.2011.131.

Powell, L. M., Szczypka, G., & Chaloupka, F. J. (2007). Exposure to food advertising on television among US children. *Archives of Pediatrics & Adolescent Medicine, 161*(6), 553–560.

Pridgen, M. D. (2011). *Consumer protection and the law* § 12:12. St. Paul, MN: Thompson West (Westlaw database, updated October 2011).

Rexha, D., Mizerski, K., & Mizerski, D. (2010). The effect of availability, point of purchase advertising and sampling on children's first independent purchases. *Journal of Promotion Management, 16*(1–2), 148–166.

Robinson, T. N., Borzekowski, D. L. G., Matheson, D. M., & Kramer, H. C. (2007). Effects of fast food branding on young children's taste preferences. *Archives of Pediatrics and Adolescent Medicine, 161*(8), 792–797.

Schmedemann, D., & Kunz, C. L. (2007). *Synthesis: Legal reading, reasoning, and writing* (3rd ed.). New York, NY: Aspen Publishers.

Sharma, L., Teret, S., & Brownell, K. (2010). The food industry and self-regulation: standards to promote success and to avoid public health failures. *American Journal of Public Health, 100*(2), 240–246.

Sheldon, A. N. (2001) *State consumer protection laws and unfair competition*, SF74 ALI-ABA, 501–528.

Swinburn, B., Sacks, G., Lobstein, T., Rigby, N., Baur, L. A., Brownell, K. D., Gill, T., Seidell, J., & Kumanyika, S. (2008). The "Sydney Principles" for reducing the commercial promotion of foods and beverages to children. *Public Health Nutrition, 11*(9), 881–886.

Underhill, P. (2008). *Why we buy: The science of shopping*. New York, NY: Simon and Schuster.

Valkenburg, P. M., & Buijzen, M. (2005). Identifying determinants of young children's brand awareness: Television, parents and peers. *Journal of Applied Developmental Psychology, 26*(4), 456–468.

Vladeck, D. (2011). Prepared statement of the FTC on the Interagency Working Group on Food Marketed to Children before the House Energy and Commerce Committee, Subcommittee on Commerce, Manufacturing, and Trade and the Subcommittee on Health, U.S. House of Representatives (October 12).

Washington Post. (1978). *The FTC as national nanny*. March 1, A22.

World Health Organization. (2010). Set of Recommendations on the Marketing of Foods and Non-Alcoholic Beverages to Children. Geneva, Switzerland. http://whqlibdoc.who.int/publications/2010/9789241500210_eng.pdf, Accessed 1 December 2011.

Chapter 7
Monitoring Food Company Marketing to Children to Spotlight Best and Worst Practices

Jennifer L. Harris, Megan Weinberg, Johanna Javadizadeh, and Vishnudas Sarda

In 2006, the Council of Better Business Bureaus and ten of the largest children's food marketers launched the Children's Food and Beverage Advertising Initiative (CFBAI), an industry self-regulatory program for the purpose of "Changing the nutritional profile of food and beverage products in child-directed advertising" (BBB, 2009). These companies' pledges were fully implemented by 2008, and as of August, 2011, 17 companies had joined the CFBAI. The food industry has declared the CFBAI a success, with companies exhibiting excellent compliance with their pledges and the number of food and beverage advertisements on children's television programming falling by 50% from 2004 to 2010 (BBB, 2010).

The public health community, however, holds a widely different perspective on the success of the CFBAI. Many advocates have expressed concerns that the program provides considerable public relations value for the food companies, but has done little to improve the obesinogenic food marketing environment that surrounds children in the USA (Harris, Pomeranz, Lobstein, & Brownell, 2008; Hawkes, 2007; Sharma, Teret, & Brownell, 2009). As discussed in Chaps. 6 and 8 (Aoki & Moore; Powell, Schermbeck & Chaloupka), numerous loopholes in the pledges allow food companies to continue to extensively market their unhealthy products to children.

We propose that independent research plays an important role in this debate to (1) define marketing outcomes that are likely to improve children's health; (2) measure progress over time in achieving these outcomes; and (3) provide support for public health actions to limit unhealthy food marketing to children. In this chapter, we first describe five case studies in which research highlighted shortcomings in CFBAI pledges. We then discuss four different research methods that can be used to monitor food marketing practices, including syndicated data analysis, content analysis, field audits and marketing impact research, and appropriate uses, strengths and

J.L. Harris (✉) • M. Weinberg • J. Javadizadeh • V. Sarda
Rudd Center for Food Policy and Obesity, Yale University, 309 Edwards Street, New Haven, CT 06511, USA
e-mail: Jennifer.harris@yale.edu

J.D. Williams et al. (eds.), *Advances in Communication Research to Reduce Childhood Obesity*, DOI 10.1007/978-1-4614-5511-0_7,

weaknesses of each method. Finally, we provide suggestions for researchers who wish to provide support for public policy and industry actions that will improve children's health.

Case Studies

The following case studies illustrate the differences in industry-defined measures of success and measures that are likely to improve children's health. These examples document the results of studies conducted by researchers who are independent of the food industry. The research described in these five case studies provide evidence that, even though companies have complied with the CFBAI pledges they have defined, the outcomes are not likely to improve children's health. Case study 1 shows that children's exposure to all food advertising on TV has increased; case studies 2 and 3 document food company advergames and other digital marketing, product placements, and event sponsorships that continue to promote foods of poor nutritional quality; case study 4 provides data to show that preschool-age children continue to view similar numbers of TV ads compared to older children who are supposed to be the audience for these ads; and case study 5 demonstrates that companies continue to promote products to children that do not meet criteria for healthful foods that children should be encouraged to consume.

Increase in Children's Exposure to TV Food Ads

Participation in the CFBAI requires companies to restrain from advertising unhealthy foods during TV programs with an audience comprised of more than a specified percentage of children (typically 35%) (CFBAI, 2011a). Companies, therefore, have placed limitations on advertising that specifically targets children, but do not address advertising that appears on general-audience programming viewed by large numbers of children. A report by the Federal Trade Commission (FTC, 2007) demonstrates that approximately half of all food ads viewed by children appear on general-audience programming. As children can be affected by any food advertisement they view, whether or not it is directed toward them exclusively, public health researchers are concerned about children's total exposure to food advertising. Total exposure is defined as the average number of food ads viewed by children, regardless of the type of programming during which they are placed.

Companies' CFBAI pledges were fully implemented by 2008 (Peeler, Kolish, & Enright, 2009). Children's exposure to all food advertising on television peaked in 2004—when the average child (ages 2–11) viewed 14.0 food ads per day—and then declined by 12% to 12.3 ads viewed per day in 2008 (Rudd Center for Food Policy & Obesity [Rudd Center], 2011). However, 2010 saw a dramatic reversal of this positive trend. In 2010, the average child viewed 13.4 food ads per day, an increase of 9% from 2008 and just 4% fewer than the 14.0 ads per day viewed in 2004 (Rudd Center, 2011). Fast-food restaurants and cereals were the largest food marketers to children, accounting for more than 40% of food ads seen by children in 2010. From 2008 to 2010, there was a 7% increase in ads viewed by children for these categories. Of additional concern, advertising for two of the least nutritious product categories, carbonated beverages and candy, increased dramatically from 2008 to 2010. Exposure to candy advertising doubled from 2008 to 2010 among all age groups and reversed the substantial declines in candy advertising from 2004 to 2008. In 2010, candy overtook prepared meals as the second most-viewed category of food advertising accounting for more than 8% of food ads seen by children. Although just 2% of children's total exposure to food advertising, carbonated beverage advertising increased by 70% from 2008 to 2010.

The initial goal of the CFBAI was "to shift the mix of advertising primarily directed to children to encourage healthier dietary choices" (BBB, 2011). In spite of this goal, children's total exposure to advertising for six of the least nutritious product categories (candy, sweet snacks, crackers/savory snacks, carbonated beverages, fast food, and other restaurants) increased by 60% from 2008 to 2010; in 2010, these categories represented 78% of all food ads viewed by children, compared to 53% in 2008 (Rudd Center, 2011). In comparison, although fruit and vegetable ads seen by children doubled from 2008 to 2010, they contributed less than 1% of total food ads. A report from Children Now in 2009 found that, after implementation of the CFBAI pledges, more than two-thirds of all advertising by participating companies participating were for the least nutritious products (i.e., "whoa" foods) which are supposed to be consumed only on special occasions, such as your birthday (Kunkel, McKinley, & Wright, 2009). The same report found that it would require viewing of about 10 h of children's TV programs to find one healthy food ad. During that same period, a child would see 55 ads for foods of low nutritional quality and 20 ads for foods of moderate nutritional quality.

The increases in candy and carbonated beverage advertising demonstrate a significant shortcoming of the CFBAI. All CFBAI participating companies have pledged that they will not advertise these products in child-targeted media, and content analyses of advertising on children's television confirm that carbonated beverages are no longer advertised on these forms of programming. However, the increase in carbonated beverage advertising viewed by children was even higher than the increase for adolescents and adults. These results indicate that companies may be placing their ads on programs viewed by disproportionately more children than older age groups, although the programs did not meet the cut-off for child targeted programming specified in their CFBAI pledges.

Also, since participating in CFBAI pledges is voluntary, nonparticipating companies have a competitive advantage as they are not restricted by advertising limitations. Across all children's food ads on television, 29% were placed by companies that did not participate in the CFBAI, such as Chuck E'Cheese restaurants and Topps candies; therefore, their marketing practices to children were not guided by the CFBAI requirements (Kunkel et al., 2009). In summary, participating companies have reduced the number of advertisements on children's TV that do not meet their criteria for "healthy dietary choices"; however, children continue to view just as many ads on TV for unhealthful products.

Food Company Advergames

In recent years, the public health community has raised concerns about food company-sponsored advergames on the internet. Advergames are designed to market products in a fun, engaging manner that is highly appealing to children (Winkler & Buckner, 2006). In addition, they commonly incorporate features that encourage children to return to the websites multiple times, thus increasing their exposure to these marketing messages (Santos, Gonzalo, & Gisbert, 2007). Food companies use advergames extensively. Approximately 80% of company websites for foods promoted on children's television networks included advergames (Culp, Bell, & Cassady 2010); and 546 games were found on food company websites (Moore & Rideout, 2007). As with television advertising, the majority (84%) of foods and beverages promoted in advergames contained high levels of sugar, fat, and/or sodium, and just 3% contained information about nutrition or health (Lee, Choi, Quilliam, & Cole, 2009). Playing advergames is an effective marketing strategy for companies. They increase positive brand associations (Winkler & Buckner, 2006; Wise, Bolls, Kim, Venkataraman, & Meyer, 2008), brand recall (Bardzell, Bardzell, & Pace, 2008; Cauberghe & De Pelsmacker, 2010; Lee & Faber, 2008; Winkler & Buckner, 2006), and brand preferences (Mallinckrodt & Mizerski 2007). In addition, playing unhealthy advergames increases consumption of other unhealthy snack foods (Harris, Speers, Schwartz, & Brownell, 2012).

To address these concerns, participating companies in the CFBAI have also pledged to advertise only "healthier products" on the internet (CFBAI, 2011a). This pledge includes restrictions on products promoted through advergames. As with pledges on TV advertising, child-targeted internet advertising is defined by participating companies as advertising on websites where the percentage of children in the audience exceeds a certain threshold. The majority of companies have set this threshold at 35%; three companies have set 30% thresholds (Burger King, Hershey, and McDonalds): and one company (Mars) has set the threshold at 25% (CFBAI, 2011b).

We utilized syndicated data from comScore, a market research company that tracks visitors to company websites and their usage of these websites, to determine whether food companies have complied with their CFBAI pledges regarding advergames (see Harris et al., 2012). As found for TV advertising, this analysis revealed that food companies have complied with their pledges to refrain from promoting foods that they have not identified as "healthy dietary choices" on company websites that meet their definitions of "child-targeted." However, this analysis also revealed that company definitions of child-targeted websites do not capture the vast majority of websites that use advergames to promote foods to children. Of the 26 websites sponsored by CFBAI participating companies that contained advergames, just one

Exhibit 7.1 Examples of child-targeted advergames from M&M and Klondike

(McDonald's McWorld.com) had a large enough audience to meet the company's definition of child-targeted advertising (see Table 7.1). None of the websites had a child audience of 35% or more, the definition of child-targeted used by the majority of CFBAI participants; and just 3 of the 26 websites had child audiences of 25% or more. As a result, companies continued to use advergames to promote products that they have not identified as healthy dietary choices, including Klondike ice cream bars and M&Ms and Wonka candies. Examination of individual websites demonstrates that even sites with audiences comprised of less than 20% children (e.g., Postopia.com, ClubBK.com, and Wonka.com) featured content that was highly appealing to children (Exhibit 7.1).

Increased attention to food company advergames appears to have had some impact on companies' marketing practices. In 2009, we conducted a comprehensive analysis of cereal companies' child-targeted marketing, including advergames (Harris, Schwartz, Brownell, et al., 2009). Immediately after publication of the report, PepsiCo discontinued their child-targeted website promoting Cap'n Crunch (TheGazette.com, 2011). In addition, in 2011 General Mills discontinued its Millsberry.com website, the largest and most frequently visited food company advergame site on the internet (Millsberry.wikia.com, 2011).

Marketing to Children "Under the Radar"

Coca-Cola has been a member of the CFBAI since 2006 and has pledged to not "place any of [the company's] brands' marketing on television, radio and print programming that is primarily directed to children under the age of 12 and where the audience profile is higher than 35% of children under 12" (Coca-Cola, 2010). Although Coca-Cola appears to have complied with this pledge, our research reveals substantial loopholes that allow the company to continue to reach large numbers of children "under the radar" using product placements on prime-time programming, event sponsorships, and digital marketing which are not covered by their pledge. In fact, across all measured media, children saw more ads for Coca-Cola in 2010 than

Table 7.1 Unique visitors and usage for company websites containing advergames for CFBAI participants: Average per month in 2009[a]

			Children (2–12 years)		Usage by visitors 2–17 years		
Website URL	Company	Category	Unique visitors	% of all visitors	Pages per visitor	Minutes per visit	Visits per visitor
CFBAI-approved products							
millsberry.com	General Mills	Cereal	284.3	17.6%	100.7	21.1	3.0
happymeal.com	McDonalds	Fast food	189.3	28.5%	8.5	6.1	1.8
mcworld.com	McDonalds	Fast food	100.9	33.0%	4.7	3.2	1.8
pfgoldfish.com	Campbell Soup Co	Crackers	74.1	34.5%	7.9	7.1	1.4
applejacks.com	Kellogg Company	Cereal	72.0	22.5%	4.3	4.7	1.4
postopia.com	Ralcorp	Cereal	60.9	17.1%	18.7	11.8	2.1
frootloops.com	Kellogg Company	Cereal	58.6	24.5%	1.9	1.3	1.1
clubbk.com	Burger King	Fast food	35.2	18.5%	13.1	7.5	1.6
luckycharms.com	General Mills	Cereal	31.5	16.2%	2.5	2.2	1.3
poptarts.com	Kellogg Company	Pastry	21.4	13.2%	14.5	2.1	2.3
ricekrispies.com	Kellogg Company	Cereal	17.1	6.0%	5.6	3.2	1.1
reesespuffs.com	General Mills	Cereal	12.4	17.8%	15.5	9.1	1.2
cornpops.com	Kellogg Company	Cereal	12.3	20.7%	3.4	2.0	1.2
Products CFBAI companies do not market to children							
klondikebar.com	Unilever	Ice cream	32.7	24.9%	2.9	1.7	1.1
wonka.com	Nestle	Candy	26.1	18.8%	2.7	2.4	1.3
mms.com	Mars	Candy	25.7	8.5%	5.3	4.3	1.2
nabiscoworld.com	Kraft Foods	Cookies, crackers	24.9	5.4%	5.5	3.3	1.5
cocacolazero.com	Coca-Cola	CSDs Diet	15.5	19.8%	2.4	1.5	1.1
mycoke.com	Coca-Cola	CSDs	15.5	10.5%	30.7	4.7	1.7
countrycrock.com	Unilever	Misc	10.9	14.8%	8.9	0.8	4.7
m-ms.com	Mars	Candy	8.6	7.7%	3.6	1.9	1.1
butterfinger.com	Nestle	Candy	6.6	13.8%	5.6	3.7	1.1
twix.com	Mars	Candy	6.3	8.5%	1.9	2.6	1.1
stridegum.com	Cadbury Adams	Gum	4.3	6.2%	13.8	6.0	1.1
pringles.com	Unilever	Chips	2.9	8.7%	N/A	N/A	N/A
cheetos.com	PepsiCo	Chips	2.6	4.5%	1.3	1.7	1.1

[a]comScore Media Metrix report

for any other sugary drink, even those that were specifically marketed to children (i.e., Capri Sun, Kool-Aid, and Sunny D) (Harris, Schwartz, Brownell, et al., 2011).

Product placement occurs when a brand is placed, either visually or audibly within mass-media programming, reaching TV audiences in a way that many may not recognize as advertising (Wilde, 2009; Stanley, 2010). Children and adolescents may be more susceptible to these disguised persuasive attempts (Auty & Lewis, 2004; Ulaby, 2008).

We conducted research using Nielsen data to examine child, adolescent, and adult exposure to food, beverage, and restaurant brand appearances on prime-time TV in 2008 (Speers, Harris, & Schwartz, 2011). Exposure to brand appearances was compared with exposure to TV advertisements for the same categories and companies using additional Nielsen data. In 2008, Coca-Cola brand appearances accounted for 15% of all appearances that occurred on TV and 70% of all appearances actually viewed by children. Coca-Cola was the only company for which exposure to brand appearances exceeded exposure to TV advertisements; children saw almost 10 times as many Coke brand appearances as traditional Coke TV commercials. The average child viewed 198 Coke appearances in 2008, nearly four times per week, and 97% of them appeared on *American Idol.* Although *American Idol* did not meet Coca-Cola's definition of child-targeted programming, nearly 2.2 million children watched each episode of *American Idol* in 2008 (Marketing Charts, 2008).

Marketing through sponsorships is not addressed by the CFBAI, but studies have shown that they positively change a consumer's willingness to buy brands (Harvey, 2010) and that sponsorship exposure has a positive impact on brand liking, trust, and loyalty (Mazodier & Merunka, 2011). Coca-Cola has sponsored the Olympic Games since 1928 and has already committed to continuing the partnership through 2020 (Olympic.org, n.d.). In 2008, Coca-Cola became "the official soft drink of the Olympic Games," when it sponsored the Beijing Summer Games, a move which proved to be very effective for the company. IEG estimated that the company spent as much as $400 million on the sponsorship and related marketing (e.g., Olympic themed packaging, local events, television advertising) (Fowler & McKay, 2008).

Among all 2008 Olympics sponsors, Coca-Cola achieved the highest spontaneous awareness with "38 percent of online consumers being able to recall the brand without prompting" (Nielsen, 2008a). Coca-Cola also had the highest unaided recall for Olympic viewers, individuals who are very interested in the Olympics, and even individuals with little or no interest in the Olympics (TNS, 2008). More than 1.4 million children (ages 2–11) watched NBC's prime-time coverage of the Beijing Olympics (Nielsen, 2008a). Given the effectiveness and breadth of Coca-Cola's Olympics marketing strategy, Coca-Cola is likely to be highly associated with the Olympics in the minds of children.

In a comprehensive analysis of sugary drink and energy drink marketing in 2010 we found that 63% of all full-calorie soda and energy drink ads on national television included sponsorship of an athlete, sports league or team, or an event or cause. Local television advertising also highlighted sponsorships of events such as athletic events, concerts, fairs, festivals, and theme park attractions (Harris et al., 2011) (Exhibit 7.2).

Exhibit 7.2 "Bird's Nest," a Coca-Cola television ad which was liked and recalled most during the 2008 Beijing Summer Games (Nielsen, 2008b)

Coca-Cola's CFBAI pledge indicates that it will not buy advertising or place marketing messages on internet sites, interactive games, or mobile phone programs where more than 35% of the audience is comprised of children under 12 (CFBAI, 2010b). As found with advergames, the brand continued to reach significant numbers of children in the digital space through its websites, social media accounts, and mobile marketing applications.

The Coca-Cola website MyCokeRewards.com was the most popular sugary drink website among young people, attracting 42,000 unique child visitors (ages 2–11) every month in 2010 (Harris et al., 2011). The site's content may not be overtly child-targeted, but many of the rewards had strong youth appeal (e.g., Disney Cruise vacations, Six Flags theme park passes) making it more popular than Capri Sun's website. In 2011, Coca-Cola had the most popular brand on Facebook and the eleventh most popular page on all of Facebook, with over 31 million fans (TheNextWeb.com, 2011). While the Facebook terms of service do not allow children under 13 to become members of the site, this prohibition is easily circumvented: five million Facebook users were younger than 13 years (Consumer Reports, 2011) and approximately 37% of 10- to 12-year-olds had a Facebook account (Pieters & Krupin, 2010). As of May 2009, 29% of teens had added a brand to their online network (Fuse Network, 2009); since then, the promotion of food brands on Facebook has skyrocketed (Braat, 2011).

Coca-Cola also has released a number of applications for the iPhone, the two most popular of which have significant youth appeal: a "Magic Coke Bottle" reminiscent of a magic 8-ball toy and "Spin the Coke" which allows users to play spin the bottle with a virtual coke. comScore does not provide data for children under age 12, but as of September 2010, 39% of all persons 12+ using the Magic Coke Bottle app were teens and 26% of all persons 12+ using the Spin the Coke app were teens (Harris et al., 2011). As these cases demonstrate, children continue to be exposed to significant advertising messages for Coca-Cola, in spite of the company's CFBAI pledge that it will not advertise to this age group.

Advertising to Very Young Children

The majority of CFBAI participating companies, including General Mills and Kellogg's, have also pledged that they will not advertise any products to children under age 6. Advertising to very young children is a concern because a large body of psychological research shows that, until age 7 or 8, children do not have the cognitive capacity to understand that advertising presents a biased point-of-view; they simply view it as another source of information (Kunkel et al., 2004; John, 1999; Ward, Wackman, & Wartella, 1977). As a result, any form of advertising to very young children is inherently unfair (Kunkel et al., 2004) and even potentially misleading or deceptive (Pomeranz, 2010). Even executives in the advertising industry believe that advertising to very young children is unethical (Geraci, 2004).

In spite of these pledges and the research supporting the need to protect very young children from advertising, recent analyses of TV food advertising using Nielsen data have demonstrated that 2- to 5-year-olds view nearly as many TV food ads as somewhat older children. For example, in our analysis of advertising for children's cereals, preschool-age children viewed just 10% fewer TV ads for these products than did elementary school-age children (Harris, Schwartz, Brownell, et al., 2009). Similarly, Powell and colleagues showed that young children (ages 2–5) continue to view 10.9 food-related ads every day, just 14% fewer than the 12.7 food-related ads viewed by older children (ages 6–11) (Powell, Szczypka, & Chaloupka, 2010). In addition, many child-targeted ads from CFBAI participating companies contain cartoon spokes-characters, toy giveaways, and other techniques designed to appeal to very young children (Harris, Schwartz, et al., 2009; Harris, Schwartz, Brownell, et al., 2010).

As with the CFBAI pledges concerning internet marketing, the reason that young children continue to view considerable amounts of television food advertising is that companies' definitions of advertising targeted to very young children do not apply to any of the advertisements viewed by this age group. Companies limit their pledges to programming in which 30–50% (varies by company) of the audience is under 6 years (CFBAI, 2011b). However, most programming that meets this definition does not allow advertising of any sort, such as children's shows on public television or NickJr (the preschool-targeted programming from Nickelodeon). We found more than 30,000 telecasts in 2010 in which young children (2–5 years) comprised 35% or more of the audience (Nielsen, 2010). However, 83% of those telecasts appeared on networks, such as Nick Jr., PBS, and Disney Channel that do not accept outside advertising. As evidenced by their high exposure to advertising for children's cereals (Harris, Schwartz, et al., 2009), preschool-age children watch considerable amounts of children's television also viewed by older children; therefore, companies can claim that they do not advertise to very young children while these youngest consumers continue to view extensive advertising for their products.

Promotion of "Healthy Dietary Choices" on Child-Targeted Programming

The CFBAI report on compliance with company pledges in 2009 detailed few instances (0.07%) where non-CFBAI-approved products appeared in advertising to children (BBB, 2010). However, examination of the content of child-directed TV advertising for products that companies have defined as healthy dietary choices demonstrates that these ads do not actually promote a healthy diet. For example, McDonald's pledged to advertise only its Happy Meals that include chicken nuggets or a hamburger, apple dippers with low-fat caramel dipping sauce, and low-fat white milk (CFBAI, 2010a). Although as of 2009, McDonald's had determined that these meals meet its criteria for healthful choices for children, they contained 610 and 680 mg of sodium respectively, and both exceeded recommended limits for sodium (544 mg) for preschoolers set by the Institute of Medicine (IOM, 2007) and the Interagency Working Group on Food Marketed to Children (IAWG, 2011). Both meals meet the IOM maximum calorie criteria for elementary school-age children (650), but the hamburger meal does not meet the calorie cutoff for preschoolers (410) (IOM).

We conducted a content analysis of McDonald's child-targeted ads to determine how the company portrayed the healthy options available in Happy Meals, including apple dippers, 100% juice, and plain low-fat milk (Harris, Schwartz, et al., 2010). Although McDonald's did feature only these healthy side options and drinks in its child-targeted advertising, the food was never the primary focus of the ads. The food was usually depicted briefly and in the background. Rather, the ads focused on the toy being given away with the Happy Meal, children playing, scenes from a movie tie-in, or just the Happy Meal box itself. Thus, the ads were focused on creating positive associations with the brands, and not on the food itself (Exhibit 7.3).

In addition, we conducted an audit of sales practices at fast-food restaurant to understand what side and beverage options were offered to customers when they ordered a kid's meals (Harris, Schwartz, et al., 2010). Field personnel disguised as customers purchased whatever was offered with the meal automatically, or the first item offered if the employee offered a choice. McDonalds and Burger King were among the five top fast-food chains included in the analysis, which was conducted at 50 locations of each chain. At McDonald's, employees automatically provided french fries with Happy Meals 86% of the time, and a cup for a soft drink 54% of the time. Therefore, even though the restaurant pictured the healthier side and beverage items in its advertising to children, parents were not even given an option to order them the majority of the time.

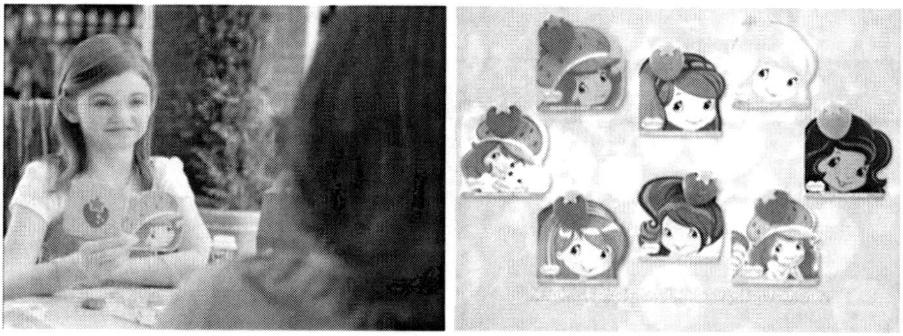

Exhibit 7.3 Kid's meal ads from McDonalds where food is not the primary focus of the ad

In response to pressure from the public health community, in 2011, McDonald's announced that it would change the default option for its Happy Meals (AboutMcDonalds.com, 2011). The new Happy Meal includes both a half serving of apple slices, 1.1 ounces of french fries, the choice of a hamburger, cheeseburger or Chicken McNuggets, and a choice of beverage, including 1% low-fat milk and fat-free chocolate milk. McDonald's press release claimed that "the impact will be an estimated 20% reduction in calories of the most popular Happy Meals, also reducing fat in those meals" (AboutMcdonalds.com, 2011).

Marketing Research Methods

Table 7.2 presents four of the methods we have used to assess food marketing to children, including syndicated data analysis, content analysis, field audits, and impact research. Each of these methods is useful in different situations, and all have advantages and disadvantages.

Syndicated Data Analysis

Syndicated data are provided by market research firms and can be useful to assess company marketing practices. Typically, these data are obtained through a variety of methods, including survey panels, monitoring systems placed on media devices, and scanned barcodes. Nielsen, comScore, and Arbitron are three of the largest providers of syndicated data to measure exposure to different media. Market research firms, such as the NPD Group and SymphonyIRI, also provide sales and purchasing data for food and beverages.

Table 7.2 Research methods that have been used to measure progress in improving the food marketing environment

Research method	Definition and use	Strengths	Weaknesses
Syndicated data analysis	Data purchased from outside market research companies (e.g., Nielsen, comScore, Symphony IRI, NPD Group) to assess marketing exposure and product sales	• Industry standard • Comprehensive	• Expensive • Limited flexibility/designed for industry purposes • Reporting restrictions • Not available for newer forms of marketing • Proprietary methods
Content analysis	Coding to assess the creative content of individual advertisements and other marketing messages	• Scientific qualitative data • Highly flexible	• Limits to coverage • Time and labor intensive • Measures incidence, not exposure • Somewhat subjective
Field audits	Individuals assess incidence and content of marketing in different geographic or other locations, for marketing that differs by location	• Representative sample of localized marketing activities • Scientific qualitative data • Highly flexible	• Expensive • Less control over data collection • Measures incidence, not exposure
Impact research	Measures the health impact of exposure to different forms of marketing using different methods, including experiments, natural experiments, and surveys	• Provides rationale for limiting food marketing • Identifies specific messages, techniques, etc. of concern • High media and public interest in findings • Relatively inexpensive	• Limited by existing marketing examples • Relatively narrow focus on specific types of marketing and/or consumers • Difficult to show long-term and/or cumulative effects

The case studies cited earlier used syndicated data extensively. Powell and colleagues also use syndicated data from Nielsen to examine exposure to food advertising on TV to children and teens and to identify the products advertised so that they can determine the nutritional quality of the foods in ads seen most often by young people (e.g., Powell et al., 2010; Powell, Schermbeck, Szczypka, Chaloupka, & Braunschweig, 2011). Syndicated data allow researchers to quantify children's and adolescents' exposure to many forms of marketing, including TV advertising, radio advertising, product placements on prime-time TV, company websites, banner advertising on third-party websites, and mobile advertising. Syndicated data are also available to measure product sales and consumption patterns.

There are a number of advantages to working with syndicated data. Nielsen, comScore, and Arbitron are considered to be the standard bearers in TV, digital media, and radio measurement, respectively. Their data are considered to be the best available, and are commonly used by advertisers to develop and assess their media plans. Pricing for advertising is based on the ratings established by Nielsen for TV, by Arbitron for radio, and, in certain instances, by comScore for the internet. Furthermore, the data these firms provide are comprehensive. For each media being measured, there is a wide range of metrics available and new ones constantly being added to respond to an evolving market. Therefore, findings of studies that use these data are less subject to criticism by the food industry.

Despite these benefits, syndicated data come with drawbacks as well, chiefly their expense. Most academic and public health researchers do not have the budgets to purchase syndicated data, which can cost tens to hundreds of thousands of dollars. Also, researchers are not the primary audience for these data; they are primarily purchased by businesses to optimize their advertising or understand competitors' activities. Therefore, working with syndicated data can be a challenge. The majority of metrics provided are of little use to public health researchers; they have been created to help advertisers attend to particular optimizations or other minute details. And uncovering the metrics or set of reports that are, indeed, useful for researchers can be challenging. Frequently, support staff at syndicated data firms do not understand the needs of researchers as well as they understand those of their traditional corporate clients. Limitations are sometimes placed on what researchers can report, such as specific company or retailer information, as market research companies do not want to offend or alienate their core customer base. We have found this to be particularly true of firms that provide food and beverage sales data.

In addition, the availability of syndicated data lags behind the adoption of new forms of marketing. For example, we have not yet identified a source of syndicated data for social media that meets our purposes. There are no data available that will provide demographic profiles for fans of food and beverage Facebook pages or Twitter accounts, nor have we found a data source that will provide us with an accurate understanding of who is watching specific videos on YouTube. As these media become more and more established forms of marketing, we expect this situation to change.

And finally, there are limitations to what syndicated data can tell researchers. For example, these data can quantify how many people viewed a particular banner ad, but cannot tell how many interacted with it. Interaction data are tracked by the advertisers themselves and not by the data providers. Syndicated data only provide half of the picture; we can get exposure numbers but not data that reveals ad effectiveness.

Content Analysis

Content analysis is used in communications research to evaluate the content of messages (Lombard, Snyder-Duch, & Campanella Bracken, 2002). It allows researchers to apply scientific principles to analyze any type of communication, such as that found on TV, in print, on the internet, or in social media. Thus, it is a systematic way of looking at qualitative data. Content analysis can be used, for example, to assess the messages portrayed in food advertising. In this way, it can help highlight industry practices which may not be obvious to most consumers.

Much research has shown that the content of food marketing has an effect on children's eating behaviors, namely that it causes children to prefer and ask for the products advertised (IOM, 2006). Given these findings, content analysis becomes an important tool to understand what kinds of foods and messages are being advertised to children. For example, content analyses repeatedly show that the majority of foods which appear on child-targeted programming are either high in fat, sodium, or added sugars or low in essential nutrients (Batada & Wootan, 2007; Folta, Goldberg, Economos, Bell, & Melzer, 2006; IOM, 2006; Reece, Rifon, & Rodriguez, 1999; Stitt & Kunkel, 2008). The same is true for food ads that appear during general-audience programming viewed most often by children (Harrison & Marske, 2005). Unhealthy eating messages also abound, such as anytime snacking (Harrison & Marske, 2005) and promotion of positive emotional associations with these unhealthy foods (Folta et al., 2006; Schor & Ford, 2007).

Content analysis begins with development of a codebook, which is a collection of both implicit (e.g., fun, cool) and explicit (e.g., value, new) messages about the advertised product that the researcher would like to capture. It is essential that a draft of the codebook be tested using actual advertisements. Once a codebook is drafted, intercoder reliability should be assessed to determine if all coders have reached a reasonable level of agreement using statistics such as Scott's Pi, Krippendorff's Alpha, or Cohen's Kappa. Without good intercoder reliability, the data are subjective interpretations and not scientifically valid (Lombard et al., 2002). Once an adequate level of agreement has been reached (typically between 0.70 and 0.90) for each variable tested, a formal and final reliability testing should be conducted during the coding of the full sample. The size of the reliability sample should be no less than 10% of the full sample (Lombard, 2010).

Content analysis is fundamental to mass communication research (Lombard et al., 2002) and has a number of strengths, including that it can be used to evaluate any type of media. As discussed, it is also a way to look at the deeper meaning or psychology behind messages in advertising in a quantifiable way. If done correctly, content analysis results can be generalized and replicated.

However, one of the major weaknesses of the method when examining TV advertising is that the researcher must either purchase copies of creative executions from a company that tracks them (e.g., Kantar Media), which can be very expensive, or limit the analysis to advertisements that can be recorded by the researchers themselves. The majority of content analyses are conducted using ads aired during a specific time period, and often during limited types of programming, such as children's programming. Content analyses can also be time- and labor-intensive, requiring many coders to assess larger-sized samples. Another limitation is that content analyses measure incidence, not exposure. Researchers can determine that 80% of all ads portrayed a "cool" message, but will not know how many children actually saw this message on TV. Lastly, if not conducted with well-defined variable codes and adequate reliability testing, content analysis can be quite subjective and arguably meaningless. Researchers decide what is important to code and a team of coders must agree on what "cool" means, for example. Implicit measures such as these are less clear-cut and researchers must identify ways to operationalize them to reach acceptable coder agreement.

Field Audits

According to the FTC (2008) report on food marketing to children and adolescents, approximately 28% of food advertising spending directed at youth (more than 457 million dollars) was at the local level, including in-store marketing, packaging and labeling, premiums, events, cross-promotion licenses, athletic sponsorships and philanthropy. Despite the substantial amount of these types of marketing, they are not tracked by traditional syndicated data providers. Therefore, researchers must design and implement their own studies to track marketing activity in local communities. In some cases, researchers can collect these data themselves. For example, (Yancey, Cole, Brown, et al., 2009) conducted an audit of food billboards to show that billboards that promote fast food and sugared beverages appear seven to nine times as often in low-income Latino and black communities than they do in white and high-income communities. In addition, researchers at the Rudd Center analyzed product packaging in local supermarkets to identify child-targeted promotions on packages (Harris, Schwartz, et al., 2010), and child features and nutrition-related claims on ready-to-eat cereals (Harris, Schwartz, et al., 2009) and sugary drink packages (Harris et al., 2011).

Another option for this type of research is to commission a company that specializes in in-store testing, distribution and shelf studies, mystery shopping, merchandising, and shop-alongs for companies to assess their own and competitors' marketing practices. These companies maintain staffs of field representatives in major markets across the country. For example, we utilized such a company to conduct an audit of in-store marketing of ready-to-eat cereals in a nationally representative sample of 400 supermarkets located in 18 metropolitan areas (Harris, Bargh, et al., 2009; Harris, Brownell, et al., 2009). Researchers developed detailed instructions and a comprehensive survey instrument for field personnel to record shelf facings, in-aisle displays, and promotional activities conducted by national cereal brands over a four-week period. The same company was used to conduct an audit of signs at fast-food restaurants, which detailed the menu items, messages, and promotions on signs located inside and outside the restaurants, as well as the examination of default side and beverage items offered with kids' meals described earlier (Harris, Schwartz, et al., 2010).

Although expensive, these types of audits of marketing practices provide several advantages. They are highly flexible and can be designed to provide exactly the type of information researchers are looking for. When using a firm with a national staff of field representative, these audits can provide a nationally-representative sample of localized marketing activities. In addition, as with content analyses, they provide a scientifically valid means to collect qualitative data. Therefore, field audits of local marketing activities add to our understanding of marketing in local communities, including at the point of purchase, and provide invaluable information that traditionally is not tracked by syndicated data providers.

Impact Studies

In a comprehensive review of the research on food marketing to youth, the IOM called for additional studies to understand the impact of food marketing to children (IOM, 2006). Since then, numerous studies have documented the extent and content of child-targeted food marketing practices; however, far less research has assessed the influence of food marketing on children's health. We propose that additional impact studies are needed to advance the case for effective public health action to reduce child exposure to unhealthy food marketing. Although the IOM report also concluded that it is likely that the high volume of marketing for calorie-dense nutrient-poor foods has a negative effect on children's health (IOM, 2006), research is needed to disprove industry claims that food marketing has no impact on high rates of childhood obesity and poor diet, as well as to increase public awareness of the harm caused by food marketing.

Food industry proponents have defended child-targeted marketing practices by stating that marketing affects brand preferences (e.g., Coke over Pepsi, or McDonald's over Burger King), but that there is no evidence that it increases consumption of unhealthy product categories (Young, 2002). In addition, the food industry commonly claims that it is parents' responsibility, not theirs, to decide what products to feed children; they are just responding to consumer demand. As a result, research that demonstrates that food marketing affects consumption of categories of unhealthy products, in addition to brand preferences, and has broader impact on children's diet and food preferences is critical to counteract these claims.

Research with parents also reveals limited understanding of how food marketing affects their children. In focus groups, most parents indicated that they found food marketing targeted to their children annoying, but essentially harmless (Ustjanauskas, Eckman, Harris, Goren, Schwartz, et al., 2010). Similarly, a survey of parents indicated moderate levels of concern with unhealthy food marketing. Parents were more concerned about sexual permissiveness and materialism in the media than they were about food marketing, but less concerned about media depictions of alcohol and tobacco use (unpublished data). However, food marketing may be one of the most dangerous forms of media influence due to its breadth of influence, as well as the difficulty that individuals of all ages have in defending against its influence (Harris, Brownell, et al., 2009). Parents' support for restrictions on food marketing to children is significantly related to beliefs that food marketing has a negative impact on children's health (Goren, Harris, Schwartz, & Brownell, 2010); therefore, research that demonstrates these negative effects is likely to increase public support for actions to limit children's exposure to this harmful influence.

Longitudinal studies that track the relationship between child exposure to food advertising and diet over time will provide the most conclusive evidence of long-term food marketing effects; but this type of research is expensive and takes many years to conduct. In the shorter term, modeling using publicly available datasets and experimental studies can provide evidence of the broader effects of food marketing exposure. For example, recent studies using syndicated advertising data and public health datasets have demonstrated that soft drink and fast-food television advertising is associated with increased total consumption of soft drinks and fast food and higher BMI among elementary children (Andreyeva, Kelly, & Harris, 2011; Chou, Rashad, & Grossman, 2008). Experimental studies have also shown that exposure to television food advertising, as well as playing unhealthy food advergames, increases children's immediate consumption of any available unhealthy snack foods (Halford, Boyland, Hughes, Oliveira, & Dovey, 2007; Harris, Bargh, et al., 2009; Harris et al., 2012); and that licensed characters on snack foods increase preschoolers' perceived taste of those foods (Roberto, Baik, Harris, & Brownell, 2010). Studies such as these tend to be fairly narrow in scope and subject to other limitations. For example, cross-sectional studies cannot prove causation, and experimental studies show only short-term effects and may not replicate in real-world situations. However, when examined together, they provide increasing proof that food advertising affects much more than brand preferences. In addition, these studies tend to receive considerable media attention and thus help raise awareness among parents and the general public about the negative effects of food advertising on children's health.

Using Research to Support Public Health Action

Academic researchers are well suited to conduct the independent studies needed to measure progress in reducing children's exposure to unhealthy food marketing. Any study that criticizes the food industry is likely to be met with accusations about "food nannies" and "junk science" (American Beverage Association, 2011; JunkScience.com, 2011). Therefore, the quality of the research is critical to its effectiveness. The peer review process that academic researchers utilize provides an extra level of quality control to ensure that research methods are transparent and meet scientific standards, and that conclusions are supported by the evidence.

Unfortunately, several obstacles limit academic researchers' ability and motivation to conduct this type of research. In addition to a thick skin, researchers need the budgets and manpower to conduct food marketing studies. As discussed, they often require purchasing expensive data or commissioned studies and/or significant numbers of individuals to collect the data. However, the number of institutions funding this type of research is limited. A few food policy researchers have received funding from the National Institutes of Health, but the Robert Wood Johnson Foundation is currently the largest funder, with its commitment to spend $500 million over 5 years to combat childhood obesity (Robert Wood Johnson, 2007). In addition, academic success is measured by numbers of papers in high status scientific journals, which may conflict with the research needs of the public health community. For example, many related academic fields, such as psychology, marketing, and economics, reward researchers who develop new theoretical models to explain human behavior; whereas, policymakers require a more "applied" approach to demonstrate outcomes from specific policy interventions or evidence of actual marketing tactics.

For those researchers who do conduct research on food marketing, we propose several steps they can take to ensure that their efforts provide the most value to the public health community. First, timely data are critical. The scientific process can take years from study proposal to academic publication; by the time the results are published, the data are no longer relevant. Researchers should consider publication in journals with faster turnaround times, such as medical journals. In cases where policymakers require the data immediately, researchers can submit commentaries, develop reports or fact sheets to be publicly available on researchers' websites, or share the data with policymakers who can use them when it is time to make their decisions. Second, researchers should use the media to raise consumer awareness about their findings and the issue, as well as to place pressure on the food industry to take action. Issuing press releases when new findings come out and being available to reporters when they are looking for comments on the issue will help establish relationships with key media. In our experience, criticism of the food industry in the media has been one of the most effective means to encourage them to take action. Finally, researchers can introduce themselves to advocates, legislators and attorneys, and maintain a dialog to identify areas in which research is most needed to set direction for future research. In addition, these discussions will help researchers understand how to communicate their findings in a way that policymakers will understand and be most useful for them.

Just as food marketers constantly seek new and innovative ways to reach children, research on food marketing to youth must be reinvented in order to compete with such a powerful entity, and ultimately, to reach consumers in a meaningful way. Traditional academic paths simply cannot spread important messages gleaned from research at a pace rapid enough or a force strong enough to be heard by consumers and policy-makers. Although the methods we have discussed are unconventional and researchers who utilize such techniques may face several obstacles to successful implementation, the possible impact that such an approach can have is tremendous.

References

AboutMcDonalds.com (2011). *McDonald's announces commitments to offer improved nutrition choices*. Retrieved November 3, 2011 from http://www.aboutmcdonalds.com/mcd/media_center/recent_news/corporate/commitments_to_offer_improved_nutrition_choices.html

American Beverage Association (2011, October 31). *Brownell is up to his old tricks this Halloween*. Retrieved November 2, 2011, from http://www.ameribev.org/blog/.

Andreyeva, T., Kelly, I. R., & Harris, J. L. (2011). Exposure to food advertising on television: Associations with children's fast food and soft drink consumption and obesity. *Economics and Human Biology.*, *9*(3), 221–233.

Auty, S., & Lewis, C. (2004). Exploring children's choice: the reminder effect of product placement. *Psychology and Marketing, 21*(9), 697–713.

Bardzell, J., Bardzell, S., & Pace, T. (2008). *Player engagement and in-game advertising. A report for One to One Interactive.* Retrieved June 26, 2009, from http://www.onetooneinteractive.com.

Batada, A., & Wootan, M. G. (2007). Nickelodeon markets nutrition-poor foods to children. *American Journal of Preventive Medicine, 33*(1), 1–3.

Better Business Bureaus [BBB] (2009). *Children's food and beverage advertising initiative.* Retrieved September 28, 2011, from http://www.bbb.org/us/children-food-beverage-advertising-initiative/

Better Business Bureaus [BBB] (2010). *Children's Food and Beverage Advertising Initiative in Action: A report on compliance and implementation during 2009.* Retrieved November 3, 2011, from http://www.bbb.org/us/storage/0/Shared%20Documents/BBBwithlinks.pdf

Better Business Bureaus [BBB] (2011). *About the initiative.* Retrieved November 2, 2011, from http://www.bbb.org/us/about-children-food-beverage-advertising-initiative/.

Braat, P. (2011). *The state of brands on Facebook.* Retrieved November 1, 2011, from http://www.viralblog.com/facebook-marketing-2/the-state-of-brands-on-facebook/

Cauberghe, V., & De Pelsmacker, P. (2010). Advergames: The impact of brand prominence and game repetition on brand responses. *Journal of Advertising, 39*(1), 5–18.

Children's Food and Beverage Advertising Initiative [CFBAI] (2010a). *McDonald's USA support: Updated February 2010.* Retrieved November, 3, 2011, from http://www.bbb.org/us/storage/16/documents/McD%20Final%20Restated%20Pledge.pdf

Children's Food and Beverage Advertising Initiative [CFBAI] (2010b). *Coca-Cola North America's pledge restated.* Retrieved November 3, 2011, from http://www.bbb.org/us/storage/0/Shared%20Documents/coke%20final.pdf

Children's Food and Beverage Advertising Initiative [CFBAI] (2011a). *The U.S. children's food and beverage advertising initiative fact sheet.* Retrieved November 3, 2011, from http://www.bbb.org/us/storage/0/Shared%20Documents/ChildrensFoodBeverageFactssingle%20v-2.pdf

Children's Food and Beverage Advertising Initiative [CFBAI] (2011b). *Audience definitions for under 12 and under age six.* Retrieved November 3, 2011, from http://www.bbb.org/us/storage/0/Shared%20Documents/bbb/audience%20definitions%20for%20under%2012%20and%20under%20age%20six-march%202011-final.pdf

Chou, S.-Y., Rashad, I., & Grossman, M. (2008). Fast-food restaurant advertising on television and its influence on childhood obesity. *Journal of Law and Economics, 51*, 599–618.

Coca-Cola (2008). *For Beijing 2008 Olympic Games, a time to "Live Olympic on the Coke side of life." Press release.* Retrieved September 29, 2011, from http://www.thecoca-colacompany.com/presscenter/presskit_olympicgames2008_global_campaign_update.pdf

Coca-Cola (2010). *Coca-Cola North America's pledge restated. CFBAI.* Retrieved September 29, 2011, from http://www.bbb.org/us/storage/0/Shared%20Documents/coke%20final.pdf

Consumer Reports (2011). *That Facebook friend might be 10 years old, and other troubling news.* Retrieved September 29, 2011, from www.consumerreports.org/cro/magazine-archive/2011/june/electronics-computers/state-of-the-net/facebook-concerns/index.htm

Culp, J., Bell, R., & Cassady, D. (2010). Characteristics of food industry web sites and "advergames" targeting children. *Journal of Nutrition Education and Behavior, 42*(3), 197–201.

Federal Trade Commission (2007). *Bureau of Economics staff report: Children's exposure to TV advertising in 1977 and 2004.* Retrieved October 22, 2007, from http://www.ftc.org.

Federal Trade Commission (2008). *Marketing food to children and adolescents: A review of industry expenditures, activities, and self-regulation. A report to Congress.* Retrieved September 13, 2011, from www.ftc.gov/os/2008/07/P064504foodmktingreport.pdf.

Folta, S. C., Goldberg, J. P., Economos, C., Bell, R., & Melzer, R. (2006). Food advertising targeted at school-age children: A content analysis. *Journal of Nutrition Education and Behavior, 38*, 244–248.

Fowler, G., & McKay, B. (2008). Coke pins China hopes on blitz in Beijing. *Wall Street Journal.* Retrieved September 29, 2011, from http://online.wsj.com/article/SB121910643955651579.html

Fuse Network (2009). *Fuse's Teen Advertising Study*. Retrieved September 29, 2011 from http://www.fusemarketing.com/pdfs/Fuse_UMASS_Teen_Advertising_Study.pdf

Geraci, J. C. (2004). What do youth marketers think about selling to kids? *Advertising & Marketing to Children,* (April–June), 11–17. www.cruxresearch.com/downloads/selling-to-kids-0404.pdf.

Goren, A., Harris, J. L., Schwartz, M. B., & Brownell, K. D. (2010). Predicting support for restricting food marketing to youth. *Health Affairs, 29*(3), 419–424.

Halford, J. C. G., Boyland, M. J., Hughes, G., Oliveira, L. P., & Dovey, T. M. (2007). Beyond-brand effect of television (TV) food advertisements/commercials on caloric intake and food choice of 5- to 7-year-old children. *Appetite, 49*, 263–267.

Harris, J. L., Bargh, J. A., & Brownell, K. (2009). The direct effects of television food advertising on eating behavior. *Health Psychology, 28*(4), 404–413.

Harris, J. L., Brownell, K. D., & Bargh, J. A. (2009). The food marketing defense model: Integrating psychological research to protect youth and inform public policy. *Social Issues and Policy Review, 3*, 211–271.

Harris, J. L., Pomeranz, J. L., Lobstein, T., & Brownell, K. D. (2008). A crisis in the marketplace: How food marketing contributes to obesity and what can be done. *Annual Review of Public Health, 30*, 5.1–5.15.

Harris, J. L., Schwartz, M. B., & Brownell, K. D. (2010). Marketing foods to children and youth: Licensed characters and other promotions on packaged foods in the supermarket. *Public Health Nutrition, 13*(3), 409–417.

Harris, J. L., Schwartz, M. B., Brownell, K. D., Sarda, V., Weinberg, M. E., Speers, S., et al. (2009). *Cereal FACTS: Evaluating the nutrition quality and marketing of children's cereals.* Retrieved December 3, 2009, from http://www.cerealfacts.org/media/Cereal_FACTS_Report.pdf.

Harris, J. L., Schwartz, M. B., Brownell, K. D., Sarda, V., Ustjanauskas, A., Javadizadeh, J. et al. (2010). *Fast Food FACTS: Evaluation of the nutritional quality and marketing of fast food to youth.* Retrieved November 2, 2011, from www.fastfoodfacts.org.

Harris, J. L., Schwartz, M. B., Brownell, K. D., Javadizadeh, J., Weinberg, M. E., Sarda, V., et al. (2011). *Sugary drink FACTS: Evaluating sugary drink nutrition and marketing to youth.* Retrieved November 2, 2011, from http://www.sugarydrinkfacts.org/resources/SugaryDrinkFACTS_Report.pdf

Harris, J. L., Speers, S. E., Schwartz, M. B., & Brownell, K. D. (2012) US Food company branded advergames on the internet: Children's exposure and effects on snack consumption. *Journal of Children and Media, 6*(1), 51–68.

Harrison, K., & Marske, A. L. (2005). Nutritional content of foods advertised during the television programs children watch most. *American Journal of Public Health, 95*, 1568–1574.

Harvey, B. (2006). Measuring the effects of true sponsorship. *Journal of Advertising Research, 41*(1), 59–65.

Hawkes, C. (2004). *Marketing food to children: the global regulatory environment.* Geneva: WHO. Retrieved from whqlibdoc.who.int/publications/2004/9241591579.pdf.

Hawkes, C. (2007). Regulating food marketing to young people worldwide: Trends and policy drivers. *American Journal of Public Health, 97*, 1962–1973.

Interagency Working Group on Food Marketed to Children [IAWG] (2011). *Preliminary proposed nutrition principles to guide industry self-regulatory efforts.* Retrieved October 4, 2011, from http://www.ftc.gov/os/2011/04/110428foodmarketproposedguide.pdf.

Institute of Medicine [IOM] (2006). National Academy of Sciences, Committee on Food Marketing and the Diets of Children and Youth. *Food marketing to children and youth: threat or opportunity?* Washington, DC: National Academies Press.

Institute of Medicine [IOM] (2007). *Nutrition standards for foods in schools: Leading the way toward healthier youth*. Washington, DC: National Academies Press.

John, D. R. (1999). Consumer socialization of children: A retrospective look at twenty-five years of research. *Journal of Consumer Research, 26*, 183–213.

JunkScience.com (2011, October 31). *Yale: 'Sugary drinks are the most unhealthy food product marketed to children.'* Retrieved November 2, 2011, from http://junkscience.com/2011/10/31/yale-sugary-drinks-are-the-most-unhealthy-food-product-marketed-to-children/.

Kunkel, D., McKinley, C., & Wright, P. (2009). *The impact of industry self-regulation on the nutritional quality of foods advertised on television to children.* Retrieved October 03, 2011, from www.childrennow.org/uploads/documents/adstudy_2009.pdf.

Kunkel, D., Wilcox, B. L., Cantor, J., Palmer, E., Linn, S., Dowrick, P. (2004). *Report of the APA task force on advertising and children.* Retrieved November 22, 2004, from http://www.apa.org/releases/childrenads.pdf.

Lee, M., Choi, Y., Quilliam, E. T., & Cole, R. T. (2009). Playing with food: Content analysis of food advergames. *The Journal of Consumer Affairs, 43*(1), 129–154.

Lee, M., & Faber, R. J. (2008). Effects of product placement in on-line games on brand memory: A perspective of the limited-capacity model of attention. *Journal of Advertising, 36*(4), 75–90.

Lombard, M., Snyder-Duch, J., & Campanella Bracken, C. (2002). Content analysis in mass communication: Assessment and reporting of intercoder reliability. *Human Communications Research, 28*(4), 587–604.

Lombard, M. (2010). *Practical resources for assessing and reporting intercoder reliability in content analysis research projects.* Retrieved October 4, 2011, from http://astro.temple.edu/~lombard/reliability/#How%20should%20content%20analysis%20researchers%20properly%20assess%20and%20report%20intercoder%20reliability.

Mallinckrodt, V., & Mizerski, D. (2007). The effects of playing an advergame on young children's perceptions, preferences, and request. *Journal of Advertising, 36*, 87–100.

Marketing Charts (2008). Nielsen measures the American Idol phenomenon. *Marketing Charts.* Retrieved September 29, 2011 from http://www.marketingcharts.com/television/nielsen-measures-the-american-idol-phenomenon-4628

Mazodier, M., & Merunka, D. (2011). Achieving brand loyalty through sponsorship: the role of fit and self-congruity. *Journal of the Academy of Marketing Science.* Retrieved November 7, 2011, from http://www.springerlink.com/content/e74631214t303115/fulltext.pdf.

Millsberry.Wikia.com. (2011). *Millsberry wiki.* Retrieved November 3, 2011, from http://millsberry.wikia.com/wiki/Millsberry

Moore, E. S., & Rideout, V. J. (2007). The online marketing of food to children: Is it just fun and games? *Journal of Public Policy and Marketing, 26*(2), 202–220.

Nielsen (2008). *Who were the real winners of the Beijing Olympics? Just ask Nielsen.* Retrieved September 29, 2011, from cn.en.nielsen.com/site/documents/Olympic_en.pdf.

Nielsen (2008). *Nielsen IAG top 10 Olympics/cultural themed ads airing during NBC primetime Olympics coverage. Nielsen Blog.* Retrieved September 29, 2011 from http://blog.nielsen.com/nielsenwire/wp-content/uploads/2008/08/top10_olympicsthemedads_8808-814081.xls.

Nielsen (2010). www.nielsen.com.

Olympic.org. (n.d.). *Coca-Cola Olympic sponsorship.* Retrieved September 29, 2011, from http://www.olympic.org/sponsor-coca-cola.

Peeler, C.L., Kolish, E.D., & Enright, M. (2009). *The children's food and beverage advertising initiative: A report on compliance and implementation during 2008.* Retrieved November 2, 2011 from www.bbb.org/us/Storage/0/shared%20Documents/finalbbs1.pdf.

Pieters, A. & Krupin, C. (2010). *Youth online behavior study for McAfee. Harris Interactive.* Retrieved September 29, 2011 from http://safekids.com/mcafee_harris.pdf

Pomeranz, J.L. (2010). Television food marketing to children revisited: The Federal Trade Commission has the constitutional and statutory authority to regulate. *Journal of Law, Medicine and Ethics* (Spring), 98–116.

Powell, L. M., Szczypka, G., & Chaloupka, F. J. (2010). Trends in exposure to television food advertisements among children and adolescents in the United States. *Archives of Pediatric and Adolescent Medicine, 164*(9), 794–802.

Powell, L., Szczypka, G., Chaloupka, F., & Braunschweig, C. (2007). Nutritional Content of Television Food Advertisements Seen by Children and Adolescents in the United States. *Pediatrics, 120*, 576–583.

Powell, L., Schermbeck, R., Szczypka, G., Chaloupka, F., Braunschweig, C. (2011). Trends in the Nutritional Content of Television Food Advertisements Seen by Children in the United States. *Archives of Pediatrics & Adolescent Medicine*

Reece, B. B., Rifon, N. J., & Rodriguez, K. (1999). Selling food to children. Is fun part of a balanced breakfast? In L. C. Machlin & L. Carlson (Eds.), *Advertising to Children: Concepts and Controversies* (pp. 189–208). Thousand Oaks, CA: Sage Publications.

Robert Wood Johnson Foundation (2007, April 4). *Robert Wood Johnson Foundation announces $500 million commitment to reverse childhood obesity in U.S.* Retrieved November 2, 2011, from http://www.rwjf.org/pr/product.jsp?id=21938.

Roberto, C., Baik, J., Harris, J. L., & Brownell, K. D. (2010). The influence of licensed characters on children's taste and snack preferences. *Pediatrics, 126*(1), 88–93.

Rudd Center for Food Policy & Obesity (2011). *Trends in television food advertising to young people: 2010 update. Rudd Report.* Retrieved September 19, 2011, from www.yaleruddcenter.org/resources/upload/docs/what/reports/RuddReport_TVFoodAdvertising_6.11.pdf

Santos, E., Gonzalo, R., & Gisbert, F. (2007). Advergames: Overview. *Information Technologies and Knowledge, 1*, 203–208.

Schor, J. B., & Ford, M. (2007). From tastes great to cool: Children's food marketing and the rise of the symbolic. *Journal of Law and Medical Ethics*, 10-21

Sharma, L. L., Teret, S. P., & Brownell, K. D. (2009). The food industry and self-regulation: Standards to promote success and to avoid public health failures. *American Journal of Public Health, 100*, 240–246.

Speers, S., Harris, J., & Schwartz, M. (2011). Child and Adolescent Exposure to Food and Beverage Brand Appearances During Prime-Time Television Programming. *American Journal of Preventative Medicine, 41*(3), 291–296.

Stanley, T. L. (2010). That's advertainment. *Brandweek.* Retrieved September 29, 2011, from www.brandweek.com/bw/content_display/esearch/e3i7f27204a864d83e70675df51a9a7dd5b.

Stitt, C., & Kunkel, D. (2008). Food advertising during children's television programming on broadcast and cable channels. *Health Communication, 23*, 573–584.

TheGazette.com (2011). *Cap'n Crunch resurfaces after anxious week in blogosphere.* Retrieved November 3, 2011, from http://thegazette.com/2011/03/12/cap%E2%80%99n-crunch-resurfaces-after-anxious-week-in-blogosphere/

TheNextWeb.com (2011). *Meet the top 20 brands on Facebook.* Retrieved September 29, 2011, from www.thenextweb.com/socialmedia/2011/-07/04/meet-the-top-20-brands-on-facebook

TNS (2008). *TNS' holistic approach shows Olympic Game sponsors go for gold in Beijing. Press release.* Retrieved September 29, 2011, from http://pilot.us.reuters.com/article/2008/08/21/idUS184288+21-Aug-2008+BW20080821.

Ulaby, N. (2008). *Taking product placement another step. NPR.* Retrieved September 29, 2011, from www.npr.org/templates/story/story.php?storyId=94851729.

Ustjanauskas, A., Eckman, B., Harris, J. L., Goren, A., Schwartz, M. B., & Brownell, K. D. (2010). *Focus groups with parents: What do they think about food marketing to their kids?* Retrieved November, 7, 2011 from http://www.yaleruddcenter.org/resources/upload/docs/what/reports/RuddReport_FocusGroupsParents_5.10.pdf

Ward, S., Wackman, D. B., & Wartella, E. (1977). *How Children Learn to Buy.* Beverly Hills, CA: Sage Publications.

Wilde, P. (2009). Self-regulation and the response to concerns about food and beverage marketing to children in the U.S. *Nutrition Reviews, 67*(3), 155–166.

Winkler, T., & Buckner, K. (2006). Receptiveness of gamers to embedded brand messages in advergames: Attitudes towards product placement. *Journal of Interactive Advertising, 7*(1), 24–32.

Wise, K., Bolls, P. D., Kim, H., Venkataraman, A., & Meyer, R. (2008). Enjoyment of advergames and brand attitudes: The impact of thematic relevance. *Journal of Interactive Advertising, 9*(1), 27–36.

Yancey, A. K., Cole, B. L., Brown, R., Williams, J. D., Hillier, A., Kline, R. S., et al. (2009). A cross-sectional prevalence study of ethnically targeted and general audience outdoor obesity-related advertising. *Milbank Quarterly, 87*, 155–184.

Young, B. (2002). Does food advertising make children obese? *International Journal of Advertising and Marketing to Children, 4*(19–26).

Part III
Measuring the Impact of Advertising Effects

Chapter 8
Children's Exposure to Food and Beverage Advertising on Television: Tracking Calories and Nutritional Content by Company Membership in Self-regulation

Lisa M. Powell, Rebecca M. Schermbeck, Glen Szczypka, and Frank J. Chaloupka

Introduction

American children have an energy imbalance that has contributed to current obesity rates of 10.4% and 19.6% for children aged 2–5 and 6–11, respectively (Ogden, Carroll, Curtin, Lamb, & Flegal, 2010). Whereas estimated energy requirements for moderately active children aged 2–5 and 6–11, respectively, are 1,300 kilocalories (kcal) and 1,733 kcal for boys and 1,250 kcal and 1,633 kcal for girls (United States Department of Agriculture, 2005), actual estimated daily intake for these respective age groups is 1,559 kcal and 2,151 kcal for boys and 1,393 kcal and 1,889 kcal for girls (Wright, Wang, Kennedy-Stephenson, & Ervin, 2003). This implies an energy gap based on moderate activity in the range of 143–418 kcal per day, on average, depending on age and gender. Recent estimates of top sources of energy show that children obtain significant empty calories from grain desserts (e.g., 138 kcal/day for ages 4–8 and 145 kcal for ages 9–13) and sugar-sweetened beverages (e.g., 121 kcal/day for ages 4–8 and 169 kcal for ages 9–13) (Reedy & Krebs-Smith, 2010). It was

L.M. Powell, Ph.D. (✉) • F. J. Chaloupka, Ph.D.
Institute for Health Research and Policy, University of Illinois at Chicago,
1747 West Roosevelt Road, Room 558, M/C 275, Chicago, IL 60608, USA

Department of Economics, University of Illinois at Chicago,
1747 West Roosevelt Road, Room 558, M/C 275, Chicago, IL 60608, USA
e-mail: powelll@uic.edu

R.M. Schermbeck, M.P.H., M.S., R.D. • G. Szczypka, B.A.
Institute for Health Research and Policy, University of Illinois at Chicago,
Chicago, IL, USA

J.D. Williams et al. (eds.), *Advances in Communication Research to Reduce Childhood Obesity*, DOI 10.1007/978-1-4614-5511-0_8,

estimated that approximately 40% of children's total energy intake (798 out of 2,027 kcal per day) came in the form of empty calories with 433 kcal from solid fat and 365 kcal from added sugar (Reedy & Krebs-Smith, 2010). Children's overall diets are less healthy than recommended and related high intakes of sugar, sugar sweetened beverages, fat, saturated fat, and sodium and have been associated with greater risk of obesity in addition to other negative health outcomes and other health consequences (Appel, Frohlich, Hall, Pearson, Sacco, Seals et al., 2011; Bray & Popkin, 1998; Gidding, Dennison, Birch, Daniels, Gillman, Lichtenstein et al., 2006; Guenther, Dodd, Reedy, & Krebs-Smith, 2006; Ludwig, Peterson, & Gortmaker, 2001).

Extensive evidence has emerged over the past few decades documenting the poor nutritional content of foods advertisements seen by children and on children's programming (Batada, Seitz, Wootan, & Story, 2008; Harris, Schwartz, Brownell, Sarda, Weinberg, Speers et al., 2009; Powell, Szczypka, Chaloupka, & Braunschweig, 2007; Powell, Schermbeck, Szczypka, Chaloupka, & Braunschweig, 2011; Schwartz, Vartanian, Wharton, & Brownell, 2008; Stitt & Kunkel, 2008). The Institute of Medicine Report on Food Marketing to Children and Youth concluded that for children aged 2–11 years old there is strong evidence that television advertising influences children's food and beverage preferences and purchase requests and short-term food consumption patterns and moderate evidence that it influences usual dietary intake. There is strong evidence that exposure to television advertising is associated with adiposity in children (Institute of Medicine, 2006; see Chap. 2). As a result there has been an emphasis on the need to address unhealthy food advertising directed at children (Federal Trade Commission, 2008; Institute of Medicine; The Henry J. Kaiser Family Foundation, 2004).

In 2006, the Council of Better Business Bureaus launched the Children's Food and Beverage Advertising Initiative (CFBAI) composed at the time of 10 major US food companies that pledged to devote at least half of their child-directed advertising to promote healthier or "better-for-you" products (as defined by each company) and/or encourage good nutrition and healthy lifestyles (Council of Better Business Bureaus, 2008). At the writing of this chapter (2011), 17 companies were members of the CFBAI and four companies (Cadbury Adams, The Coca-Cola Company, Hershey Company, and Mars) pledged not to engage in any advertising of food or beverage products on programming primarily directed to children under the age of 12, while the remaining companies pledged to engage in 100% "better-for-you" advertising (Council of Better Business Bureaus, 2009; Council of Better Business Bureaus, 2011a; see Chaps. 6 and 7).

Several recent studies have assessed changes in the volume of food advertising and the nutritional content of ads seen by children or those on children's programming post-implementation of the CFBAI. An examination of the nutritional content of food ads aired on a sample of children's programming on broadcast and cable television channels found that 72.5% of ads were for high-calorie low-nutrient products, 26.6% were for products high in fat or sugar that should be consumed only in moderation and just 0.9% of ads were for low calorie nutrient rich food products (Kunkel, McKinley, & Wright, 2009). Another recent study examined children's exposure to cereal ads using an international nutrient profile method and found that cereal companies mostly market their least nutritious cereals to children, and that none of the brands marketed directly to children in the USA received a nutrient score high enough to advertise to children on TV in the UK (Harris, Schwartz, & Brownell, 2009).

In our previous work, we found that although children were exposed to fewer food and beverage ads between 2003 and 2009 (pre- and post-CFBAI), decreased from 10.1 ads to 6.8 ads daily for children aged 2–5 and decreased 10.1–7.9 ads daily for children aged 6–11, among those ads seen, there was only a modest improvement in nutritional content (Powell et al., 2011). In 2003, pre-CFBAI, 94% of food and beverage ads seen by children were high in either saturated fat, sugar, or sodium as compared to 88% in 2009. Our previous study also documented a substantial increase in fast-food advertisements seen by children aged 2–5 and 6–11 which increased 21.1% and 30.8%, respectively. Other previous research also reported large increases in children's exposure to fast-food advertising and has documented its poor nutritional content (Harris, Schwartz, & Brownell, 2010).

This study builds on our previous research by examining detailed nutritional content information for saturated fat, sugar and sodium as well as trends in caloric content of food and beverage product ads for each CFBAI member company. Analyses are presented by age, product categories and by parent company. The results are assessed in the context of the self-regulatory CFBAI based on a detailed nutritional analysis of exposure for each CFBAI member company.

Methods

Children's exposure to food and beverage television advertisements was assessed using television ratings data from Nielsen Media Research for television advertisements in calendar years 2003 and 2009, pre- and post-CFBAI self-regulation. We used annual age-specific targeted rating points for children aged 2–5 and 6–11 to capture exposure to broadcast network, cable network, syndicated and spot television food advertising from all programming (except Spanish language programming). The food and beverage product advertisements were assessed by five broad categories including cereals, sweets, snacks, beverages, and other food products, and by parent company based on membership in the CFBAI. This study assessed caloric and nutritional content of all food and beverage products which accounted for 6.8 out of 10.9 and 7.9 out of 12.7 food-related ads, including restaurant ads seen per day by children aged 2–5 and 6–11, respectively. The caloric and nutritional content of fast-food and full-service restaurant ads were not assessed given that many ads did not market a specific product, sources for nutritional information on restaurants are limited, and nutritional content of fast-food restaurants was recently assessed in another study (Harris et al., 2010).

Calories (kcal) were assessed per product advertisement with related measures of exposure to total calories from all food and beverage products per day, and by product categories and parent company. Nutrient content was assessed for total grams (g) of saturated fat and sugar, and total milligrams (mg) of sodium. Caloric and nutritional content data were determined by one of four methods, in the following order: (1) the Minnesota Nutrient Data System; (2) US Department of Agriculture (USDA) Nutrient Data base; (3) nutrition facts panels on the product's label; and, (4) manufacturer's website. Using these data for each age group, we assessed exposure to food product advertising in terms of mean percentage of kcal from saturated fat and sugar and mean sodium content (mg) per 50 g serving. Nutrient content of products was classified as high in saturated fat or sodium using USDA standards for foods sold in competition with the school meal program (National Academy of Science & Institute of Medicine, 2007). A food was classified as "high saturated fat" if it contained >10% of total calories from saturated fat (nuts, nut butter, and seeds were exempted). Products containing >200 mg of sodium per 50 g serving were classified as "high sodium." High sugar products were defined based on recommendations contained in the dietary reference intakes report from the National Academy of Sciences that no more than 25% of total calories come from added sugars and thus we classified products as "high sugar" if >25% of kcal came from sugar (whole fruits, 100% juice, and plain white milk were exempted).

Results

Table 8.1 shows that, in 2009, children aged 2–5 and 6–11 years, respectively, were exposed, on average, to a total of 962 and 1,123 calories from food and beverage product ads on television, daily. With the 32.5% decrease in food and beverage advertisements seen by children aged 2–5 from 10.1 to 6.8 ads per day, exposure to calories fell proportionately by 32.6% from 1,427 to 962 kcal from 2003 to 2009. For children aged 6–11, total calories seen daily fell by 21.5% from 1,431 to 1,123 kcal, parallel to the 21.7% drop in ads seen. Average kcal per ad seen by 2–5 and 6–11 year olds, respectively, remained constant at 141 and 142 kcal for each age group over the 2003–2009 period. However, there was substantial variation in changes in the caloric content of ads by product category.

As compared to 2003, calories per ad in 2009 were higher for cereal and snacks, about the same for sweets, and decreased for beverages and other products. For both age groups, the average number of calories per cereal ad increased by almost 25%, from approximately 120 kcal per ad to 149 kcal per ad. Previous work showed that a smaller proportion of cereal ads seen in 2009 compared to 2003 were high in sugar (decreased from 92.6% to 86.5% among 2–5 year olds and down from 91.6% to 85.8% for children aged 6–11), while ads for cereals high in saturated fat remained at less than 1%, and fiber content in cereal ads seen increased by approximately 75% (Powell et al., 2011). This suggests that the additional calories found in cereal ads are, in part, likely from fiber-related content.

For snacks, calories per ad increased modestly, by 11% in ads seen by children 2–5 and 9% among 6–11 year olds. Again, given lower levels of sugar and saturated

Table 8.1 Children's exposure to food and beverage television advertisements and calories by age, by product category, and by year

	# of Ads/day			# of Calories/day			# of Calories/ad/day		
	2003	2009	%Change 2003–2009	2003	2009	%Change 2003–2009	2003	2009	%Change 2003–2009
All children aged 2–5 years									
Beverages	1.5	0.9	–43.0%	170.5	63.3	–62.9%	114.4	74.5	–34.9%
Cereal	2.6	1.8	–30.4%	308.0	266.8	–13.4%	119.9	148.8	+24.1%
Snacks	1.3	0.7	–43.5%	143.9	90.1	–37.4%	110.0	121.5	+10.5%
Sweets	2.3	1.0	–55.1%	364.7	167.0	–54.2%	160.9	163.9	+1.9%
Other	2.5	2.4	–2.0%	440.2	374.6	–14.9%	177.2	153.8	–13.2%
All food and beverage product ads	10.1	6.8	–32.5%	1427.4	961.8	–32.6%	141.0	140.6	–0.3%
All children aged 6–11 years									
Beverages	1.7	1.0	–40.9%	198.2	75.7	–61.8%	116.3	74.9	–35.6%
Cereal	2.3	2.1	–11.5%	281.7	309.5	+9.9%	120.5	149.1	+23.7%
Snacks	1.3	0.9	–32.0%	143.2	105.5	–26.3%	111.8	121.5	+8.7%
Sweets	2.3	1.3	–44.0%	372.0	210.6	–43.4%	160.6	162.4	+1.2%
Other	2.5	2.7	+8.1%	435.7	422.0	–3.1%	176.6	158.0	–10.5%
All food and beverage product ads	10.1	7.9	–21.7%	1430.9	1123.4	–21.5%	141.6	141.8	+0.2%

@ The Nielsen Company 2009. Note: % Change calculations were based on two decimal points

fat and higher fiber content previously documented for snack ads, similar to cereal, the increased caloric content is likely related to increased fiber content in many of these products. Calories per ad for sweets remained stable (up 1–2%). Calories, on average, per beverage ad seen by children decreased from about 115 kcal to 75 kcal per ad in both age groups. This reduction stemmed in part from the reduction in the proportion of beverage ads that were for high-sugar products which, as previously documented, fell from 85.7% to 62.7% for children aged 2–5 and from 85.6% to 64.1% for children aged 6–11 (Powell et al., 2007).

Examining exposure to calories on the basis of membership in the CFBAI, Tables 8.2 and 8.3 show that among the CFBAI companies, on average, the number of calories seen per day fell by a slightly lesser extent than the number of ads per day (−34.9% versus −37.5% for 2–5 year olds and −21.8% versus −25.1% for 6–11 year olds). Therefore, on average, the number of calories per ad viewed per day increased between 2003 and 2009 by 4.1% among children aged 2–5 and by 4.4% among 6–11 year olds. In 2009, calories per ad seen from CFBAI companies ads versus non-CFBAI companies were, on average, 148.0 kcal per ad versus 111.7 kcal for children aged 2–5, and, similarly, 149.1 kcal per ad versus 111.3 kcal per ad for children aged 6–11.

In terms of the nutritional content of ads seen by children in 2003 and 2009, as shown in Tables 8.4 and 8.5, there were larger reductions in ads for products containing high saturated fat and high sugar among CFBAI companies compared to non-CFBAI companies. In 2003, about 30–31% of both CFBAI and non-CFBAI ads seen were for products high in saturated fat, but by 2009 this fell to about 23% for the CFBAI companies compared to about 27–28% for non-CFBAI companies across the two age groups. The proportion of ads for high-sugar products also fell to a larger extent among CFBAI versus non-CFBAI companies, but such ads nonetheless remained higher among CFBAI versus non-CFBAI companies in 2009. In 2009, among 2–5 and 6–11 year olds, respectively, 63.3% and 62.9% of CFBAI ads seen were for high sugar products compared to 50.0% and 50.9% of non-CFABI company ads seen. The relatively larger reductions in ads for products high in saturated fat and sugar by CFBAI companies were offset with increases in ads for products with high sodium (+10.3% for 2–5 years old and +14.9% for 6–11 year olds), whereas the reductions in ads for products high in saturated fat and sugar from the non-CFBAI were complemented by reductions in ads for products high in sodium. As a result, from 2003 to 2009, for both age groups of children, non-CFBAI companies had about 15% fewer ads seen that were for foods high in saturated fat, sugar or sodium compared to a smaller reduction of about 6% for the CFBAI companies.

Between 2003 and 2009, the largest advertiser to children, General Mills, had an 18.8% and 18.1% increase in calories per ad seen by children aged 2–5 and 6–11, respectively. Correspondingly, as shown from the detailed nutrient content analyses in Tables 8.4 and 8.5, although about 10% fewer of these ads were for high-sugar products, roughly one quarter (23.3% and 27.9% for aged 2–5 and 6–11, respectively) more ads between 2003 and 2009 were for products high in saturated fat. Additionally, the proportion of ads seen that were for products high in sodium increased by about 21% for both age groups of children. As a result, in addition to the increased exposure

Table 8.2 All children aged 2–5 years' exposure to food and beverage advertising and calories by parent company, by age, by year

	# of Ads/day			# of Calories/day			# of Calories/day		
	2003	2009	% Change 2003–2009	2003	2009	% Change 2003–2009	2003	2009	% Change 2003-09
CFBAI companies									
Cadbury	0.1	0.1	+16.7%	0.4	2.0	+363.6%	7.1	30.1	+324.7%
Campbell	0.3	0.3	+3.4%	26.4	24.1	−8.7%	92.0	80.6	−12.3%
Coca-Cola	0.2	0.1	−57.9%	22.1	5.0	−77.2%	118.6	63.1	−46.9%
ConAgra	0.3	0.3	+3.8%	71.0	66.4	−6.5%	276.7	241.8	−12.6%
Dannon	0.2	0.2	+22.2%	20.6	20.8	+0.7%	112.7	93.9	−16.7%
General Mills	2.4	2.0	−16.0%	277.0	275.9	−0.4%	116.9	138.9	+18.8%
Hershey	0.3	0.2	−34.5%	47.6	45.4	−4.7%	165.8	234.8	+41.6%
Kellogg	1.5	0.7	−50.7%	213.4	115.4	−46.0%	145.9	161.2	+10.5%
Kraft	1.3	0.6	−51.6%	176.1	86.8	−50.7%	139.8	141.9	+1.5%
Mars	0.7	0.3	−64.3%	138.8	43.6	−68.6%	197.2	175.1	−11.2%
Nestle	0.4	0.3	−35.7%	88.2	52.9	−40.0%	207.7	197.7	−4.8%
Pepsi	0.6	0.2	−70.7%	74.4	18.0	−75.8%	128.0	106.6	−16.7%
Post	0.4	0.2	−46.5%	52.1	36.5	−30.0%	120.3	157.4	+30.9%
Unilever	0.2	0.1	−65.0%	27.7	12.0	−56.5%	136.9	177.1	+29.3%
CFBAI companies' food and beverage products subtotal	8.7	5.4	−37.5%	1236.0	804.9	−34.9%	142.1	148.0	+4.1%
Non CFBAI companies' food and beverage products subtotal	1.4	1.4	−1.4%	194.3	156.7	−19.3%	136.7	111.7	−18.3%
Total food and beverage companies' products	10.1	6.8	−32.7%	1430.2	961.5	−32.8%	141.3	140.6	−0.5%

@ The Nielsen Company 2009. Note: % Change calculations were based on two decimal points

Table 8.3 All children aged 6–11 years' exposure to food and beverage advertising and calories by parent company, by age, by year

	# of Ads/day			# of Calories/day			# of Calories/ad/day		
	2003	2009	% Change 2003–2009	2003	2009	% Change 2003–2009	2003	2009	% Change 2003–2009
CFBAI companies									
Cadbury	0.1	0.1	+42.9%	0.5	3.9	+704.2%	7.1	40.2	+466.3%
Campbell	0.3	0.3	+17.2%	26.6	27.6	+3.5%	91.9	81.2	−11.6%
Coca-Cola	0.2	0.1	−54.5%	27.4	6.3	−76.9%	122.7	66.4	−45.9%
ConAgra	0.2	0.3	+25.0%	65.0	70.3	+8.1%	269.0	236.9	−12.0%
Dannon	0.2	0.2	+27.8%	20.2	21.6	+7.3%	112.8	93.7	−16.9%
General Mills	2.2	2.3	+6.5%	256.2	321.8	+25.6%	118.7	140.2	+18.1%
Hershey	0.3	0.2	−20.0%	49.3	56.8	+15.2%	165.6	233.6	+41.1%
Kellogg	1.4	0.9	−36.8%	201.2	138.6	−31.1%	147.5	161.6	+9.6%
Kraft	1.3	0.8	−40.8%	180.7	109.0	−39.7%	138.8	142.0	+2.3%
Mars	0.8	0.3	−56.0%	146.8	55.2	−62.4%	196.4	169.8	−13.6%
Nestle	0.4	0.3	−33.3%	86.9	59.4	−31.6%	207.9	214.9	+3.3%
Pepsi	0.7	0.2	−67.7%	83.0	22.6	−72.8%	128.1	107.6	−16.0%
Post	0.4	0.3	−32.6%	52.2	45.9	−12.1%	120.9	158.4	+31.1%
Unilever	0.2	0.1	−55.6%	24.4	15.0	−38.7%	132.5	192.1	+45.0%
CFBAI companies' food and beverage products subtotal	8.6	6.4	−25.1%	1220.4	953.9	−21.8%	142.7	149.1	+4.4%
Non CFBAI companies' food and beverage products subtotal	1.6	1.5	−2.6%	213.2	169.4	−20.5%	137.1	111.3	−18.8%
Total food and beverage companies' products	10.1	7.9	−21.7%	1433.6	1123.4	−21.6%	141.8	141.8	0.0%

@ The Nielsen company 2009. Note: % Change calculations were based on two decimal points

Table 8.4 Nutritional indicators for advertised food and beverage products for children aged 2–5 years by parent company, by year

	% of Ads high in saturated fat			% of Ads high in sugar			% of Ads High in Sodium			% of Ads High in Saturated Fat, Sugar or Sodium		
	2003	2009	% Change 2003–2009	2003	2009	% Change 2003–2009	2003	2009	% Change 2003-2009	2003	2009	% Change 2003-2009
CFBAI companies												
Cadbury	0.0%	0.0%	–	0.0%	17.2%	–	0.0%	0.0%	–	0.0%	17.2%	–
Campbell	28.9%	8.2%	−71.8%	39.2%	26.0%	−33.5%	54.2%	46.7%	−13.8%	88.2%	70.7%	−19.8%
Coca-Cola	0.0%	0.0%	–	82.9%	41.4%	−50.1%	0.0%	0.0%	–	93.9%	41.4%	−56.0%
ConAgra	40.6%	20.8%	−48.8%	13.0%	9.8%	−24.5%	25.9%	48.4%	+86.9%	63.9%	63.1%	−1.2%
Dannon	83.4%	11.3%	−86.4%	100.0%	99.9%	−0.1%	0.0%	0.0%	–	100.0%	99.9%	−0.1%
General Mills	14.8%	18.3%	+23.3%	92.7%	83.3%	−10.1%	50.5%	61.1%	+20.9%	97.2%	97.4%	+0.2%
Hershey	67.9%	89.1%	+31.1%	81.5%	100.0%	22.7%	0.0%	0.0%	–	81.5%	100.0%	+22.7%
Kellogg	14.3%	12.0%	−16.0%	72.2%	67.4%	−6.7%	75.6%	61.1%	−19.1%	98.8%	89.2%	−9.8%
Kraft	41.2%	30.1%	−26.8%	65.8%	36.2%	−45.0%	37.4%	60.1%	+61.0%	97.7%	94.3%	−3.5%
Mars	61.9%	54.6%	−11.8%	93.5%	72.9%	−22.1%	2.7%	1.3%	−50.9%	95.5%	75.1%	−21.4%
Nestle	72.2%	55.2%	−23.6%	57.8%	18.6%	−67.9%	16.0%	16.3%	+1.6%	91.0%	72.3%	−20.5%
Pepsi	16.7%	3.2%	−81.1%	66.4%	58.2%	−12.3%	44.8%	23.4%	−47.8%	91.7%	81.6%	−11.0%
Post	0.0%	0.0%	–	86.6%	82.6%	−4.6%	90.0%	96.7%	+7.4%	95.2%	96.7%	+1.5%
Unilever	66.5%	65.6%	−1.4%	32.0%	37.7%	18.0%	59.8%	37.0%	−38.2%	95.1%	92.2%	−3.1%
CFBAI companies food and beverage products subtotal	30.3%	23.0%	−24.1%	74.9%	63.4%	−15.4%	43.6%	48.1%	+10.3%	94.0%	88.2%	−6.2%
Non CFBAI companies food and beverage products subtotal	31.4%	27.6%	−12.0%	56.1%	50.0%	−10.9%	38.5%	30.2%	−21.4%	93.3%	79.1%	−15.3%
Total food and beverage companies' products	30.4%	23.9%	−21.4%	72.4%	62.0%	−14.4%	42.9%	44.4%	3.5%	93.9%	86.3%	−8.1%

@ The Nielsen Company 2009. Note: % change calculations were based on two decimal points. % change calculations could not be computed for cases where the 2003 value was 0%.

Table 8.5 Nutritional Indicators for Advertised Food and Beverage Products for Children Aged 6–11 Years by Parent Company, by Year

	% of Ads High in Saturated Fat			% of Ads High in Sugar			% of Ads High in Saturated Sodium			% of Ads High in Saturated Fat, Sugar or Sodium		
	2003	2009	% Change 2003–2009	2003	2009	% Change 2003–2009	2003	2009	% Change 2003–2009	2003	2009	% Change 2003–2009
CFBAI companies												
Cadbury	0.0%	0.0%	–	0.0%	24.3%	–	0.0%	0.0%	–	0.0%	24.3%	–
Campbell	28.5%	8.0%	–71.9%	40.5%	25.1%	–38.0%	52.9%	46.1%	–12.9%	88.5%	69.6%	–21.4%
Coca-Cola	0.0%	0.0%	–	84.0%	44.8%	–46.7%	0.0%	0.0%	–	94.5%	44.8%	–52.6%
ConAgra	42.1%	19.5%	–53.7%	13.1%	8.7%	–33.3%	27.1%	49.3%	82.2%	66.3%	62.8%	–5.2%
Dannon	80.7%	13.0%	–83.9%	100.0%	99.9%	–0.1%	0.0%	0.0%	–	100.0%	99.9%	–0.1%
General Mills	14.9%	19.1%	+27.9%	90.5%	81.6%	–9.8%	50.4%	60.8%	+20.6%	96.6%	97.3%	+0.7%
Hershey	67.0%	89.0%	32.8%	79.6%	100.0%	+25.7%	0.0%	0.0%	–	79.6%	100.0%	+25.7%
Kellogg	15.4%	11.9%	–22.8%	71.8%	66.5%	–7.5%	73.9%	60.4%	–18.3%	98.7%	88.7%	–10.1%
Kraft	40.5%	30.6%	–24.5%	64.9%	36.8%	–43.2%	38.0%	60.0%	+57.9%	97.6%	94.9%	–2.7%
Mars	60.8%	50.1%	–17.6%	93.4%	72.1%	–22.9%	2.5%	1.4%	–43.4%	95.3%	74.0%	–22.3%
Nestle	70.7%	55.5%	–21.4%	60.1%	18.7%	–68.9%	17.1%	20.2%	+18.1%	92.6%	73.7%	–20.5%
Pepsi	15.2%	3.0%	–80.5%	66.3%	57.4%	–13.4%	37.8%	25.0%	–34.0%	90.8%	82.4%	–9.3%
Post	0.0%	0.0%	–	85.2%	83.7%	–1.8%	89.8%	96.9%	+8.0%	94.7%	96.9%	+2.4%
Unilever	64.0%	66.3%	+3.6%	36.9%	39.6%	+7.3%	56.8%	31.7%	–44.2%	96.8%	91.8%	–5.2%
CFBAI companies food and beverage products subtotal	30.3%	23.3%	–23.3%	74.0%	62.9%	–15.0%	41.8%	48.1%	+14.9%	93.7%	88.2%	–5.8%
Non CFBAI companies food and beverage products subtotal	31.4%	27.1%	–13.5%	55.5%	50.9%	–8.2%	38.5%	29.1%	–24.4%	93.6%	79.4%	–15.2%
Total food and beverage companies' products	30.5%	24.0%	–21.3%	71.4%	61.8%	–13.3%	41.4%	44.4%	7.5%	93.6%	86.5%	–7.6%

@ The Nielsen company 2009. Note: % Change calculations were based on two decimal points. % change calculations could not be computed for cases where the 2003 value was 0%

to calories per ad, the overall proportion of ads that were seen for products high in saturated fat, sugar or sodium remained virtually unchanged at 97%.

Kellogg Company, the next largest advertiser, also had an increase in calories per ad by about 10% for both age groups. The detailed nutritional indicators showed that there were declines in the proportion of ads that were for products high in saturated fat and high in sugar, indicating that these components were not the contributors to the higher caloric content per advertisement. Given that Kellogg Company is a large cereal producer, as noted earlier these additional calories likely stemmed from fiber-related ingredients. Almost three quarters (73%) of Kellogg Company ads seen were for cereal. Further, sodium levels in Kellogg Company ads seen by children also decreased (−19.1% for children aged 2–5 and −18.3% for children aged 6–11). As a result of declines across all three indicators of saturated fat, sugar and sodium (although with relatively smaller declines in sugar), the overall proportion of products high in saturated fat, sugar or sodium fell by 9.8% and 10.1% for children aged 2–5 and 6–11, respectively.

Kraft Foods Global, Inc. (Kraft), the third of the top three advertisers to children, had virtually no change in calories per ad seen by children between 2003 and 2009, although similar to Kellogg Company, overall ad exposure fell substantially. Among ads that were viewed by children aged 2–5 and 6–11, respectively, 26.8% and 24.5% fewer were high in saturated fat and 45.0% and 43.2% fewer were high in sugar between 2003 and 2009. Unfortunately, this progress was offset by an increase in exposure to high sodium ads (+61.0% for 2–5 and +57.9% for 6–11 year olds). As a result of this increase in sodium, there was only a modest reduction in overall exposure to products high in saturated fat, sugar or sodium which was decreased by just 3.5% among 2–5 year olds and 2.7% among 6–11 year olds.

Nestle USA was another company where there were reductions in the proportions of high saturated fat and high sugar ads seen, but there was an increase in ads seen that were high in sodium between 2003 and 2009. Of note, Nestle USA had the largest percentage decrease in high sugar ads seen by children (−67.9% for ages 2–5 and −68.9% for ages 6–11). Overall, the proportion of ads that were high in saturated fat, sugar or sodium fell by 20.5% for children in both age groups. Post Foods, whose advertisements were all for cereal products, had a 30.9% and 31.1% increase in calories per ad (in line with the changes reported for cereal above). Post Foods cereal ads continued to have no high-saturated fat content, were down slightly in high-sugar content, and up slightly in sodium with almost no resultant change in overall nutritional content.

As we saw from Table 8.1, there was a substantial reduction in exposure to calories from beverage advertisements between 2003 and 2009. Correspondingly, the largest reductions among CFBAI companies came from The Coca-Cola Company and PepsiCo, Inc. with a 77.2% and 75.8% respective fall in total daily calories seen by 2–5 year olds and a 76.9% and 72.8% respective fall in total calorie exposure among 6–11 year olds. Among children aged 2–5 and 6–11, respectively, calories per ad seen fell by 46.9% and 45.9% for The Coca-Cola Company and by 16.7% and 16.0% for PepsiCo, Inc. These reductions in calories were related to the reductions in exposure to high-sugar ads from these companies as shown in Tables 8.4 and 8.5.

The product ads seen from ConAgra Foods continued to be those with the highest number of calories per ad in 2009 for both 2–5 year olds at 241.8 kcal (down by 12.6% from 2003) and 6–11 year olds at 236.9 kcal (down by 12.0%). Compared to other companies these products were more likely to be entrees (about 75%) and thus had higher total calories per product. The prevalence of both high-saturated fat and high-sugar product ads from ConAgra Foods fell over the 2003–2009 period; among 2–5 and 6–11 year olds, respectively, the proportion of product ads seen that were high in saturated fat ads was down 48.8% and 53.7% and those that were high in sugar were down 24.5% and 33.3%. On the other hand, there were substantial increases in sodium levels: between 2003 and 2009, there was an 82.2% and 86.9% increase in the number of high-sodium product ads seen by 2–5 and 6–11 year olds. As a result, similar to the findings for Kraft, these increases in sodium offset the positive reductions in saturated fat and sugar, such that, between 2003 and 2009 there was only a modest reduction in the proportion of product ads that were viewed that were high in saturated fat, sugar or sodium (−1.2% for ages 2–5 and −5.2% for ages 6–11). Unilever's product ads, on the other hand, either increased or stayed approximately the same for saturated fat and higher in sugar, but substantially fewer of their ads seen by children both ages 2–5 (−38.2%) and 6–11 (−44.2%) were high in sodium.

In 2009, Cadbury Adams, Campbell Soup Company, The Dannon Company, and The Coca-Cola Company advertisements seen by children aged 2–5 and 6–11 were for products, on average, with less than 100 kcal per advertisement. The Campbell Soup Company also had significant reductions in ads for products high in saturated fat, and its ads were also less likely to be for high-sugar or high-sodium products in 2009 as compared to 2003. For The Dannon Company, whereas there were also substantial reductions in high-saturated fat ads seen (−86.4% for ages 2–5 and −83.9% for ages 6–11), virtually all of its advertised products continued to be high in sugar in 2009. Some new high-sugar ads from Cadbury Adams were seen, but, despite this development, overall advertising exposure remained very low as did calories, on average, at 30 kcal per advertisement.

Discussion

Children saw fewer nonrestaurant food and beverage product ads between 2003 and 2009. As a result, they were exposed to fewer ads for unhealthy products and fewer total calories from nonrestaurant food and beverage products daily. Over this period, calories per ad seen remained relatively constant at 141 kcal per advertisement. Where calories per ad for cereal and snacks increased, the evidence suggested that this did not stem from increased fat or sugar content. In particular, increases in caloric content of cereal ads were likely related to higher fiber content. In terms of the detailed nutritional content of ads seen by children, between 2003 and 2009, among CFBAI versus non-CFBAI companies there were relatively larger reductions, on average, in high-saturated fat and high-sugar product ads seen.

However, among CFBAI companies these reductions in saturated fat and sugar were offset by increases in high-sodium ads, whereas among the non-CFBAI companies these reductions were complemented by reductions in high sodium product ads. The increases in sodium that offset positive changes in reductions in saturated fat and reductions in sugar occurred for a number of companies, particularly ConAgra Foods and Kraft. Overall, the largest advertiser, General Mills, not only had an increase in high-sodium product ads but also an increase in the proportion of their ads seen that were for products high in saturated fat. Overall, the majority of ads, 88% and 79%, respectively, of CFBAI and non-CFBAI company ads seen by children in 2009, continued to be for products high in saturated fat, sugar or sodium.

Between 2009 (the last year of exposure data analyzed in this study) and 2011, eight companies made changes to their individual pledges. For example, the Campbell Soup Company strengthened their pledge and added new sodium guidelines for their products, General Mills added a sugar guideline for their products, and The Dannon Company streamlined their total fat requirements from age specific to one general requirement. PepsiCo was the only company to change their policy to be less restrictive than in previous years, but did include language requiring positive nutrients/food groups to be present in food and beverages advertised on programming primarily directed toward children less than 12 years. A number of other companies (ConAgra Foods, Nestle USA, Post Foods) made changes to their food categories or made changes to "and/or" statements that did not actually affect the strength of the guidelines (Kraft Foods) (Council of Better Business Bureaus, 2011b).

Despite these changes, the CFBAI pledges continue to lack uniformity. In July 2011, CFBAI addressed this concern by announcing that by January 1, 2014 any company wishing to be a part of the CFBAI will follow a uniform set of nutrition criteria developed by the CFBAI and a "participant committee" that included nutritionists and scientists. The CFBAI has noted that approximately one-third of the products currently advertised to children under the existing company-specific nutrition standards do not meet the new uniform criteria. Thus, the participants will have to change their recipes for these products if they wish to continue advertising them after these new criteria go into effect. Companies that are unable to reformulate products or choose not to reformulate products by January 1, 2014 will not advertise those products any longer on programming directed at children under the age of 12.

These proposed CFBAI guidelines have some benefits over the company-specific guidelines aside from being uniform. Currently, among the 17 food and beverage companies that are part of the CFBAI there are 25 different food categories with various nutritional standards (i.e., soup, canned pasta, meals, cereals, 100% fruit juices, popsicles, etc.). The uniform guidelines have only 10 major food categories (juice; dairy products; grain, fruit and vegetable products and items not in other categories; soup and meal sauces; seed, nuts, nut butters and spreads; meat, fish, poultry products; mixed dishes; main dishes and entrees; small meals; meals, entrée and other items including a beverage) with dairy products separated out into four subcategories (milk and milk substitutes; yogurt and yogurt type products; dairy-based desserts; cheese and cheese products). Additionally, food and beverage products no longer will qualify for advertising simply for meeting a "reduced" claim (i.e., ≥ 25% less sodium) or being sold in a portion controlled package (i.e., 100 calorie packs). Finally, all product categories have calorie limits, and will have to meet criteria for nutrients to limit (saturated fat, sodium and total sugars), and nutrition components to encourage (i.e., dairy, fruits, vegetables, whole grains and/or nutrients, i.e., fiber, calcium, potassium, iron, vitamin A, vitamin C, and/or vitamin D) (Council of Better Business Bureaus, 2011c).

These new uniform voluntary guidelines can be expected to change the nutritional quality of foods and beverages advertised on children's programming starting in 2014 and hopefully will have led to the reformulation of food and beverage products. However, some companies may not have to reformulate products or they may only make minimal changes to the product lines advertised to children because the current company-specific guidelines already meet or exceed the uniform guidelines. For example, The Campbell Soup Company currently has three product categories they advertise on children's programming (1) baked snacks, (2) soup, and (3) canned pasta. For all the "nutrients to limit" categories Campbell Soup Company has the same guidelines or exceeds the guidelines that will be in effect starting 2014. The only categories that will require Campbell Soup Company to address are total sugars and saturated fat in the soup and saturated fat in canned pasta. Companies that have pledges that cover the entire product line (i.e., all products advertised will be ≤175 kcal, ≤15% kcal from sat fat, ≤480 mg of sodium, and ≤12 g of total sugar), such as General Mills, Kellogg Company and PepsiCo, Inc. may have to make more substantial changes in order to comply with the uniform guidelines. For example, General Mills and Kellogg Company have one sodium limit that all their products must meet in order to be eligible to advertise to children: ≤480 mg and ≤230 mg, respectively. The new guidelines have a range of sodium limits for the 10 categories from ≤110 mg for dairy-based desserts to ≤740 mg for meals (entrée and other items including a beverage). Overall, the uniform guidelines address the product categories that the companies have targeted since the inception of the initiative. Of the ten product categories only two address beverage advertisement (juices and dairy products which includes a milk and milk substitute subcategory). All other potentially advertised beverages, including bottled waters, must meet FDA regulations for "low calories" and "very low sodium." However, diet sodas may not be advertised (Council of Better Business Bureaus, 2011c).

Parallel to the industry-level changes, in 2009, Congress directed the Interagency Working Group (IWG) made up of the Federal Trade Commission (FTC), Centers for Disease Control and Prevention (CDC), Food and Drug Administration (FDA) and the USDA to develop model, voluntary guidelines addressing food and beverage marketing directed towards children. By April 2011, IWG had developed nutrition standards based on the Dietary Guidelines for American, the Institute of Medicine, the Daily Reference Intakes the USDA's food pyramid and the FDA's food-labeling rules. The IWG voluntary guidelines divide foods into three categories (individual foods, main dishes, and meals) and have two parts (Principle A and B) which must be met for a food to be advertised to children. Principle A relates to the provision of food groups that make a meaningful contribution to a healthful diet and Principle B addresses nutrients including saturated fat, trans fat, added sugars and sodium that should be limited due to their negative impact on health or body weight.

Overall, IWG's proposed guidelines are stronger than CFBAI's uniform guidelines. For example, sodium restrictions for CFBAI vary from ≤110 mg to ≤740 mg per serving size across the 10 product categories. IWG only has three product categories with a sodium limit ≤210 mg per serving size and ≤450 mg per serving size for main dishes and meals. These recommendations become stronger effective 2021; ≤140 mg/RACC (reference amount customarily consumed) for individual foods and ≤300 mg/RACC for main dishes and meals. Total sugar guidelines (no more than 13 g of added sugars per RACC for individual foods; per serving size for main dishes and meals) are generally stronger for IWG guidelines than the CFBAI guidelines with a few exceptions such as cheese and cheese products; soups and meal sauce; seeds, nuts, nut butters and spreads. Other differences include that IWG has a limit for trans fats in food and beverage products, while the CFBAI guidelines do not and that CFBAI includes a limit on calories while the IWG does not.

A recent study conducted by the Center for Science in the Public Interest (CSPI) found that many of the currently CFBAI-approved products do meet the IWG guidelines for saturated fat (71%), trans fat (100%), added sugar (75%) and the interim sodium guideline (66%) for individual items; although, only one-third of current pledge-approved products will meet the final sodium recommendation that will be in effect as of 2021 (Wootan, Vickroy, & Pokress, 2011). The CSPI report indicated that where companies have problems meeting the IWG guidelines is in providing a positive nutritional component such as 0.5 cups of fruit or fruit juice in the product, 0.6 cups vegetable or vegetable juice, 1 egg or egg equivalent, etc.

Despite the recent reductions in children's television advertising exposure to unhealthy food and beverage ads, the study results from this chapter show that children continue to be exposed to food and beverage advertising for products that are high in saturated fat, sugar and sodium. The development of new uniform CFBAI pledges can be expected to improve exposure starting in 2014. If the IWG recommendations were to be adopted by the CFBAI, we can expect even further improvements in the nutritional content of foods ads seen by children. As companies reformulate products and change their advertising practices directed at children, we nonetheless need to continue to be cognizant of the extent to which advertising for unhealthy products reaches children. Companies may be 100% compliant in their child-directed advertising but many ads for unhealthy products may continue to reach substantial numbers of children. Previously, the definition of what constitutes child-directed advertising was set by each company. In 2010, the CFBAI created a uniform definition for "child-directed advertising" of 35% or greater share of children 2–11 in the audience for all participating companies to utilize (Council of Better Business Bureaus, 2011a). The IWG recommends for children aged 2–11 years, the audience share for consideration as "directed" to children should be 30% as measured on an annual basis. In this regard, overall exposure and exposure based on different measures of children's audience share need to be monitored closely to ensure that children are safeguarded from ads that promote products that are high in empty calories.

Acknowledgement January, 2012 We gratefully acknowledge research support from the Robert Wood Johnson Foundation (RWJF) through the Bridging the Gap program for the ImpacTeen project, the National Institutes of Health (NIH), National Cancer Institute (NCI) award number 1R01CA138456-01A1, and the Centers for Disease Control and Prevention (CDC) award number 11IPA1102973. The content is solely the responsibility of the authors and does not necessarily represent the official views of the RWJF, the NCI, the NIH, or the CDC.

Reference

Appel, L. J., Frohlich, E. D., Hall, J. E., Pearson, T. A., Sacco, R. L., Seals, D. R., et al. (2011). The importance of population-wide sodium reduction as a means to prevent cardiovascular disease and stroke: A call to action from the American Heart Association. *Circulation, 123*(10), 1138–1143.

Batada, A., Seitz, M. D., Wootan, M. G., & Story, M. (2008). Nine out of 10 food advertisements shown during Saturday morning children's television programming are for foods high in fat, sodium, or added sugars, or low in nutrients. *Journal of the American Dietetic Association, 108*, 673–678.

Bray, G. A., & Popkin, B. M. (1998). Dietary fat intake does affect obesity! *The American Journal of Clinical Nutrition, 68*, 1157–1173.

Federal Trade Commission. (2008). *Marketing food to children and adolescents: A review of industry expenditures, activities, and self-regulations*. Washington, DC: FTC. Available at: http://www.ftc.gov/os/2008/07/P064504foodmktingreport.pdf.

Council of Better Business Bureaus (2008). Changing the landscape of food and beverage advertising: the children's food and beverage advertising initiative in action a progress report on the first six months of implementation: July–December 2007. Available at: http://www.bbb.org/us/storage/16/documents/CFBAI/ChildrenF&BInit_Sept21.pdf [On-line].

Council of Better Business Bureaus (2009). BBB *children's food and beverage advertising initiative: food and beverage products that meet participants' approved nutrition standards*. Available at: http://www.bbb.org/us/storage/0/Shared%20Documents/Aug_Product_List_final1.pdf [On-line].

Council of Better Business Bureaus (2011a). *The children's food and beverage advertising initiative in action. A report on compliance and implementation during 2010 and a five year retrospective: 2006–2011*. Available at http://www.bbb.org/us/storage/16/documents/cfbai/cfbai-2010-progress-report.pdf [On-line].

Council of Better Business Bureaus (2011b). *BBB children's food and beverage advertising initiative: Synopsis of participants' nutrition standards*. Available at http://www.bbb.org/us/children-food-beverage-advertising-initiative [On-line].

Council of Better Business Bureaus (2011c). The children's food & beverage advertising initiative white paper on cfbai's uniform nutrition criteria. Available at http://www.bbb.org/us/children-food-beverage-advertising-initiative [On-line].

Gidding, S. S., Dennison, B. A., Birch, L. L., Daniels, S. R., Gillman, M. W., Lichtenstein, A. H., et al. (2006). Dietary recommendations for children and adolescents: A guide for practitioners. *Pediatrics, 117*, 544–559.

Guenther, P. M., Dodd, K. W., Reedy, J., & Krebs-Smith, S. M. (2006). Most Americans eat much less than recommended amounts of fruits and vegetables. *Journal of the American Dietetic Association, 106*, 1371–1379.

Harris, J. L., Schwartz, M. B., & Brownell, K. D. (2009). *Cereal F.A.C.T.S.:Nutrition and marketing ratings of children's cereals*. Yale University: Rudd Center foe Food Policy and Obesity.

Harris, J. L., Schwartz, M. B., & Brownell, K. D. (2010). *Fast food F.A.C.T.S.: Evaluating fast food nutrition and marketing to youth*. Yale University: Rudd Center for Food Policy and Obesity.

Harris, J., Schwartz, M., Brownell, K., Sarda, V., Weinberg, M., Speers, S. et al. (2009). Cereal FACTS. Evaluating the nutrition quality and marketing of children's cereals. http://www.cerealfacts.org [On-line]. Available: http://www.cerealfacts.org.

Institute of Medicine. (2006). *Food marketing to children and youth: Threat or opportunity?* Washington, DC: The National Academies Press.

Kunkel, D., McKinley, C., & Wright, P. (2009). *The impact of industry self-regulation on the nutritional quality of foods advertised on television to children.* Oakland, CA: Children Now.

Ludwig, D. S., Peterson, K. E., & Gortmaker, S. L. (2001). Relation between consumption of sugar-sweetened drinks and childhood obesity: A prospective, observational analysis. *The Lancet, 357*, 505–508.

National Academy of Science and Institute of Medicine. (2007). *Nutrition standards for foods in school: leading the way toward healthier youth.* Washington, DC: National Academies Press.

Ogden, C. L., Carroll, M. D., Curtin, L. R., Lamb, M. M., & Flegal, K. M. (2010). Prevalence of high body mass index in US children and adolescents, 2007–2008. *JAMA: The Journal of the American Medical Association, 303*, 242–249.

Powell, L. M., Schermbeck, R. M., Szczypka, G., Chaloupka, F. J., & Braunschweig, C. L. (2011). Trends in the nutritional content of television food advertisements seen by children in the United States: Analyses by age, food categories, and companies. *Archives of Pediatrics and Adolescent Medicine, 165*(12), 1078–1086.

Powell, L. M., Szczypka, G., Chaloupka, F. J., & Braunschweig, C. L. (2007). Nutritional content of television food advertisements seen by children and adolescents in the United States. *Pediatrics, 120*, 576–583.

Reedy, J., & Krebs-Smith, S. M. (2010). Dietary sources of energy, solid fats, and added sugars among children and adolescents in the United States. *Journal of the American Dietetic Association, 110*, 1477–1484.

Schwartz, M. B., Vartanian, L. R., Wharton, C. M., & Brownell, K. D. (2008). Examining the nutritional quality of breakfast cereals marketed to children. *Journal of the American Dietetic Association, 108*, 702–705.

Stitt, C., & Kunkel, D. (2008). Food advertising during children's television programming on broadcast and cable channels. *Health Communication, 23*, 573–584.

The Henry J. Kaiser Family Foundation. (2004). *The role of media in childhood obesity.* Menlo Park: The Henry J. Kaiser Family Foundation.

United States Department of Agriculture (2005). MyPyramid food intake pattern calorie levels. http://www.choosemyplate.gov/foodgroups/downloads/MyPyramid_Calorie_Levels.pdf [On-line]. Available at: http://www.choosemyplate.gov/foodgroups/downloads/MyPyramid_Calorie_Levels.pdf

Wootan, M. G., Vickroy, L. C., & Pokress, B. H. (2011). *Putting nutrition into nutrition standards for marketing to kids: How marketed foods measure up to the interagency working group's proposed nutrition principles for food marketed to children?* Center for Science in the Public Interest. Available from http://cspinet.org/new/pdf/iwg-report.pdf

Wright, J. D., Wang, C. Y., Kennedy-Stephenson, J., & Ervin, R. B. (2003). *Dietary intake of ten key nutrients for Public Health, United States: 1999–2000.* Hyattsville, MA: National Center for Health Statistics.

Chapter 9
The Role of Advertising on Attitudes and Consumption of Food and Beverage Products

Gary B. Wilcox, Jerome D. Williams, Sara Kamal, and Kyung Ok Kacy Kim

Introduction

Advertisements are a central feature of life in the late twentieth and early twenty-first centuries. Despite the difficulty of measuring what advertising does, critics sometimes suggest that it is self-evident that the combined effects of advertising expenditures in markets will lead to more sales of the product category in question, whether or not this is the intention. So the argument goes, alcohol advertising in the aggregate makes us drink more than we would otherwise as does food advertising make us eat more. These arguments are not just academic; from a public policy perspective advertising bans in individual product areas are present around the world.

Advertising and promotion have become important elements of the marketing mix of food and beverage products in the USA. Through advertising in digital and nondigital media, couponing, in-store displays and promotions consumers are surrounded with almost an unending flow of food and beverage product offerings (Chester & Montgomery, 2009). In addition, food and beverage companies spend considerable sums promoting their brands directly to the retailer through discounts, allowances, incentives, and slotting fees. Food marketers even make use of food

G.B. Wilcox, Ph.D. (✉) • K.O.K. Kim
Department of Advertising and Public Relations, The University of Texas at Austin, Austin, TX, USA
e-mail: burl@mail.utexas.edu; kyungok.kim@gmail.com

J.D. Williams, Ph.D.
Department of Management and Global Business, Rutgers Business School-Newark and New Brunswick, 1 Washington Park Room 1040, Newark, NJ 07102, USA
e-mail: jeromew@business.rutgers.edu

S. Kamal, Ph.D.
School of Business Administration, American University, Dubai, P.O. Box 28282, Dubai, U.A.E.
e-mail: skamal@aud.edu

J.D. Williams et al. (eds.), *Advances in Communication Research to Reduce Childhood Obesity*, DOI 10.1007/978-1-4614-5511-0_9,

stylists to help make the food that appears in the advertisements look especially appetizing.

With this ever presence of food and beverage advertising comes criticisms that have suggested it encourages consumption of unhealthy products, over influences children's food choices, and contributes to epidemic levels of obesity in the USA (Harrison, 2009; Oren & Dodson, 2010). Most of the criticisms have focused on the promotion of fast food, soft drinks, and sugar-related products.

While most of these critics view advertising as an overpowering marketing tool that companies use to manipulate consumers, this chapter presents information from both a theoretical and empirical view that offers a different perspective. In this chapter, theoretical issues are examined regarding the intended effects of advertising in the US economic system from a macro perspective. Next, empirical evidence is presented regarding the effects of aggregate advertising on the consumption of two food and beverage products—soft drinks and fast food. Then, research is reviewed that investigates the effects of advertising and product placement on the attitudes of kids and mothers for popular food and beverage brands. Finally, conclusions and implications of this research are summarized and thoughts for future study are presented.

How Advertising Works

Advertising's role and effects have been examined through the perspective of many domains including history, economics, management, and psychology (Packard, 1957; Borden, 1942a, b; Holt, 2002; Levy, 1963; McCracken, 1988; Lears, 1994; Jhally, 1987; Batra, Meyers, & Aaker, 1995). These varying and often contradictory approaches envision the role of advertising as dialectical and symbolic to wasteful and damaging. While advertising primarily plays an economic role, it may also impact society in social and psychological ways, thus making it hard to measure all of its effects quantitatively.

In the early twentieth century, modern communication technologies as well as enhancements in transportation systems encouraged the use of large-scale brand advertising. Those processes led to a wider discussion of advertising as a topic for economic thought and debate. Early economic analysis of advertising can be traced back to this time with works of Marshall (1890, 1919) and Chamberlin (1933). Marshall (1890) established a distinction between the two specific roles that advertising played within the economy. First, he noted that advertising has a "constructive" role in the economy in that it provided consumers with purchase-related information such as product price and product quality. By imparting pertinent information to the consumer, advertising increased the consumers' knowledge about the product and reduced their search costs.

Marshall also proposed an alternative view—advertising may have a "combative" role in the marketplace whereby it provided little new information to consumers and mainly redistributed consumers from one brand to another. The incorporation of the combative and constructive roles of advertising into economic theory was done by Chamberlin (1933) who was the first scholar to integrate the role of advertising within his theory of monopolistic competition.

The underlying assumption in Chamberlin's theory is that within a given industry, individual firms sell differentiated products. As a consequence, each firm is subject to a downward-sloped demand curve, meaning that as the price of a product decreases, the demand for that good will increase. Chamberlin identified advertising as a means for firms to further distinguish their products from competing firms. Thus, advertising allows companies to differentiate their products from rival companies and doing so helps the advertised company expand its market.

These early works mark the beginnings of the economic analysis of advertising. A seminal study on the economic effects of advertising was executed by Borden (1942a, b). On the basis of extensive intra-industry data, Borden noted that that the relationship between advertising and the demand for a product may vary by the nature of the market and the maturity of the product advertised. Specifically, in markets that are expanding, advertising will have a positive effect on the demand at the aggregate level. However, in mature or declining markets, advertising is less likely to have an effect at the aggregate level. Instead, advertising will impact the selective demand in this market. Thus, advertising for a given firm is likely to have an effect on the sales for that firm, but typically at the expense of rival firm's market share. In addition, Borden argues that in new industries advertising will have the "greatest influence" on stimulating demand (Borden, 1942b, p. 97).

Almost 40 years following Borden's work, Albion and Farris (1981) offered two similar economic perspectives of advertising's role in the marketplace—the market power view and the information view. In discussing a wide range of the effects of advertising, they agree with Borden's view that advertising may be useful increasing the consumption of a particular product but only within a favorable social and economic climate. In expanding markets, advertising will contribute to the market expansion as well as the market share of the companies that advertise. On the other hand, they believe that in a declining market, advertising reallocates the market share of firms in a given industry and would not increase the overall consumption of the product category.

Empirical Evidence

Translating theory into practice many times is a difficult and laborious process. A majority of studies that have examined the advertising–sales relationships have focused on declining or mature industries such as tobacco or alcohol while only a few have examined markets that are growing or expanding. The following section briefly examines this literature in the tobacco and alcohol markets and may provide insight for the role of advertising in the food and beverage markets.

Tobacco Products

Borden (1942a) examined aggregate and selective demand for cigarettes in an expanding market from the late 1800s to the late 1930s and found that advertising was an important factor increasing both the aggregate and selective demand for cigarettes. However, studies that have examined the relationship of aggregate cigarette advertising to consumption since the 1950s have produced inconsistent findings. Several studies indicate that aggregate advertising does not have an impact on the aggregate consumption of tobacco products (Grabowski, 1976; Schneider, Klein & Murphy, 1981; Yuclet & Kaynak, 1984; Baltagi & Levin, 1986; Johnson & Oksanen, 1974; Godfrey, 1986; Hoffman, 1987; McAuliffe, 1988; Baltagi & Levin, 1992; Wilcox & Vacker, 1992; Duffy, 1991; Franke, 1994; Duffy, 1995; Goel & Morey, 1995; Duffy, 1996; Gallet, 1999).

On the other hand, there are some studies that have found that advertising does have a positive effect on aggregate consumption for tobacco products (Fujii, 1980; Witt & Pass, 1981; Young, 1983; Bishop & Yoo, 1985; Radfar, 1985; Leeflang & Reuijl, 1985; Abernethy & Teel, 1986; Porter, 1986; Chetwynd, Coope, Brodie & Wells, 1988; Kao & Tremblay, 1988; Harrison, Chetwynd & Brodie, 1989; Sheldon & Doroodian, 1989; Tegene, 1991; Smee, 1992; Valdes, 1993; Tremblay & Tremblay, 1995).

While there is controversy regarding the aggregate effects, there is however consistent empirical evidence to support a positive relationship between brand level advertising and brand sales since the 1950s (Wilcox, 1991; Nguyen, 1987; Pollay, Siddarth & Siegel, 1996). These relationships seem consistent with both Borden (1942a, b) and Albion and Farris (1981) in that advertising is likely to impact brand sales in a more mature market (since 1950s) and impact aggregate consumption in an expanding market (1800s to 1930s).

Alcohol Products

A review of the econometric studies examining the effects of advertising on consumption of alcohol beverages reveals findings consistent with the cigarette market. Johnson (1986) found that beer and wine advertising had significant association with both beer and wine demand but that spirits advertising had no effect on spirits demand. Selvanathan (1991) found that beer advertising had a significant association with beer, wine, and spirits demand and that wine and spirits advertising reduced the demand for beer. Blake and Nied (1997) noted that alcohol advertising had weak effects in their study of demand in the UK market from 1952 to 1991. A similar study in the USA was conducted by Franke and Wilcox (1987) using quarterly data from 1964 to 1984 and found no evidence of a significant relationship between total advertising and consumption of beer, but found statistically significant although weak relationships between consumption and advertising of wine and distilled spirits.

Fisher and Cook (1995) using data from 1970 to 1990 found that consumers choose between categories of alcohol beverages such as beer and wine and these products are seen as similar alternatives in the overall alcohol category. This cross category similarity can be further explained as a give-and-take relationship in that beer consumption increases when wine and liquor advertising is low and vice versa. Nelson and Moran (1995) also observed significant relationships between categories of alcohol beverages. Specifically distilled spirits consumption decreased as wine advertising increased and distilled spirits consumption increased when wine advertising was reduced. These authors noted that advertising had little impact on total consumption of alcohol beverages but instead served to alter individual brand shares. Most recently, Gius (1996) examined brand advertising and brand consumption and provided empirical support that advertising for a distilled spirits brand had a significant positive effect on brand sales. He concluded that brand-level spirits advertising results only in brand switching and does not increase the size of the spirits market.

To summarize, the main purpose of alcohol advertising over the last 40 years appears to be to enhance or defend category or market share. Wilcox and Gangadharbatla (2006) confirmed this point of view in a study of the beer market in the USA from 1970 to 2003. The findings in his study were consistent with previous research indicating that aggregate beer advertising expenditures in the USA have had little or no effect on aggregate consumption, but were important to beer brand market share instead (Wilcox, 2001). The findings for the alcohol market while similar to those in the cigarette market also seem consistent with both Borden (1942a, b) and Albion and Farris (1981) in that advertising is likely to impact brand sales in the more mature alcohol market.

Using this theoretical perspective to examine the effect of advertising on food and beverage products will provide additional insight to an area where advertising has been criticized not unlike the alcohol and tobacco industries. The following sections present a summary of three studies. The first two studies provide evidence of the macro effects of advertising on soft drinks and fast foods to the US population as a whole. The third study takes a different approach by examining the effects of advertising on brand ratings by kids and moms in the USA instead of sales or market share.

Advertising and Soft Drinks: A Declining Market Example

In the recent years, the carbonated soft drink (CSD) industry has come under a lot of criticism from consumer advocacy and special interest groups for producing and marketing a product that is considered one of the causes of obesity. Critics point to advertising as one of the major contributing factors for increased CSD consumption, particularly among children and teens.

National dietary studies indicate that carbonated soft drink consumption more than doubled in youths from about five ounces per day in the late 1970s to 12 ounces in the mid to late 1990s. Soft drink consumption more than tripled during those years among teenage boys' (Collins, 2004).

Public policy remedies have been suggested by special interest groups who have petitioned the FDA to require a series of rotating health notices on containers of all nondiet soft drinks. Others have called for a tax on sugary soft drinks to make them much more expensive in hopes of shifting demand to diet or less sugary drinks. However, most critics of the CSD industry point to intense marketing and advertising efforts of CSD manufacturers as a chief contributing factor for increased CSD consumption. They claim that soft drink companies spend billions of dollars on advertising much of which is targeted at children and youth.

On the other hand, CSD manufacturers respond that the huge amounts of dollars spent on CSD advertising is to steal and/or maintain market share more so than to increase aggregate consumption. In reality, the relationship between advertising and consumption is a complex economic, social, and cultural issue, making it difficult to identify a direct relationship between advertising and increased consumption. Critics point to advertising as the "cause" of these problems, but provide minimal scientific evidence at best. The study reviewed here provides an analysis of the relationship between annual advertising expenditures and consumption for carbonated soft drinks sold in the USA from 1984 to 2007.

In the 1970s and 1980s, consumption of CSDs grew as did expenditures for advertising and promotion. The per capita consumption of CSDs peaked in 1998 and has been slowly declining since. Overall consumption declined 12% to 49.3 gallons in 2007. It is generally thought that the CSD market is in a decline period that may be attributed to health concerns related to sugar content of regular sodas. Advertising spending is also down during this period. In 2007, expenditures fell nearly 26% from 2006 to $381 million (Media Economy, 2008).

Perhaps the most widely discussed factor influencing CSD consumption among adolescents is advertising even though very few studies provide evidence suggesting an increase in aggregate-level consumption of CSD. Grimm et al. (2004) used television viewing as a proxy measure for exposure to soft drink advertising and suggested that the odds of drinking soft drinks almost daily was twice as likely for those who watched 3.5 hours or more of television each day than those that watched less television.

Other studies have linked food advertising directly to actual food consumed by children. For instance, Hitchings and Moynihan (1998) found that children exposed to a set of food commercials were more likely to choose the advertised items than those who had not been exposed to the commercials. A similar experiment conducted by Borzekowski and Robinson (2001) using preschool children also found that children exposed to a video with embedded commercials were significantly more likely to choose the advertised item than children who saw the same videotape without commercials. These findings suggest that advertising is influential in the choice of a particular brand over another but they do not address the aggregate increases or decreases in consumption.

Studies that link advertising to increases in individual-level consumption of soft drinks have one major limitation. These studies use either cross-sectional data

Table 9.1 US Soft Drinks. Variables and Sources

Variables	Time period
Soft drink consumption	1984–2007
Source: Beverage Marketing Corporation, NY	
Advertising Expenditures	1984–2007
Source: Advertising figures in millions of 1982–1984 dollars, Leading National Advertisers, Inc./ Nielsen AdViews deflated using McCann-Erickson Media Unit Cost Index	
Socioeconomic variables	
Producer Price Index Soft Drinks	1986–2007
Source: http://www.economagic.com	
Consumer Price Index Soft Drinks	1984–2007
Source: http://www.economagic.com	
US Population	1984–2007
Source: US Department of Commerce, Bureau of the Census	

(survey methodology) or controlled experiments to identify advertising as one of the possible factors influencing CSD consumption. While such cross-sectional studies may be helpful in linking individual-level choice of beverage to advertising and/or television viewing as noted above, these studies fail to provide evidence for the existence of a link between advertising and aggregate-level CSD consumption, particularly among adolescents.

The study discussed here used longitudinal data from 1984 to 2007 to provide insight into the relationship between advertising and consumption of soft drinks (Wilcox, Gangadharbatla & Kamal, 2009). In this time series regression analysis, seven variables were analyzed—one soft drink consumption variable, one soft drink advertising variable, and five socio-economic variables—Producer Price Index for Soft Drinks, Consumer Price Index for Soft Drinks, Population Age groups 10–14 and 15–19 expressed as fractions of total US population. The advertising expenditure variable consisted of deflated media totals for newspaper, magazines, network television, spot television, radio, outdoor, cable and syndicated television for the carbonated soft drink (CSD) industry reported on an annual basis. The advertising expenditures consisted of media totals for newspaper, magazines, network television, spot television, radio, outdoor, cable and syndicated television for the carbonated soft drink (CSD) industry reported on an annual basis (see Table 9.1).

The major finding in this study is that aggregate advertising expenditures and aggregate consumption for soft drinks in the USA were not significantly related from 1984 to 2007 (see Table 9.2 for the full and final regression models). While this may seem counterintuitive given the expenditures by CSD companies on advertising, much of these expenditures may be attributed to maintaining or increasing market share. CSD advertising might influence consumers, especially teens, in choosing a particular brand of soft drink but likely not have much influence in their decision to drink soda. Perhaps the decision to consume CSDs may be more influenced by family and upbringing, friends, and healthy eating habits more so than a mere exposure to soda advertising as has been suggested by Grimm et al. (2004).

Table 9.2 Full/Final consumption model

Predictor	*B* value	*t* value	P-level
Intercept	4,233,264	0.29	0.7735
pop Age10–14	−6,672,266	−1.27	0.2213
pop Age15–19	−56,079,442	−1.16	0.2643
Population	94.1547	2.02	0.0605
PPI Softdrink	22,469	o.53	0.6042
CPI Softdrink	−96,691	−1.72	0.1047
Advertising 0.00415	1.19	0.2524	
Total RSQ=0.9903. DFE= 16			
Intercept	−10,527,594	−1.33	0.1981
Population	118.7735	3.02	0.0067
CPISoftdrink −74282	−2.20	0.0397	
Total RSQ=0.9879. DFE=20			

Two of the socio-demographic variables used in the analysis were significantly related to CSD consumption. Population was a significant, positive predictor in the final model suggesting that increases in population were associated with increases in consumption of carbonated soft drinks. The Consumer Price Index for soft drinks was also significantly related to consumption, but the relationship was negative indicating that increases in the Consumer Price Index were associated with decreases in per capita soft drink consumption. It is also interesting to note that neither of the population age groups 10–14 or 15–19 exhibited a significant relationship with soft drink consumption. These age groups are felt by critics of soft drink advertising to be targeted by soft drink advertising.

As noted previously in this chapter, Borden (1942a, b) concluded that with expanding markets, advertising may play a role in its more rapid expansion, but results of this analysis indicate that advertising expenditures did not play a significant role in this market expansion. The market for CSD over the period in this study expanded rapidly until 1998 however has been declining since. Perhaps this 10-year declining market is the reason why advertising was not significantly related to aggregate consumption levels (see Exhibit 9.1).

Advertising and Fast Food: An Expanding Market Example

The fast-food industry is a major business sector in the US economy, with an approximate value of $66.2 billion by the end of 2011. It is also an expanding market, since 2006 the fast-food industry as a whole has increased by roughly 20% (Datamonitor, 2009; Hoovers, 2009). Additionally, from the standpoint of international economics, the fast-food sector in the USA represents over 53.8% of the global fast-food market's value (Datamonitor, 2009).

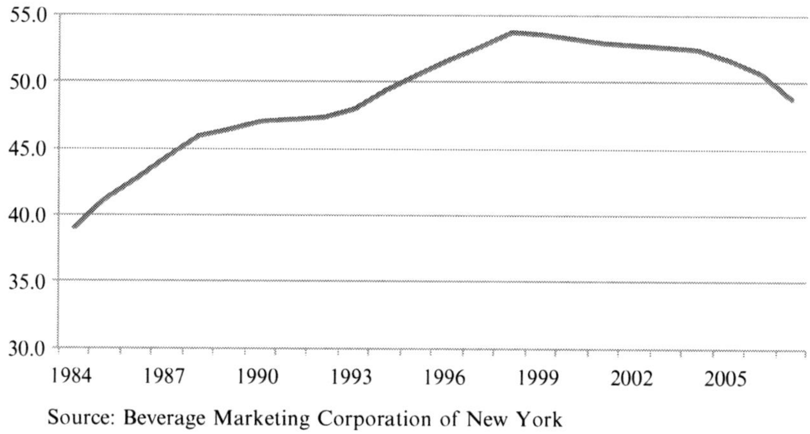

Exhibit 9.1 Soft drink Per capita Consumption in gallons. Source: Beverage Marketing Corporation of New York

The predominant segment within the fast-food industry is the Quick Service Restaurants (QSR) category, which corresponds to over 73% of the entire fast-food industry in the USA (Datamonitor, 2009). QSRs are defined as those restaurants that: (1) primarily sell limited lines of refreshments and prepared food items (typically offering food items such as pizza, barbecued chicken, and hamburgers); (2) have minimal table service; and (3) offer food for consumption either on or near the premises or take-away (Chou, Rashad, & Grossman, 2005).

In terms of national aggregate restaurant sales, QSR firms accounted for over 41% of sales in 2007. Scholars such as Kara, Erdener, and Orsay (1997) have noted that even in recessionary times, the sales of fast-food franchises have grown as high as 11%. Certainly, the QSR market is a lucrative and important market for the national economy, it is also a growing market with aggregate sales estimated at $59.7 billion dollars in 2008 (Datamonitor, 2009).

The study discussed in this chapter examined the relationship between advertising expenditures and sales revenue at the aggregate level for the Quick Service Restaurant (QSR) industry in the USA from 1986 to 2007. The main objective of this study was to provide an analysis of the relationship between advertising expenditures and sales revenues for the category of QSR firms, in the USA during the observed period.

Based on prior empirical research, in order to examine the relationship between advertising expenditures and sales it is important to control for price, inflation and population effects which have been associated with sales revenues (Bass, 1969; Telser, 1962; Franke & Wilcox, 1987). Thus, the database included one QSR consumption variable: annual sales revenues; four advertising variables: aggregate advertising expenditures, electronic advertising expenditures, print advertising expenditures, outdoor advertising expenditures; two socio-economic variables: CPI for Food Away from Home (FAFH), Annual Expenditure on FAFH; and one demographic variable: population size.

Table 9.3 US QSR. Variables and sources time frame (Reported in USD Millions)

Variables	Time period
Advertising Expenditures	1986–2007
Source: Leading National Advertisers (LNA), Inc. deflated using Media Unit Cost Index	
Sales Revenues per capita	1986–2007
Source: Technomic, Inc.	
Socioeconomic Variables	1986–2007
US Population	
Source: US Bureau of Census	
Consumer Price Index—Food Away from Home (FAFH) Annual	
Expenditure for Food Away from Home	
Source: US Bureau of Labor and Statistics (BLS)	

Because no reliable and consistent record of QSR prices exists, the CPI for FAFH was deemed as the best measure of price available. Previous research has also used CPI as a proxy measure for price. For example, in a similar study about cigarette consumption and advertising, Bass (1969, p.293) stated that: "although it might have been desirable to include prices of the filter and non-filter cigarettes as variables, the non-filter price is available as a component of the consumer price index." The CPI for Food Away from Home (FAFH) measures the average price paid for food items purchased away from home by an average US consumer and compares it to the average price paid for the same items in an earlier base year. As the CPI for FAFH is a weighted average of actually paid prices, it captures the price promotional effects within the market (Franses, 1991).

Annual aggregate expenditures from 1986 to 2007 for sales of Food Away From Home (FAFH) were also included in this study. The FAFH variable includes the total sales from eating and drinking places, hotels and motels, retail stores and direct selling, recreational places, schools and colleges, and all others. The rationale of including annual expenditure for FAFH was to examine the relationship between annual expenditures in the FAFH categories and sales revenues of QSR companies over the observed period. To adjust for inflationary changes in FAFH expenditures, the annual expenditures for FAFH were converted to constant dollar scale (Base 1982–1984 = 100). All advertising series were deflated using the McCann-Erickson Media Unit Cost Index to obtain consistent aggregation of expenditures. Table 9.3 provides an overview of the variables, sources, and time periods.

The relationships between advertising expenditures and sales revenues were explored for the overall QSR industry. These regression equations aimed to explicate the macro-level effect and relationship between aggregate QSR advertising expenditures and total QSR sales revenues. Regression analysis was preformed with

Table 9.4 Full/Final consumption—Aggregate advertising model

Predictor	*B* value	*t* ratio	p-level
Intercept	−4,311	−8.76	<0.0001
Aggregate Advertising	1.092E-6	2.51	0.0215
FAFH Annual Expenditures	0.0264	10.99	<0.0001
Total RSQ=0.9953; DFE=19 Durbin-Watson=1.3206			

aggregate advertising expenditures and annual expenditures for FAFH as the independent variables and per capita sales revenues as the dependent variable. The regression model is presented in Table 9.4.

Taking into account significant autocorrelations at one and two years, the study results suggested that aggregate advertising expenditures had a positive and significant relationship with sales revenues for the category of QSR firms ($t=2.51$, $p=0.0215$). Additionally, annual expenditures for FAFH have a positive and significant relationship with sales revenues for the category of QSR firms ($t=10.99$, $p=<0.0001$). This suggests that as the annual expenditures for FAFH categories increased so did the on sales revenues of QSR companies over the observed period.

In addition, the relationship between advertising expenditures by types of media and aggregate sales revenue was also examined. The advertising variables in this study were also analyzed by media outlet type: electronic, print, and outdoor. Results from this set of analysis are shown in Tables 9.5 and 9.6. Taking into account significant autocorrelations at one and two years, outdoor advertising expenditures exhibited a significant positive relationship with per capita sales revenues ($t=2.89$, $p=0.0093$). Similarly, annual expenditures for food away from home (FAFH) showed a significant positive relationship with per capita sales revenues ($t=30.04$, $p=<0.0001$). The models explained over 99% of the variance in the time series.

The major finding of this study was that the relationship between aggregate level advertising and industry wide sales showed a significant and positive relationship in the USA from 1986 to 2007. These results are consistent with studies that report the presence of a positive and significant relationship between advertising expenditures and consumption variables across numerous expanding industries (Borden, 1942a, b; Walsh, 1982; Wilcox, 1991, 2001; McGuinness and Cowling, 1975; Hamilton, 1977; Abernethy & Teel, 1986; Leeflang and Revijl, 1985; Ippolito & Mathios, 1995; Yiannaka, Giannakas, & Tran, 2002; Duffy, 1999).

It is important to note that although aggregate advertising expenditures are significantly related to QSR sales revenues, the coefficient values are small and thus have a minimal impact on sales revenues. As seen in Table 9.3 advertising has a point of estimate of 1.092E-6, which means a 1% increase in advertising of QSR is associated with an increase in the per capita sales revenues of QSR by 1.092E-6 percent. For outdoor advertising, the coefficient values are also small. For example, outdoor advertising has a point of estimate of 0.000218, which means a 1% increase

Table 9.5 Full consumption—Aggregate Advertising by Media type model

Predictor	*B* value	*t* ratio	p-level
Intercept	−4,555	−8.29	<0.0001
Electronic Advertising	4.3941E-7	0.73	0.4781
Print Advertising	5.8451E-6	0.70	0.4905
Outdoor Advertising	0.000111	0.93	0.3632
FAFH Annual Expenditures	0.0277	9.98	<.0001
Total RSQ = 0.9962; DFE = 17 Durbin-Watson = 1.3634			

Table 9.6 Final consumption—Aggregate Advertising by Media type model

Predictor	*B* value	*t* ratio	p-level
Intercept	−4,986	−8.29	<0.0001
Outdoor Advertising	0.000218	2.89	0.0093
FAFH Annual Expenditures	0.0297	30.04	<0.0001
Total RSQ = 0.9957; DFE = 19 Durbin-Watson = 1.3898			

in outdoor advertising of QSR is associated with an increase in the per capita sales revenues of QSR by 0.000218%.

Interestingly, when examined by individual media, the findings revealed some surprising relationships. Neither electronic nor print advertising expenditures were significantly associated with the per capita sales revenues. This is a surprising finding, given that spending for electronic advertising tends to be the highest in the QSR category and that these media are the mostly visible targets of the critics of fast-food advertising. On the other hand, aggregate outdoor advertising expenditures had a positive relationship with sales revenues, suggesting that tactically this medium may play an important role in the QSR category.

It may also be important to consider that billboard and other outdoor advertising do double service—they serve as advertising to remind and influence consumer's brand choice; and may also act like signage, or directions indicating the outlet location. Thus, billboard advertising may be persuasive in its nature but may also be informative because it imparts information to the consumers such as location at the time of purchase.

Figures 9.1 and 9.2 provide a visual understanding of the positive relationship found by the current study. The plots of aggregate advertising from 1986 to 2007 in constant dollar scale (Fig. 9.1) show a positive trend indicating an increase of sales over time. That is, advertising expenditures for the industry have been on the rise for the observed period of time (1986–2007). Similarly, the plot for aggregate sales for the category of QSR firms (Fig. 9.2) also shows an increase in aggregate sales over the past 22 years in the USA.

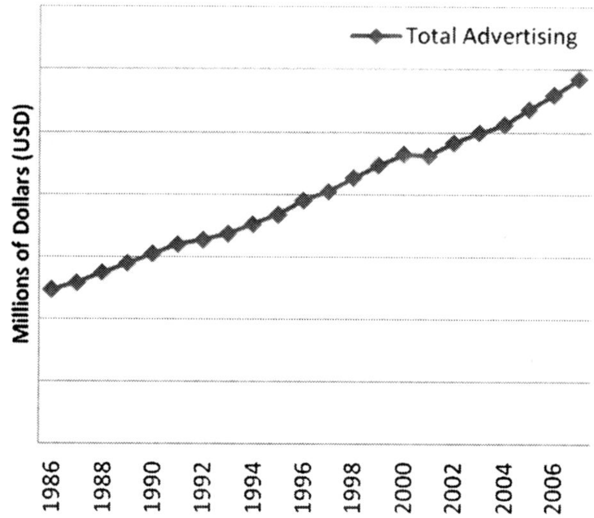

Fig. 9.1 Aggregate Advertising Expenditures for QSR in the USA 1986–2007

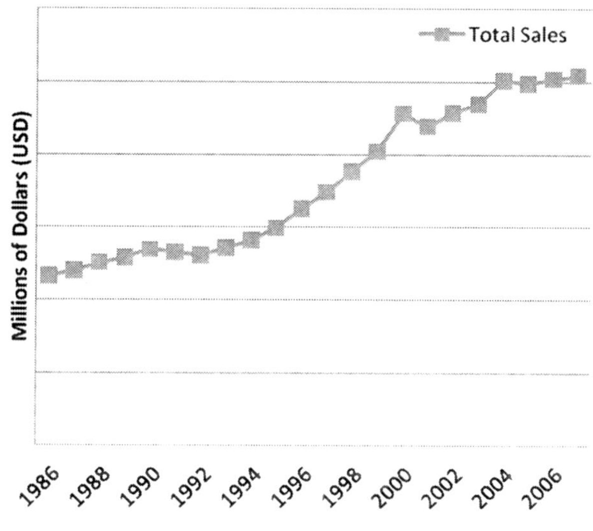

Fig. 9.2 Aggregate Sales for QSR in the USA 1986–2007

The finding that aggregate advertising expenditures were positively related to aggregate sales revenues provides empirical support for Borden's (1942a, b, 1952) classical studies. Specifically, Borden predicted that in industries that are expanding, advertising will have a positive effect on sales. Also, Borden stated that if macro trends (such as population, usage habits, lifestyles, etc.) are supportive of market growth advertising is likely to increase the macro trend.

Advertising's Impact on Kid's/Mom's Attitudes of Popular Food and Beverage Brands

Because of growing concerns regarding the effects of this food and beverage advertising on children and parents as can be noted previously as well as in other chapters in this book, this final study examined the relationship between advertising expenditures and children/mother's perceptions of popular brands in the USA.

In less than 30 years, the prevalence of overweight children and adolescents in the USA has more than doubled. In the 1963–1970 period, 4% of children aged 6–11 years and 5% of adolescents aged 12–19 were defined as being overweight. The percentage of children who are overweight had more than tripled by 1999, reaching 13%. For adolescents, the incidence of being overweight has nearly tripled in the same period, reaching 14% (Centers for Disease Control and Prevention, 2001). The increased availability of highly palatable and convenience foods has been thought to contribute to rising rates of childhood obesity.

According to the Federal Trade Commission report (2008), overall expenditures promoting food and beverages to children and adolescents in the USA were more than $1.6 billion annually by the 44 reporting companies. The companies spent $870 million on food marketing directed toward children under 12 and over $1 billion to adolescents, aged 12–17, with about $300 million of these expenditures addressed to both age groups.

Carbonated beverages, fast food, and breakfast cereals accounted for 63% of the total food and beverages marketing expenditure. In terms of promotional strategies, 46% of the $1.6 billion was spent on television advertising, 7% accounted for other traditional measured media such as radio and print advertising, and new media—company websites, Internet, word-of-mouth, and viral—represented 5%. Since marketing communication of fast food and beverages, many of which are fatty and of low nutritional value, is often identified as an influencing factor of children's weight and obesity, it is critical to analyze the degree to which such advertising can influence children, and especially when it has the potential to have a negative impact from a public health perspective.

It has been argued that young children may not recall advertisements due to their limited memory capacity; therefore, they will be relatively immune to an advertiser's message (Macklin, 1994). Other critics of food and beverage advertising argue that young children experience difficulty when they interpret and understand a persuasive message in advertisements because of their undeveloped cognitive mechanism.

Pine and Nash (2002) examined whether children are influenced by the sales messages of advertisers via television. Children ages 4–7 were divided into two groups, English children with considerable access to television and Swedish children with legal protection from advertising on television. Considering a Christmas wish list, English children referenced specific brand name products, which are marketed under a proprietary trademark or registered names, such as Barbie doll, as opposed to generic terms, while Swedish counterparts requested "significantly fewer items" and "more generalized products."

These findings imply that advertising to children may be more effective at creating brand awareness and recognition as opposed to producing desire for advertised items themselves. This study also highlighted that children in this age group are likely to have higher trust, lower recall, and lower understanding of commercial messages than older children, and that would lead us to expect these children to have a higher vulnerability to advertising, although perhaps with a lower recall of brand names.

If the degree of recall and preference differ by brands, advertisers may feel they need to concentrate on influencing one or the other. Even though high recall and high preference and low recall and low preference tended to be associated, there were some similarities and differences in the results for these two factors.

The research presented here examined the relationship between advertising expenditures, product placement, and children's and mother's perception of popular food and beverage brands in the USA The findings provide further insight into the controversial relationship between advertising's and children's brand perceptions for these products.

The analysis focused on the correlation between advertising expenditures and the most popular food and beverage brands of children and mothers to determine the importance that advertising might have on how children and mothers rank the brands in terms of what could be call "likeability." A marketing research firm, *Smarty Pants*, conducts an annual online survey of brand "likeability" by children and mothers, which includes a wide variety of brands, not just food and beverage brands.

This study presented an analysis of the results of the *Smarty Pants* survey for 2009 and 2010. The survey polled a representative sample of 4,500 US families with children aged 6–12. The study evaluated more than 270 consumer brands in 20 categories, resulting in the "Top 100 Kids' Most Loved Brands" list (see Exhibits 9.2 and 9.3). In addition to these "most loved" brands, annual advertising expenditures and product/brand placement data for these brands were used as independent variables in the regression analysis.

This research found that magazine advertising exhibited a positive and significant relationship with brand affinity scores to kids and moms while other advertising, such as electronic advertising and other print advertising, had either a negative or insignificant relationship with brand affinity scores (see Tables 9.7 and 9.8). Furthermore, this research also examined the correlation between exposure times through product/brand placement and brand affinity scores, and the results were very similar to advertising expenditure analysis. Product placement did not present any positive and significant relationship with brand affinity scores of either kids or moms (see Tables 9.7 and 9.8).

After the statistical analysis was completed, the data were examined from a qualitative perspective. Specifically, a visual comparison of the combined (2009 and 2010) Top 5 rated brands and media expenditures from both the Kids' and the Moms' Brand Affinity scores was preformed. Results from this analysis revealed that only two of the brands appeared on both lists—Oreo and M&Ms. The top rated brand for the Kids' Most Loved Beverage and Food Brands was McDonald's with

Ranking	Brand	2009 Score	2010 Score
1	Air Heads	776	785
2	BurgerKing	831	771
3	CapriSun	821	848
4	Cheetos	849	844
5	Chipsahoy	835	856
6	Chuck E. Cheese	794	783
7	Cinnamon Toast Crunch	748	765
8	Coca-Cola	790	787
9	Doritos	860	871
10	Drumstick	810	796
11	Easy Mac	767	782
12	Eggo	801	803
13	Froot Loops	765	795
14	Frosted Flakes	742	751
15	Fruitbyfoot	814	769
16	Fruitrollups	809	831
17	Go-GURT	771	776
18	Goldfish	789	833
19	Hubba Bubba	777	758
20	KFC	753	766
21	Koolaid	805	832
22	Kraftmac/cheese	857	828
23	Lucky Charms	759	758
24	Lunchables	824	801
25	M&Ms	875	884
26	McDonald's	880	898
27	Minute Maid	758	756
28	Nerds	780	791
29	Oreo	887	877
30	Pepsi	798	766
31	Pizza hut	834	820
32	Pop-Tarts	799	822
33	Popsicle	846	870
34	Pringles	821	845
35	Reese's	839	852
36	Ring Pop	795	780
37	Skittles	828	835
38	Snickers	772	794
39	Sour Patch	752	749
40	Sprite	774	779
41	Starburst	829	823
42	Subway	789	789
43	SunnyD	760	769
44	SweeTarts	737	783
45	Toaster Strudel	739	737
46	Totino's	726	764
47	Trix	752	744
48	Tropicana	763	739
49	Twix	798	814
50	Wendy's	765	806

Exhibit 9.2 Food & Beverage in Kids' Top 100 Most Loved Brands

	Brand	2009 Score	2010 Score
1	CapriSun	833	827
2	Cheetos	849	825
3	Cinnamon Toast Crunch	777	767
4	Coca-Cola	794	805
5	Doritos	844	870
6	Drumstick	849	843
7	Easy Mac	780	775
8	Eggo	837	819
9	Froot Loops	782	795
10	Frosted Flakes	807	797
11	Fruitrollups	784	812
12	Go-GURT	763	781
13	Goldfish	853	869
14	KFC	773	786
15	Kraftmac/cheese	841	850
16	M&M	893	894
17	McDonalds	796	796
18	Minute Maid	844	854
19	Oreo	860	860
20	Pepsi	777	786
21	Pizza hut	837	794
22	Popsicle	809	861
23	Pringles	845	819
24	Reeses	873	860
25	Skittles	809	811
26	Snickers	818	799
27	Sprite	794	790
28	Starburst	823	833
29	Subway	852	873
30	Totino's	763	782
31	Tropicana	851	819
32	Twix	846	847
33	Wendy's	800	789

Exhibit 9.3 Food & Beverage in Moms' Top 100 Most Loved Brands

media expenditures over five times higher than the third ranked brand—M&Ms. For the Mothers, however, the top rated brand was M&Ms, whose media expenditures were less than half of the third ranked brand—Subway.

When media expenditures were examined by medium, interestingly all of the brands were heavy users of electronic media with the percentages ranging from a low of 57% for Oreo to 99% for Doritos. McDonald's by comparison spent slightly over 90% of their expenditures in the electronic media. From this final visual examination of total advertising expenditures and individual media, it is clear that the advertising media expenditures by individual media were not important factors in determining the Brand Affinity scores for either the children or mothers.

Table 9.7 Average Advertising Expenditure and Average Kid's Brand Affinity Scores for 2009 and 2010

Predictor	*B* Value	t-ratio	Probability
Intercept	784.9	133.12	<2e-16*
Electronic Advertising	3.23e-05	0.53	0.60
Other Print Advertising	−6.27e-03	−0.79	0.43
Magazines	2.53e-03	3.92	3.01e-04*
Product Placement (PPL)	6.51e-04	0.54	0.60

(R^2=0.31, df=46)

Table 9.8 Average Advertising Expenditure and Average Mom's Brand Affinity Scores for 2009 and 2010

Predictor	*B* Value	t-ratio	Probability
Intercept	814.10	119.79	<2e-16*
Electronic Advertising	−9.25e-05	−1.56	0.13
Other Print Advertising	1.52e-03	0.21	0.84
Magazines	1.88e-03	2.89	0.01*
Product Placement (PPL)	−4.45e-04	−0.40	0.69

(R^2=0.24, df=28)

Discussion and Implications

The primary purpose of this chapter was to present information on relationships of advertising and consumption of soft drinks and fast foods in the USA Two studies were discussed that examined this relationship using over 20 years of longitudinal data. These analyses were important because they illustrate from a macro perspective the varying role advertising has in the promotion of products and services. From a theoretical perspective, the advertising relationships for soft drinks and fast food produced consistent findings—in declining or mature markets, advertising exhibited little or no impact on aggregate consumption while in expanding markets advertising was shown to positively impact the expansion. Additional evidence is provided of advertising's minimal role on the formation of attitudes of popular brands of food and beverages for both kids and moms.

When examined from this perspective, it appears that the criticisms leveled at advertising's role in the promotion of soft drinks and fast foods are unwarranted. For both of these industries, advertising has become an important element in the marketing mix. As the most visible element in the promotion of these types of products it is also the most convenient target for critics.

Further research is needed to provide a more in depth understanding of the relationship of advertising/promotion to consumption of soft drinks and fast food.

Specifically, it would be important to examine the relationship of brand advertising on brand consumption or market share. Other more social science approaches could provide insight into the role CSD and fast-food advertising and promotion are hypothesized to have on youth and obesity.

While it was the purpose of this study to offer as much insight as possible, other types of promotion methods employed such as toys, cartoons, movies, contests, etc. were not captured by the advertising expenditure data used in these analyses. To the best of the authors' knowledge, information on these types of marketing expenditures were not available for the period examined. It may be that other types of promotional methods may have contributed to increases in CSD and fast-food consumption.

One of the purposes of this study was to provide policy recommendations for an effective control of the obesity problem that our nation faces. Although the direct link between childhood obesity and CSD/fast-food consumption is hotly debated both in academia and industry, consumption of CSD/fast food in large quantities may not be beneficial to anyone in the long run. However tempting, the proposed restrictions or regulations on CSD/fast-food advertising cannot be justified based on the results of these studies. While criticism of CSD/fast-food advertising and promotional methods abound, implementation of remedies that would restrict or regulate such activities may not have the desired effect of reducing consumption.

As noted above, this study only examined advertising expenditure levels. The creative appeals used by the advertisers play a critical role by interacting with expenditure levels to result in effective advertising. There was no attempt here to measure such interaction effects. Furthermore, advertising expenditures used in our model do not include promotions such as incentives in the distribution channel and trade discounts.

It is also important to note that the relationships detected in these studies are correlational, not necessarily causal. Other factors not included in the analysis such as changing attitudes toward soft drink or fast-food consumption or personal preferences for other shifts in product category choice may no doubt have had an impact on consumption of these products. It may be, in many cases, that product consumption drives advertising expenditures.

Another area of research is to investigate the motivations why individuals consume fast food and soft drinks. Advertising may be a reason why people choose a particular brand but it appears unlikely that it is the reason why they choose to consume the product in the first place or to over indulge. There may be other reasons such as eating habits and economics that are important predictors of this behavior. Soda consumption and fast food are inexpensive and maybe the only viable option for many low income and economically disadvantaged populations. This rings particularly true given that the obesity problem facing our nation is higher for low income and minority groups. In such circumstances, it may not be advertising that is to blame and banning or restricting it may not do much to address this issue.

References

Abernethy, A. M., & Teel, J. E. (1986). Advertising regulation's effect upon demand for cigarettes. *Journal of Advertising, 15*(4), 51–55.

Albion, M. S., & Farris, P. W. (1981). *The advertising controversy: evidence on the economic effects of advertising*. Boston, MA: Auburn House Publishing Company.

Baltagi, B. H., & Levin, D. (1986). Estimating demand for cigarettes using panel data: the effects of bootlegging, taxation and advertising reconsidered. *The Review of Economics and Statistics, 68*(1), 148–155.

Baltagi, B. H., & Levin, D. (1992). Cigarette taxation: Raising revenues and reducing consumption. *Structural Change and Economic Dynamics, 3*(2), 321–335.

Bass, F. M. (1969). A simultaneous equation regression study of advertising and sales of cigarettes. *Journal of Marketing Research, 6*(3), 291–300.

Batra, R., Meyers, J., & Aaker, D. (1995). *Advertising management* (5th ed.). Upper Saddle River, NJ: Prentice Hall.

Bishop, J. A., & Yoo, J. H. (1985). Health scare, excise taxes and advertising ban in the cigarette demand and supply. *Southern Economic Journal, 52*, 402–411.

Blake, D., & Nied, A. (1997). The demand for alcohol in the United Kingdom. *Applied Economics, 29*, 1655–1672.

Borden, N. H. (1952). *Economic effects of advertising*. Homewood, IL: Richard D. Irwin.

Borden, N. H. (1942a). *The economic effects of advertising*. Chicago, IL: Richard Irwin, Inc.

Borden, N. H. (1942b, April). Findings of the Harvard study on the economic effects of advertising. *Journal of Marketing, 6*(4), Part 2, 89–99.

Borzekowski, B., & Robinson, T. (2001). The 30-second effect: an experiment revealing the impact of television commercials on food preferences of preschoolers. *Journal of American Diet Association, 101*(1), 42–46.

Centers for Disease Control and Prevention. (2001). Overweight Among U.S. Children and Adolescents, National Center for Health Statistics.

Chamberlin, E. (1933). *The theory of monopolistic competition*. Cambridge, MA: Harvard University Press.

Chester, J., & Montgomery, K. (2009). Interactive food and beverage marketing: Targeting children and youth in the digital age. Berkeley, CA: Berkeley Media Studios Group. http://digitalads.org/documents/digiMarketingFull.pdf.. Accessed 5 Aug 2009.

Chetwynd, J., Coope, P., Brodie, R. J., & Wells, E. (1988). Impact of cigarette advertising on aggregate demand for cigarettes in New Zealand. *British Journal of Addiction, 83*, 409–414.

Collins, K. (2004). The soft drink explosion among kids. October 1, 2004. http://www.msnbc.msn.com/id/6142711/ns/health-diet_and_nutrition/t/soft-drink-explosion-among-kids/#.ToCccU9pi6V.

Chou, S., Rashad, I., & Grossman, M. (2005) *Fast-food restaurant advertising on television and its influence on childhood obesity*. NBER Working Paper No. W11879. Available at SSRN http://ssrn.com/abstract=875730.

Datamonitor. (2009). Fast food in the United States, Industry Report. Retrieved April 6, 2009, from Business Monitor International (BMI) database.

Duffy, M. (1991). Advertising and the consumption of tobacco and alcoholic drink: A system-wide analysis. *Scottish Journal of Political Economy, 38*(4), 369–385.

Duffy, M. (1995). Advertising in demand systems for alcoholic drinks and tobacco: A comparative study. *Journal of Policy Modeling, 17*(6), 557–577.

Duffy, M. (1996). An econometric study of advertising and cigarette demand in the United Kingdom. *International Journal of Advertising, 15*(3), 262–284.

Duffy, M. (1999). The influence of advertising on the pattern of food consumption in the UK. *International Journal of Advertising, 18*(2).

Fisher, J. C., & Cook, P. A. (1995). *Advertising, alcohol consumption, and mortality: An empirical investigation*. Westport, CT: Greenwood Press.

Food CPI, Prices, and Expenditures: Expenditure Tables. Economic Research Service. Retrieved online on September 30, 2008, from http://www.ers.usda.gov/briefing/CPIFoodAndExpenditures.

Franke, G. R., & Wilcox, G. B. (1987). Alcoholic beverage advertising and consumption in the United States 1964–1984. *Journal of Advertising, 16*, 22–30.

Franke, G. R. (1994). U.S. cigarette demand, 1961–1990: Econometric issues, evidence, and implications. *Journal of Business Research, 30*(1), 33–41.

Franses, P. H. (1991). Primary demand for beer in the Netherlands: An application of ARMAX model. *Journal of Marketing Research, 28*(2), 240–245.

Fujii, E. T. (1980). The demand for cigarettes: Further empirical evidence and its implications for public policy. *Applied Economics, 12*, 479–489.

Gallet, C. A. (1999). The effects of the 1971 advertising ban on behavior in the cigarette industry. *Managerial and Decision Economics, 20*, 299–303.

Gius, M. P. (1996). Using panel data to determine the effect of advertising on brand-level distilled spirits sales. *Journal of Studies on Alcohol, 57*, 73–76.

Godfrey, C. (1986). *Price and advertising elasticities of demand for tobacco*. Working paper, ESRC Addiction Research Centre, University of York.

Goel, R. K., & Morey, M. J. (1995). The interdependence of cigarette and liquor demand. *Southern Economic Journal, 62*, 451–459.

Grabowski, H. G. (1976). The effect of advertising on the inter-industry distribution of demand. *Explorations in Economic Research, 3*, 21–75.

Grimm, G. C., Harnack, L., & Story, M. (2004). Factors associated with soft drink consumption is school-aged children. *Journal of the American Dietetic Association, 104*(8), 1244–1249.

Hamilton, J. L. (1977). *The effect of cigarette advertising bans on cigarette consumption*. Proceedings of the 3rd World Conference on Smoking and Health (pp. 829–840). Washington, DC: U.S. Department of Health, Education and Welfare.

Harrison, J. (2009). New study levels new criticisms at food industry, University communications, December 13, 2009, from http://uanews.org/node/29055.

Harrison, R., Chetwynd, J., & Brodie, R. J. (1989). The influence of advertising on tobacco consumption. *British Journal of Addiction, 84*, 1241–1246.

Hitchings, E., & Moynihan, J. (1998). The relationship between television food advertisements recalled and actual foods consumed by children. *Journal of Human Nutrition and Dietetics, 11*, 511–517.

Hoffman, V. H. J. (1987). The effect of advertising on cigarette consumption in the Federal Republic of Germany. *Jahrbucher fur Nationalokonomie und Statistik, 203*, 257–273.

Holt, D. B. (2002). Do brands cause trouble? A dialectical theory of consumer culture and branding. *Journal of Consumer Research, 29*, 70–90.

Hoovers. (2009). Fast-food & quick-service restaurants industry overview. Retrieved online at http://industries.hoovers.com/leisure/restaurants-and-cafes/fast-food-and-quick-service-restaurants.

Ippolito, P. M., Mathios, A. D. (1995, May). *Information and advertising: The case of fat consumption in the United States, The American Economic Review, Vol. 85, No. 2*. Papers and Proceedings of the Hundredth and Seventh Annual Meeting of the American Economic Association, Washington, DC, January 6–8, 1995, pp. 91–95.

Jhally, S. (1987). *The codes of advertising: Fetishism and the political economy of meaning in the consumer society*. New York, NY: St. Martin Press, Inc.

Johnson, L. W. (1986). Advertising expenditure and the aggregate demand for cigarettes in Australia. *International Journal of Advertising, 1*, 45–58.

Johnson, J. A., & Oksanen, E. H. (1974). Socio- economic determinants of the consumption of alcoholic beverages. *Applied Economics, 6*, 293–301.

Kao, K., & Tremblay, V. J. (1988). Cigarette "health scare", excise tax and advertising ban: Comment. *Southern Economic Journal, 54*, 770–776.

Kara, A., Erdener, K., & Orsay, K. (1997). Marketing strategies for fast-food restaurants: A customer view. *International Journal of Contemporary Hospitality Management, 7*(4), 16–22.

Lears, J. (1994). *Fables of abundance: A cultural history of advertising in America*. New York: Basic Books.

Leeflang, P. S. H., & Reuijl, J. C. (1985). Advertising and industry sales: An empirical study of the West German cigarette market. *The Journal of Marketing, 49*, 92–98.

Levy, S. J. (1963). Symbolism and life style. In D. W. Rook (Ed.), *Brands, consumers, symbols, & research*. Beverly Hills, CA: Sage.

Macklin, C. (1994). The effects of an advertising retrieval cue on young children's memory and brand evaluations. *Psychology and Marketing, 11*(3), 291–311.

Marshall, A. (1890). *Principles of economics*. London: MacMillan and Co.

Marshall, A. (1919). *Industry and trade: A study of industrial technique and business organization; and of their influences on the conditions of various classes and nations*. London: MacMillan and Co.

McAuliffe, R. (1988). The FTC and the effectiveness of cigarette advertising regulations. *Journal of Public Policy and Marketing, 7*, 49–64.

McCracken, G. D. (1988). *Culture and consumption*. Bloomingdale and Indianapolis: Indiana University Press.

McGuinness, T., & Cowling, K. (1975). Advertising and the aggregate demand for cigarettes. *European Economic Review, 6*, 311–328.

Media Economy Newsletter (2008, May 29). Issue eight hundred-ninety-eight.

Nelson, J. P., & Moran, J. R. (1995). Advertising and US alcoholic beverage demand system-wide estimates. *Applied Economics, 27*, 1225–1236.

Nguyen, D. (1987). Advertising, random sales response, and brand competition: Some theoretical and econometric implications. *Journal of Business, 60*, 259–279.

Oren, R., Dodson, H. (2010). *Fast food restaurants dish up unhealthy marketing to youth*. Researchers Release Unprecedented Report on Fast Food Nutrition and Marketing. November 8, 2010, http://opac.yale.edu/news/article.aspx?id=7981.

Packard, V. (1957). *The hidden persuaders*. London: Penguin.

Pine, J. K., & Nash, A. (2002). Dear Santa: The effects of television advertising on young children. *International Journal of Behavioral Development, 26*(6), 529–539.

Pollay, R. A., Siddarth, S., & Siegel, M. (1996). The last straw? Cigarette advertising and realized market shares among youth and adults, 1979–1993. *Journal of Marketing, 60*, 1–16.

Porter, R. H. (1986). The impact of government policy on the United States cigarette industry. In P. M. Ippolito & D. T. Scheffman (Eds.), *Empirical approaches to consumer protection economics*. Washington, DC: United States Government Printing Office.

Radfar, M. (1985). The effect of advertising on total consumption of cigarettes in the UK: A comment. *European Economic Review, 29*, 225–231.

Schneider, L., Klein, B., & Murphy, K. (1981). Government regulation of cigarette health information. *Journal of Law and Economics, 24*, 575–612.

Selvanathan, E. A. (1991). Cross-country alcohol consumption comparison: An application of the Rotterdam demand system. *Applied Economics, 23*, 1613–1622.

Sheldon, B. J., & Doroodian, K. (1989). A simultaneous model of cigarette advertising: Effects on demand and industry response to public policy. *Review of Economics and Statistics, 71*, 673–677.

Smee, C. (1992). *Effects of tobacco advertising on tobacco sponsorship: A discussion document reviewing the Evidence*. London: Economics and Operational Research Division, Department of Health.

Tegene, A. (1991). Kalman filter and the demand for cigarettes. *Applied Economics, 23*, 1175–1182.

Telser, L. (1962). Advertising and cigarettes. *Journal of Political Economy, 70*, 471–499.

Tremblay, C. H., & Tremblay, V. J. (1995). The impact of cigarette advertising on consumer surplus, profit, and social welfare. *Contemporary Economic Policy, 13*, 113–124.

Valdes, B. (1993). Cigarette consumption in Spain: Empirical evidence and implications for public policy. *Applied Economics, 20*, 149–156.

Walsh, B. (1982). The demand for alcohol in the UK: A comment. *The Journal of Industrial Economics, 30*(4), 439–446.

Wilcox, G. B. (1991). Cigarette brand advertising and consumption in the United States, 1949–1985. *Journal of Advertising Research, 31*, 61–67.

Wilcox, G. B., & Gangadharbatla, H. (2006). What's changed? Does beer advertising affect consumption in the United States? *International Journal of Advertising, 25*(1), 35–50.

Wilcox, G. B., & Vacker, B. (1992). Cigarette advertising and consumption in the United States, 1961–1990. *International Journal of Advertising, 11*(3), 269–78.

Wilcox, G. B., Gangadharbatla, H., & Kamal, S. (2009). Soft drink advertising and consumption in the United States: 1984–2007. *International Journal of Advertising, 28*(2).

Wilcox, G. B. (2001). Beer brand advertising and market share in the United States: 1975 to 1998. *International Journal of Advertising, 20*(2), 149–168.

Witt, S. F., & Pass, C. L. (1981). The effects of health warnings and advertising on the demand for cigarettes. *Scottish Journal of Political Economy, 28*(1), 86–91.

Yiannaka, A., Giannakas, K., & Tran, K. C. (2002). Medium, message, and advertising effectiveness in the Greek processed meats industry. *Applied Economics, 14*, 1757–1763.

Young, T. (1983). The demand for cigarettes: Alternative specifications of Fujii's model. *Applied Economics, 15*, 203–211.

Yuclet, U., & Kaynak, E. (1984). A study of measuring influence of advertising and forecasting cigarette sales. *Managerial and Decision Economics, 5*, 213–218.

Chapter 10
The Digital Food Marketing Landscape: Challenges for Researchers

Kathryn C. Montgomery, Sonya A. Grier, Jeff Chester, and Lori Dorfman

In 2008, when Frito-Lay's Doritos brand wanted to re-launch two older flavors that had been discontinued in the 1980s, the company created a digital marketing campaign called "Hotel 626." Part of a Halloween promotion to bring the defunct chips "back from the dead," the campaign was aimed squarely at teenagers, using a variety of under-the-radar techniques to entice them to "check in" to the online hotel (which was only open from 6 p.m. to 6 a.m.). By entering their names and email addresses, teens were immediately immersed in a nightmarish movie, from which they could escape only through a series of unpleasant challenges that asked them to use their webcams, microphones, and mobile phones. Live Twitter feeds enabled users to share their experiences in real time, and they were encouraged to post and share photos of themselves as they participated. A custom Facebook app prompted teens to "send a scare" to friends in their social networks. With a budget of less than $1 million, the Hotel 626 campaign had a significant impact—even though the site

K.C. Montgomery, Ph.D. (✉)
School of Communication, American University,
4400 Massachusetts Ave, NW Washington DC 20016
e-mail: kcm@american.edu

S.A. Grier, MBA, Ph.D.
Department of Marketing, Kogod School of Business,
American University, 4400 Massachusetts Ave,
NW Washington DC 20016
e-mail: sonya.grier@american.edu

J. Chester, MSW
Center for Digital Democracy, 1621 Connecticut Ave,
NW Washington, DC 20089
e-mail: jeff@democraticmedia.org

L. Dorfman, DrPH
Berkeley Media Studies Group, 2130 center st. #302
Berkeley, CA 94704
e-mail: dorfman@bmsg.org

J.D. Williams et al. (eds.), *Advances in Communication Research to Reduce Childhood Obesity*, DOI 10.1007/978-1-4614-5511-0_10,

never mentioned the name of the product itself. By the following spring, more than four million people in 136 countries had visited the site and played the game, with an average stay of 13 minutes. The re-launched flavors sold out, selling two million bags in just 3 weeks, and Hotel 626 was awarded the Cyber Lion at the 2009 Cannes Advertising awards—perhaps the most prestigious prize in marketing (Hotel626.com, 2010; Inspiration Room, 2009). The campaign was so successful that it spawned an even more elaborate and terrifying sequel the following year, called "Asylum 626" (Diaz, 2009).

Frito-Lay's two 626 campaigns are typical of digital food marketing in the twenty-first century, featuring immersive, engaging, interactive environments, in which the traditional hard sell gives way to more subtle forms of community building, with social media at the center of that process. Not surprisingly, young people are a favored target, as they represent an especially lucrative market for advertisers. According to an August 2010 meeting of the Advertising Research Foundation, "Kids Purchasing Influence" was $700 billion in 2009, up from $50 billion in 2000 (Chester & Montgomery, 2007). Along with other youth marketers, the food and beverage industries are investing large sums of money in research examining the ways that digital media have become so integrated into the social relationships, behaviors, and buying habits of children and teenagers (Microsoft Advertising & Carat, 2010).

The health implications of this advertising juggernaut are grave. Over the past four decades, the level of obesity among US adolescents has grown at an alarming rate, quadrupling from 4.5% in the mid-sixties to 17.6% by 2006. Today, one of every three teens is either overweight or obese. Rates are significantly higher for African-American and Hispanic adolescents than for white adolescents (Grier, 2009). Food marketing—particularly for "high-calorie, low-nutrient" products—is a key environmental factor, and a major "default" affecting adolescent health. The teen years are a critical developmental period, during which long-term consumer habits and eating behaviors are established and reinforced (Brownell, Schwartz, Puhl, Henderson, & Harris, 2009; Story, Sallis, & Orleans, 2009).

Digital food marketing is advancing rapidly, and is poised to reach a crucial tipping point in the very near future, as expenditures for Internet and mobile advertising continue to rise. Major food and beverage companies are investing heavily in global research and development strategies to enhance their ability to promote brands through interactive media—with particular focus on social media, online video, mobile and location marketing. Yet despite this rapid growth in the digital marketplace, academic research concerned with the impact of food marketing on children and adolescents has failed to stay abreast of these developments, or to grasp fully the nature and scope of the impact of such marketing on young people's behaviors.

The ongoing transformation of food and beverage marketing poses serious threats to the health and wellbeing of young people, and requires both new thinking and comprehensive agendas for policy intervention and research. This chapter presents a conceptual framework for understanding how digital marketing differs from more conventional forms of advertising and marketing. We identify the challenges such marketing raises for researchers, and offer an agenda for future studies that can support evidence-based policymaking. In addition to highlighting the new metrics that industry has developed to measure the effectiveness of interactive food advertising, we also call attention to the most problematic marketing practices that threaten to cross the boundary between commercial messaging and consumer manipulation.

In the course of carrying out this research, we relied on several different sources, including (1) ongoing analysis of trends and contemporary practices in the digital marketing industry, including reports, trade publications, academic articles, and other materials, with a particular focus on the food and beverage sector; (2) in-depth investigation of marketing campaigns by several major corporations in the food and beverage industry; and (3) review of relevant scientific literature regarding marketing impact, child and adolescent development, racial and ethnic minorities, and health.

The Research Gap

Compared to the available research on children, relatively few studies have examined adolescent exposure to food advertising (Brownell et al., 2009; Story et al., 2009). One reason for this gap is that the framework for US children's advertising regulation, established during the 1970s, applies only to children who are under the age of 12 or 13 (depending upon the particular regulation) (Kunkel, 1990, 2001, 2006; Montgomery, 2008). This tradition has continued in the present policy debate over food marketing and childhood obesity. The recent marketing guidelines developed by food and beverage companies remain focused on younger children, as the advertising industry's self-regulatory guidelines do (Chester & Montgomery, 2007; Children's Advertising Review Unit, 2006). (These self-regulatory programs are discussed in detail in Chap. 6.) As a consequence, adolescents have been understudied by scholars and largely ignored by policy makers in both government and self-regulatory arenas.

This research gap is further widened by a dearth of academic studies of contemporary digital food marketing, especially regarding teens (Kunkel & Castonguay, 2012). Today's adolescents are growing up at the center of an exploding digital media culture (Montgomery, 2007, pp. 107–139). According to the Pew Internet & American Life Project, "93% of teens use the Internet, and more of them than ever are treating it as a venue for social interaction" (Lenhart, Madden, & Macgill, 2007; Pew Research Center, 2010). Seventy-three percent of online youth between the ages of 12 and 17 use social networking sites (Lenhart, Purcell, Smith, & Zickuhr, 2010; Williamson, 2008). Mobile phone ownership among 8- to 18-year-olds has soared during the past 5 years, from 39% to 66% (Kaiser Family Foundation, 2010). Adolescents, because of their role as "early adopters" of new media practices and their steadily rising spending power, are prime targets for interactive marketing. A 2008 survey found that 58% of youth between the ages of 13 and 17 have made a purchase online, spending an average of $46 per month, with more than a quarter of teens spending $50 or more (OTX, 2008).

A large infrastructure of ad agencies, market research firms, and trend analysis companies has been studying how teens incorporate digital media into their daily lives, and developing marketing strategies tailored to key psychosocial needs of adolescence (Montgomery & Chester, 2009). Digital marketing is increasingly regarded as one of the most cost-effective ways to reach and engage young people. The major food and beverage brands are employing a panoply of digital marketing practices to target teenagers across a variety of platforms—social networks, videogames, mobile services, online videos, instant messaging, and even virtual worlds (Chester & Montgomery, 2007; Montgomery & Chester).

Six Unique Concepts Define a Framework for Digital Marketing

Intensive digital marketing campaigns for fast food, snacks, and sweetened beverages feature an integrated set of digital practices designed to engage children and youth, regardless of time or location. We have identified six defining concepts that constitute unique features of digital media and marketing.

Ubiquitous Connectivity. Children and teens now move seamlessly, and often simultaneously, across a spectrum of platforms—from laptops to desktop computers to cell phones to televisions (Rideout, Foehr, & Roberts, 2010). The "360-degree strategy" is one of the core principles of contemporary marketing, aimed at reaching viewers and users repeatedly at multiple "touchpoints" on various platforms (Tsirulnik, 2010). Such campaigns can be highly complex, combining mobile, online video, interactive television, and social networks, and creating a powerful multiplier effect by spreading messages extensively throughout and among social groups (Chester & Montgomery, 2007, 2008). Major media companies are now offering cross-platform marketing opportunities where, in a single buy, advertisers can target customers across a company's media properties, online and off.

One of the most significant developments is the growth of mobile marketing, viewed by industry observers as "the next great advertising medium," given mobile's near-ubiquitous status among consumers (Interactive Advertising Bureau, 2008). Mobile and location marketing are quickly reshaping the entire advertising landscape, offering new means of pinpoint ad targeting (Hansen, 2010; Vdopia, n.d.). New interactive, "call-to-action" formats foster instantaneous results, such as the delivery of a mobile coupon through text messaging, scanning a barcode, or clicking on a banner ad (Apsalar, 2011; Mobile Marketing Association, 2011).

Coca-Cola, Pepsi, McDonald's, Kellogg's, Burger King and other food and beverage companies are playing a leading role in both the mobile and location marketing arenas (Interactive Food & Beverage Marketing, n.d.). For example, the location-based game MyTown, which gives points for checking in at stores, reported that quick-service restaurant chains (including Subway, McDonald's, Burger King, Taco Bell, Pizza Hut, Domino's, and Wendy's) made up eight of the top ten places favored by its users (Patel, 2010). McDonald's also reported a 33% jump in traffic in the spring of 2010 and generated additional press when it piloted an event using

Foursquare, the loyalty-based program that relies on mobile use and rewards consumers as they "check-in" at a restaurant or retail store. Extending the reach of mobile campaigns still further, many of these applications tie together one's friends through a variety of social media techniques (Keane, 2010).

Engagement. In the world of digital marketing, "engagement" is a widely invoked concept and one of the fundamental goals of today's contemporary campaigns. It is related to other, more traditional marketing concepts, such as "involvement" and "experiential marketing," which capture consumers' interest in and interaction with a brand. For the past several years, the Advertising Research Foundation (ARF) has conducted research and consulted with various advertisers, agencies, media companies, and research firms to clarify definitions and develop measurement approaches. Rather than simply exposing consumers to a particular marketing message, product, or service, one of the key goals of engagement is to create an environment in which consumers actually interact with a brand, befriending the product and integrating it into their personal and social relationships. While the definitions vary considerably, there are a number of key themes that are useful for understanding what marketers mean by engagement. These include, for example, the length of time one spends involved with an advertisement, the amount of interaction, and whether or not a consumer takes a specific action regarding the brand (Advertising Research Foundation, 2006).

Thus McDonald's "strategic guiding principle" for its Avatar campaign (discussed more fully in the "Immersive Environments" section below) was to "leverage 'digital' as the cornerstone to drive brand engagement." The goal was to provide its targeted customers an experience "true to the film's vision; at the same time, to deliver an experience exclusive to McDonald's customers" (Promotion Marketing Association, 2010). Viewing the engagement concept more broadly, Coca-Cola's My Coke Rewards website has been aptly described as the soft drink giant's "relationship building network," in which offline and online engagements are woven together (Henneges, La Kier, & Geller, 2009).

User-generated Content. Digital technologies make it possible for marketers to enlist youth in creating and distributing brand-related content, including products, packaging, and advertisements for their favorite brands. In this way, youth are no longer passive viewers of commercial messages, but active practitioners in the marketing enterprise. User-generated-media campaigns employ a variety of techniques to encourage consumers to become involved in creating marketing messages. In most cases, companies create a template and provide incentives to foster participation. Mountain Dew's DEWmocracy campaign encourages its youthful fan base to become "co-creators" of the brand, to interact with it on multiple levels, and to promote it among their friends ("Commentary: DEWmocracy and Mountain Dew's Online Marketing," 2008; Kahn, 2008; Mountain Dew, 2010). Using a combination of savvy street PR and online promotion, the innovative campaign attracted millions of consumers to its website and led to the creation of the brand's first "fan created flavor"—Mountain Dew Voltage, which quickly sold 11 million cases. According to Christian Dietrich, director of the Pepsi client business at Tribal DDB, the viral campaign succeeded in "...maximizing the reach of a program towards greater participation.... The consumers do the work for us" (Burns, 2009). In the process, Mountain Dew managed to turn the conventional model of advertising on its head, transforming young people from mere viewers of commercials into ad producers and distributors themselves.

Personalization. Through ongoing data collection and tracking, digital marketers can create personalized marketing and sales appeals based on a customer's unique preferences, behaviors, and psychological profile. Personalized marketing evolved from "customer relationship marketing" (CRM), a practice that predated the advent of the World Wide Web, but has become exponentially more sophisticated in the Digital Age with the advent of a new generation of media platforms, software, and measurement tools (Hanson, 1999). For example, behavioral targeting has become a core strategy of contemporary marketing, a linchpin of many digital media campaigns targeting young people—not only online but also on cell phones, video games, and other new platforms (Hallerman, 2008; Khan, Weishaar, & Polinsky, 2009). The practice uses a range of online methods—including cookies and invisible data files—to track the online behaviors of individuals (Center for Digital Democracy & U.S. PIRG, 2006, 2007, 2009a, b; EPIC, Center for Digital Democracy, & U.S. PIRG, 2007a, b). Marketers then use this data to create personalized marketing and sales appeals designed to tap into an individual young person's interests, identity, or concerns, and raising an entirely new set of issues that were not part of the traditional advertising and marketing paradigm (Hallerman, 2008; Khan, Weishaar, & Polinsky, 2009).

Data are collected online from youth through such techniques as contests, sweepstakes, "free" offers, and "point" schemes, delivering detailed information on a particular user (e.g., name, address, email, cell phone number). Immersive, interactive applications, such as games, online video, and so-called "rich media," are often designed to engage in "data capture"—collecting personal details as well as measuring user responses to online content. "Passive" data collection through the use of cookies, IP addresses, and other data that the industry considers "non-personally identifiable" enables marketers to track and target individual users (Center for Digital Democracy, 2010).

Behavioral targeting is routinely used in the digital campaigns of food and beverage marketers. Fast-food company websites, such as Denny's, Chuck E Cheese, Dominos, and Jack in the Box, as well gaming sites that display fast-food ads, use data collection and behavioral targeting (AOL Advertising, 2011; Brightkite, 2011; Mattis, 2010; Wyman, 2011). Youth can be lured to any site for ad targeting using video, music, or other applications (Butterfinger—Comedy Network, n.d.). AOL Advertising tells clients they can "find households with teens that have the greatest propensity to purchase specific products or brands.... Find your ideal teenage audiences on the sites they are most likely to visit.... Find people who are searching for information about music or fashion.... Explicitly target households with teenagers present...." AOL claims to reach 83% of all teens, and targets them when they visit the "AOL Youth Super Channel" and its gaming sites, or when they "chat and listen to music" (AOL Advertising, 2010; Lotame, 2010). Coca-Cola has been at the forefront of companies harnessing the capabilities of digital media to collect data from users, creating online forms of "loyalty" and "direct-response" marketing. Its My Coke Rewards campaign has proven highly successful in promoting the company's soft drink brands to youth. The campaign's website "blends brand content and transactional interactions" and incorporates advertising, including messages from such fast-food company partners as McDonald's, Wendy's, and Carl's Jr. (Henneges et al., 2009; Kruse, 2008).

Social Graph. Participatory Web 2.0 platforms—particularly social networking sites such as Facebook—are further enhancing marketers' ability to know the nature and extent of an individual's social relationships, and to use that information for highly sophisticated social media marketing campaigns. Online social networks are among the most popular digital media platforms for teens, with more than three-fourths of US online youth aged 12–17 participating in them (Lenhart, Purcell, Smith, & Zickuhr, 2010; Owyang, 2010). Social media resonate strongly with many of the fundamental developmental tasks of adolescence, such as identity exploration, social interaction, and autonomy (Buckingham, 2007).

Social networking platforms have added a feature to digital marketing that is distinct and important: the ability to tap into the *social graph*—the complex web of relationships among individuals facilitated and tracked online—enabling marketers to access and influence both individuals and their communities in ways that were never before possible (Iskold, 2007). Using a host of new techniques and measurement tools, social media marketers can know the breadth and depth of these online social relationships, as well as how they function, understanding who influences whom, and how the process of influence works. These social media campaigns target teens at a point in their lives when they are relying less on their parents and family and more on friends.

Companies such as Coca-Cola, Pepsi, Burger King, and McDonald's are among the pioneers of social media marketing, which offers "brand-building opportunities far beyond what's available through traditional advertising" (Interactive Advertising Bureau, 2008, 2009). PepsiCo, for example, has restructured its overall marketing approach to focus on social media, enabling it to take advantage of the more extensive and deeper connections the online environment provides to those marketing to youth (Daniels, 2010; Ostrow, 2010; "PepsiCo Names 10 Tech Start-Ups," 2009; Ritchie, 2009). Coca-Cola, Kellogg's, General Mills, Hershey's, Pizza Hut, Dominos, Jack in the Box, and McDonald's are also playing a significant role ("Come From Behind Victory," 2011; Lingeris, 2010; Tobin, 2011). Coca-Cola, for example, has more than 21 million fans on Facebook, and is developing its campaigns shaped by and using social media (Coca-Cola Company, 2010; "New Coca-Cola Ads Debuting," 2010; "Retail Sector Facebook 'Fan' Winners and Losers," 2011).

Multicultural social media marketing is also growing, reflecting the participation of diverse communities with social sites. Food marketers (including Pepsi, Unilever, and McDonald's) are developing social media campaigns targeting African Americans, Hispanics, and Asian Americans especially (eMarketer, 2010). Hispanics, given their early adoption of new digital communications services, are viewed as a particularly important market that can be influenced by social media

(Carter, 2010; Garcia, 2011; "Hispanic Social Media Insights," n.d.). McDonald's, for example, recently sponsored a major meeting of Latina and Latino bloggers ("two hours worth of intense blogger with brand and agency speed dating") ("Sessions—Hispanicize 2011," 2011). Pepsi funds "Pepsiweinspire.com," aimed at African-American women, as social media marketing has become a key component of the advertising arsenal (Pepsico, n.d.).

Immersive Environments. State-of-the-art animation, high-definition video, and other multimedia applications are spawning a new generation of immersive environments, including interactive games and three-dimensional virtual worlds, which marketers are using for brand promotion. Immersive environments surround and engross a person with powerful, realistic images and sounds, creating an experience of being inside the action, a mental state that is frequently accompanied by "intense focus, loss of self, distorted time sense, effortless action" (Vamey, 2006). These environments often trigger a sense of "presence," which is defined as "being there," a subjective feeling as if one is actually physically in the virtual environment (Li, Daugherty, & Biocca, 2002). Immersive marketing techniques routinely integrate advertising and "content" in such a way as to make the two indistinguishable (Dickson, 2011; Hoffman & Novak, 1996; Wang, 2010). Marketers seamlessly incorporate brands into the flow of the immersive experience, using a highly sophisticated, finely tuned strategy that combines product placement, behavioral targeting, and viral marketing to foster deep, ongoing relationships between brands and individuals.

The industry is carefully monitoring the impact of immersive environments on receptivity to marketing. As one report explained, advertising in the popular XBox LIVE gaming format produces significant results in consumer behavior: "The context—(a deeply immersive, HD entertainment experience)—and the behavior (a desire to engage and interact with the content that is being delivered through that immersive experience, usually gaming but increasingly advertiser-sponsored content) can combine to create a double-whammy of sorts. That's why we consistently see double digit brand lifts and industry-leading CTRs [click-through-rates]" (Kroese, 2010; Microsoft Advertising, n.d.). Microsoft conducted research on the impact of Doritos and other products in games, finding that "video game ad campaigns evoke stronger emotional connections with consumers and more positive emotional association from the brands" (Microsoft, 2009; Microsoft Advertising, 2011). Another study concluded that "the more immersive an environment is, the more likely a player is to have intent to buy a product they see." Virtual worlds are particularly effective at inducing a state of flow, because they "create opportunities for participants to lose track of time in enjoyable brand related activities." This mental state "contributes to a participant's attitude about a brand. Ultimately, this strongly influences the participant's intention to purchase a product from that brand" ("Researchers Find Link," 2010).

McDonald's cross-promotion campaign involving the blockbuster movie *Avatar* is considered the "most extensive deployment" of augmented reality ever used in a marketing effort, utilizing some of the most advanced techniques for linking immersive, online gaming environments to real-world products ("McDonald's Orders Up

Augmented Reality," 2009). The fast-food restaurant collaborated with *Avatar's* production team to develop a "digital platform" for the delivery of "an immersive digital experience centered around Pandora, the mythical planet of Avatar." The campaign began in the restaurants on December 1, 2009, with hundreds of millions of McDonald's boxes featuring the Avatar images. Food purchases for both Big Macs and Happy Meals were at the core of the Avatar effort. Buying Big Macs gave the consumer a way to access online Avatar experiences created by the company, and also enabled access to higher levels of game play. In the store, Happy Meals featured Avatar toy characters—"highly innovative Happy Meal toys" that "light up via touch, sound or motion" (McDonald's, n.d.; "McDonald's Brings Customers," 2009; Total Immersion, n.d.). In this manner, the McDonald's brand was fully integrated into the virtual reality experience ("McDonald's Big Mac Joins Fox's 'AVATAR,'" 2010).

Challenges for Researchers

Researchers will need to take into account the six concepts discussed above when designing studies of how young people respond to digital marketing, addressing, for example, the role that flow, presence, and subjective experience might play in making young people susceptible to food and beverage promotions. An important challenge for research on digital marketing campaigns will be understanding how the components interact in a unified framework with each other and with traditional media marketing. Moreover, the ubiquitous nature of new media makes it difficult for researchers to take into account the entirety of an individual's interaction with marketing; neither the "medium" nor the "message" can easily be identified or isolated. While it is still important to understand how youth respond to individual media platforms and marketing appeals, they cannot be examined in isolation. Rather, researchers will need to find ways of assessing synergies across platforms, as well as how these platforms and the marketing content within them reinforce each other and create multiplier effects. The role of peer influence in brand promotion needs to be studied, as well the intersection of online social interactions with eating behaviors. For example, is participation in an online game likely to encourage "mindless eating," and can this tendency be exacerbated by interaction with friends during the game, as well as the presence of brands?

New Metrics

In meeting these challenges—and especially because the field of interactive advertising is so new—scholars will need to adopt and adapt the metrics that industry has developed to assess the impact of their investments in the digital domain. Many of these new forms of monitoring and measurement were simply not possible before the advent of digital media, and the advertising industry is developing an array of new metrics to refine still further the nuances of interactions between users and digital marketing.

The new generation of social media marketing tools, for example, tracks and measures a broad range of "events" that have quickly become a new way to evaluate the effectiveness of campaigns. Such events might include "ads to acquire fans, user shares offer in newsfeed, 'Like' buttons for sharing website links to drive traffic, wall posts to build community, influencer relations for promoting content, Facebook connect for identity pooling" (Webtrends, 2011). Social media metrics, similarly, might include "virality of spread," "most influential," "velocity," and "purchase intent"—information used to help foster engagement with interactive content (e.g., "apps"), which are increasingly used by food marketers to target youth (trueAnthem, n.d; Webtrends). Food and beverage marketers, who increasingly view advertising on Facebook as essential, understand the economic value of capturing a "fan." One recent study found that a fan for a top brand marketing on Facebook is estimated to be worth $136.38, "based on a combination of how much they spend on products, loyalty, recommendations and earned media" ("Facebook Fans More Valuable Customers," 2010).

Measurement has been incorporated into content, delivery systems, and user interactions. Through web analytics, conversation monitoring, and other forms of surveillance, marketers can now track individuals online, across media, and in the real world, following their interactions, social relationships, and locations. Increasingly, these various forms of analysis can take place in real time, tracking users' movements and behaviors from moment to moment and assessing their reactions to marketing techniques. As a result, these techniques can be tested, refined, and tailored for maximum impact. Through the use of neuroscience, which is able to monitor brain activity with increasing precision, marketers are further developing their abilities to tap into and elicit subconscious responses.

In this manner, the concept of engagement is being deployed as a measurable set of user behaviors. Engagement metrics include concepts such as "dwell time," the duration a user spends with an online object (such as a "widget") and the manner in which the user interacts with that object. Social media analytics measure both users and marketing across the social networking landscape, to assess "how the users are socially linked, and what social interactions occur among the site's users," and to arrive at various indexes—such as the "social influence marketing score" or SIM—to assess the lines of influence in social media and viral marketing campaigns. Measurement systems are also being designed to evaluate 360-degree campaigns, which link online and offline marketing efforts. These include methods of identifying the impact of real-time online marketing with retail product sales. An entirely new range of measurements is being developed, finally, for mobile and location-based marketing. Scholars concerned with the youth obesity crisis should examine all of these tools, both as industry practices themselves, and as another means of assessing the public health implications of new media.

Rethinking the Research Paradigm

With the increasing concern over childhood and adolescent obesity, a few scholars have begun to turn their attention to food marketing in digital media. Several studies have analyzed the content and effects of digital food marketing, for example, documenting certain forms of interactive content and assessing children's responses to some of the new interactive advertising techniques (Alvy & Calvert, 2008; American Academy of Pediatrics Committee on Communications, 2006; Calvert, 2008; Calvert, Jordan, & Cocking, 2002; Harris, Schwartz, Brownell, et al., 2009; Kaiser Family Foundation, 2004; Kunkel, Wilcox, Cantor, et al., 2004; Moore, 2006; Moore & Rideout, 2007; Quilliam, Rifon, Lee, Paek, & Cole, 2009; Story & French, 2004; Valkenburg, 2000). For the most part, however, these studies have been based on traditional methods (e.g., content analysis) and standard theoretical models of child development. Drawing from Piaget's theories, three successive developmental stages have been identified during which children acquire increased abilities to understand advertisers' intentions to persuade them. It is not until children reach the age of 7 or 8 that they have the cognitive ability to recognize the persuasive intent behind a television advertisement (Kunkel et al., 2004; Roedder-John, 1999). By age 12, children are able to articulate a more critical comprehension of advertising intent and become more skeptical (Livingstone & Helsper, 2006). According to this age-based, "cognitive defense" approach, regulatory safeguards are necessary only for the younger segment of the youth population (Kunkel, 2001, 2006; Montgomery, 2007; Nairn, 2009; Nairn & Fine, 2008).

In recent years, however, some scholars have begun to critique the cognitive model, suggesting other theoretical approaches for assessing the impact of contemporary marketing. For example, Harris et al., examined a large body of research on what is known about how children and adolescents respond to marketing, concluding that the psychological models traditionally applied to food marketing research do not explain many of the demonstrated effects of such marketing (Harris, Brownell, & Bargh, 2009). Wright and his colleagues (2005) argue that the emphasis on cognitive understanding of intent has oversimplified the ways in which advertising works. By focusing on only one aspect of the persuasive process, the model fails to take into account "the multiple psychological effects that are instrumental in persuasion."

The conventional models for studying advertising effects are ill equipped to address the latest marketing techniques. No one theory can fully explain the complex ways in which contemporary food marketing influences the health behaviors of children and adolescents. However, we see several theoretical models and approaches that may provide a useful foundation on which scholars can build a better understanding of how digital marketing works.

For example, according to theories of dual process models of persuasion, two separate and distinct sets of mental processes—explicit and implicit—are at work in persuasive communication. Explicit processes are consciously accessible, while implicit processes "are activated automatically and effortlessly, without intention or awareness, and are thus difficult to control" (Nairn & Fine, 2008). Implicit persuasion is a fundamental aspect of many digital marketing efforts, especially when brands are woven seamlessly into the highly engaging content and social interactions of the online environment, where they can still be influential without being consciously recognized or recalled (Auty & Lewis, 2003; Harris, Brownell, & Bargh, 2009; Law & Braun, 2000). Recent research has suggested that dual process models of persuasion may be a more appropriate approach for understanding new media marketing strategies (Moses, 2009; Nairn, 2009). Many elements of digital marketing are purposefully designed to elicit emotional responses and to circumvent the deliberate elaboration or conscious processing of product attributes. Exploring the role of affect as a mediator in dual process models may be particularly helpful in understanding how many contemporary food marketing campaigns work (Eagly & Chaiken, 1993; Harris, Brownell, & Bargh, 2009; Livingstone & Helsper, 2006). A number of scholars have proposed that unconscious, or automatic, processes may underlie responses to emotionally oriented advertising (Bargh, 2002; Fitzsimons, Hutchinson, Williams, et al., 2002). This may be particularly important with children and adolescents (Harris, Brownell, & Bargh, 2009).

Given the ubiquity of digital media, researchers may also want to draw from models of familiarity and norms to study how marketing functions in the digital context. According to the mere exposure effect model (also called the familiarity principle in social psychology), people exhibit a preference for things because they are familiar with them (Zajonc, 1968). In today's cross-platform, 24/7 media environment, exposure to marketing has become frequent and commonplace, engendering a level of familiarity that may go unnoticed, yet result in significant marketing effects (Harris, Brownell, & Bargh, 2009). Repeated exposure to marketing stimuli—especially stimuli that are processed less consciously—may lead to perceived norms regarding specific foods and beverages. When the ubiquity of marketing brands and icons is combined with various forms of engagement and integrated into social interactions, the impact of familiarity and social norms may be even further intensified. Researchers need to understand the effect of synergy across digital platforms, as well as digital synergy with other (traditional) marketing methods. Finally, contextual factors must also be taken into account. Individual behavior is influenced by the context in which the behavior is enacted; thus real-life contexts help shape how digitally marketed messages are interpreted, integrated, and influence behavior (Cockerham, Rütten, & Abel, 1997). This is especially important when researching ethnic minority youth and other cultural subgroups (Grier & Kumanyika, 2008).

Beyond these theories and models are other theoretical approaches that could be explored in order to gain further insights for guiding the study of digital food marketing. For example, the obesity research paradigm developed by the African American Collaborative Obesity Research Network (AACORN) is framed as an ecological model that includes variables specifically focused on studying African-American communities and may be adapted to examine other subcultural groups (Kumanyika, Whitt-Glover, Gary, et al., 2007). It is also important to consider the theories that digital marketers themselves cite as influential in developing their strategies (McPhersony, Smith-Lovin, & Cook, 2001). For example, social media marketers have drawn from social network theory to design their efforts for influencing consumers through online social networking platforms (Honig & Steckler, n.d.; McPhersony et al.).

Developing a Research Agenda

The growth of digital media and marketing requires fresh thinking and new agendas for research. Several areas of inquiry deserve particular focus:

Adolescent vulnerabilities. While adolescents are at serious risk for obesity, they have not received the same level of scholarly attention that has been focused on younger children, particularly with regard to food marketing (McGinnis, Gootman, & Kraak, 2005). Because of the emphasis on cognitive theory in much of the advertising effects research, scholars have viewed adolescents as more knowledgeable about marketer intentions, and thus better able to resist advertising and marketing influences (Goldberg, Niedermeier, Bechtel, & Gorn, 2006). With the prevailing policy emphasis focused on younger children, there is a dearth of studies on adolescents (Livingstone & Helsper, 2006). Recent research suggests, however, that biological and psychosocial attributes of the adolescent experience may play an important role in how teens respond to marketing, making them more vulnerable than they have been thought to be in the past (Leslie, Levine, Loughlin, & Pechmann, 2009; Pechmann, Levine, Loughlin, et al., 2005). Factors such as brain development, hormonal changes, mood variations, and social stresses may make teens more susceptible to the kinds of marketing techniques that are becoming pervasive in the digital media (Collins, Ellickson, McCaffrey, et al., 2007; Giedd, 2008; McAnarney, 2008; McCreanor, Barnes, Gregory, et al., 2005; Pechmann et al.; Steinberg, 2007, 2008).

Identity. A related area involves the role of identity formation in the commercial digital context. Consumer researchers have begun to examine how marketing contributes to "self-brand connections" among children and adolescents, with very little attention to the role of digital marketing in this process (Chaplin & Roedder-John, 2005). Many digital marketing strategies purposefully seek to exploit this nexus of self-identity and brand identity. But we still do not know enough about how these interrelationships influence young people. The intersections of brand identity and personal identity may be particularly influential with ethnic minority youth, who must develop an ethnic identity in addition to developing a personal identity and fitting in with peers like other youth (Castro, 2004; Grier, 2009). Products, including foods and beverages, can contribute to identity development, and since research suggests that adolescent self-consciousness can make them more receptive to image advertising for frequently promoted brands, ethnically targeted social media marketing may be particularly effective among minority youth (Grier, 2009 ; Levy, 1959; Pechmann et al., 2005). For example, research among elementary school students indicates that viewing African-American programs among African Americans is associated with higher self-esteem, and suggests how targeted ads may be used in this manner (McDermott & Greenberg, 1984). Thus, since ethnic-targeted marketing may serve identity development purposes among minority youth, the relationship may support enhanced responsiveness to digital target marketing.

Targeted digital marketing to ethnic minority groups. The high levels of obesity among African-American and Hispanic youth are especially alarming. Not only are Hispanic and African-American youth at greater risk for obesity but also more immersed in many aspects of the digital media culture, and are subjected to an increasing amount of targeted marketing based on ethnicity and race. Some 2.5 million US Hispanic teens aged 12–17 subscribe to mobile phone service, and that group is projected to have a subscriber growth rate of two to three times that of the overall US teen market over the next 5 years. African-American and Hispanic youth use many mobile tools more than the general population (Briabe Media, 2007).

Digital marketers have made understanding and reaching minority youth a priority given their numeric growth, favorable usage patterns, and cultural trendsetting. Target marketing to African-American and Hispanic youth influences their consumption choices by affecting the awareness and availability of food-related information and options and can contribute to perceived norms (Grier & Kumanyika, 2008; Grier, Mensinger, et al., 2007). Further, research suggests that ethnic minority youth are more interested in, positive towards, and influenced by marketing than non-Hispanic whites (Grier, 2009).

Food marketing encountered by African-American and Hispanic youth tends to promote less healthful foods, and is less likely to support positive nutrition, although few studies have focused specifically on digital marketing efforts (Bang & Reece, 2003; Grier & Kumanyika, 2008; Harrison, 2006; Outley & Taddese, 2006; Powell, Szczypka, & Chaloupka, 2007). Moreover, minority youth are important cultural models who influence the behaviors of the larger youth population (Bush, Smith, & Martin, 1999; Korzenny, Korzenny, McGavock, & Inglessis, 2006; Moschis, 1987; Singh, Kwon, & Pereira, 2003; Stroman, 1991; Woods, 1995). As a consequence, minority youth may be subject to multiple layers of vulnerability, given family circumstances, normative exposures to obesity, and the contexts in which they live (Grier & Kumanyika, 2008, 2010; Grier, Mensinger, et al., 2007; Kumanyika & Grier, 2006). Unfortunately, there is very limited research on ethnic minority youth and marketing, especially of direct relevance to the digital environment (Grier, 2009).

Impulsivity and addictive behaviors. Food and beverage manufacturers continually research and perfect combinations of flavors and tastes in order to maximize their appeal to consumers, inserting high quantities of sugars, fats, and salts, which can alter the biological circuitry in the brain. Cues may include emotional memories of a particular kind of food or other kinds of positive associations, triggering responses that, over time, become habitual (Drewnowski, 1995; Kessler, 2009). These ingredients, as well as other food additives, may also trigger an addictive process in the brain in ways that are similar to how drugs of abuse work (Gearhardt, Corbin, & Brownell, 2009). So far, researchers have not examined the role of digital media and marketing in any of these processes, which is an area that deserves focused attention. When products with compelling and addictive properties are marketed to young people through contemporary digital techniques, their impact on health behaviors may be compounded.

If current obesity trends among children and adolescents are to be reversed, the public health community will need to develop an aggressive, fast-tracked, targeted program of research. To begin understanding the complex ways that youth are interacting with this new commercial media culture, it will be necessary to develop flexible and innovative methodological approaches. Much of this research will need to be collaborative and interdisciplinary, combining expertise from various fields to pose hypotheses that cut across disciplines and across levels of influence (Huang, Drewnowski, Kumanyika, & Glass, 2009). The research methods that academic scholars are employing to study youth engagement with digital media culture—including qualitative, ethnographic investigations of youth subcultures—provide models for exploring digital marketing (Livingstone, 2007; MacArthur Foundation, n.d.). Many researchers across academic fields, as well as within industry, are adapting ethnographic techniques—now dubbed "netnography"—to study behavior online, in order to understand how youth use and are influenced by social networks and other digital media (Kozinets, 2009).

Finally, studies undertaken on youth and digital marketing must also be grounded in the real-world practices of the contemporary marketplace, which is not static but constantly evolving. This will require close, ongoing monitoring of market research, theories, platforms, and techniques. Industry's new metrics are a clear departure from more traditional types of measurement, and need to be fully understood in order to design research methods that academics can use for testing the health impacts of food and beverage marketing in the digital media. Similarly, various techniques that digital market researchers now use to assess youth consumer behavior could also be adapted for academic researchers, as long as these techniques are employed in accordance with academic standards for ethical research. Specific measures could be developed for assessing each of the key concepts; these measures, in turn, could be incorporated into a model for understanding the impact of digital food marketing on attitudes and behaviors.

References

Advertising Research Foundation. (2006). Engagement: Definitions and anatomy. Retrieved from http://my.thearf.org/source/Orders/index.cfm?section=unknown&task=3&CATEGORY=PUB&PRODUCT_TYPE=SALES&SKU=PUB_ENGDA_E&DESCRIPTION=Publications&FindSpec=&CFTOKEN=73112952&continue=1&SEARCH_TYPE=find&StartRow=1&PageNum=1.

Alvy, L. M., & Calvert, S. L. (2008). Food marketing on popular children's web sites: A content analysis. *Journal of the American Dietary Association, 108*(4), 710–713.

American Academy of Pediatrics Committee on Communications. (2006). Policy statement: Children, adolescents, and advertising. *Pediatrics, 118*(6), 2563–2569.

AOL Advertising. (2010). Audiences: Teens. Retrieved from http://advertising.aol.com/audiences/teens.

AOL Advertising. (2011). Teens. Retrieved from http://advertising.aol.com/audiences/teens.

Apsalar. (2011). ApTimizer. Retrieved from http://apsalar.com/documentation/aptimizer/.

Auty, S., & Lewis, C. (2003). The 'Delicious Paradox': Preconscious processing of product placements by children. In L. J. Shrum (Ed.), *The psychology of entertainment media: Blurring the lines between entertainment and persuasion* (pp. 117–133). London: Psychology Press.

Bang, H.-K., & Reece, B. B. (2003). Minorities in children's television commercials: New, improved, and stereotyped. *Journal of Consumer Affairs, 37*(1), 42–66.

Bargh, J. A. (2002). Losing consciousness: Automatic influences on consumer judgment, behavior and motivation. *The Journal of Consumer Research, 29*(2), 280–286.

Briabe Media. (2007). Briabe media offers multicultural mobile marketing assessments for brands seeking to better connect with Hispanic and African American customers. Retrieved from http://www.prwebdirect.com/releases/2007/2/prweb507171.htm.

Brightkite. (2011). Advertise with Us: Ultra-targeted advertising. Retrieved from http://brightkite.com/pages/bk_ad_targeting_capabilities.html

Brownell, K. D., Schwartz, M. B., Puhl, R. M., Henderson, K. E., & Harris, J. L. (2009). The need for bold action to prevent adolescent obesity. *The Journal of Adolescent Health, 45*(3), S8–S17.

Buckingham, D. (Ed.). (2007). *Youth, identity, and digital media*. Cambridge, MA: MIT Press.

Burns, E. (2009). Mountain Dew plugs into online campaign for new drink. *ClickZ*. Retrieved from http://www.clickz.com/3632466.

Bush, A. J., Smith, R., & Martin, C. (1999). The influence of consumer socialization variables on attitude toward advertising: A comparison of African-Americans and Caucasians. *Journal of Advertising, 28*(3), 13–24.

Butterfinger – Comedy Network. (n.d.). Retrieved from http://comedy.video.yahoo.com/

Calvert, S. L. (2008). Children as consumers: Advertising and marketing. *The Future of Children, 18*(1), 205–234.

Calvert, S. L., Jordan, A. B., & Cocking, R. R. (Eds.). (2002). *Children in the digital age: Influences of electronic media on development*. Westport, CT: Praeger.

Carter, J. F. (2010). 8 Social media strategies to engage multicultural consumers. *Mashable*. Retrieved from http://mashable.com/2010/04/21/social-media-multicultural/.

Castro, F. G. (2004). Physiological, psychological, social, and cultural influences on the use of menthol cigarettes among Blacks and Hispanics. *Nicotine & Tobacco Research, 6*(Suppl. 1), S29–S41.

Center for Digital Democracy. (2010). Written comments: Promotion of food and drug administration-regulated medical products using the Internet and social media tools. Retrieved from http://www.democraticmedia.org/files/u1/2010-02-28-FDAcomments.pdf.

Center for Digital Democracy & U.S. PIRG. (2006). Complaint and request for inquiry and injunctive relief concerning unfair and deceptive online marketing practices. Federal Trade Commission Filing. Retrieved from http://www.democraticmedia.org/files/pdf/FTCadprivacy.pdf.

Center for Digital Democracy & U.S. PIRG. (2007). Supplemental statement in support of complaint and request for inquiry and injunctive relief concerning unfair and deceptive online marketing practices. Federal Trade Commission Filing. Retrieved from http://www.democraticmedia.org/files/FTCsupplemental_statement1107.pdf.

Center for Digital Democracy & U.S. PIRG. (2009a). Complaint and request for inquiry and injunctive relief concerning unfair and deceptive mobile marketing practices. Retrieved from http://www.democraticmedia.org/current_projects/privacy/analysis/mobile_marketing.

Center for Digital Democracy & U.S. PIRG. (2009b). Supplemental statement in support of complaint and request for inquiry and injunctive relief concerning unfair and deceptive online marketing practices. Retrieved from http://www.democraticmedia.org/files/FTCsupplemental_statement1107.pdf.

Chaplin, L. N., & Roedder-John, D. (2005). The development of self brand connections in children and adolescents. *Journal of Consumer Research, 32*(119–129).

Chester, J., & Montgomery, K. (2007). Interactive food & beverage marketing: Targeting children and youth in the digital age. Retrieved from http://www.digitalads.org/documents/digiMarketingFull.pdf.

Chester, J., & Montgomery, K. (2008). Interactive food & beverage marketing: Targeting children and youth in the digital age: An update. Retrieved from http://digitalads.org/documents/NPLAN_digital_mktg_memo.pdf.

Children's Advertising Review Unit. (2006). Self-Regulatory Program for children's advertising. Retrieved from http://www.caru.org/guidelines/guidelines.pdf.

Coca-Cola Company. (2010). Coca-Cola's expedition 206 kicks off with new years celebration in Madrid. Retrieved from http://www.thecoca-colacompany.com/presscenter/nr_20100104_exp206.html.

Cockerham, W. C., Rütten, A., & Abel, T. (1997). Conceptualizing contemporary health lifestyles: Moving beyond Weber. *The Sociological Quarterly, 38*(2), 321–342.

Collins, R. L., Ellickson, P. L., McCaffrey, D., & Hambarsoomians, K. (2007). Early adolescent exposure to alcohol advertising and its relationship to underage drinking. *The Journal of Adolescent Health, 40*(6), 527–534.

Come From Behind Victory: Domino's Pizza president and CEO will keynote Multi-Unit Franchising Conference. (2011). Retrieved from http://www.franchising.com/articles/come_from_behind_victory.html.

Commentary: DEWmocracy and Mountain Dew's Online Marketing. (2008). Retrieved from http://www.bevreview.com/2008/02/27/commentary-dewmocracy-and-mountain-dews-online-marketing/.

Daniels, T. (2010). Q&A with Pepsico's Chief Consumer Engagement Officer, Frank Cooper. Retrievedfromhttp://socialmediaweek.org/blog/2010/01/30/qa-with-pepsicos-chief-engagement-officer-frank-rose/.

Diaz, A.-C. (2009). Goodby and B-Reel Enter the Asylum for the sequel to Doritos Hotel 626. Creativity Online. Retrieved from http://creativity-online.com/news/goodby-and-breel-step-into-the-asylum-for-the-sequel-to-doritos-hotel-626/139224.

Dickson, D. (2011). New Research Study: Advertising engagement in digital magazines. Retrieved from http://blogs.adobe.com/digitalpublishing/2011/01/ad-engagement.html.

Drewnowski, A. (1995). Energy intake and sensory properties of food. *The American Journal of Clinical Nutrition, 62*(5 Suppl), 1081S–1085S.

Eagly, A. E., & Chaiken, S. (1993). Process theories of attitude formation and change: The elaboration likelihood model and heuristic systematic models. In A. E. Eagly & S. Chaiken (Eds.), *The psychology of attitudes* (pp. 305–325). Fort Worth, TX: Harcourt Brace Jovanovich.

eMarketer. (2010). CPG marketers target Hispanic shoppers in-store and online. July 2010. Retrieved from http://www.emarketer.com/(S(ppu3fi55jxxhdv45cqq3xo2k))/Reports/All/Emarketer_2000677.aspx.

EPIC, Center for Digital Democracy, & U.S.PIRG. (2007a). In the matter of Google, Inc. and DoubleClick, Inc., Complaint and Request for Injunction, Request for Investigation and for Other Relief, before the Federal Trade Commission. Retrieved from http://www.epic.org/privacy/ftc/google/epic_complaint.pdf.

EPIC, Center for Digital Democracy, & U.S.PIRG. (2007b). In the matter of Google, Inc. and DoubleClick, Inc., Second Filing of Supplemental Materials in Support of Pending Complaint and Request for Injunction, Request for Investigation and for Other Relief. Retrieved from http://epic.org/privacy/ftc/google/supp2_091707.pdf.

Facebook Fans More Valuable Customers. (2010). Retrieved from http://www.marketingcharts.com/direct/facebook-fans-more-valuable-customers-13274/.

Fitzsimons, G., Hutchinson, J. W., Williams, P., Alba, J., Chartrand, T. L., & Huber, J., et al. (2002). Non-conscious influences on consumer choice. *Marketing Letters, 13*(3), 269–279.

Garcia, T. (2011). Latino influence on social media growing. *PRNewser.* Retrieved from http://www.mediabistro.com/prnewser/latino-influence-on-social-media-growing_b12769.

Gearhardt, A. N., Corbin, W. R., & Brownell, K. D. (2009). Preliminary validation of the Yale Food Addiction Scale. *Appetite, 52*. Retrieved from http://www.yaleruddcenter.org/resources/upload/docs/what/addiction/FoodAddictionScaleArticle09.pdf.

Giedd, J. N. (2008). The Teen Brain: Insights from neuroimaging. *The Journal of Adolescent Health, 42*(4), 335–343.

Goldberg, M., Niedermeier, K., Bechtel, L., & Gorn, G. (2006). Heightening adolescent vigilance toward alcohol advertising to forestall alcohol use. *Journal of Public Policy and Marketing, 25*(2), 147–159.

Grier, S. (2009). African American & Hispanic youth vulnerability to target marketing: Implications for understanding the effects of digital marketing. Second NPLAN/BMSG Meeting on Digital Media and Marketing to Children. Retrieved from http://digitalads.org/documents/Grier%20NPLAN%20BMSG%20memo.pdf.

Grier, S., & Kumanyika, S. (2008). The context for choice: Health implications of targeted food and beverage marketing to African Americans. *American Journal of Public Health, 98*(9), 1616–1629.

Grier, S. A., & Kumanyika, S. (2010). Targeted marketing and public health. *Annual Review of Public Health, 31*(1), 349–369.

Grier, S. A., Mensinger, J., Huang, S. H., Kumanyika, S. K., & Stettler, N. (2007). Fast food marketing and children's fast food consumption: Exploring parental influences in an ethnically diverse sample. *Journal of Public Policy and Marketing, 26*(2), 221–235.

Hallerman, D. (2008). Behavioral targeting: Marketing trends. *eMarketer.*

Hansen, E. J. (2010). How to optimize mobile marketing efforts with targeting. Retrieved from http://www.mobilemarketer.com/cms/opinion/columns/8347.html.

Hanson, W. (1999). *Principles of internet marketing*. Cincinnati, OH: Southwestern College Publishing.

Harris, J. L., Brownell, K. D., & Bargh, J. A. (2009). The Food Marketing Defense Model: Integrating psychological research to protect youth and inform public policy. *Social Issues and Policy Review, 3*(1), 211–271.

Harris, J. L., Schwartz, M. B., Brownell, K. D., Sarda, V., Weinberg, M. E., & Speers, S., et al. (2009). Cereal FACTS: Evaluating the nutrition quality and marketing of children's cereals. Retrieved April 10, 2010, from http://www.cerealfacts.org/media/Cereal_FACTS_Report.pdf.

Harrison, K. (2006). Fast and sweet: Nutritional attributes of television food advertisements with and without Black characters. *Howard Journal of Communications, 17*(4).

Henneges, M., La Kier, M., & Geller, M. (2009). How Coca-Cola is blurring the lines between online advertiser and publisher. Retrieved from http://www.imediaconnection.com/summits/23153.asp.

Hispanic Social Media Insights. (n.d.). Retrieved from http://www.hispanicprblog.com/category/hispanic-social-media-insights/.

Hoffman, D. L., & Novak, T. P. (1996). Marketing in hypermedia computer-mediated environments: Conceptual foundations. *The Journal of Marketing, 60*(3), 50–68.

Honig, D., & Steckler, L. (n.d.). Who do you know. Retrieved from http://m6d.com/wp-content/themes/md6/documents/who-do-you-know.pdf.

Hotel626.com. (2010). Retrieved from http://www.cyberentries.com/hotel626/.

Huang, T. T., Drewnowski, A., Kumanyika, S., & Glass, T. A. (2009). A systems-oriented multilevel framework for addressing obesity in the 21st century. *Preventing Chronic Disease, 6*(3), 1–10.

Inspiration Room. (2009). Doritos Hotel 626. Retrieved from http://theinspirationroom.com/daily/2009/doritos-hotel-626/.

Interactive Advertising Bureau. (2008). IAB Platform Status Report: A mobile advertising overview. Retrieved from http://www.iab.net/media/file/moble_platform_status_report.pdf.

Interactive Advertising Bureau. (2009). Social media metrics definitions. Retrieved from http://www.slideshare.net/womarketing/iab-social-media-metrics-definitions.

Interactive Food & Beverage Marketing: Targeting Children and Youth in the Digital Age. (n.d.). Retrieved from http://www.digitalads.org/.

Iskold, A. (2007). Social graph: Concepts and issues. *ReadWriteWeb.* Retrieved from http://www.readwriteweb.com/archives/social_graph_concepts_and_issues.php.

Kahn, M. A. (2008). PepsiCo launches branded mobile widget for Mountain Dew. *Mobile Marketer*. Retrieved from http://www.mobilemarketer.com/cms/news/gaming/996.html.

Kaiser Family Foundation. (2004). The role of media in childhood obesity. Retrieved from http://www.kff.org/entmedia/upload/The-Role-Of-Media-in-Childhood-Obesity.pdf.

Kaiser Family Foundation. (2010). Daily media use among children and teens up dramatically from five years ago. Retrieved from http://www.kff.org/entmedia/entmedia012010nr.cfm.

Keane, M. (2010). Case Study: McDonald's ups foot traffic 33% on Foursquare Day. *Econsultancy.* Retrieved from http://econsultancy.com/us/blog/6582-case-study-mcdonald-s-and-foursquare.

Kessler, D. A. (2009). *The end of overeating: Taking control of the insatiable American appetite.* New York: Rodale.

Khan, I., Weishaar, B., & Polinsky, L. (2009). Nothing but Net: 2008 Internet Investment Guide. Retrieved from https://mm.jpmorgan.com/stp/t/c.do?i=2082C-248&u=a_p*d_170762.pdf*h_-3ohpnmv.

Korzenny, F., Korzenny, B. A., McGavock, H., & Inglessis, M. G. (2006). The multicultural marketing equation: Media, attitudes, brands, and spending.

Kozinets, R. V. (2009). *Netnography: Doing ethnographic research online*. Newbury Park, CA: Sage.

Kroese, M. (2010). Is It What You Watch… or Who You Are?—IAB Mixx 2010. Retrieved from http://community.microsoftadvertising.com/blogs/advertising/archive/2010/09/10/is-it-what-you-watch-or-who-you-are.aspx.

Kruse, C. (2008). Coca-Cola vice president for global interactive marketing, speaker profile. Retrieved from http://www.emarketingassociation.com/2008/SF/speaker_bios.htm.

Kumanyika, S., & Grier, S. (2006). Targeting interventions for ethnic minority and low-income populations. *The Future of Children, 16*(1), 187–207.

Kumanyika, S. K., Whitt-Glover, M. C., Gary, T. L., Prewitt, T. E., Odoms-Young, A. M., & Banks-Wallace, J., et al. (2007). Expanding the obesity research paradigm to reach African American communities. *Preventing Chronic Disease*, 4(4), 1–22.

Kunkel, D. (1990). The role of research in the regulation of children's television advertising. *Knowledge: Creation, Diffusion, Utilization, 12*(1), 101–119.

Kunkel, D. (2001). Children and television advertising. In D. G. Singer & J. L. Singer (Eds.), *Handbook of children and the media* (pp. 375–393). Thousand Oaks, CA: Sage.

Kunkel, D. (2006). Kids media policy goes digital: Current development in children's television regulation. In J. A. Bryant & J. Bryant (Eds.), *The children's television community: Institutional, critical, social systems, and network analyses* (pp. 203–228). Mahwah, NJ: Lawrence Eribaum Associates.

Kunkel, D., & Castonguay, J. (2012). Children and advertising: Content, comprehension, and consequences. In D. G. Singer & J. L. Singer (Eds.), *Handbook of children and the media* (2nd ed.). Thousand Oaks, CA: Sage.

Kunkel, D., Wilcox, B. L., Cantor, J., Dowrick, P., Linn, S., & Palmer, E. (2004). Report of the APA Task Force on advertising and children. Retrieved October 2, 2008, from http://www.kff.org/entmedia/upload/The-Role-Of-Media-in-Childhood-Obesity.pdf.

Law, S. & Braun, K. A. (2000). I'll have what she's having: Gauging the impact of product placements on viewers. *Psychology and Marketing, 17*(12), 1059–1075.

Lenhart, A., Madden, M., & Macgill, A. R. (2007). Teens and social media. Retrieved from http://www.pewinternet.org/PPF/r/230/report_display.asp.

Lenhart, A., Purcell, K., Smith, A., & Zickuhr, K. (2010). Social media and young adults. Retrieved from http://www.pewinternet.org/Reports/2010/Social-Media-and-Young-Adults.aspx.

Leslie, F. M., Levine, L. J., Loughlin, S. E., & Pechmann, C. (2009). Adolescents' psychological & neurobiological development: Implications for digital marketing. Memo prepared for the Second NPLAN/BMSG Meeting on Digital Media and Marketing to Children for the NPLAN Marketing to Children Learning Community. Retrieved from http://digitalads.org/documents/Leslie_et_al_NPLAN_BMSG_memo.pdf.

Levy, S. J. (1959). Symbols for sale. *Harvard Business Review, 37*, 117–124.

Li, H., Daugherty, T., & Biocca, F. (2002). Impact of 3-D advertising on product knowledge, brand attitude, and purchase intention: The mediating role of presence. *Journal of Advertising, 31*(3).

Lingeris, A. (2010). S'mores 'Snacktivity' Suite. Retrieved from http://www.slideshare.net/GasPedal/blogwell-philadelphia-social-media-case-study-the-hershey-company-presented-by-anna-lingeris.

Livingstone, S. (2007). Do the media harm children? Reflections on new approaches to an old problem. *Journal of Children and Media, 1*(1), 5–14.

Livingstone, S., & Helsper, E. J. (2006). Does advertising literacy mediate the effects of advertising on children? A critical examination of two linked research literatures in relation to obesity and food choice. *The Journal of Communication, 56*(3), 560–584.

Retail Sector Facebook 'Fan' Winners and Losers—December 2010. (2011). Retrieved from http://seekingalpha.com/instablog/667722-retail-geeks/125257-retail-sector-facebook-fan-winners-and-losers-december-2010.

Lotame. (2010). Lotame's Statement on The Wall Street Journal Article Dated July 31, 2010. Retrieved from http://www.lotame.com/2010/08/lotames-statement-on-the-wall-street-journal-article-dated-july-31-2010/.

MacArthur Foundation. (n.d.). Building the field of digital media and learning. Retrieved from http://www.digitallearning.macfound.org/site/c.enJLKQNlFiG/b.2029199/k.BFC9/Home.htm.

Mattis, M. (2010). Reaching your teens. Retrieved from http://www.yadvertisingblog.com/blog/2010/01/22/reaching-your-teens/.

McAnarney, E. R. (2008). Adolescent brain development: Forging new links? *The Journal of Adolescent Health, 42*(4), 321–323.

McCreanor, T., Moewaka Barnes, H., Gregory, M., Kaiwai, H., & Borell, S. (2005). Consuming identities: Alcohol marketing and the commodification of youth experience. *Addiction Research and Theory, 13*(6), 579–590.

McDermott, S., & Greenberg, B. (1984). Parents, peers and television as determinants of Black children's esteem. In R. Bostrom (Ed.), *Communication yearbook* (pp. 164–177). Beverly Hills, CA: Sage.

McDonald's Big Mac Joins Fox's 'AVATAR' to Thrill Fans Nationwide. (2010). Retrieved from http://www.prnewswire.com/news-releases/mcdonaldsr-big-macr-joins-foxs-avatar-to-thrill-fans-nationwide-78680402.html.

McDonald's Brings Customers. (2009). Retrieved August 3, 2010, from to Another Planet in Partnership With James Cameron's Movie Masterpiece 'Avatar' 1, http://www.aboutmcdonalds.com/etc./medialib/aboutMcDonalds/mediacenter/EPK_-_Avatar.Par.53996.File.tmp/AVATAR%20Global%20Release%20FINAL.pdf.

McDonald's Orders Up Augmented Reality from Total Immersion in Global Promotion For Fox's Avatar. (2009). Retrieved from http://seriousgamesmarket.blogspot.com/2009/12/serious-games-as-ar-extensive.html.

McDonald's. (n.d.). Competition FAQs. Retrieved August 4, 2010, from http://www.mcdonalds-avatar.com/faqs.aspx.

McGinnis, J. M., Gootman, J. A., & Kraak, V. I. (Eds.). (2005). *Food marketing to children and youth: Threat or opportunity?* Washington, DC: Institute of Medicine.

McPhersony, J. M., Smith-Lovin, L., & Cook, J. M. (2001). Birds of a feather: Homophily in social networks. *Annual Review of Sociology, 27*, 415–444.

Microsoft. (2009). Games advertising strikes an emotional chord with consumers. Retrieved from http://www.emsense.com/press/game-advertising.php.

Microsoft Advertising. (2011). Doritos Xbox Live Arcade Game Smashes Records. Retrieved from http://advertising.microsoft.com/europe/doritos-xbox-live-arcade-game.

Microsoft Advertising & Carat. (2010). The new shopper: Today's purchase path and the media that influences it. Retrieved from https://docs.google.com/viewer?a=v&pid=gmail&attid=0.0&thid=12e590fee34ee131&mt=application/pdf&url=https://mail.google.com/mail/?ui%3D2%26ik%3D483c01c2dc%26view%3Datt%26th%3D12e590fee34ee131%26attid%3D0.0%26disp%3Dsafe%26zw&sig=AHIEtbTjycviXEx1tIOv1ljGie05Iy_GSw.

Microsoft Advertising. (n.d.). Xbox. Retrieved from http://advertising.microsoft.com/gaming/xbox-advertising.

Mobile Marketing Association. (2011). MMA mobile advertising guidelines. Retrieved from http://www.mmaglobal.com/mobilecouponguidelines.pdf.

Montgomery, K. (2007). *Generation digital: Politics, commerce and childhood in the age of the Internet*. Cambridge, MA: MIT Press.

Montgomery, K. (2008). Creating a media policy agenda for the digital generation. In A. M. Scheiter (Ed.), *And communications for all: A policy agenda for the new administration* (pp. 281–300). Lanham, MD: Lexington Books.

Montgomery, K., & Chester, J. (2009). Interactive food & beverage marketing: Targeting adolescents in the digital age. *The Journal of Adolescent Health, 45*, S18–S29.

Moore, E. S. (2006). It's child's play: Advergaming and the online marketing of food to children. Retrieved October 2. 2008, from http://www.kff.org/entmedia/upload/7536.pdf.

Moore, E. S., & Rideout, V. J. (2007). The online marketing of food to children: Is it just fun and games? *Journal of Public Policy & Marketing, 6*(2), 202–220.

Moschis, G. P. (1987). *Consumer socialization: A life-cycle perspective*. Lexington, MA: Lexington Books.

Moses, L. J. (2009). Research on child development: Implications for how children understand and cope with digital media. Memo prepared for the Second NPLAN/BMSG Meeting on Digital Media and Marketing to Children for the NPLAN Marketing to Children Learning Community. Retrieved from http://www.digitalads.org/documents/Moses_NPLAN_BMSG_memo.pdf.

Mountain Dew. (2010). *Wikipedia*. Retrieved from http://en.wikipedia.org/wiki/Mountain_Dew.

Nairn, A. (2009). Changing the rules of the game: Implicit persuasion and interactive children's marketing. Second NPLAN/BMSG Meeting on Digital Media and Marketing to Children for the NPLAN Marketing to Children Learning Community. Retrieved from http://www.digitalads.org/documents/Nairn_NPLAN_BMSG_memo.pdf.

Nairn, A., & Fine, C. (2008). Who's messing with my mind? The implications of dual-process models for the ethics of advertising to children. *International Journal of Advertising, 27*(3), 447–470.

New Coca-Cola Ads Debuting During Broadcast of Super Bowl XLIV are Part of Something Bigger. (2010). Retrieved from http://www.thecoca-colacompany.com/dynamic/press_center/2010/01/new-coca-cola-ads-debuting-during-broadcast-of-super-bowl-xliv-are-part-of-something-bigger.html.

Ostrow, A. (2010). Inside Gatorade's Social Media Command Center. *Mashable*. Retrieved from http://mashable.com/2010/06/15/gatorade-social-media-mission-control/.

OTX. (2008). Teens would rather have their lockers vandalized than homepage, but prefer shopping in store to online: New research from OTX and Intelligence Group Looks at Teens' Online Behavior. Retrieved from http://www.otxresearch.com/documents/PressReleases/2008/06-18-08_Teens_and_Internet.pdf.

Outley, C. W., & Taddese, A. (2006). A content analysis of health and physical activity messages marketed to African American children during after-school television programming. *Archives of Pediatrics & Adolescent Medicine, 160*(4).

Owyang, J. (2010). A collection of social network stats for 2010. Retrieved from http://www.web-strategist.com/blog/2010/01/19/a-collection-of-social-network-stats-for-2010/.

Patel, K. (2010). Fast-food chains grab most location-based check-ins. *Advertising Age*. Retrieved from http://adage.com/digital/article?article_id=145413.

Pechmann, C., Levine, L., Loughlin, S., & Leslie, F. (2005). Impulsive and self-conscious: Adolescents' vulnerability to advertising and promotion. *Journal of Public Policy and Marketing, 24*(2), 202–221.

PepsiCo Names 10 Tech Start-Ups for Pilot Digital Marketing Programs. (2009). Retrieved from http://www.pepsico.com/PressRelease/PepsiCo-Names-10-Tech-Start-Ups-for-Pilot-Digital-Marketing-Programs09092010.html.

Pepsico. (n.d.). Pepsi we inspire. Retrieved from http://www.pepsiweinspire.com/.

Pew Research Center. (2010). Teen Internet use. Retrieved from http://pewresearch.org/millennials/teen-internet-use-graphic.php.

Powell, L. M., Szczypka, G., & Chaloupka, F. (2007). Adolescent exposure to food advertising on television. *American Journal of Preventitive Medicine, 33*(4), S51–S56.

Promotion Marketing Association. (2010). 2010 REGGIE Awards: McDonald's Avatar Program. Retrieved from http://www.omnicontests3.com/pma_reggie_awards/omnigallery/entry/gallery_item_info.cfm?child=1&client_id=1&entry_id=312&competition_id=1&entrant_id=97&gallery_item_id=135.

Quilliam, E. T., Rifon, N. M., Lee, M., Paek, H.-J., & Cole, R. (2009). *Food Advergames targeting children: Prevalence, effects, and policy implications*. Paper presented to the Conference, Consumer Culture and the Ethical Treatment of Children: Theory, Research & Fair Practice, East Lansing, MI.

Researchers Find Link Between Immersion and Virtual Buying Habits. (2010). Retrieved from http://games.ign.com/articles/110/1103374p1.html.

Rideout, V. J., Foehr, U. G., & Roberts, D. F. (2010). Generation M2: Media in the Lives Of 8-18-Year-Olds. Retrieved from http://www.kff.org/entmedia/upload/8010.pdf.

Ritchie, K. (2009). Doritos Continues Interactive Horror Franchise with Asylum 626. Retrieved from http://www.boardsmag.com/articles/online/20090922/asylum626.html.

Roedder-John, D. (1999). Consumer socialization of children: A retrospective look at twenty-five years of research. *The Journal of Consumer Research, 26*(3), 183–213.

Sessions—Hispanicize 2011—2nd Annual Hispanic PR and Social Media Conference. (2011). Retrieved from http://www.hispanicizeconference.com/sessions.html.

Singh, N., Kwon, I.-W., & Pereira, A. (2003). Cross-cultural consumer socialization: An exploratory study of socialization influences across three ethnic groups. *Psychology & Marketing, 20*(10).

Steinberg, L. (2007). Risk taking in adolescence: New perspectives from brain and behavioral science. *Current Directions in Psychological Science, 16*(2), 55–59.

Steinberg, L. (2008). A social neuroscience perspective on adolescent risk-taking. *Developmental Review, 28*(1), 78–106.

Story, M., & French, S. (2004). Food advertising and marketing directed at children and adolescents in the U.S. *International Journal of Behavioral Nutrition and Physical Activity, 1*, 1–3.

Story, M., Sallis, J., & Orleans, T. (2009). Adolescent obesity: Toward evidence-based policy and environmental solutions. *The Journal of Adolescent Health, 45*(3), S1–S5.

Stroman, C. A. (1991). Television's role in the socialization of African American children and adolescents. *The Journal of Negro Education, 60*(3), 314–327.

Tobin, J. (2011). SXSW Panel recap: Marketing budgets have gone social—Is it working? Retrieved from http://www.ignitesocialmedia.com/conferences/sxsw-panel-recap-marketing-budgets-have-gone-social-is-it-working/.

Total Immersion. (n.d.). Behind the Augmented Reality Magic: McDonald's, Avatar & Total Immersion. Retrieved from http://www.aboutmcdonalds.com/etc./medialib/aboutMcDonalds/mediacenter/EPK_-_Avatar.Par.88064.File.tmp/TI%20Fact%20Sheet.pdf.

trueAnthem. (n.d.). Retrieved from http://www.trueanthem.com/.

Tsirulnik, G. (2010). Why brands must have a 360-degree mobile web strategy. Retrieved from http://www.mobilemarketer.com/cms/news/advertising/6191.html.

Valkenburg, P. M. (2000). Media and youth consumerism. *Journal of Adolescent Health, 27*(S), 52–56.

Vamey, A. (2006). Immersion unexplained. *The Escapist.* Retrieved from http://www.escapistmagazine.com/articles/view/issues/issue_57/341-Immersion-Unexplained.

Vdopia. (n.d.). Retrieved from http://www.ivdopia.com/?page=insights.

Wang, A. (2010). Digital Ad engagement: Perceived interactivity as a driver of advertising effectiveness. Retrieved from http://blogs.adobe.com/digitalpublishing/files/2011/01/digital_magazine_ad_engagement.pdf.

Webtrends. (2011). Engage 2011: Measuring Facebook. Retrieved trueAnthem, from http://www.trueanthem.com/.

Williamson, D. (2008). Kids and teens: Communication revolutionaries. Retrieved from http://www.emarketer.com/Report.aspx?code=emarketer_2000539.

Woods, G. B. (1995). *Advertising and marketing to the new majority*. Belmont, CA: Wadsworth Publishing Company.

Wright, P., Friestad, M., & Boush, D. M. (2005). The development of marketplace persuasion knowledge in children, adolescents, and young adults. *Journal of Public Policy and Marketing, 24*(2), 222–233.

Wyman, K. (2011). Mobile social next big teen trend—Mimi Ito at Imagine 2011. Retrieved from http://community.microsoftadvertising.com/blogs/advertising/archive/2011/03/30/mobile-social-is-the-next-big-teen-trend-shared-by-mimi-ito-at-imagine-2011.aspx.

Zajonc, R. B. (1968). Attitudinal effects of mere exposure. *Journal of Personality and Social Psychology, 9*, 1–27.

Chapter 11
A Multi-Method Study to Understand How Youth Perceive and Evaluate Food and Beverage Advertisements

Keryn E. Pasch, Cayley E. Velazquez, and Sara E. Champlin

As a formal practice, advertising has been in existence for over 100 years, most often with the purpose of creating consumer excitement for, and the voluntary purchase of, company products and goods (Grier & Kumanyika, 2010). While advertising is meant to drive consumption, the purchase of certain products, especially among specific groups, may be problematic. Recent literature suggests that there may be a link between food and beverage advertising and the prevalence of childhood obesity among youth in the USA (IOM, 2006). Because of the dramatic increase in the prevalence of obesity over the past 30 years (Ogden, Carrol, Curtin, Lamb, & Flegal, 2010), investigating factors that may contribute to weight gain among children and adolescents is essential. While overweight and obesity is influenced by many factors, food and beverage advertising, and its resulting influence on the dietary preferences and choices of youth, is thought to be a key factor (Story & French, 2004; IOM, 2006). The amount and type of advertising that is directed toward youth has grown considerably in recent years, with marketers using an increasing number of techniques and outlets to promote their products. Greater media use among youth (Rideout, Foehr, & Roberts, 2010), in combination with advertising that extends to a variety of media channels, has resulted in increased exposure to unhealthy food and beverage products.

Given that youth encounter increasingly more advertisements, it is not surprising that a systematic review of the literature conducted by the Institute of Medicine Committee on Food Marketing and the Diets of Children and Youth found that food and beverage advertising, most often in the form of television commercials, influences the dietary preferences, choices, and behaviors of youth (IOM, 2006, see Chap. 2). Moreover, this evidence is particularly apparent for children (2–11 years), whereas in many cases, it remains insufficient for adolescents (12–18 years) (IOM, 2006). Building on the previous research on the influence of food and beverage advertising on youth, the purpose of this chapter is twofold. First, we will provide a

K.E. Pasch (✉) • C.E. Velazquez • S.E. Champlin
Department of Kinesiology and Health Education, University of Texas at Austin, 1 University Station, D3700 Austin, TX 78712, USA
e-mail: kpasch@austin.utexas.edu; cayley.velazquez@ubc.ca; sara.champlin@gmail.com

J.D. Williams et al. (eds.), *Advances in Communication Research to Reduce Childhood Obesity*, DOI 10.1007/978-1-4614-5511-0_11,

brief overview of the amount and type of food and beverage advertising to which youth are exposed, as well as discuss examples of common techniques employed by marketers to gain the attention of youth and ultimately engage them in what is being offered. Second, we describe a multi-method study that aimed to determine how youth perceive and evaluate food and beverage advertisements using objective measures of attention. We end the chapter by proposing implications of this work, as well as ideas and suggestions for future research.

Food and Beverage Advertising to Youth

Data shows that companies spent approximately $9.6 billion dollars marketing foods and beverages in the US during 2006. Out of that total amount, $1.6 billion was used to market foods and beverages directly to youth (FTC, 2008), which suggests that companies use 17% of their marketing expenditures to promote their products directly to youth consumers (FTC). In order to target this young audience, television remains the dominant channel in which marketers advertise. It is estimated that children view over 30,000 television advertisements each year, of which 7,600, or 25%, are for food and beverage products (Gantz, Schwartz, Angelini, & Rideout, 2007). Of food and beverage advertisements that target youth, a large percentage are for unhealthy items, including candy and snacks (34%), sugar cereals (28%), and fast food (10%). In comparison, dairy products and real fruit juices comprise only 4% and 1% of television advertisements, respectively. Rarely, if ever, are television advertisements for fruits or vegetables (Gantz et al.), which is inconsistent with national dietary recommendations. This unequal representation of unhealthy foods and beverages likely provides mixed messages to youth as to the frequency with which these products should be consumed, especially as compared to healthy products.

Other studies suggest similar findings in regards to the amount and type of advertisements seen by youth (Bell, Cassady, Culp, & Alcalay, 2009; Powell, Szczypka, & Chaloupka, 2007; Powell, Schermbeck, Szczypka, Chaloupka, & Braunschweig, 2011; see also Chap. 8). For example, using national data, Powell and colleagues (2007) found that advertisements for food items accounted for over 25% of the total advertisements seen by adolescents on television, and, of these food-related advertisements, 23% were for fast-food restaurants, 22% were for sweets, 17% were for beverages, 11% were for cereals, and 9% were for snacks (Powell et al., 2007). In a content analysis of Saturday morning and weekday afternoon television programs, Bell and colleagues (2009) found similar results, in that one-fifth of all advertisements were for food products, of which 70% were for high fat and/or high sugar items. Moreover, less than 2% of advertisements were for fruits and vegetables, and only one out of every 63 food advertisements was a public service announcement for a nutrition-related product (Bell et al.).

While it is clear that television advertising is prominent in the lives of youth, the reach of advertising extends to a variety of other media channels including movies, the Internet, and billboards/posters, resulting in increased exposure to unhealthy food and beverage items. In an effort to describe the number and types of food and beverage items advertised in the top 20 grossing movies each year from 1996 to 2005, researchers found that most were for energy-dense, nutrient-poor products (Sutherland, MacKenzie, Purvis, & Dalton, 2010). In addition, close to 70% of movies contained at least one food, beverage, for those containing at least one brand placement, there was an average 8.6 placements per movie, (Sutherland et al., 2010). Candy and snacks were the most prevalent food items advertised (47%), while sugar-sweetened beverages were the most prevalent beverage items advertised (76%), indicating that movies can provide considerable exposure to a number of unhealthy food and beverage items.

In a recent examination of popular children's websites, researchers found, that while not extensive on many of the sites, 70% of websites contained food advertising (Alvy & Calvert, 2008). Of these advertisements, most were for candy, sweetened breakfast cereals, snacks, and fast-food restaurants (Alvy & Calvert). Popular children's websites were analyzed for the nutritional content of the food and beverage items and the majority of products were not in alignment with current dietary recommendations (Lingas, Dorfman, & Bukofzer, 2009). Of the 77 advertised items, only five met the Institute of Medicine's criteria of foods to encourage. Moreover, 49 advertisements were for items classified as items to avoid, and 23 advertisements were for items classified as ones to neither encourage nor avoid (Lingas et al.). With the increase in online and social media, youth are likely exposed to advertising in many additional venues (see Chap. 10).

Outdoor food and beverage advertising, such as billboards and posters, is another channel in which marketers are able to reach youth (see Chap. 14). In Australia, Kelly and colleagues (2008) examined the number and content of advertisements surrounding elementary schools and found that approximately 25% were for food and beverage items. Moreover, 80% of these advertisements were for non-core products (i.e., sugar sweetened beverages, fast food, chocolate, ice cream) (Kelly, Cretikos, Rogers, & King, 2008). Maher, Wilson, and Signal (2005) studied the number and content of outdoor advertisements surrounding secondary schools and found the prevalence to be even higher, with around 60% of advertisements being for food and beverage items of which approximately 70% were for unhealthy products (i.e., 22% for soft drinks, 16% for frozen confectionary, 11% for savory snacks) (Maher et al., 2005). Moreover, the density of outdoor advertisements for high-calorie, low nutrient-dense food and beverage items has been found to be greatest among lower income and minority neighborhoods (Yancey et al., 2009; see Chaps. 16 and 18), which may put these individuals at higher risk for experiencing diet and obesity-related health issues over the long term.

Techniques of Food and Beverage Advertising

Advertising techniques used to target specific audiences include the use of branding, developing branded logos, and a variety of characters, most of which are animated. These efforts appear to be commonplace among youth-oriented advertisements and are often used as a means of attracting the attention of young people and engaging them in what is being offered (Kelly, Hattersley, King, & Flood, 2008; see also Chap. 15). Moreover, the use of these concepts in advertisements tends to provide visual cues which represent the attributes of the brand (i.e., fun, excitement), and are often used in an attempt to build awareness, generate product recognition, establish loyalty, and create perceived product value (IOM, 2006). Therefore, such strategies are likely to be highly influential in promoting the desire for and purchase of food and beverage products, particularly among youth who may not recognize the intent of such tactics.

Branding, the process of using a name or symbol to identify or differentiate a product from items within the same product category (IOM, 2006), is a technique that is often used to create recognition and to assist in the process of communicating product attributes to consumers (Connor, 2006; Lawrence, 2003). Because one goal of marketers is to create lifelong customers, and given that product awareness is thought to lead to stronger brand loyalty as children grow older (Connor), establishing brand awareness at an early age is particularly important. Children are aware of brand names and logos beginning at an early age. For example, in a study designed to examine the development of brand awareness among young children, researchers found that children aged 2–3 years recognized 8 out of 12 brand logos presented, including M&Ms, Cheetos, Lay's and McDonalds, along with other nonfood products (Valkenburg & Buijzen, 2005). Almost all children aged 8 years were able to recognize 100% of the brand logos (Valkenburg & Buijzen).

Recognition of branded logos is also thought to lead to brand preference for food and beverage items (Pine & Nash, 2003). Children, as young as preschool age, have been asked to choose which product they preferred between both branded and non-branded items (e.g., a chocolate bar) and found that the branded product was chosen 68% of the time (Pine & Nash). Branding has also been shown to influence food preferences and taste perceptions among youth. After being presented with pairs of fast-food items, the only difference being the wrapping, one of which was packaged in McDonald's wrapping and the other in plain wrapping, and then sampling the items, children showed a stronger preference for the branded item (Robinson, Borzekowski, Matheson, & Kramer, 2007). Given the pervasive use of these techniques, it is important to better understand how such tactics might influence youth.

The use of animated characters in advertising to youth is prevalent in a wide variety of food and beverage product advertising domains. For instance, Tony the Tiger (Frosted Flakes cereal), Lucky the Leprechaun (Lucky Charms cereal), and Ronald McDonald (McDonald's restaurant), are all examples of spokes-characters that were created for the sole purpose of promoting a product to children. Spokes-characters tend to be considered an effective method of establishing a favorable brand–consumer relationship among children (Lawrence, 2003).

Licensed characters, on the other hand, are characters that have been created specifically for children's television shows and/or movies (Garretson & Niedrich, 2004), and are loaned to other companies for a fee (IOM, 2006). Marketers often rely on coupling a product with an existing well-known character to influence the food and beverage product purchases of youth (Palmer & Carpenter, 2006).

For example, Spiderman, Scooby-Doo, and Winnie the Pooh are all licensed character images that companies have used to promote unhealthy food and beverage products (IOM, 2006). In a recent study of cross-promotions on packaged foods advertised in the supermarket, researchers found that over half of all promotions were targeted toward children, and 71% involved licensed characters. Moreover, products with cross-promotions were considerably less healthy, containing nearly 40% of energy from added sugar and nearly 20% of energy from fat (Harris, Schwartz, & Brownell, 2009). Other work suggests that branding food packages with licensed characters significantly influences the taste preferences and snack choices that children make for unhealthy food items (Lapierre, Vaala, & Linebarger, 2011; Roberto, Baik, Harris, & Brownell, 2010).Whether a spokes-character or a licensed characters is used, these animated images in advertisements targeting children are prevalent in today's media and may influence the products used by this audience.

While previous research has documented associations between exposure to food and beverage advertising with food preferences and choices, research that explores how youth interpret messages and images in advertisements is still needed. Additionally, much of the previous research has focused on either self-reported or objectively documented exposure. However, these types of measures do not indicate whether youth actually pay attention to advertisements. As a result, it is unclear as to whether mere exposure is enough to influence youth or whether attention must actually be paid to advertising for negative health outcomes to result. As such, additional measures are needed. One possible method to objectively record attention to advertising is through the use of eye-tracking technology to document eye movements, as eye movements are thought to "provide a physiological assessment of attention that is linked directly to cognitive processing (Fox, Krugman, Fletcher, & Fischer, 1998, p.60)." Therefore, the purpose of the present study was to use a multi-method approach, including the use of eye-tracking technology, to explore how youth perceive and evaluate food and beverage advertisements. The relationships between attention/perception and evaluation and beliefs, attitudes, and opinions about foods and beverages were also explored.

Using Multiple Methods to Evaluate Youth Attention and Evaluation of Food and Beverage Advertisements: The MEDIA Study

The Measuring and Evaluating the Determinants and Influence of Advertising (MEDIA) study, was a cross-sectional, observational study that aimed to explore how youth perceive and evaluate the content of food and beverage advertising through the use of: quantitative surveys, eye-tracking technology, written stories/descriptions of advertisements, and focus groups. Participants for this study included a sample of children and adolescents, who were recruited through the use of flyers, university sponsored summer camps, and university-based website postings. Initial recruitment strategies consisted of posting flyers throughout the surrounding community, for example, post offices, libraries, pools, and recreation centers. Later recruitment strategies involved providing all willing university summer camp directors with flyers to distribute to their campers, in addition to posting an announcement on the university website for community members to access. Informed consent was obtained from parents in the manner of a written consent form and from children in the manner of a written youth assent form. Prior to coming to the university for the first study visit, parents were mailed or emailed a "welcome package" which included the consent and assent forms. Participants were brought into the laboratory on two separate occasions, both of which lasted approximately 1–1½ h. Participants were given an incentive of $15 per visit and the parent was given an additional $12 per visit to cover travel and parking. The study took place between April and November 2010. The Institutional Review Board at the University of Texas at Austin approved the study.

Participants

Participants included a sample of 102 children and adolescents between the ages of 8 and 15 years old. Participants were 56.4% Caucasian, 18.8% Hispanic, 6.9% Asian, 1.0% American Indian, and 16.8% Mixed (students who indicated being more than one race/ethnicity, of these, four students indicated they were African-American and another race/ethnicity). The average age of participants was 11.6 years, with grade in school ranging from second grade (6.9%) to tenth grade (2%); however, most students were between fourth and sixth grade. Approximately 43.1% of participants were female, 93.1% spoke English most often in their home, 71.6% were from two parent families, 18.8% reported receiving free or reduced price lunches while at school, and 23.2% were classified as overweight or obese. For the focus groups and written stories, a subsample of the large study, 75 students, provided data.

Measures

Quantitative Surveys

In order to obtain information about beliefs, behaviors, and exposures related to food and beverage advertising, self-report surveys were completed by participants in the study laboratory. Surveys consisted of 83 questions which assessed participants' beliefs, attitudes, and opinions about food and beverage advertising, as well as their self-reported exposure to food and beverage advertising, their food and beverage preferences, and their typical food and beverage choices.

Survey Measures

Exposure to Food and Beverage Advertising. Exposure to food and beverage advertising was measured with two items that assessed self-reported exposure to fast-food advertisements (i.e., food from a restaurant where you order at a counter) and to sugar-sweetened beverage advertisements (i.e., sweetened teas, sports drinks, soda) in the past week. Participants selected what type of advertising channel (billboards, inside and outside of stores, at community events, in magazines, on television, on radio, and on the computer or Internet) they were exposed. Each participant was given a point for each type of advertising they had seen, for a total possible score of 14. The mean of this score was 6.1 (SD=3.3), meaning that, on average, the study sample was exposed to slightly more than six different types of food and beverage advertising in the past week.

Susceptibility to Food and Beverage Advertising. Susceptibility to food and beverage advertising was a summary of three items: exposure to food and beverage advertising (as described above), ownership of food and beverage-branded merchandise, and willingness to wear and/or use food and beverage-branded merchandise. Similar measures (i.e., ownership of and willingness to wear branded merchandise) have been used in alcohol and tobacco research with youth (McClure, Stoolmiller, Tanski, Worth, & Sargent, 2009; Pierce et al., 2010).

Ownership of food and beverage-branded merchandise was measured with two items assessing whether the participant owned or collected food and beverage-branded merchandise. The questions asked "Do you own or collect anything that has the name of a fast-food company on it, like a t-shirt, hat, poster, or water bottle?" and "Do you own or collect anything that has the name of a sugar-sweetened beverage on it, like a t-shirt, hat, poster, or water bottle?" The response options were "yes" or "no." Seventy-two percent of participants reported that they did not own fast food or sugar-sweetened beverage branded merchandise, 10% of participants reported ownership of fast food-branded merchandise only, 12% of participants reported ownership of sugar-sweetened beverage branded merchandise only, and 7% of participants reported owning both fast food and sugar-sweetened beverage branded merchandise.

Willingness to wear and/or use food and beverage-branded merchandise was measured with two items assessing if the participant would be willing to wear and/or use food and beverage-branded merchandise. The questions asked "Would you ever wear or use an item that has the name of a fast-food company on it, like a t-shirt, hat, poster, or water bottle?" and "Would you ever wear or use an item that has the name of a sugar-sweetened beverage on it, like a t-shirt, hat, poster, or water bottle?" The response options were "yes" or "no." While 49% of participants reported that they were not willing to wear and/or use fast food or sugar-sweetened beverage branded merchandise, 5% of participants reported being willing to wear and/or use fast-food branded merchandise only, 12% of participants reported being willing to wear and/or use sugar-sweetened beverage branded merchandise only, and 35% of participants reported being willing to wear and/or use both fast food and sugar-sweetened beverage branded merchandise.

Each of these three variables was combined to create one overall index of food and beverage advertising susceptibility. The susceptibility to food and beverage advertising index ranged from 0 to 18 and the mean was 7.3 (SD=3.5). A higher score on the index indicates increased risk as a higher value represents greater susceptibility to food and beverage advertising.

Food and Beverage Preferences. Food and beverage preferences were measured by self-report of food and beverage preferences. Thirty items were used to assess preferences for fruits, vegetables, dairy, and snack foods. Participants were given a list of food and beverage items and asked to circle whether they liked, disliked, or had never tasted the selected items. Items were coded as 0 (dislike/never tasted) and 1 (like). A composite score of unhealthy food and beverage items was then created to measure overall unhealthy food and beverage preferences. The unhealthy eating preference index summed responses to 12 questions measuring consumption of snack foods, with a possible response range of 0–12. The mean of the unhealthy food and beverage preferences index was 10.0 (SD=2.1). The food and beverage preference questions were adapted from previous research that has been deemed as having acceptable internal consistencies and test–retest reliabilities (Domel et al., 1993). A higher score on the index indicates a greater preference for unhealthy food and beverage items.

Food and Beverage Choices. Food and beverage choices were measured by self-report of foods eaten on a regular weekday (usual consumption). Thirteen items were used to assess consumption of fruits, vegetables, milk, snack foods, and sugar sweetened beverages. An example item is "On a regular weekday, how often do you usually … eat French fries or chips? (Include potato chips, tortilla chips, Cheetos, corn chips or other snack food)." Another example item is "On a regular weekday, how often do you usually … drink any regular (NOT diet) soda or soft drink?" Response options were "I don't usually eat this food" "less than one time a day (for example, 1 or 2 times per week)" "1 time a day" "2 times a day" "3 times a day" "4 times a day" or "5 or more times a day." Items were coded as 0 (I don't usually eat this food), 0.5 (less than one time a day (for example, 1 or 2 times per week), 1 (1 time a day), 2 (2 times a day), 3 (3 times a day), 4 (4 times a day) or 5 (5 or more times a day) to get a measure of daily consumption. A composite score of unhealthy eating was created to measure overall unhealthy food choices. The unhealthy eating index summed responses to eight questions measuring consumption of snack foods and sugar-sweetened beverages, with a possible response range of 0–40. The mean of the unhealthy eating index was 4.7 (SD=4.6). A higher score on the index indicates a greater consumption of unhealthy food and beverage items. The food and beverage choice questions were adapted from the School Physical Activity and Nutrition (SPAN) questionnaire (CATCH, 2010), which has been previously evaluated for reproducibility and validity with this age group (Hoelscher, Day, Kelder, & Ward, 2003; Penkilo, George, & Hoelscher, 2008; Thiagarajah et al., 2008).

Overweight and Obesity. BMI was calculated from self-reported height and weight, using a standard equation (weight in kilograms divided by height in meters squared and then plotted on a BMI-for-age chart) to determine a child's BMI percentile (Ogden, Yanovski, Carroll, & Flegal, 2007; Kuczmarksi et al. 2002). While self-reported

BMI has its limitations, it has been shown to be highly correlated with objectively measured height and weight, and is thus a reliable indicator of body fatness for most children (Goodman, Hinden, & Khandelwal, 2000; Sherry, Jefferds, & Grummer-Strawn, 2007). Using current weight status categories, a BMI between the 85th and 95th percentile for age and gender was considered overweight, while a BMI greater than or equal to the 95th percentile for age and gender was considered obese (Flegal, Tabak, & Ogden, 2006). BMI z-score was then calculated for participants. BMI z-score is calculated in order to make comparisons across ages and to better describe the weight status of youth at the extreme ends of the distribution (Kuczmarksi et al., 2002). Since participants in this study reported age, but not birth date, child age was assigned the midpoint (i.e., 11 years was assigned 11 years and 6 months) for classification purposes, a method that research suggests has little effect on overweight and obesity prevalence estimates (Flegal, 2000). Thus, BMI z-score was calculated based on age, gender, height, and weight.

Eye-Tracking

Eye-tracking technology is a computer-based technology that provides an unobtrusive, real time descriptive analysis of an individual's point of gaze, sequence of gaze, and length of attention for each advertisement. Essentially, eye tracking data indicates which parts of an advertisement gained attention, when, and for how long. Having this type of information is useful to better understand what components of advertising are appealing to youth, as well as which components gain attention first and for the longest amount of time.

The objective measures of attention to food and beverage advertising that were used in this study are thought to reflect the moment-to-moment cognitive processing of individuals (Rayner, 1998), because "the eye fixates on a word or phrase as long as it is being cognitively processed (Fox et al., 1998, p.60)." Thus, the time a participant spends looking at a particular component of an advertisement represents their level of cognitive processing (Fox et al., 1998). As such, a fixation occurs when an individual pauses to examine or interpret a specific component or feature of an advertisement (Just & Carpenter, 1980; Rayner, 1998). The total number of fixations (total number of times a person stops to examine or interpret specific components or features in an advertisement and/or the return of fixations to a particular element) is thought be an indicator of the level of cognitive processing, where a greater number of fixations suggests a greater amount of processing for that element of the visual stimulus (Just & Carpenter, 1980; Rayner, 1998). For a full description of eye-tracking technology see Holmqvist et al., 2011.

In the present study, participants were asked to view a series of 40 static food and beverage advertisements and 15 food and beverage commercials (grouped into three segments to imitate standard commercial blocks) on the eye tracking monitor. In order to record participants' pattern of attention to the food and beverage advertisements, their eye movements were captured using a Tobii T60 Eye

Tracker. The eye tracker requires that youth sit in a chair and view a monitor that resembles a computer screen. The monitor displays an advertisement (print or video) and youth view the advertisement on the screen as they would any other type of document on a computer.

Participants were brought into the laboratory and asked to sit in front of the eye tracking monitor, at which time participants were asked to view each advertisement in the same manner they would watch TV, look at a magazine, or play on the computer, and instructed to look at each advertisement for as long as they wanted, at which point they were to click the mouse to move to the next advertisement. Prior to viewing the advertisements, participants' eye movements were calibrated with the machine, which required them to follow (in other words track) a red dot on the screen with their eyes. Once complete, participants began viewing the study advertisements and commercial blocks which were presented in a random order.

Attention Measures

Recorded attention variables from the eye-tracking session used for this study included total time, fixation length, and fixation count. *Total time* was calculated for total time, in seconds, spent on all advertisements. *Total unhealthy time* was also calculated for total time, in seconds, spent on all unhealthy food and beverage advertisements. These measures were calculated based on the length of time a participant took between mouse clicks (i.e., to move from one advertisement to the next advertisement). Thus, total time was the length of time a participant spent viewing the first through the last advertisement, whereas total unhealthy time was a summary measure of the length of time a participant spent on all unhealthy advertisements.

In addition to the viewing time measures, fixation length and fixation count were also obtained. To begin, each advertisement was coded for the specific advertising components such as those described previously (i.e., animated characters, branded logos, and unhealthy food and beverage items) that, based on the previous research (Kelly et al., 2008; Palmer & Carpenter, 2006; Lapierre et al., 2011; Roberto, Baik, Harris & Brownell, 2010; Pine & Nash, 2003; Robinson et al., 2007), were thought to be most important for this study. In doing this, areas of interest for each advertisement were designated, which was done by outlining the specific advertising components that were of interest to the study by using a pen tool in the Tobii eye tracking software. The areas of interest were then used to measure *fixation length* (amount of time spent on the specific area of interest) and *fixation count* (number of times each area of interest was fixed upon, including return fixations where a participant returned to look at a particular area of interest).

A summary of the attention measures used for this study are as follows: (1) total time for all advertisements (2) total time for unhealthy advertisements (3) fixation length for unhealthy food and beverage items (4) fixation length for animated characters, (5) fixation length for branded logos (6) fixation count for unhealthy food and beverage items (7) fixation count for animated characters and, (8) fixation count for branded logos. Similar attention measures have been used in previous research (Peterson, Thomsen, Lindsay, & John, 2010; Fox et al., 1998).

Focus Groups

In order to obtain qualitative information about what youth thought about several food and beverage advertisements, focus groups were conducted with youth. Participants took part in a 60-minute focus group session with approximately 6–8 other youth, where they discussed a variety of food and beverage advertisements (healthy and unhealthy). At the start of each focus group, participants were instructed to answer the questions as honestly as possible. Each focus group began with two ice-breaker questions, followed by four general questions, and eight specific questions that were repeated for each advertisement. Focus group questions were based on previous advertising research (Pasch, Komro, Perry, Hearst, & Farbakhsh, 2007; Grube & Waiters, 2005), and adapted where necessary. All focus groups were audio recorded and transcribed verbatim.

Written Stories

To gain a better understanding of what youth think about food and beverage advertising, participants were also asked to sort, in order of preference, several food and beverage advertisements and then provide written stories/descriptions for two of the food and beverage advertisements. Each participant received a package of seven laminated advertisements, which they were asked to place in order of preference from most favorite to least favorite. Advertisement preferences were recorded by the study staff. After completing this task, participants were asked to write two short stories, one for each of their two favorite advertisements (approximately one page in length each). The participants were instructed to write about what they believed the advertisements were about, however, if they were unable to do this, participants described the chosen advertisements and wrote what they liked and did not like about them.

Data Analysis for Quantitative Data: Descriptive Statistics and Correlational Analyses

In order to describe attention to unhealthy advertising, food and beverage product logos, and the use of animated characters, means, standard deviations, and ranges were calculated for each of the eye tracking variables. Additionally, to document associations between the eye-tracking variables, self-reported advertising susceptibility, and food/beverage preferences and choices, Pearson Correlations were calculated.

Results

Youth spent an average of 235.3 s (3.9 min) viewing all 40 advertisements, of which, 188.4 s (3.1 min) were spent viewing the 32 unhealthy advertisements (an average of 6 s each). In total, there were 30 unhealthy food and beverage items, 20 characters, and six logos coded in the 32 unhealthy advertisements. Youth spent an average of 32.1 s viewing unhealthy food and beverage items (an average of 1.1 s for each item), 10.7 s viewing animated characters (0.5 s per character), and 4.6 s viewing branded logos (0.8 s per logo). In addition, the average fixation count for unhealthy food and beverage items was 97 (on average each food and beverage item was fixated on 3.2 times). For animated characters, the average fixation count was 33 (1.7 times per character) and for logos the average was 14 (2.3 times per logo).

Self-reported susceptibility to food and beverage advertising was strongly and positively associated with self-reported exposure to food and beverage advertising ($r=0.93$ $p<0.01$), as well as weakly and positively associated with unhealthy food and beverage preferences ($r=0.28$, $p<0.01$) and unhealthy choices ($r=0.31$ $p<0.01$). These findings suggest that higher levels of self-reported susceptibility to food and beverage advertising (i.e., greater exposure to food and beverage advertising, owning or willingness to own food and beverage branded merchandise) tend to be associated with higher levels of self-reported exposure to food and beverage advertising, unhealthy food and beverage preferences, and unhealthy eating behavior (see Table 11.1).

Self-reported susceptibility to food and beverage advertising was also weakly and positively associated with fixation length on unhealthy food and beverage items ($r=0.20$, $p<0.05$), suggesting that youth who reported higher susceptibility also spent more time looking at unhealthy food and beverage items. Self-reported exposure to food and beverage advertising was weakly and positively associated with fixation length on unhealthy food and beverage items ($r=0.19$, $p=0.05$) and unhealthy preferences ($r=0.19$, $p=0.05$), suggesting that youth who reported seeing more food and beverage advertisements spent more time on unhealthy food and beverage items.

Qualitative Findings

Focus Groups

In order to better understand how youth evaluate or think about food and beverage advertising, a subsample of the larger study ($n=75$) also participated in a focus group session. Obtaining qualitative data through focus groups provided us with insight into how food and beverage advertisements make youth think about the products presented. To start the focus groups, participants were asked to recall some advertisements they had recently seen. Participants were then shown a series of five advertisements (as time permitted) and asked several questions about each one. The advertisements included: Oreos, Minute Maid Fruit Juice (four different types of

Table 11.1 Means, standard deviations, and correlations for all study variables

	1	2	3	4	5	6	7	8	9	10	11	12	13
1. Susceptibility to FB advertising	–												
2. Exposure to FB advertising	0.93*	–											
3. Total time on all advertisements	0.09	0.10	–										
4. Total time on unhealthy advertisements	0.08	0.08	0.99*	–									
5. Fixation length on unhealthy FB items	0.20*	0.19*	0.83*	0.82*	–								
6. Fixation length on characters	0.14	0.14	0.81*	0.80*	0.87*	–							
7. Fixation length on logos	0.14	0.14	0.75*	0.74*	0.81*	0.75*	–						
8. Fixation count on unhealthy FB items	0.16	0.16	0.81*	0.81*	0.97*	0.82*	0.79*	–					
9. Fixation count on characters	0.12	0.12	0.81*	0.80*	0.84*	0.96*	0.71*	0.83*	–				
10. Fixation count on logos	0.13	0.12	0.73*	0.72*	0.81*	0.72*	0.93*	0.84*	0.73*	–			
11. Unhealthy preferences	0.28*	0.19*	0.11	0.12	0.15	0.12	0.05	0.16	0.11	0.08	–		
12. Unhealthy choices	0.31*	0.19	–0.07	–0.06	0.07	–0.02	–0.03	0.07	–0.02	0.02	0.16	–	
14. BMI z-score	–0.16	–0.13	–0.00	–0.00	–0.03	–0.05	0.01	–0.04	–0.07	–0.06	0.02	0.06	–
N	101	101	100	100	100	100	100	100	100	100	101	96	81
Mean	7.34	6.12	235.32	188.37	32.07	10.68	4.58	96.76	33.00	13.99	10.04	4.74	0.13
Standard deviation	3.48	3.34	125.96	99.47	19.30	8.11	3.36	49.87	20.85	8.64	2.11	4.60	1.36

*p≤0.05

juice, only some 100% juice), Cheetos, Tropicana Orange Juice, and Starbucks Frappuccino. Presented below are some of the statements provided by youth during the focus group sessions.

Recent Advertisements and Advertising in General

In almost every focus group, participants mentioned seeing fast food or sugar-sweetened beverage advertisements. Fast-food advertising was the most mentioned advertising recently seen and McDonalds advertising was the most commonly mentioned fast-food advertisement. However, some participants did not like McDonalds advertising. For example, one participant said, *"Well, I don't like the McDonald's commercials, there's a creepy clown."* Some participants also commented on the unhealthy products promoted by McDonalds, for example, *"I don't like it because they're trying to get you to buy something that's bad for your health."*

While sugar-sweetened beverages were mentioned frequently as advertisements participants had seen recently, most participants did not elaborate on what they liked or did not like about these advertisements. However, one participant commented on a recent advertising campaign by Coca-Cola, *"They used to have these old Coke commercials with coke and polar bears. I love coke now."*

In one focus group, participants talked about the purpose of commercials and advertisements. Participants seemed aware of the persuasive nature of advertising and the use of characters and logos by the advertisers to promote products. For example, one participant said *"Sometimes they use cartoon characters to make people buy it. And want to get people familiar and they use Nickelodeon characters, and may mimic SpongeBob to buy Nickelodeon."* Another participant talked about the inaccuracies sometimes present in advertising, *"For people to spread the word about a specific product or multiple products about the company so that people can buy more of their products instead of other products otherwise they'll lose the competition to get the most products. Also for the facts on it, lying you can actually get sued for, but some companies just plain out tell lies, even though they can get sued because they make enough money off of the lies. Also, wording it in a specific way with commercials seem that you can get away with some lying if you can word it correctly."*

Focus Group Advertisements

When asked about the specific advertisements, it was surprising that the Oreo and Cheetos Advertisements were not as popular among the participants as was expected. For example, many students commented on the implausibility and confusing nature of the Oreo advertisement which showed a glass of milk with a straw and an Oreo inside the straw as if the milk was drinking the Oreo. One participant commented,

"I get it. It just makes me think hard and I don't like commercials. Just show it in the milk for Pete's sake, not shove it in the straw" Researcher: So you don't like that it is confusing? You don't like that you have to think about it?

Yeah I like to get it, like get the point. I don't like to think about it.

For the Cheetos advertisement, which was for Flaming Hot Cheetos, many participants did not like the advertisement. Overall, they did not like the image of the open bag with a scorched out grass field alluding to the spicy nature of the product. For example, "*It's like open a bag of flaming hot Cheetos and you will burn. It's just not realistic.*" Several participants thought the advertisement was depressing and boring, however, they still thought the advertisement would appeal to children and teenagers, particularly boys.

While the Oreo advertisement had many negative comments, a few participants did like the advertisement. One participant said *"I like it because it's like kind of funny because the milk is eating the cookie and it's kind of ironic I guess."* Another commented, "*Well an Oreo kind of reminds me of, like, family. Like when I saw that commercial it reminded me of the father and son relationship. And they have a good bond so I guess that could be a positive thing.*" Similar to the Cheetos advertisement, while the participants did not personally like the Oreo advertisement, most did say that this advertisement would appeal to kids their age.

Some participants were skeptical of the "healthier" advertisement presented for Minute Maid Fruit Juice. For example, *"Well one thing that I dislike about this ad is probably because of the people who made it because it probably has like 3% real fruit inside it because this is mostly just sugar because minute maid is known to do that."* Another participant commented, *"It's not exactly, like, healthy because they don't show, like, all the extra ad in things like that is all behind the scenes."* These comments suggest that some youth are aware of the difference between 100% juice and fruit juice beverages. However, for the Tropicana Orange Juice advertisement, many students commented on the healthful nature of the product but they also thought the advertisement was boring. For example, *"I think it's kind of boring, it just shows juice. I mean, smaller, compact sizes isn't a brand new thing. It's been around."*

Written Stories

In addition to qualitative information provided in focus groups, each participant was asked to write a response to two of their favorite advertisements (out of a group of seven). The purpose of this component of the study was to better understand what types of images and ideas these advertisements elicited among youth, as well as which elements of the advertisements were most favorable and why. Of the seven advertisements, two advertised Coca-Cola, one Red Bull, one Skittles, one "Got Milk" advertisement (with a popular television and movie star as the central figure in the advertisement), one All Bran cereal (with Snow White as the main feature of the advertisement), and one Fruit Plus 100% juice.

Overall, a total of 150 written stories were recorded with varying levels of completeness (four stories had unclear content and were excluded from analysis). The four unhealthy products were the most popular advertisements to write about, suggesting that these products were within the top two favorite advertisements for approximately 80% of the participants. The two Coca-Cola advertisements were ranked the most highly with 44 participants writing about one of the Coca-Cola advertisements and 34 writing about the other. The Red Bull advertisement followed with 24 participants choosing to write about this advertisement and 17 participants wrote about the Skittles advertisement. The three healthy products were written about 27 times in total. The most popular healthy advertisement was for milk, followed by Fruit Plus 100% juice, and All Bran.

Similar to the focus group component of the study, included below is a sample of statements written by participants in response to the advertisements, grouped by advertisement.

Coca-Cola Advertisements

Many participants wrote about the positive feelings elicited by the two Coca-Cola advertisements. Below are some excerpts from several written stories, each describing happiness and the opportunity for possibilities, both themes that were present in the advertisements.

> *'Open up to the coke side of life.' Pretty much saying open up to a better life. It makes see things in a better way. A positive way. Looking at all of the creative things like rainbow bears, makes me feel really happy.*
>
> *In this picture, I think that Coca-Cola is trying to advertise that Coke will make you feel happy and energetic.*
>
> *I think that it is trying to bring out all the fun, and show you that there is a lot of excitement in drinking it, and that there is a lot of fun in drinking it, and that there is a lot happening when you drink it.*
>
> *When you open up a coke, all sorts of happiness flows out. It will remind you of all the happy things in life! The colors of the rainbow come out. Teddy bears dance and play. Cars 'fly' out. Drinks of happiness dance out. Bubbles fizz out happily. Ideas are able to flow.*
>
> *I like the picture! It reminds me of fun times and pretty things. Happy stuff is able to be free in you. Also, when you taste that first sip, that 'ahh…' tells everyone around you, 'Hello all! I have had a coke and I am very happy about it!"*
>
> *A magical coke bottle has life inside of it like teddy bears and school buses and lights and music. It shows that coke has real life inside of it and if you drink it you can experience real life. It also shows that coke and life is sort of like a tree, connected together, just branching out.*
>
> *The coke ad was my favorite advertisement because it makes you think that when you open a coke bottle, you open a world of possibilities.*

Red Bull Advertisement

The advertisement for Red Bull elicited discussions of Einstein, who was pictured in the advertisement. Several participants linked Einstein to positive qualities of the product, especially his intelligence. For example, one participant wrote "... *how they used Albert Einstein to show because he was a very famous scientist and people tend to doubt themselves. So, when its says, 'Einstein knows energy. Do you think you know better than Einstein?' People automatically think that the product is good. In the actual picture it shows Einstein thinking very hard and carefully about something and it shows in a bubble that a Red Bull equals mc², so it makes me think that a Red Bull really is energy and that it is the best way to get energy.*"

Another participant commented *"The ad is trying to imply Red Bull is a really good energy drink, so when you drink it you'll know a lot more about the meaning of energy than Albert Einstein ever would."*

A third participant also wrote, *"This ad is humorous because it does a play off of a well known physicist (Albert Einstein), saying that Einstein thinks Red Bull is pure, awesome energy, and then challenges the reader by asking if they would go against Einstein's word, him being an extremely talented and smart man, therefore forcing the reader to accept this fact out of a form of guilt for going against the smartest man that has ever lived."*

"Got Milk" Advertisement

The most popular healthy advertisement was for milk and it featured a popular television and movie star. A total of 14 stories were written about this advertisement and many focused on the healthfulness of the product and several commented on the use of a celebrity to promote the product. For example one participant wrote, *"In this Got Milk? Ad, it shows Hayden Panettiere holding a glass of milk which is being smashed. Below the photo, it says that you don't have to be a hero to be invincible. This is because milk helps build muscles. In the photo, the glass that the milk is in is breaking. Maybe it suggests that milk helps you be strong because it is strong itself? In the photo, they show a wide known celebrity which can be used to convince people to drink milk because she drinks it, too. Also, the phrase "got milk?" is quite catchy."*

Another participant commented, *"I think this is an effective ad, and is probably directed to all ages. Boys would like it because the girl on the ad is attractive. Girls could like it because they would want to strive to look as good as the girl, and milk drinkers or people who want to drink milk because it utilizes the logical appeal by adding statistics and factual information about the benefits of drinking milk. It also uses the emotional appeal by using a pop star figure that is well known to appeal to a larger variety of people."*

Discussion

Food and beverage advertising is prominent in the lives of children (IOM, 2006; Gantz et al., 2007). While the previous studies suggest that increased exposure to food and beverage advertising is associated with greater preferences for and choices of unhealthy food and beverage products (IOM, 2006; Lapierre et al., 2011; Pine & Nash, 2003; Roberto et al., 2010; Robinson et al., 2007; Valkenburg & Buijzen, 2005), few studies have used objective measures of attention to determine what components of these advertisements gain the greatest attention of youth. In addition, the use of a multi-method study to better understand how youth perceive and evaluate food and beverage advertising allows for a nuanced look at what it is about advertising that may be so appealing to this audience. Through the present study, we were able to document that youth who reported greater susceptibility to food and beverage advertising (i.e., exposure to food and beverage advertising and owning and/or willingness to own food and beverage branded merchandise) also reported more unhealthy food and beverage preferences as well as made more unhealthy food and beverage choices. These findings are similar to the previous research on food and beverage preferences and choices; however, they extend this work to include a measure of overall susceptibility similar to previous work in the alcohol and tobacco fields. In particular, cross-sectional research from McClure, Dal Cin, Gibson, and Sargent (2006) found that individuals who owned at least one alcohol-branded merchandise item were significantly more likely to have begun using alcohol than their non-owning counterparts. Additionally, in longitudinal research, ownership of alcohol-branded merchandise predicted both initiation of alcohol use and binge drinking at follow-up (McClure et al., 2009). Other work also suggests that individuals who were more receptive to tobacco marketing (i.e., had a favorite cigarette advertisement and/or owned or were willing to use a tobacco promotional item) were more likely to start smoking as teenagers (Pierce et al., 2010) and be established smokers in young adulthood (Gilpin, White, Messer, & Pierce, 2007). Given these similarities, continued work with measures of food and beverage susceptibility is warranted. Additionally, unlike tobacco and alcohol, parents are the likely purchasers of many of the food and beverage products consumed by youth aged 8–15 years. As such, future work should include measures of parenting to better understand the role parents play in these associations.

We also found that youth with greater food and beverage advertising susceptibility spent more time looking at unhealthy food and beverage items within advertisements. Additionally, youth who reported greater exposure to food and beverage advertising also reported greater unhealthy food and beverage preferences and spent more time looking at unhealthy food and beverage items. These findings, while self-report based, are similar to the previous work which has documented associations between exposure to advertising and preferences (IOM, 2006). Extending this research, we also found that greater self-reported exposure was associated with an objective measure of attention, specifically, time spent on unhealthy food and beverage items. Additionally, the measure of exposure used in this study included a comprehensive list of several channels of advertising including billboards, inside and outside of stores, at community events, in magazines, on television, on radio, and on the computer or Internet. Overall, the quantitative findings of this study suggest further research is warranted in this area to continue to explore these associations among larger, more diverse groups of youth. Additionally, future research should explore if differences in attention vary by important moderators such as age, gender, and weight status.

The results of the qualitative findings indicate that youth are aware of food and beverage advertising and can readily recall seeing advertisements for fast food and sugar-sweetened beverages. Additionally, youth are aware of many of the advertising tactics used such as the placement of logos and the use of popular celebrities to promote the product. When asked to write stories about their favorite advertisements from a set of advertisement given to them, 80% of the stories focused on the unhealthy product advertisements and many participants wrote about the feelings elicited by these images. Moreover, participants described advertisements for unhealthy food and beverage products with enthusiasm and suggested that the products may bring them (and others) happiness. While some youth did choose the healthy advertisements to write about, most commented on the use of a popular celebrity or Disney character and cited that as a reason for liking that advertisement. Further research is needed that continues to explore differences in healthy and unhealthy advertisements, in both objective attention paid to the components of the advertisement as well as qualitative preferences and descriptions of the advertising.

While this study was one of the first to use a multi-method approach it does have some limitations. The small sample size may have limited the quantitative findings; however, for both qualitative and eye-tracking data, the sample size was adequate, given that some studies include as few as 30 participants. Additionally, as this study is cross-sectional, we were not able to assess whether attention to advertising is a predictive factor of the food and beverage preferences and choices of youth, as well as their weight status. The relationship may in fact be the converse, in that youth who have a higher weight status develop preferences for advertisements which contain unhealthy food and beverage products and, thus, spend greater amounts of time attending to these advertisements. Future longitudinal research is needed that elucidates this relationship. Finally, this study is also limited in its methodology, in particular, by the artificial lab setting as it does not take into account the multi-tasking reality of real life, which could have resulted in some participants looking at the advertisements for longer or shorter than they would if they were allowed to look as they would when alone or in familiar settings. However, given that the previous research has focused on self-reported measures of exposure, using an objective measure, such as those provided by eye-tracking technology, is an important step in better understanding how and why food and beverage advertising influences youth.

While there are limitations to this study, several strengths should be noted. Much of the current evidence for the relationship between food and beverage advertising and diet and obesity-related outcomes is for young children (aged 2–11 years); however, this study also included older adolescents (aged 12–15 years) to begin to document associations among this group as well. Additionally, although researchers have begun to examine the influence of exposure to food and beverage advertising on youth, much of the literature remains focused on how exposure to television advertising affects young people, with few studies examining the structural components of an advertisement that actually gain the attention of youth. As such, this study is also strengthened by the fact that the exposure variable included an objective measure of attention to food and beverage advertising. Finally, this study also incorporated the use of both quantitative and qualitative methods to better understand how youth perceive and evaluate food and beverage advertising.

Implications/Practical Lessons

The use of a multi-method study to better understand how youth perceive and evaluate food and beverage advertising can provide important insight into how this at-risk group develops favorable attitudes towards unhealthy food and beverage products via these prevalent visual stimuli. Using several methodologies not only allows us to understand the exposure levels and attention paid to advertisements for consumable products by youth but it also incorporates potential qualitative explanations behind these quantitative values. The combination of these research strategies maximizes our potential to document and describe how perceptions are formed and how these perceptions play out in the preferences for and purchases of these products, where greater exposure and attention to these advertisements could result in increased consumption of unhealthy products, leading to long-term, negative health outcomes.

However, future studies are needed that continue to build the evidence base on the influence of food and beverage advertising on youth. By providing additional findings to the scientific evidence base, the information gained from this study may also be used to support current policy initiatives aimed at changing the landscape of food and beverage advertising. For example, the Interagency Working Group on Food Marketing to Children has proposed nutrition principles to guide industry self-regulatory efforts (Federal Trade Commission, n.d.). In particular, the Working Group recommends that new food products be designed and existing food products be reformulated to "make a meaningful contribution to a healthful diet (FTC, n.d., p.4)" focusing specifically on the foods most heavily marketed to children and adolescents (i.e., cereals, sugar-sweetened beverages). Additionally, the Children's Food and Beverage Advertising Initiative (CFBAI) (Council of Better Business Bureaus, 2012; see Chap. 6) is a voluntary self-regulation program that includes several large food and beverage companies in the USA. The core principles of CFBAI include establishing nutrition standards that are consistent with scientific/government standards and limiting the use of third-party licensed characters, for example.

While voluntary self-regulation is a notable first step, as Sharma, Teret, and Brownell (2010) point out, it still remains unclear as to whether such initiatives will be helpful or harmful; thus, additional research that demonstrates the influence of food and beverage advertising on youth is needed so as to put continued pressure on the food and beverage industry, especially those companies that are members of the CFBAI, to make significant changes to the way they advertise to youth. If findings from this study are replicated with larger and more diverse samples, policy changes could include regulating the size and placement of unhealthy food and beverage items and their corresponding branded logos and animated characters.

Future studies should also include a deeper analysis of the online environment inhabited by youth and their potential exposure to unhealthy consumable products via this rapidly developing media source. In addition, youth continue to spend an increasing amount of time using social media websites such as Facebook and Twitter, which, due to the site's reliance on user-generated content, do not abide by the same marketing standards as do product websites. Future research is needed that documents the content of this online and digital marketing to better understand what types of messages and content youth are exposed to through these channels. Youth also comprise a large user base of mobile device applications; future studies should also investigate the prominence of food and beverage advertising on this new platform.

Finally, findings from the current study may have important implications for future use in media literacy or other intervention programs. Specifically, given the potential influence of attention to advertising on the food and beverage preferences of youth, interventions may consider addressing ways in which to teach youth about the advertising techniques that marketers use. Moreover, teaching youth critical thinking skills and/or providing them with opportunities to analyze and question the content of advertising messages may help them to understand the purpose behind these marketing techniques and perhaps make changes to their food and beverage preferences and choices as a result. Additionally, using effective strategies to create advertising messages that can be used to promote healthy food and beverage items that appeal to youth would be important. In particular, the use of appealing healthy food and beverage items, as well as relevant and age appropriate animated characters/branded logos within healthy food and beverage advertisements could be important to explore as an influence on the healthy food and beverage preferences of youth. Continued research in this area will help us to further our knowledge on the most influential components of advertising in order to develop the most effective counter-marketing and media literacy campaigns.

Overweight and obesity among youth has risen to levels not seen before in this country and in many nations of the world. As rates of obesity-related diseases and negative health outcomes continue to grow, especially among youth, continued research is needed to better understand the multi-factorial causes of obesity. The promotion of foods and beverages through advertising is one such contributing factor. Through further research and intervention efforts, we can better understand the exposure and influence of food and beverage advertising and we can provide youth and parents with the knowledge and skills they need to navigate and resist these influences.

References

Alvy, L. M., & Calvert, S. L. (2008). Food marketing on popular children's websites: A content analysis. *Journal of the American Dietetic Association, 108*, 710–713.

Bell, R. A., Cassady, D., Culp, J., & Alcalay, R. (2009). Frequency and types of foods advertised on Saturday morning and weekday afternoon English- and Spanish-Language American television programs. *Journal of Nutrition Education and Behavior, 41*, 406–413.

Connor, S. (2006). Food-related advertising on preschool television: Building brand recognition in young viewers. *Pediatrics, 118*, 1478–1485.

Coordinated Approach to Child Health (CATCH). (2010). School physical activity and nutrition (SPAN) questionnaire. Retrieved June 2, 2011, from http://www.sph.uth.tmc.edu/catch/catch_em/MeasureToolsDesc_01.htm.

Council of Better Business Bureaus (2012). Children's food and beverage advertising initiative. Retrieved January 18, 2012, from http://www.bbb.org/us/children-food-beverage-advertising-initiative/.

Domel, S. B., Baranowski, T., Davis, H., Leonard, S. B., Riley, P., & Baranowski, J. (1993). Measuring fruit and vegetable preferences among 4th and 5th grade students. *Preventive Medicine, 22*, 866–879.

Federal Trade Commission. (2008). *Marketing food to children and adolescents: A review of industry expenditures, activities, and self-regulation. A report to Congress*. Retrieved June 19, 2012, from http://www.ftc.gov/os/2008/07/P064504foodmktingreport.pdf.

Flegal, K. M. (2000). The effects of age categorization on estimates of overweight prevalence for children. *International Journal of Obesity, 24*, 1636–1641.

Flegal, K., Tabak, C., & Ogden, C. (2006). Overweight in children: Definitions and interpretation. *Health Education Research, 21*(6), 755–760.

Fox, R. J., Krugman, D. M., Fletcher, J. E., & Fischer, P. M. (1998). Adolescents' attention to beer and cigarette print ads and associated product warnings. *Journal of Advertising, 27*(3), 57–68.

Gantz, W., Schwartz, N., Angelini, J., & Rideout, V. (2007). *Food for thought: Television food advertising to children in the United States*. Menlo Park, CA: Henry J. Kaiser Foundation.

Garretson, J., & Niedrich, R. (2004). Spokes-characters: Creating character trust and positive brand attitudes. *Journal of Advertising, 33*(2), 25–36.

Gilpin, E., White, M., Messer, K., & Pierce, J. (2007). Receptivity to tobacco advertising and promotions among young adolescents as a predictor of established smoking in young adulthood. *American Journal of Public Health, 97*(8), 1489–1495.

Goodman, E., Hinden, B., & Khandelwal, S. (2000). Accuracy of teen and parental reports of obesity and body mass index. *Pediatrics, 106*, 52–58.

Grier, S. A., & Kumanyika, S. (2010). Targeted marketing and public health. *Annual Review of Public Health, 31*, 349–369.

Grube, J. W., & Waiters, E. (2005). Alcohol in the media: Content and effects on drinking beliefs and behaviors among youth. *Adolescent Medicine Clinics, 16*(2), 327–343.

Harris, J. L., Schwartz, M., & Brownell, K. D. (2009). Marketing foods to children and adolescents: Licensed characters and other promotions on packaged foods in the supermarket. *Public Health Nutrition, 13*(3), 409–417.

Hoelscher, D. M., Day, R. S., Kelder, S. H., & Ward, J. L. (2003). Reproducibility and validity of the secondary level School-Based Nutrition Monitoring student questionnaire. *Journal of the American Dietetic Association, 103*(2), 186–194.

Holmqvist, K., Nystrom, M., Andersson, R., Dewhurst, R., Jarodzka, H., & Van De Weijer, J. (2011). *Eye tracking: A comprehensive guide to methods and measures*. New York, NY: Oxford University Press.

Institute of Medicine. (2006). *Food marketing to children and youth: Threat or opportunity*. Washington, DC: National Academies Press.

Just, M. A., & Carpenter, P. A. (1980). A theory of reading: From eye fixations to comprehension. *Psychological Review, 87*, 329–354.

Kelly, B., Cretikos, M., Rogers, K., & King, L. (2008). The commercial food landscape: Outdoor food advertising around primary schools in Australia. *Australian and New Zealand Journal of Public Health, 32*(6), 522–528.

Kelly, B., Hattersley, L., King, L., & Flood, V. (2008). Persuasive food marketing to children: Use of cartoons and competitions in Australian commercial television advertisements. *Health Promotion International, 23*(4), 337–344.

Kuczmarksi, R. J., Ogden, C. L., Guo, S. S., Grummer-Strawn, L. M., Flegal, K. M., Mei Z. (2002). 2000 CDC growth charts for the United States: Methods and development. National Center for Health Statistics. *Vital Health Statistics, 11*(246).

Lapierre, M. A., Vaala, S. E., & Linebarger, D. L. (2011). Influence of licensed spokescharacters and health cues on children's ratings of cereal taste. *Archives of Pediatric Adolescent Medicine, 165*(3), 229–234.

Lawrence, D. (2003). The role of characters in kids marketing. *Advertising and Marketing to Children*, 43–48.

Lingas, E. O., Dorfman, L., & Bukofzer, E. (2009). Nutrition content of food and beverage products on Web sites popular with children. *American Journal of Public Health, 99*, S587–S592.

Maher, A., Wilson, N., & Signal, L. (2005). Advertising and availability of 'obesogenic' foods around New Zealand secondary schools: a pilot study. *The New Zealand Medical Journal, 118*(1218).

McClure, A., Dal Cin, S., Gibson, J., & Sargent, J. (2006). Ownership of alcohol-branded merchandise and initiation of teen drinking. *American Journal of Preventive Medicine, 30*(4), 277–283.

McClure, A., Stoolmiller, M., Tanski, S., Worth, K., & Sargent, J. (2009). Alcohol-branded merchandise and its association with drinking attitudes and outcomes in US adolescents. *Archives of Pediatric Adolescent Medicine, 163*(3), 211–217.

Ogden, C. L., Carroll, M. D., Curtin, L. R., Lamb, M. M., & Flegal, K. M. (2010). Prevalence of high body mass index in US children and adolescents, 2007–2008. *Journal of the American Medical Association, 303*(3), 242–249.

Ogden, C., Yanovski, S., Carroll, M., & Flegal, K. (2007). The epidemiology of obesity. *Gastroenterology, 132*, 2987–2102.

Palmer, E., & Carpenter, C. (2006). Food and beverage marketing to children and youth: Trends and issues. *Media Psychology, 8*, 165–190.

Pasch, K. E., Komro, K. A., Perry, C. L., Hearst, M. O., & Farbakhsk, K. (2007). Outdoor alcohol advertising near schools: Where is it located, what does it advertise and how is it related to intentions and use among young adolescents? *Journal of Studies on Alcohol and Drugs, 68*(4), 587–596.

Penkilo, M., George, G. C., & Hoelscher, D. M. (2008). Reproducibility of the School-Based Nutrition Monitoring Questionnaire among fourth-grade students in Texas. *Journal of Nutrition Education and Behavior, 40*(1), 20–27.

Peterson, E. B., Thomsen, S., Lindsay, G., & John, K. (2010). Adolescents' attention to traditional and graphic tobacco warning labels: An eye-tracking approach. *Journal of Drug Education, 40*(3), 227–244.

Pierce, J., Messer, K., James, L., White, M., Kealey, S., & Vallone, D. (2010). Camel No.9 cigarette-marketing campaign targeted young teenage girls. *Pediatrics, 125*(4), 619–626.

Pine, K., & Nash, A. (2003). Barbie or Betty? Preschool children's preference for branded products and evidence for gender-linked differences. *Developmental and Behavioral Pediatrics, 24*, 219–224.

Powell, L. M., Schermbeck, R. M., Szczypka, G., Chaloupka, F. J., Braunschweig, C. L. (2011). Trends in the nutritional content of television food advertisements seen by children in the United States: Analyses by age, food categories, and companies. *Archives of Pediatric and Adolescent Medicine, 165*(12), 1078–1086. Epub 2011 Aug 1.

Powell, L. M., Szczypka, G., & Chaloupka, F. J. (2007). Adolescent exposure to food advertising on television. *American Journal of Preventive Medicine, 33*(4), S251–S256.

Rayner, K. (1998). Eye movements in reading and information processing: 20 years of research. *Psychological Bulletin, 124*(3), 372–422.

Rideout, V. J., Foehr, U. G., & Roberts, D. F. (2010). *Generation M2: Media in the lives of 8-to18-year-olds*. Menlo Park, CA: The Henry J. Kaiser Family Foundation.

Roberto, C., Baik, J., Harris, J., & Brownell, K. (2010). Influence of licensed characters of children's taste and snack preferences. *Pediatrics, 126*(1), 88–93.

Robinson, T., Borzekowski, D., Matheson, D., & Kraemer, H. (2007). Effects of fast food branding on young children's taste preferences. *Archives of Pediatric and Adolescent Medicine, 161*, 792–797.

Sharma, L. L., Teret, S. P., & Brownell, K. D. (2010). The Food Industry and Self-Regulation: Standards to Promote Success and to Avoid Public Health Failures. *American Journal of Public Health, 100* 240–246.

Sherry, B., Jefferds, M. E., & Grummer-Strawn, L. M. (2007). Accuracy of adolescent self-report of height and weight in assessing overweight status: A literature review. *Archives of Pediatric Adolescent Medicine, 161*(12), 1154–1161.

Story, M., & French, S. (2004). Food advertising and marketing directed at children and adolescents in the US. *International Journal of Behavioral Nutrition and Physical Activity, 1*(3), 1–17.

Sutherland, L. A., MacKenzie, T., Purvis, L. A., & Dalton, M. (2010). Prevalence of food and beverage brands in movies: 1996–2005. *Pediatrics, 125*, 468–474.

Thiagarajah, K., Fly, A. D., Hoelscher, D. M., Bai, Y., Lo, K., & Leone, A. (2008). Validating the food behavior questions from the elementary school SPAN questionnaire. *Journal of Nutrition Education and Behavior, 40*(5), 305–310.

Valkenburg, P., & Buijzen, M. (2005). Identifying determinants of young children's brand awareness: Television, parents, and peers. *Applied Developmental Psychology, 26*, 456–468.

Yancey, A. K., Cole, B. L., Brown, R., Williams, J. D., Hillier, A., & Kline, R. S. (2009). A cross-sectional prevalence study of ethnically targeted and general audience outdoor obesity-related advertising. *The Milbank Quarterly, 87*(1), 155–184.

Part IV
A Global Perspective of Food Marketing and the Role of Place

Chapter 12
Adolescents' Response to Food Marketing in Delhi, India

Melissa H. Stigler, Jose Medina, Monika Arora, Gaurang Nazar, Lindsay M. Rodrigues, K. Srinath Reddy, and Cheryl L. Perry

Background

The majority of this book relays research specific to the effects of media and communication, generally, on *reducing* childhood obesity. This chapter considers, instead, how media—and food marketing practices in particular—might be increasing childhood obesity, or at least contributing to this epidemic (Harris, Pomeranz, Lobstein, Brownell, 2008), which is now growing on a global scale (Wang & Lobstein, 2006). The chapter reports the results of a study from Delhi, India. In large cities of India now, like Delhi, the prevalence of obesity among affluent adolescents is comparable to youth in other developed nations in the West, like the USA and the UK (Wang, Chen, Shaikh, & Mathur, 2009). Compared to other countries in the West, however, the negative health sequelae of obesity, like diabetes, occur a decade earlier in the life course (UK Prospective Diabetes Study, 1994) and at lower BMI values (Misra, 2003), suggesting the problem of obesity may ultimately prove more challenging to ameliorate in India, when compared to the West. This may be further complicated by the evolving landscape of food marketing across India, given the relatively recent entrance of multinational food corporations into this country and increasing aspiration for Western lifestyles among its citizens (Goddard, 2009), especially by youth (or "Youngistans") (Robinson, De Vera, & Witt, 2008).

Globally, food promotion and advertising is the most common type of marketing practices geared towards youth. A growing body of research from the West confirms that young people not only recall, enjoy, and engage with these marketing campaigns

M.H. Stigler (✉) • J. Medina • L.M. Rodrigues • C.L. Perry
Michael & Susan Dell Center for Healthy Living, School of Public Health, University of Texas Health Science Center, Austin, TX, USA
e-mail: Melissa.H.Stigler@uth.tmc.edu

M. Arora • G. Nazar • K.S. Reddy
HRIDAY (Health-Related Information Dissemination Amongst Youth), Delhi, India

J.D. Williams et al. (eds.), *Advances in Communication Research to Reduce Childhood Obesity*, DOI 10.1007/978-1-4614-5511-0_12,

but also change their food preferences, purchasing behavior, and consumption as a result of them (Cairns, Angus, & Hastings, 2009, Hastings et al., 2006). Since most advertised foods contrast sharply with that recommended by public health professionals, this is cause for concern. To date, the majority of research on food marketing to young people has been conducted in developed countries like the USA and the UK (Cairns et al., 2009). Few studies from developing nations like India exist Hastings et al., 2006).

India's Food Industry and Food Marketing

India is the second largest producer of food worldwide, and its food processing industry is growing rapidly (IBEF, 2011), driven, in large part, by the entry of Western corporations like McDonalds into this market (Kulkarni, Lassar, Sridhar, & Venkitachalam, 2009). By 2015, the food industry in India is predicted to grow to $300 billion USD, up from $200 billion USD in 2007 (IBEF, 2011). Recently, increased trade liberalization has opened new, larger market opportunities for many multinational companies in this area of the world, including food companies (Goddard, 2009). "India is special in terms of existing opportunities and market potential," according to the Global CEO for Domino's Pizza (IBEF, 2011). These multinational companies are inspired by an economy in India that continues to grow (unlike many other countries worldwide at present) and large and increasing numbers of middle and upper class consumers, including young people (Goddard). Although estimates vary, more than 250 million people belong to the middle and upper classes in India (Tharoor, 2007), and these consumers are currently purchasing at a higher rate than most countries, worldwide (Saha, 2009). Although the Indian middle class is less affluent than middle classes in the West or China, the sheer size of this market may someday exceed the buying power of the American middle class. By 2030, India will be home to almost 20% of the world's population (Bijapurkar, 2007).

The extent of food marketing has increased in recent years in India (Nawathe, Gawande, & Dethe, 2007). From 2003 to 2005, for example, the money spent on marketing food to young people in India rose by more than 150% (Hawkes, 2007). By 2007, over 50% of the food industry's budget in India was spent on food marketing alone, compared to only 2% on research and development (Nawathe et al.). Further, the nature of food marketing in India is not unlike that in other parts of the world, such as the USA. Television advertising dominates food marketing in India and other parts of Asia, like it does in the USA and the UK (Escalante de Cruz, Phillips, Visch, & Bulan Saunders, 2004). In 2004, 40–50% of advertisements displayed during children's programming were about food (Escalante de Cruz et al.). For each hour of children's programming reviewed in this study, 15 min were devoted to advertising, overall (Escalante de Cruz et al.). At that time, Coca Cola, PepsiCo, Britannia, Parle, and Nestle sponsored the majority of food advertisements, promoting soft drinks, confectionary, and biscuits (i.e., cookies) (Escalante de Cruz et al.).

In 2010, Hindustan Unilever Ltd topped these charts, with the largest commercial volume, overall (Businessworld, 2010). This company originated in the UK and, in addition to home and personal care products, offers Knorr's soups and Wall's ice cream locally, as a leading food company in India (HUL, 2011).

Although the marketing strategies that these food companies employ in India and other parts of Asia are similar to those they use in developed countries (Robinson et al., 2008), their impact might be different, given the fast pace at which they are being implemented. Food advertising messages directed to youth stress fun, excitement, and taste, while messages to parents note health benefits (Hastings et al., 2006). However, the food products being promoted are mainly energy dense and nutrient poor, as they are high fat, salt, and sugar (HFSS) foods (Lobstein, Macmullan, McGrath, & Witt, 2008). Globally, the most commonly advertised food products are sugar-sweetened breakfast cereals, soft drinks, savory snacks, fast food, and confectionary—also known as the "Big Five" (Cairns et al., 2009). In India, ready-to-eat breakfast cereals are only beginning to emerge, so that they are not (yet) heavily advertised. However, the majority of food products that are currently marketed to younger consumers in India, like other parts of the world, are micro-nutrient poor and not in compliance with national dietary guidelines for Indians (National Institute of Nutrition, 2011); in fact, they are inversely related to them. The speed with which many multinational food companies and their marketing campaigns have arrived, executed, and prospered in India has been swift. For example, in 1997, only 5,172 min of soft drink advertisements aired on television. By 2000, this had risen to over 30,000 min—an increase of more than 500% (Escalante de Cruz et al., 2004). Though no more recent data could be found for comparison, it is likely that the extent of these advertisements has grown even further over a decade later, given the continued prominence of Coca-Cola and PepsiCo in the food and advertising sectors of India today.

Despite the increased pervasiveness of food marketing in India, few studies have evaluated how children and adolescents have responded to it. Only three such studies were identified in the most recent comprehensive reviews of this literature (Cairns et al., 2009; Hastings et al., 2006), and they were conducted over a decade ago. Two other more recent and relevant studies from India (Bhattacharyya & Kohli, 2007; Nawathe et al., 2007) and one of immigrants from India in the USA (Mahima & Puja, 2008) were identified in preparation for this chapter, but they focus on parent perspectives. Given the changes over the last decade, youth perspectives need to be considered, too.

"Youngistans" and "Westernization"

India is uniquely situated worldwide, with an especially large and potentially lucrative target market of youth. More than 400 million children and adolescents call this country home, which is 40% of India's current population and the most of any country worldwide (Youthreach, 2004). The youth segment in India will continue to grow in coming years, such that over half of its population will remain under the age of 25 years (Bansal, 2004). By 2050, India will have the largest working age population, worldwide (Pant, 2008). Many multinational companies are attracted to this potential market, as these youth want to spend and have access to monies to do so (Goddard, 2009). This younger generation is referred to by many as Youngistans or Youngistans, being a blend of young and Hindustan, another name for India. Their image, in large part, has not only been created by the media (Sen, 2010) but is perpetuated by it (see PepsiCo's website for these youth, http://www.youngistaan.com/wow/p2/index.php) and will, no doubt, ultimately change the way many products are advertised (Sen).

Although young people may not yet have the purchasing power comparable to their Western counterparts, they are the center of the Indian family and, as such, can heavily influence purchasing decisions of parents, in addition to purchasing products on their own (Kaur & Singh, 2006). To date, most studies of their purchasing power have focused on the influence on the family, in regards to purchases for durable goods, like televisions, refrigerators, and cars (Kaur & Singh), though studies are beginning to emerge specific to food (e.g., Mahima & Puja, 2008). Regardless of product category, most of these purchases are geared towards consuming Western goods, as there is a strong desire—among the old and young alike (but, especially, among the young)—to emulate the West and its affluent lifestyle (Goddard, 2009). Western brands are status symbols in India and are increasingly available, given globalization of the Indian market.

Like many emerging economies, India is changing quickly. Globalization is changing the ways these young people live and the social environments in which they reside, in ways that affect their health (Beaglehole & Yach, 2003). Globalization refers to the increasing connectivity of our world and its cultures, driven by the exchange of ideas and goods, often through media outlets and marketing efforts (Tomlinson, 1999). According to Arnett (2002), adolescents can play a central role in globalization, as they are integrally involved in and affected by it. Compared to adults, adolescents are more receptive to novel ideas and new products and can be more exposed to different types of media, like television and the Internet. As a result, they can often be the target of specific marketing efforts increasingly focused on selling these "global brands" to "global teens," given similar patterns of consumption by urban youth worldwide (UNDP, 1998).

The majority of "global brands" originate in the West and include a variety of multinational food companies like Coca-Cola, Kellogg's, and Nestlé. Indeed, the most pervasive "global" influence in contemporary India is that of the West, especially that from the USA and the UK. McDonalds and Pizza Hut are prolific now, offering consumers vegetarian versions of their usual fare, like the Maharaja Mac (Pingali, 2007), to appeal to the Indian consumer. The growth of the Western-style fast-food industry in India has been phenomenal. Kentucky Fried Chicken and Pizza Hut, for example, entered the Indian market with 1 restaurant in 1995. By 2003, there were 70 restaurants; by 2005, there were 127; and 1000 are planned for 2014 (India Franchise Blog, 2011). Thus, in this country, as in many others in Asia, globalization has become synonymous with "westernization." No studies of the effects of food marketing to young people in India have considered this evolving and increasingly "westernized" landscape.

The purpose of this study is to document young adolescents' response to food marketing in contemporary India. In doing so, their recall of favorite food advertising is considered, in addition to their preferred characteristics of food marketing campaigns and perceived impact. The influence of "westernization" on their response is examined, too, so the literature that has already appeared from India can be updated in this way. Globally, few studies have considered the exposure to and effects of food advertising on adolescents, compared to the large body of research on children (Brownell, Schwartz, Puhl, Henderson, & Harris, 2009). Thus, this study extends the body of literature on this key developmental phase of life, as well. Adolescence is a critical period in the life course, since consumer socialization takes on new meaning (Kaur & Singh, 2006) and key health-related behaviors like eating are established during this time and ultimately track into adulthood (Kelder, Perry, Klepp, & Lytle, 1994).

Methods

Study Setting and Participants

This is a qualitative study, cross-sectional by design. Fifteen focus groups were conducted in five Private schools in Delhi, India, between September and December, 2009. A total of 151 students enrolled in 6th and 8th grades (10–14 years old) were recruited through purposive sampling and agreed to participate. In India, Private schools typically cater to families of middle to high socio-economic status (Sharma, 1999). English is the medium of instruction in these schools. Each focus group included 10–12 participants, with equal numbers of boys and girls present. Ethical clearances for the study were obtained from appropriate institutional review boards in India and the USA. Active parent consent and active student assent were required for study participation.

Data Collection and Interview Guide

Each focus group was led by one moderator, assisted by two note-takers. All field staff were trained by a social scientist in appropriate techniques (Mishra et al., 2005). At the start of each focus group, the moderator explained the purpose of and procedure for the discussion, followed by a short ice-breaker. Then, they facilitated the discussion, using an interview guide. Each discussion lasted about 60 min and was audio taped. Teachers were not present. All focus groups were conducted in English.

Table 12.1 Interview guide for focus groups—food marketing campaigns

1. Of all the advertising campaigns for food or drink, which one do you like the best? What is the product being advertised? How often have you seen this campaign?
2. Thinking about this campaign, where have you seen the ad? Who are the models in the ad? What are the models doing?
3. Thinking about this campaign, what is the main message of the campaign? What did you understand from this message?
4. Thinking about this campaign, is the ad in a local Indian language or in English? Which language should the ad be in? Would you say the ad is more "Indian" or more "Western" in flavor? Why? Which would you prefer?
5. Did this campaign make you feel like trying the product it advertised? If/when you tried the product, did it meet your expectations based on the advertising campaign? Would you recommend it to your friends/family?

Among other questions, the interview guide included queries specific to food marketing campaigns. Table 12.1 provides the list of questions used to guide discussion.

Data Coding and Analysis

Data analysis began concurrently with data collection. Each focus group was transcribed from the audiotapes by the note-takers on the same day the discussion was conducted. A detailed account of each discussion that included non-verbal cues and gestures was also prepared from notes. This was integrated with the detailed transcripts so that minute details of the focus groups were not missed. After all transcripts were ready, they were transferred to the US team where further analysis was done. At this stage, data were coded and organized into particular themes relevant to the research questions of interest. This was done with software for qualitative data analysis (NVivo 9; QSR International, 2011). Responses were organized by grade level and school type, to be able to detect and interpret differences, if any. Once analyzed, the results were returned to India, where they went through verification checks with field staff to ensure interpretations of student responses were reasonable and accurate.

Results

No differences in these responses were noted by grade level or school type. Therefore, results are presented in narrative and summative form, for all participants. Where appropriate, narratives are made more concrete with actual responses from student participants. These responses are *italicized* and "quoted" when they appear.

Exposure to Food Advertising

Students reported seeing food advertisements primarily on television, on both adult and children's television channels alike. They reported watching their favorite ad four to five times, daily. The frequency of advertisements during television shows did not go unnoticed. "*When we see any [half-hour] program [on TV], the program is only of 15–20 minutes. And if the program is of 1 hour, half an hour these channels spend on advertising to earn money. So that is a major problem.*" Although television was the main outlet for these food advertisements, students reported seeing advertisements for food in newspapers, magazines, billboards, and cinema halls. Students also reported watching them on the Internet, though this communication channel was least common.

Recall of Food Advertising

A large majority of these students were able to easily recall a favorite food advertisement. For most types of foods, their recall was strongly linked to particular brand names. This included advertisements for pre-sugared breakfast cereals (e.g., Kellogg's), soft drinks (e.g., Thums Up, Coca Cola), savory snacks (e.g., Kurkure), fast foods (e.g., McDonalds), and other types of processed foods (e.g., Maggi noodles). Although students could recall favorite advertisements for a variety of confectionary products (e.g., chocolates, cookies, ice cream), brand awareness was not as strong.

Overall, students remembered more advertisements for Western-style foods (e.g., pizza, burgers) than for Indian-style foods. Although students recalled favorite advertisements for Eastern-style foods (e.g., noodles) too, they recalled advertisements for a much wider variety of Western foods. Several students noted, "*Ninety percent of advertisements are for Western foods*"; "*We see more advertisements of chips, burgers, soft-drinks, pizzas*"; and "*No, they are not Indian foods. They are more Western foods. But now they are available in India, too.*" When asked about advertisements for Indian foods, only two were mentioned: "badam pista" (an energy powder added to milk, also called Complan) and "chayavanprash" (an ayurvedic paste used as an immune booster). Advertisements for Maggi noodles were the most popular Eastern-style food advertised, and one of the most popular campaigns, overall. Maggi is discussed further, below.

Students were cognizant that Western-style food was increasingly finding its way into the Indian subcontinent. "*It has been adopted from the Western culture because [parents] don't have time to prepare [Indian] foods for them or their children. Now-a-days, Western culture is coming to India; it results in consumption of [this kind] of food.*" Notably, when students discussed traditional Indian fare, they almost always referred to food types by name (e.g., roti, dal, idli). However, when students referred to Western foods, they mainly referred to brand names, not food types (e.g., 7Up, Lays, Pizza Hut). As well during interviews, some students named Western (e.g., macaroni, hot dogs) and Eastern (e.g., noodles, momos) food products as Indian, blurring demarcation in origin.

Western brand recognition was strongest in the fast food (e.g., McDonalds, Pizza Hut) and pre-sugared cereal (e.g., Kellogg's) categories, while Indian brand recognition was strongest in the savory snacks (e.g., Kurkure, a cheeto-like snack) and confectionary (e.g., Amul ice cream) categories. Western and Indian brands were equally endorsed in regards to beverages. All Western brands were for carbonated soft drinks (e.g., Coca Cola, Pepsi), except Tropicana juice. Indian brands included carbonated soft drinks (e.g., Limca), non-carbonated health drinks (e.g., Complan, Horlicks), and other types of non-carbonated drinks (e.g., Maaza). Adverts for Indian brand fruit juices were popular, too.

Favorite Characteristics of Food Advertising

Several characteristics of the advertising campaigns were especially appealing to these students. Most notably, the use of popular actors and actresses to advertise food products drew close attention from students. Students easily associated celebrity names with certain brand names of food: Aamir Khan with Coca-Cola, Juhi Chawla with Kurkure, Katrina Kaif with Slice, Javed Jaffery with Maggi ketchup, and Saif Ali Khan with Pepsi, among others. The impact of this technique seemed strong. "*If they [celebrities] are eating it, then we should also do it.*" A good example of this advertising technique is the campaign for Thums Up, which was by far the most popular campaign reported by these students. Advertisements for this cola-flavored soft drink feature Akshay Kumar, a famous actor, whizzing through city streets, doing death-defying stunts to get to his Thums Up (e.g., see http://www.desihits.com/news/view/akshay-kumar-in-thums-up-cola-commercial-20100413; "If you want me, come and get me" commercial for 2010). Students discussed how celebrities were portrayed as being "*cool*," and that students, therefore, could be "*cool-er*" if they ate/drank the products being advertised. "*Through celebrities, they allure teenagers to buy these items and portray them as tasty and cool.*"

The other most popular advertising campaign was for Maggi noodles. These commercials feature non-celebrity spokespersons, like parents and children, preparing and consuming them (e.g., http://www.youtube.com/watch?v=Uf67yrJ7y6Q&NR=1). Students were aware of and responded favorably to Maggi's slogan, "*taste bhi health bhi [provides both taste and health].*" They knew, too, that "*Maggi is quick to make (in 2 minutes).*" Taste, convenience, and health effects, therefore, were key messages in these commercials that students enjoyed. Like Maggi, advertising campaigns for other food products, like Complan and Horlicks, often resonated with students for their health claims, too—that their product was high in protein, or that it would make one strong.

Students preferred watching television commercials that were conveyed in Hindi, the national language of India. According to these students, about 80% of food advertisements are in Hindi, even when seen on Western television channels, like HBO or Star. "*[It should be in] Hindi, so it can be easily understood.*" "*Because the language of the other country [English] and the language we speak [local English] is bit different. It is faster, and sometimes there are very tough English words we don't understand. We understand it only after [an advertisement] appears 4–5 times. It is difficult sometimes."*

Students mentioned other characteristics of these food marketing campaigns that they enjoyed, though did so less often compared to the factors mentioned above. For instance, innovation was perceived as effective at getting the attention of children. As one 6th grader said, *"Children do not get attracted by masalas and all these [more traditional] things. Children already know about all this, they want to know about new things."* Offering toys as part of the campaign was also noted as a successful strategy. *"There is a gift in the packet which also attracts." "Sir, there is one ad of Boost [a health drink]. A flying saucer is given free with them. Sir, some students, they collect them."*

Impact of Food Advertising

These food promotion campaigns had an impact not only on students' attitudes towards a particular food but also on their food purchase and consumption behavior. Given that these were their most favorite campaigns, the students' attitude change was generally favorable towards the food. *"If we see interesting ads, then we think they [products] are good for us."* Students reported that these advertisements made them feel like they must purchase the food product. However, once they reflected on the advertisement, some students understood that the particular food might not be in their best interest. *"Sir, first we feel like buying it, but then afterwards we understand these are not healthy foods, so we should not buy it."* Other students reported purchasing food and drinks (e.g., Horlicks, Maggi, Coca-Cola) after watching these advertisements. Students also reported eating or drinking products, given the advertisements. One student noted, *"We like Akshay Kumar's advertisement for Thums Up on TV, so we buy and drink it."* Another said, *"After seeing the Maggi ad … we feel like eating Maggi—and I will eat it."*

The effects of the advertisements extended beyond the effects on the child. Many children reported further promoting food items to others such as family, friends, and peers if they have a pleasant experience with the product, after trying it. *"Yes, we do tell them if we like it. We tell them that it tastes nice and they should also get it."* Some students reported their parents would yield to their demands for certain food products, given "pester power," while others said their mothers would refuse to buy.

Discussion

The food marketing landscape in India appears to have undergone substantial changes in the last decade, when considered from the perspective of young people. The effect of globalization, or "westernization," seems strong and can change the way that adolescents behave (Arnett, 2002). This study provides evidence to support that school-going youth in India engage with and enjoy food marketing initiatives that are geared towards Western products but are promoted in ways that are inherently Indian. The use of local language and local celebrities are especially effective strategies. This study suggests campaigns are changing food purchasing and consumption in Delhi, India, too.

Students recalled favorite advertisements in each of the "Big Five" frequently advertised categories of food—pre-sweetened breakfast cereals, soft drinks, savory snacks, confectionary, and fast food. Advertisements for noodles, which fall outside of the "Big Five," were favorites, also. Compared to earlier studies in Maharashtra and Delhi, a wider range of products were represented here. Advertisements for soft drinks were especially preferred in past studies (Unnikrishnan & Bajpai, 1996; Vaipeyi, 2001), in addition to adverts for noodles and confectionary (e.g., biscuits, chocolate) (Radkar & Mundlay, 2001). In one of these past studies, children had higher levels of recall than parents for all products, except the noodles (Radkar & Mundlay). This, of course, cannot be directly compared here. Still, it is notable that, a decade later in Delhi, India, youth of the same age (10–14 years old) are reporting a larger repertoire of favorite food advertisements. It is unclear whether their exposure to these food advertisements has increased in breadth—or their receptivity to them has changed. Given the expansion of food marketing over the last decade, it may be a combination of both. Regardless, all of the food products recalled here, except fruit juices, were nutrient poor, energy dense.

Notably, youth recall of favorite advertisements was strongly linked to brand names. This is a departure from past research, where brand names for soft drinks, alone, were identified. In the late 1990's, young adolescents were only aware of the "war" in advertising between Coca-Cola and PepsiCo (Vaipeyi, 2001), the two biggest soft-drink companies in India. Brand recognition in the present study extended across many food categories and was particularly strong for Western brands (e.g., McDonalds) and Western-style foods (e.g., pizza), although certain Indian brands (e.g., Thums Up) and Eastern-style foods (e.g., Maggi noodles) were prominent, as well. India appears to be geographically and metaphorically stuck in the middle between Western and Eastern food landscapes. The strongest influence at present seems to be from the West, as the large majority of advertisements are for Western-style foods and for Western brands. It is interesting to note that, for some students, the distinction between Western, Eastern, and Indian foods is increasingly blurred, as these new foods enter this market in India.

In earlier studies in India, young people were conscious of the use of celebrity endorsement to promote products (Vaipeyi, 2001). The use of this marketing strategy to promote food has expanded over time in developing countries (Cairns et al., 2009; Hastings et al., 2006). It appears to be an especially effective means for multinational companies to "think global, act local" (Vignali, 2001) in order to reach young audiences in India. In this study, youth readily associated numerous celebrity names with all kinds of food products. The majority of the celebrities that students named were actors or actresses in *Bollywood* movies. Famed sports persons were also referred to by students, but much less frequently. In prior market research,

PepsiCo's higher recognition status was attributed to its long-standing affiliation with cricket, a favorite past-time in India. Endorsement by famous cricketers and high visibility of products at cricket matches was more effective than Coca-Cola's big spend on television advertising (LODESTAR, 2002).

Though students were aware that not all food products being advertised were healthy, they still reported purchasing and consuming them. None of the prior studies from India documented changes in these children's behaviors (Radkar & Mundlay, 2001; Unnikrishnan & Bajpai, 1996; Vaipeyi, 2001), although parents reported in two studies that their children's demand for a particular food product substantially influenced their own buying decisions (Radkar & Mundlay, 2001; Vaipeyi, 2001). The potential strength of "pester power" is underscored from the child's perspective in this study. This study provides some evidence, too, that children are a potential vehicle for food promotion, in regards to reaching out to family and friends. Other studies corroborate that children in developing countries are targeted not only as potential consumers but also as critical bridgeheads into the wider society and local culture, facilitating the introduction of new or innovative products, like food (Arnett, 2002; Cairns et al., 2009; Hastings et al., 2006).

Parent perspectives were not considered in this study, but would be important, given that much of the purchasing power still lies within their domain, especially in India (Kaur & Singh, 2006). Traditionally, women (e.g., mothers, aunts, and grandmothers) were the sole food purchasers within an extended family structure that defined much of India. Today, extended joint families are being replaced more often by nuclear families, and these nuclear families are characterized by dual-career heads-of-household, where both the mother and father work. Increasingly, then, their children have become more influential in regards to purchasing decisions, which can be driven by food marketing campaigns (Kaur & Singh). Parents now actively seek out their child's opinions in this setting, because they are more knowledgeable of "brands, models, and the latest trends" (Kaur & Singh). "Pester power" may be taking on a new (less annoying) meaning in this setting, as parents are genuinely interested in their child's opinion on buying products, especially those from the West (Goddard, 2009). Alternatively, or in addition, parents in India may be more permissive in acquiescing to purchase requests, given their desire to provide a certain lifestyle for their children that their own parents could not afford for them. In a recent cross-cultural study of American parents and Indian parents, no significant differences between cultures were found in regards to children bringing in new information about packaged food products (Mahima & Puja, 2008). However, the influence of children on the actual buying decisions regarding the packaged food products was significantly higher among Indian parents than American parents (Mahima & Puja). These authors blame the "invasive marketing practices targeted at children" (p. 32, Mahima & Puja). Most Indian parents are aware of the changing food marketing landscape in India and their questionable practices geared towards children. In one study from India, 86% of parents felt the government should regulate food advertisements, 41% thought food marketing should be regulated during children's television programming, and 7% felt that any food advertisements directed at children should be banned outright (Nawathe et al., 2007). In another study, 95% of parents believed that advertisers were doing a disservice to society and favored Government regulation of food advertisements. Unfortunately, little to no regulation exists in India.

In fact, there is little regulation in food marketing across Asia, despite the need for the same (Robinson et al., 2008). Self-regulation is common practice in this part of the world, even in the most recent update of laws from the Food Safety and Standards Authority of India (2010) (Vadehra, 2010; Vashishtha, 2010). Seven multinational food companies (Coca-Cola, General Mills, Kellogg's, Nestlé, Mars, PepsiCo, and Unilever) recently came together to pledge to change their food advertising to children, effective January 1, 2011 (see http://www.hul.co.in/Images/Signed%20India%20Pledge_tcm114-257148.pdf). As part of this pledge, they promised not to advertise their products to children under 12 years old (defined as advertising to media audiences with minimum 50% of children under 12 years), nor to advertise in primary schools. It is unclear what impact, if any, this will have on food promotion in India, or on children's consumption of these food products. Self-regulation in the USA has failed to achieve desired changes to marketing practices (see Chaps. 6, 7, and 8). As is clear in this study, the effects of food promotion extend beyond the age of 12 years, into at least early adolescence. Last year (in 2010), the World Health Organization (WHO) released a set of recommendations regarding the marketing of food and nonalcoholic beverages to children (WHO, 2010). In this global document, the first of its kind, WHO (and its 193 Member States) does consider the marketing of food and nonalcoholic beverages to children to be an international issue and a global phenomenon (WHO). A set of twelve different recommendations were made, to support the implementation and enforcement of policies in Member States to reduce the exposure to and effectiveness of food marketing geared towards children (WHO). Unfortunately, however, the age range for "children" was never made explicit, as was hoped, so that these recommendations would cover children and adolescents up to at least the age of 16 years (Robinson et al., 2008). Research shows that older adolescents are able to understand the marketing messages in relation to product pricing and possess the intellectual capacity to be more resistant to "persuasive advertising" (Brownell et al., 2009; Kaur & Singh, 2006). However, this ability to perceive the messages behind advertising of products does not negate adolescents' vulnerability (Brownell et al., 2009). This level of intellect and critical thinking among adolescents is clear to marketers who are therefore now driven to market messages to "de-activate" any potential resistance, so adolescents remain a target market (Eisenberg, McDowell, Berestein, Tsiantar, & Finan, 2002).

It is not yet clear what will happen in India, and whether adolescents will ultimately be protected by regulation, like children. Future studies should inform the development of national regulation specific to food marketing in India, since children and adolescents in the developing world may be more susceptible to influences of food marketing and promotion, compared to their counterparts in the Western world (Cairns et al., 2009).

This study focused only on urban, affluent school-going youth attending Private schools. Future studies should include less affluent youth, too. Marketing messages do not discriminate on the basis of income, and rich and poor youth alike have access to these messages, via television, in India. Across all of India, over 85% of households, or 229 million households, now have access to a television, and this is growing annually (TAM Annual Universe Update, 2011). Access to television (and even the electricity to run it) is not problematic for less affluent families in this setting. In Tamil Nadu (a state in southern India), the government was involved in a program to provide free color TVs to each household in its state (7.5 million), with the goal of ensuring every household has access to a television by the end of 2011 (National Portal Content Management Team, 2009). In practice, over 16 million televisions were distributed in this widely popular scheme, particularly to those living below the poverty line (The Hindu, 2011). Although this may have positive effects on some segments of society (e.g., improving the status of women in rural settings; Jensen & Oster, 2008), others may suffer because of it, instead. In India, 50% of advertising on children's television is for food (Escalante de Cruz et al., 2004). In addition to being nutrient poor and energy dense, advertised foods are typically inexpensive and as such are easily accessible to those of low socioeconomic status. Critics, therefore, are concerned that these advertised foods may become the regular diet of the less affluent, widening the nutrition gap that already exists in much of the developing world (Hawkes, 2006). This may be reinforced by globalization and the effects of westernization. Not all Indians are able to afford to be or appear as Western, though many still yearn to do so, especially in lower classes (Goddard, 2009). Compared to other durable goods, Western foods are available and easily accessible to those less affluent, making them highly desirable, with the potential for negative health outcomes.

This study was cross-sectional and qualitative, by design. Causality, of course, cannot be inferred. Prior research in the developed world finds modest, but consistent evidence for a causal link between food marketing and related behaviors (Cairns et al., 2009). The evidence is strongest for the link with food purchasing. Prior reviews of this literature suggest these findings can be extrapolated to developing countries, since the marketing activity here mirrors that in the developed world (Cairns et al.). Future, more sophisticated studies shall be required to confirm this hypothesis in developing country contexts like India. As India faces its nutrition transition, a more westernized diet is emerging, driven in large part by the aggressive food marketing campaigns that India experienced a tremendous increase in over the last decade. This new diet can be characterized as having higher fat, sugar, and salt content than before. In a country like India, which faces a large double burden of under- and overnutrition, the problem can easily be seen to explode in the next decade, with additional micronutrient deficiencies that affect both children and adolescents (Hu, 2008; Ramachandran, 2006). The need for additional research—and especially intervention—is critical in this part of the world.

References

Arnett, J. J. (2002). The psychology of globalization. *The American Psychologist, 57*(10), 774–783.

Bansal, R. (2004, June 28). Urban youth. *Business World*. Available from http://www.businessworldindia.com/june2804/coverstory05.asp. Accessed 5 Oct 2011.

Beaglehole, R., & Yach, D. (2003). Globalisation and the prevention and control of non-communicable disease: The neglected chronic diseases of adults. *The Lancet, 362*(9387), 903–908.

Bhattacharyya, R., & Kohli, S. (2007). *Targeting marketing to children – The ethical aspect*. Paper presented at the International Marketing Conference on Marketing and Society, 8–10 April 2007.

Bijapurkar, R. (2007). *We are like this only: Understanding the logic of consumer India*. New Delhi: Portfolio by Penguin Books India.

Brownell, K. D., Schwartz, M. B., Puhl, R. M., Henderson, K. E., & Harris, J. L. (2009). The need for bold action to prevent adolescent obesity. *Journal of Adolescent Health, 45*, S8–S17.

Businessworld. (2010). In J. S. Pocha (Ed.), *The Marketing Whitebook 2009–2010*. New Delhi: ABP Pvt. Ltd., n.a.

Cairns, G., Angus, K., & Hastings, G. (2009). The extent, nature and effects of food promotion to children: A review of the evidence to December 2008. Prepared for the World Health Organization. Stirling: Institute for Social Marketing.

Eisenberg, D., McDowell, J., Berestein, L., Tsiantar, D., & Finan, E. (2002). It's an ad, ad, ad, ad world. *Time, 160*(10), 38–42.

Escalante de Cruz, A., Phillips, S., Visch, M., & Bulan Saunders, D. (2004). *The junk food generation. A multi-country survey of the influence of television advertisements on children*. Kuala Lumpur, Malaysia: Consumers International Asia Pacific Office.

Goddard, A. (2009). *Consumption as a lifestyle: The use of western lifestyle as a status symbol in multinational corporations' advertising in India*. Retrieved from ISP Collection (Paper 811). Accessed http://digitalcollections.sit.edu/isp_collection/811.

Harris, J. L., Pomeranz, J. L., Lobstein, T., & Brownell, K. D. (2008). A crisis in the marketplace: How food marketing contributes to childhood obesity and what can be done. *Annual Review of Public Health, 30*, 211–225.

Hastings, G., McDermott, L., Angus, K., Stead, M., & Thomson, S. (2006). *The extent, nature and effects of food promotion to children: A review of the evidence*. Technical Paper prepared for the World Health Organization. Geneva: World Health Organization.

Hawkes, C. (2006). Uneven dietary development: Linking the policies and processes of globalization with the nutrition transition, obesity, and diet-related chronic diseases. *Globalization and Health, 2*(4), 1–18.

Hawkes, C. (2007). Marketing food to children: Changes in the global regulatory environment 2004–2006. International Food Policy Research Institute. Geneva: World Health Organization.

Hindustan Unilever Limited. (2010). India pledge: We will change our food advertisement to children. http://www.hul.co.in/Images/Signed%20India%20Pledge_tcm114-257148.pdf Accessed 4 Mar 2011.

Hindustan Unilever Limited. (2011). Home page. http://www.hul.co.in. Accessed 5 Oct 2011.

Hu, F. B. (2008). Globalization of food patterns and cardiovascular risk. *Journal of the American Heart Association, 118*, 1913–1914.

India Brand Equity Foundation. (2011). Food industry. http://www.ibef.org/industry/foodindustry.aspx. Accessed 12 Sep 2011.

India Franchise Blog. (2011). Pizza Hut, Dominos, KFC, McDonalds, Taco Bell all in the race for the no. 1 restaurant franchise brand in their respective categories. http://indiafranchiseblog.blogspot.com/2011/01/pizza-hut-dominos-kfc-mcdonalds.html.

Jensen, R., & Oster, E. (2008). *The power of tv: Cable television and women's status in India*. (NBER Working Papers 13305). Cambridge, MA: National Bureau of Economic Research. http://home.uchicago.edu/eoster/tvwomen.pdf. Accessed 5 Oct 2011.

Kaur, P., & Singh, R. (2006). Children family purchase decision making in India and the west: A review. *Academy of Marketing Science Review, 2006*(8), 1–30.

Kelder, S. H., Perry, C. L., Klepp, K. I., & Lytle, L. L. (1994). Longitudinal tracking of adolescent smoking, physical activity, and food choice behaviors. *American Journal of Public Health, 84*(7), 1121–1126.

Kulkarni, S., Lassar, W., Sridhar, C., & Venkitachalam, A. (2009). McDonald's ongoing marketing challenge: Social perception in India. *Online Journal of International Case Analysis, 1*(2), 1–19.

Lobstein, T., Macmullan, J., McGrath, T., & Witt, J. (2008). *Cereal Offences: A wake-up call on the marketing of unhealthy food to children*. London, UK: Consumers International.

LODESTAR. (2002). "How Cricket Works." A LODESTAR media study. http://www.excahnge-4media.com/e4m/others/e4m_bt.asp. Accessed 4 Apr 2006.

Maggi Noodles commercial on YouTube.com. (2007). Taste Bhi Health Bhi. http://www.youtube.com/watch?v=Uf67yrJ7y6Q&NR=1. Accessed 4 Mar 2011.

Mahima, S. T., & Puja, K. (2008). Relationship between parental overindulgence and buying behavior in the context of invasive marketing: A comparative study of the cultures. *Seoul Journal of Business, 14*(1), 31–53.

Mishra, A., Arora, M., Stigler, M. H., Komro, K. A., Lytle, L. A., Reddy, K. S., et al. (2005). Indian youth speak about tobacco: Results of focus group discussions with school students. *Health Education & Behavior, 32*(3), 363.

Misra, A. (2003). Revisions of cutoffs of body mass index to define overweight and obesity are needed for the Asian-ethnic groups. *International Journal of Obesity, 27*(11), 1294–1296.

National Institute of Nutrition. (2011). *Dietary guidelines for Indians: A manual*. Hyderabad, India: National Institute of Nutrition.

National Portal Content Management Team. (2009). Free colour television distribution scheme: Tamil Nadu. http://india.gov.in/govt/viewscheme.php?schemeid=1332. Accessed 5 Oct 2011.

Nawathe, A., Gawande, R., & Dethe, S. (2007). Impact of advertising on children's health. *International Marketing Conference on Marketing & Society*, 8–10 Apr 2007, IIMK.

Pant, V. (2008). India: Meet a billion of your newest customers. *Nielsons Consumer Insight, 9*, 14–17.

Pingali, P. (2007). Westernization of Asian diets and the transformation of food systems: Implications for research and policy. *Food Policy, 32*(3), 281–298.

QRS International. (2011). NVivo 9. http://www.qsrinternational.com/products_nvivo.aspx. Accessed 4 Mar 2011.

Radkar, A., & Mundlay, A. (2001). Impact of TV food advertisements on buying decisions: Joint project by Consumers' International (ROAP) and Mumbai Grahak Panchayat – India. Results of a Survey from Maharashtra, India. *Pune, Centre for Research and Education* http://www.ciroap.org/food. Accessed 4 Apr 2006.

Ramachandran, P. (2006). *The double burden of malnutrition in India*. Rome, Italy: Food & Agricultural Organization.

Robinson, E., De Vera, A., & Witt, J. (2008). *The junk food trap marketing unhealthy food to children in Asia Pacific*. London, UK: Consumers International.

Saha, A. (2009). India retail forum: The talking points of a historic year – 1. *Images Retail, 8*(10), 42–77.

Sen, A. S. (2010). The many Youngistans in young India. http://www.financialexpress.com/news/the-many-youngistans-in-young-india/681211/3. Accessed 5 Oct 2011.

Sharma, N. (1999). *Understanding adolescence*. Delhi, India: National Book Trust.

TAM Annual Universe Update. (2011). *TAM Annual Universe Update*. http://www.tamindia.com/tamindia/Images/Overview_Universe_update_2011.pdf Accessed 5 Oct 2011.

Tharoor, S. (2007). *The elephant, the tiger, and the cellphone*. New Delhi: Viking by Penguin Books India.

The Hindu. (2011, June 4). Remaining colour tv sets to be given away to government institutions. *The Hindu*. http://www.thehindu.com/news/states/tamil-nadu/article2093442.ece. Accessed 5 Oct 2011.

Thums Up commercial on DesiHits.com. (2010). If you want me come and get me. http://www.desihits.com/news/view/akshay-kumar-in-thums-up-cola-commercial-20100413. Accessed 4 Mar 2011.

Tomlinson, J. (1999). *Globalization and culture*. Chicago: The University of Chicago Press.

UK Prospective Diabetes Study. (1994). XII: Differences between Asian, Afro-Caribbean and white Caucasian type 2 diabetic patients at diagnosis of diabetes. *UK Prospective Diabetes Study Group. Diabetic medicine, 11*(7), 670–677.

United Nations Development Programme. (1998). *Human development report*. New York: Oxford University Press.

Unnikrishnan, N., & Bajpai, S. (1996). Children's advertising. In N. Unnikrishnan & S. Bajpai (Eds.), *The impact of television advertising on children* (pp. 252–277). New Delhi: Sage.

Vadehra, S. (2010). Advertising to children in India. *Young Consumers, 11*(2), 153–156.

Vaipeyi, R. (2001). *Impact of tv food advertisement parents and children survey*. India: Voice.

Vashishtha, V. M. (2010). Advertisement of food products for children: A tale of legality, ethics, and indifference. *Indian Pediatrics, 47*, 857–859.

Vignali, C. (2001). McDonald's: 'think global, act local' – The marketing mix. *British Food Journal, 103*(2), 97–111.

Wang, Y., Chen, H. J., Shaikh, S., & Mathur, P. (2009). Is obesity becoming a public health problem in India? Examine the shift from under-to overnutrition problems over time. *Obesity Reviews, 10*(4), 456–474.

Wang, Y., & Lobstein, T. (2006). Worldwide trends in childhood overweight and obesity. *International Journal of Pediatric Obesity, 1*(1), 11–25.

World Health Organization. (2010). *Set of recommendations on the marketing of foods and non-alcoholic beverages to children*. Geneva, Switzerland: World Health Organization.

Youthreach. (2004). If I were rain: Profiles of disadvantaged youth in India. New Delhi, India.

Chapter 13
The Role of Schools in Food and Beverage Marketing: Significance, Challenges, Next Steps

Lara A. Latimer, Joanne Delk, Andrew E. Springer, and Keryn E. Pasch

Introduction

The potential detrimental effects of food and beverage advertising through television and print have been documented (e.g., Institute of Medicine [IOM], 2006; Holt, Ippolito, Desrochers, & Kelley, 2007; see also Chap. 8), however less research has examined this type of advertising in schools. It is necessary to further the literature in this area, because children spend a great deal of time in schools (Frumkin, 2006) and begin to form lifelong habits during these age periods (Birch, 1999). In order to further our understanding of the influence of in-school food and beverage marketing and promotion, the current chapter aims to do the following (1) present a brief review of the current literature on in-school food and beverage promotion; (2) describe the development of a tool to assess in-school food and beverage promotion (as defined as advertising and product promotion); (3) present data from a pilot study that used the new in-school observation tool; and (4) highlight challenges and future goals in this area of research.

L.A. Latimer • J. Delk • A.E. Springer
University of Texas at Austin, Department of Kinesiology and Health Education, 1 University Station, D3700, Austin, TX 78712
e-mail: lara.a.latimer@gmail.com

Michael & Susan Dell Center for Advancement of Healthy Living, University of Texas School of Public Health-Austin Regional Campus

K.E. Pasch (✉)
University of Texas at Austin Department of Kinesiology and Health Education, 1 University Station, Austin, TX 78712
e-mail: kpasch@austin.utexas.edu

J.D. Williams et al. (eds.), *Advances in Communication Research to Reduce Childhood Obesity*, DOI 10.1007/978-1-4614-5511-0_13,

The School Environment and Child Health

Children in the USA spend more time at school than in any other environment outside of the home (Frumkin, 2006). Over 48 million students attend 94,000 elementary, middle, and high schools daily (Wirt et al., 2005). Most youth eat at least one meal or snack at school a day, and some estimates show that children may consume approximately 26–47% of daily energy at school (Briefel, Crepinsek, Cabili, Wilson, & Gleason, 2009). Healthy eating and physical activity lessons are key components in public school curriculum, and school settings provide opportunities for students to make food-related decisions and engage in physical activity. While the obesity epidemic may not singlehandedly be reversed by school-based interventions, it is likely that any major strides in decreasing obesity among children and adolescents will involve changes in the school environment (Evans, Finkelstein, Kamerow, & Renaud, 2005; Waters et al., 2011). Despite the promising role of schools in promoting children's health, there appears to be room for improvement. For instance, a recent review of child-targeted obesity interventions concluded that significant changes in body mass index have resulted (Waters et al.). However, these changes were small and the effectiveness of specific intervention components was not established.

The School Food Environment

The school food and beverage environment is one area that may need to be addressed in order to make strides in reducing childhood obesity. The school food environment is composed of food availability, accessibility, and advertising. Foods available in schools are provided primarily through national school breakfast and lunch programs and through competitive outlets, or those that offer food outside of the standardized school menu. Foods offered through the National School Lunch Program (NSLP) and the School Breakfast Program (SBP) must meet federally regulated standards for energy, macronutrients, and key vitamins and minerals (IOM, 2007). The school lunch menu and associated marketing techniques (e.g., signs promoting certain menu items) constitute the promotion of this program and the foods it provides.

Competitive foods are those foods that are available in schools that compete with the federal meal programs. These foods and beverages may be sold in vending machines, a la carte lines by the cafeteria during meal periods, snacks bars, classrooms, school stores, and canteens, through fundraisers, or at sporting events and concession stands. Competitive foods are typically low in nutrient density and contain high levels of fat, sugar, and calories (Gordon, Crepinsek, Nogales, & Condon, 2007). At the federal level, competitive foods are not regulated, with the exception of foods of minimal nutritional value (FMNV). FMNVs include chewing gum, soft drinks, certain candies, and water ices (Gordon et al.). Under federal guidelines, if a school participates in the federal meal program, FMNVs cannot be sold in the cafeteria during meal periods. However, although individual states may have additional rules concerning competitive foods, accessibility of FMNVs is still an issue in the school food environment, as students may purchase these items sold outside of the cafeteria during, before, and after meal times.

It is possible that children see the school as an endorser of these types of foods simply because of their presence in the school environment, regardless of explicit support by the school or school staff. Research suggests that restrictions on unhealthy competitive foods in schools may help decrease middle- and high school students' daily intake of these products at school (e.g., Cullen & Zakeri, 2004; Cullen, Watson, Zakeri, & Ralston, 2006; Hartstein et al., 2008; Neumark-Sztainer, French, Hannan, Story, & Fulkerson, 2005). Additionally, qualitative data show that elementary children view a high number of unhealthy foods available in school stores as a barrier to healthy eating at school (Hesketh, Waters, Green, Salmon, & Williams, 2005), and parents and teachers feel that schools should prioritize students' nutritional health, but feel that schools do not adequately address student nutrition (Kubik, Lytle, & Story, 2005).

In addition to food availability and accessibility, food and beverage advertising is common in the school environment. In 2006, The Federal Trade Commission (FTC) found that approximately $870 million was spent on promoting food to children in marketing channels other than traditional television advertisements, with $186 million of that allocated to advertising in schools (FTC, 2008). Examples of food advertising in the school environment include posters and other signage, advertising in school newspapers, and corporate-sponsored classroom activities, lessons, and book covers (IOM, 2005). Newscasts and other broadcasting (i.e., Channel One) and beverage contracts are also forms of school-based food and beverage advertising. Although it is common for this type of commercialism to exist in school, it is likely shaping students' views on food and beverage products and is not necessarily what school stakeholders advocate. For instance, parents and teachers feel that the advertisements displayed in schools influence students to purchase the advertised product (Kubik et al., 2005), and teachers believe that food and beverage advertisements should be prohibited in schools (Kubik et al., 2005).

The Significance of the School Food Environment

It is not surprising that food and beverage companies find schools an ideal environment to promote their products. Children are required to attend and spend about 7–8 h in school daily, and they constitute a captive audience who is less likely to play an active role in types of product promotions they are exposed to. Specifically, while children may have input on the types of items that are purchased for the home and the opportunity to change channels when television advertisements appear, they have less input in what is promoted in the school environment. As such, it is hard to ignore the pervasiveness of commercial products in competitive food outlets in schools, including the presence of product logos and brand promotion. As students are repeatedly exposed to these products and images in school, they may choose these items both in- and outside of the school environment. There is evidence to show that repeated exposure to unhealthy advertising may influence children's requests for, attitudes toward, and selection of similar foods (e.g., Goldberg, Gorn, & Gibson, 1978, Gorn & Goldberg, 1982, Borzekowski & Robinson, 2001, Dixon, Scully, Wakefield, White, & Crawford, 2007). While most advertising exposure research has predominantly focused on television, it is plausible that a similar relationship exists between in-school food and beverage promotion exposure and related choices and preferences. Additionally, in-school product promotion may be all the more persuasive, since previous qualitative research shows that children may view things promoted in the school environment as inherently healthy (Hesketh et al., 2005). Specifically, children may view unhealthy items available in schools as relatively healthy because of the environment in which they are promoted, despite contradictions with school-based nutrition education (Hesketh et al.) and may associate certain products with the power and prestige of school officials, teachers, or coaches (Palmer et al., 2004).

Schools may also provide a beneficial environment for commercial companies to market products. Marketers gain access to a large, captive group of young consumers whose attendance is required. In turn, food and beverage promotion often fills a funding gap for schools, because they receive incentives from companies for selling and promoting certain products (IOM, 2006), which may replace some of the funding cuts many schools have experienced. Contracts between companies and schools typically involve the sale and promotion of energy dense/low nutrient foods, such as sodas. Schools of lower socioeconomic level may be more dependent on incentives provided by commercial food companies, which is especially disconcerting because of the disproportionate effects of obesity among this population (Palmer et al., 2004).

The School Food Environment: Current State of the Literature

While the potential negative effects of television advertisements on youth food and beverage choices and weight-related outcomes are well documented (e.g., Halford, Gillespie, Brown, Pontin, & Dovey, 2004; IOM, 2006; Halford, Boyland, Hughes, Oliveira, & Dovey, 2007; Chou, Rashad, & Grossman, 2008; Risvas, Panagiotakos, & Zampelas, 2008), a paucity of research exists on in-school marketing specifically, and its association with food preferences, choices, and obesity-related outcomes. Research that has been conducted in this area, however, points to the likelihood that children's exposure to food and beverage marketing in the school environment influences them to choose products similar to those promoted and available in the same environment. For example, the availability of snacks and drinks sold in schools has been associated with higher student intake of total calories, fat, saturated fat, and soft drinks, and with lower intake of milk, fruits and vegetables, and vital nutrients (Cullen, Eagan, Baranowski, Owens, &

de Moor, 2000; Kubik, Lytle, Hanna, Perry, & Story, 2003; Cullen & Zakeri, 2004; Cullen & Thompson, 2005).

Much of the research on the school environment has focused primarily on the existence of competitive foods (i.e., vending machines, a la carte lines), and has found that students who have access to a la carte lines in school may have a lower intake of fruits and vegetables (Kubik et al., 2003; Cullen & Zakeri, 2004), and a higher intake of sweetened beverages (Cullen & Zakeri, 2004). Additionally, the availability of vending machines has been positively associated with student BMI z-scores (Fox, Hedley-Dodd, Wilson, & Gleason, 2009).

Little has been done to examine food and beverage promotion in schools, either through traditional advertising channels, such as posters displaying commercial brands, or through products as a form of promotion. One study documented the existence, locations, and prevalence of soft drink advertisements in over 200 Pennsylvania high schools from food service director reports (Probart, McDonnell, Bailey-Davis, & Weirich, 2006). Specifically, participants indicated the existence of a pouring-rights contract, average daily lunch participation, incentives from soft drink companies, Channel One subscriptions, time of the first lunch period, locations of soft drink advertisements, and the extent of access to vending machines. About 63% of schools had soft drink machines owned by a commercial company that provides funding to the school based on revenue percentage, and 48.5% of schools had an exclusive pouring-rights contract with a soft drink bottler. Sixty-two percent of respondents reported soft drink advertisements were present on vending machines. Twenty-seven percent of schools reported soft drink advertisements on school grounds (i.e., on the exterior of the school, but not on the building itself, such as playing fields), 10.6% were in cafeterias, and 9.3% were in other areas of the school building. The majority of respondents (66.5%) indicated that soft drink advertisements existed in at least one location in the school. Analyses showed that average number of daily National School Lunch Program participants was significantly and inversely associated with the number of advertisement locations, indicating that the higher the number of advertisement locations, the lower the level of average daily participation. Given the positive associations of exposure to advertising and food preferences among youth, such that youth tend to prefer advertised products over other items (IOM, 2006), these findings are cause for concern.

Mazur et al. (2008) explored the impact of food advertising in schools on food purchases in a sample of about 15,000 primary and secondary students in forty-four schools in Poland. Data were collected from food shop workers on student food purchases in the shop for the preceding week. The types of foods displayed in the shop were documented and categorized by researchers as "healthy" (those recommended by the US Department of Agriculture's My Pyramid) or "unhealthy." These food types were then placed into categories based on if they were advertised and/or purchased in the school. Additionally, any direct corporate advertising present in the school was documented. Alarmingly, results showed that more than half of the schools did not offer any type of "healthy" food in the school food shop and, even in the shops that did offer "healthy" foods, sales of these types of foods were low. Significant correlations between advertisement of a specific food and purchasing of the specific product were found, which showed that increased advertising of specific foods was associated with an increased purchase rate of those foods. There was no significant difference in purchasing behavior and location of advertisements (near the food shop versus elsewhere on campus) and no commercial advertisements for "healthy" foods were found in any school. These results suggest that any advertising for and availability of "unhealthy" foods in schools likely contributes to student purchases of these foods.

Recently, cross-sectional data on school food environment characteristics and student dietary behavior from 287 schools in seven different US geographical regions were examined (Briefel et al., 2009). School environment was measured through surveys of principals and food service employees, lunch menus, and on-site observations. Child dietary behavior was measured by consumption of the following: low-nutrient/energy-dense foods, sugar-sweetened beverages, and fruits and vegetables. Results for over 2,300 students in grades one through 12 showed that attending a school without snack bars significantly reduced kilocalorie intake from sugar-sweetened beverages in middle- and high school students by 22 and 28 kcal/day, respectively. Significantly less energy came from sugar-sweetened beverages among students who attended middle schools with no pouring rights contract, a la carte lines with no low-nutrient energy-dense items, and no a la carte lines. A significant and positive relationship was found between the absence of low-nutrient, energy-dense foods in a la carte lines and vegetable intake (excluding French fries) among middle-school students. Overall, study results indicate that students who are not exposed to low-nutrient energy-dense foods in school may be less likely to consume similar types of food and may be more likely to consume healthier options.

Minaker, Storey, Raine, et al. (2011) conducted a study that examined associations between the school food environment, specifically vending machine availability and the presence of food/beverage logos, and students' BMI and food behaviors among Canadian students in grades 7–10. Students were also asked if snack and beverage vending machines and logos were present in their school, with response options of "yes," "no," or "don't know." The majority of students reported the presence of snack and/or beverage vending machines, about 40% reported snack logo presence, and 57% reported beverage logo presence in their schools. Even after adjusting for possible confounding variables (consumption of items from vending machines, overall soda or sugar consumption, presence of snack vending machines, and snack or beverage logo presence), students who reported the presence of beverage vending machines had a 27% greater chance of being overweight or obese, compared with students who reported no beverage vending machines. Additionally, students who indicated the presence of snack and/or beverage logos in school were significantly more likely to consume snacks from a vending machine than students who reported no logos, and the presence of snack logos was significantly associated with a higher likelihood of candy and salty snack consumption. The authors posited that the mere presence of vending machines in the school environment implies that it is acceptable for students to consume items traditionally sold in vending machines, even if they are not purchasing these items in school. Additionally, they suggested that the finding that snack and beverage logo presence, but not the presence of vending machines, was associated with soda, salty snack, and candy consumption may reflect the effects of brand marketing in that logos oftentimes exist in areas of the school other than vending machines (e.g., logos on clocks or scoreboards, branded items that are available in a la carte lines).

Summary

The literature reviewed here supports the hypothesis that food and beverage promotion in schools may encourage consumption of unhealthy foods while deterring the intake of healthy options. However, due to the lack of empirical evidence to show the effects of in-school food promotion, broadly defined to include both advertisements placed in the school as well as commercial foods that are promoted in the school, research is needed in this environment. Few studies have incorporated direct observations of the school food environment, and most have been dependent on information provided by school administration or cafeteria staff. Additionally, most of this research has not examined all forms of advertisements and signage, including product logos and products in the schools as a form of promotion.

Given these limitations of the current body of research described above, the development of practical and effective assessment methods are needed in order to study the prevalence and effects of in-school food and beverage promotion. Ideally, assessment methods should be discreet, allow for efficient data collection in order to minimize disruption in schools, and increase the precision of measurement. The following section describes the development of an observational method for assessing the food-promoting environment in schools based on the experience of researchers working with school-based health promotion efforts in elementary and middle school students in central Texas. The description includes the history, iterations, challenges, and future directions of developing a food and beverage promotion assessment method.

Measuring the In-School Food Promotion Environment: Experiences from CATCH

The Need for an Assessment Tool

Given the importance of the in-school promotion environment and the limited research in the area, it was decided in the spring of 2007, while developing a process evaluation framework for the Travis County CATCH (Coordinated Approach to School Health) elementary school dissemination research study in central Texas, that there was a need for a method to document food and beverage signage within schools. CATCH is an evidenced based coordinated school health program aimed at increasing healthy eating, and physical activity and reducing the prevalence of obesity (Luepker, Perry, McKinlay, et al., 1996; Nader, Stone, Lytle, et al., 1999, Coleman et al., 2005; Hoelscher et al., 2010). As part of implementing the CATCH Program, schools were provided CATCH promotional materials, including a banner and various posters to hang in the school. Additionally, schools were encouraged to create a CATCH bulletin board and to use nutrition and physical activity (PA) promotion signage provided by other organizations. The signage checklist was created as a process measure to record if schools were implementing this portion of the program, and to assess the relationship between health promotion signage and study outcomes, such as the prevalence of obesity and overweight, student fruit and vegetable consumption, and student physical activity levels.

The elementary schools where the CATCH dissemination study was conducted had very little food and beverage promotion signage, as the school districts and State of Texas have policies in place to limit unhealthy food sales, which in turn had the effect to limit signs promoting these foods. As we entered into a subsequent study with middle schools known as the Central Texas CATCH Middle School Project (Springer et al., in press), we discovered the policies on food sales were more lenient for middle schools. Due to the volume of food promotion signs and the impact these professionally created signs are designed to have, we realized the checklist would have to be modified to capture the extent of food marketing and promotion within the schools.

Instrument Development

Many versions of the checklist have been created, with many similarities, in order to find the optimal version. The main objective that guided checklist development was a need to find a balance between recording all the data of interest with the amount of time and staff it would take to gather. For the original checklist, we decided to only look for signage in the school's gym, cafeteria, and main hallways as this was where the majority of students gathered, had access to, or passed through regularly. There were several reasons for the decision to limit locations in the school to document. First, recording signage in all hallways would be time consuming, and the research study was not budgeted for this. Second, it was assumed that signage placed in grade-level hallways would not be observed by all students at the school; therefore, we could not assess the reach of those signs. Finally, with the exception of the gym, we did not want to go into individual classrooms because we (1) did not want to interrupt classes and (2) we could only enter classes when they were not being used. These procedures for locations to document remained consistent under all versions of the checklist.

With these criteria in mind, our CATCH team created the "School Health Promotion Signage Observation Checklist," which comprised a data collection tool and data collection protocol. The data collection tool included specific categories for signage as well as the locations in which the signage is observed (i.e., main hallway, gym, or cafeteria). Signage categories included nutrition, physical activity, other public health (e.g., smoking, hand washing), and Whoa Foods. Whoa Foods stem from the Go, Slow Whoa classification system in CATCH and refer to low nutrient, energy dense foods that students are encouraged to limit their consumption (Perry et al., 1997; see Table 13.2). Additionally, the observer would record if CATCH signs were posted. A response of yes or no was recorded for each area of the school, indicating whether or not the specific signs were present. This version worked well as a process measure for the implementation of the CATCH program, as we could document if signage provided by the program had been posted. However, we wanted to be able to investigate if students at schools with higher amounts of signage had healthier eating habits, participated in more physical activity and had lower rates of obesity than students at schools with less signage. It seemed unlikely that the dichotomous responses would be sensitive enough to correlate with difference in these behaviors.

The next version consisted of a checklist where the original dichotomous (yes/no) scale was expanded to a 4-point scale. Specifically, the scale points were none, low, medium, and high, and for each area of a school the observer would record the amount of signage for each category. When the definitions for the categories were first created they were solely based on the number of signs present. For instance, "low" was recorded if one sign was present, "medium" if there were two to three signs, and "high" was recorded for more than three signs. However, this purely objective scale did not take into account the visibility of the signs. Some schools' have much larger cafeterias, gyms, and especially main hallways than others. This scale also did not take into account that a small school may not have to have as many signs posted to reach the same level of visibility as a large school. The main hallways posed another problem, in that they can represent a very large area. It was often the case that one corner of a hallway, such as immediately outside the gym, would have more than three physical activity promoting signs, but the rest of the hallway was void of any physical activity signage. According to the objective definitions, this would be recorded as high. However, students would only be exposed to these signs when they went to physical education class. We wanted to set a higher bar for the high category. To address this, subjective definitions were added for low, medium, and high. "None" was defined as "no signs are present." "Low" was defined as "one sign is present and/or the signs are not very visible. It is very easy to miss or ignore promotional messages." "Medium" signified that "two to three signs are present and/or signs are moderately visible or dense," and "high" was classified as "more than three signs are present and/or the sign(s) are highly visible. It is hard to ignore the signs due to their volume or their size". In general, this checklist could be completed in less than 20 min, which was similar to the time required for the previous version with the dichotomous scale. Additionally, when inter-rater reliabilities were performed the measurement performed well, despite the scale's slight subjectivity. In general, the ratings assigned for the cafeteria and gym used the numerical definition of the scale. However, when rating the main hallways, the observer would often employ the subjective definition.

With the new version of the checklist, for the middle school study, several descriptors for each sign of interest were included. The first descriptor was the location—gym, cafeteria, or main hallway. The second was the size—small, medium, or large. Third was a place to mark whether the message on the sign was passive or direct. Signs defined as direct contained a message encouraging or directing people to action, or providing them with knowledge concerning the main category (e.g., consuming vegetables prevents heart disease). Additionally, food logos were classified as direct. This was based primarily on previous research with children and food branding, which indicates that children can recognize logos and associate them with products (Arredondo, Castaneda, Elder, Slymen, & Dozier, 2009) and that food branding has the potential to influence children's food preferences (Robinson, Borzekowski, Matheson, & Kraemer, 2007). Signs defined as passive contained messages where the explicit intent was not to provide knowledge or promote an activity that would improve an individual's health. However, the sign may indirectly do this through images, such as pictures of sports equipment, fruit and vegetables, families eating together, or people exercising. The fourth attribute was if the sign was CATCH branded. Fifth, the data collector could indicate if the sign was printed professionally or not. If a sign was printed in color on glossy paper, then it was recorded as being professionally printed. If the printing of the sign was of a lesser quality, or if the sign was hand-made, it was recorded as not professionally printed. The sixth attribute was a list of all the CATCH-provided signs, where the observer would mark if the sign was present or, in the case of a bulletin board, how many signs were present. The last section was a series of boxes where the general content of the sign could be recorded (e.g., nutrition, physical activity, water promotion, food promotion/advertising, etc.). In these boxes, the observer would check off if the content was present and what percentage of the sign was devoted to that specific content. To make data collection more efficient, each row on the data collection tool contained a space to indicate how many of each type of sign was observed as schools often had multiple versions of the same sign.

Pilot Assessment of the In-School MEDIA DOT

As a first step toward assessing the food and beverage and PA promotion environment in middle schools, we conducted a pilot assessment with the newly developed In-School Measuring and Evaluating the Determinants and Influence of Advertising Direct Observation Tool (In-School MEDIA DOT). This tool is based on the most recent version of the CATCH School Health Promotion Signage Observation Checklist described in the previous section of this chapter. The primary purposes of the pilot assessment were to: (1) determine the logistics and feasibility of conducting a similar, larger scale study; (2) develop an electronic version of the data collection tool, based on the previously described iterations,

Table 13.1 Descriptive data for pilot schools ($n=5$)

Mean SES (average % on free/reduced lunch)	41.62
Ethnicity	
African-American	14.7%
Asian/Pacific Islander	4.175%
White	49.2%
Hispanic	31.275%
Mean number of students in each school (SD)	1,041 (200)

to use in a larger study; and (3) obtain preliminary data to gain a better understanding of the prevalence and type of in-school food and beverage promotion and the prevalence of CATCH-specific signage. Five schools in central Texas were chosen for the pilot study (Table 13.1). These schools were chosen by a CATCH team member based on availability and the likelihood that the sample would provide an accurate and diverse picture of all the middle schools that would be used for a larger project.

Pilot Data Collection Methods

Two research team members went to each of the five schools, and the duration of data collection ranged from approximately 20 to 75 min per school. Both team members worked together to methodically move through the school and identify food, beverage, and PA signage in the main hallways, gym, and cafeteria (including the dining room, main, and a la carte lines) at each school. We defined food and beverage promotion as any type of signage that had a picture of foods or beverages, words that advertised a product, or a food/beverage-related behavior. We also documented any commercial products we encountered, defined as those packaged with a visible logo or product name and unpackaged a la carte items (e.g., whole fruit such as apples and bananas). We walked through every major hallway, which varied between the schools. For instance, we did not limit observations to halls in or outside of the gym or cafeteria necessarily. We looked at each school map as a whole to see how the halls were arranged and determined which would logically be the busiest. We documented types of signage if they could be seen without moving objects or opening doors. As signage was identified, the researchers would discuss categorization, description, and other pertinent details. One person took a picture of the sign and the other recorded information with pencil and paper.

Several key lessons were identified with this first pilot data collection. First, it became apparent that, while the data collection was feasible for one person to do, it would be more efficient and streamlined for two data collectors to work together. Because one of the goals of a larger scale project is to collect data with as little interruption in the schools as possible, limiting the amount of time data collectors spend in the school is of primary importance. Second, the pilot study was conducted with a pencil and paper version of the preliminary tool; however, an electronic measure of data collection would allow for quicker data collection and for taking pictures of the advertisements and products. Therefore, an iPod Touch® will be used for the next study phase in order to enhance efficiency with collecting data. The iPod Touch® is a handheld device, about the size of a cell phone, which has a touch screen and capabilities for photographs and electronic applications. Thus, some of the feasibility issues (e.g., taking time to write descriptions for each sign or product) will be reduced or eliminated. Conducting pilot data collection allowed researchers to gain a better understanding of what may be encountered in the school environment, some potential obstacles, ideas for improvement of an electronic-based tool, and key aspects of a research protocol for a future, larger scale study.

Pilot Study Results

Many of the signs and items were consistent between all of the pilot schools. For instance, all schools had at least one "multi-sign board," a label we assigned to a freestanding, moveable board that displayed multiple signs. The contents of the multi-sign boards varied between schools, but all of the signs were related to nutrition and/or PA. Often the nutrition signs displayed on the multi-sign board contradicted each other, promoting "healthy" foods on some signs and "unhealthy" foods on others. For instance, one school had a multi-sign board that included a sign promoting green vegetables and one promoting lean protein sources, both of which are healthy choices. On the same multi-sign board, there was a promotion for "epic burgers," which displayed large pictures of hamburgers with various toppings, but no vegetables, and a promotion for Chick-Fil-A, a popular fast-food chain restaurant that offers a limited menu in most middle school cafeterias in this district.

Many of the signs promoting unhealthy items in the pilot schools were found in the cafeteria, which is noteworthy since this is where most of the students' food-related decisions are made. Most schools had advertisements, menus, and/or price lists for Otis Spunkmeyer cookies, Blue Bell ice cream, and Tyson chicken, as well as non-commercial products such as pizza, chicken strips, popcorn chicken, cookies, and burgers sold in the main or a la carte cafeteria lines. Some schools had advertisements for Dasani water and Coca-Cola, usually on the side of a drink cooler or vending machine (vending machines did not contain Coca-Cola but the advertisements still remained on the machines).

Additionally, every pilot school had foods and drinks for sale and openly displayed in the a la carte and/or main lines. Products included snack foods (e.g., Doritos, Chex Mix, cereal bars, pretzels, Rice Krispie Treats) and drinks (e.g., Gatorade, V8 Splash, Milk, Sweet Leaf Tea, water, 100% juice). Because of the associations between product branding and children's food preferences (e.g.,

Table 13.2 CATCH Go, Slow, Whoa criteria

Go

- "Whole foods," or those that are minimally processed, and low in salt, sugar, and unhealthy fats
  Examples
- Fresh or frozen fruit
- Fresh, frozen, or canned vegetables
- Whole-grain bread, pasta, rice, crackers; corn tortillas, baked tortilla chips
- Unsweetened skim/1% milk, low-fat cheese, unsweetened or 100% fruit-juice sweetened yogurt

Slow

- These foods are moderate, relative to "go" and "whoa" foods
  Examples
- Fruit canned in light syrup, dried fruit with added sugar
- Baked French fries or fresh/frozen/canned vegetables prepared with vegetable oil
- From refined, white flour: bread, pasta, rice, low-sugar cereal, and low-fat crackers
- Baked potato chips, pretzels, cereal/fruit bars
- 2% milk, flavored fat-free milk, low-fat yogurt (sweetened), low-fat ice cream or frozen yogurt

Whoa

- Generally the most processed and highest in unhealthy fats, added sugar, and/or salt
  Examples
- Fresh/frozen/canned vegetables prepared with solid fats, battered, and/or fried
- Fruit canned in heavy syrup or fruit roll-ups
- Muffins, donuts, pancakes, waffles, and French toast made with solid fats
- Potato chips, cheese puffs, high-fat crackers, high-sugar cereal
- Whole milk, flavored 2% milk, whole-milk yogurt, processed cheese, ice cream, whole-milk cheese

Robinson et al., 2007; Arredondo et al., 2009), these displayed products likely serve as a form of food and beverage promotion. Every school had large, fountain-type drink machines that contained food-colored fruit juice offered with the NSLP meal and/or a fruit juice slushy sold a la carte (juices range from 50 to 100% fruit juice).

Very few signs were found in the school gyms, and the signs that were posted in gyms promoted healthy foods and beverages and PA predominantly. CATCH signage was found posted throughout the building in most of the pilot schools. Information on these signs included the general promotion of staying healthy by eating nutritious foods, being physically active, and drinking more water. Most schools displayed at least one CATCH banner, which promoted physical activity and healthy eating through pictures.

Based on CATCH Go, Slow, Whoa criteria (Table 13.2), data provided in Table 13.3 show preliminary categorization of signs and items documented in the pilot schools as healthy or unhealthy. These preliminary results indicate that every school has Slow/Whoa food and beverage signs posted, and, among three of the five schools, Slow/Whoa food and beverage signs were more prevalent than Go signs. All schools have more Slow/Whoa items available than Go items, and only one school had more than 1% of documented items available that were healthy.

Table 13.3 Categorizations of food and beverage promotion in five middle schools in central Texas

	Items		Signs	
	"GO" Items	"Slow & Whoa" Items	"Go" Signs	"Slow & Whoa" Signs
School				
1	0.02%	97.4%	30.4%	69.5%
2	0.02%	97.6%	52.1%	74.9%
3	0%	100%	36.6%	63.3%
4	0.06%	93.6%	75%	25%
5	21.9%	78.1%	60.9%	39.1%

Challenges

In addition to the difficulties encountered in creating and using the checklist, there are some general limitations to this method of data collection. First, simply posting a sign does not mean that it is in a prominent location. We tried to address this by recording signs in areas where we believed all students travel. However, without studying the traffic patterns and policies of a school (e.g., where students are supposed to wait for buses, or where students congregate in the morning), we do not know if we are observing high-traffic locations of a school or if we are observing places where students rarely travel. A second challenge, which is much more difficult to address, is that we do not know which signs are the most effective. We are using sizes and counts as proxies for a sign's impact. While this may not be completely unreasonable, it is possible that it does not capture the true effectiveness of a sign. One factor may be that a sign may have more impact if is complemented by messages or advertising students are receiving elsewhere. For instance, the CATCH program provides schools with nutrition education signage meant to complement CATCH classroom lessons. The impact of the signs may be compromised if the lessons are not being taught. Also, even a small food product logo posted in a school may have a large impact if the logo is used in a national advertising campaign.

Another challenge is accurately recording the size of the signs. Data collectors are prompted to record the size as small, medium, or large, where the definitions for each category are, index card to tabloid poster, 24″×36″ to 48″×72″, and greater than 48″×72″, respectively. The definitions established here are common dimensions of posters and bulletin boards found in schools. Through pilot testing, we found most data collectors where good at identifying these dimensions. However, when signage was encountered that had different proportions it could be difficult to identify the correct size category. To be completely accurate, the sign definitions would need to be given in square inches instead of dimensions, for instance instead of 24″×36″ it would be 864 in.^{2}. However, few people can visualize 864 in.^{2}, and we did not want to have to measure each poster. Additionally, most data collectors had difficulty distinguishing between small and medium. A possible solution may be to have data collectors carry a tabloid sheet of paper to use as a size reference.

Beyond documenting food and beverage promotion, in-school data collection efforts present some specific challenges. For instance, taking quality pictures of types of food/beverage and PA promotion quickly and without including students, proved to be difficult in some cases. Working around school schedules and interacting with staff were also challenging in some instances. Additionally, minimizing time spent in schools without sacrificing quality of the data collected was also a challenge. In some schools, timing was an issue, as the cafeteria staff stocks the main and a la carte lines before the first lunch period. Specifically, if data collectors arrived before the first lunch period, there were more items to document; for later data collections or those that took place during a lunch period (when students had already purchased many of the items), the amount of items documented may not be representative of what some children are exposed to. In most schools, staff replenished items between lunch periods. These circumstances indicate that representative data may be best collected just prior to a lunch period beginning. However, it should be noted that this requires quick data collection, as there is a small window of time when the cafeteria is stocked and open for data collectors before students are present. This also reinforces the need for a new, faster data collection tool, which we aim to accomplish with the development of the electronic In-School MEDIA DOT.

Next Steps

Electronic In-School MEDIA DOT Development

For the pilot study, data collectors used the paper and pencil version of the In-School MEDIA DOT. Based on the pilot study, we were able to better determine which aspects were most useful and those that needed to be modified or deleted, which will be discussed below. For next steps, an electronic data collection tool will be developed in FileMaker®, database software that allows for data collection and entry to occur simultaneously. Data may be managed through this software and accessed on multiple devices, including an iPod Touch® through the use of the FileMaker Go® application, which can be used for future data collections.

Data collectors wrote a lot of information freehand because the collection tool lacked appropriate ways to document the a la carte items and signs that were found primarily in the cafeteria. A descriptive, useful, and discreet way to estimate the size and space available for a la carte items is needed in the final tool. Also, preset categories and options, based on the pilot data, will be included in the FileMaker® program.

Additionally, a larger study will be conducted to assess the in-school food and beverage advertising environment in 30 middle schools. Through this study we will be able to link in-school advertising findings with the behaviors and obesity status of eighth grade middle school students to determine if students in schools with more unhealthy in-school advertising are more likely to make unhealthy choices and be overweight or obese.

Conclusions

Although schools have particular aspects that present research challenges, there is a clear need to assess this environment and its possible effects on child health. This chapter provides a place from which to build regarding the assessment and evaluation of food and beverage promotion in schools. Further examination of the school food and beverage environment is necessary to gain a clearer picture of the prevalence, type, and range of this type of promotion that is aimed at children. Other research in this area may include identifying possible policy implications regarding food and beverage promotion in schools and using the In-School MEDIA DOT to assess other environments where children spend time.

Schools are unique in that they represent a setting where children spend a significant amount of time, have limited food and beverage options, make food-related decisions, and develop habits that may track into adulthood. While the school environment has been understudied with regard to food and beverage promotion, previous research on the possible health-related outcomes associated with food and beverage advertising in other environments provides evidence that the effects of the school atmosphere should be further examined. Given the current childhood obesity crisis, it is necessary to examine all surroundings where youth may be exposed to food and beverage promotion, in an attempt to find promising solutions.

References

Arredondo, E., Castaneda, D., Elder, J. P., Slymen, D., & Dozier, D. (2009). Brand name logo recognition of fast food and healthy food among children. *Journal of Community Health, 34*, 73–78.

Birch, L. L. (1999). Development of food preferences. *Annual Review of Nutrition, 19*, 41–62.

Borzekowski, D. G., & Robinson, T. N. (2001). The 30-second effect: An experiment revealing the impact of television commercials on food preferences of preschoolers. *Journal of the American Dietetic Association, 101*(1), 42–46.

Briefel, R. R., Crepinsek, M. K., Cabili, C., Wilson, A., & Gleason, P. M. (2009). School food environments and practices affect dietary behaviors of US public school children. *Journal of the American Dietetic Association, 109*, S91–S107.

Chou, S., Rashad, I., & Grossman, M. (2008). Fast-food restaurant advertising on television and its influence on childhood obesity. *Journal of Law and Economics, 51*, 599–618.

Coleman, K. J., Tiller, C. L., Sanchez, J., Heath, E. M., Sy, O., Milliken, G., et al. (2005). Prevention of the epidemic increase in child risk of overweight in low-income schools the El Paso coordinated approach to child health. *Archives of Pediatrics & Adolescent Medicine, 159*, 217–224.

Cullen, K. W., Eagan, J., Baranowski, T., Owens, E., & de Moor, C. (2000). Effect of a la carte and snack bar foods at school on children's lunchtime intake of fruits and vegetables. *Journal of the American Dietetic Association, 100*, 1482–1486.

Cullen, K. W., & Thompson, D. I. (2005). Texas school food policy changes related to middle school à la carte/snack bar foods: Potential savings in kilocalories. *Journal of the American Dietetic Association, 105*(12), 1952–1954.

Cullen, K. W., Watson, K., Zakeri, I., & Ralston, K. (2006). Exploring changes in middle-school student lunch consumption after local school food service policy modifications. *Public Health Nutrition, 9*(6), 814–820.

Cullen, K. W., & Zakeri, I. (2004). Fruits, vegetables, milk, and sweetened beverages consumption and access to a la carte/snack bar meals at school. *American Journal of Public Health, 94*, 463–467.

Dixon, H. G., Scully, M. L., Wakefield, M. A., White, V. M., & Crawford, D. A. (2007). The effects of television advertisements for junk food versus nutritious food on children's food attitudes and preferences. *Social Science & Medicine, 65*, 1311–1323.

Evans, W. D., Finkelstein, E. A., Kamerow, D. B., & Renaud, J. M. (2005). Public perceptions of childhood obesity. *American Journal of Preventive Medicine, 28*(1), 26–32.

Federal Trade Commission (FTC). (2008). *Marketing food to children and adolescents. A review of industry expenditures, activities, and self-regulation*. Available online at http://www.ftc.gov. Accessed 9 May 2012.

Fox, M. K., Hedley-Dodd, A., Wilson, A., & Gleason, P. M. (2009). Association between school food environment and practices and body mass index of US public school children. *Journal of the American Dietetic Association, 109*, S108–S117.

Frumkin, H. (2006). Introduction: Safe and healthy school environments. In H. Frumkin, R. J. Geller, L. L. Rubin, & J. Nodvin (Eds.), *Safe and healthy school environments*. New York: Oxford University Press.

Goldberg, M. E., Gorn, G. J., & Gibson, W. (1978). TV messages for snack and breakfast foods: Do they influence children's preferences? *The Journal of Consumer Research, 5*, 73–81.

Gordon, A. R., Crepinsek, M. K., Nogales, R., Condon, E. (2007). *School nutrition dietary assessment study-III. Vol. I: School foodservice, school food environment, and meals offered and served*. Final report. Princeton, NJ: Mathematica Policy Research, Inc.

Gorn, G. J., & Goldberg, M. E. (1982). Behavioral evidence of the effects of televised food messages on children. *The Journal of Consumer Research, 9*(2), 200.

Halford, J. C. G., Boyland, M. J., Hughes, G., Oliveira, L. P., & Dovey, T. M. (2007). Beyond-brand effect of television (TV) food advertisement/commercials on caloric intake and food choice of 5–7-year-old children. *Appetite, 49*, 263–267.

Halford, J. C. G., Gillespie, J., Brown, V., Pontin, E. E., & Dovey, T. M. (2004). Effect of television advertisements for foods on food consumption in children. *Appetite, 42*, 221–225.

Hartstein, J., Cullen, K. W., Reynolds, K. D., Harrell, J., Resnicow, K., & Kennel, P. (2008). Impact of portion-size control for school à la carte items: Changes in kilocalories and macronutrients purchased by middle school students. *Journal of the American Dietetic Association, 108*(1), 140–144.

Hesketh, K., Waters, E., Green, J., Salmon, L., & Williams, J. (2005). Healthy eating, activity and obesity prevention: A qualitative study of parent and child perceptions in Australia. *Journal of Health Promotion International, 20*(1).

Hoelscher, D. M., Springer, A. E., Ranjit, N., Perry, C. L., Evans, A. E., Stigler, M., et al. (2010). Reductions in child obesity among disadvantaged school children with community involvement: The Travis County CATCH Trial. *Obesity, 18*, S36–S44.

Holt, D. J., Ippolito, P. M., Desrochers, D. M., & Kelley, C. R. (2007). *Children's exposure to TV advertising in 1977 and 2004: Information for the obesity debate*. Bureau of Economics Staff Report. Washington, DC: Federal Trade Commission.

Institute of Medicine (IOM). (2005). *Preventing childhood obesity-health in the balance*. Washington, DC: The National Academies Press.

Institute of Medicine (IOM). (2006). *Food marketing to children and youth: Threat or opportunity?* Washington, DC: National Academies Press.

Institute of Medicine (IOM). (2007). *Nutrition standards for foods in schools: Steps toward healthier youth in America*. Washington, DC: National Academies Press.

Kubik, M. Y., Lytle, L. A., Hanna, P. J., Perry, C. L., & Story, M. (2003). The association of the school food environment with dietary behaviors of young adolescents. *American Journal of Public Health, 93*(7).

Kubik, M. Y., Lytle, L. A., & Story, M. (2005). Soft drinks, candy, and fast food: What parents and teachers think about the middle school food environment. *Journal of the American Dietetic Association, 105*, 233–239.

Luepker, R. V., Perry, C. L., McKinlay, S. M., Nader, P. R., Parcel, G. S., Stone, E. J. et al. (1996). Outcomes of a field trial to improve children's dietary patterns and physical activity. *JAMA: The Journal of the American Medical Association, 275*, 768–776.

Mazur, A., Telega, G., Kotowicz, A., Malek, H., Jarochowicz, S., Gierczak, B., et al. (2008). Impact of food advertising on food purchases by students in primary and secondary schools in south-eastern Poland. *Public Health Nutrition, 11*(9), 978–981.

Minaker, L. M., Storey, K. E., Raine, K. D., Spence, J. C., Forbes, L. E., Plotnikoff, R. C. et al. (2011). Associations between the perceived presence of vending machines and food and beverage logos in schools and adolescents' diet and weight status. *Public Health Nutrition, 14*(8), 1350–1356.

Nader, P. R., Stone, E. J., Lytle, L. A., Perry, C. L., Osganian, S. K., Kelder, S. et al. (1999). Three year maintenance of improved diet and physical activity, The CATCH Cohort. *Archives of Pediatrics & Adolescent Medicine, 153*, 695–704.

Neumark-Sztainer, D., French, S. A., Hannan, P. J., Story, M., & Fulkerson, J. A. (2005). School lunch and snacking patterns among high school students: Associations with school food environment and policies. *International Journal of Behavioral Nutrition and Physical Activity, 2*(1), 14.

Palmer, E., Cantor, J., Dowrick, P., Kunkel, D., Linn, S., Wilocx, B. (2004). Report of the APA task force on advertising and children: Psychological issues in the increasing commercialization of childhood. Section: Psychological implications of commercialism in schools. Washington, DC: American Psychological Association.

Perry, C. L., Sellers, D. E., Johnson, C., Pedersen, S., Bachman, K. J., Parcel, G. S., et al. (1997). The Child and Adolescent Trial for Cardiovascular Health (CATCH): Intervention, implementation, and feasibility for elementary schools in the United States. *Health Education & Behavior, 24*(6), 716–735.

Probart, C., McDonnell, E., Bailey-Davis, L., & Weirich, E. (2006). Existence and predictors of soft drink advertisements in Pennsylvania high schools. *Journal of the American Dietetic Association, 106*, 2052–2056.

Risvas, G., Panagiotakos, D. B., & Zampelas, A. (2008). Factors affecting food choice in Greek primary-school students: ELPYDES study. *Public Health Nutrition, 11*(6), 639–646.

Robinson, T. N., Borzekowski, D. L., Matheson, D. M., & Kraemer, H. C. (2007). Effects of fast food branding on young children's taste preferences. *Archives of Pediatrics & Adolescent Medicine, 161*(8), 792–797.

Springer, A. E., Kelder, S., Byrd-Williams, C., Pasch, K. E., Ranjit, N., Delk, J., et al. (in press). Promoting energy-balance behaviors among ethnically diverse adolescents: Overview & baseline findings of the Central Texas CATCH Middle School Project. *Health Education & Behavior.*

Waters, E., de Silva-Sanigorski, A., Hall, B. J., Brown, T., Campbell, K. J., Gao, Y., et al. (2011). Interventions for preventing obesity in children. *Cochrane Database of Systematic Reviews*, (12).

Wirt, J., Rooney, P., Hussar, B., Choy, S., Provasnik, S., Hampden-Thompson, G. (2005). The condition of education. Available online at http://nces.ed.gov/pubsearch/pubsinfo.asp?pubid=2005094. Accessed 5 Sep 2011.

Chapter 14
Outdoor Food and Beverage Advertising: A Saturated Environment

Keryn E. Pasch and Natalie S. Poulos

Overweight and obesity have been increasing among youth, with the prevalence of overweight among children and teens in the US tripling since 1980 (Ogden & Carroll, 2010). While the prevalence rates have leveled off in recent years (Ogden, Carroll, Curtin, Lamb, & Flegal, 2010; Ogden, Carroll, Kit, & Flegal, 2012), the rates of obesity-related diseases continue to rise (Knip et al., 2008), and health disparities exist in the prevalence of overweight and obesity across racial/ethnic groups, with African American and Hispanic youth at higher risk of being overweight or obese (Ogden et al., 2012). One factor that has been associated with obesity is exposure to food and beverage advertising (Institute of Medicine, 2006). Additionally, racial ethnic minorities have been disproportionately targeted and exposed to this type of advertising (see Chaps. 16, 17, and 18). One form of food and beverage advertising that has received less attention is outdoor advertising. As such, the purpose of this chapter is to review the literature on outdoor food and beverage advertising and provide researchers and community practitioners with a tool to document and describe this type of advertising in their own communities. We will also present pilot data from our study designed to document and describe food and beverage advertising around schools and end with a discussion on policy implications and future directions for research in this area.

Food and Beverage Advertising

A systematic review of the literature, conducted by the Institute of Medicine Committee on Food Marketing and the Diets of Children and Youth, found that children's food and beverage advertising exposure was related to food preferences,

K.E. Pasch (✉) • N.S. Poulos
University of Texas at Austin, Department of Kinesiology and Health Education,
1 University Station, D3700, Austin, TX 78712, USA
e-mail: kpasch@austin.utexas.edu;natalie.poulos@utexas.edu

J.D. Williams et al. (eds.), *Advances in Communication Research to Reduce Childhood Obesity*, DOI 10.1007/978-1-4614-5511-0_14,

purchasing attempts, food choices, and obesity (Institute of Medicine, 2006) (see Chap. 2). Children are key market segments as they not only purchase their own foods and beverages but also solicit purchase requests from parents (Institute of Medicine; Linn, 2004; McNeal, 1992; Schor, 2004), and may consume foods as adults they learned to prefer as children. Specifically, youth have considerable influence on the purchases of sugar-sweetened beverages, candy, salty snacks, and breakfast cereals (Institute of Medicine; Schor, 2004). In addition, youth are most likely to cite snacks, beverages, breakfast cereal, and food from fast-food restaurants as the top items they are allowed to buy without parental consent (Chaplin, 1999; Institute of Medicine; Schor, 2004). In fact, books have been written to help marketers capitalize on the youth segment of the population (Acuff & Reiher, 1997; Del Vecchio, 1997; McNeal, 1992). These marketing efforts are used to develop interest in products so that youth can develop brand loyalty (Acuff & Reiher, 1997; Hawkes, 2002; McNeal, 1992). Because brand loyalty is highest for carbonated soft drinks and quick serve restaurants, marketers have tried to increase their efforts targeting youth in order to develop brand loyalty at earlier ages. Marketers also use advertising to associate foods and beverages with pleasurable experiences and try to make the product more desirable (Hawkes, 2002; Institute of Medicine), which may then influence children's norms and beliefs about unhealthy food.

Food and beverage advertising is prominent in the lives of youth. Overall, in 2006, $1.6 billion dollars was spent in the US alone to promote foods and beverages targeted toward youth (Federal Trade Commission, 2008). When considering where foods and beverages are advertised, the focus has been on traditional measured media, newer (e.g., online) media, in-store packaging and labeling, in-school, premiums such as toys or contests, and other traditional promotions such as product placements (Federal Trade Commission). Additionally, much of the research on the influence of food and beverage advertising on obesity-related outcomes (i.e., unhealthy food preferences and choices as well as obesity) has focused on television advertising (Institute of Medicine, 2006). While research on these traditional media outlets is valuable, one important outlet which has been understudied is the outdoor food and beverage advertising environment.

Outdoor Food and Beverage Advertising

Outdoor advertising is commonplace in the US and many countries around the world. In order to encourage purchases and create brand recognition, businesses frequently advertise their products on storefronts and billboards, as well as other outdoor surfaces such as buildings, bus stands, and benches. In 2006, $3.83 billion was spent on measured outdoor advertising in the USA (Advertising Age, 2007). Of that, $76.5 million was spent by the food, beverage, and candy industries, and, of the top 25 advertisers in the US, three (Kraft Foods, Pepsi Co, and Nestle) were food, beverage, or candy companies (Advertising Age). Nestle spent $2.5 million on outdoor advertising in 2006 while Kellogg Co., a leading manufacturer of children's sugared cereals, spent $1.7 million (Advertising Age). Pepsi Co. and Coca-Cola spent a combined $30.5 million dollars on outdoor advertising (Advertising Age), and Cadbury Schweppes increased their outdoor advertising expenditures in the period from 2005 to 2006 from $1.97 million to $6.8 million. McDonald's Corporation, classified as a restaurant and not included in the food, beverage, and candy totals, spent $48.7 million dollars on outdoor advertising (Advertising Age). These advertising budgets suggest that youth may be exposed to a large, disproportionate amount of outdoor food and beverage advertising, particularly for unhealthy foods and beverages.

Outdoor advertising, particularly around schools or other areas where children frequent, may be especially problematic as children are exposed to advertising around schools on a daily basis. Previous research with alcohol advertising has shown that increased exposure to alcohol advertising around schools influences adolescent's intentions to use alcohol (Pasch, Komro, Perry, Hearst, & Farbakhsh, 2007). In addition, advertising research suggests that repetitive exposure to advertising over time can lead to low-involvement learning, or learning that occurs when a person is a passive participant (Mazis, 1995). This passive learning, due to repetitive exposure, is important as youth may encounter advertising around schools multiple times a day, going to and from school, as well as time spent outdoors if the advertising is close enough to the school. Additionally, adolescents have been found to create associations between alcohol use and important values, goals, and lifestyles even when they do not like or are skeptical of the alcohol advertisements (Mazis). Similar processes may also occur for food and beverage advertising. As such, it is crucial to document and describe the prevalence and content of this type of advertising to begin to further our understanding of how outdoor food and beverage advertising influences youth.

Many studies have examined the density of food outlets around schools (Austin et al., 2005; Babey, Wolstein, & Diamant, 2011; Davis & Carpenter, 2009; Day & Pearce, 2011; Kipke et al., 2007; Larson & Story, 2009; Laska, Hearst, Forsyth, Pasch, & Lytle, 2010; Simon, Kwan, Angelescu, Shih, & Fielding, 2008; Tester, Yen, & Laraia, 2010; Walton, Pearce, & Day, 2009; Zenk & Powell, 2008). In a recent review, it was suggested that neighborhood residents who have better access to supermarkets and limited access to convenience stores tend to have healthier diets and lower levels of obesity. There is also some evidence to suggest that residents with limited access to fast-food restaurants have healthier diets and lower levels of obesity (Larson & Story, 2009). While the presence of food outlets may have important implications for diet quality and other obesity-related outcomes, and does in fact serve as a form of product promotion (i.e., a McDonalds sign is an important form of branding children may see on a daily basis), little attention has been given to the larger outdoor advertising environment. The limited research that has focused on outdoor food and beverage advertising has primarily been conducted in countries outside of the US (Adams, Ganiti, & White, 2011; Kelly, Cretikos, Rogers, & King, 2008; Maher, Wilson, & Signal, 2005; Walton et al., 2009), with the exception of two studies which explored outdoor advertising in the US (Hillier et al., 2009;

Yancey et al., 2009) and one which focused on exterior marketing of fast-food restaurants (Powell, Rimkus, Isgor, Barker, & Chaloupka, 2012).

In a study of the outdoor food advertising environment within 500 m around 40 primary schools in Australia, Kelly and colleagues (2008) documented and coded all food advertisements. Advertisements were coded based on type of food, defined as core foods or foods needed to meet daily requirements, non-core foods or foods that are extra to daily requirements, and miscellaneous drinks defined as coffee or tea (Kelly et al., 2008). The study found 2,286 food advertisements around the 40 schools with 80% of the food advertisements for non-core foods and only 5% for core foods, with soft drinks the most frequently advertised products.

A New Zealand study documented food outlets and advertisements within a 2 km (2,000 m) buffer of four primary schools in New Zealand (Walton et al., 2009). The average number of advertisements around each school ranged from 2.9 to 22.0 and approximately 21-88% of students (depending on school) passed a food outlet or advertisement on their way to or from school each day. In another study conducted in New Zealand, outdoor advertising within 1 km (1,000 m) of ten schools (grades 9–13) was documented. A total of 1,408 product advertisements were documented, with 61.5% of those advertisements for food; 70.2% of those food advertisements were classified as unhealthy (Maher et al., 2005). Similar to the study conducted by Kelly et al., soft drinks were the most commonly advertised product. Interestingly, higher socio-economic status (SES) neighborhoods had significantly more unhealthy food advertisements than lower SES neighborhoods (Maher et al.).

In a recent study conducted in a Northern England city, all outdoor advertisements within city boundaries were documented, photographed, and classified as food or non-food (Adams et al., 2011). Advertisements were then coded for size and nutritional content (percentage of energy from protein, carbohydrate, sugar, fat, and saturated fat, total energy, fiber, and sodium) based on producers' websites. A total of 1,371 advertisements were found, with 15% of the advertisements for food products. Additionally, the greatest number of advertisements, as well as a greater proportion of advertising space (i.e., larger advertisements), was found in the least affluent areas. Nutritional content analysis found that foods advertised tended to be high in fat and sugar. However, similar to findings in the studies conducted by Maher and colleagues (2005), foods advertised in the highest SES tertile were the least healthy as compared to foods advertised in the lowest SES tertile, while those advertised in the middle SES tertile tended to be the healthiest (Adams et al.).

In contrast to the findings that higher SES communities have more unhealthy outdoor advertising in both New Zealand and Northern England, a recent study in the US, which explored the clustering of unhealthy outdoor advertising (e.g., alcohol, tobacco, sugar-sweetened beverages, and fast food) around child-serving institutions in several zip code areas of four major cities (i.e., Los Angeles, Philadelphia, New York, and Austin), found that out of all outdoor advertisements documented, 14.9% were for obesity-related products or services, and advertisements of energy-dense, low-nutrient products were twice as likely to be found in low-income zip code areas (Yancey et al., 2009). Additionally, in another study, advertisements for unhealthy products did not cluster around the child-serving institutions in Austin, but they did cluster in Los Angeles and Philadelphia. The most common products advertised around child-serving institutions were alcohol in Austin and Philadelphia, and alcohol and fast food in Los Angeles (Hillier et al., 2009).

In a study which documented exterior marketing of 2,442 fast-food restaurants in 154 communities in the US, 80% of fast-food restaurants advertised with exterior signage, and, on average across all the communities, fast-food restaurants had an average of five exterior advertisements (Powell et al., 2012). This exterior advertising was significantly more likely in lower income communities as compared to higher income communities, as well as communities that are majority Black or Latino as compared to White communities. Price promotion was common on more than half of exterior advertising and more common in lower income and Latino neighborhoods (Powell et al., 2012).

It is clear that childhood obesity is a problem in the US and worldwide. Given that outdoor food and beverage advertising is prevalent, likely to be unhealthy, and has found to cluster around child-centered institutions such as schools, the outdoor advertising of unhealthy foods and beverages should be considered as one of the contributing causes. Additionally, in the US, it appears that outdoor food and beverage advertising is more prevalent in lower income and minority communities. Therefore, it is critical that we determine how the outdoor food and beverage-advertising environment influences children's behaviors and choices and ultimately their rates of obesity, as well as how this environment may disproportionately affect youth at greatest risk of obesity and obesity-related diseases. Furthermore, given that children are repeatedly exposed to outdoor food and beverage advertising around schools on a daily basis, studies are needed which document and describe this form of advertising so that we can not only inform schools, communities, and policy makers about the prevalence and influence of these advertisements but also enable us to create interventions which will reduce the exposure and influence of this type of advertising. In the remaining sections of this chapter, we will describe a study designed to document food and beverage advertising around schools as well as provide pilot results for data collected around four middle schools in the US. We hope this chapter can provide researchers and community practitioners with a tool for documenting and describing outdoor food and beverage advertising to build the evidence base on this type of advertising as well as provide support for policy initiatives to reduce youth exposure to food and beverage advertising.

Documenting and Describing the Outdoor Food and Beverage Advertising Environment: The Outdoor MEDIA Study

The Outdoor MEDIA (Measuring and Evaluating the Determinants and Influence of Advertising) Study was designed to document and describe the prevalence of outdoor food and beverage advertising around Central Texas middle schools. The Outdoor MEDIA study will also document and describe food and beverage advertising and establishments within half a mile of 34 middle schools, 13 high schools, and 9 hospitals. In addition to documenting prevalence, the Outdoor MEDIA study will also code advertisements for content to better understand the themes used in outdoor food and beverage advertising. For this chapter, however, we will describe the pilot study in which we documented food and beverage advertising and establishments within one mile (i.e., 1,600 m) of four middle schools. To do this, we created maps and directions outlining all streets within a one-mile radius of each school. Data collection teams subsequently documented the location of and photographed each food or beverage advertisement within the one-mile data collection area. An electronic data collection tool was developed to make data collection more rapid and less intrusive when out in the field, as well as to allow for reduced data entry and coding time and errors once the data were collected. Documenting and coding each advertisement will allow for future analysis of prevalence, density, clustering, and content of the outdoor food and beverage advertisements. Below, we describe the development of the mapping and data collection protocols as well as the results from this pilot study.

Creating Maps

ESRI ArcGIS (Environmental Systems Resource Institute, 2010) was used to create maps that represented the streets located within 1,600 m of each data collection school. Street files were downloaded from a comprehensive set of downloadable GIS (Geographic Information System) data for Austin, TX (City of Austin, 2012). Street files included all streets in Travis County and were last updated July 8, 2011. School location files were downloaded from the Texas Education Agency and were last updated July 2010 (Texas Education Agency, 2012). This file contained locations for all of the schools in Texas. Both of these files were brought into ArcMap as data layers. The coordinated system used for this series of layers was the North American Datum 1984 State Plane Central Texas. The projection was set to a Lambert Conformal Conic projection to minimize distortion from East to West.

First, all schools defined as data collection schools were selected by name within the Texas Education Agencies layer of school locations and exported as a new layer. In addition, all Austin Independent School District elementary schools and high schools were selected by district and school type (elementary, middle, or high school) and exported to individual layers. This was done to allow for the possibility of additional data collection. The location chosen for school placement was based on street addresses on the street layer as well as comparison with Google Maps (Google, 2011). To create the 1,600-m radius around each middle school, the Buffer tool was used. To print maps for each school, each school was selected manually and centered on the screen. The display was then changed to page view to allow for the school to be centered on a page as zoomed in as possible with the buffer intact. Maps were then printed for each school and included the name of the school, address, and scale bar to assist in later driving direction creation.

Creating Driving Directions

Directions for data collection for each map were created based on a protocol developed for use with outdoor alcohol advertising (Pasch et al., 2007). Turn-by-turn driving directions were created to ensure that every possible street in the 1,600-m radius around the school was documented. All directions began at the school and then continued down each street located within the 1,600-m radius of the school. Streets located within neighborhoods were only driven down once in a single direction because each side of the street was easily visible. Larger streets and highways were driven down twice (e.g., north and south or east and west) to allow data collectors to view each side of the street separately. When the 1,600-m buffer intersected a street, the directions continued to the next most appropriate stopping point, often to the next block. In order to ease data collection burden, directions were created to flow as continuously as possible. When this was not possible, directions would suggest to data collectors to return to the school and start going down another street.

Due to the scale of the street file, not all street names were printed on the map used for reference. In order to accurately create the directions for streets not named specifically on ArcGIS printed maps, Google Maps was used. The address of the school was typed into Google Maps, and the zoom tool was used to identify street names and traffic flow on streets unnamed by the ArcGIS printout. Google Street View was particularly useful in creating the map directions because it allowed data collectors to determine appropriate stopping locations, identify discrepancies between the ArcGIS map and Google Maps, and identify traffic flow of streets.

Directions were created for each of the four schools used for pilot data collection. Directions were typically 13 pages long (range = 6–20 pages) and took approximately 9.6 h (range = 6–20 h) to complete for each school. Length of directions greatly varied according to the number of streets located within each data collection area.

Data Collection Protocol

The data collection protocol was based on a protocol used for Project Northland Chicago (PNC) (Pasch et al., 2007; Pasch, Komro, Perry, Hearst, & Farbakhsh, 2009), a similar project documenting alcohol advertising around schools. Key components of the data collection protocol included the research objective and how the objective would be accomplished, instructions on what to look for while in the field, safety while working in the field, materials needed to complete data collection, descriptions and directions of how to use all data collection materials, a team overview and description of responsibilities for each team member, as well as a detailed description of how to systematically collect data while in the field.

The Outdoor MEDIA Direct Observation Tool

While planning the methods for performing data collection, we decided to collect all data electronically, as this would minimize manual data entry and, therefore, increase the efficiency of data collection and entry as well as decrease the likelihood of human error during manual entry. Therefore, we created the Outdoor MEDIA Direct Observation Tool, or Outdoor MEDIA DOT. In order to do this, an iPod Touch® was selected as an appropriate means of data collection for a variety of reasons. Primarily, the iPod Touch® has access to FileMakerGo, an application that allows for the creation of a customized database, is relatively inexpensive, easy to use, and has the ability to take photographs (FileMaker, 2011). The use of FileMakerGo allows for separate databases to be created for each school. Additionally, these files could be used while in the field to collect all data in an organized fashion. FileMakerGo also has the ability to insert photographs taken by the iPod Touch® directly into the file. This removes the problem of manually linking a digital camera photo to the data collection record of a particular advertisement after returning from field data collection. Finally, as many people own smart phones, the use of this device to document food and beverage advertising in public areas, such as outside gas stations or fast-food restaurants, was not disruptive and did not attract attention when entering data or taking photos since it is commonplace to see people typing on or taking photos with their smart phones in many different settings.

In order to create the mobile databases with FileMakerGo, both FileMaker Pro and FileMakerGo were used. FileMaker Pro allowed for the creation and merging of the databases (FileMaker, 2011) to be used with FileMakerGo. Due to the fact that multiple people in the field would use these database files, we opted to create separate files for each school. This ensured that only the data for each school would be modified at one time and would also prevent all data from being lost if something were to happen while in the field. An additional database file was created to document what researchers call a "Line of Sight." This file was used to document what could be seen from each side of the school. Once the data was collected in separate database files, each file was merged together into one comprehensive database.

Basic information such as school id, address, name, latitude and longitude, date, start and end time, and team member's names were included on the main data collection form of the Outdoor MEDIA DOT. In addition, information such as advertisement type, category, location, description, and photograph were included. Finally, a notes section was added in order to document any additional information that was determined to be important. For the Line of Sight file, a description box and two photographs were used to document what was seen from each side of the school (Front, Right, Back, and Left).

Creation of databases first began with creating labels for each of the items to be collected. Once in place, a layout was designed to incorporate each label. A header was included, which automatically populated the fields for the school address, id, longitude, latitude, date, starting time, ending time, and data collection team information. Below the header, variables were inserted with drop down boxes that provided appropriate options. Options were decided based on categories and types used in previous research and knowledge of the area. In addition, photo boxes were inserted to allow for direct collection of photographs, both wide angle and zoomed. Finally, a description and notes box was placed at the bottom of the layout to provide a place for additional notes. After creation of the database files, all files were synced to the computer with the iPod Touch®. In all, three files were created for each data collection school: a primary data collection file, a backup data collection file, and a line of sight file. This was done to ensure there was at least one working file for primary data collection while in the field. All files were then synced with the iPod Touch® FileMakerGo application.

During field application of FileMakerGo, data collectors began with the line of sight database. Data collectors were instructed to begin facing the school and take a photograph of the school sign as well as any visible advertisements. Data collectors then proceeded counterclockwise around the school noting any advertisements visible from the school grounds. Data collectors then proceeded out of the school grounds to follow the turn-by-turn driving directions to document all food and beverage advertisements and establishments within a one-mile radius of the school.

Pilot Data Collection

Pilot data collection was conducted for four middle schools in a variety of locations around Austin, TX. Four schools were randomly selected and resulted in a sample of schools located in south, central, east and west Austin. Data collection was completed in August and September 2011. The pilot data collection indicated that collecting data within a 1,600-m buffer of the schools may be too large of a distance from the school for students to reasonably walk. This was determined after only approximately 50% of the buffer area was completed for the first pilot school by two data collectors over a 4-h period.

Several additions were made to the protocol after the pilot data collection. It was determined that directory signs as well as street signs should be documented, as they typically include well-known images and branding for food and beverage establishments. In addition, it was determined that data collectors should proceed into shopping centers and strip malls to collect data because it is reasonable to believe students would still walk to these food and beverage establishments and observe the advertising. Furthermore, all logos of fast-food restaurants were to be documented as they are well-known and recognizable brand promotion and advertisements for these food and beverage establishments.

Additionally, through pilot data collection it was decided three overall categories would be used to document all advertising and establishments: advertisement, establishment, and advertisement establishment. Advertisement included all advertisements that are free standing, located on something other than a building (e.g., A-frame), or billboards. Establishment included the physical building of the business selling foods and beverages. Establishment advertisement included any advertisement that was directly attached to the building. These new categories were added to the electronic data collection tool for future data collection.

Given the variety of locations of schools used in our pilot data collection, it is likely the majority of concerns and questions related to future data collection were addressed. Pilot data collection allowed for refinement of the electronic tool and for the development of appropriate measures. After reviewing the pilot data, new protocols for categories of advertisements, types of advertisements, and subjects of advertisements were implemented. In addition, it was decided the buffer regions would be reduced to 800 m (i.e., one half mile) to allow for increased efficiency during data collection, and for providing a more realistic distance for students to walk to and purchase foods or beverages.

Pilot Results

Overall, a total of 563 food and beverage advertisements were found within 1,600 m of the four middle schools. Of the 563 advertisements, 427 were directly attached to establishments (median = 116 per school), and 136 were free-standing advertisements (median = 10 per school). The most common type of advertisements were located on or at a convenience store and/or gas station (56%, median = 77 per school). Other common types included advertisements associated with restaurants (21%, median = 22 per school), particularly fast-food restaurants (11%, median = 13 per school). Additional types of advertisements included street-side advertisements (8%, median = 8.5 per school), liquor store advertisements/establishments (4%, median = 1.5 per school), directory boards (the logo of a restaurant on a sign that indicated what stores were in a shopping area) (9%, median = 2.5 per school), grocery stores (1%, median = 0 per school), billboards (<1%, median = 0 per school), and other (2%, median = 2.5 per school).

In addition to advertisement information, the line of sight was completed for all schools. From three of the four schools, only residential property, fields, or park land was visible. From one school, a variety of food and beverage establishments were visible from the back of the school, where the playground was located, and included Starbucks, a frozen yogurt shop, a Chinese food restaurant, and a take-out pizza restaurant.

Conclusion

In the present study, we have highlighted the development of an electronic tool to document and describe outdoor food and beverage advertising as well as provided a review of the research on this type of advertising. Based on our pilot results, as well as previous research (Adams et al., 2011; Hillier et al., 2009; Kelly et al., 2008; Maher et al., 2005; Yancey et al., 2009), outdoor food and beverage advertising appears to be prevalent, especially around schools, with some having extreme amounts of this type of advertising. As such, outdoor food and beverage advertising should be considered when discussing the influence of advertising on youth, as well as a factor likely related to overweight, obesity, and obesity-related diseases. Future research should consider replicating this work in additional geographic areas to better understand the prevalence across different types of communities and to determine if there are differences by the type of school (elementary, middle, and high schools). Given that research in the US has found that there are differences in the prevalence of outdoor food and beverage advertising by race/ethnicity (Yancey et al., 2009), and that previous work in tobacco and alcohol advertising has found that outdoor advertising is more prevalent in minority areas (Alaniz, 1998; Alaniz & Wilkes, 1998; Altman & Schooler, 1991; Hackbarth et al., 2001; Hackbarth, Silvestri, & Cosper, 1995; Harwood et al., 2003; Mitchell & Greenberg, 1991; Pasch et al., 2009; Schooler, Basil, & Altman, 1996), additional research is needed to further document these relationships for food and beverage advertising. Future research which links exposure to obesity-related outcomes is also needed.

Using procedures as outlined above and described in the pilot study, both researchers and community practitioners will be able to develop effective outdoor data collection tools for a variety of topics. For example, these procedures could be used for community regional planning to document the prevalence, use, and conditions of parks, green spaces, and public spaces to better understand how to build and develop these areas to promote physical activity. In addition, the prevalence and type of food outlets including neighborhood grocery stores, local farmers markets, as well as larger grocery stores and fast-food outlets can be documented along with the types of food that may be offered there. Using techniques to objectively document the outdoor environment will add to our understanding of exposure to advertising as well as food and physical activity options in communities. The Outdoor MEDIA DOT can also be used in other research domains such as tobacco and alcohol research to document the prevalence of tobacco point of purchase advertising as well as alcohol-related outdoor advertising. As such, further research is needed to continue to create additional data collection protocols to implement this tool in a variety of settings.

Given the prevalence of food and beverage advertising to youth, documented associations with obesity-related outcomes, and limited research on outdoor food and beverage advertising, continued studies documenting and describing the outdoor advertising environment are greatly needed. Through this chapter, we have tried to provide an overview of the research on outdoor food and beverage advertising, discuss the importance of this environment, provide a background on the development of the Outdoor MEDIA DOT, an electronic data collection tool, and share data from a pilot study with four middle schools. We hope researchers and community practitioners will be able to use the information presented in this chapter to continue to document the outdoor environment and use the information gained to support policy initiatives to reduce youth exposure to unhealthy food and beverage advertising.

References

Acuff, D. S., & Reiher, R. H. (1997). *What kids buy and why: The psychology of marketing to kids*. New York: Free Press.

Adams, J., Ganiti, E., & White, M. (2011). Socio-economic differences in outdoor food advertising in a city in Northern England. *Public Health Nutrition, 14*(6), 945–950.

Advertising Age. (2007). 100 leading national advertisers. *2007 Marketer Profiles Yearbook*. Retrieved from http://adage.com/images/random/lna2007.pdf.

Alaniz, M. L. (1998). Alcohol availability and targeted advertising in racial/ethnic minority communities. *Alcohol Health and Research World, 22*(4), 286–289.

Alaniz, M. L., & Wilkes, C. (1998). Pro-drinking messages and message environments for young adults: The case of alcohol industry advertising in African American, Latino, and Native American communities. *Journal of Public Health Policy, 19*(4), 447–472.

Altman, D. G., & Schooler, C. (1991). Alcohol and cigarette advertising on billboards. *Health Education Research, 6*(4), 487–490.

Austin, S. B., Melly, S. J., Sanchez, B. N., Patel, A., Buka, S., & Gortmaker, S. L. (2005). Clustering of fast food restaurants around schools: A novel application of spatial statistics to the study of food environments. *American Journal of Public Health, 95*(9), 1575–1581.

Babey, S. H., Wolstein, J., & Diamant, A. L. (2011). Food environments near home and school related to consumption of soda and fast food. *Policy Brief UCLA Center for Health Policy Research* (PB2011-6), 1–8.

Chaplin, H. (1999). Food fight! *American Demographics*, 64–65.

City of Austin. (2012). City of Austin GIS Data Sets. Retrieved June 18, 2012, from ftp://ftp.ci.austin.tx.us/GIS-Data/Regional/coa_gis.html.

Davis, B., & Carpenter, C. (2009). Proximity of fast-food restaurants to schools and adolescent obesity. *American Journal of Public Health, 99*(3), 505–510.

Day, P. L., & Pearce, J. (2011). Obesity-promoting food environments and the spatial clustering of food outlets around schools. *American Journal of Preventive Medicine, 40*(2), 113–121.

Del Vecchio, G. (1997). *Creating ever-cool: A marketer's guide to a kid's heart*. Gretna, LA: Pelican Pub. Co.

Environmental Systems Resource Institute. (2010). *ArcMap*. Redlands, CA: ESRI.

Federal Trade Commission. (2008). Marketing food to children and adolescents: A review of industry expenditures, activities, and self-regulation. A report to Congress. Washington, DC: Author. Retrieved from http://www.ftc.gov/os/2008/07/P064504foodmktingreport.pdf.

FileMaker. (2011). FileMaker Pro 12: Apple Inc.

Google. (2011). Google Maps.

Hackbarth, D. P., Schnopp-Wyatt, D., Katz, D., Williams, J., Silvestri, B., & Pfleger, M. (2001). Collaborative research and action to control the geographic placement of outdoor advertising of alcohol and tobacco products in Chicago. *Public Health Reports, 116*(6), 558–567.

Hackbarth, D. P., Silvestri, B., & Cosper, W. (1995). Tobacco and alcohol billboards in 50 Chicago neighborhoods: Market segmentation to sell dangerous products to the poor. *Journal of Public Health Policy, 16*(2), 213–230.

Harwood, E. M., Erickson, D. J., Fabian, L. E., Jones-Webb, R., Slater, S., & Chaloupka, F. J. (2003). Effects of communities, neighborhoods and stores on retail pricing and promotion of beer. *Journal of Studies on Alcohol, 64*(5), 720–726.

Hawkes, C. (2002). Marketing activities of global soft drink and fast food companies in emerging markets: A review. In *Globalization, diets, and non-communicable diseases*. Geneva: World Health Organization.

Hillier, A., Cole, B. L., Smith, T. E., Yancey, A. K., Williams, J. D., Grier, S. A., et al. (2009). Clustering of unhealthy outdoor advertisements around child-serving institutions: A comparison of three cities. *Health & Place, 15*(4), 935–945.

Institute of Medicine. (2006). *Food marketing to children and youth: Threat or opportunity?* Washington, DC: National Academies Press.

Kelly, B., Cretikos, M., Rogers, K., & King, L. (2008). The commercial food landscape: Outdoor food advertising around primary schools in Australia. *Australian and New Zealand Journal of Public Health, 32*(6), 522–528.

Kipke, M. D., Iverson, E., Moore, D., Booker, C., Ruelas, V., Peters, A. L., et al. (2007). Food and park environments: Neighborhood-level risks for childhood obesity in east Los Angeles. *The Journal of Adolescent Health, 40*(4), 325–333.

Knip, M., Reunanen, A., Virtanen, S. M., Nuutinen, M., Viikari, J., & Akerblom, H. K. (2008). Does the secular increase in body mass in children contribute to the increasing incidence of type 1 diabetes? *Pediatric Diabetes, 9*(3 Pt 2), 46–49.

Larson, N., & Story, M. (2009). A review of environmental influences on food choices. *Annals of Behavioral Medicine, 38*(Suppl 1), S56–S73.

Laska, M. N., Hearst, M. O., Forsyth, A., Pasch, K. E., & Lytle, L. (2010). Neighbourhood food environments: Are they associated with adolescent dietary intake, food purchases and weight status? *Public Health Nutrition, 13*(11), 1757–1763.

Linn, S. E. (2004). *Consuming kids: The hostile takeover of childhood.* New York: New Press.

Maher, A., Wilson, N., & Signal, L. (2005). Advertising and availability of 'obesogenic' foods around New Zealand secondary schools: A pilot study. *The New Zealand Medical Journal, 118*(1218), U1556.

Mazis, M. B. (1995). Conducting research on nontraditional media in the marketing of alcoholic beverages. In S. E. Martin (Ed.), *The effects of mass media on the use and abuse of alcohol* (Vol. 28, NIH Publication No. 95–3743). Bethesda, MD: National Institute on Alcohol Abuse and Alcoholism, U.S. Department of Health and Human Services.

McNeal, J. U. (1992). *Kids as customers: A handbook of marketing to children.* New York: Lexington Books.

Mitchell, O., & Greenberg, M. (1991). Outdoor advertising of addictive products. *New Jersey Medicine, 88*(5), 331–333.

Ogden, C., & Carroll, M. (2010). Prevalence of obesity among children and adolescents: United States, trends 1963–1965 through 2007–2008. (June 19, 2012). Retrieved from http://www.cdc.gov/nchs/data/hestat/obesity_child_07_08/obesity_child_07_08.htm.

Ogden, C. L., Carroll, M. D., Curtin, L. R., Lamb, M. M., & Flegal, K. M. (2010). Prevalence of high body mass index in US children and adolescents, 2007–2008. *Journal of the American Medical Association, 303*(3), 242–249.

Ogden, C. L., Carroll, M. D., Kit, B. K., & Flegal, K. M. (2012). Prevalence of obesity and trends in body mass index among US children and adolescents, 1999–2010. *Journal of the American Medical Association, 307*(5), 483–490.

Pasch, K. E., Komro, K. A., Perry, C. L., Hearst, M. O., & Farbakhsh, K. (2007). Outdoor alcohol advertising near schools: What does it advertise and how is it related to intentions and use of alcohol among young adolescents? *Journal of Studies on Alcohol and Drugs, 68*(4), 587–596.

Pasch, K. E., Komro, K. A., Perry, C. L., Hearst, M. O., & Farbakhsh, K. (2009). Does outdoor alcohol advertising around elementary schools vary by the ethnicity of students in the school? [Comparative Study]. *Ethnicity and Health, 14*(2), 225–236.

Powell, L. M., Rimkus, L. M., Isgor, Z., Barker, D., & Chaloupka, F. J. (2012). Exterior marketing practices of fast-food restaurants. Retrieved from http://www.bridgingthegapresearch.org/_asset/2jc2wr/btg_fast_food_pricing_032012.pdf.

Schooler, C., Basil, M. D., & Altman, D. G. (1996). Alcohol and cigarette advertising on billboards: Targeting with social cues. *Health Communication, 8*(2), 109–129.

Schor, J. (2004). *Born to buy: The commercialized child and the new consumer culture.* New York: Scribner.

Simon, P. A., Kwan, D., Angelescu, A., Shih, M., & Fielding, J. E. (2008). Proximity of fast food restaurants to schools: Do neighborhood income and type of school matter? *Preventive medicine, 47*(3):284–8.

Tester, J. M., Yen, I. H., & Laraia, B. (2010). Mobile food vending and the after-school food environment. *American Journal of Preventive Medicine, 38*(1), 70–73.

Texas Education Agency. (2012). School District Locator – Data Download. Retrieved June 18, 2012, from http://ritter.tea.state.tx.us/SDL/sdldownload.html.

Walton, M., Pearce, J., & Day, P. (2009). Examining the interaction between food outlets and outdoor food advertisements with primary school food environments. *Health & Place, 15*(3), 811–818.

Yancey, A. K., Cole, B. L., Brown, R., Williams, J. D., Hillier, A., Kline, R. S., et al. (2009). A cross-sectional prevalence study of ethnically targeted and general audience outdoor obesity-related advertising. *The Milbank Quarterly, 87*(1), 155–184.

Zenk, S. N., & Powell, L. M. (2008). US secondary schools and food outlets. *Health & Place, 14*(2), 336–346.

Chapter 15
Exploring Marketing Targeted at Youth in Food Stores

Diana S. Grigsby-Toussaint, Kristen Harrison, Michelle R. Nelson, Barbara H. Fiese, and Mary J. Christoph

Overview

Childhood obesity is a major public health problem in the USA, with youth at all stages of development at increasing risk (Health, 2008). Between 1976 and 2004, increases in overweight prevalence ranged from 5.0% to 12.4% for 2-to-5-year olds, 6.5% to 17% for 6-to-11-year olds, and 5.0% to 17.6% for 12- to– 19-year olds (Ogden, Carroll, &, Flegal, 2008; Ogden et al., 2006; Ogden & Carroll, 2010). These statistics are particularly alarming as overweight youth disproportionately suffer from chronic conditions such as hypertension and diabetes, thus resulting in

D.S. Grigsby-Toussaint (✉)
University of Illinois at Urbana-Champaign, Department of Kinesiology and Community Health and Division of Nutritional Sciences, 2019 Huff Hall, 1206 S Fourth Street, USA
e-mail: diana.grigsby@gmail.com

K. Harrison
University of Michigan, Department of Communication Studies, 5389 North Quad, 105 South State Street, Ann Arbor, MI 48109-1285, USA

M.R. Nelson
University of Illinois at Urbana Champaign College of Media, 810 South Wright Street, 102 Gregory Hall, Urbana, IL 61801, USA

B.H. Fiese
University of Illinois, Department of Human and Community Development, Family Resiliency Center, 1016 B Doris Christopher Hall, MC-81, 904 W Nevada Street, Urbana, IL 61801, USA

M.J. Christoph
University of Illinois at Urbana-Champaign, Department of Kinesiology and Community Health, 80B Huff Hall, 1206 South Fourth Street, Champaign, IL 61820, USA

J.D. Williams et al. (eds.), *Advances in Communication Research to Reduce Childhood Obesity*, DOI 10.1007/978-1-4614-5511-0_15,

reduced quality of life at an early age (Anderson & Butcher, 2006). Overweight children are also at high risk for becoming overweight adults with the attendant comorbid conditions, including osteoarthritis and certain forms of cancer (Freedman, Dietz, Srinivasan, & Berenson, 1999; Dietz, 1998; Khaodhiar, McCowen, & Blackburn, 1999). As a consequence, a sense of urgency exists to disentangle the complex, multifactorial interactions between individual and environmental factors that lead to child weight imbalance and obesity (Johnson-Taylor & Everhart, 2006; Papas et al., 2007; Sallis & Glanz, 2006; Wang & Beydoun, 2007).

From the environmental perspective, exposure to food marketing and advertising has been identified as a major determinant of family food choices and habits that influence childhood obesity (Story & French, 2004; Institute of Medicine, 2006; Harris et al., 2009). Due to the ubiquitous marketing of high-sugar, high-fat obesogenic foods (Moore, 2006), it has become more challenging than ever for families to make informed and healthful choices that promote lifelong healthy eating and exercise habits among children (Harris et al., 2009). A study by the Kaiser Family Foundation (Moore 2006), for example, found that in the course of a year, an average American child will spend more hours watching television than in school, and the average 2-to-7-year old will be exposed to more than 4,000 food advertisements. Unfortunately, most of these advertisements are for high-calorie convenience foods, fast foods, and soda, with very few for fruits and vegetables (Harrison & Marske, 2005; Moore; Stitt & Kunkel, 2008). This trend is not likely to change as the budgets for food marketers dwarf those of government fruit and vegetable marketing programs such as "5-a-day"—$1.6 billion per year versus $2 million per year, respectively (FTC, 2008; USDA, 2010). As a result, youth are more likely to develop brand loyalty to nutrient-poor foods that influence family food purchasing and consumption behaviors (Robinson, Borzekowski, Matheson, & Kraemer, 2007; Dijksterhuis, Smith, van Baaren, & Wigboldus, 2005; Halford, Boyland, Hughes, Oliveira, & Dovey, 2007; Halford, 2004; Harris et al., 2009; Hastings, Stead, McDermott, Forsyth, et al., 2003; Institute of Medicine, 2006).

While the research literature supports the association between exposure to food marketing and increases in childhood obesity (Harris et al., 2009; Kunkel et al., 2004; Wiecha et al., 2006), empirical attention has focused on television as a vehicle of marketing to children in the home, with limited attention to the broader nutrition environment in which families are embedded (Connor, 2006; Institute of Medicine, 2006; Story, Kaphingst, & French, 2006; Crespo et al., 2001; Elliott, 2007; Fiese & Schwartz, 2008). The focus on children's direct exposure to television does not take into account the various social contexts in which children and families are exposed to food marketing and promotion, thus limiting the potential for effective interventions in multiple spaces and places that shape family purchasing and dietary behaviors. One critical social context that has received limited attention in the documentation of food marketing on childhood obesity is the retail food store environment. While an emerging body of literature suggests that improving the availability and accessibility of healthful food options via the retail food environment has great potential for creating sustainable dietary change in communities (NAEYC & SRCD 2008), few studies have explored how food marketing mediates this relationship. Previous studies report that shopping at or living in close proximity to a large supermarket or grocery store is associated with increased fruit and vegetable intakes while convenience store proximity is negatively associated with fruit and vegetable consumption, even after controlling for individual- or family-level characteristics (Rose & Richards, 2004; Morland, Wing, & Diez-Roux, 2002; Zenk et al., 2005; Zenk et al., 2009; Pearce, Hiscock, Blakely, & Witten, 2008). Most of these studies, however, have not included food marketing as an explanatory variable. Due to the increasing amount of time children spend shopping with their parents (~3 h per week for 3-to-8-year olds) (O'Daugherty, Story, & Stang, 2006; Hofferth & Sandberg, 2001) and the influence of children's requests on family purchasing habits (O'Daugherty et al.; Atkin, 1978; Galst & White, 1976), it is clear that this omission constrains a more complete understanding of the role the retail food environment plays in shaping dietary behaviors. A study by O'Dougherty et al. (2006) found that 50% of children shopping in supermarkets with their parents initiated a request for specific foods, and that the majority of these requests were for sweets or snacks influenced by brand loyalty and marketing techniques. The authors noted effective refusal strategies by parents most of the time, but found that the shopping experience was not used to educate children about food and nutrition, and that in some instances, parents initiated the purchase of nutrient-poor foods (O'Dougherty et al.). This illustrates the importance of the retail food store environment as a setting where families negotiate the influence of food and beverage marketing on purchasing practices that influence dietary behaviors. Additionally, this also suggests that retail food stores might be an important component of novel and systematic approaches for tackling childhood obesity in the USA.

The focus on the retail food environment is also important for addressing the disproportionately higher rates of overweight and obesity among low income and racial/ethnic minority groups. From an environmental perspective, these groups are at elevated risk for obesity due to higher media use (e.g., TV viewing) and residence in neighborhoods saturated with commercial food advertising and limited healthy food options (Strum, 2005; Yancey et al., 2009; Larson, Story, & Nelson, 2009; Zenk et al., 2006). As low-income families may have inadequate resources to overcome the environmental barriers that contribute to poor dietary choices, studies examining how marketing influences these choices in the retail food environment will be critical for developing effective interventions and advocating for policy changes that reduce childhood obesity rates.

A potentially confounding effect may be the different types of parenting strategies effective in low-income families as compared to strategies used in middle class families. If parents are to be empowered to be effective gatekeepers of the food that comes into their home, it is important to recognize that there are cultural variations in how families interact around food choice and manage eating behaviors. Although there is a longstanding tradition in developmental science that parents that are highly involved, provide considerable verbal reasoning to their children about their parenting decisions, and encourage autonomy will have children who fare better both emotionally and physically (Petit, Bates, & Dodge, 1997). However, recent research suggests that there is considerable variation across ethnic groups in parenting practices such that some groups may take more permissive or authoritarian approaches and their children still fare well (McWayne, Owsianik, Green, & Fantuzzo, 2008; Rodriquez, Donovick, & Crowley, 2009). When considering guidance for parents to take charge of their food environment, it will be important to consider not only the marketed environment but also how they connect with food and their families.

A particular concern is the omnipresence of televisions in the areas where children eat. Families who routinely watch television during their mealtimes have children and adolescents who tend to consume less nutrient-rich foods (Coon, Goldberg, Rogers, & Tucker, 2001; Feldman, Eisenberg, Neumark-Sztainer, & Story, 2007). There are several possible explanations for this relation. First, sheer exposure to food advertisements while eating may promote choice of less healthy foods even at an early age (Borzekowski & Robinson, 2001). Over time, the combination of television during meals and exposure to food advertising may create menus dense in fast foods, sweetened beverages, and lean in vegetables. A second possible mechanism is that the presence of television detracts from positive forms of interaction during meals. Emerging research indicates that families that are able to communicate positively during meals are less likely to have children who are overweight or obese (Jacobs & Fiese, 2007). Although the precise mechanism has not been fully explicated, it is possible to speculate that meals that include measured conversation are also more evenly paced and less likely to include rushed eating habits. Finally, it is important to consider why families find it necessary or soothing to have the television on during meals. Embedded in a survey conducted by the Centers for Disease Control and Prevention, mothers with young children who reported that they had the television on during meals said they often did so to reduce conflict at the table (Centers for Disease Control and Prevention, 2007). Thus, as a behavior management strategy, television becomes a distractor and rather than having parents monitor children's behavior (and perhaps their eating behaviors), the television is the center of attention.

In sum, while the literature demonstrates an association between food and beverage marketing and dietary behavior (Kunkel et al., 2004), most studies have been limited to the role of the television inside the home (Institute of Medicine, 2006; Fiese & Schwartz, 2008; Harrison & Marske, 2005; Elliott, 2007). Little is understood, however, about how food and beverage marketing to children and their families in the broader nutrition environment shapes purchasing behavior and ultimately, dietary intake. In this chapter, we hope to address this gap in the literature by (a) examining mechanisms used by marketers to influence food preferences among children, including exposure to food marketing via television and digital media; (b) exploring the reinforcement of marketing exposure via visual cues in food stores, and (c) exploring options for policy and environmental interventions/solutions.

Mechanisms of Persuasion

Theoretical Framework

While several theories have been used to explain the mechanisms through which marketing influences children, social cognitive theory (SCT), with the emphasis on triadic reciprocity, seems to best capture the interaction between environmental stimuli ("marketing") and children's cognitive ability to process their exposure. The mechanisms behind this relationship require some elaboration. Jordan and Robinson (2008) compared research on four different mechanisms proposed to link television viewing to child obesity (i.e., metabolic slowdown, displacement of physical activity, excessive energy intake due to eating while viewing, and excessive energy intake due to advertising of obesogenic foods) and concluded that the strongest and most consistent evidence to date exists for advertising obesogenic foods, followed by excessive energy intake due to eating while viewing. Regarding advertising effects, social cognitive theory (Bandura, 2002) offers a description of how observational learning via exposure to rewarded or unpunished behaviors on the part of media characters or models may encourage modeling of the depicted behaviors. In the case of food advertising, plentiful and visually appealing depictions of delicious-looking foods enjoyed by happy, satisfied people present an alluring vision of the rewards to be had by consuming advertised foods. Content analysis shows that even in advertisements aimed at children, foods are depicted as having addictive properties (i.e., producing exaggerated pleasure sensations and dependency), especially high-sugar foods (Page & Brewster, 2009). Further, preschool children are developmentally limited in their ability to distinguish commercials from program content (Kunkel et al., 2004), so they are unlikely to view food advertising with a critical eye. Even for those who do have some sense of advertising's purpose, it is the rare preschooler who can buy his or her own food. Rather, preschoolers exert their power over their dietary intake primarily in the form of refusals and requests (a.k.a. the "nag factor," see Morton, Stanton, Zuppa, & Mehta, 2005). These requests are not inconsequential; the national purchase influence of 2- to 14-year-old children is estimated at $500 billion annually (Institute of Medicine, 2006). Still, it is the parents and other caregivers who stock the pantry and provide the universe of foods from which young children may choose.

Accordingly, there are several ways parents may act as intermediaries between household media exposure and preschooler dietary habits. First, consistent with social cognitive theory (Bandura, 2002), parents also may engage in observational learning of eating behaviors via the advertisements they see when viewing child-oriented content with their children, or when viewing adult-oriented content with or without their children. In this case, one would expect exposure to stimulate increased parental purchasing of advertised foods, which are largely obesogenic and unhealthful. Second, regardless of the route by which unhealthful foods make their way into the family pantry, the mechanism described by Jordan and Robinson (2008) as "excessive energy intake due to eating while viewing" identifies a process by which screen media exposure may increase the likelihood that these foods are chosen by both parents and children over healthier alternatives for consumption during and after viewing. Harris, Bargh and Brownell (2009) found support for TV effects on appetitive priming in a study showing that children exposed to snack food advertisements ate more of a non-advertised snack food while viewing the program in which the advertisements had been embedded than did children who had been exposed to nonfood advertisements embedded in the same program. A follow-up study with adults showed that those who had been exposed to snack food advertisements ate more of a variety of foods, especially obesogenic foods, during a post-exposure taste test than those who had been exposed to advertisements for healthful foods (who actually ate less than a no-advertising control group; Harris et al., 2009). Third, what appears to be a causal relationship between child media exposure and child consumption of unhealthful foods may in fact be a spurious one produced by a third factor, one we might call "parental indulgence." Parents who have trouble limiting their children's media consumption may also have trouble limiting their children's intake of sugar-sweetened beverages, snack foods, sweets, and other enjoyable but unhealthful foods. These effects may be compounded when education and race are taken into account. African-American children and children of parents who have a high-school education or less are more likely to watch four or more hours of television per weekday. (Trends, 2010)

In all likelihood, these mechanisms (and others) are operating simultaneously. The first two (social learning leading to increased parental food purchasing and appetitive priming leading to increased child food intake during and after media exposure) have been supported by ample research (see Institute of Medicine, 2006, and Jordan & Robinson, 2008, for summaries). The third mechanism is harder to isolate and observe. If "parental indulgence" was largely responsible for the link between child TV exposure and child consumption of unhealthful foods, then children's use of multiple media—not just TV—should be correlated with their dietary habits, because parents who are reluctant to set dietary limits should also be reluctant to set limits on *all* types of media use (e.g., DVD/VHS, video games, and computer/Internet). However, with the possible exception of video game playing, which has been correlated with BMI in children aged 1–12 (Vandewater, Shim, & Caplovitz, 2004), TV has been more strongly and consistently linked to child overweight than any other medium. However, the association between various forms of digital media and child weight status has not been explored as extensively in the literature. There is evidence to suggest, however, that the digital environment is increasingly serving as a medium for influencing food choices among children.

With advergames, for example, the persuasion effects of embedded brands in games are mainly based on two different processes. First, on conditioning, where the positive experience of the game is frequently combined with the brand. Therefore, evaluative (emotional) conditioning is happening (De Houwer, 2007; De Houwer, Baeyens, & Field, 2005; De Houwer, Thomas, & Baeyens, 2001; Kroeber-Riel, 1984), where an emotional stimulus (the enjoyable gaming situation) is combined with a neutral stimulus (brand). When conditioned, every time the brand is seen, the emotional experience will also be remembered and a positive feeling towards the brand increases. A separate but related process may occur when persons in a good mood or feeling positive tend to evaluate subjects and objects more positively (Bagozzi, Gopinath, & Nyer, 1999). As the gaming situation usually is pleasing, game players will evaluate not only the game more positively, but they may also evaluate the embedded brand more positively. This classic affect transfer is also well known in traditional advertising research (e.g., Bagozzi, Gopinath, & Nyer, 1999; Batra & Stayman, 1990; Brown & Stayman, 1992; Lutz, McKenzie, & Belch, 1983; MacKenzie, Lutz, & Belch, 1986).

Another way that games may more implicitly persuade is related to the procedural rhetoric of the game (Bogost, 2007). The basic idea of this concept is that compared to explicit messages of traditional media, games offer the possibility of integrating the message less explicitly and in the winning conditions. In essence, the persuasive claims can be inserted into the games via interaction. For instance, Pringles promotes the flavors of the potato chips by asking players to collect ingredients (http://www.groovyglider.com), which is a winning condition, as the player gathers the most points when collecting the correct ingredients. Through this activity, the player learns the different flavors and establishes related brand beliefs (Waiguny, Nelson, & Terlutter, 2012).

Cartoon and Spokes-Characters

In order to engender brand loyalty among children, many advertisers use anthropomorphized cartoon and spokes-characters (Calcott & Lee, 1994; Phillips, 1996; Phillips & Gyoerick, 1999) that evoke positive emotions associated with various products. Briefly, branded spokes-characters can be defined as "fictional, animate beings or animated objects that have been created for the promotion of a product, service or idea"; Phillips, 1996, p.146. Popular cartoon characters such as Dora the Explorer or SpongeBob SquarePants® from children's television shows or movies are also licensed to market foods to children (Roberto, Baik, Harris, & Brownell, 2010). In commercial practice, original spokes-characters such as Tony the Tiger™ or licensed characters such as Spiderman® are used to attract attention and convey the unique attributes of the character to the brand. For instance, the Pillsbury Doughboy™ was found to be exciting, whereas Aunt Jemima™ was viewed as nurturing (LeBel & Cooke, 2008). Marketers carefully craft the image of the character with the attributes desired among the target audience. Research shows that such strategies impact memory and purchases. In a free recall task among children, the most frequently mentioned characters were for sugary cereals such as Tony the Tiger™, Toucan Sam®, and Captain Crunch (LeBel & Cooke, 2008). Some research with children in experimental studies shows additional impact of characters on health claims and perceived product taste. For example, children aged 5–7 who saw a character on the box liked the cereal more than the identical cereal in a box without a character (Lapierre, Vaala, & Linebarger, 2011). Further, Waiguny, Nelson, and Terlutter (2010) asked children aged 7–10 to play an advergame (custom-made digital games designed especially to promote a company's brand or products; Youn & Lee, 2005) for Nesquik cereal featuring a bunny spokes-character who gained power by collecting the cereal grain symbols. They found that liking the advergame influenced children's attitude towards the Nesquik brand directly. The children also believed that the brand was healthy because the spokes character avatar became more powerful from the cereal which children attributed toward health in real life. In sum, research suggests that spokes characters can attract attention, convey, and transfer personality qualities to the food product, and influence perceived taste and product choice.

Exposure

Television

Although young children today are inundated with various forms of media in the home, the television remains the primary medium through which they are exposed to marketing messages (Roberts & Foehr, 2004). This is not surprising, as almost all children in the US live in a home with a television, with approximately 71% of them having access to one in their bedrooms (Rideout, Vandewater, & Wartella, 2003; Anderson & Butcher, 2006). As a consequence, the average American child spends more hours watching TV than in school, with the youngest children (aged 0–6) spending as much time watching TV (73%) as they do reading or being read to by an adult or other caregiver (79%) on a typical day (Rideout et al., 2003). While a reduction in the exposure to food advertisements to children and adolescents decreased between 2003 and 2009, most advertisements are still for high-calorie convenience foods, fast foods, and soda, with very few for fruits and vegetables (Powell, Schermbeck, Szczypka, Chaloupka, Braunschweig, 2011; Harrison & Marske, 2005; Stitt & Kunkel, 2008). In a content analysis of food advertisements that aired during television shows heavily viewed by children, Harrison and Marske (2005) found that convenience foods and sweets comprised 83% of all advertised foods. Additionally, "snacking" was the most common "meal" depicted in most ads, with few for ads breakfast, lunch, or dinner (Harrison & Marske, 2005). Most disconcerting, however, was the finding that if children were to consume the foods most commonly advertised to them, they would exceed USDA recommended daily values (RDVs) of sodium, and add up to a cup of sugar to their daily diets (Harrison & Marske, 2005).

In addition to marketing nutrient-poor foods, TV also provides an opportunity for food and beverage companies to introduce cartoon and spokes characters, as well as company logos to children (Institute of Medicine, 2006; Kinsky & Bichard, 2011). Since most young children cannot read, the television allows companies to use symbolism to educate children about their brands and ingrain a sense of loyalty at an early age (Institute of Medicine, 2006; Kinsky & Bichard, 2011). This may occur through product tie-ins with television shows or movies, as well as product placement (Moore, 2006; Speers, Harris, & Schwartz, 2011). A recent analysis by Speers et al. (2011) of food and beverage product placement on television in 2008 showed that over the course of the year, Cocoa Cola products were seen almost 200 times by young children.

Digital Media

Increasingly, food marketers are looking to digital environments to promote their products. One popular way to do so is by sponsoring games. Advergames are specially designed to promote a company's brand or products (Youn & Lee, 2005), which combine two key elements: the brand and entertainment (Kretchmer, 2004). The main aims of advergames are to deliver a message for the advertised brand and to achieve higher traffic on brand websites (Santos, Gonzalo, & Gisbert, 2007). Advergames are usually offered free of charge and are downloadable from the company's website. They are "casual games": easy to learn, simple to play, offering quick rewards with forgiving game play, which makes for a quick, fun experience (Kuittinen, Kultima, Niemelä, & Paavilainen, 2007). Hence, advergames are branded casual games, which can be downloaded or played for free from a company's website or a high-traffic website.

An analysis of websites of the top 100 companies in the US revealed that more than half of the games featured food products (Lee & Youn, 2008). Other content analysis studies have reported that advergames on food brand websites (Lee, Yoonhyeung, Quilliam, & Cole, 2009; Moore, 2006; Moore & Rideout, 2007) are primarily targeting children with "less healthy" foods. Most of these games are created with fun as the main objective to build consumer relationships with the game and the brand (Lee & Youn; Santos et al., 2007). Critics and regulators have placed increased attention on the use of advergaming to promote (unhealthy) food products to children (Institute of Medicine of the National Academies 2006; Moore, 2004; Thomson, 2010).

From Television and Digital Media to Food Stores

Although food marketing targeted at children has been more extensively studied via television and the internet, there are several reasons to conduct extensive marketing evaluations of the retail food store environment. First, children are exposed to marketing in food stores at a very young age. According to John (1999), children begin:

> their exposure to the marketplace…as soon as they can be accommodated as a passenger in a shopping cart at the grocery store. ….infants and toddlers are exposed to a variety of stimuli and experiences, including aisles of products, shoppers reading labels and making decisions, and the exchange of money and goods at the checkout counter. These experiences, aided by developing cognitive abilities that allow them to interpret and organize their experiences, result in an understanding of marketplace transactions (John, 1999, p. 192).

In fact, several studies suggest an increase in the amount of time children spend shopping with their parents (~3 h per week for 3-to-8-year olds) (O'Daugherty et al., 2006) and the influence of children's requests on family purchasing habits (O'Daugherty et al., 2006; Ebster, Wagner & Neumueller, 2009). A study by O'Dougherty et al. (2006) found that 50% of children shopping in supermarkets with their parents initiated a request for specific foods and that the majority of these requests were for sweets

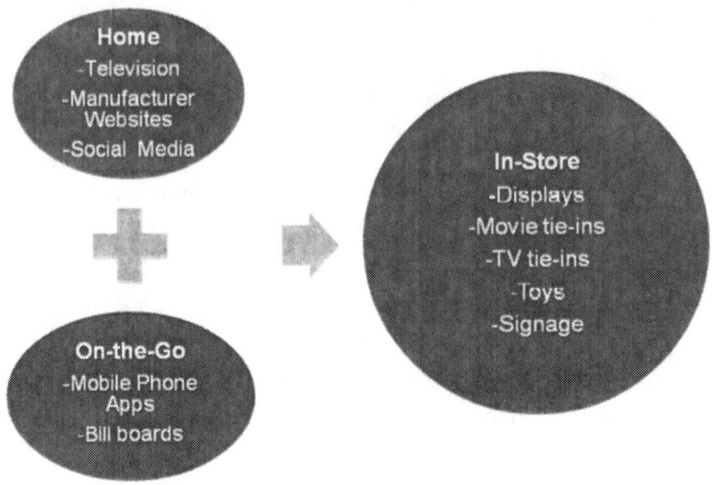

Fig. 15.1 Sectors of influence and marketing techniques used to reach consumers before and during in-store purchases based on examples from a 2009 Grocery Manufacturers Association Report

or snacks influenced by brand loyalty and marketing techniques. Additionally, Ebster et al. (2009) found that children are more persuasive in their requests for food items in supermarkets if they are easily consumed (e.g., candy) or include giveaways such as toys. These studies illustrate the importance of the retail food store environment as a setting where families negotiate the influence of food and beverage marketing on purchasing practices that influence dietary behaviors.

Second, food and beverage companies increasingly view the retail environment as a critical medium for content delivery, with a goal towards reaching people when they are in a buying mode. A 2009 Grocery Manufacturers Association Report describes "shopper marketing" – programs and promotions that collectively influence consumers "on the path to purchase" in the retail environment (Grocery Manufacturers Association, 2009). Specific sectors of influence and marketing techniques include the *home environment* (e.g., television), *on-the-go* (e.g., mobile phone apps, billboards), and *in-store* (e.g., displays, movie-tie ins) (Fig. 15.1).

These shopper-marketing programs are considered to be effective with respect to purchasing food and beverage in the retail environment due to influences on brand selection and shopping behaviors in and out of the store environment. Survey research indicates that 67% of the consumers are influenced by various marketing techniques out-of-the store (TV commercials/shows/movies: 32%, online coupons: 45%, websites: 17%, blogs: 16%, social media: 12%) when selecting specific brands to purchase in-store (Grocery Manufacturers Association, 2009). Companies also have an opportunity to influence food and beverage purchases in-store, as consumers also indicate that product displays (28%) and signage (40%) may influence whether they actually purchase a specific product in the retail environment (Grocery

Manufacturers Association, 2009). Shopper marketing has become so successful, a 2011 Robert Wood Johnson Foundation/The Food Trust report noted, that it is one of the fastest growing areas in the food retail marketing budget, and accounted for about 21% of the budget for manufacturers and 26% for retailers (Robert Wood Johnson Foundation, 2011). As the VP of Shopper Marketing for ConAgra noted in the trade publication, Advertising Age, more people are exposed to point of purchase advertising and promotions than major television events, suggesting that while major sitcoms had finales once a year, people are…."walking through Walmart every week." (Bryson, 2010) ConAgra now spends 20% of their advertising and promotions budget on shopper marketing, shopper insights, and in-store marketing, Saatchi has a psychologist and anthropologist on staff to understand shopper behavior, and Kraft, Campbell's Soup, and Wal-Mart have all rolled out research programs to gain insights into how shoppers interact with brands and promotions in-store (Bryson, 2010).

Third, although several companies have signed on to the Children's Food and Beverage Advertising Initiative (CFBAI) to either refrain from marketing to children under 12, or to market healthier foods to this age group, retail food stores are not included as one of the settings for this initiative (Better Business Bureau, 2011). Consequently, food and beverage companies are free to continue "marketing as usual" to children and adolescents without any oversight.

In sum, food and beverage companies are increasing their efforts to use the retail food store environment to market their products to consumers. Brand cues such as in-store signage and displays, as well as other marketing techniques have been shown to influence point-of-purchase selections. Although most empirical evidence linking food marketing to child weight status has focused on television, and more recently, digital media, the retail food store is an important medium, as young children are being exposed to marketing techniques as part of family shopping routines.

Case Study- Investigating Food Marketing in Retail Food Stores in Illinois

Given the increased importance of retail food stores as a critical medium for marketing targeted to children and families, (Grigsby-Toussaint et al., 2011) investigated the presence or absence of 78 items commonly marketed to youth on television or the internet across 118 food stores located in Central Illinois. Stores were classified either as grocery stores (i.e., stores with both fresh produce and meat sections) or convenience/corner stores for data analysis. Following similar procedures from a previous study (Grigsby-Toussaint et al., 2010), stores were designated as being in Black or *White* neighborhoods (census block groups) based on US census 2010 estimates (U. S. Census Bureau 2010). On average, 76% of the residents of *White* neighborhoods were White, while the mean concentration of Blacks in *Black* neighborhoods was 53%.

In order to investigate marketing techniques, packaging on food items were evaluated for specific claims (e.g., nutrition or taste), the presence of cartoon characters, information on giveaways, the inclusion of toys, or statements regarding suggested use (e.g., "great as a lunchbox treat"), or convenience (e.g., "ready-to-eat pudding snacks").

Audit Instrument and Data Collection Procedures

Adapted from an existing instrument by Chapman, Nicholas, Banovic and Supramaniam (2006), an audit tool was developed and tested for use in the study area. The 78 items included on the instrument were based on competitive media reports and a literature review of items commonly advertised to youth on television and the internet (Institute of Medicine, 2006; FTC, 2008; Moore, 2006). Items were categorized as (1) breads and pastries, (2) breakfast cereals, (3) candy and gum, (4) chips, (5) cookies and crackers, (6) dairy, (7) fruit and cereal bars, (8) ice cream, (9) prepared foods (e.g., lunchables), (10) sodas, and (11) non-carbonated drinks (e.g., juices).

Data Analysis

A *marketing to availability (M:A)* ratio was calculated to determine how often marketing techniques were utilized when an item was available. Chi-square tests were used to test for differences in the *M:A* ratio between store types and neighborhoods. SPSS version 16.0 was used to run all analyses.

Results

Figure 15.2 summarizes how often items were available and had marketing techniques (M:A ratio) observed on packaging across neighborhoods and store types. Grocery stores (57.5%) and stores located in Black neighborhoods (56.6%) were the most likely to have marketing techniques on the packaging of items targeted at youth and families (Grigsby-Toussaint, et al., 2011). Given the wide selection of foods available at grocery stores, this observation was not unexpected. Although Black neighborhoods did not have as many grocery stores, a higher prevalence of available items with evidence of marketing was observed compared to stores in White neighborhoods (Grigsby-Toussaint et al., 2011).

Figure 15.3 summarizes the distribution of marketing techniques on selected items that were evaluated as part of the study. Overwhelmingly, non-carbonated drinks (97.7%) were most likely to have some marketing technique present on packaging, followed by fruit and cereal bars (76.9%), soda (62.2%), dairy products (55.5%) and prepared foods (49.5%). Although not presented in figure 15.2 or 15.3, across all

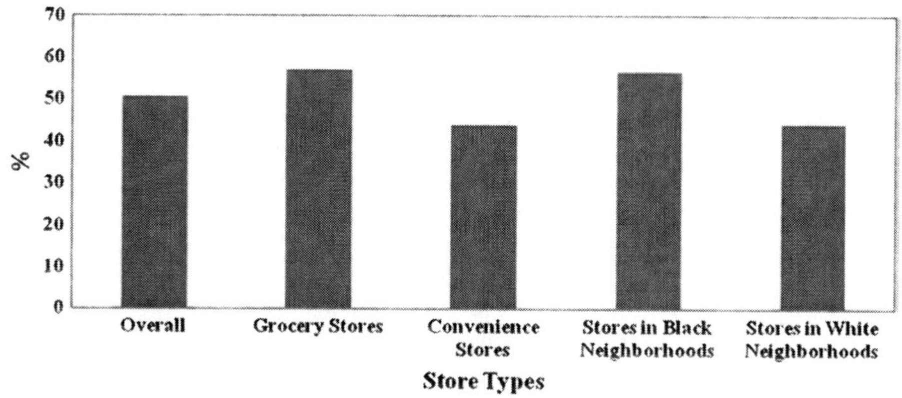

Fig. 15.2 Percent of available items with marketing techniques targeted to youth across store types and neighborhoods

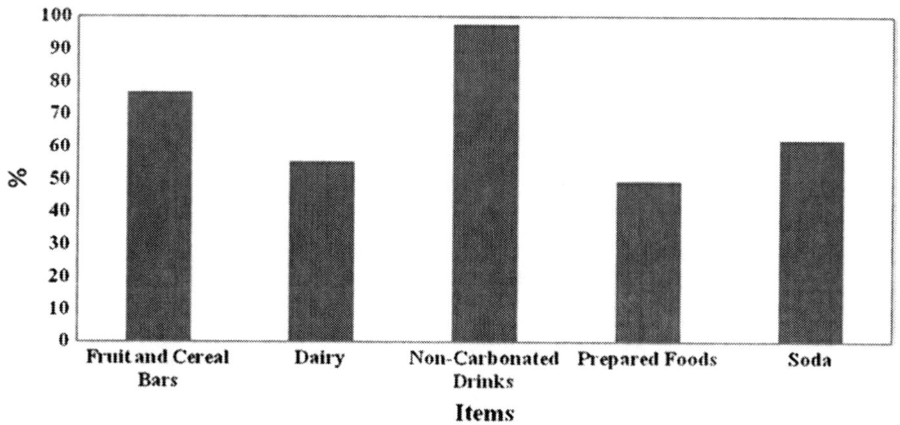

Fig. 15.3 Percent of selected items with marketing techniques targeted to youth in retail food stores

stores, nutrition (92%) and taste (90%) claims were the most common. Tie-ins for television shows (72%) were observed more often than tie-ins for movies (63.5%), but this was not significantly different between store types or neighborhoods.

Case Study Summary

This investigation of marketing in food stores in Central Illinois found that foods commonly promoted to youth on television and the internet were often available and marketed in food stores. Given estimates that some youth are exposed to more than 4000 advertisements via television per year, primarily for foods of poor nutritional content (Harris et al., 2009; Moore 2006), the retail food store environment may conceivably reinforce preferences for energy dense foods. A study by Borradaile et al. (2009), for example, showed that urban elementary school children were most likely to purchase energy-dense foods from corner stores (Borradaile et al., 2009), further bolstering the importance of food stores as sites for targeted childhood obesity interventions (e.g., working with stores to change the placement of certain items). Additionally, the observation that specific foods are more commonly marketed in stores located in Black neighborhoods is also of particular concern. This finding suggests that youth residing in these neighborhoods have increased exposure to food marketing, in addition to limited healthy food options (Grigsby-Toussaint et al., 2010), thus placing them at higher risk for obesity.

Areas for Intervention

In order to effectively counter marketing targeted at children and families, public health advocates will have to work in all areas utilized by major food and beverage companies to influence purchasing behaviors (Fig. 15.4). For example, in the food store environment, retailers can increase the marketing of healthier food alternatives, while parents can reduce screen time in the home environment. Specific examples for potential interventions are highlighted below.

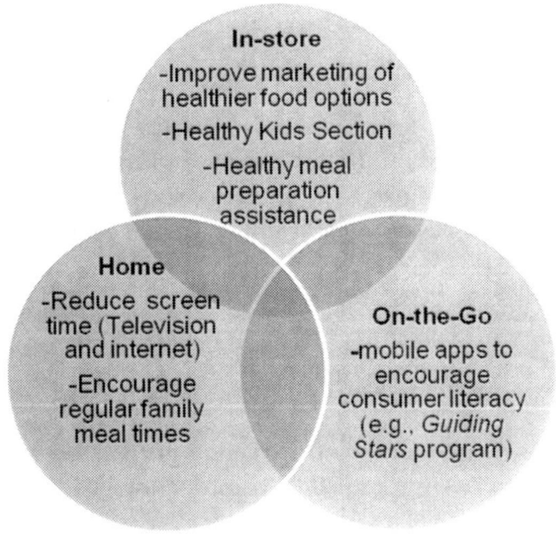

Fig. 15.4 Potential areas for intervention to counter shopper marketing programs that influence consumer choices in the retail food store environment

Food Stores

A Robert Wood Johnson/Food Trust (2011) report highlighted several successful interventions in the retail food store environment to encourage healthy eating. These include the Snack Smart program in Philadelphia, where community partnerships resulted in the development of marketing material that could be placed on doors and windows inside food stores to highlight healthier snacks and beverages. In another example, the Baltimore Healthy Stores project successfully negotiated the promotion of specific food items at different times based on the needs of both community residents and store owners (Gittelsohn, Suratkar, Song, Sacher, et al., 2010). In this case, foods were promoted around specific themes, e.g., healthy breakfast (low-sugar cereals), healthy beverage (water), rather than having all food types promoted at the same time (Gittelsohn et al., 2010).

Another interesting food store intervention, undertaken by Hannaford supermarkets, involves using a front-of-package nutrition labeling system to assist consumers with locating healthy food options (Robert Wood Johnson Foundation, 2011). The *Guiding Stars®* system uses a star rating system to indicate foods with the highest nutritional value, and is currently undergoing licensing procedures for use on social media websites in addition to mobile application formats.

Although these are successful examples of in-store interventions intended to improve the consumption of healthier food options, each community would be well served to hold discussions to determine which modifications to food stores would also reap (financial) benefits for store owners. In the study area of the lead author, displays for children's lunches were typically elaborate and bereft of fruits and vegetables (Fig. 15.5), while on rare occasions, fruits and vegetables were found with some targeted marketing for families (Fig. 15.6). Discussions in this community then could conceivably focus on reversing this trend, with community-based organizations highlighting stores encouraging fruit and vegetable consumption, and stores using sales data to examine potential improvements in their bottom line.

Media/Advertising Literacy

Media literacy can help children to critically evaluate commercial messages and then, quite possibly, circumvent persuasion influences. According to Moses and Baldwin (2005), in order to understand advertising, children need to (1) know when they are viewing advertisements to guard against them; and (2) recognize the purpose of advertising, with the understanding that there are many purposes in mind (e.g., selling intent, preference, etc.). Such knowledge has been encapsulated in the persuasion knowledge model (Friestad & Wright, 1994), which predicts that as audiences gain knowledge about persuasion attempts, they may be able to ignore or counter argue against the attempt as a way to cope.

Fig. 15.5 Nabisco's popular Oreo cookies are advertised in the familiar setting of a children's school bus. The "Pack a smile" logo encourages parents to include Oreo cookies in their children's lunch to make them happy. These elaborately designed and appealing packages and kiosks are rarely used to advertise fresh fruits and vegetables

Fig. 15.6 The Chiquita bananas pictured here are relatively free of advertising, although Chiquita, somewhat unique to fruit and vegetable suppliers, does include labels with slogans on their fresh fruit

A handful of studies have tested the influence of advertising literacy ("persuasion knowledge") on persuasion with children. For instance, after children aged 8–11 played a Nesquik chocolate cereal advergame, their recognition that the advergame was an advertisement and their recognition of the specific brand were assessed (i.e., persuasion knowledge) (Waiguny, Nelson, & Terlutter, 2012). However, the results showed that persuasion knowledge (understanding the advergame's commercial intent) only negatively influenced brand attitudes for the featured brand when the children were under-challenged by the game (Waiguny, Nelson, & Terlutter, 2012). For those children who were optimally challenged and having fun, critical evaluation of the brand did not occur. This finding suggests that the fun of the game may supersede any literacy effects.

One of the ways to increase media literacy of a specific persuasion attempt is to create clear and conspicuous disclosures of the advertising. In digital settings such as advergames, disclosures come in the form of an 'ad break' (e.g., from Applejacks.com *KIDS:* This page may contain a product or promotion advertisement).

A study by An and Stern (2011) tested whether persuasion knowledge would be activated when children (aged 8–11) saw or heard an "ad break" (disclosure) while playing an advergame. Their results showed that even though the ad breaks did not increase children's persuasion knowledge, the breaks did reduce the children's recall of and preference for the embedded brand.

Using Media to Create Preferences for Healthy Foods

Another way to promote healthy food is to use the same successful persuasion techniques used by marketers of junk food (e.g., advergames; Dias & Agante, 2011; Hernandez & Chapa, 2010; Pempek & Calvert, 2009). For example, researchers have found that after children (aged 9–10) played a healthier version of Pac-Man (where players were awarded/penalized points for consuming nutritious/less nutritious snacks), they were more likely than those who played a less healthy version to select and eat more healthier snacks after game play than those in the less healthy condition (Pempek & Calvert). Similar results were obtained among children (aged 7–8) in Portugal (Dias & Agante). That is, directly after playing a game that featured healthy or unhealthy foods, children were more likely to choose the type of food featured in the game. Therefore, the growing body of research on the persuasive power of advergames, especially with children, seems to suggest a direct response of playing the game on more favorable attitudes, preference, and choice for the embedded products or brands – at least in the short term directly after game play.

Family Mealtimes

Families can play an important role in reducing the effects of food marketing on their children. Taking charge of mealtimes has the potential to have profound effects. Families that regularly eat together reduce their child's odds of being overweight by 12% and increases their odds of eating healthy foods by 24% (Hammons & Fiese, 2011) Yet, these are difficult settings for many parents to manage. In surveys of barriers to sharing meals together, parents report that being able to plan ahead, controlling children's behavior, dealing with picky eating, and conflict at the table often get in the way of a pleasant mealtime (Fulkerson, Story, Neumark-Sztainer, & Rydell, 2008; Quick, Fiese, Anderson, Koester, & Marlin, in press). In order to convince parents to turn off the television while eating together, it will be important to give them the tools to more effectively manage behaviors commonly experienced during mealtimes. An initiative developed by the Family Resiliency Center at the University of Illinois has created public service announcements and supporting materials to address common mealtime dilemmas such as sibling conflict (http://familyresiliency.illinois.edu/MealtimeMinutes.htm). Other programs to promote positive mealtimes have identified the need to include tips on how to reduce TV watching during meals (Fulkerson et al., 2011). In order to fully capture the health potential of mealtimes, it is essential to give families the tools they require to regain control of this important event. It may not be sufficient to tell families to turn off the TV if they are overwhelmed with work responsibilities, have inadequate cooking skills, and feel powerless in controlling their children's behavior. A proactive stance in recognizing these barriers may assist families in making healthier choices for their children.

Summary

Emerging empirical evidence suggests that the retail food store environment is increasingly becoming an important medium for the food and beverage industry to target children and families with various marketing techniques. Due to family routines which involve food shopping, young children may more often be exposed to marketing via the retail environment, even if parents prohibit television and digital media exposures. Improving our understanding of in-store marketing, as well as other promotions undertaken outside of the stores, is critical for curbing the purchase of energy-dense foods with low-nutritional value that increase obesity risk among children and their families.

References

An, S., & Stern, S. (2011). Mitigating the effects of advergames on children. *Journal of Advertising, 40*(1), 43–56.

Anderson, P. M., & Butcher, K. F. (2006). Childhood obesity: Trends and potential causes. *The Future of Children, 16*, 19–46.

Applejacks.com. http://www.applejacks.com. Accessed 25 Sep 2011.

Atkin, C. (1978). Observation of parent–child interaction in supermarket decision making. *The Journal of Marketing, 42*, 41–45.

Bandura, A. (2002). Social cognitive theory of mass communication. In J. Bryant & D. Zillmann (Eds.), *Media effects: Advances in theory and research* (2nd ed., pp. 121–154). Mahwah, NJ: Erlbaum.

Bagozzi, R., Gopinath, M., & Nyer, P. (1999). The role of emotions in marketing. *Journal of the Academy of Marketing Science, 27*(2), 184–206.

Batra, R., & Stayman, D. M. (1990). The role of mood in advertising effectiveness. *The Journal of Consumer Research, 17*(2), 203–214.

Bogost, I. (2007). *Persuasive games: The expressive power of video games*. Cambridge: MIT Press.

Borradaile, K. E., Sherman, S., Vander Veur, S. S., McCoy, T., Sandoval, B., Nachmani, J., et al. (2009). Snacking in children: The role of corner stores. *Pediatrics, 124*(5), 1293–1298.

Borzekowski, D. L., & Robinson, T. N. (2001). The 30-second effect: An experiment revealing the impact of television commercials on food preferences of preschoolers. *Journal of the American Dietetic Association, 101*(1), 42–46.

Brown, S. P., & Stayman, D. M. (1992). Antecedents and consequences of attitude toward the ad: A meta-analysis. *The Journal of Consumer Research, 19*, 34–51.

Calcott, M. F., & Lee, W. (1994). A content analysis of animation and animated spokes-characters in television commercials. *Journal of Advertising, 23*, 1–12.

Chapman, K., Nicholas, P., Banovic, D., & Supramaniam, R. (2006). The extent and nature of food promotion directed to children in Australian supermarkets. *Health Promotion International, 21*, 331–339.

Child Trends. (2010). *Watching television*. Retrieved from http://www.childtrendsdatabank.org/?q=node/261. Conference summary: The Wingspread Conference on Childhood Obesity, Healthy Eating and Agriculture Policy (2007). Retrieved January 5, 2009, from http://www.healthyeatingresearch.org/images/stories/her_wingspread/1wingspreadsummary.pdf.

Control, C. f. D. (2007). Childhood obesity. Retrieved from http://www.cdc.gov/nccdphp/dnpa/obesity/childhood.

Connor, S. M. (2006). Food-related advertising on preschool television: Building brand recognition in young viewers. *Pediatrics, 118*(4), 1478–1485.

Coon, K. A., Goldberg, J., Rogers, B. L., & Tucker, K. L. (2001). Relationships between use of television during meals and children's food consumption patterns. *Pediatrics, 107*, e7.

Council of Better Business Bureaus (CBBB). (2011). The children's food and beverage advertising initiative in action. The US children's food and beverage advertising initiative fact sheet. http://www.bbb.org/us/children-food-beverage-advertising-initiative/. Accessed 25 Sep 2011.

Crespo, C. J., Smit, E., Troiano, R. P., Bartlett, S. J., Macera, C. A., & Andersen, R. E. (2001). Television watching, energy intake, and obesity in US children: Results from the Third National Health and Nutrition Examination Survey, 1988–1994. *Archives of Pediatric Medicine, 155*, 360–365.

De Houwer, J. (2007). A conceptual and theoretical analysis of evaluative conditioning. *The Spanish Journal of Psychology, 10*(2), 230–241.

De Houwer, J., Baeyens, F., & Field, A. P. (2005). Associative learning of likes and dislikes: Some current controversies and possible ways forward. *Cognition and Emotion, 19*(2), 161–174.

De Houwer, J., Thomas, S., & Baeyens, F. (2001). Associative learning of likes and dislikes: A review of 25 years of research on human evaluative conditioning. *Psychological Bulletin, 127*(6), 853–869.

Dias, M., & Agante, L. (2011). Can advergames boost children's healthier eating habits? A comparison between healthy and non-healthy food. *Journal of Consumer Behaviour, 10*(3), 152–160.

Dietz, W. H. (1998). Health consequences of obesity in youth: Childhood predictors of adult disease. *Pediatrics, 101*(3 Pt 2), 518–525.

Dijksterhuis, A., Smith, P. K., van Baaren, R. B., & Wigboldus, D. H. J. (2005). The unconscious consumer: Effects of environment on consumer behavior. *Journal of Consumer Psychology, 15*(3), 193–202.

Ebster, C., Wagner, U., & Neumueller, D. (2009). Children's influences on in-store purchases. *Journal of Retailing and Consumer Services, 16*(2), 145–154.

Elliott, C. (2007). Against happiness. *Medicine, Health Care, and Philosophy, 10*(2), 167–171.

Federal Trade Commission. (2008, July). *Marketing food to children and adolescents: A review of industry expenditures, activities, and self-regulation* [Report to Congress]. Retrieved from http://www.ftc.gov/opa/2008/07/foodmkting.shtm.

Feldman, S., Eisenberg, M., Neumark-Sztainer, D., & Story, M. (2007). Associations between watching TV during family meals and dietary intake among adolescents. *Journal of Nutrition Education and Behavior, 39*, 257–263.

Fiese, B. H., & Schwartz, M. B. (2008). *Reclaiming the family table: Mealtimes and children's health and wellbeing*. Washington, DC: Society for Research In Child Development.

Freedman, D. S., Dietz, W. H., Srinivasan, S. R., & Berenson, G. S. (1999). The relation of overweight to cardiovascular risk factors among children and adolescents: The Bogalusa Heart Study. *Pediatrics, 103*, 1175–1182.

Friestad, M., & Wright, P. (1994). The persuasion knowledge model: How people cope with persuasion attempts. *The Journal of Consumer Research, 21*(1), 1–31.

Fulkerson, J. A., Story, M., Neumark-Sztainer, D., & Rydell, S. (2008). Family meals: Perceptions of benefits and challenges among parents of 8- to 10-year-old children. *Journal of the American Dietetic Association, 108*, 706–709.

Fulkerson, J. A., Kubik, M. Y., Rydell, S., Boutelle, K., Garwick, A. W., Story, M., et al. (2011). Focus groups with working parents of school-aged children: What's needed to improve family meals? *Journal of Nutrition Education and Behavior, 43*(3), 189–193.

Galst, J. P., & White, M. A. (1976). The unhealthy persuader: The reinforcing value of television and children's purchase-influencing attempts at the supermarket. *Child Development, 47*, 1089–1096.

Gittelsohn, J., Suratkar, S., Song, H., Sacher, S., Rajan, R., Rasooly, I.R., et al. (2010). Process evaluation of Baltimore health stores: A pilot health intervention program with supermarkets and corner stores in Baltimore City. 1–10. *Health Promot Pract, 11*(5) 723–732.

Grigsby-Toussaint, D. S., Zenk, S. N., Odoms-Young, A., Ruggiero, L., & Moise, I. (2010). Availability of commonly consumed and culturally specific fruits and vegetables in African-American and Latino neighborhoods. *Journal of the American Dietetic Association, 110*, 746–752.

Grigsby-Toussaint, D., Moise, I. K., & Geiger, S. D. (2011). Observations of marketing on food packaging targeted to youth in retail food stores. *Obesity, 19*(9), 1898–1900.

Grocery Manufacturers of America. (2009). Shopper Marketing 3.0: Unleashing the Next Wave of Value. http://www.gmaonline.org/downloads/research-and-reports/Booz_Ci_GMA_Shopper_Marketing_3.0.FIN_LR.PDF. Accessed online Sept 2011.

Groovyglider.com. http://www.groovyglider.com/. Accessed 25 Sep 2011.

Halford, J. C. (2004). Clinical pharmacotherapy for obesity: Current drugs and those in advanced development. *Current Drug Targets, 5*(7), 637–646.

Halford, J. C., Boyland, E. J., Hughes, G., Oliveira, L. P., & Dovey, T. M. (2007). Beyond-brand effect of television (TV) food advertisements/commercials on caloric intake and food choice of 5-7-year-old children. *Appetite, 49*(1), 263–267.

Hammons, A., & Fiese, B. H. (2011). Is frequency of shared family meals related to the nutritional health of children and adolescents? A meta-analysis. *Pediatrics, 127*(6), e1565–e1574.

Health, T. f. A. s. (2008). *F as in fat: How obesity policies are failing in America*. Washington, DC: Trust for America's Health.

Harris, J. L., Bargh, J. A., & Brownell, K. D. (2009). Priming effects of television food advertising on eating behavior. *Health Psychology, 28*(4), 404–413.

Harris, J. L., Pomeranz, J. L., Lobstein, T., & Brownell, K. D. (2009). A crisis in the marketplace: How food marketing contributes to childhood obesity and what can be done. *Annual Review of Public Health, 30*, 211–225.

Harrison, K., & Marske, A. L. (2005). Nutritional content of foods advertised during the television programs children watch most. *American Journal of Public Health, 95*(9), 1568–1574.

Hastings, G., Stead, M., McDermott, L., Forsyth, A., MacKintosh, A. M., Rayner, M. et al. (2003). *Review of the research on the effects of food promotion to children*. Glasgow, Scotland: Center for Social Marketing.

Hernandez, M. D., & Chapa, S. (2010). Adolescents, advergames and snack foods: Effects of positive affect and experience on memory and choice. *Journal of Marketing Communications, 16*, 59–68.

Hofferth, S. L., & Sandberg, J. F. (2001). How American children spend their time. *Journal of Marriage and Family, 63*, 295–308.

Institute of Medicine (U.S.), & Committee on Health Food Marketing and the Diets of Children and Youth. (2006). *Food marketing to children and youth: Threat or opportunity?* Washington, DC: National Academy Press.

Jacobs, M. P., & Fiese, B. H. (2007). Family mealtime interactions and overweight children with asthma: Potential for compounded risks? *Journal of Pediatric Psychology, 32*(1), 64–68.

John, D. R. (1999). Consumer socialization of children: A retrospective look at 25 years of research. *The Journal of Consumer Research, 26*, 183–213.

Johnson-Taylor, W. L., & Everhart, J. E. (2006). Modifiable environmental and behavioral determinants of overweight among children and adolescents: Report of a workshop. *Obesity, 14*(6), 929–966.

Jordan, A. B., & Robinson, T. N. (2008). Children, television viewing, and weight status: Summary and recommendations from an expert panel meeting. *The Annals of the American Academy of Political and Social Science, 615*, 119–132.

Khaodhiar, L., McCowen, K. C., & Blackburn, G. L. (1999). Obesity and its comorbid conditions. *Clinical Cornerstone, 2*(3), 17–31.

Kinsky, E. S., & Bichard, S. (2011). Mom! I've seen that on a commercial!" US preschoolers' recognition of brand logos. *Young Consumers: Insight and Ideas for Responsible Marketers, 12*(2), 145–158.

Kretchmer, S. B. (2004). Advertainment: The evolution of product placement as a mass media marketing strategy. *Journal of Promotion Management, 10*(1/2), 37–54.

Kroeber-Riel, W. (1984). Emotional product differentiation by classical conditioning (with consequences for the "low-involvement hierarchy"). *Advances in Consumer Research, 11*, 538–453.

Kuittinen, J., Kultima, A., Niemelä, J., & Paavilainen, J. (2007). *Casual games discussion*. Paper presented at the Proceedings of the 2007 Conference on Future Play.

Kunkel, D., Wilcox, B. L., Cantor, J., Palmer, E., Linn, S., & Dowrick, P. (2004). *Psychological issues in the increasing commercialization of childhood.* Report of the APA Task Force on Advertising and Children. Washington, DC: American Psychological Association.

Lapierre, M. A., Vaala, S. E., & Linebarger, D. L. (2011). Influence of licensed spokescharacters and health cues on children's ratings of cereal taste. *Archives of Pediatrics & Adolescent Medicine, 165*(3), 229–234.

Larson, N. I., Story, M. T., & Nelson, M. C. (2009). Neighborhood environments: Disparities in access to healthy foods in the US. *American Journal of Preventive Medicine, 36*, 74–81.

LeBel, J. L., & Cooke, N. (2008). Branded food spokescharacters: consumers' contributions to the narrative of commerce. *The Journal of Product and Brand Management, 17*, 143–153.

Lee, M., Yoonhyeung, C., Quilliam, E. T., & Cole, R. T. (2009). Playing with food: Content analysis of food advergames. *Journal of Consumer Affairs, 43*, 129–154.

Lee, M., & Youn, S. (2008). Leading national advertisers' uses of advergames. *Journal of Current Issues & Research in Advertising, 30*, 1–13.

Lutz, R. J., Mackenzie, S. B., & Belch, G. E. (1983). Attitude toward the ad as a mediator of advertising effectiveness: Determinants and consequences. *Advances in Consumer Research, 10*, 532–539.

Mackenzie, S. B., Lutz, R. J., & Belch, G. E. (1986). The role of attitude toward the ad as a mediator of advertising effectiveness: A test of competing explanations. *Journal of Marketing Research, 23*(2), 130–143.

McWayne, C., Owsianik, M., Green, L. E., & Fantuzzo, J. W. (2008). Parenting behaviors and preschool children's social and emotional skills: A question of the consequential validity of traditional parenting constructs for low-income African Americans. *Early Childhood Research Quarterly, 23*, 173–192.

Morland, K., Wing, S., & Diez-Roux, A. (2002). The contextual effect of the local food environment on residents' diets: The atherosclerosis risk in communities study. *American Journal of Public Health, 92*, 1761–1767.

Morton, H., Stanton, R., Zuppa, J., & Mehta, K. (2005). Food advertising and broadcasting legislation: A case of system failure? *Nutrition and Dietetics, 62*(1), 26–32.

Moore, E. S. (2004). Children and the changing world of advertising. *Journal of Business Ethics, 52*, 161–167.

Moore E. S. (2006). *It's child play: Advergaming and the online marketing of food to children*. Kaiser Family Foundation: Menlo Park, CA. http://www.kff.org/entmedia/entmedia071906pkg.cfm. Accessed 30 September 2012.

Moore, E. S., & Rideout, V. J. (2007). The online marketing of food to children: Is it just fun and games? *Journal of Public Policy & Marketing, 26*, 202–220.

Moses, L. J., & Baldwin, D. A. (2005). What can the study of cognitive development reveal about children's ability to appreciate and cope with advertising? *Journal of Public Policy & Marketing, 24*, 186–201.

NAEYC & SRCD (2008). Using research to improve outcomes for young children: A call for action. Final report of the Wingspread Conference, September 18–20, 2007. *Early Childhood Research Quarterly, 23*(4), 591–596.

O'Daugherty, M., Story, M., & Stang, J. (2006). Observations of parent–child co-shoppers in supermarkets: Children's involvement in food selections, parental yielding, and refusal strategies. *Journal of Nutrition Education and Behavior, 38*, 183–188.

Ogden, C. L., & Carroll, M. (2010). Prevalence of obesity among children and adolescents: United States, trends 1963–1965 through 2007–2008. National Center for Health Statistics. Retrieved June 30, 2011 from http://www.cdc.gov/nchs/data/hestat/obesity_child_07_08/obesity_child_07_08.htm.

Ogden, C. L., Carroll, M. D., & Flegal, K. M. (2008). High body mass index for age among US and adolescents, 2003–2006. *Journal of the American Medical Association, 299*, 2401–2405.

Ogden, C. L., Carroll, M. D., Curtin, L. R., McDowell, M. A., Tabak, C. J., & Flegal, K. M. (2006). Prevalence of overweight and obesity in the United States, 1999–2004. *Journal of the American Dietetic Association, 295*, 1549–1555.

Page, R. M., & Brewster, A. (2009). Depiction of food as having drug-like properties in televised food advertisements directed at children: Portrayals as pleasure enhancing and addictive. *Journal of Pediatric Health Care, 23*(3), 150–157.

Papas, M. A., Alberg, A. J., Ewing, R., Helzlsouer, K. J., Gary, T. L., & Klassen, A. C. (2007). The built environment and obesity. *Epidemiologic Reviews, 29*, 129–143.

Pearce, J., Hiscock, R., Blakely, T., & Witten, K. (2008). The contextual effects of neighbourhood access to supermarkets and convenience stores on individual fruit and vegetable consumption. *Journal of Epidemiology and Community Health, 3*, 198–201.

Pempek, T. A., & Calvert, S. L. (2009). Tipping the balance: Use of advergames to promote consumption of nutritious foods and beverages by low-income African American children. *Archives of Pediatrics & Adolescent Medicine, 163*, 633–637.

Petit, G. S., Bates, J. E., & Dodge, K. A. (1997). Supportive parenting, ecological context, and children's adjustment: A seven-year longitudinal study. *Child Development, 68*, 908–923.

Phillips, B. J., & Gyoerick, B. (1999). The cow, the cook, and the Quaker: Fifty years of culture. *The Journal of Popular Culture, 29*(4), 143–156.

Phillips, B. J. (1996). Defining trade characters and their role in American popular culture. *The Journal of Popular Culture, 29*(4), 143–156.

Powell, L. M., Schermbeck, R. M., Szczypka, G., Chaloupka, F. J., Braunschweig, C. L. (2011). Trends in the nutritional content of television food advertisements seen by children in the United States. *Arch Pediatr Adolesc Med, 165*(12):1078–86.

Quick, B. L., Fiese, B. H., Anderson, B., Koester, B., & Marlin, D. W. (in press). A formative evaluation of family mealtime for parents of toddlers and young children. *Health Communication, 26*(7):656–66.

Rideout, V. J., Vandewater, E. A., & Wartella, E. A. (2003). *Zero to six: Electronic media in the lives of infants, toddlers, and preschoolers.* A Kaiser Family Foundation Report. Menlo Park, CA: Kaiser Family Foundation.

Robert Wood Johnson Foundation Report. (2011). *Harnessing the power of supermarkets to help reverse childhood obesity*. http://www.rwjf.org.

Roberts, D. F., & Foehr, U. G. (2004). *Kids and media in America.* Cambridge, UK: Cambridge University Press.

Roberto, C. A., Baik, J., Harris, J. L., & Brownell, K. D. (2010). Influence of licensed characters on children's taste and snack preferences. *Pediatrics, 126*, 88–93.

Robinson, T. N., Borzekowski, D. L., Matheson, D. M., & Kraemer, H. C. (2007). Effects of fast food branding on young children's taste preferences. *Archives of Pediatrics & Adolescent Medicine, 161*(8), 792–797.

Rodriquez, M. M. D., Donovick, M. R., & Crowley, S. L. (2009). Parenting styles in cultural context: Observations of "protective parenting" in first-generation Latinos. *Family Process, 48*, 195–210.

Rose, D., & Richards, R. (2004). Food store access and household fruit and vegetable use among participants in the US Food Stamp Program. *Public Health Nutrition, 7*, 1081–1088.

Sallis, J. F., & Glanz, K. (2006). The role of built environments in physical activity, eating, and obesity in childhood. *The Future of Children/Center for the Future of Children, the David and Lucile Packard Foundation, 16*(1), 89–108.

Santos, E., Gonzalo, R., & Gisbert, F. (2007). Advergames: Overview. *International Journal Information Technologies and Knowledge, 1*, 203–208.

Schrammel, J., Mattheiss, E., Döbelt, S., Paletta, L., Almer, A., & Tscheligi, M. (2011). Attentional behavior of users on the move towards pervasive advertising media. In J. Müller, F. Alt, & D. Michelis (Eds.), Proceedings of Pervasive Advertising. London: Springer.

Speers, S. E., Harris, J. L., & Schwartz, M. B. (2011). Child and adolescent exposure to food and beverage brand appearances during prime-time television programming. *American Journal of Preventive Medicine, 41*(3), 291–296.

Stitt, C., & Kunkel, D. (2008). Food advertising during children's television programming on broadcast and cable channels. *Health Communication, 23*(6), 573–584.

Story, M., & French, S. (2004). Food advertising and marketing directed at children and adolescents in the US. *International Journal of Behavioral Nutrition and Physical Activity, 1*(3), 1–17.

Story, M., Kaphingst, K. M., & French, S. (2006). The role of schools in obesity prevention. *The Future of Children/Center for the Future of Children, the David and Lucile Packard Foundation, 16*(1), 109–142.

Strum R. (2005). Childhood obesity—What we can learn from existing data on societal trends, part 1. *Preventing Chronic Disease* [serial online] 2005 Jan [May 30, 2009]. Available from http://www.cdc.gov/pcd/issues/2005/jan/04_0038.htm.

Thomson, D.M. (2010). Marshmallow power and frooty treasures: Disciplining the child consumer through online cereal advergaming. *Critical Studies in Media Communication*, August, 1–17.

U. S. Census Bureau. (2010). *Race data.* Retrieved July 26, 2010, from http://www.census.gov/population/www/socdemo/race/racefactcb.html

U.S. Department of Agriculture. (2010). *Part D Section 1: Energy balance and weight management. Report of the dietary guidelines advisory committee of the dietary guidelines for Americans, 2010.* Retrieved August 10, 2010 from http://www.cnpp.usda.gov/dietaryguidelines.htm.

Waiguny, M. K. J., Nelson, M. R., & Terlutter, R. (2010). Persuading playfully? The effects of persuasion knowledge and positive affect on children's attitudes, brand beliefs and behaviors. In W.-N. Lee (Ed.), *Proceedings of the 2010 Conference of the American Academy of Advertising* (pp. 67–70). Minneapolis: AAA.

Waiguny, M. K. J., Nelson, M. R., & Terlutter, R. (2012). Entertainment matters! The relationship between challenge and persuasiveness of an advergame for children. *Journal of Marketing Communications, 18*:1, 69–89.

Wang, Y., & Beydoun, M. A. (2007). The obesity epidemic in the united states–gender, age, socio-economic, racial/ethnic, and geographic characteristics: A systematic review and meta-regression analysis. *Epidemiologic Reviews, 29*, 6–28.

Wiecha, J. L., Peterson, K. E., Ludwig, D. S., Kim, J., Sobol, A., & Gortmaker, S. L. (2006). When children eat what they watch: Impact of television viewing on dietary intake in youth. *Archives of Pediatrics & Adolescent Medicine, 160*(4), 436–442.

Vandewater, E. A., Shim, M., & Caplovitz, A. G. (2004). Linking obesity and activity level with children's television and video game use. *Journal of Adolescence, 27*(1), 71–85.

Yancey, A. K., Cole, B. L., Brown, R., Williams, J. D., Hillier, A., Kline, R. S., et al. (2009). A cross-sectional prevalence study of ethnically targeted and general audience outdoor obesity-related advertising. *Milbank Quarterly, 87*(1), 155–84.

York, Emily Bryson. (April 15, 2010). Shopping aisles at cutting edge of consumer research and tech. *Advertising Age*

Youn, S., & Lee, M. (2005). Advergame playing motivations and effectiveness. In M. R. Stafford & R. J. Faber (Eds.), *Advertising, promotion and new media* (pp. 320–347). Armonk: M.E.Sharpe.

Zenk, S. N., Schulz, A. J., Israel, B. A., James, S. A., Bao, S., & Wilson, M. L. (2006). Fruit and vegetable access differs by community racial composition and socioeconomic position in Detroit. *Michigan, Ethnicity and Disease, 16*, 275–280.

Zenk, S. N., Schulz, A. J., Hollis-Neely, T., Campbell, R. T., Holmes, N., Watkins, G., et al. (2005). Fruit and vegetable intake in African-Americans: Income and store characteristics. *American Journal of Preventive Medicine, 29*, 1–9.

Zenk, S. N., Lachance, L. L., Schulz, A. J., Mentz, G., Kannan, S., & Ridella, W. (2009). Neighborhood retail food environment and fruit and vegetable intake in a multiethnic urban population. *American Journal of Health Promotion, 23*, 255–264.

Zenk, S.N., Grigsby-Toussaint, D. S., Curry, S.J., Berbaum, M., Schneider, L. Short-Term Temporal Stability in Observed Retail Food Characteristics. (2010). Journal of Nutrition, Education and Behavior, 42, 26–32.

Part V
Racial/Ethnic Minorities and Community Empowerment

Chapter 16
Understanding Community Perspectives: A Step Towards Achieving Food Marketing Equity

Sonya A. Grier and Vikki C. Lassiter

Introduction

This chapter will examine how historical and social factors impact community perspectives, receptivity, and potential motivation to improve food marketing environments. We explore the diversity of Black Americans' perspectives of marketing and the contextual factors that support different beliefs and responses. Given the nature and history of Black Americans as consumers, it is no surprise that de-marketing unhealthy food and beverages proves to be quite challenging. Insights from the community perspective are necessary in order to develop social and counter-marketing activities to support healthy food environments.

First, we briefly overview obesity rates and then describe how food marketing environments may contribute to these disparities. We define "food marketing environment" from not only the marketer perspective but also from the consumer and community perspective. Subsequently, we summarize key historical points that provide context for understanding consumer response to current targeted marketing efforts. We then discuss qualitative research examining Black consumer perceptions of marketing, and how they navigate inequitable marketing environments. We end with a discussion of results and related implications for increased understanding of how to shift Black consumer demand towards healthier foods.

S.A. Grier, Ph.D. M.B.A. (✉)
American University, Kogod School of Business,
4400 Massachusetts Avenue, DC 20016-8044, NW Washington
e-mail: sonya.grier@american.edu

V.C. Lassiter M.S.
African American Collaborative Obesity Research Network,
University of Pennsylvania, 3401 Market St., Suite 202, PA 19104, Philadelphia
e-mail: vlassite@mail.med.upenn.edu

J.D. Williams et al. (eds.), *Advances in Communication Research to Reduce Childhood Obesity*, DOI 10.1007/978-1-4614-5511-0_16,

Obesity and African Americans

Obesity rates are alarmingly high among African Americans, especially women and girls. In 2007–2008, 46.3% of African-American girls between the ages of 12 and 19 (as compared to 29.9% of White adolescent girls) were overweight or obese (Ogden, Carroll, Curtin, Lamb, & Flegal, 2010). Further, although the prevalence of high BMI is declining for some groups, this is not uniformly observed in data on Black girls (Madsen, Weedn, & Crawford, 2010). If current trends continue, African-American teens will have some of the largest increases (a 1.8-fold increase) in overweight and obesity (Wang, Beydoun, Liang, Caballero, & Kumanyika, 2008). And with African Americans, we do not see the same inverse relationship between youth obesity and parental increases in education or income (Ogden, Carroll, & Flegal, 2008). In fact, among girls aged 10–17 years old research has found that obesity rates are highest among African-American girls at the highest socioeconomic status level (Wang & Beydoun, 2007). Nonetheless, the effects of income on obesity among Blacks may be more pronounced given that significant numbers of Blacks are lower income.

Overweight and obesity are often preludes to serious chronic conditions and increase the risk of diabetes, asthma, cardiovascular disease, and other health complications (Caprio et al., 2008). Further, childhood obesity increases the risk of adult obesity (Daniels, 2006) and Black Americans generally face a disproportionate amount of diet-related diseases. The observed differences in overweight and obesity also manifest among adults, as Black adults, especially women, also have higher rates of overweight and obesity than White adults (Flegal, Carroll, Ogden, & Curtin, 2010). The elevated rates among adults may present to black youth a heavily biased weight norm.

The high rates, significant racial disparities in obesity, as well as the grave consequences, underscore the need for more tailored interventions and policies that target high-risk groups. Food marketing has proved an important area to consider in terms of these disparities given that strategies may focus on specific groups and support unhealthy food marketing environments (Grier & Kumanyika, 2008).

The Food Marketing Environment

It should come as no surprise that food marketing is implicated in the obesity epidemic as it is a system designed to affect consumption. Marketing is perceived as influencing the awareness of, attitudes about, and availability of food, beverages, and related information. The American Marketing Association defines marketing as "the activity, set of institutions, and processes for creating, communicating, delivering, and exchanging offerings that have value for customers, clients, partners, and society at large" (AMA, 2008). Central to the definition is a notion of self-interest as people buy and consume products out of their own perceptions of value. Food marketers thus design strategies to create perceptions of value among consumers so that they will think positively about, buy, and consume their products.

Although advertising is often the most visible aspect of marketing, this is less than one-quarter of the story. Marketing efforts are also implemented through the integration of product, distribution, price, and promotion strategies, known as "the four P's" or the "marketing mix". The first "p", *product,* reflects what is offered to a market, including tangible goods or services, Distribution strategies encompass the next "p" of *place* which refers to how products are made available to consumers. The p*rice* "p" refers to the cost that is exchanged for the product, in absolute terms and relative to alternatives while the *promotion* "p" involves persuasive communications that convey product benefits, prices, and availability. Advertising is just one promotional tool used to reach consumers. There are a wide array of promotional strategies beyond advertising, including sales promotions, food sampling, direct mail, digital marketing, corporate sponsorship, and product placement. Marketing strategy involves coordinating these four "P's" for optimal effect, so one cannot consider them solely in isolation.

Target marketing, where research-based strategies are aimed at a particular subset of consumers is the basis of contemporary marketing (Kotler, 1997). Targeted marketing strategies affect the products people in the subgroup are exposed to, that are promoted and available to them, and the prices they pay. It is in this way that marketing may contribute to obesity disparities. Specifically, the cross-cutting strategies among the marketing mix of product, price, promotion, and place result in a particular food marketing environment for target consumers, one that may challenge or support people's ability to eat healthfully. The targeted marketing environment may also counteract the effect of general initiatives as commercial marketing messages often overshadow public health messages that encourage healthier behaviors.

Research supports the notion that targeted food marketing may contribute to food marketing environments that challenge the ability of Black consumers to eat healthy. A systematic review of empirical research on targeted food marketing to Black consumers examined the evidence that describes what food products Black Americans are made aware of, have access to, and the cost (Grier & Kumanyika, 2008). Articles were identified through a search for empirical literature in eight major databases across disciplines over a 14-year time period. Only studies that compared marketing practices directed towards a Black versus a White or general market were included to help understand if the marketing practices differed by group.

The search identified twenty articles over the 14-year period; eight were content analysis of ad messages, one was an assessment of in-store promotions, eleven studies were of food outlet locations, and three were comparisons of food prices. Analysis of the identified articles demonstrated that products marketed to Black consumers are dominated by low-cost foods that are high in sugar and low in nutrition (Grier & Kumanyika, 2008). Black consumers saw more in-store promotions although they were less likely to be for healthy items, and they also saw fewer positive nutritional messages and healthier foods than other target markets. One study focused on children found that ads with Black characters were more likely to promote convenience and fast foods instead of foods consistent with dietary recommendations, depict more snacking between meals, and less likely to have overweight characters or adult supervision (Harrison, 2006). Additionally, results show that Black consumers tend to have less access to supermarkets and greater access to fast food restaurants than their White consumers. Other recent studies are consistent with these findings (Hillier et al., 2009; Yancey et al., 2009).

Marketing not only promotes behaviors but also reinforces them and contributes to the development of norms. Norms, like attitudes, may serve as a belief mechanism through which marketing activities influence consumption on an ongoing basis. Social norms encompass shared beliefs about behavior and capture the social influence that a consumer perceives regarding consumption behavior (Fishbein & Ajzen, 1975). The social influence may come from one of two types of norms. First, subjective norms involve people's perceptions of what is appropriate behavior, based on their beliefs that people important to them believe that they should perform a particular behavior (Fishbein & Ajzen).

Second, descriptive norms pertain to people's perceptions of the actual behavior of people important to them (Fishbein & Ajzen, 1980). The high prevalence of a behavior or perceived approval of the behavior among important reference groups influences a person's performance of that behavior (Bagozzi, Wong, Abe, & Bergami, 2000; Cialdini, Kallgren, & Reno, 1991). In this way, norms can either support or inhibit particular choices.

Marketers strategize to develop positive attitudes and norms so that they support product and brand consumption. Of course many factors besides marketing influence normative behavior, such as news and entertainment, family, other people, and personal experiences. However, marketing can reinforce existing behavioral patterns by convincing consumers of specific product benefits and the pervasiveness of consumption. For example, a consumer's preference can be influenced by price promotions which elicit product trial, encourage repeat purchases, and contribute to beliefs that the promoted items are frequently eaten (Hoek & Gendall, 2006). Thus, marketing efforts can send an implicit message that certain consumption behaviors are socially supported and facilitate the likelihood of the behavior.

Research among an ethnically diverse sample of parents of 2- to 12-year-old children in medically underserved communities found that greater exposure to fast food promotion is associated both with beliefs that eating fast food is normative and with more frequent fast food consumption by their children (Grier, Mensinger, Huang, Kumanyika, & Stettler, 2007). Furthermore, parents' perceptions of more favorable social norms mediated the relationship between fast food promotional exposure and children's more frequent fast food consumption. If fast food marketing contributes to perceived social norms about fast food consumption in a community, differences in the amount and content of targeted food marketing may create, or support differences in the healthfulness of attitudes and norms toward fast food and its consumption. This is especially important given the attenuated access to affordable and healthy foods in Black communities which challenges attempts at healthy eating (Kumanyika et al., 2007).

While the described research does not establish a direct link between marketing and food consumption, it illustrates how the food marketing environment of Black consumers is more likely to challenge healthy eating. A food marketing environment that encourages consumption of sugar-sweetened beverages and high energy dense foods in preference to healthier and lower calorie food and beverage options may contribute to overconsumption of calories. Thus, inequities in food marketing environments merit particular concern given the higher risk of obesity in the Black community, especially among Black youth.

The "food marketing environment" from the consumer and community perspective involves the set of factors that influence consumers' preferences for, ability to acquire, and actual acquisition and consumption of food, including not only the traditional "4 P's" of marketing but also the psychobiological, ethnic and cultural, social, and setting-based factors that influence the interactions of individuals, families, and communities at large with these marketing variables. Further, inequities in food marketing also relate to what marketers have done historically and consumer response to these strategies.

Historical Foundations of Target Marketing to Black Consumers

Marketers have historically targeted Blacks, although how they have been targeted and how they have been represented has shifted. A full description of the history of Black consumers and marketing is beyond the scope of this chapter, and more detailed and comprehensive treatments of the topic are available (Branchik & Davis, 2009; Weems, 1998).

Nonetheless, some historical remnants highlight points that help provide context for the target marketing that we see today. Although a variety of factors contributed to the growth in Black consumerism over the past decades since slavery, the civil rights and Black power movements were especially significant events (Weems, 1998). In both social movements, the struggle for racial equality encompassed consumption equality, and target marketing was desired and in fact demanded as a signal of citizenship. As a result, for Black consumers, consumption is perceived as a means of expressing mainstream social participation, marketplace equality, and ethnic pride (Branchik & Davis, 2009; Chambers, 2006; Lamont & Molnár, 2001; Tharp, 2001). Some scholars argue that consumer rights are as important as labor and production rights to African Americans (Mullins, 1999). A study of marketing professionals who specialize in the African-American market found that they viewed Black consumption behavior as motivated by a desire for societal inclusion, and cultural distinctiveness, and this perception underlies their developed target marketing approaches (Lamont & Molnár, 2001). Further, they note that the use of consumption in this way is reinforced because, as a Senior Black ad executive noted, "branded consumer goods may be obtained more easily than employment, housing or membership in certain groups and organizations" (page 38). Nonetheless, the discrimination observed in employment and housing markets is also a significant issue in the consumer goods context (Williams, Henderson, & Harris, 2001).

Marketers thus frequently target Blacks using strategies to convince them that purchasing power is an expressive collective tool to signal being a full member of society (Lamont & Molnár, 2001). Such motivations may be reflected in political ideologies which undergird African-American strategies to allocate resources amid disadvantage, such as in the case of attenuated access to food (Crockett & Wallendorf, 2004). The current day "food deserts" which exist in many Black communities and relate to marketing distribution strategies have emerged from supermarket flight which started over 50 years ago. In addition, the use of specific strategies and tactics including an emphasis on celebrity advertising, the importance of Black radio as a media vehicle, and corporate sponsorships of community activities also reflect historical patterns. Overall, many practices and perceptions observed in the Black community today have emerged from the specific history of the relationship between Black consumers and the marketplace.

Black Consumer Exposure and Response to Targeted Marketing

The persistence of historical factors related to the promotion and availability of food contributes to the continuity of social and cultural adaptations developed in Black communities in response to these factors. Marketers recognize Black consumers as a distinctive market and work to exploit preferences that may have developed over time for specific food and beverage options. Even highly motivated individuals must continually work against the tide of commercial marketing forces that promote unhealthy eating and perpetuate the norms of unhealthy eating. A comprehensive understanding of the effects of target marketing must include an understanding of how consumers respond to the marketing efforts, especially as a precursor to integrating community perspectives. Consumer behavior, i.e., what people buy, what they purchase, how often, how much, etc. is influenced by marketing strategy in two important ways: marketing exposure and consumer response.

Frequent media exposure can increase the influence of marketing messages on consumer behavior. Viewing the same or similar messages has been found to increase belief in the message, suggest certain behaviors as normal, and affect how quickly people spread the message to others (Hornik, 2002). Thus, repeated exposure to food-related marketing messages can influence the awareness and meaning of specific types of foods, affect brand attitudes, and contribute to food-related norms (Grier, 2009). Increased media usage, especially TV, is associated with increased caloric intake and weight (Escobar-Chaves & Anderson, 2008; Institute of Medicine, 2005). A study of adolescents 10 to 15 years old found that the odds of being overweight were almost five times greater for those who viewed 5 h of TV per day vs. those who viewed two or less hours (Gortmaker et al., 1996).

Research shows that Blacks consumers have high rates of media use, especially TV. Black youth average about 13 h of media exposure daily, almost 5 h more than the 8½h among White youth (Rideout, Foehr, & Roberts, 2010). The biggest differences are among television time, where Black youth spend almost 6 h daily watching TV compared to 3½h among White youth and are also significantly more likely to report that the TV is on during meals (78% for Blacks vs. 58% for Whites). The most recent figures reflect increased differences in media use by race and ethnicity over the past five years. Similarly high rates of media usage, especially Television, have been noted among adults. This heavy media usage also extends to certain digital media which are a core strategy of modern targeting efforts (Grier, 2009). The increased media exposure translates to increased food marketing exposure. For example, research has shown that African Americans aged 12–17 view 14% more food product advertisements than their White peers (Powell, Szczypka, & Chaloupka, 2007).

The orientation of Black consumers, especially Black youth, to the marketing they are exposed to is also positive and strong. Black consumers appear more favorable towards marketing generally, and especially towards targeted marketing that "speaks" to them. Research suggests that Black consumers are more likely to pay more attention to identify with and trust spokespersons of similar ethnicity and to have more positive attitudes and purchase intentions towards a brand when it features ethnic cues (Aaker, Brumbaugh, & Grier, 2000; Appiah, 2001, 2004; Grier & Brumbaugh, 1999). Black consumers are also more favorable to in-store sales promotions (Green, 1995). Black consumers have also been characterized as highly brand loyal, are seen as new product trendsetters, and will readily spread word of mouth about products within their networks. Further, as a member of a minority group, Black youth also encounter and may respond positively to marketing targeted to all youth, to other minority youth (e.g., Latinos), to minority adults, to marketing efforts targeted at White consumers, and to efforts based on other segmentation criteria besides race.

The frequency and resonance of identity-linked targeted marketing which promotes less healthful products may support the development of less healthful eating patterns and result in adverse health effects. Thus, in many ways public health views marketing as "bad", i.e., as a force not working to support health. Of course, marketing is not all bad, although those concerned with the health effects of frequently promoted unhealthy products might see it that way. Marketing can also be a positive force for health, both in terms of social marketing, as well as conscious and responsible commercial marketing activities. The positive use of targeted food and beverage marketing to Black consumers appears an open opportunity in light of what has been observed and documented.

The Black Consumer Market and Targeted Food Marketing

Black consumers continue to be a vital demographic in terms of market growth and profitability, and very important target markets for food and beverage marketing. Black Americans' buying power has increased from $316.3 billion in 1990 to

$946.6 billion in 2010 and is projected to climb to $1.3 trillion in 2017 (Humphries, 2012). Black consumers comprise one of the fastest growing segments of the youth population (Frey, 2003; Humphreys, 2006; Zhou, 1997) and ethnic minority families are also growing at a faster rate than the total population (The Nielsen Company, 2009). Spending on target marketing geared to Black consumers was $2.3 billion for 2006–2007 (Nielsen, 2008). Specific to food and beverages, Black consumers are a very desirable market as they shop for food more often, and spend more money per food shopping trip compared to the rest of the population (Grier & Kumanyika, 2008).

Food and beverage advertising expenditures represent a significant proportion of overall ethnically targeted marketing. Although it is often argued that any food and beverage can be part of a balanced meal, fast food and soda are seen as two likely contributors to the obesity epidemic and Black youth are heavy consumers of both products. Marketers are aware of this and their targeting strategies reflect this knowledge. Ad spending in African-American media fared better than overall ad market in 2009 with fast food restaurants increasing ad spend by 19.2% in Black-oriented media (Bachman, 2010). And soda companies continue targeting efforts directed to African-American youth which began in earnest in the 1940s (Grocery Manufacturer, 1971; Tharp, 2001). For example, in 2006, Coca-Cola re-established a dedicated African-American marketing group in order to better connect with "key consumers, including teens, moms and multicultural consumers" (Zmuda, 2009).

Marketers design strategies to specifically reach Black youth, while also reaching them with their general youth targeting efforts. Food marketers use techniques that have been observed historically to reach Black consumers, including the use of popular Black celebrities, ethnic symbols, and music to link the consumption of specific products with Black culture (Grocery Manufacturer, 1971). Fast food marketing targets Black children and teens with TV advertising, targeted websites, and banner ads, and Black children and teens see at least 50% more fast food ads than other children and teens (Harris, Schwartz, & Brownell, 2010). For example, Pepsi used hip-hop singer Busta Rhymes to increase relevance and awareness of Mountain Dew and Code Red and reported that the results of their campaign led to "all-time highs in awareness and conversion of the two brands among African-Americans and Latinos" (Radio Advertising Bureau). Sprite, part of Coca-Cola's soda portfolio, has a consumer base that is about 30% African American, and the company targets them with customized promotions including digital marketing (Khan, 2009; MacArthur & Neff, 2004).

A campaign entitled "365 Black" by McDonald's demonstrates a variety of marketing tools working together. The campaign includes a targeted website that promotes the year-round celebration of African-American culture and achievement. The campaign uses ads that feature Black celebrities such as Venus Williams, communicates "little known Black history facts" to over 122 million listeners on a daily radio show, displays posters in the fast food outlets, distributes Black history booklets in schools in collaboration with Coca-Cola, and supports community events including a Black college tour and an academic achievement program for middle school students (McDonald's Corporation). The use of ethnic cues in the campaign (e.g., Black celebrities, African cultural symbols, support of cultural institutions) and ethnic media (e.g., Black radio) can increase favorable responses towards the campaign.

Fast food marketers are also cognizant that their products serve a particular need among low income and minority consumers, so price-based marketing is also a common strategy (Warner, 2006). *See Table 16.1 for a description of marketing techniques and examples of how markers use these techniques.* The diversity of marketing strategies highlights the complexity likely inherent in consumer perceptions of marketing. For example, corporations provide product information, as well much needed funds such as through sponsorship and support of Black media, yet at an often unacknowledged cost of increased exposure to less healthy food and beverage products.

In the age of new technologies, consumers are not just recipients of marketing messages but also message creators such as through blogging, word of mouth, and even the creation of marketing campaigns (Montgomery & Chester, 2009). Companies no longer solely control product messaging; instead they are facilitators of the conversation. Marketing is a three-way conversation in which the food marketer and public health perspective need to integrate community perspectives in order to develop "win-win" business and community health solutions. Although marketers have integrated new technologies, data, and analytical know-how to engage in marketing focused on particular communities, the power of the consumer-driven marketing paradigm has yet to be fully realized in support of the health of Black communities. Thus, it is important to understand how Black consumers perceive the food and beverage marketing they encounter.

Engaging Communities to Address Childhood Obesity

There is a growing focus on policy and environmental interventions (e.g., food taxation, restrictions on targeted unhealthy food and beverage marketing, zoning to increase access to healthy foods and to encourage physical activity, etc.) to help address the childhood obesity epidemic and particularly in high-risk populations (Dietz, Bland, Gortmaker, Molloy, & Schmid, 2002). However, the importance of rapid population-based action to address childhood obesity should not outweigh understanding the unintended consequences of establishing policies without evidence of their potential effectiveness with specific populations. Understanding the current challenges in implementing evidence-based practices and existing policies will also be critical for developing future interventions.

Limited data exists on community-level interventions with sustainable outcomes for Black children at risk or currently affected by childhood obesity. Examples of community-level interventions, including the Girls health Enrichment Multi-site Studies GEMS (Robinson et al., 2003), the Central California Regional Obesity Prevention Program (Schwarte et al., 2010), Shape Up Somerville: Eat Smart, Play Hard (Economos et al., 2001), and Hip Hop to Health Jr. (Fitzgibbon et al., 2011)

Table 16.1 Examples of ethnic marketing techniques used to market foods and beverages to Black consumers

Technique	Definition	Example
Advertising	Any paid form of nonpersonal communication about an organization, product, service, or idea by an identified sponsor[a]	McDonald's and KFC targeted African American youth with TV advertising, websites, and banner ads. The African American teens saw 75% more TV ads for McDonald's and KFC than white teens[b]
Event Sponsorship	A type of promotion where a company provides financial support in return for the right to display a brand name, logo, or advertising message and be identified as an event supporter[c]	In order to increase engagement with multicultural college-age consumers, Sprite sponsored and hosted a step dance competition open to step troupes from college campuses across the nation.[d] Stepping is an ages-old tradition of African-American sororities and fraternities
Product Placements	References to or inclusion of a product or service within some media (e.g., movie, song) in return for payment or other benefits[e]	McDonald's Corp. hired an entertainment marketing firm to design strategies to encourage hip-hop artists to integrate the Big Mac sandwich into their songs. Artists receive $1–$5 each time their song is played on the radio[f]
Street Teams	A group or organization called upon to promote and advertise an event or venture[g]	Pepsi sent six vans and six trucks carrying disc jockeys and soda products to Black and Hispanic neighborhoods in 22 cities. The vans and trucks went to schools, parks, and basketball courts, and asked audiences to sing and rap for Mountain Dew items. They also distributed 20-ounce bottles which included offers under the cap for another free bottle[h]
Giveaways, Scholarships	A product given away to potential customers without demanding any payment for it[i]	Coca Cola awards $125,000 in scholarships to five Historically Black Colleges and Universities (HBCUs) in Louisiana to support women's empowerment and education initiatives[j]
Internet Websites	An organization makes information available about their product on the internet. The website allows for use of additional marketing techniques	On the Reese's Puffs cereal website one can listen to a predominately Black youth band rap about the taste of Reese's Puffs, or create one's own mixes with the online mixing board (reesepuffs.com)
Mobile Marketing	The use of mobile medium as a marketing vehicle. May involve text messages, delivery of coupons, or access to internet marketing	Coca-Cola's and Church's chicken collaborated on the "Be Heard" mobile promotion allows customers to text a code on their mobile devices for coupons and to enter a sweepstakes for a chance to win cash awards[k]

(continued)

Table 16.1 (continued)

Technique	Definition	Example
Social Media Marketing	Social media involves an online platform or site that focuses on building and reflecting on social relations among people, who for example, share interests and/or activities.[l] Social Media Marketing involves activities directed at these networks	Sprite developed the Sprite Yard program for mobile phones to interact with its "mostly African American youth target audience" by letting them download information, share pictures, and text with friends.[m] The Sprite Yard example reflects the use of a social media for marketing on a mobile platform
Community Relations	Community Relations is the process that an organization uses to connect with its various constituents such as clients, volunteers, donors, community partners, and peers[n]	General Mills created the "Feeding Dreams" program to recognize everyday people in the Black community who positively impact their communities.[o] The program gives cash prizes and donations to the recognized individuals' favorite charities

[a]Belch, G., & Belch M. (2012). Advertising and promotions: An integrated marketing communications perspective. 9e

[b]Harris, J. L., Schwartz, M. B., & Brownell, K. D. (2010). *Fast Food F.A.C.T.S.: Evaluating Fast Food Nutrition and Marketing to Youth.* Rudd Center for Food Policy & Obesity

[c]Belch, G., & Belch M. (2012). Advertising and promotions: An integrated marketing communications perspective. 9e

[d]Sprite Step Off. (2010). Promo Magazine, Jul 3, 2010. Accessed 4 Oct. 2011, from http://promomagazine.com/pro_awards/sprite-step-off/

[e]Percy, Larry. (2008). Strategic integrated marketing communications, new media and other IMC options (pp.131–132). Oxford, UK: Elsevier

[f]Graser, M. (2005, March 23). McDonald's buying way into Hip-Hop Song Lyrics. *Advertising Age*

[g]News Marketing Group. Street Team. Found on October 5, 2011, from http://newsmarketing-group.com/site/earning-while-learning/street-team/

[h]Adage. (2000). Urban warfare; Hip-hop and street savvy are soda marketers' weapons in the battle for minority kids. Found on http://www.highbeam.com/doc/1G1-65103765.html.

[i]The Internet Marketing Dictionary. Giveaway. Found on October 5, 2011, from http://www.internetmarketing-dictionary.com/Give-Away.html

[j]Coca Cola jazzes up the Essence music festival with $125,000 in scholarships to schools in Louisiana. Found at http://www.eurweb.com/2011/07/coca-cola%C2%AE-jazzes-up-the-essence-music-festival%E2%84%A2-with-125000-in-scholarships-to-schools-in-louisiana/

[k]Butcher, Dan. (2009) Church's Chicken, Coca-Cola use SMS to connect with urban youth, (January 28), Accessed 1 Oct, 2011. http://www.mobilemarketer.com/cms/news/messaging/2532.print

[l]Mashable. Social networking. Found October 5, 2011, from http://mashable.com/follow/topics/social-networking/

[m]Khan, M. A. (2007). Coca-Cola debuts ambitious mobile push for Sprite *DM News, June 06.* Retrieved from http://www.dmnews.com/Coca-Cola-debuts-ambitious-mobile-push-for-Sprite/article/95828/

[n]Marketing and Community Relations Module. Found on October 5, 2011, from http://www.nonprofitinclusiveness.org/files/Module%2015.pdf

[o]General Mills expands its Feeding Dreams programs to honor heroes in 10 markets, (August 3, 2010). Accessed 7 Oct 2011. http://www.targetmarketnews.com/storyid08041001.htm

have engaged Black children in healthy eating and/or active living demonstrating modest improvements in outcomes. Still, clearly additional research is needed to elucidate both the targets (e.g., school settings, family-based, etc.) for interventions and the community processes whereby changes can be accomplished.

Collaborating and working with members of the community is fundamental for efforts to improve the health status of communities, and particularly in communities of color. Communities have been described as physical or social entities that are sufficiently defined to support focused interventions (Robinson, 2005). History, culture, context, and geography provide the core basis for understanding the consciousness, experience, and social boundaries of communities as well as how and why people are exposed to particular factors. Communities are complex systems and understanding how communities are organized and operate may increase researchers as well as community-based research partners' ability to take a holistic or integrated approach to the design of programs to address food, activity, and weight.

A universal definition does not exist for community-centered approaches. However, community-centered strategies similar to community engagement approaches have been described as strategies that utilize community assets, community capacity and research to develop effective interventions (Lindau et al. 2011; Wandersman, 2003). The value of community-centered approaches is their ability to strengthen communities from the inside out. Community-centered approaches are highly effective because they do not merely address the impact of environmental factors on an individual's health and lifestyle, but on the community as a whole.

Utilizing community-centered approaches can be a powerful contributor in generating endogenous solutions to combat childhood obesity. Successfully addressing childhood obesity will also require integration and collaboration from all sectors (e.g., education, government, business, faith-based, public health, etc.) and interests or providers that work within specific areas to meet community needs. As we work towards eradicating childhood obesity we must have well-connected, interdependent sectors that share responsibility for recognizing and resolving environmental factors that impact community health.

The *Community-centered View of Influences on Eating, Activity, and Body Weight* (see Fig. 16.1) was developed by Dr. Shiriki Kumanyika, Founder and Chair of the African American Collaborative Obesity Research Network (AACORN) based at the University of Pennsylvania Perelman School of Medicine. This model is based on a systems-oriented framework and was developed for communities and researchers to think through approaches to intervening on obesity in people-oriented rather than problem-oriented terms. The model is geared to a collective or group perspective, i.e., what are the environmental or behavioral issues "on average" or that tend to be the most common in communities. Key questions to understand the dynamics of eating, activity, and body weight include:

- How do eating, physical activity, and weight reflect the opportunities, constraints, and issues in people's everyday lives?
- What aspects of people's everyday lives and circumstances must be considered in order to develop appropriate, effective, and sustainable intervention approaches?

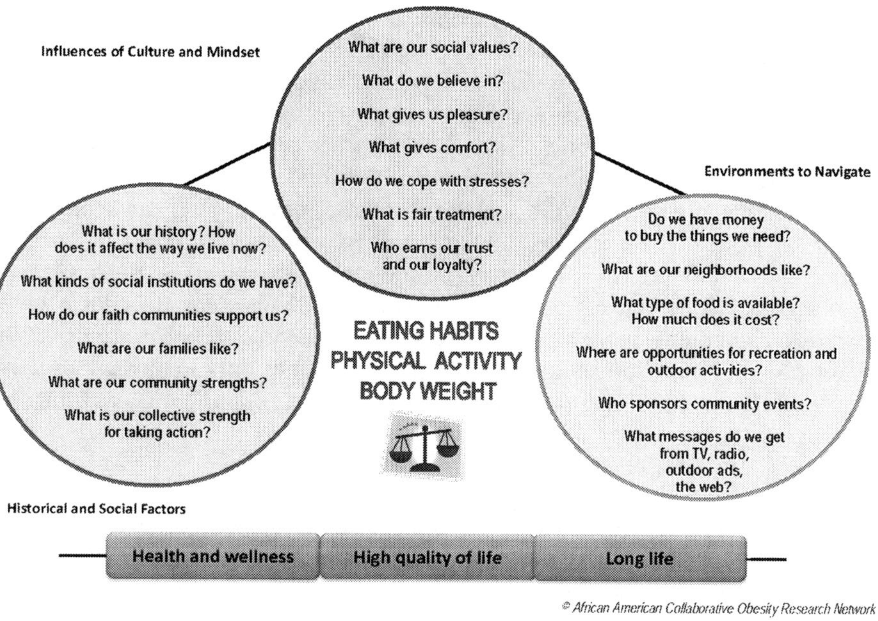

Fig. 16.1 A community-centered view of influences on eating, activity, and body weight

- How can interventions on obesity support high quality of life and community priorities that are broader than food, activity, or weight?

In other words, it is not simply a matter of teaching people about how many calories are in their food or how long they would have to exercise in order to burn a certain number of calories. The issue is much more complicated, as many people in Black communities already know this information. To elicit reflection on the complexity of the issue, the model shown in the diagram calls for reflection of several different types of community-level factors that influence (1) eating habits and physical activity and, ultimately, body weight and body fatness; and (2) resources available to take positive actions to address social or health issues that may be associated with eating or activity habits or weight.

This approach recognizes that individuals within a community have a lot of variation in what they eat, how active they are, or whether they are overweight, but focuses on the concept that improvements on these fronts are needed to foster health and wellness and, therefore, high quality of life and longevity. Identifying processes whereby Black communities undergo positive structural and cultural changes and how these processes might apply to food-related and physical activity behaviors is still needed. This model also reiterates the need for endogenous, community-driven solutions that are congruent with community perspectives and preferences.

To understand the community response and perceptions of the food marketing environment, particularly responses by Blacks, it is important to first understand some of the issues facing these consumers. Ultimately food purchases and intake are a matter of individual choice that is greatly influenced by exposure to food marketing strategies and tactics. As described earlier, research suggests that Blacks face challenges with all four components of the food marketing system; namely, place (i.e., geographic location, types of outlets), product (i.e., food attributes, quality and quantity), price (i.e., amount charged, discounts offered), and promotion (i.e., advertising and consumer promotion) (Drewnowski, 2009; Grier & Kumanyika, 2008; Yancey et al., 2009). These challenges are embedded within complex community processes and involve business practices that are driven by profitability of many unhealthy foods. The issue is not only marketers targeting Blacks for unhealthy food and beverages but the perception that Blacks only eat certain foods that may be less healthful. Therefore, marketing continually targets these products to Black consumers.

If current consumer demand has been shaped by marketing and marketing continues to reinforce certain types of demand, even highly motivated individuals are constantly challenged to work against the multitude of commercial marketing forces that promote unhealthy eating and perpetuate the norms of unhealthy eating. One could argue that marketers are only marketing what individuals are willing to buy and ultimately want. However, from an historical perspective we recognize that certain food and beverage products have been aligned with certain ethnic groups over time and since it has been done over time it has shaped individuals' preferences (Birch, 1999; James, 2004). Thus, individual preferences are shaped by the marketing system that reinforces in many cases the unhealthy preferences we want people to avoid. As noted, beyond shaping individual preferences, marketing creates the environments in which individuals interact with food and beverages and therefore influences community norms regarding eating behaviors (Grier & Kumanyika, 2008; Grier et al., 2007; Story, Neumark-Sztainer, & French, 2002). Thus, without ameliorative environmental changes, success in changing community preferences will continue to be limited or absent.

From a public health perspective, certain groups, such as children and youth, and for different reasons, Black consumers, may be considered vulnerable to aspects of marketing (Grier & Kumanyika, 2010; Mello, Studdert, & Brennan, 2006). However, we have limited knowledge of how members of groups targeted for marketing that can be considered harmful view the marketing they encounter. Do various segments within the Black community view certain marketing strategies and tactics directed towards them as fair or unfair? Also, how do individuals relate these marketing practices to their food marketing environments? Acknowledging the heterogeneous nature of Black communities (Kumanyika et al., 2007) is critical when examining potential answers to these questions.

Examining Black Adult and Youth Perceptions of Food Marketing

Research in marketing pertaining to Black consumers' perceptions of their food marketing environment is fairly scarce. In 2009, AACORN conducted a pilot study to ascertain Black adult and youth perceptions of social injustices, with respect to targeted marketing as a foundation for the development of community-centered approaches to improve food marketing environments. The purpose of this study was to inform the development of a multi-site study that would further examine whether framing adverse marketing practices as social justice issues would be effective as a basis for community mobilization to change demand or stimulate counter-marketing campaigns. Understanding community perceptions of the environments individuals have to navigate in their day-to-day lives is an important first step in determining the trigger points for generating support in terms of what is most needed and desired to sustain the health and well-being of the community.

Six semi-structured focus groups (90 min sessions) were conducted by trained moderators at various community locations (e.g., community center, church, etc.). The study design, which focused on understanding responses of this specific target population for food and beverage marketing, only engaged participants who self-identified their race as "Black" to participate in the study. Stratified sampling by age, gender (youth only), and recent exposure to lifestyle weight loss programs was used based on the expectation that these groups may have different responses to food and beverage marketing practices and that this level of group homogeneity would facilitate focused discussions. Key study inclusion criteria also required adult participants to have at least one child (3–18 years of age) in the household to increase the likelihood that participants would have opinions about scenarios that involve marketing to children and youth.

The focus group respondents included: adolescent males ($N=5$), adolescent females ($N=6$), male and female adult caregivers ($N=9$), adult caregivers who participated in a weight loss program ($N=10$), and older adults ($N=7$). Study participants' education varied from the highest level of education completed being 8th grade to completing a graduate degree. Income data was not collected from study participants. However, all study participants were from the same zip code areas in West and Southwest Philadelphia, PA. Recruitment for this study occurred through AACORN's community partners in these neighborhoods known to have ongoing involvement with the types of participants needed and with facilities suitable for conducting group interviews.

The focus groups explored respondent reactions to brief scenarios designed to reflect the types of marketing practices that might be perceived as unfair, including examples of marketing to both youth and adults. Focus group data was collected through a demographic survey and electronic auto response software. During the focus group sessions, questions and scenarios of different marketing strategies and tactics were presented and individuals responded independently using the auto response software keypads. Individual responses were tabulated and presented during the focus group to motivate further discussion of individual and group perceptions. All of the focus group discussions were audio taped and transcribed.

The analysis of the pilot study data examined the following questions: would respondents consider any of the scenarios to represent unfair or unjust practices; what the characteristics of those scenarios were; the nature of any specific perceived injustice; what types of actions the injustice would warrant, and by whom; what language and concepts the participants use when discussing these issues; and what demographic or consumer characteristics were associated with particular responses.

The results presented below are based on a data-driven content analysis of partial data (qualitative data only) from the six semi-structured focus groups ($N=37$). Consequently, the data presented should be regarded as providing preliminary insights rather than summary conclusions about the entire data set. Dimensionalizing techniques (Graneheim & Lundman, 2004) were used to examine a group of codes that were emerging in the data as a category or theme and how the dimensions that emerged from the data were different or similar. Text segments that are most representative of each focus group's theme describing Black adult and youth responses (in the participants' voices) to the marketing system of price, promotion, product, and placement/distribution, and the use of ethnic target marketing strategies are presented in Fig. 16.2.

Marketing Tactic/ Strategy	**Price Variation**	**Placement/ Channels of Distribution**	**Product**	**Promotion- Celebrity Endorsement**		**Cultural References and Cues**
Question	*Smaller neighborhood stores tend to have higher prices than larger supermarkets or "big box" stores (e.g., Wal-Mart). Do you think this is fair to the consumer?*	*Do you know of neighborhoods that don't have supermarkets?*	*Does it matter to you that companies target you to sell certain foods and beverages?*	*Lil Wayne headlining a Coco Cola concert or Burger King family fun days with Mario (R & B singer) - Do you see this as marketing?*	*Popular artists' songs (e.g., Chris Brown - Doublemint gum) and images are used to promote specific product brands. Does this type of ad influence what people buy? [youth: "... what you buy"]*	*Does it matter to you if advertisers appeal to your ethnicity or cultural ties?*
Responses from Female Youth (16-21 years of age)	**Sue** "I said it is not fair to the consumer because even though their stores are smaller they might need more money so they can make it better or make it bigger. But it is unfair to the customer that they have to pay more rather than the bigger companies."	**Heather** "Yes, and you are not getting the most for your money, if you don't have a supermarket in your neighborhood." **Carrie** "Yes, people got to travel to go get their food."	**Heather** "I put no, because it really don't matter to me. I am still going to eat the food or whatever. I mean food is food to me…I really don't take into consideration all that healthy stuff. Do what you are going to do. "	**Sue** "Yes, because he is advertising something and trying to sell it." **Ashley** "Yes, because he is hot and people will like to buy stuff from him."	**Ashley** "I was going to say that I don't really care what they wear or whatever. I wear what I want to wear." **Heather** "Yeah it does matter about the product."	**Sue** "It don't matter because I'm still going to eat what I want." **Christie** "Yes and no, you know what I am saying? They just want to make themselves look better."
Responses from Male Youth (16-21 years of age)	**Ned** "Corner stores are there to meet the needs of the consumer and if the corner store did sell things like a box of cereal for, like, two-fifty, it wouldn't be able to make that much of a profit to actually renew its stock…like, larger stores can sell it at a, like, cheaper price because they buy in bulk, but a corner store doesn't make as much money. I could be wrong; I have the right to be wrong, but that's just what I think." **Bob** "The corner stores are selfish."	**Mike** "I've never had to catch the bus with groceries and I hope I'd never have to but I imagine it would be pretty annoying to have to take bags on public transportation. You know, if there's not a supermarket, there is, like they showed in the picture, a gas station or a corner store which seem to, most of the time, have a lot lesser quality when it comes to the care that is used with the food."	**Ned** "I say 'yes it does matter' because it's you specifically. How could it not, like, matter to you if it doesn't pertain to you. But it affects me and it has me in the category." **Phil** "Well, I guess I'm neutral in that because… they're targeting me to sell foods and beverages, if I don't want them, I won't get them so it's not really hurting me."	**Bob** "People like to go with what one person is doing so if they see Lil Wayne, somebody that is famous for being, like, kind of a leader even though he is a horrible leader, doing something like drinking Coca Cola, they are going to think…they are going to try and play on that."	**Ned** "Because I don't buy it either way. If I don't like, I don't like it, so I will not buy it."	**Ned** "Yes…it's modern-day racism because what they're blatantly saying is that I want to do something that goes directly to this one minority or one, like, group - period."

Fig. 16.2 Black consumer responses to marketing tactics and strategies. Pseudonyms have been added to all comments presented in the figure

Responses from Male Parents/ Caregivers (22 to 65 years of age)	**Steve** "It's a fact that smaller businesses have to pay more for their products than a larger establishment does. Such as if you were to shop at ShopRite, what they're getting for a gallon of milk versus your corner store getting for a gallon of milk, it's going to be almost a dollar difference for that same gallon of milk. Therefore, that corner store, for them to make any profit, may have to charge fifty cents more than ShopRite because they're paying a dollar more to start with."	**Jason** " I'll go with the fact that would make you have to go to a corner store which can jack up the price for a little more. I won't say a lot more, but it's going to be more for you to have that product, whatever it is that you're looking for, in their store. So, you're at their mercy. It's not like there's a...the word eludes me however, but there's no. competition. "	**George** "Yes, I guess it shouldn't because ... I'm going to eat what I want to eat. It doesn't matter, you know, what you promote. If I don't like it, it won't get bought."	**Gary** "I think anytime you have sponsorships, that's a form of marketing because you know that when any type of production, Family Fest, you'll have a lot of different companies and they advertise. If their brand name is there, it's advertising."	**Steve** "...To me it doesn't matter what the product is because... I won't say the average person, but there's going to be somebody out there that's going to purchase a product that you endorse because you're famous."	**Gary** "I think there are just certain products that we all use, certain products that we don't all use. I chose that vein because that seems to be the thing that for years...I've been involved in a lot of discussions with a lot of different people, but that is the one thing that has always been plagued or pushed in our neighborhoods because that is one thing that they know people will run after and go after."
Responses from Female Parents/Caregivers (22 to 65 years of age)	**Mary** "I put 'no' because I figure they know it's unfair, and we can't get to the big market. So lower your prices, so more people can probably come to your store." **Anne** "I answered 'yes.' The only reason I feel that it is fair to the consumer is because they put the corner stores there for convenience. So therefore in order for the corner stores to be able make their profit, they do have to jack things up a little bit higher than the supermarkets."	**Joan** "In the first place, they are making you go to a corner store which is higher and it's inconvenient... So you are not getting the most for your money, if you don't have a supermarket in your neighborhood."	**Lisa** "I agree that it does depend on what they are selling, but at the same time, if you're targeting me, that means that you are targeting the things that I like – what I'm going to the store to buy on a regular basis. If it's not just to me...if it's something that's going to make me obese, that's my decision. They are more interested in money, what can they do to make a profit off of everybody."	**Mary** "When you bring a group of people together and they're having fun and stuff, you are really putting that advertisement out. So, sooner or later, somebody in the group or family is going to buy some Burger King."	**Anne** "Yes, if they idolize that certain singer or actor. A lot of times you have young people...or sometimes older people... You might see something and say, "That's nice, I like that." It influences all age groups. It might sound crazy, but some people think that if they dress like that person, they might even be able to sing or dance like that person." **Kim** "I don't care what the product is...Most of the time it costs too much."	**Lisa** "I chose 'No' because I feel like a lot of the companies don't care what your ethnic background is, their whole motive is to try to pull you in. You're trying to get everybody to promote it...but you're talking about 'creeping.' If you didn't know that was a commercial, you would think that they were talking about someone cheating on him or something like that. They don't care what your background is; they are just trying to get you to come in and to spend that money."
Responses from Adults with experience in weight loss program (22 to 65 years of age)	**Eve** "I took into account your point of view that they have less stuff. They have to charge more for profit but I still said that it was unfair because I felt the unfairness is in...when there's no option. When you go to the corner store because it's convenient and you want to pay more for convenience, that's fine, but if you are going there because it is the only store, then it becomes unfair because you don't have an option."	**Roxy** "Yeah, I mean, if I want to walk to the market, it's not convenient for me to walk to Super Fresh, Fresh Grocer or ShopRite." **Val** "And If you go on SEPTA, you can't get everything you want."	**Melanie** "I think it matters simply when they get their facts right."	**Celeste** "Well basically it's just to promote more business for Burger King...to show what more they might be offering or something like that. That is basically all that I see it as, just something to promote, you know you either go more to Burger King than say, McDonalds or any other place."	**Rose** "They are the ones promoting this, because these children don't know nothing about that until you brainwash them with this. I believe basically, that's all it is: brainwashing."	**Celeste** "If it's a negative product, then I would be concerned if it's targeted toward us, but overall it was just something to catch you, and to get you, it doesn't matter to me. But, if it's something like targeting children and is negative and it's targeted to my child, then it would be a problem."
Responses from Seniors (65 years of age or older)	**Jen** "Because most senior citizens are on a fixed income and you cannot afford to be spending extra money, is what I feel." **Lynn** "People don't go to them so they have to jack their prices up to make ends meet with rent and...you know you got to pay the government tax and all that. They pass right by their stores and go on to the market."	**Nicole** "Well I said 'yes' because a lot of stores that had been supermarkets, they closed down because they were not doing the business like they should do and did not have the people to work in it. The prices were too high, so they had to shut down." **Joan** "You have to go too far to try and shop and then maybe you might settle for whatever is in the way..."	**Nicole** "I look at it like this now. For instance, say if I had a store and they wanted to get me to sell this or sell that, I don't have to get that product in my store because that is my store, I don't have to take it. Now if I know I can't sell it, nobody's going to buy, why should I put it in stock in my place?"	**Chloe** "I see what they did as a kind of advertising ...something to make people to buy more from them."	**Nicole** "Well I said 'yes' because now I have quite a few grands and great-grands, I had an eleven-year-old who wanted Nikes, and then another one, the thirteen-year-old one said, "I want both of them." So it influences the younger kids too."	**Courtney** "I said 'yes, it bothers me' because I remember when they used to have the Colt 45 ads on the TV and it was always in our neighborhood. You know, some of us, they want us to buy ...it bothers me. I have been noticing that. It does bother me."

Fig. 16.2 (continued)

Preliminary Findings: A Summary of Respondents' Views on Marketing Tactics and Strategies

Price was viewed as very important and respondents were aware of differences in food prices among different types of food outlets. Interestingly, even access to food outlets were described by respondents in terms of price. Respondents associated smaller food outlets closer to home, with higher prices and the cost of accessing food that is not accessible in your neighborhood. However, several of the respondents, particularly male youth and male caregivers, also appreciated the need for businesses to make a profit. In terms of products, views ranged from product marketing having no effect or some effect on consumers to a desire for marketers to direct certain products towards them. The use of celebrities in promotion was viewed as a positive strategy for businesses but some respondents also found it less favorable for children or individuals easily influenced by others. In general, respondents provided more comments about how the various food and beverage marketing scenarios affected others than about how the marketing directly affected their own actions or behaviors. The data also demonstrated how segments of the community, particularly adolescents and adults, may perceive the same marketing environment in different ways.

The data suggests that although respondents acknowledged and had specific opinions on the use of cultural and ethnic target marketing there was no consensus of viewing these marketing strategies as positive or negative. In general, respondents recognized ethnic marketing and the use of cultural references and cues as the norm. Differences in perceptions were also dependent on the product being directed to certain groups. Products viewed as less healthful or more harmful elicited a strong negative reaction whereas less harmful types of products elicited a neutral response with the use of cultural references and ethnic target marketing.

The findings from this pilot study demonstrate that Blacks of various ages, gender, and life experiences view marketing both favorably and with concerns. The concerns voiced focused on how marketing impacts consumers' choices or lack of choice. The data suggest that respondents may not fully appreciate the interplay between community supply and demand and have accepted the current marketing tactics and strategies directed towards them as part of their overall experience as consumers. However, the opportunity to amplify the consumer voice and have marketers as well as food and beverage companies respond to meet a new consumer demand also exist (Denegri-Knott, Zwick, & Schroeder, 2006).

Respondents are aware that they are reacting to a set of circumstances related to their food marketing environment; however, they seem less conscious of their potential role in changing elements of their food environment that they may believe are not truly working in their favor. The complexity of what individuals perceive as acceptable to the extent that they are not seeking opportunities to change the marketing system but yet still recognize the need for some degree of change is the public health dilemma that necessitates additional research in the domain of consumer response to food marketing environments.

Discussion and Future Directions

Our preliminary findings highlight the diversity of views towards marketing among even a small sample of Black consumers. The semi-structured focus group approach used for this study works well for uncovering individuals' perceptions of marketing by providing them a forum to share personal experiences as well as other peoples' experiences in a narrative format. The narratives revealed the complex and in some cases misguided perceptions of consumer power. Therefore, the immediate opening for changing the relationship between marketers and consumers may lie in increasing or facilitating opportunities for consumers to recognize their role in the co-creation of marketing.

As mentioned earlier, advances in technology have made it possible for nearly everyone to have an active voice in the conversation and engagement of marketing. This increasing shift in power is regarded as beneficial for consumers (Denegri-Knott et al., 2006). The use of data illuminating the tactics and strategies used in the food marketing system similar to techniques used in tobacco counter-marketing may also prove to be a powerful organizing tool in Black communities and the news media that serve them (Yerger, Daniel, & Malone, 2005).

Additional analyses of the data will provide insights about specific communication strategies to shift community responses to the current food marketing environment towards a demand for marketing of more healthful food and beverages. Often, interventions are framed as actions taken in the "best interests" of the community. An understanding of the best interests of the community in relation to inequitable food marketing environments may be used to develop communication strategies to engender community awareness, interest, and action regarding changing food demand and supply. A critical first step appears to involve increasing the importance of the issue of food marketing to both youth and adults with other major day-to-day interests and priorities in Black communities.

An applicable model that is specifically designed to activate community members using a marketing mind-set is the Community-Based Prevention Model (CBPM). CBPM is a framework for community-directed social change that utilizes marketing strategies and theories to create and evaluate health promotion and disease prevention programs. In the CBPM framework, "prevention" refers to promoting positive health behaviors and minimizing negative health behaviors. "Marketing" refers to the key distinguishing features of commercial marketing normally used to sell a product or service in the consumer marketplace (Bryant et al., 2007). The primary goal of CBPM is to enhance a community's ability to work together to pursue evidence-based strategies to address public health concerns as well as to empower the community by placing community members in control of the issues investigated.

Precedent for solving other public health issues that are similarly woven into the social fabric suggests that the elements of solutions essentially constitute a social movement (Economos et al., 2001). Young people, in particular, are at the center of social change and have a critical voice in helping to improve community environments for healthful eating with reciprocal benefits for youth development and well-being (Millstein & Sallis, 2011). Youth organizing draws on the power of youth to create the change they want to see in their community (Deschenes, McLaughlin, & Newman, 2008). The benefits of having youth actively engaged in decision making about the institutions and systems that affect their communities are numerous. However, the inclusion of youth perspectives, especially from Black youth, in the development and implementation of solutions to address the obesity epidemic has been largely overlooked. One of the greatest pleasures in working with youth may be the simple, honest, yet unexpected responses they give to complicated problems. Youth have the ability to influence their peers and think creatively in ways adults cannot conceptualize, while adults are able to think systemically and identify unintended consequences of change. Therefore, the need for creative and innovative youth-adult partnered approaches in developing communication strategies and interventions to address childhood obesity is greater than ever. Additionally, further research is still needed on the marketing environment as a comprehensive system, i.e., where all of the components of marketing are examined together. This is critical since this is the way businesses develop their strategies, and this is a way we can understand the marketing context in which consumers make choices and act.

The approach and findings from AACORN's research also suggest that data on ethnic target marketing approaches can be made comprehensible to communities and injected meaningfully into public debates over exposure to marketing practices that can have negative effects on health. The role of public policy with regards to the food marketing environment suggests an important relationship between decisions at all levels of government and the social environment of communities that support, encourage, and promote healthful eating among its members. Determining which policies will be effective in which populations requires evidence in not only objective but also subjective aspects of consumer food purchasing and consumption behavior in relation to food cost availability and promotion.

Conclusions

Given the multifaceted nature of childhood obesity, a multidisciplinary approach, involving collaborative efforts, across fields will be required. In addition to innovative and cross-cutting approaches, funding to support research, interventions and policy initiatives in communities as well as evaluation, will also be necessary. The need for community-centric research questions and the role of community-partner approaches is clear. Integrating community perspectives to develop interventions is an important component of childhood obesity prevention efforts. To a large extent, the literature provides little guidance on communication strategies related to food marketing for obesity prevention in communities of color, and specifically Black communities. This lack of evidence and the complexity of implementing a comprehensive approach to childhood obesity prevention that includes the use of marketing and media communication channels create challenges in moving communities from awareness to action (Swinburn, Gill, & Kumanyika, 2005). Generating endogenous, community-driven solutions that are congruent with community perspectives and preferences is essential for addressing the current inequities in food marketing.

The path to solutions is a two-way street. The current food marketing environment is a result of controllable strategies that businesses develop, therefore proactive corporate interventions, such as increased targeting of healthful foods and beverages, are also needed. Communities and specifically Black communities must embrace their power to push back on a system that fully recognizes and expects them to participate in co-creation. While a shift in community demand can motivate such changes, companies will need to alter the supply in these communities and ultimately focus on value in terms of community health and choice in relation to food marketing environments.

References

Aaker, J. L., Brumbaugh, A. M., & Grier, S. A. (2000). Nontarget markets and viewer distinctiveness: The impact of target marketing on advertising attitudes. *Journal of Consumer Psychology, 9*(3), 127–140.

American Marketing Association (2007). "AMA Definition of Marketing," Retrieved from September 20, 2012, http://www.marketingpower.com/Community/ARC/Pages/Additional/Definition/default.aspx].

Appiah, O. (2001). Ethnic identification on adolescents' evaluations of advertisements. *Journal of Advertising Research* (Vol. 41, p. 7): Cambridge University Press, UK.

Appiah, O. (2004). Effects of ethnic identification on web browsers' attitudes toward and navigational patterns on race-targeted sites. *Communication Research, 31*(3), 312–337.

Bachman, K. (2010). Multicultural Ad spend fared better in '09. *Mediaweek*. Retrieved from http://www.mediaweek.com/mw/content_display/news/media-agencies-research/e3i888c20be761d1d659a7ad31dc4dc5c0c.

Bagozzi, R. P., Wong, N., Abe, S., & Bergami, M. (2000). Cultural and situational contingencies and the theory of reasoned action: Application to fast food restaurant consumption. *Journal of Consumer Psychology, 9*(2), 97–106.

Birch, L. L. (1999). Development of food preferences. *Annual Review of Nutrition, 19*, 41–62.

Branchik, B. J., & Davis, J. F. (2009). Marketplace activism. *Journal of Macromarketing, 29*(1), 37–57.

Bryant, C. A., Brown, K. R., McDermott, R. J., Forthofer, M. S., Bumpus, E. C., Calkins, S. A., et al. (2007). Community-based prevention marketing: Organizing a community for health behavior intervention. *Health Promotion Practice, 8*(2), 154–163.

Caprio, S., Daniels, S. R., Drewnowski, A., Kaufman, F. R., Palinkas, L. A., Rosenbloom, A. L., et al. (2008). Influence of race, ethnicity, and culture on childhood obesity: Implications for prevention and treatment. *Diabetes Care, 31*(11), 11.

Chambers, J. (2006). Equal in every way: African Americans, consumption and materialism from reconstruction to the civil rights movement. *Advertising & Society Review, 7*(1).

Cialdini, R. B., Kallgren, C., & Reno, R. (1991). A focus theory of normative conduct – A theoretical refinement and reevaluation of the role of norms in human-behavior. *Advances in Experimental Social Psychology, 24*, 201–234.

Crockett, D., & Wallendorf, M. (2004). The role of normative political ideology in consumer behavior. *The Journal of Consumer Research, 31*(3), 511–528.

Daniels, S. R. (2006). The consequences of childhood overweight and obesity. *The Future of Children, 16*(1), 47–67.

Denegri-Knott, J., Zwick, D., & Schroeder, J. E. (2006). Mapping consumer power: An integrative framework for marketing and consumer research. *European Journal of Marketing, 40*(9/10), 950–971.

Deschenes, S., McLaughlin, M., & Newman, A. (2008). Community organizing and youth advocacy. *New Directions for Youth Development* (117), 1–4.

Dietz, W. H., Bland, M. G., Gortmaker, S. L., Molloy, M., & Schmid, T. L. (2002). Policy tools for the childhood obesity epidemic. *The Journal of Law, Medicine & Ethics, 30*(3 Suppl), 83–87.

Drewnowski, A. (2009). Obesity, diets, and social inequalities. *Nutrition Reviews, 67*(Suppl 1), S36–S39.

Economos, C. D., Brownson, R. C., DeAngelis, M. A., Novelli, P., Foerster, S. B., Foreman, C. T., et al. (2001). What lessons have been learned from other attempts to guide social change? *Nutrition Review, 59*(3 Pt 2), S40–S56. discussion S57–S65.

Escobar-Chaves, S. L., & Anderson, C. A. (2008). Media and risky behaviors. *The Future of Children, 18*(1), 147–180.

Fishbein, M., & Ajzen, I. (1975). *Belief, attitude, intention, and behavior: An introduction to theory and research*. Reading, MA: Addison-Wesley.

Fishbein, M., & Ajzen, I. (1980). *Understanding attitudes and predicting social behavior*. Englewood Cliffs, NJ: Prentice-Hall.

Fitzgibbon, M. L., Stolley, M. R., Schiffer, L. A., Braunschweig, C. L., Gomez, S. L., Van Horn, L., et al. (2011). Hip-Hop to Health Jr. obesity prevention effectiveness trial: Postintervention results. *Obesity (Silver Spring), 19*(5), 994–1003.

Flegal, K. M., Carroll, M. D., Ogden, C. L., & Curtin, L. R. (2010). Prevalence and trends in obesity among US adults, 1999–2008. *JAMA: The Journal of the American Medical Association, 303*(3), 235–241.

Frey, W. (2003). Married with children. *American Demographics, 25*, 17–19.

Gortmaker, S. L., Must, A., Sobol, A. M., Peterson, K., Colditz, G. A., & Dietz, W. H. (1996). Television viewing as a cause of increasing obesity among children in the United States, 1986–1990. *Archives of Pediatrics & Adolescent Medicine, 150*(4), 356–362.

Graneheim, U. H., & Lundman, B. (2004). Qualitative content analysis in nursing research: Concepts, procedures and measures to achieve trustworthiness. *Nurse Education Today, 24*(2), 105–112.

Green, C. L. (1995). Differential responses to retail sales promotion among African-American and Anglo-American consumers. *Journal of Retailing, 71*(1), 83–92. doi:10.1016/0022-4359(95)90014-4.

Grier, S. (2009). *African American & Hispanic youth vulnerability to target marketing: Implications for understanding the effects of digital marketing*. Berkeley, CA: NPLAN Marketing to Children Learning Community.

Grier, S. A., & Brumbaugh, A. M. (1999). Noticing cultural differences: Ad meanings created by target and non-target markets. *Journal of Advertising, 28*(1), 79.

Grier, S. A., & Kumanyika, S. K. (2008). The context for choice: Health implications of targeted food and beverage marketing to African Americans. *American Journal of Public Health, 98*(9), 1616–1629.

Grier, S. A., & Kumanyika, S. (2010). Targeted marketing and public health. *Annual Review of Public Health, 31*, 349–369.

Grier, S. A., Mensinger, J. L., Huang, S. H., Kumanyika, S. K., & Stettler, N. (2007). Fast food marketing and children's fast food consumption: Exploring parental influences in an ethnically diverse sample. *Journal of Public Policy & Marketing, 26*(2), 221–235.

Grocery Manufacturer. (1971). Negro consumers are waiting. In G. Joyce & N. Govoni (Eds.), *The Black consumer: Dimensions of behavior and strategy* (pp. 49–59). New York: Random House.

Harris, J. L., Schwartz, M. B., & Brownell, K. D. (2010). *Fast food F.A.C.T.S.: Evaluating fast food nutrition and marketing to youth*. Rudd Center for Food Policy & Obesity.

Harrison, K. (2006). Fast and sweet: Nutritional attributes of television food advertisements with and without Black characters. *Howard Journal of Communications, 17*(4), 16.

Hillier, A., Cole, B. L., Smith, T. E., Yancey, A. K., Williams, J. D., Grier, S. A., et al. (2009). Clustering of unhealthy outdoor advertisements around child-serving institutions: A comparison of three cities. *Health Place, 15*(4), 935–945.

Hoek, J., & Gendall, P. (2006). Advertising and obesity: A behavioral perspective. *Journal of Health Communication, 11*, 409–423.

Hornik, R. (2002). Exposure: Theory and evidence about all the ways it matters. *Social Marketing Quarterly, 8*(3), 31–36.

Humphreys, J. M. (2006). *The multicultural economy 2006* (Vol. 66, No. 3). Atlanta: The University of Georgia, Selig Center for Economic Growth.

Humphries, J. M. (2012). The multicultural economy 2012 report. University of Georgia Selig Center for Economic Growth.

Institute of Medicine. (2005). *Food marketing to children and youth: Threat or opportunity?* Retrieved from Citation http://www.nap.edu/catalog/11514.html.

James, D. (2004). Factors influencing food choices, dietary intake, and nutrition-related attitudes among African Americans: Application of a culturally sensitive model. *Ethnicity and Health, 9*(4), 349–367.

Khan, M. A. (2009). Coca-Cola debuts ambitious mobile push for Sprite. Retrieved May 18, 2009, from http://www.dmnews.com/Coca-Cola-debuts-ambitious-mobile-push-for-Sprite/article/95828/.

Kotler, P. (1997). *Marketing management: Analysis, planning, implementation and control* (9th ed.). Englewood Cliffs, NJ: Prentice-Hall, Inc.

Kumanyika, S. K., Whitt-Glover, M. C., Gary, T. L., Prewitt, T. E., Odoms-Young, A. M., Banks-Wallace, J., et al. (2007). Expanding the obesity research paradigm to reach African American communities. *Preventing Chronic Disease, 4*(4), A112.

Lamont, M., & Molnár, V. (2001). How Blacks use consumption to shape their collective identity. *Journal of Consumer Culture, 1*(1), 31–45.

Lindau, S. T., Makelarski, J. A., Chin, M. H., Desautels, S., Johnson, D., Johnson, W. E., Jr., et al. (2011). Building community-engaged health research and discovery infrastructure on the South Side of Chicago: Science in service to community priorities. *Preventive Medicine, 52*(3–4), 200–207.

MacArthur, K., & Neff, J. (2004). Sprite shifts gears in quest for street cred. *Advertising Age, 75*(4).

Madsen, K. A., Weedn, A. E., & Crawford, P. B. (2010). Disparities in peaks, plateaus, and declines in prevalence of high BMI among adolescents. *Pediatrics, 126*(3), 434–442.

McDonalds Corporation. What is McDonald's 365 Black? Retrieved May 29, 2009, from http://www.365black.com/365black/whatis.jsp.

Mello, M. M., Studdert, D. M., & Brennan, T. A. (2006). Obesity–The new frontier of public health law. *The New England Journal of Medicine, 354*(24), 2601–2610.

Millstein, R., & Sallis, J. (2011). Youth advocacy for obesity prevention: The next wave of social change for health. *Translational Behavioral Medicine*, 1–9.

Montgomery, K. C., & Chester, J. (2009). Interactive food and beverage marketing: Targeting adolescents in the digital age. *The Journal of adolescent health: official publication of the Society for Adolescent Medicine, 45*(3), S18–S29.

Mullins, P. R. (1999). Race and the Genteel consumer: Class and African-American consumption, 1850–1930. *Historical Archaeology, 33*(1), 22–38.

Nielsen. (2008). Advertising spending targeting African-Americans exceeds $2.3B a year. *Marketing Charts*. Retrieved from http://www.marketingcharts.com/television/advertising-spending-targeting-african-americans-exceeds-23b-a-year-3243/.

Ogden, C. L., Carroll, M. D., Curtin, L. R., Lamb, M. M., & Flegal, K. M. (2010). Prevalence of high body mass index in US children and adolescents, 2007–2008. *JAMA: The Journal of the American Medical Association, 303*(3), 242–249.

Ogden, C. L., Carroll, M. D., & Flegal, K. M. (2008). High body mass index for age among US children and adolescents, 2003–2006. *JAMA: The Journal of the American Medical Association, 299*(20), 2401–2405.

Powell, L. M., Szczypka, G., & Chaloupka, F. J. (2007). Adolescent exposure to food advertising on television. *American Journal of Preventive Medicine, 33*(4 Suppl), S251–S256.

Radio Advertising Bureau. Pepsi pumps the vibe on the streets Retrieved March 8th, 2010, from http://www.rab.com/public/ncs/pdfs/pepsi.pdf.

Rideout, V. J., Foehr, U. G., & Roberts, D. F. (2010). *Generation M2: Media in the lives of 8–18 year olds*. Menlo Park, CA: Kaiser Family Foundation.

Robinson, R. G. (2005). Community development model for public health applications: Overview of a model to eliminate population disparities. *Health Promotion Practice, 6*(3), 338–346.

Robinson, T. N., Killen, J. D., Kraemer, H. C., Wilson, D. M., Matheson, D. M., Haskell, W. L., et al. (2003). Dance and reducing television viewing to prevent weight gain in African-American girls: The Stanford GEMS pilot study. *Ethnicity & Disease, 13*(1 Suppl 1), S65–S77.

Schwarte, L., Samuels, S. E., Capitman, J., Ruwe, M., Boyle, M., & Flores, G. (2010). The Central California Regional Obesity Prevention Program: Changing nutrition and physical activity environments in California's heartland. *American Journal of Public Health, 100*(11), 2124–2128.

Story, M., Neumark-Sztainer, D., & French, S. (2002). Individual and environmental influences on adolescent eating behaviors. *Journal of the American Dietetic Association, 102*(3 Suppl), S40–S51.

Swinburn, B., Gill, T., & Kumanyika, S. (2005). Obesity prevention: A proposed framework for translating evidence into action. *Obesity Reviews, 6*(1), 23–33.

Tharp, M. (2001). *Marketing and consumer identity in multicultural America*. Thousand Oakes: Sage.

The Nielsen Company. (2009). Nielsen projects older, multi-cultural, and low-income consumers driving consumer packaged goods trends in 2020. Retrieved May 12, 2009.

Wandersman, A. (2003). Community science: Bridging the gap between science and practice with community-centered models. *American Journal of Community Psychology, 31*(3–4), 227–242.

Wang, Y., & Beydoun, M. A. (2007). The obesity epidemic in the United States – Gender, age, socioeconomic, racial/ethnic, and geographic characteristics: A systematic review and meta-regression analysis. *Epidemiological Review*, mxm007.

Wang, Y., Beydoun, M. A., Liang, L., Caballero, B., & Kumanyika, S. K. (2008). Will all Americans become overweight or obese? Estimating the progression and cost of the US obesity epidemic. *Obesity, 16*(10), 2323–2330.

Warner, Melanie (2006). "Salads or No, Cheap Burgers Revive McDonald's." in The New York Times. New York.

Weems, R. E. (1998). *Desegregating the Dollar: African American consumerism in the twentieth century*. New York: New York University Press.

Williams, J., Henderson, G., & Harris, A.-M. (2001). Consumer racial profiling: Bigotry goes to market. *The New Crisis, 108*, 22–24.

Yancey, A. K., Cole, B. L., Brown, R., Williams, J. D., Hillier, A., Kline, R. S., et al. (2009). A cross-sectional prevalence study of ethnically targeted and general audience outdoor obesity-related advertising. *The Milbank Quarterly, 87*(1), 155–184.

Yerger, V. B., Daniel, M. R., & Malone, R. E. (2005). Taking it to the streets: Responses of African American young adults to internal tobacco industry documents. *Nicotine & Tobacco Research, 7*(1), 163–172.

Zhou, M. (1997). Growing up American: The challenge confronting immigrant children and children of immigrants. *Annual Review of Sociology, 23*, 63–95.

Zmuda, N. (2009). How coke is targeting black consumers. Retrieved March 8, 2010, from http://adage.com/bigtent/post?article_id=137716.

Chapter 17
Latino Youth and Obesity: Communication/ Media Influence on Marketing

Amelie G. Ramirez, Kipling Gallion, and Rebecca Adeigbe

Introduction

Increasing childhood obesity rates have led many public health researchers, child health advocates, and policymakers to carefully examine the strategies food and beverage companies use to target children (Larson & Story, 2008; Nestle, 2006).

Latino youth are quickly becoming an attractive and accessible target for food and beverage companies because of their heavy use and early adoption of digital media (Leopold, 2011; Lopez & Livingston, 2010). The link between increased media use and childhood obesity is apparent among the Latino population (Gordon-Larsen, 2003; Rosas et al., 2011; Thompson, 2010).

Marketers are aware of Latino youths' consumption of media and they are beginning to incorporate strategies that integrate the family roles, beliefs, and behaviors of the Latino culture (Cable Television Advertising Bureau, 2008; Valdes, 2005).

In this chapter, we will first introduce the Latino youth demographics, followed by the marketing strategies food and beverage companies use to target US youth and the pervasiveness of media among youth. We will then discuss Latino youths' media consumption behaviors and the marketing strategies used to target Latino youth and its influence on Latino youth obesity.

A.G. Ramirez • K. Gallion (✉) • R. Adeigbe
The Institute for Health Promotion Research,
The University of Texas Health Science Center at San Antonio, USA
e-mail: gallion@uthscsa.edu

J.D. Williams et al. (eds.), *Advances in Communication Research to Reduce Childhood Obesity*, DOI 10.1007/978-1-4614-5511-0_17,

Latino Youth Demographics

Latino youth are part of the largest, youngest, and fastest rising US minority group. The Latino population grew by 14.2 million people between 2000 and 2010—accounting for more than half the entire US population growth in that span. Latinos now account for nearly 51 million people or 16% of the US population (Humes, Jones, & Ramirez, 2011).

For the first time in 20 years, the rate of Latino births has surpassed the rate of immigration. This increase can be attributed to the significant increase in the Mexican-American population. Mexican Americans accounted for 11.4 million of the 14.2 million Latino growth (Taylor et al., 2011). This shift is changing the cultural makeup of the Latino population. Latinos younger than age 18 make up 22% of all US youth, up from 17.1% a decade ago. One in five school children and one in four newborns are Latino (Taylor, Kochhar, Livingston, Lopez, & Morin, 2009). In less than 15 years, Latinos will make up more than 30% of all US youth (Fry & Passel, 2009).

Latino youth are not homogenous and can be either native born or foreign born. Native-born Latinos are individuals born in the USA with two US born parents or born in the USA where at least one parent is foreign born (Suro & Passel, 2003). Foreign-born Latinos, those born outside the USA, can be naturalized US citizens, legal immigrants, or undocumented immigrants. Within the past decade, the number of native-born Latinos has increased by nearly 44% (13.1 million) while the foreign-born population grew by only 28% (9.2 million) (Dockterman, 2009; Passel, Cohn, & Lopez, 2011; Passel & Taylor, 2010).

The native born and foreign born status of Latino youth have an effect on their overall acculturation; that is, their adoption of American culture behaviors. Acculturation among the Latino population is not instantaneous but is dependent on many cultural, behavioral, and socioeconomic factors (Cable Television Advertising Bureau, 2008). Acculturation for Latino youth is highly dependent on not only their native or foreign born status, but also by their household, community, and school environment (Cable Television Advertising Bureau). The pace of acculturation for Latino youth can be slowed if they live in communities and attend schools with larger Latino populations and cultural influences (Cable Television Advertising Bureau). Acculturation among households can vary and native-born Latino youth or those who migrated early tend to be more acculturated and surpass the acculturation level of their parents and grandparents.

The majority of Latino youth are native born (89%) and the generational status, whether first, second, or third, has an impact on the overall acculturation of this population (Lopez & Livingston, 2010; Taylor et al., 2011).

Native-born Latino youth are usually second or third generation (both parents born in the USA) and are considered to be in the "fast-lane" for becoming acculturated (Cable Television Advertising Bureau, 2008; Fry & Passel, 2009). Foreign-born Latinos are considered first generation and least acculturated (Suro & Passel, 2003).

About 69% of first-generation Latino, 73% of second-generation Latino youth, and 52% of third-generation Latino youth live in married-couple families. Nearly

43% of first-generation, 40% of second-generation, and 15% of third-generation Latino youth have parents with less than a high school education. About 26% of second-generation and 16% of third-generation Latino youth live in poverty, while most native-born Latino youth live in a household with an annual income around \$40,000. Compared to 34% of foreign-born Latino youth who live in poverty and other foreign-born Latino youth live in a household with an annual income around \$35,000 (Saenz, 2010).

Almost 80% of second-generation and 95% of third-generation Latino youth are fluent in English while nearly 50% of foreign-born Latino youth are not (Fry & Passel, 2009). It is reported that native-born Latino youth today are encouraged to speak Spanish more so than the older native-born population (51% versus 40%). In addition, fewer than one-third of native-born Latino youth say their parents talk about solely being American, but emphasize their Latino origin and culture (Taylor et al., 2009). In comparison, for foreign-born Latino youth, citizenship and length of time in the USA is more closely associated with identifying themselves as American (only 29% of foreign-born youth refer to themselves as American). Today, foreign-born Latino youth are being encouraged more by their parents to speak Spanish compared to older foreign-born Latinos (84% versus 69%), and, like native-born youth, foreign-born youth are reminded of their Latino origin and culture frequently (Taylor et al.).

Acculturation is a vital issue because it influences many Latino social, economic, and demographic situations and subsequent behavioral and psychosocial factors (e.g., language fluency in both English and Spanish, parental education attainment, and poverty levels). As the Latino youth population continues to grow and they begin to embrace aspects of the American culture and behavior, these youth are becoming a relevant and appealing target for marketers. For example, scientific evidence suggests that, as US acculturation increases, eating, purchasing, and physical activity behaviors change (Gordon-Larsen, 2003). These changes are shown to be associated with increasing obesity rates (Rosas et al., 2011), solidifying the notion that acculturation is likely a contributor to high obesity rates among Latino youth and an influencing factor in marketing strategies applied to Latino youth and their families (Fry & Passel, 2009).

Comorbidities Due to Obesity Among Latino Youth

Currently, 38.2% of Latino children ages 2–19 are overweight or obese, compared with 31.7% of all US children those ages, placing them at higher risk of developing chronic diseases (Leadership for Healthy Communities, 2010). Latinos have an increased risk of several obesity-related comorbidities, such as diabetes, hypertension, cardiovascular disease, dyslipidemia, and certain cancers (CDC, 2007; Haboush, Phebus, Tanata Ashby, Zaikina-Montgomery, & Kindig, 2011; Ogden, Carroll, Curtin, Lamb, & Flegal, 2010).

Other factors contribute to these Latino obesity disparities and comorbidities. Nearly 34% of all Latino children live in poverty and most lack health insurance and a primary care doctor. Low socioeconomic status, lack of primary care, and access to health systems may contribute to Latino children's obesity rates and sedentary lifestyles. Latino youth living in low-income neighborhoods have social and environmental factors that contribute to higher overweight and obesity rates (Fana, 2010; Leadership for Healthy Communities, 2010; Zambrana, 2000).

Latino communities often have approximately one-third as many chain supermarkets as other communities, spawning "food deserts"—areas that lack access to healthy food and increase dependability on fast-food restaurants and corner stores that typically offer nutritionally poor choices. Latinos are more likely not to have affordable access to healthy options in their communities and may pay 40% more than the national average for the healthier option (Mikkelsen & Chehimi, 2007; National Council of La Raza, 2010). Latino youth tend to participate in less physical activity for reasons associated with their built environments. About 41% of Latino parents identify concern for safety as a barrier for allowing youth to be physically active in their neighborhood (compared to 8% of white parents), and only 26% of Latino youth participate in organized physical activity (compared to 47% white youth) (Fana, 2010; Leadership for Healthy Communities, 2010).

Marketing's Impact on Foods and Beverages Consumed by Children and Adolescents

To better understand the impact of marketing on Latino youths food and beverage consumption, it is first important to understand the market's use of evolving technology and the marketing strategies used to target youth. While these strategies impact children and adolescents in general, they particularly impact Latinos because of the numbers they represent in the US youth population and because of their increasing appeal to food and beverage marketers. As you will read later in this chapter, there are similarities between the types of media used by Latino youths and US youths; however, differences arise in the exposure and consumption of food and beverage marketing.

Food and beverage marketing is increasingly recognized as a contributing factor to the rapid growth of overweight and obese children and adolescents. As the food industry increases its marketing budgets to target younger audiences, childhood and adolescent obesity rates continue to rise (Roberto, 2010). The food industry's marketing toward children and adolescents is proving problematic because the quality of food and beverage items advertised are usually of poor nutritional value and are typically the antithesis of dietary recommendations (Nicklas, 2011). For decades, the food and beverage industry has used third-party agreements—licensing with children's TV characters, sponsorships, etc.—to expand their advertisement efforts to appeal to child and parent audiences. Using popular characters essentially makes certain foods and beverages "branded" and well recognized by children and adolescents (Harris, Schwartz, & Brownell, 2010; Roberto, 2010).

Due to increased exposure and use of media and electronic devices among youth, energy expenditure is on the decline and energy consumption is increasing, both key contributors to the US childhood obesity epidemic. Physical activity levels tend to decrease due to use of media (TVs, video games, or computers) (Utter, 2003). Also, youth who watch TV, play video games, or use a computer for an extended period of time tend to consume more energy. Several studies have reported the associations between media use and increased food intake and unhealthy eating patterns. Some researchers have made the association between this energy consumption behavior and the constant bombardment of unhealthy food and beverage advertisements (Utter).

Marketing and Technology Advancements

The food industry's use of cross promotion is becoming increasingly popular as technology advancements allow for more sharing across multimedia channels. Industries now have the option of marketing not only through the traditional TV market and product packaging but also now can advertise in "digital markets" like the Internet, social media, and sharing networks (Harris, Schwartz, & Brownell, 2010). These digital markets include the Internet, mobile applications, mobile ads, Internet banner ads, and pop-up ads which all direct consumers to websites which have multiple interactive features that offer blog spots, upload areas, games, and promotions (Harris, Schwartz, Brownell, Sarada, et al., 2010). The interactive nature of this technology has provided market researchers the opportunity to continually monitor and study the trends of youth while gathering feedback on media usage and brand preference, which is used to expand their marketing strategy (Montgomery, 2009).

New technologies allow digital marketing to increasingly engage consumers, who interact with and adopt products into their daily lives (Montgomery, 2009). These strategies, even though the consumer may be unaware, are cultivating a personal connection to the consumer product while also appealing to a generation of consumers who use digital marketing and media as a form of self-expression (Montgomery).

Digital Marketing Strategies

The fast-food and beverage industry is most prominently recognized for utilizing these new digital marketing campaigns to promote their products among youth of all ages (Harris, Schwartz, Brownell, Sarada, et al., 2010). Reports have examined the strategies used by some of the top food and beverage companies to cast light on this growing market. The use of web banners, websites, advergames, mobile ads, mobile applications, and social media networks has become an important avenue for marketers to target youth (Harris, Schwartz, Brownell, Sarada, et al.; Korzenny & Korzenny, 2011; Montgomery, 2009).

Food and beverage marketers have been able to target children by incorporating targeted messages and features into their websites or by creating child-specific sites. (Alvy & Calvert, 2008; Harris, Schwartz, Brownell, Sarada, et al., 2010; Weber, 2006). Child-specific websites provide children with an opportunity to play games, create avatars, virtual worlds, chat with friends, and allow for cross-promotional advertisements with popular children movies and television shows. These websites also offer, videos, polls, quizzes, and allow for users to enter promotional codes found on their products to win prizes or receive coupons (Harris, Schwartz, Brownell, Sarada, et al.). A few, fast-food-related child websites now offer educational counting and alphabet games to appeal to the parents which allows for product branding and brand loyalty for both the child and parent. In one study, looking at digital marketing exposure for children on these child-targeted websites, children between the ages of 2 and 11 were noted for visiting most often and spent on average 12 minutes a month interacting with the more popular fast-food restaurant websites (Harris, Schwartz, Brownell, Sarada, et al.).

Unlike child-specific websites, food and beverage companies are marketing to youth by incorporating features most used by this age group (Harris, Schwartz, Brownell, Sarada, et al., 2010; Weber, 2006). The main websites for these companies offer many of the elaborate features seen on child sites (music, videos, games, quizzes, polls, etc.). However, youth and adult targeted websites offer more humor, celebrity, entertainment, and viral content. They also offer users the ability to view and upload photos and download product content such as wallpapers and ringtones. These websites tend to also offer more information on nutritional facts, specific menu items, and special promotions (Harris, Schwartz, Brownell, Sarada, et al.). These teen and adult targeted websites tend to have more viewership than the child focused websites. In one analysis, these main websites, targeted mainly to youth, averaged around 430,000 visitors every month and users viewed the site on average, 8 minutes (Harris, Schwartz, Brownell, Sarada, et al.).

Marketers are using banner ads on websites to advertise to young consumers (Harris, Schwartz, Brownell, Sarada, et al., 2010). Web banners allow marketers to target specific groups and in specific languages based on the third-party websites they advertise on. These ads are becoming increasingly popular and use elaborate flash animations, bright colors, and large text to draw consumers to their advertisements. This strategy is commonly used to target youth between the ages of 2 and 17 (Harris, Schwartz, Brownell, Sarada, et al.). Food and beverage companies promote their brand and items on websites visited most by youth. For example, one in four banner ads found on youth websites are for fast-food restaurants and almost all food and beverage ads direct the viewer back to their websites (Harris, Schwartz, Brownell, Sarada, et al.; Weber, 2006). Youth ads focus more on menu items that convey a single, straightforward message, such as taste and size and highlight special offers, value, and new and improved products. For child-targeted banner ads, they generally do not focus on a food or beverage product, but use characters and promotional tie ins (i.e., upcoming movies and toys) to attract the viewer to their child-targeted website (Harris, Schwartz, Brownell, Sarada, et al.).

Marketers are also capitalizing on social media networks, primarily Facebook. Most fast-food marketers are using Facebook to capture the feedback of the consumers by placing polls on their page to seek product feedback, determine customer preference, and introduce new items (Harris, Schwartz, Brownell, Sarada, et al., 2010). Marketers post on average five times a week on Facebook and change their profile pictures to promote menu items and special offers. About 29% of teenage youth currently have at least one fast-food, food, or beverage company as a friend on Facebook (Harris, Schwartz, Brownell, Sarada, et al.). These marketers use these types of relationships on social networking sites to entice consumers to register their cell phone numbers and emails to receive exclusive deals and join fan clubs to receive points and coupons (Harris, Schwartz, Brownell, Sarada, et al.).

Posting videos on video-sharing websites, primarily YouTube, is another strategy used by the food industry to promote its products. An analysis of 50 fast-food restaurant videos in 2009 found that each video averaged 5,000 views and the majority of videos highlighted a specific menu item, depicted the item being consumed and used humor or cool, hip scenarios (Harris, Schwartz, Brownell, Sarada, et al., 2010). For example, fast-food restaurant, Taco Bell, created a Hip-Hop inspired music video to tie in with its TV commercial advertisements to promote its less than a dollar menu and received over 100,000 views in 2009. The Sonic Drive-In restaurant is also known to post humorous videos usually depicting individuals engaging conversation centered around their menu items. Other fast-food restaurants such as Domino's post videos of their companies' chief executive officers their goal to make customers happy with their products and encourage viewers to upload in pictures, videos, and feedback on the website so they can improve their product and keep customers happy (Harris, Schwartz, Brownell, Sarada, et al.).

Marketers are increasingly placing banner ads on mobile phone applications and mobile device websites. Fast-food restaurants, in particular, place their mobile ads on entertainment, sport, video sharing, and music websites. These ads are usually less graphic but offer easy promotional messages or coupons and, when clicked, direct consumers to their website (Harris, Schwartz, Brownell, Sarada, et al., 2010). Mobile ads mainly target the youth audience (11–18) and usually target fewer than 10 websites. Marketers use mobile applications to target youth because youth are the main downloaders of these applications (Harris, Schwartz, Brownell, Sarada, et al.). Most applications are distributed for fast-food restaurants and offer users the ability to find locations, play games, order online, and offered special deals and nutrition information. For example, in 2010, eight fast-food restaurants offered mobile applications, 12- to 17-year-olds accounted for 90% of the Taco Bell locator application, 41% downloaded the Burger King Now application, and 16% downloaded Pizza Hut's application (Harris, Schwartz, Brownell, Sarada, et al.).

Marketing strategies are always evolving to keep up with technology and the demand of youth and the level of exposure to these strategies is dependent on youth's consumption of media. The accessibility youth have to digital media has been beneficial to marketers. Marketers have found a way to create a "360 strategy," to target youth and the way they interact with technology (Montgomery, 2009). This strategy allows marketers to reach viewers wherever they are. The digital media platform becomes more enticing to food and beverage companies as advertising agencies, market research firms, and new media creations develop new ways to interact with youth (Montgomery).

Media's Pervasiveness in Children's Lives

Traditional TV advertising and product labeling and packaging remain food and beverage marketers' most effective means of targeting children ages 12 and younger, but with the increased use of digital media within this age group, exposure to advertisement is on the rise (Bell, 2009; Harris, Schwartz, Brownell, 2010; Roberto, 2010).

For example, children younger than 6 do not just have TV, they are increasingly using digital media (videos, DVDs, video games, computers, etc.). About 68% of children younger than 2 use screen media (i.e., TV, video games, computers) an average of 2 hours a day, and 43% watch TV daily. Further, 36% of children younger than 6 have a TV in their bedroom, and 10% have their own game console. Nearly half of all 4-6-year-olds have played video games and 70% have used a computer. Of those 70% who have used a computer, more than half have used the computer alone, 40% can load a CD-ROM, and 37% can turn on a computer by themselves (Rideout, Vanderwater, & Wartella, 2003).

Media's Pervasiveness in Adolescents' Lives

Regarding adolescents ages 12–17, food and beverage companies are increasingly using digital media and marketing to take advantage of this new growing subset of consumers by appealing to their attraction to social networks, video games, online gaming, and mobile communication devices (Montgomery, 2009).

Today's adolescents typically own three or four electronic gadgets, such as mobile communication devices (cell phones), mp3 music players, computers, video game consoles, and portable gaming devices (Lenhart, Purcell, Smith, & Zickuhr, 2010). Four of five adolescents have an iPod or mp3 music player, four of five have a video gaming console, and nearly half of all teens have a portable gaming device. About seven of every 10 adolescents have access to a computer (Lenhart, Purcell, et al.).

Computers remain teens' most popular way to access the Internet. Over the past decade, Internet use among adolescents has increased to 93%. Nearly two-thirds of adolescent Internet users go online every day, with about half of those going online several times a day (Lenhart, Purcell, et al., 2010).

About 75% of US adolescents have a cell phone. Phone ownership is constant regardless of race/ethnicity, but socioeconomic status plays a more significant role in ownership levels among adolescents (Lenhart, Purcell, et al., 2010). Cell phones are used most often for text messaging—about 88% of adolescent cell phone users use text messaging—and talking. The use of cell phones to access the Internet also is becoming increasingly popular among this age group. About 27% of adolescents access the Internet with their phones; those with a household income less than $30,000 use their phones to access the Internet more frequently (41%) (Lenhart, Ling, Campbell, & Purcell, 2010).

The use of social networks continues to climb among adolescents and young adults; this cohort accounts for the largest group to use and create accounts with these services. Currently, about 75% of online adolescents use a social network site. Adolescents are using these sites to network and communicate with friends on a daily basis, half are using these sites to send group messages and two-thirds use these sites to send messages. The most popular function, with 86% of teen use, is the ability to post comments and pictures on friends' pages and walls (Lenhart, Ling, et al., 2010). The frequency of use has also increased dramatically, and more than half of adolescents are logging on more than once a day and 22% of teenagers report logging into their favorite social media site more than 10 times a day (Media, 2009).

The ability to create, modify, and share content online, such as photos, videos, artwork, and stories, is one of digital media's most appealing factors for this age group. About 12 million teens used the Internet to watch a video online in 2009. Adolescents view more than 3 hours of online videos a month. Adolescents, 12–17 years old, account for about 15% of online video watching, while children aged 2–11 account for 8%. Nearly 40% of adolescents share content online via venues such as YouTube and BlogSpot. Increasingly, however, most adolescents are using social networking to share videos and blog (Lenhart, Purcell, et al., 2010).

Factors Related to Latino Youth, Media Usage and Obesity

So, how do Latino youth digital media consumption compare to US youth? Although some may say access to electronic devices hinge on socioeconomic status and race/ethnicity, more and more evidence indicates that access is increasingly available to most minority adolescents, including Latino youth (Montgomery, 2009). Minority youth (ages 8–18) on average consume 13 hours of media content a day, and Latino youth consumed four times as much media than their white counterparts in the past decade (Leopold, 2011).

Latinos Youth and TV Use

On average, Latino youth report watching 28 hours of TV a week, about 2 hours more than the 26 hours a week among all US youth (Cosio, Spadoni, Caplinger, Solana, & Marquez, 2005). Latino youth TV consumption increases with the availability of TV viewing technologies (i.e., TiVo, instant demand, online viewing, and mobile viewing), and Latino youth are more likely to have a TV in their bedroom compared to white youth (77% versus 64%) and eat their meals while in front a TV (67% versus 58%) (Leopold, 2011; Sisson, 2011).

Some reports indicate Latino youth, as early as 24 months of age born to English-speaking Latino mothers, watch significantly more TV than children of non-English speaking Latino mothers (Thompson, 2010). On average, a child of an English-speaking Latino mother will watch around 2 hours of TV a day, compared to an hour-and-a-half for Spanish-only speaking mothers. As Latino children get older, the amount of time spent watching TV increases. A 2- or 3-year-old Latino child with a Spanish-speaking mother will watch less than 2 hours, while a Latino child with an English-speaking mother watches more than 3 hours. This supports the notion that, as Latino families become more acculturated, TV and media usage increases (Thompson).

Just under half (48%) of foreign-born Latino youths report watching TV primarily in Spanish, and this number drops to 9% among native second-generation Latino youth, and 2% among third-generation Latino youth (Taylor et al., 2009). About 26% of foreign-born Latino youth report watching TV equally in both languages and 15% among native born. As acculturation increases among Latino youth, 26% of foreign-born youth report watching TV primarily in English, second generation youth jumps to 70% and by the third generation, 91% of Latino youths report watching TV primarily in English (Taylor et al.).

Latino Youth and Mobile Devices

Latino youth are also avid users of mobile communications (e.g., cell phones) cellular phones, making them a "significant sub-market" for food and beverage marketers (Montgomery, 2009). The US Latino youth subscriber rate is as many as three times that of the overall US youth market. Latino youth ages 12–17 represent 2.5 million subscribers; by age 15, wireless subscription rates increase to 64%, and by age 17, 78% of Latino youth have a cellular phone (Tornoe, 2008).

Half of Latino youth say they text message daily and nearly half say they talk to friends daily. Latino youth on average send and receive 112 text message, slightly less than African American youth (117) and very similar to white youth (111). The average phone calls made per day for Latino youth are 17 more than both African American (13) and white youth (7) (Lenhart, Ling, et al., 2010). Latino youth do not typically use landlines or traditional email as a form of communication (Lopez & Livingston, 2010).

Use of mobile communications by Latino youth varies based on foreign or native status, the level of English fluency, and acculturation. Eight of every 10 native-born Latino youth use a cell phone, more so than foreign-born youth. About 65% of native-born Latino youth text on a daily basis compared to 26% of foreign-born youth. While 68% of English-dominant and half of bilingual young Latinos use text messaging daily for communication, only 19% of Spanish-dominant young Latinos do the same. A reason for the differences between native and foreign born mobile phone use can be attributed to the fact that native-born youth are more likely to own a mobile phone compared to foreign-born youth (84% versus 70%) (Lopez & Livingston, 2010).

Latino Youth Internet and Social Media Use

Internet usage among Latino youth continues to rise. About 95% of Latino youth currently go online, more than all other ethnic groups. And unlike other groups, Latinos primarily access the Internet via mobile devices. Internet use among Latinos has grown fastest among households with incomes of less than $30,000, a 17% increase from 2006 (71%), compared to 2% for $30,000–$49,000 income households (79%), and no change in Latino households with incomes more than $50,000 (85%) (Livingson, Parker, & Fox, 2009; Livingston, 2011; Watkins, 2010).

Latino youth are also the leading users of social networking. More than 85% of young Latinos report having a social networking page, and about 25% of Latino youth say they use social networking sites daily to talk and network with friends. Latino females are more likely than Latino males to use social networking sites for communication (27% versus 19%). In contrast, Latino females are less likely than males to communicate face to face outside of school, work or with friends (15% versus 26%) (Gray, 2008; Lopez & Livingston, 2010).

Key Research Results on Latino Youth Target Marketing, Media Influence and Obesity

As media consumption increases among US youth, even more so in Latino youth, research has found that each additional hour of TV viewing, above the recommended amounts, increases the risk of obesity by 2%. The use of other forms of media, such as electronic games, increases the risk of obesity nearly twofold for every additional hour spent daily. One study found that the odds of being overweight were almost five times greater for youth ages 10–15 who watched 5 hours of TV per day compared to those who watch 2 hours or less (Stettler, 2004). Thus, effects of media exposure are more pronounced among the most frequent viewers, such as Latino youth (Dietz & Gortmaker, 1985; Stettler, 2004).

Levels of media exposure are important to understand because repeated exposure can increase a marketing message's significance to the consumer, suggest behaviors, and affect the diffusion of the message. "Multi-faceted campaigns that entice this market with interactive content, contests, and ringtones are doing more than simply moving product: They're making themselves vital to young Latinos' everyday experiences, and establishing strong footholds for their brands in the process (Portada, 2007)."

Understanding Latino Youth Marketing

Marketers understand that, to effectively appeal to the Latino population, they must have an understanding of the deep-rooted Latino culture and family dynamic (Cable Television Advertising Bureau, 2008). Marketing in Spanish or infusing Spanish words in English messages may be effective in gaining the attention and awareness of the Latino consumer, but may not be enough to entice the Latino population to buy their product. Past English language marketing campaigns that have been directly translated into Spanish have led to misunderstood, ineffective, and in some cases insulting messaging (Cable Television Advertising Bureau; Carona & McCabe, 2011).

The importance of family among Latinos is powerful and plays a significant part in shaping the roles and behaviors of all family members (Valdes, 2005). The multidisciplinary model used to describe the Latino culture and family dynamic is now being used in marketing strategies for Latinos. This model segments the Latino family into four areas: (1) *Familismo,* which is the foundation of the Latino family and places an emphasis on the well-being of the immediate and extended family; (2) *Machismo,* which describes the man's role as a leader, provider, and protector of the family; (3) *Marianismo,* which defines the woman's role as the mother, spouse, supporter, and care taker for the family; and (4) *Chicoismo*, which defines the child's role as to carry on the family legacy and be grateful, respectful due to their provision of more opportunities than his/her parents (Cable Television Advertising Bureau, 2008; Valdes).

The *familisimo* concept focuses on the importance of family and tends to adopt more of the American values and cultures as families become acculturated; however, this shift is most commonly seen among native born generations and those foreign born who have spent most of their lives in the US. Native-born Latino youth are most commonly seen as acculturating to the America culture, but their parents still hold root to the *familismo* concept (Valdes, 2005). Because *familismo* is long lasting among the Latino culture, advertisers focus their strategies around the family both explicitly and implicitly (Cable Television Advertising Bureau, 2008). For example, fast-food marketers are using culturally tailored digital marketing strategies to appeal to Latino youth and their family. Most Spanish web banner ads promote value/price, new and improved products, and increased quality of food as their selling point and unlike other consumer groups, commercials and videos targeted at Latinos focus more attention to the inclusion of family and large groups to again, address the *familisimo* concept. These ads generally convey a pleasant experience with ordering menu items and stick to more recognized and traditionally favorite items compared to other consumer group ads which highlight new or limited time items (Harris, Schwartz, Brownell, Sarada, et al., 2010). The *Chicoismo* concept plays a pivotal role among the Latino family and has the ability to influence many of the decisions parents make for their Latino youth. For many native-born Latino youth, parents may state that their main reason for immigrating to the USA was to provide their children with opportunities they themselves did not have (Passel &

Taylor, 2010; Valdes). Because of this, many Latino parents will indulge their children to make them happy and to provide them with a piece of the US culture (Korzenny & Korzenny, 2011; Valdes). One research study found that 78% of Latino children and adolescents have an influence on where families go for fast food and Latino parents often take pride in taking their families to fast-food restaurant because it shows a sign of status and financial well-being while satisfying their children's request (Grier, Mensinger, Huang, Kumanyika, & Stettler, 2007; Kraak, 1998; Valdes).

Marketers who understand the importance of *Familisimo* have now begun to target the Latino parent both directly and indirectly through mediums recognized most by adult Latinos (i.e., magazines, newspapers, commercials, and Internet websites and ads) (Carona & McCabe, 2011). More specifically, food marketers are now capitalizing on the *marianismo* concept and targeting the Latina mother, who is seen as the caretakers and decision makers for products bought for their children. Latina mothers are seen as brand loyal and more likely to purchase heritage brands that resonate emotionally; they do not mind paying more for a food or beverage product that the family enjoys and are seen as less price sensitive than the general public (Angrisani, 2005; Cortez, 2009). In addition, Latino parents, particularly Latina mothers, are more inclined to purchase foods and prepare meals their children have become accustomed to or grown up with in the USA. As Ricalo of Panavista, a specialized retail and shopper marketing agency focused on the Latino community states, "Lasagna may not be a meal that was part of their original family custom but, since their kids are experiencing Italian foods here, Hispanic moms want to satisfy their children's food cravings (Angrisani, 2005)." Additionally, Latina mothers are more inclined to purchase items for their children if the advertisement has Latino actors/actresses and shows the mother interacting with the child (Baby Center, 2011; Cable Television Advertising Bureau, 2008; Valdes, 2005). With Latinas becoming one of the fastest-growing groups to go online, marketers are also targeting this group by creating websites, such as General Mills' *Que Rica Vida*, which aims to "gain awareness and trial by positioning General Mills as a trusted source of information for Latina moms who need help navigating life in the United States" and offers Latino recipes and sweepstakes for all their General Mills products (Berkeley Media Studies Group, 2010). This type of strategy is not only effective at attracting the Latina consumer, but is also playing on the vulnerability of less acculturated Latinas and building brand loyalty (Berkeley Media Studies Group; Valdes; Wentz, 2009).

Marketing Products to Latino Youth

Beverage companies are beginning to tap into the Latino market with most companies using different creative strategies. Soda companies such as Coca-Cola have rolled out marketing campaigns such as "Batea La Sed" (Beat the Thirst) in the past to target Latino youth between the ages of 13 and 16 by teaming up with popular Latino baseball players and offering changes to win baseball game tickets and autographed baseballs (Howard & Lefton, 2000). The soda brand Dr. Pepper also rolled out its own campaign to target Latino youth by using a more product familiarity and language approach. The company reported that acculturated Latinos drink 62% more Dr. Pepper than the general market (Wentz, 2005). Dr. Pepper marketers created commercials for their English audience by using blindfolded teenagers who were able to pick out the "unmistakable" taste of Dr. Pepper. To market the Spanish speaking audience, which were thought to be less familiar with their product, commercials showed individuals tasting Dr. Pepper for the first time and showing surprise and delight with the taste. As one Dr. Pepper marketing member, Mr. Ramirez states, "For both audiences, it's about inducing trial. Get the ones who have never tried it and, on the other side, those who haven't had Dr. Pepper in a long time (Wentz)."

Pepsi has also joined the ranks of marketing to Latinos. One of Pepsi's campaigns, "Pepsi Generation," created an ad which took place at a quinceañera, a coming of age party for Latino girls to resonate with not only the young Latino population but Latino parents as well (Herbig & Yelkur, 1997). In the past Pepsi has also joined ranks with popular chip manufacturer, Frito Lay's, to create a joint campaign, "The Power or One," using popular novella (Spanish soap-opera) stars and Latino musicians to cross promote their products on Latino television networks and other campaigns such as the "Movimiento Pepsi" (The Pepsi Movement) featuring the Latina musician Shakira, popular with Latino youth to promote their product on both English and Spanish networks (Charski, 2002; Hill, 2001).

Fast-food companies such as McDonald's create marketing strategies specifically for Latinos as well such as their Latino banner "points of pride" which included a drawing contest for young children and its "Lo Maximo de la Musica Latina" (The Best of Latin Music) campaign in the early 2000s which encouraged aspiring singers to submit audio and video performances for a chance to record a song and star in a music video which would air the Univision television network during Hispanic Heritage Month (Bertagnoli, 2000). Less common fast-food chains among Latinos, such as Wendy's, created a marketing campaign a few years ago using a more general message "En Wendy's comer es mas rico" (At Wendy's eating is more enjoyable/tastes better) for its TV and radio ads (Macarthur & Wentz, 2002).

As its been reported, 10% of Latino households' food purchases are spent on sweets (Pacyniak, 2003). Mars Snack Food US, the manufacturers of the candy brand M&M's, expanded its larger "Inner M" campaign a few years ago to target Latinos. Their campaign focused on featuring Latino stars whose personalities reflect M&M's fun nature (Lee, 2008). The campaign launch featured young Latino stars Wilmer Valderrama and Cristina Saralegui animated to resemble M&M's characters. The commercials intended purpose was to drive consumers to their website where they could create their own personal characters and create buzz for the product (Lee).

Marketing Latino-Specific Products

Not only are food and beverage companies creating marketing campaigns to target Latino youth, but they are also capitalizing on their opportunities to create and market products which resonate with both the native- and foreign-born Latino youth and parent. For example, Hostess, the manufacturer of packaged snacks has created a line of products to target Latinos, their product line named "Las Delicias de Hostess" incorporates flavors and textures appealing and familiar to the Latino population and offers bilingual packaging (Angrisani, 2005). General Mill's has also targeted the Latino youth population by distributing "La Lechera Flakes" a popular cereal in Mexico into the USA and by also creating their "Para Su Familia" (For your Family) line of cereal brands which resemble similar cereals such as Frosted Corn Flakes, Fruits and Cinnamon Corn Stars, and other Latin food favorites such as Arroz Con Leche (rice pudding) and Flan (caramel custards) (Bernstein, 2001; Wentz, 2006). General Mills' campaign to promote their products used a bilingual approach and aired commercials on Latino television networks (Reyes, 2000). The Gamesa Cookie, a cookie brand favored by consumers in Mexico, attempted to revitalize its product for the "new" Latino consumer by creating a product for teenagers the Blaster poprock cookies and appealing to mothers by introducing a "mother's make-over" sweepstake both which launched commercial advertising in both English and Spanish (Reyes, 2002).

The soda brand Coca-Cola has also launched an apple-flavored "Manzana Mia" soda, Coca-Cola Lime, Diet Coke with Lime, and increased marketing for its Fanta soda products to by launching Spanish-language commercials appearing during primetime Spanish language shows (Fuhrman, 2005). Other more Latino recognized brands such as Goya and Tampico continue to introduce products to retain their Latino consumer market. Goya's "refrescos" (refreshments) continue to roll out new soda flavors such as tamarind, coconut, mango, and pear and Tampico has launched a line of flavored waters with a Latin twist such as pina-colada, grapefruit, and tangerine (Chura, 2001; Zegler, 2006). Similar efforts have been replicated by beverage manufactures such as Campbell with their V8 Splash and Minute Maid with their Mifruta Flavored drinks which infuse natural fruit flavors popular with Latinos (Fuhrman; Reyes, 2003; Zegler).

Latino Youth Marketing's Role in the High Risk of Overweight Among Latino Children

With the recent growth of the young Latino population and the newly rising number of Latino youth watching, interacting with and using multimedia devices, the effects of food and beverage companies' marketing strategies to Latino youth and how Latino youth respond by changing their behaviors (or not) are not well known (Bell, 2009).

As Latino youth become more acculturated, consumption of fast food increases, eating habits change, and physical activity levels decrease (Sisson, 2011). According to one report, Latino youth, age 16-17, visit fast-food restaurants on average 21 times per month and are more likely to eat inside a restaurant than other consumers their age (28% versus 23%). Latino youth (16–17) are also twice as likely to choose a burger or pizza to satisfy their hunger and are more often to choose these foods as a lunch meal (Hume, 2007). This combined with Latino youth's increasing time spent using media devices are likely the contributors to the high obesity rates among Latino youth. The more frequently Latino youth are exposed to product advertisements while using media, the more they become interested in a product and take a more positive view of the product. Marketers are investing much of their resources into understanding the Latino youth population in order to better appeal to this group (Grier, 2010).

The Latino youth population is vulnerable to targeted food marketing partly due to their increased media use. Marketers understand that, when appealing to this young Latino market, high levels of media exposure, promotion of unhealthy foods, audience receptiveness, and the importance of ethnic identifiers are critical factors (Grier, 2010). Tailored messages from marketers that include Latino models with similar language styles, music, symbols, values, and beliefs are said to attract Latino youth most. Latino youth are more likely to pay attention, have a positive association and purchase a product if it is presented by someone who resembles them (Grier). In addition, foreign-born Latino youth are more likely to purchase brands that are advertised specifically toward them in Spanish and are more likely to use brands recommended and used by family and friends. Latino youth for a variety of reasons rely on advertisement as a source of information and are said to be more interested in advertisements than other ethnic groups. Latinos are considered trendsetters, willing to try new products and brand loyal (however, with acculturation brand loyalty tends to diminish) (Grier).

Marketers are beginning to capitalize on the media behaviors and wants of this Latino youth consumer group. As mentioned, most Latino youth are bilingual. Native-born Latino youth watch both English and Spanish TV, while foreign-born Latino youth are most likely to watch more Spanish TV. Latino youth who watch Spanish TV see at least one fast-food ad every two days, while preschool-aged children who watch Spanish language TV see one ad a day (Harris, Schwartz, Brownell, Sarada, et al., 2010). Latino youth are more likely to see a fast-food ad on Spanish TV than English TV (Bell, 2009).

Current and Anticipated Growth of the Latino Youth Spending Market

Latino youth being the youngest and fastest growing population in the USA and heavy consumers of digital media, marketers have started and will continue to target this group. Latino youths' brand loyalty, trendsetting ways, and diversified taste in entertainment have given food and beverage marketers an en route to foster brand loyalty and taste preference that they hope will continue into adulthood.

Current reports indicate Latino youth (ages 6–14) have an annual income of $1,191 (lunch money, allowance, gifts, earned income, etc.) and have a strong purchasing power influence not only on their peers but also their family and overall society (Grier, 2010). Young Latinos' rising consumerism will influence how all manufacturers, including food and beverage companies, develop and promote their products. Latino youth spending patterns will affect the success or failure of many products and services tailored for youth (Humphreys, 2009). It is projected that the Latino youth overall spending market will grow 32% in the next 15 years. Although the monetary consumption patterns of digital, media, and technologically advanced communication products seen among Latino youth is currently similar to that of all US youth, increased spending power and discretionary income may allow young Latinos to begin to spend more in this arena (Cosio et al., 2005).

Future Directions

Food and beverage marketing strategies that target Latino youth are dynamic and will continue to be reframed as the Latino youth cultural and sociodemographic profile changes (Gray, 2008; Grier, 2010; Montgomery, 2009; Roberts, 2000). Marketers are catching on to this booming Latino consumer segment and Latino youth are at the forefront for receiving their messages.

Marketers continue to conduct consumer research to target Latino youth. In most cases the research methods and results are proprietary with methods and outcomes reported in summary form. This lack of research information makes it difficult for third parties to anticipate marketers' next moves or to mount counter-marketing campaigns. Regardless, Latino youth are being exposed to a wide assortment of messages on many fronts that encourage youth consume unhealthy foods and beverages. If public health authorities do not invest more in understanding how to protect vulnerable populations like Latino youth from the predatory marketing practices of food and beverage corporations, our society will face another health crisis of increased chronic illness among Latino youth in America.

References

Alvy, L. M., & Calvert, S. L. (2008). Food marketing on popular children's web sites: A content analysis. *Journal of the American Dietetic Association, 108*(4), 710–713. doi:10.1016/j.jada.2008.01.006.

Angrisani, C. (2005). Latino loyalty. [Article]. *SN: Supermarket News, 53*(40), 34–39.

Baby Center. (2011). Baby Center releases acculturation study about Latina Moms. Retrieved from http://marketingtolatinosentertainment.blogspot.com/2011/02/babycenter-releases-acculturation-study.html.

Bell, R. A. (2009). Frequency and types of foods advertised on saturday morning and weekday afternoon English- and Spanish-Language American television programs. *Journal of Nutrition Education and Behavior, 41*(6), 406–413.

Berkeley Media Studies Group. (2010). The soda and fast-food industries target their marketing towards mothers of color. Retrieved from http://www.bmsg.org/pdfs/bmsg_cchc_target_marketing_ethnic_moms.pdf.

Bernstein, R. (2001). Food for thought. *American Demographics: Marketing Tools Sourcebook 2002*, D47–D49.

Bertagnoli, L. (2000). Marketing, Latin style. *Restaurants & Institutions, 110*(31), 53–60.

Cable Television Advertising Bureau. (2008). *Hispanic marketers' guide to cable: Hispanic cable facts & cultural cues*. New York, NY: Cabletelevision Advertising Bureau.

Carona, R., & McCabe, M. B. (2011). Acculturation in marketing to Latinos in the US. [Article]. *Journal of Business & Economics Research, 9*(9), 67–70.

CDC. (2007). The surgeon general's call to action to prevent and decrease overweight and obesity. Retrieved from http://www.cdc.gov/nccdphp/dnpa/obesity/childhood/defining.htm.

Charski, M. (2002). Pepsi gets a Latino 'Movement'. [Article]. *Adweek Southeast Edition, 23*(31), 2.

Chura, H. (2001). Sweet spot. (cover story). [Article]. *Advertising Age, 72*(46), 1–16.

Cortez, A. (2009). Meet today's Latino Shoppers. [Article]. *Natural Foods Merchandiser, 30*(9), 64.

Cosio, J. T., Spadoni, V., Caplinger, M., Solana, J., & Marquez, C. (2005). The U.S. HispanTelligence (Firm). (2005). The U.S. Hispanic economy in transition: Facts, figures, and trends. Santa Barbara, Calif: HispanTelligence.

Dietz, W. H., & Gortmaker, S. L. (1985). Do we fatten our children at the television set? Obesity and television viewing in children and adolescents. *Pediatrics, 75*(5), 807–812.

Dockterman, D. (2009). Population change by race and ethnicity: 2000 and 2009. Retrieved from http://pewhispanic.org/files/factsheets/hispanics2009/Table%202.pdf.

Fana, C. (2010). *Hispanic obesity: An American crisis*. Washington, DC: The National Hispanic Caucus of State Legislators.

Fry, R., & Passel, J. S. (2009). *Latino children: A majority are U.S.-born offspring of immigrants*. Washington, DC: Pew Research Center.

Fuhrman, E. (2005). Latin flair in bebidas for the masses. [Article]. *Beverage Industry, 96*(8), 44–47.

Gordon-Larsen, P. (2003). Acculturation and overweight-related behaviors among Hispanic immigrants to the US: The National Longitudinal Study of Adolescent Health. *Social Science and Medicine. Part E, Medical Psychology, 57*(11), 2023.

Gray, L. (2008). The Intelligence Group Releases 2008 Latino Lifestyle Study(R): Subscription-based study offers marketers a comprehensive look at the fast-growing young Latino market. Retrieved from http://www.prweb.com/releases/latino/intelligence/prweb897294.htm.

Grier, S. (2010). Targeted marketing and public health. *Annual Review of Public Health, 31*, 349.

Grier, S., Mensinger, J., Huang, S. H., Kumanyika, S. K., & Stettler, N. (2007). Fast-food marketing and children's fast-food consumption: Exploring parents' influences in an ethnically diverse sample. [Article]. *Journal of Public Policy & Marketing, 26*(2), 221–235. doi:10.1509/jppm.26.2.221.

Haboush, A., Phebus, T., Tanata Ashby, D., Zaikina-Montgomery, H., & Kindig, K. (2011). Still unhealthy 2009: Building community research to identify risk factors and health outcomes in childhood obesity. *Journal of Community Health, 36*(1), 111–120. doi:10.1007/s10900-010-9288–8.

Harris, J. L., Schwartz, M. B., & Brownell, K. D. (2010a). Marketing foods to children and adolescents: Licensed characters and other promotions on packaged foods in the supermarket. *Public Health Nutrition, 13*(3), 409–417. doi:doi:10.1017/S1368980009991339.

Harris, J. L., Schwartz, M. B., Brownell, K. D., Sarada, V., Ustjanauskas, A., Javadizadeh, J., et al. (2010b). *Rudd Center for Food Policy and Obesity. (2010)*. Fast food facts: Evaluating fast food nutrition and marketing to youth. New Haven, Ct: Yale University Rudd Center for Food Policy & Obesity. Retrieved from http://www.fastfoodmarketing.org/media/FastFoodFACTS_Report.pdf.

Herbig, P., & Yelkur, R. (1997). Differences between Hispanc and Anglo consumer expectations. *Managment Decision, 35*(2), 125–132.

Hill, J. D. (2001). Dieste Pairs Pepsi, Doritos as 'The Power of One.'. [Article]. *Adweek Southwest Edition, 23*(24), 6.

Howard, T., & Lefton, T. (2000). Latino Players Star in 'Familia de Beisbol'. [Article]. *Brandweek, 41*(31), 49.

Hume, S. (2007). Los adolescentes. *Restaurants & Institutions, 117*(12), 71.

Humes, K., Jones, N. A., Ramirez, R. R., & Census Bureau U. S. (2011). *Overview of race and Hispanic origin, 2010*. Washington, D.C.: U.S. Dept. of Commerce, Economics and Statistics Administration, U.S. Census Bureau. Retrieved from http://www.census.gov/prod/cen2010/briefs/c2010br-02.pdf.

Humphreys, J. M. (2009). The multicultural economy 2009. *Georgia Business and Economic Conditions, 69*(3).

Korzenny, F., & Korzenny, B. A. (2011). *Hispanic marketing: Connecting with the New Latino consumer*. Amsterdam: Butterworth-Heinemann.

Kraak, V. (1998). The influence of commercialism on the food purchasing behavior of children and teenage youth. *Family Economics and Nutrition Review, 11*(3), 15.

Larson, N., & Story, M. (2008). Food and Beverage Marketing to Children and Adolescents: What Changse are Needed to Promote Healthy Eating Habits? Retrieved from http://www.healthyeatingresearch.org/images/stories/her_research_briefs/her%20food%20mktg_brief110308final.pdf.

Leadership for Healthy Communities. (2010). Overweight and obesity among Latino youths.

Lee, E. (2008). M&M's get sweet on Hispanics. [Article]. *njbiz, 21*(34), 17.

Lenhart, A., Purcell, K., Smith, A., & Zickuhr, K. (2010). *Social media & mobile Internet use among teens and young adults*. Washington, DC: Pew Research Center.

Lenhart, A., Ling, R., Campbell, S., & Purcell, K. (2010). *Teens and mobile phones*. Washington, DC: Pew Research Center.

Leopold, W. (2011). Study: Stark differences in media use between minority and white Youth. Retrieved from http://www.northwestern.edu/newscenter/stories/2011/06/media-usa-youth-wartella.html.

Livingson, G., Parker, K., & Fox, S. (2009). *Latinos online, 2006–2008: Narrowing the gap*. Washington, DC: Pew Research Center.

Livingston, G. (2011). *Latinos and digital technology, 2010*. Washington, DC: Pew Research Center.

Lopez, M. H., & Livingston, G. (2010). *How young Latinos communicate with friends in the digital age*. Washington, DC: Pew Research Center.

Macarthur, K., & Wentz, L. (2002). Beefing up Hispanic. [Article]. *Advertising Age, 73*(9), 28.

Media, C. S. (2009). Is technology networking changing childhood? A national poll. Retrieved from http://www.commonsensemedia.org/sites/default/files/CSM_teen_social_media_080609_FINAL.pdf.

Mikkelsen, L., & Chehimi, S. (2007). *The links between the neigborhood food environment and childhood nutrition*. Oakland, CA: Prevention Institute.

Montgomery, K. C. (2009). Interactive food and beverage marketing: Targeting adolescents in the digital age. *The Journal of Adolescent Health: Official Publication of the Society for Adolescent Medicine, 45*(3 Suppl), S18–S29.

National Council of La Raza. (2010). Profiles of Latino health: A closer look At Latino child nutrition. Retrieved from http://www.nclr.org/images/uploads/publications/250_profiles_latino_healthFINAL.pdf.

Nestle, M. (2006). Food marketing and childhood obesity—A matter of policy. *The New England Journal of Medicine, 354*(24), 2527–2529. doi:doi:10.1056/NEJMp068014.

Nicklas, T. A. (2011). Impact of commercials on food preferences of low-income, minority preschoolers. *Journal of Nutrition Education and Behavior, 43*(1), 35–41.

Ogden, C. L., Carroll, M. D., Curtin, L. R., Lamb, M. M., & Flegal, K. M. (2010). Prevalence of high body mass index in US children and adolescents, 2007–2008. *JAMA: The Journal of the American Medical Association, 303*(3), 242–249. doi:10.1001/jama.2009.2012.

Pacyniak, B. (2003). Taking a full-circle approach to Hispanic marketing. [Article]. *Candy Industry, 168*(7), 14.
Passel, J. S., Cohn, D. V., & Lopez, M. H. (2011). *Census 2010: 50 million Latinos Hispanics account for more than half of nation's growth in past decade*. Washington, DC: Pew Hispanic Center.
Passel, J. S., & Taylor, P. (2010). *Unauthorized immigrants and their U.S.-born children*. Washington, DC: Pew Research Center.
Portada. (2007). Tracking the expansion of Hispanic print and digital media. Retrieved from http://www.portada-online.com/html/services/Portada26.pdf.
Reyes, S. (2000). Betty Crocker Says Hola! in TV Ads, Twin Entries, Seeking 'Authenticity'. [Article]. *Brandweek, 41*(21), 4.
Reyes, S. (2002). Gamesa, mother's cookies seek to satisfy kids' snacktime cravings. [Article]. *Brandweek, 43*(26), 9.
Reyes, S. (2003). Campbell looks to make a splash with Hispanics. [Article]. *Brandweek, 44*(45), 9.
Rideout, V., Vanderwater, E., & Wartella, E. (2003). Zero to six: Electronic media in the lives of infants, toddles and preschoolers. Retrieved from http://www.kff.org/entmedia/loader.cfm?url=/commonspot/security/getfile.cfm&PageID=22754.
Roberto, C. A. (2010). Influence of licensed characters on children's taste and snack preferences. *Pediatrics, 126*(1), 88.
Roberts, D. F. (2000). Media and youth: Access, exposure, and privatization. *The Journal of Adolescent Health: Official Publication of the Society for Adolescent Medicine, 27*(2 Suppl), 8–14.
Rosas, L., Guendelman, S., Harley, K., Fernald, L., Neufeld, L., Mejia, F., et al. (2011). Factors associated with overweight and obesity among children of Mexican descent: Results of a Binational Study. *Journal of Immigrant and Minority Health, 13*(1), 169–180. doi:10.1007/s10903-010-9332-x.
Saenz, R. (2010). *Latinos in the United States 2010*. Washington, DC: Population Refrence Bureau.
Sisson, S. B. (2011). TVs in the bedrooms of children: Does it impact health and behavior? *Preventive Medicine, 52*(2), 104–108.
Stettler, N. (2004). Electronic games and environmental factors associated with childhood obesity in Switzerland. *Obesity Research, 12*(6), 896.
Suro, R., & Passel, J. (2003). *The rise of the second generation: Changing patterns in Hispanic population growth*. Washington, DC: Pew Research Center.
Taylor, P., Kochhar, R., Livingston, G., Lopez, M. H., & Morin, R. (2009). *Between two worlds: How young Latinos come of age in America*. Washington, DC: Pew Hispanic Center.
Taylor, P., Lopez, M. H., Livingston, G., Passel, J., Parrado, E., & Kochhar, R. (2011). *The Mexican-American boom: Births overtake immigration*. Washington, DC: Pew Research Center.
Thompson, D. A. (2010). Television viewing by young Hispanic children: Evidence of heterogeneity. *Archives of Pediatrics & Adolescent Medicine, 164*(2), 174–179.
Tornoe, J. G. (2008, October 22). Hispanic teens set for strong mobile growth. Retrieved from http://juantornoe.blogs.com/hispanictrending/2008/10/hispanic-teen-1.html.
Utter, J. (2003). Couch potatoes or french fries: Are sedentary behaviors associated with body mass index, physical activity, and dietary behaviors among adolescents? *Journal of the American Dietetic Association, 103*(10), 1298–1305.
Valdes, M. I. (2005). Hispanics: In-Culture Marketing to Reach the Fastest-Growing Youth Culture in the U.S. Palo Alto, CA: Isabel Valdes Consulting. Retrieved from http://www.isabelvaldes.com/articles/QRCAViewsFall05.pdf.
Watkins, S. C. (2010). Understanding the mobile lives of black and Latino youth. Retrieved from http://www.theyoungandthedigital.com/mobile/understanding-the-mobile-lives-of-black-and-latino-youth/.
Weber, K. (2006). Internet food marketing strategies aimed at children and adolescents: A content analysis of food and beverage brand Web Sites. *Journal of the American Dietetic Association, 106*(9), 1463.

Wentz, L. (2005). Getting Hispanics to be a pepper, too. [Article]. *Advertising Age, 76*(25), 27.

Wentz, L. (2006). General Mills cooks up magazine for Hispanics. [Article]. *Advertising Age, 77*(32), 25.

Wentz, L. (2009). Study: Latinas are Technically Savvy, Brand-Loyal 'Cheif Household Officers'. Retrieved from http://adage.com/article/hispanic-marketing/latinas-technically-savvy-chief-household-officers/136162/.

Zambrana, R. E. (2000). Latino child health: Need for inclusion in the US national discourse. *American Journal of Public Health and the Nation's Health, 90*(12), 1827.

Zegler, J. (2006). Loving Latinos. [Article]. *Beverage Industry, 97*(9), 52–54.

Chapter 18
Targeted Marketing of Junk Food to Ethnic Minority Youth: Fighting Back with Legal Advocacy and Community Engagement

Karen Kramer, Liz Schwarte, Mariah Lafleur, and Jerome D. Williams

Introduction

The youth obesity epidemic is well known and documented. Far less attention, however, has been given to the "tragic realit[y]" that childhood obesity is "most severe and rising fastest in low-income populations and communities of color, which have the fewest resources to intervene or cope with the consequences."[1] Since many ethnic minority youth are also low income, these youth are the hardest hit by the epidemic. For example, 27.5% of Mexican-American and 18.6% of African-American[2] boys ages 6–11 are obese compared to 15.5% of non-Hispanic White boys of the same age. Among 6–11-year-old girls, the statistics are 19.7% for Mexican Americans, 24% for African Americans and 14.4% for non-Hispanic Whites. Similar discrepancies exist among children ages 2–5 and 12–19.[3]

---

[1] Sallis, J. F., Story, M., & Orleans, C. T. (2007). A research perspective on findings from bridging the gap. *American Journal of Preventive Medicine, 33*(4S), 169–171, at 169.

[2] The terms African American and Black are used interchangeably in this chapter to refer to descendants of Africa and the African Diaspora.

[3] Grier, S. (2009). *African American & Hispanic youth vulnerability to target marketing: Implications for understanding the effects of digital marketing*. Berkeley, CA: Berkeley Media

K. Kramer, J.D. (✉)
ChangeLab Solutions
e-mail: kkramer@changelabsolutions.org

L. Schwarte, M.P.H.

M. Lafleur, M.P.H.
Samuels & Associates

J.D. Williams, Ph.D.
Department of Management and Global Business,
Rutgers Business School-Newark and New Brunswick,
1 Washington Park Room 1040, Newark, NJ 07102, USA
e-mail: jeromew@business.rutgers.edu

J.D. Williams et al. (eds.), *Advances in Communication Research to Reduce Childhood Obesity*, DOI 10.1007/978-1-4614-5511-0_18,

Given that ethnic minority youth are "ground zero" of the obesity epidemic, the issue of targeted marketing[4] of junk food to this subpopulation takes on particular importance. Yet while the marketing of junk food to youth in general is the subject of much research and exploration, little has been done with respect to the targeted marketing of junk food to ethnic minority youth in particular. Efforts to study and limit junk food advertising to youth in general will of course benefit ethnic minority youth as well. It is appropriate, however, to consider whether there are ways in which legal and community engagement strategies can be harnessed on behalf of ethnic minority youth in particular.

This chapter first summarizes the existing data on the targeted marketing of junk food to ethnic minority youth, and the reasons such advertising may have a particularly potent effect on this group. Second, it examines whether federal civil rights or state consumer rights laws provide a potential basis for challenging the targeted marketing of junk food to ethnic minority youth. Third, it discusses the importance and efficacy of using community engagement to address the targeted marketing of unhealthy food and beverages to ethnic minority youth, whether as a complement to legal action or as a stand-alone approach.

Existing Data on the Targeted Marketing of Junk Food to Ethnic Minority Youth

Existing data regarding the targeted marketing of junk food to minority youth is scarce. Sonya Grier, one of the few academics who have written about the issue, recently observed that "with all this concern about food marketing to children, there

Studies Group, at 12, Appendix, Table 1. Available at http://www.nplanonline.org/system/files/Targeted_marketing_to_Hisp_and_AA_youth.pdf. *See also* Berkeley Media Studies Group ("BMSG"). (2006). *Fighting junk food marketing to kids: A toolkit for advocates*. Berkeley, CA: BMSG, at 10 (noting that while only 28.2% of White children ages 6–19 are overweight or at risk for overweight, statistics grow to 35.4% for Black children and 39.9% for Mexican-American children); Williams, J. D., Achterberg, C., & Sylvester, G. P. (1993). Target marketing of food products to ethnic minority youth. *Annals of the New York Academy of Sciences, 699*, 107–114, at 107–08. To date, the research relating to ethnic minority youth, obesity, and junk food advertising concerns African-American and Hispanic youth; no data on Asian or Native American youth has been uncovered. For the sake of simplicity, however, this memo will use the term "ethnic minority youth" to refer to African-American and Hispanic youth. The term Hispanic refers to region, not race, and describes any person whose origins are Mexican, Puerto Rican, Cuban, Central or South American, or of some other Hispanic origin.

[4] Targeted marketing "refers to a general strategy through which a firm identifies consumers sharing similar characteristics (e.g., social economics status, gender, age ethnicity, sexual orientation, or a combination) and strives to reach them using those characteristics." Johnson, G., & Grier, S. (2011). Targeting without alienating: Multicultural advertising and the subtleties of targeted advertising. *International Journal of Advertising, 30*(2), 233–258, at 235.

should be a heavy emphasis on looking more carefully at food marketing to ethnic minority youth and you don't see that."[5]

When Jerome Williams wrote an article on targeted food marketing to minority youth in 1993, he "could not identify any studies that dealt specifically with the effects of food advertising on obesity in ethnic minority children."[6] As of 2010, there are still no published studies that specifically link marketing efforts to obesity outcomes with a sample of African-American or Hispanic youth. Researchers, however, are beginning to explore this issue.[7] The Federal Trade Commission is also starting to collect, for the first time, data on food and beverage marketing directed toward ethnic youth, which should be released in early 2012. In contrast to the dearth of academic research and government data, there is a "burgeoning commercial market research industry that studies ethnic minority youth" but the results are of course proprietary.[8] Existing available data does indicate, however, that ethnic minorities, as a group, are subject to a disproportionately large amount of junk food advertising on television, billboards, and other traditional media, relative to the general public,[9] as a result of both targeted marketing to ethnic minorities and higher exposure to television.[10] Indeed, studies consistently show that the "most frequently

---

[5] Grier, S. (2010, June 1). The health impact of targeted marketing: An interview with Sonya Grier. *Corporations and Health Watch*. Available at http://www.corporationsandhealth.org/news/117/59/The-Health-Impact-of-Targeted-Marketing-An-Interview-with-Sonya-Grier. Last visited Jan 13, 2012.

[6] Williams, J., et al. *supra* note 3, at 110.

[7] The African American Collaborative Obesity Research Network (AACORN) has a five year RWJ-funded project underway which will include this issue. More information is available at http://www.aacorn.org/AbouTest-1394.html. Last visited Jan 17, 2012.

[8] Grier, S. *African American & Hispanic youth vulnerability*, *supra* note 3, at 5. In fact, given that ethnic minority youth are the fastest growing segments of the child/adolescent population, food marketers are focusing on this market. *See* Food Marketing to Children Workgroup. "Comment to FTC re: Food marketing to children and adolescents study; Project No. P094511." (2009), at 4. Available at http://www.ftc.gov/os/comments/foodmktgkids-2/543668-00007.pdf. Last visited Jan 13, 2012.

[9] Grier, S., & Kumanyika, S. (2008). The context for choice: Health implications of targeted food and beverage marketing to African Americans. *American Journal of Public Health, 98*(9), 1616–1629. (Systematic review of studies indicated that African Americans are consistently exposed to food promotion and distribution patterns with relatively greater potential adverse health effects than are Whites). In one study, ads with Black characters were "more likely to promote convenience and fast foods, to depict snacking vs. meals, and were less likely to include adults, overweight characters or food in line with dietary recommendations." Grier, S. *African American & Hispanic youth vulnerability*, *supra* note 3, at 2. Studies also show that TV shows aimed at African-American audiences tend to feature more junk food commercials than general audience shows. *Id.*

[10] Harris, J. L., Schwartz, M. B., Brownell, K. D., Sarda, V., Ustjanauskas, A., Javadizadeh, J. et al. (2010). *Fast food F.A.C.T.S.: Evaluating fast food nutrition and marketing to youth*. New Haven, CT: Yale Rudd Center for Food Policy and Obesity. Available at http://www.fastfoodmarketing.org/media/FastFoodFACTS_Report.pdf; Grier, S., & Lassiter, V. (2012). Understanding community perspectives: A step towards achieving food marketing equity. In J. D. Williams, K. E. Pasch, & C. A. Collins (Eds.), *Advances in communication research to reduce childhood obesity* (Chap. 16 at 345–349). New York, NY: Springer.

promoted and most accessible products to African Americans, relative to White Americans, [are] high-calorie and low-nutrition foods and beverages."[11] The same holds true for Hispanics.[12] The data also shows that African-American children, in particular, have 60% more exposure to food-related TV advertising (particularly fast-food advertising) than White children because of targeted marketing (far more junk food commercials appear on prime time shows with large African-American audiences than those with more general audiences)[13] and higher television viewing rates.[14] And since 2003, "advertising to African-American children of items such as cookies and fast food has risen substantially in comparison to White children."[15]

These trends will likely carry over to new forms of digital and interactive advertising, particularly given that African-American and Hispanic children have higher cell phone use rates than non-Hispanic White children.[16] As an example, marketers can now send (via cell phone) a digital coupon for a fast-food restaurant when the cell phone user is identified as being in the vicinity of that restaurant. Ethnic minority teens are likely to receive a disproportionate number of such coupons not only because of higher cell phone usage but also because fast-food restaurants are more highly concentrated in minority neighborhoods.[17] Another example is the Coca Cola Company's "Sprite Yard" advertising campaign (a cell phone application that allows users to share pictures and chat with friends), which was specifically designed to

---

[11] Grier, S. *African American & Hispanic youth vulnerability*, *supra* note 3, at 2; Berkeley Media Studies Group. (2011). *Food and beverage marketing to children and adolescents: An environment at odds with good health*. Berkeley, CA: BMSG. Available at http://www.bmsg.org/pdfs/BMSG_HER_Food_Marketing_11_Mar_31.pdf.

[12] Agency Information Collection Activities, 75 Fed. Reg. 29,344 (May 25, 2010) (pointing to research indicating that "African-American and Hispanic youth are exposed to more food marketing for less nutritious foods than youth in the general population").

[13] Berkeley Media Studies Group. *Fighting junk food marketing to kids*, *supra* note 3, at 12.

[14] Yancey, A. K., & Kumanyika, S. K. (2007). Bridging the gap: Understanding the structure of social inequities in childhood obesity. *American Journal of Preventative Medicine*, *33*(4S), 172–174, at 172. Both African-American and Hispanic children spend more hours watching television than White children. Story, M., & French, S. (2004) Food advertising and marketing directed at children and adolescents in the U.S. *The International Journal of Behavioral Nutrition and Physical Activity*, *1*, 3.

[15] Berkeley Media Studies Group. *Food and beverage marketing to children and adolescents*, *supra* note 11, at 5–6.

[16] Grier, S., & Kumanyika, S. (2010). Targeted marketing and public health. *Annual Review of Public Health*, *31*, 11.1–11.21, at 11.6.

[17] Regina Austin, *Super Size Me and the Conundrum of Race/Ethnicity, Gender, and Class for the Contemporary Law-Genre Documentary Filmmaker*, 40 Loy. L.A. L. Rev. 687, 704, n. 66 (2007) (citing Block, J. P., Scribner, R. A., & DeSalvo, K. B. (2004). Fast food, race/ethnicity, and income: A geographic analysis. *American Journal of Preventive Medicine*, *27*(3), 211–217, at 214 ("finding that predominately black neighborhoods had 2.4 fast-food restaurants per square mile as compared with 1.5 in white neighborhoods, which meant that 'for an average neighborhood shopping area,' blacks were 'exposed to' six more fast food restaurants than Whites)); Yancey, A., & Kumanyika, S. *Bridging the gap*, *supra* note 14, at 172. Notably, African-American and Hispanic students in urban schools near fast food restaurants are three times as likely to have a higher body mass index. Grier, S. *African American & Hispanic youth vulnerability*, *supra* note 3, at 3.

"interact with [Sprite's] 'mostly African-American youth target audience.'"[18] Indeed, "[m]arketers are recognizing both that ethnic minority youth are leaders in the use of a lot of digital media and also that they are fast becoming the majority of the US population, so marketers are putting a lot of money and effort into marketing [through digital media] to ethnic minority youth."[19]

Not only are ethnic minority youth more exposed to both traditional and newer forms of junk food[20] marketing than their non-Hispanic White counterparts, but researchers also indicate that such advertising may have a more potent impact on this particular segment of the population.[21] First, African-American and Hispanic youth may be particularly responsive to targeted marketing. Surveys show that "minority youth are more interested in, and positive towards, media and marketing than non-Hispanic Whites." [22] Ethnic minority youth also "respond more favorably to ethnically targeted marketing than majority youth."[23] This may be because an ad that features ethnic cues (such as African-American or Hispanic celebrities or cultural symbols) may resonate particularly strongly with ethnic minority children—who are drawn to an ad that feels designed for them and suggests a sensitivity to their ethnic group. In contrast, a marketing campaign aimed at non-Hispanic White children, who have not experienced racial discrimination and routinely see ads featuring White cultural symbols and role models, would probably not strike as powerful a chord.[24] Indeed, "minority youth may use consumption to combat social stigma and economic marginalization."[25]

Second, while all children must establish a personal identity, targeted advertising may be particularly effective with minority youth because they are also in the process of developing a racial or ethnic identity. Advertisers typically seek to have their product associated with certain images. Minority youth confronting racial or ethnic identity issues may be particularly responsive to product images that are specifically targeted to their ethnic group. "[A]dolescent self-consciousness makes them more

---

[18] Grier, S., & Kumanyika, S. *Targeted marketing and public health*, *supra* note 16, at 11.14.

[19] Grier, S. "An interview with Sonya Grier," *supra* note 5; Berkeley Media Studies Group. *Food and beverage marketing to children and adolescents*, *supra* note 11, at 6.

[20] For purposes of this chapter, the term "junk food" shall refer to calorie-dense, nutrient-poor food products.

[21] Grier, S., & Lassiter, V., *supra* n. 10 at 348–49.

[22] Grier, S. *African American & Hispanic youth vulnerability*, *supra* note 3, at 3.

[23] *Id. See also* Petty, R. D., Harris, A. G., Broaddus, T., & William, B.M. *Regulating target marketing and other race-based advertising practices. Michigan Journal of Race & Law*, *8*, 335, 349 (2003) ("A 1997 study shows that Black Americans who have a strong cultural identity vividly remember [advertising with ethnic cues] and evaluate it more favorably than advertising without ethnic cues.").

[24] Research indicates that a "favorable target market effect" (i.e. a positive response to a targeted ad) has been mostly found among consumers belonging to a numeric or ethnic minority group. Johnson, G., & Grier, S. Targeting without alienating, *supra* note 4, at 235.

[25] Grier, S. *African American & Hispanic youth vulnerability*, *supra* note 3, at 4.

accepting of image advertising and frequently promoted brands, [thus] we might expect ethnically targeted marketing to play an enhancing role in ethnic identity development and minority youth response."[26]

Finally, there is a substantial amount of research regarding advertising to children generally, including marketing of food and beverages. The available evidence indicates that junk food advertising targeted toward youth generally is ubiquitous, effective, and leads to increased consumption of unhealthy foods and higher levels of obesity.[27]

In sum, more research on targeted marketing of junk food to ethnic minority youth is clearly needed. It can be inferred, however, from existing research regarding targeted junk food advertising to (1) ethnic minorities, and (2) youth, that ethnic minority youth are likely the most heavily targeted segment of the population. Further, while food marketing to children generally is known to be effective, it is likely to be even more potent with respect to ethnic minority children. Ethnic minority children also suffer, by far, the highest rates of obesity. While the causes of this disparity are complex, the targeted marketing of junk food to ethnic minority youth likely plays some contributing role.[28]

Fighting Back with Legal Advocacy

Targeted marketing to specific demographic groups is accepted as a fundamental principle of sound marketing strategy and is routinely employed. Thus, there is nothing unlawful about targeted marketing per se. No one would question the marketing of arthritis remedies to seniors, for example. Assume, however, a campaign to intensively target youth of a particular ethnic minority for the sale of an unhealthy food strongly linked to obesity and its adverse health effects, despite ample documentation that the targeted children are already suffering disproportionately high obesity relative to non-Hispanic White youth, who are not racially targeted for sales. Such activity raises issues of racial discrimination, ethics, and fundamental fairness.

As our laws currently stand, however, such activity does not fit neatly into any recognized legal claim. First, antidiscrimination laws in this country largely focus on government conduct. In the private sector, there are specific remedies aimed at a few subsectors, such as employment and housing (including remedies against

---

[26] *Id.*

[27] *See*, e.g., Berkeley Media Studies Group. *Fighting junk food marketing to kids*, *supra* note 3, at 11–12,14; Grier, S. *African American & Hispanic youth vulnerability*, *supra* note 3, at 2 (noting that increased media usage is associated with increased consumption of junk foods and higher weight); Grier, S., & Kumanyika, S. *Targeted marketing and public health*, *supra* note 16, at 11.9–11.10 (discussing the Institute of Medicine report on influence of food and beverage marketing to children); Story, M., & French, S., *supra* note 14. White House Childhood Obesity Task Force. *Solving the problem of childhood obesity in a generation*. May 2010, at 28. Available at http://www.letsmove.gov/sites/letsmove.gov/files/TaskForce_on_Childhood_Obesity_May2010_FullReport.pdf.

[28] Grier, S., & Kumanyika, S. *Targeted marketing and public health*, *supra* note 16, at 11.09–11.10 (discussing evidentiary link between junk food marketing, consumption, and obesity).

employment or housing advertisements that discriminate on the basis of race or gender).[29] Currently, however, there is no antidiscrimination law that covers advertising in general or food marketing in particular. Further, much of consumer protection law focuses on activities that are false or misleading—rather than fundamentally unfair or offensive to public policy. As discussed below, however, there are federal civil rights and state consumer laws that could potentially be drawn upon to press these issues on the legal front. The viability of such challenges, however, would turn on the willingness of courts to plow new ground.

The Civil Rights Act of 1866

In the 1990s, the cigarette maker, Phillip Morris, racially targeted the sale of mentholated tobacco products to African Americans, despite knowing that such products were significantly more harmful than other tobacco products and were causing higher cancer rates among African Americans.[30] In an effort to challenge this conduct on legal grounds, a class of African-American smokers filed suit against Phillip Morris in the case of *Brown v. Phillip Morris, Inc.* The plaintiffs argued, among other things, that Phillip Morris had violated Sections 1981 and 1982 of the Civil Rights Act of 1866,[31] which prohibits intentional racial discrimination in private contracts and the purchase and selling of personal and real property.[32,33] The Civil Rights Act of 1866 embodied "Congress's intent to enact sweeping legislation implementing the thirteenth amendment to abolish all the remaining badges and vestiges of the slavery system."[34]

While it is well established that a defendant cannot, under Sections 1981 and 1982, refuse to sell a home or product to African Americans based on race (or sell

---

[29] *See,* e.g., Civil Rights Act of 1964, 42 U.S.C. § 2000(e) (2006); Fair Housing Act, 42 U.S.C. §§ 3601 et seq. (2006).

[30] *See Brown v. Phillip Morris Inc.*, 250 F.3d 789, 795 (3rd Cir. 2001).

[31] 42 U.S.C. §§ 1981, 1982 (2006).

[32] *See generally* Petty, R. D., Harris, A.g., Broaddus, T., William, B.M. *Regulating Target Marketing, supra* note 23, at 366–371.

[33] In order to state a claim under section 1981, a plaintiff "must allege facts in support of the following elements: (1) that plaintiff is a member of a racial minority; (2) intent to discriminate on the basis of race by the defendant; and (3) discrimination concerning one or more of the activities enumerated in the statute, which includes the right to make and enforce contracts." *Brown v. Phillip Morris,* 250 F.3d at 797 (internal citation omitted). The requirements under section 1982, although "not identical" are "quite similar." *Id.* Notably, discriminatory advertising that violates civil rights laws does not qualify as protected commercial speech under the First Amendment. *Ragin v. The New York Times Company*, 923 F.2d 995, 1002–1003 (2nd Cir. 1991).

[34] *Brown v. Phillip Morris*, 250 F.3d at 797 (internal citations omitted).

it to them at different prices or terms),[35] the *Brown* case essentially involves the flip side of such scenarios—the "over offering" of a product to African Americans that is known to have adverse impacts. The appellate court refused to embrace such a claim, finding that it failed to readily fit within established precedent. As it explained, the prior cases were distinguishable "because they involved either a naked racially motivated restriction on dealing or a race-based variation of the terms of the contract at issue."[36] It specifically distinguished a case in which African Americans were targeted for sales of defective burial vaults (while Whites was were sold a nondefective version) on the ground that the burial vaults being marketed to African Americans and Whites were not identical, whereas in *Brown*, the exact same menthol products were available and sold to both racial groups at the same prices.[37] Clams of "discriminatory advertising," the court concluded, are simply not cognizable under Sections 1981 and 1982.[38]

Importantly, however, *Brown* represents only one decision, and it was decided by a split 2–1 panel of three judges. The third judge, Judge Shadur, issued a forceful dissenting opinion which could lay a foundation for another challenge in a court willing to look beyond the four corners of existing precedent. Judge Shadur argued that the decision improperly focused on the too narrow question of whether there were *unequal products* rather than whether there was intentional *unequal treatment* of different racial groups involved in the commercial transactions at issue.[39] Finding the majority opinion's attempts to distinguish prior cases "hollow," he observed:

> [W]hat I believe is...prohibited by [Sections 1981 and 1982] is using [racially targeted] advertising to deny Blacks the same treatment as Whites–the rights to contract and to purchase under the *same conditions*–by deliberately subjecting Blacks to the far greater impact of the seriously (often fatally) deleterious effects of the advertised product –effects well known to but undisclosed by the tobacco companies.[40]

Indeed if the touchstone of Sections 1981 and 1982 is rooting out intentional discrimination in the market place, then the focus should properly be on the existence of intentional unequal (and in this case, harmful) treatment on the basis of race—regardless of whether this intent is manifested through the refusal to offer a benign product or the "over offering" of a detrimental product. The *Brown* case, of course, presented particularly compelling facts; the targeted product not only caused fatal cancers but this information was concealed. And proving intent to discriminate is often a difficult challenge, absent an admission. In a case with compelling

---

[35] *Jones v. Alfred H. Mayer Co.*, 392 U.S. 409, 413 (1968) (holding that Section 1982 protects African-Americans from private discriminatory refusals to sell them real estate); *Clark v. Universal Builders, Inc.*, 501 F.2d 324, 331 (7th Cir. 1974) (involving practice of selling houses to African-American purchasers on worse terms than offered to non-African Americans).

[36] *Brown v. Phillip Morris*, 250 F.3d at 799–800.

[37] *Id.* at 798 (*citing Roper v. Edwards*, 815 F.2d 1474 (11th Cir. 1987)).

[38] *Id.* at 800.

[39] *Id.* at 807–11 (Shadur, J., dissenting).

[40] *Id.* at 810 n. 4.

plaintiffs and facts, however, the *Brown* dissent could provide a framework for renewing a challenge to racially discriminatory advertising.

Consumer Rights Remedies

Virtually every state has, in one form or another, consumer protection laws that prohibit "deceptive" trade practices, which includes misleading advertisements.[41] There are also business practices, however, that are not false or deceptive but which "state legislatures feel should be prohibited because they unfairly take advantage of consumers."[42] Thus, over half the states' consumer rights laws also prohibit "unfair" acts or practices. As of yet, however, no court has addressed whether racially targeted advertising of harmful products can ever be actionable under "unfair" state consumer rights laws.

Unlike "deception" claims which focus on the attributes of the product itself, "unfair practice" claims often focus on how the consumer is being treated. In roughly half of the states with unfairness laws, courts will find a business practice "unfair" if it (1) offends public policy under statutes, the common law or otherwise, (2) is immoral, unethical, oppressive, or unscrupulous, and/or (3) the practice causes substantial injury to consumers.[43]

Most consumer cases assert deception claims so the law regarding "unfair practices" is much less developed and more unpredictable. Given, however, that unfair practice cases focus on the treatment of the consumer, they do provide an opening to make arguments regarding business practices that are particularly harmful to ethnic minority youth.

As noted above, targeted marketing is a well-accepted practice and thus there is nothing inherently "offensive" or "unethical" about targeted marketing per se. This general proposition, however, does not preclude the possibility that a specific, harmful marketing campaign that exploits a uniquely vulnerable population could constitute an unfair trade practice.

---

[41] National Policy & Legal Analysis Network ("NPLAN"). (2010). *Consumer protection: An overview of state laws and enforcement*. Oakland, CA: NPLAN, at 1. Available at http://www.nplanonline.org/sites/phlpnet.org/files/Consumer_Protection-_An_Overview_of_State_Laws_and_Enforcement_FINAL_20100624.pdf.

[42] Pridgen, M. D. (2009). *Consumer protection and the law*. West, § 3:15.

[43] NPLAN. *Consumer protection, supra* note 41, at 2. How these three criteria are balanced may vary among the states. In Connecticut, for example, "[a]ll three criteria do not need to be satisfied to support a finding of unfairness. A practice may be unfair because of the degree to which it meets one of the criteria or because to a lesser extent it meets all three." *Keller v. Beckenstein*, 979 A.2d 1055, 1065 (Conn. App. Ct. 2009) (internal citation omitted). Also, there is debate over whether the injury to the consumer must be purely economic or can include physical injury as well. Pridgen, M.D., *supra* note 42, § 4.9.

Further, an argument could be made, particularly as the research develops, that ethnic minority youth are a uniquely vulnerable population. First, it is well documented that children in general, and particularly children under 12, are especially vulnerable to marketing campaigns and less able to distinguish advertisements from other types of information. Second, as discussed above, ethnic minority youth may be especially susceptible to marketing, not because of the cognitive limitations that affect all children, but because advertisers can exploit issues relating to historic discrimination against minority groups and the development of ethnic and racial identity among minority children. Third, ethnic minority children are probably the segment of the population with the least political or economic resources to address the consequences of targeted advertising of unsafe products.

The question then arises whether it is unethical or offensive to public policy to deliberately target ethnic minority children for the sale of a product known to increase their risk of obesity, given that ethnic minority children are a uniquely vulnerable population that already suffers disproportionately from obesity. If so, an unfair trade practice could be established under various state laws.

To date, there have not been any attempts to challenge targeted marketing as "unfair" under state consumer protection laws; thus, this type of claim is wholly untested.[44] Notably, however, the absence of precedent is less important in this area of the law than in some others. "Even more than in defining deceptive trade practices, state courts wish to retain their flexibility when it comes to determining the meaning of 'unfair'… The Massachusetts Supreme Court has stated that this process of case by case development permits the court to 'discover and make explicit those unexpressed standards of fair dealing which the conscience of the community may progressively develop.'"[45]

The First Amendment could also present a hurdle for such a claim. While courts have long held that false or misleading advertising falls outside the constitutional protection afforded commercial speech, it is less clear how restrictions on advertising found to violate state consumer protection "unfairness" laws will fare.[46]

---

[44] One case, brought under New York consumer protection laws, argued that McDonald's misleading marketing of fast food as nutritious led to the plaintiffs' obesity-related health problems, but it asserted a "deceptive," not an "unfairness," claim. *See Pelman v. McDonald's Corp.*, 396 F.3d 508, 510 (2nd Cir. 2009). And although the named plaintiffs in that case were primarily African-American youth, that fact was not been made an issue in the case. Rather, the case was brought on behalf of all New York residents. *See* Ashley B. Antler, *Note, The Role of Litigation in Combating Obesity Among Poor Urban Minority Youth: A Critical Analysis of* Pelman v. McDonald's Corp., 15 Cardozo J. L. & Gender 275, 275–76 (2009). In 2010, the court held that the case could not proceed as a class action, *Pelman v. McDonald's Corp.*, 272 F.R.D. 82 (S.D.N.Y. 2010), and in February 2011 the parties filed a voluntary stipulation dismissing the case with prejudice.

[45] Pridgen, M. D., *supra* note 42, § 3:15 (quoting *Commonwealth v. DeCotis*, 316 N.E.2d 748, 754 (Mass. 1974)).

[46] In *Central Hudson Gas & Electric Corp. v. Public Service Commission of New York*, 447 U.S. 557, 566 (1980), the Court articulated a 4-part test to determine whether a ban on advertising for reasons not related to deception was valid under the First Amendment. "First, in order to merit any

Some state attorney general's offices with strong consumer rights units have begun looking to state consumer protection laws to address food marketing abuses. Both "deceptive" and "unfair" consumer laws can be enforced by state attorney general offices, which generally have substantial authority and discretion in this area.[47] So far, such efforts have generally focused on deceptive practices. A resourceful attorney general, however, could, if so desired, attempt to break new ground in this area by invoking the unfair practice laws to challenge a racially targeted marketing campaign of unhealthy food or beverage to ethnic minority youth.[48]

---

constitutional protection, the commercial speech in question 'must at least concern lawful activity and not be misleading.' Second, the government must assert a 'substantial' interest that is, third, 'directly advance[d]' by the restriction at issue, and finally, the restriction itself must not be 'more extensive than is necessary.'" Pridgen, M. D., *supra* note 42, § 12:38 (quoting *Central Hudson*, 447 U.S. at 566). Since then, the Supreme Court has struck down two advertising bans in non-deception cases. In *44 Liquormart v.Rhode Island*, 517 U.S. 484, 516 (1996), the Court overturned a ban on price advertising of alcoholic beverages because the evidence did not sufficiently demonstrate that the ban directly advanced the state's interest in reducing alcohol consumption. In *Lorillard Tobacco Co. v. Reilly*, 533 U.S 525, 556 (2001), the Court overturned a ban on outdoor advertising of tobacco products within 1,000 ft of a school or playground. While the evidence that the ban directly advanced the state's interest was adequate in that case, the state failed to prove that the ban was not "more extensive than necessary." *Id.* at 565. To the extent that the remedy sought for an unfair business practice involves a restraint on commercial speech, defendants may raise the First Amendment as a defense. "These arguments have met with mixed success." Pridgen, M.D., *supra* note 42, § 7:29.

[47] NPLAN. *Consumer protection*, *supra* note 41, at 1–2. In some states, individuals can also sue, acting as a "private" attorney general, but the available remedies may be more limited, and the evidentiary burdens higher. *Id.*

[48] Putting aside for a moment the viability of directly challenging the targeted marketing of junk food to ethnic minority youth in particular, it is worth noting that the available research discussed above could also be used to buttress any legal efforts to attack the targeted marketing of junk food to children generally on grounds that the marketing is either deceptive or unfair under consumer protection laws.

A junk food marketing campaign targeted at children may or may not also include subtargeting to ethnic minority youth (e.g., include African-American or Hispanic characters or other cultural symbols). If it does, then the currently available evidence, while limited, provides a sufficient basis for arguing that the problems associated with the targeted marketing of junk food to youth generally are accentuated in every way for ethnic minority youth. Ethnic minority youth (1) are exposed to even more junk food advertising than other youth, (2) are more vulnerable to targeted marketing for the reasons explained earlier in this chapter, (3) suffer disproportionately high rates of obesity, and (4) have the least political or economic resources to address the consequences of targeted advertising of harmful products.

In short, if the targeted marketing to youth is challenged as "deceptive," the impact of that deception will likely be felt even more acutely among ethnic minority youth. If a marketing campaign is challenged as "unfair," the unfairness is heightened with respect to ethnic minority youth given their unique vulnerability and higher obesity rates. Even if a junk food marketing campaign does not include subtargeting to ethnic minority youth, it can still be argued that ethnic minority children are particularly harmed by such marketing given (1) their increased exposure to advertising, (2) the substantial health disparities, and (3) their lack of political or economic resources.

Fighting Back with Community Engagement

Overview of Community Engagement Approach

A community engagement approach is based on the premise that efforts to achieve public health changes in a community are more likely to be effective and sustainable if the community[49] is directly involved in the effort. This involvement is usually initiated through use of community organizing strategies to raise awareness and understanding of the issue, and ultimately develop support for policy change. A community engagement approach then builds on this support by developing in residents the capacity to act as advocates[50] for change, for example by participating in the political process, relevant administrative procedures, or other lobbying efforts or media campaigns. Importantly, a community engagement approach can be either a stand-alone strategy or employed as a precursor or complement to legal advocacy.

While there is substantial precedent for the community engagement model in the area of environmental justice,[51] recent experience also demonstrates that it is an effective tool in the public health arena as well. A case in point is Healthy Eating Active Communities (HEAC) and the Central California Regional Obesity Prevention Program (CCROPP), which, together, pioneered multisector initiatives focused on obesity prevention in low income, ethnically diverse communities. Community and youth engagement were instrumental to achieving a variety of recent policy and environmental change successes such as removal of soda from school campuses, acceptance of WIC and EBT benefits at farmers markets, parks renovation to ensure access to physical activity opportunities, and the incorporation of health language in general plans.

Similarly, community engagement was influential in a successful campaign to improve physical education in the Los Angeles Unified School District (LAUSD), the second largest school district in the nation, serving more than 675,000 students, 90% of whom are students of color and three-quarters of whom qualify for free/

[49] "Community" is broadly defined to include community members and youth, community-based organizations, advocacy organizations, public institutions, and businesses.

[50] Samuels, S., Schwarte, L., Clayson, Z., & Casey, M. (2009). *Engaging communities in changing nutrition and physical activity environments*. Oakland, CA: Samuels & Associates. Available at http://samuelsandassociates.com/samuels/upload/ourlatest/HEAC_CCROPP_EngagingCommunities.Updated5.pdf.

[51] *See*, e.g., Richard Drury, R. T. (2007). Moving a mountain: The struggle for environmental justice in southeast Los Angeles. In C. Rechtschaffen, & D. Antolini (Eds.), *Creative common law strategies for protecting the environment* (pp. 173–196). Washington, DC: Environmental Law Institute, at 195 (case study suggesting that "hybrid legal-political strategies are often most effective for achieving environmental justice. It is possible to achieve results by combining sound legal strategies with direct community organizing that might not be possible through either approach alone.").

reduced price meals.[52] A 2007 community organizing campaign provided fliers, online videos, news articles, speakers, and other messaging that mobilized the community to become involved in improving physical education for LAUSD students. Advocates relied heavily on evidence-based social science research documenting the value of physical education to educate the community, and they were able to present the information in clear and accessible formats. (This research was also used to educate school board members). All of these efforts were critical to bringing the community on board and forging a diverse and effective alliance between parents, teachers, health advocates, community activists, and lawyers. As a result of this community engagement, complemented by the legal strategy of filing an administrative complaint (and the threat of litigation), the school board adopted an implementation plan to ensure that LAUSD students received a physical education consistent with governing education and civil rights laws.[53]

In short, experience demonstrates that community engagement can be a very effective strategy in health promotion[54, 55] and achieving policy changes that improve access to healthy foods and physical activity in communities for obesity prevention.[56, 57]

Applying Community Engagement Approach to the Targeted Marketing of Junk Food to Ethnic Minority Youth

Using a community engagement approach to address the targeted marketing of junk food to ethnic minority youth will help ensure that the community "owns" the response to the problem and may also provide a hedge against challenges on this controversial issue. The public may be concerned that taking action against the junk

---

[52] Dauter, L., & Fuller, B. (2011). *How diverse schools effect student mobility: Charter, magnet, and newly built institutions in Los Angeles*. Berkeley, CA: Policy Analysis of California Education, at 16, Table 2. Available at http://www.scribd.com/doc/60445122/PACE-LAUSD-STUDY-How-diverse-schools-affect-student-mobility.

[53] Garcia, R., & Fenwick, C. (2009). Social science, equal justice, and public health policy: Lessons from Los Angeles. *Journal of Public Health Policy*, 30: S26–S32.

[54] Yoo, S., Weed, N. E., Lempa, M. L., Mbondo, M., Shada, R. E., Goodman, R. M., et al. (2004). Collaborative community empowerment: An illustration of a six-step process. *Health Promotion Practice*, *5*(3), 256–265.

[55] Fawcett, S. B., Paine-Andrews, A., Francisco, F. T., Schutz, J. A., Richter, K. P., Lewis, R. K., et al., (1995). Using empowerment theory in collaborative partnerships for community health and development. *American Journal of Community Psychology*, *23*(5), 677–697.

[56] Samuels, S. E., Craypo, L., Boyle, M., Crawford, P. B., Yancey, A., & Flores, G. (2010). The California Endowment's Healthy Eating Active Communities (HEAC) program: A midpoint review. *American Journal of Public Health*, *100*(11), 2114–2123.

[57] Schwarte, L., Samuels, S. E., Capitman, J., Ruwe, M., Boyle, M., & Flores, G. (2010). The Central California Regional Obesity Prevention Program: Changing nutrition and physical activity environments in California's heartland. *American Journal of Public Health*, *100*(11), 2124–2128.

food industry could jeopardize donations to the community, employment opportunities in low-income communities, or positive portrayals of minorities in junk food advertising. As was also the case in the areas of tobacco and obesity prevention, restrictions on targeted marketing may be viewed as paternalistic interferences with individual choice. Thus, while community engagement is an important element of public health work generally, in the case of targeted marketing of unhealthy products to ethnic minority youth, it is particularly critical to ensuring that the public is aware of the negative aspects of the issue and supports the healthy choice for communities.[58]

An example of successfully engaging the community around improving the food environment is found in South Los Angeles, where most of the residents are low-income, ethnic minorities, and 72% of the restaurants are fast-food spots, in contrast to the primarily White neighborhood of West L.A., where only 41% of eating establishing serve fast food.[59] In 2009, the Los Angeles City Council agreed to a moratorium on new stand-alone, fast-food restaurants in South Los Angeles.[60] The moratorium was aimed at halting new fast-food development in the area and creating an incentive package to attract healthy food retail offered by the Redevelopment Agency.[61]

The fast-food moratorium was controversial for some of the same reasons that challenging the targeted advertising of junk food to minority ethnic youth would likely be controversial (i.e., jeopardizing donations and employment opportunities in the community, and imposing paternalistic interferences on individual choice). Thus, developing community support was crucial. Those leading the movement around the moratorium were able to involve community residents and youth in the advocacy process through skills-based training, creating community engagement opportunities, and identifying engagement opportunities for local advocates.

For example, using Photovoice, community residents documented the pervasiveness of fast food in their environment, and illustrated their day-to-day experiences, struggles, and successes. These images were then shared with key stakeholders. Some community members and youth also participated in training on public speaking and advocacy and were able to testify publicly in front of their local representatives to share their perspectives and support for the fast-food moratorium. Hearing the voices of and seeing the images taken by actual community residents in a concerted, organized

---

[58] Grier, S. & Lassiter, V., *supra* n. 10 at 354, 356, 362.

[59] MacVean, M. *Planning Commission OKs rules for fast-food eateries in South L.A: Plan to limit stand-alone fast-food restaurants in the area still must be approved by the full City Council*. Los Angeles Times. October 15, 2010.

[60] *Id.*

[61] Aboelata, M. J., & Navarro, A. M. (2010). Emerging issues in improving food and physical activity environments: Strategies for addressing land use, transportation, and safety in 3 California-wide initiatives. *American Journal of Public Health, 100*(11), 2146–2148.

effort was a powerful tool to persuade decision makers that the fast-food moratorium was supported by the larger community and the right path to take.

Many of the strategies utilized in South Los Angeles (as well as in the other examples of community engagement described above involving HEAC, CCROPP, and the LAUSD) could be applied to address the targeted marketing of unhealthy food to ethnic minority youth in a particular community. For example, social science research could be utilized to document for the community the racial disparities in targeted advertising of junk food to ethnic minority youth and the worse health outcomes suffered by ethnic minority youth as a result of disproportionately high obesity rates. Such documentation may lead residents to see the issue as a matter of food justice, or "racial profiling" in advertising, rather than just an issue of personal choice. Ethnic minority youth could utilize Photovoice or other digital media, such as creation of YouTube videos, to capture images of the ubiquitous junk food marketing in their communities, or images of a junk food campaign particularly targeted at them. They could also be involved in data collection to document how pervasive junk food marketing is in their day-to-day lives, and how it affects their food purchases.

Once the public is more aware of and supportive of the issue, community resident leaders could participate in public speaking and training to advocate to their city government or school board for responsive action, such as removal of targeted junk food advertising to ethnic minority youth on city-owned billboards or at schools or school sporting events. Such advocacy could also contribute to other public health policy changes, media attention, "spotlighting" of unfair advertising practices, product boycotts, and development of a groundswell of public support for legal challenges.[62] On a broader scale, community residents could lend their voices to boycotts organized by national advocacy organizations focused on marketing of unhealthy foods to youth. Over time, organized efforts such as these could create strong public awareness among ethnic populations of the negative health impacts of targeted junk food marketing. Ultimately, the ubiquitous targeted marketing of junk food to ethnic minority youth could become much less acceptable.

Addressing the targeted marketing of junk food to youth may seem daunting, but the same was said of tobacco usage and marketing, and concerted efforts around this issue eventually achieved a larger awareness in the population of the dangers of consuming tobacco that resulted in a dramatic shift in social norms around tobacco in the USA.[63] Indeed, in 1997, R.J. Reynolds Tobacco Company stopped using the cartoon image of Joe Camel to market its cigarettes to youth after facing legal action

[62] Notably, some researchers have observed that "the politically sensitive aspects of targeting ethnic minority populations [for sale of unhealthy products] may include accusations of racial bias, exploitation or lack of social responsibility, which may cause problems for marketers with respect to image and may trigger boycotts or other countering strategies." Grier S., & Kumanyika, S. *Targeted marketing and public health*, *supra* note 16, at 11.15.

[63] For a list of regulations restricting the sale and distribution of cigarettes and smokeless tobacco to protect children and adolescents, see the following U.S. Food and Drug Administration website: http://www.fda.gov/TobaccoProducts/ProtectingKidsfromTobacco/RegsRestrictingSale/ucm204589.htm.

and pressure from anti-tobacco advocates.[64] Similarly, the ability to threaten legal action, combined with strong community support, could also result in a reduction of the targeted marketing of unhealthy food and drinks to ethnic minority youth.

Conclusion

The targeted marketing of junk food to ethnic minority youth, already prevalent, is only likely to increase in future years. African-American and Hispanic youth are the fastest growing population segments, and ethnic minorities are predicted to comprise almost half of all American youth by 2050.[65] Thus, junk food marketers are likely to focus increasingly on this population. Indeed, ethnic minority youth are "an attractive market segment within the overall child-focused market," not only because of their increasing size but because of their spending power (African-American and Hispanic teens spend more than the average teen),[66] media use patterns, and influence on the broader youth culture. Moreover, as public awareness decreases demand for junk food in the general market, the targeted marketing of junk food to ethnic minorities, including ethnic minority youth, may increase—in the same manner the tobacco industry shifted its marketing efforts to minority communities (and developing countries) once attitudes in the general population toward smoking began to shift.[67]

The confluence of all of these factors is likely to not only intensify the obesity epidemic overall but also exacerbate the disparities between ethnic minority youth and their White counterparts. Thus, the issue of targeted marketing of junk food to ethnic minority youth will only take on greater importance in coming years.

While existing legal avenues for addressing this issue are limited, state consumer protection laws do provide a potential opening in the event that state attorney generals and legal advocates are willing to forge new ground. Similarly, legal advocates willing to take on the Third Circuit's precedent established in *Brown v. Phillip*

[64] Coughlin, P. J., & Janecek, F. Jr. (1997). *A Review of R. J. Reynolds' Internal Documents Produced in Mangini* vs. *R. J. Reynolds Tobacco Company, Civil Number 939359: The Case that Rid California and the American Landscape of "Joe Camel."* Available at http://legacy.library.ucsf.edu/tid/ioq76b00/pdf.

[65] *See* U.S. Census Bureau, *Press Release: An Older and More Diverse Nation by Midcentury*, Aug 14, 2008. Available at http://www.census.gov/newsroom/releases/archives/population/cb08-123.html.

[66] According to surveys, African-American teens spend 6% more than the average teen and Hispanic teens spend 4% more than non-Hispanic teens. Mediamark Research. (2004). *Teen market profile*. New York, NY: Magazine Publishers of America, at 12. "With a current spending power of $20 billion and a projected growth rate six times higher than the rest of the teen market, Hispanic teens are a force in and of themselves." Davis, T., *The teen spending game: The complex marketing strategy*, Examiner.com, Aug 31, 2001 (citing Mediamark Research. (2007). *Drawing on diversity for successful marketing: Hispanic/Latino market profile*. New York, NY: Magazine Publishers of America, at 11). Available at http://www.examiner.com/small-business-in-philadelphia/the-teen-spending-game-the-complex-marketing-strategy.

[67] Yancey, A., & Kumanyika, S. *Bridging the gap*, *supra* note 14, at 173.

Morris could assert a challenge under federal civil rights law based on the strong dissenting opinion by Judge Shadur. Regardless of whether such challenges ultimately prevail, they can help bring much needed attention to the disparate obesity rates for ethnic minority youth.

An equally, if not more important vehicle, however, is community engagement. As discussed above, community engagement should form the foundation of any effort to address the targeted marketing of junk food to ethnic minority youth, whether as a precursor or complement to litigation or a stand-alone strategy. Not only does community engagement ensure that the community is fully informed on the issues, but it enables them to develop ownership over the response and build the necessary support to withstand likely controversy and sustain any successes over the long term.

The experience to date with community engagement in the public health arena provides valuable lessons and suggests that community engagement could also be effectively harnessed to start addressing the oft-ignored issue of targeted marketing of junk food to ethnic minority youth. Finally, any efforts to address this issue should be coupled with efforts to reduce the actual presence of junk foods in schools, neighborhoods, and other environments, while increasing the availability of healthy foods and beverages. Indeed, given the urgency of the issue, it is important to consider all possible strategies for drawing attention to the obesity disparities suffered by ethnic minority children.

Part VI
Communicating About Physical Activity

Chapter 19
Physical Activity, Media, and Marketing: Advances in Communications and Media Marketing

Toni Yancey, William J. McCarthy, Brian Cole, and Jerome D. Williams

Introduction

Information about Americans' growing waistlines, poor diet, lack of physical activity, and the toll these have on our health is ubiquitous, but progress in changing direction has been slow and inconsistent. On the positive note, Americans are slowly moving towards more healthful eating patterns (Frazão, 1999), although there is still plenty of room for improvement. In no small part these changes have been fueled by food marketers and diet promoters seeing new opportunities for profit, a deeply embedded cultural preoccupation with diet as the path to moral rectitude and physical well-being, and a vast industry of government- and corporate-funded nutrition research.

When it comes to physical activity, however, it has been more difficult to translate information into action. Based on objective measurement, only 8% of adolescents and 5% of adults meet physical activity guidelines (Troiano et al., 2008). These rates vary greatly by age, gender, and race/ethnicity, but reflecting other health disparities, are generally lower for African American and lower income individuals (Belcher et al., 2010; Hawkins et al., 2009; Ham & Ainsworth, 2010). It is not simply a lack of motivation. Competing demands for time in our increasingly busy schedules, innovations that engineer physical activity out of our lives, and the

T. Yancey, M.D., M.P.H. (✉) • W.J. McCarthy, Ph.D.
Department of Health Policy and Management, UCLA Fielding School of Public Health, Los Angeles, CA, USA
e mail: ayancey@ucla.edu

B. Cole, Dr.P.H.
Department of Environmental Health Sciences, UCLA Fielding School of Public Health, Los Angeles, CA, USA

J.D. Williams
Department of Management and Global Business, Rutgers Business School-Newark and New Brunswick, 1 Washington Park Room 1040, Newark, NJ 07102, USA
e-mail: jeromew@business.rutgers.edu

J.D. Williams et al. (eds.), *Advances in Communication Research to Reduce Childhood Obesity*, DOI 10.1007/978-1-4614-5511-0_19,

simple fact that physical activity requires effort all conspire to make it easier to sit instead of move, both individually and collectively as a society. This chapter examines the challenges to translating information about physical activity into action, what kinds of messages are most effective, and how moving can be made more fun and compelling and restore movement to everyday living.

Why a Marketing Perspective?

Marketers have been creative in luring us to sedentary pursuits (Fig. 19.1). To get people to move, you have to seduce them a bit—sell them on its attractiveness and immediate utility in their lives. And *immediate* for most people rarely involves their health until catastrophe strikes and they have a heart attack or stroke or cancer diagnosis. "Need an energy boost?" "Want to be sexy?" If these appeals work for sports drinks and granola bars, they can work for physical activity—*if* the costs and convenience are comparable. It is important to match apples and apples. If the sports drink with the eye-catching label is in the break room vending machine, a stone's throw from your desk, or the tantalizing aroma of coffee beckons from the reception area espresso machine around the corner, but the walking path is on the other side of the parking lot and there's nary a sign to remind you that it is there, or the barren stairs smell musty and are tucked away in the building interior, far from the entrance…those are obviously apples and oranges! The cornerstone of health promotion is making the healthy choice *easy* and the unhealthy choice increasingly difficult. This is how the battle against the tobacco industry has been waged successfully. Social marketing addresses socially beneficial behavior change, behaviors that contribute to the public good individually and collectively. It offers a framework for understanding human desires and other drivers of behavior change, how they compare with actual human needs, and how to intervene effectively, in this case, in getting people moving. Unlike commercial marketing, however, which aims to convince people to purchase something whether or not they need it, social

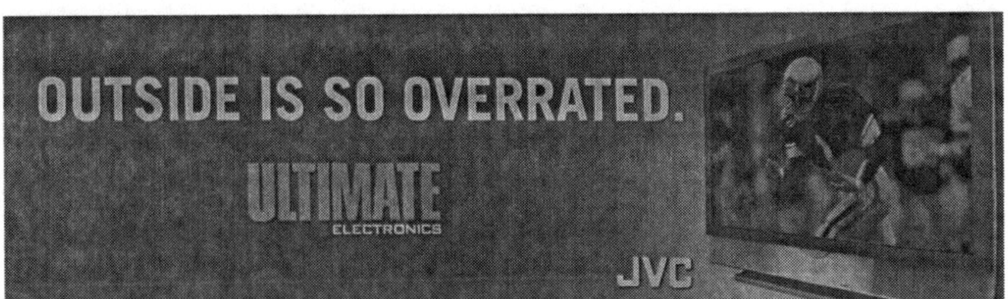

Fig. 19.1

marketing sells a needed product, service, or idea (Grier & Bryant, 2005). Social marketing borrows from commercial marketing its customer orientation, and the 4 P's, in hierarchical order: *product* (what is being offered—the benefit), *price* (what the consumer can exchange for the benefit,) *place* (where services are provided, products distributed, or information received), and *promotion* (how services or products are offered). The customer represents a defined population or target audience, and may be considered a fifth " P." Since the audience is rarely homogeneous, audience segmentation is necessary to understand and reach different groups.

There is little commercial mass marketing for physical activity (Yancey, 2009). Even targeted marketing of tennis rackets, tee times, therapy balls, and personal trainers is limited to upscale venues and vehicles, e.g., in-flight airline magazines, affluent neighborhoods, university alumni magazines, and TV shows catering to high income demographics. Just think about frequency of ads for rackets, balls, and club memberships during televised golf and the tourneys compared to the frequency of comparable products advertised during basketball and soccer games. Sedentary pursuits, on the other hand, are aggressively marketed but nothing like the $33 billion tallied annually by the food industry (Institute of Medicine (U.S.), 2006). This leaves a definite niche for the mass marketing of physical activity.

Evolution of the Public Face of Physical Activity

In its earliest incarnation more than half a century ago, any exertion beyond work, chores, or travel was synonymous with exercising—either to "reduce" (the polite term for middle-aged society women who were actually obese attempting to lose weight, not the current striving to look like a 13-year-old Barbie doll) or to enhance sex appeal. Exercises consisted of calisthenics to enhance the bust line, melt cellulite from cottage cheese thighs, or build Charles Atlas biceps and pecs to escape embarrassment and bullying on the beach. Sales appeal for gimmicks, gadgets, and potions supporting these activities came in the ladies' magazine ads for vibrator belts (see Fig. 19.2), and pulp magazine ads for muscle stimulators, diet pills, and supplements aimed at teenagers and young adults. These entreaties were augmented by early offerings from an embryonic stage of the now-booming fitness book industry. Just as is true today, these books were a mixed bag of sound advice, common sense, quackery, manipulation, and misrepresentation.

Early fitness icons, more embodiments of physical ideals of masculinity and femininity than "pitch" men and women, were generally established film stars and pin-up models of the period such as Johnny Weismuller and Jane Russell. Media representations of exercise and fitness subsequently diverged. The bodybuilding movement spun off as a sideshow, epitomized by the success of Lou Ferrigno and Arnold Schwarzenegger. Meantime Jack LaLanne, who mixed aerobic-type exercises, calisthenics, weight training, and good nutrition on his TV show, became the poster boy for the modern lifestyle gurus dominating the mainstream media, as illustrated in Fig. 19.3.

Beauty Machine Removes Excess Flesh Without Exercise

FASHION moguls have decreed that the boyish figure is passé, and that graceful curves are to be the coming mode. So, anticipating a need among the women, a far-sighted inventor has devised an instrument which literally rolls these curves into the body, getting rid of excess flesh without developing unsightly bundles of muscles, which exercising gave.

An important feature of the new device, however, is that developing these curves requires no work, for milady can become stylish in this new machine while reading a book, smoking a cigarette, or even gossiping. Hips, the chief point of attack, are reduced by means of rollers which massage the flesh, as illustrated in the accompanying photo.

Milady can smoke, read and gossip while this unique machine rolls off excess pounds of flesh around the hips, giving graceful curves, which fashion experts have decreed to be the coming mode. Massaging is performed by the rollers.

Fig. 19.2

The promotion of physical activity in the private sector through both nonprofit and commercial establishments has since been on the rise. Spa retreats and country clubs catering to the wealthy and elite have always maintained a background profile, the former in the tradition of the Western Health Reform Institute founded in the mid-1800s by the early Seventh Day Adventists and later transformed by John Harvey Kellogg into the Battle Creek Sanitarium. Private health clubs began to expand beyond social register clientele in the 1980s, when aerobics became popular and has continued into the present day. For-profit health clubs and YMCA-type gyms that were formerly considered the domain of older boys and men now include franchises marketed towards specific segments of the population such as women, secondary school youth, older folks, and young children, spanning the range from Gold's Gym (young fitness buffs) to Curves (overweight middle-aged women) to My Gym (preschoolers).

Fig. 19.3

Aerobic equipment was generally introduced in health clubs—from treadmills, punching bags, jump ropes, and bicycle ergometers to sport riders, stair climbers, skiing simulators, steps, recumbent cycles, elliptical cross-trainers, and stability balls—and then mass marketed to individual users. Of course, the same snake oil salesmen from decades earlier, in modern guise, continue to promise youth, vigor, and sex to gullible marks with too-good-to-be-true offers. How many exercycles end up getting more use as clothes-drying racks than as fitness equipment?

Ironically, the commercial promotion of physical activity has recently begun to include the providers of sedentary entertainment. Video games such as Dance Dance Revolution, Sony Eye Toy, Wii, and Kinect offer a more active option for recovering couch and mouse potatoes. Some proof of this mobilization of the sedentary may be seen in the spate of injuries specific to any exercise fad, especially among weekend Wii warriors (Das, 2009).

The early social marketing of physical activity was pioneered four decades ago at the Cooper Institute for Aerobics Research. The prior public health focus on physical activity from the 1950s was on the increased risk of heart disease and premature death associated with long periods of occupational sitting, e.g., among working class bus drivers and mail sorters in the UK (Brown, Bauman, & Owen, 2009). The Cooper Institute led the shift to a scientific focus on the benefits of activity in the form of structured leisure time exercise. The aerobics movement grew out of an affluent American white male sensibility and a medical vs. public health perspective, which persists in physical activity promotion circles to the present day. Today's dominant paradigm reflects those cultural values and opportunities, namely, individualism, an inclination toward sports over dance, ample discretionary time and income, and a strong preference for thin women. Attention to culture is key, and that's why the aerobics movement was quite successful in its mass marketing efforts to mobilize these men—through mainstream media, the workplace (e.g., executive wellness), and other social institutions serving that demographic.

Women were left behind initially, because vigorous exercise and its sweating and panting and heavy weights and baggy workout clothing was incompatible—tacitly, if not explicitly—with their feminine socialization process. However, the commercial market represented by middle and upper class women, and the opening of amendment sports opportunities to girls by the women's rights movement and passage of Title IX promoting gender equity in sports, has spawned a burgeoning culture of physical activity participation. This has been spurred on and reinforced by tailored clothing and equipment proportioned for women's bodies, group activity usually incorporating dance or music (aerobic dance, step, spinning, boxercise, and Pilates classes), and media representations of women exercising as normative. The early faces of this "market," Jane Fonda and Bridgette Nielson, have been succeeded by more recent exercise impresarios, including both men and women—Richard Simmons, Madonna, Billy Blanks, Oprah, and even Gwyneth Paltrow. Activity levels of younger adult white women are now similar to men's, though this is attributable, in part, to declining physical activity among males.

But those responding to these marketing appeals are still in the minority, and leisure time physical activity has never really penetrated the masses of adults in America, particularly less affluent communities and communities of color. Most large corporations have on-site fitness facilities available for employee use before or after work, during lunchtime. City, county, and state governments, the largest employers in many locales, together with small- and medium-sized private companies, consistently offer free or reduced-price memberships to health clubs with broad geographic reach. For example, 24 Hour Fitness has partnered with celebrity NBA athletes to establish high-quality gyms in low income, ethnic minority neighborhoods. Besides providing facilities that were previously in short supply, these gyms have demonstrated latent demand for and economic viability of sports and recreation facilities in these neighborhoods. While certainly a success from a business perspective, in terms of public health these efforts have only a modest impact since they tend to attract those who already regularly engage in activity on their own time and at their own expense. The mere presence of active recreation facilities and spaces does not engage the sedentary majority. To reach and engage those who participate in little if any physical activity, something more is needed. This is where social marketing comes in.

Promotion is the most visible component of social marketing, which feeds the misconception that social marketing relies primarily on advertising to achieve its aims. However, if an initiative stops at communications approaches, it is nothing more than a media campaign—information, perhaps some catchy ads that generate some buzz but not necessarily any action. The limits of a media campaign were demonstrated by the federally funded "Small Step" campaign launched to encourage physical activity. Pudgy white mens' love handles and pot bellies were mysteriously found on the beach, lost and abandoned after they took up walking. The program, however, gained little traction and was essentially abandoned. Attention to place, product, and price are crucial to mounting an effective social marketing campaign. Lack of sufficient resources to mount a comprehensive social marketing campaign, not merely a series of clever ads, was a crucial limitation of the Small Step. In contrast, John F. Kennedy's fitness promotion initiative for schoolchildren translated the President's youth and popularity into rallying, monitoring, and incentives on the ground floor—at the school. Kennedy's approach is resurfacing in a newer form, with advocacy groups using the Cooper Institute-derived FitnessGram as a source of data to apprise legislators, school officials, and parent of students' fitness performance and progress.

Why Marketing? Why Now?

Adherents to physical activity promotion orthodoxy express concern that emphasizing the benefits of brief bouts of exercise will erode the 30-min + per day message. First of all, if the message isn't getting through, there *is* no message. The traditional paradigm is built upon the flawed assumption that knowledge is both necessary and sufficient for behavior change—get the 30-min per day message out in enough media and with enough frequency and people will be active. Some academics also assert that multiple recommendations from expert panels confuse the public and deter activity. This concern may be exaggerated by experts' belief in how much the public attends to and values their opinion. When it comes to behavior change that takes effort and costs time and money, expert opinion probably doesn't matter much. Fear of aging, concern about expanding waistlines, and desire to fit in with friends are undoubtedly much more potent motivators.

On the other hand, neither knowledge nor concern about health drives activity among the majority, as should be intuitively obvious from the dismal failure of all of this education to keep people active after research studies end or program funds run out...or even after the first few months of a study or program. The private sector provides a window, vis-à-vis fitness industry operations, on the behavior of people more advantaged and motivated to get active than the average person. Most health clubs' business plan is dependent upon selling the same workout space over and over again. According to the National Health Club Association, during the first year after joining, median "burn-out" time for new members is 3–4 months, at which time approximately 50% discontinue regular attendance and payments. It is a misconception, perpetuated by aggressive health club advertising, that all or even most individuals joining gyms exercise at recommended levels. Most of those consistently attending are not meeting federal guidelines. Of the 50% attrition (those not completing their initial contract), 25% are inconsistent attenders and 25% are nonattenders. In subsequent years, loss rates (those completing initial contract but not renewing) are 65–80% nationally, with "good" clubs averaging 40–55%. However, much depends on the club's organizational philosophy, e.g., Bally's nearly exclusive focus on new recruitment. New sales necessitate attrition or tremendous overcrowding of facilities would occur. This is supported by data from UCLA's Fighting Cancer with Fitness pilot study—more than a third of the participants had been members of gyms or weight loss centers in the past year.

A vocal minority on the national Physical Activity Guidelines Advisory Committee tried and failed to push beyond the committee's charge to focus on the easy questions of how much, what and why, and instead to grapple with the more critical and less clear-cut questions of when, where, and how—practical, rather than academic questions, that could have helped encourage more people to be physically active. The roll-out of the report in October 2008 represented a critical missed opportunity to draw attention to the latter topics and present a thoughtful digest of the best evidence available. The release apparently excited the public health community, as evidenced by the standing-room-only crowds when we presented the guidelines at professional meetings in the aftermath of the release. But the public health community splash barely registered as a blip on the mass media radar screen.

Much behavior must be changed en route to an active nation. Ways to influence voluntary behavior change include education and communication, marketing, policy, or some combination of these. Education and communication involve activities that change the information environment for the purpose of informing people or organizations about options they currently have. Education and communication change knowledge, but simply knowing doesn't equate to doing. Marketing refers to activities that change the competitive market environment for the purpose of providing people or organizations with new options that are intended to be more attractive than their current options. Policy and legal advocacy encompass activities that change—or are intended to change—regulations and laws for the purpose of providing incentives for or mandating certain options and disincentives for or prohibiting other options.

Which of these tools for encouraging behavior change to use and when depends on several factors: gauging people's inclination to behave as desired, judging how readily benefits can be conveyed, and assessing the level of competition (Abroms & Maibach, 2008). Education and communication work fine if people are prone to behave as desired, self-interest or benefits are easy to convey, and there's little or weak competition. Marketing can be employed when people are neither prone nor resistant to the behavior promoted, when self-interest can be conveyed by pumping up the offer (i.e., incentives like free samples or short-term discounts to get them started and hopefully reaping intrinsic benefits like cost savings, and feeling or looking better), and when there's active competition. Changes in policies and laws are the last recourse, when the people are resistant to adopting the behavior, self-interest can't be readily conveyed and the competition is unmanageable.

Competition comes from within and without in the case of physical activity. People are resistant to the desired behavior by nature—genetic programming to avoid unnecessary caloric expenditure that was adaptive for most of the million years of human existence. And the outside competition is fierce, probably unmanageable—cars, gaming, and increasingly mobile screens. Self interest *can* be conveyed by enhancing the offer (what people get for their time, money, or effort), but that has yet to be done in a way that moves the masses of adults, i.e., by targeting the offers to organizations rather than individuals, and exploiting the organizational infrastructure—social networks, communications, performance measures, the physical plant, market competition, leader competitiveness, culture, and values.

Current Activity Marketing Campaigns

There are several recent examples of successful physical activity mass marketing campaigns. Not coincidentally, the private sector played a central role, with public health providing direction on content and commercial marketing or PR driving the dissemination.

Public Social Marketing

VERB™ It's what you do!

VERB was the brainchild of the US Centers for Disease Control (CDC). This was a chance to do it right. Campaign developers took a lot of heat for the substantial level of funding, which was for once sufficient to get the job done. The VERB campaign focused on "tweens" (9- to 13-year-old pre-/early-adolescents) who were encouraged to participate in physical activity by choosing a verb, e.g., run, bike, dance, skate as a starting point. A TV ad message was "Everywhere you go, everywhere you look, there are verbs out there just waiting for you to get into..."

The VERB™ campaign vividly demonstrated that culture counts. Marketers ignored the disdain of adult public health academicians and practitioners, and grounded its campaign messages in hip-hop culture. A huge budget by public health standards—in excess of $150 million by a direct Congressional appropriation—was invested, mostly in engaging a top advertising firm. Unfortunately, as soon as brand visibility was achieved and successful outcomes demonstrated, the campaign was sacrificed to make room for a round of tax cuts. The organizers tried hard to tie the campaign to ongoing youth group activities, as well as state and local health department and parks and recreation programs that provide active leisure opportunities. In contrast to most public health interventions, effects were greatest among ethnic minority populations, African-American girls in particular (Huhman, Heitzler, & Wong, 2004).

Private Marketing and Community Benefit

Kaiser Permanente's Thrive™

The Thrive™ ad campaign, aimed at getting people to live healthier and happier lives, and not incidentally, differentiating the company from its competitors with "warm and fuzzy" associations, complements its Healthy Eating Active Living (HEAL) Initiative funded in part by its Community Benefit program. *Thrive* communicates KP's philosophy of prevention and health promotion, and influences social norms with radio, TV, outdoor, and online spots. Colorful and fast-moving images against varied backdrops of energetic and upbeat people of both genders and varying ages, sizes, classes, and ethnicities dancing and playing, with mouth-watering shots of fruits and vegetables, convey KP's commitment to helping everyone "thrive." The few clinical settings depicted are of happy doctors and healthy patients getting routine physicals with death and disease nowhere in sight!

Public–Private Partnership in Activity Marketing

RWJF's investment in active gaming

Robert Wood Johnson Foundation (RWJF) played an active role in the development of physical gaming. Aggressive foundation support of the electronic gaming industry in developing physical or active video games represents a public-private partnership model that may have applications for recess breaks. This support came in the form of sponsoring interdisciplinary conferences, offering scholarships and awards, underwriting the development or expansion of university computer science gaming programs, and grant-making to speed commercial application. These activities and opportunities raised the profile of physical gaming, attracting talented young scientists.

The Real Gatekeepers

One group whose role in health promotion has been grossly underappreciated is journalists. They feel a professional responsibility to document the culture of the population that they're writing about (e.g., the "embedded" journalists of the Gulf War who likely compromised their objectivity for eyewitness accounts and real-time reporting). Public health professionals are starting to zero in on the cultures of business and politics to understand what drives the decisions of these gatekeepers and influencers. But only a few public health investigators (Hinnant, Oh, Caburnay, & Kreuter, 2011) and even fewer public health practitioners are talking about journalists and their culture—motivation, drivers, constraints, etc. The Fig. 19.4 excerpt from a front page story in the Los Angeles Times Lifestyle section illustrates how journalism can improve the reach of ongoing community research.

The Messenger and the Medium

Health-related social marketing tries to reach or penetrate a target audience with a message that is effective in inducing a desirable behavior change. That change must be amplified or adopted widely, fully implemented, and maintained and sustained over a sufficient period of time to create lasting change in sociocultural norms, practices, and policies.

The most important aspect of that message is its resonance with the target audience and the credibility of its messenger for the product or service being marketed.

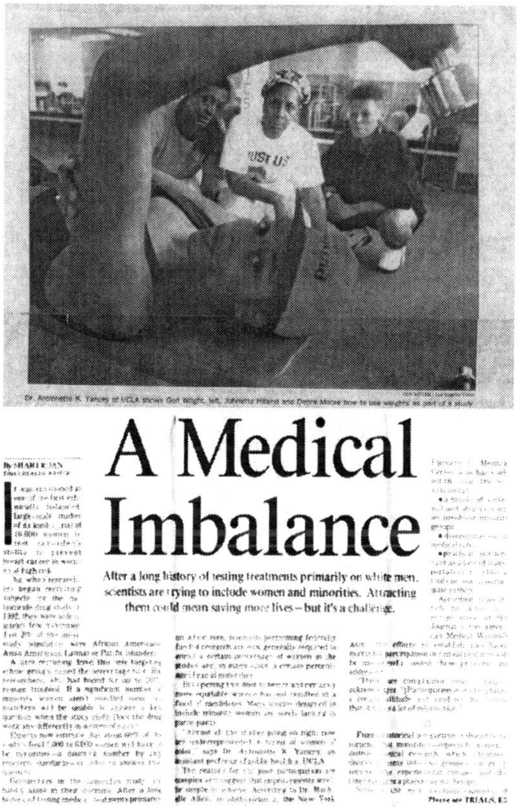

A Medical Imbalance

After a long history of testing treatments primarily on white men, scientists are trying to include women and minorities. Attracting them could mean saving more lives—but it's a challenge.

Fig. 19.4

Marketing people refer to the latter as *homophily*—degree of similarity between messenger and audience. For example, the TV show *ER*, in consultation with University of Southern California's "Hollywood, Health and Society" project, created a multiepisode storyline around a young, overweight, black male character recurring over several episodes who regularly consumed fast food and ended up in the intensive care unit in congestive heart failure. Recall of those *ER* episodes in a subsequent opinion poll among African Americans and among men was significantly more likely to result in some evidence of behavioral change, such as self-reported increases in fruit and veggie intake and reported increases in walking a few blocks, than other demographic groups (Valente et al., 2007). Those demographic segments, notoriously difficult to engage in health promotion efforts, would have been unlikely to respond to messages from real doctors, patients, and hospitals, even if they had appeared in ads or public service announcements during the same popular show. Interestingly, exposure to this *ER* storyline among African Americans was not associated with greater knowledge or more favorable attitudes toward physical activity compared with those not exposed.

Instant Recess®: A Case in Point

An Ancient Idea Whose Time Has Come—Again!

In 1999 three organizations acting independently introduced similar 10-min exercise break interventions integrating the activity into organizational routine as a way of operationalizing the CDC/ACSM guidelines updated in 1996. These organizations included the Mexican Ministry of Health in Mexico City (Mexico's CDC equivalent), a nonprofit health education institute in Atlanta, and the Los Angeles Department of Health Services' Public Health Branch. The resonance of certain cultural factors in communities of color became apparent in the reception of this model, e.g., family- and community-centered activities, the church as a political and social as well as religious institution, and, of course, the importance of music and dance. Frequent reminders have since appeared that these types of interventions have long been institutionalized in other countries such as Japan and China (Wile, 1996)—in corporations, mass media, schools, and city squares, as exemplified in Fig. 19.5. The obesity epidemic is prompting their revival in some places (Gu, 2010).

The concept of group exercise to enhance alertness and prevent injury is also not uncommon in corporate America. For example, mandatory stretch breaks have been implemented for more than 30 years at Maine-based apparel and equipment retailer

Fig. 19.5

L.L. Bean, headquartered in Freeport, ME. Their wellness coordinator equates incorporating activity breaks to requiring safety glasses for eye protection (Simon, 2006). Similarly, Minneapolis-based construction company M.A. Mortenson Co instituted mandatory stretching in 1999, and it now holds a place with tie lines, hard hats, reflective vests, and dozens of other strictly enforced safety rules, according to its operating group safety director (Rumbach, 2007).

Public health priority populations' high rates of inactivity demanded an intervention approach that could *active*-ate unfit and overweight folks not very far along the path toward adopting fitter lifestyles (if they'd even found the path). First, they needed to feel competent. Unlike eating—not terribly challenging for most – dance involves movement skills coming into *play*. And a lot of these folks had been on the short end of the stick in childhood games, with some pretty bad memories of being taunted, teased, or excluded.

But at the same time, the approach also had to excite and motivate people with a range of fitness levels, athleticism, and functional abilities, including exercise buffs and gym rats who might help "carry the water" in pushing for and implementing such changes. One way to do this was to weave in specific dance movements and rhythms, sports traditions, and activity-linked themes and icons with cultural resonance. Another was to invoke the notion of these breaks as an entitlement—similar to what many people feel about coffee or smoking breaks. After all, most active people don't get as much exercise as they want or feel they need. Of course, there are the naysayers—the holier-than-thou types that run or lift everyday and dismiss such modest amounts of activity as a waste of time.

Models for the Social Marketing of Instant Recess®

Demonstrating that Instant Recess® (IR) could get otherwise sedentary people moving and that it was sustainable was important, but to really make a difference it needed to be more broadly disseminated. The success of several other social marketing campaigns offers lessons for scaling up IR from a demonstration project to a movement.

California 5-A-Day

The same agency that developed the 5-A-Day promotion for fruit and vegetable consumption, the California Department of Health Services,(Foerster et al., 1995) now the Department of Public Health, supported the development of IR and its *Lift Off* predecessor. Although it may seem like we're comparing apples to oranges—or rather apples to modified jumping jacks—bear with me. The parallels between the evolution of 5-A-Day and the emergence of IR are striking. Recess breaks could be seen as a promotional message for physical activity comparable to that associated with the 5-A-Day message for fruit and vegetable intake. Like 5-A-Day, IR conveys a simple, easily recalled and understood, and immediately do-able action. Each of the two products may be attractively packaged. Also like 5-A-Day, the recess message is consistent with the incremental nature of behavior change. Adding 10 min to the typical US adult's 6–10 min a day of at least moderate intensity activity is within reach, in the same way that adding a serving or two to the average adult's three or four per day is not a huge leap.

IR may actually have a few advantages over 5-A-Day—the product is cheaper and could well be as profitable as the competition (sedentary behavior-promoting products and services, e.g., traditional video games), the competition is not mobilized in opposition, and its success is aligned with the goals of several deep-pocket private industries who could profit from increased population interest and engagement in physical activity—manufacturers and retailers of sporting goods and equipment and fitness apparel, gyms and health clubs, field and court rental facilities, and personal training and fitness instruction companies. This may also create more of an appetite for spectator sports and its collateral product sales (e.g., teens who watch sports, for example, also play more sports than nonspectators (Taveras et al., 2004)).

Recess breaks also do not present the problem of maldistribution from a public equity standpoint. They may be done anywhere, anytime, any place, in any attire. The delivery mechanism (CD, DVD) may be distributed at minimal, if any, cost and reused (i.e., can be made available for streaming and downloading from the Internet). Fruits and vegetables are typically much more available in affluent than in poor neighborhoods. Recess breaks may be more readily picked up and disseminated by the private sector—the profit margin is there and existing distribution networks may be exploited (e.g., bookstores, DVD rental businesses, fitness industry retailers, wellness contractors).

The main disadvantage of IR compared with 5-A-Day is that it flies in the face of physical activity promotion orthodoxy—instead of individually motivated and initiated solo or team activity, it focuses on socially obligatory group activity in amounts less than the officially recommended level of 30 min per day. Some in the scientific bureaucracy have been adamant that a public focus on the recess message undermines the chances of Americans achieving regular physical activity by implying that bouts of less than 30 min per day are insufficient. As explained above, this really shouldn't be a concern, since so few Americans are even close to achieving this recommendation, nor are they particularly tuned into official recommendations anyway.

A 20-year veteran of exercise break implementation at L. L. Bean, wellness coordinator Susan Tufts concurred that a more modest recommendation would be empowering for people who aren't meeting the guidelines. She indicated that, in her experience, people tune out the 30-min message as daunting and unattainable. She also said she'd often seen employees start small and build up almost automatically, as a natural progression accompanying physiological conditioning. The Bean employee population is mostly blue-collar white men, a large and largely overlooked overweight and inactive population segment that's "hidden in plain sight." Many assume these men get lots of exercise as construction workers, mechanics, and longshoremen. But most of those jobs have become much more mechanized and much less strenuous, as in the rest of society—requiring a lot more fine motor finger movement than large muscle contraction and ambulation.

Active Gaming

Key commonalities between physical gaming and the dissemination of activity breaks are the clear public-private partnership opportunities, the exploitation of new electronic information technologies, and the opportunities for rapid and mass diffusion. Several differences are also noteworthy. Active video gaming's emphasis is on individual and family participation, aside from some marketing to schools for use in physical education and to video arcades, e.g., "Dance Dance Revolution." The ability to try out active games is also somewhat limited because a relatively expensive upfront purchase is required, though this may be offset by opportunities to sample the products at the homes of friends and extended family. Another challenge to electronic gaming is estimating demand and matching supply—Nintendo's *Wii* often sold out at retail outlets after its introduction, which may have suppressed sales and hampered distribution.

Structured activity breaks, on the other hand, require little to no upfront investment, are unlimited in supply, encourage innovation especially by youth, and may be immediately acted upon after exposure to the promotional message. The motivation for adoption of active gaming mostly operates at the individual level, as is true for the traditional physical activity promotion paradigm. Gaming does drive motivation beyond individual enjoyment or health improvement to social interaction and reinforcement—fun, competition, and camaraderie. Activity breaks, however, usually require organizational practice change motivation, in leadership driven by existing incentives and disincentives for performance outcomes, visibility or political expediency.

Active Dissemination

Most requests for materials and technical assistance through 2006 were responses to lectures given by Yancey, particularly keynotes and plenary talks at large annual meetings, e.g., Grantmakers in Health, Society of Behavioral Medicine and California Childhood Obesity Conference. Among the early adopters of IR, a majority were health departments and health care organizations, but schools, universities, local government agencies, and religious organizations also pursued technical assistance and implementation support materials.

In 2007, clips of the original *Lift Off!* video and the first IR DVD became available for streaming online from the California Department of Health Services website. Web 2.0 technologies that increase the depth of consumer engagement, e.g., webinars (including Skype video augmentation), YouTube, Flikr, Facebook, LinkedIn, and Twitter,(Bernhardt, Mays, & Kreuter, 2011) have since been used increasingly to fuel Instant Recess® diffusion. With the release of the book, *Instant Recess: Building a Fit Nation 10 minutes at a Time* by the University of California Press in August 2010, media coverage—radio, print, TV, and blog—has been the primary driver of diffusion (Table 19.1).

Table 19.1 Instant Recess® Dissemination Timeline

Time period	External sources of support	Internal sources of support	Major partners	CDs and DVDs distributed; downloads	Media impressions (via Google search)
1999–2001	USDA-funded CA DHS Nutrition Network	LAC DHS	Community Health Councils	Not available	0
2002–2006	The California Endowment, RWJF		California WIC, Community Health Councils	1338[a] (2006 data only)	30
2007–2011	NIH, CDC, RWJF	UCLA KP Center for Health Equity	LAC DPH, Sparks, Padres, California WIC, FAME, UCC, KEEN	4815 direct[b]; 460 IR downloads/month	17,500

[a]Incomplete because electronic tracking of sales and distribution did not begin until March 2006

[b]Distributed by UCLA—does not include purchases and distribution by state and local health or education depts

Now in its 13th year, IR includes a library of more than 50 breaks (on CD and DVD), including American Indian powwow, Latin salsa, cumbia, reggae, hip hop, line and African dance, along with basketball, baseball, football, boxing, and soccer moves. Active and passive diffusion efforts have included more than 1,500 worksites—primarily ethnic minority-serving health and human services agencies in the Greater Los Angeles area and statewide by the CA state health department & CA WIC Association—and thousands of schools—particularly those affiliated with the USDA-funded Network, Alliance for a Healthier Generation, and The California Endowment's Healthy Eating Active Living and Building Healthy Communities initiatives. IR materials have been purchased by organizations in 45 states, Washington DC and 10 foreign countries.

We have partnered with athletes and sports teams to promote the IR model, concentrating on the settings in which they have the greatest sway or leverage, namely sports venues and schools or other youth-serving programs. IR-focused community fitness initiatives have been implemented with two professional teams, the MLB San Diego Padres (*FriarFit*) since April 2008 (Fig. 19.6 captures some of the Padres' efforts), and for two seasons (2009 and 2010) with the WNBA LA Sparks (*SPARKing* Motion) (Fig. 19.7 shows the DVD of the Spark's version of Instant Recess). A large-scale IR implementation effort in the Winston-Salem/Forsyth Co., NC Schools engaged high school athletes in peer modeling for younger students and developing their own breaks, e.g., "Got Moves?" contests (Whitt-Glover, Ham, & Yancey, 2011).

The first to engage a media outlet as a partner, a Washington DC IR initiative, was launched in the summer of 2010, with three months of daily IR broadcasts on the public radio station WPFW, including choreography and production of a local line dance (Wobble Dance) IR break. The local health department and several community-based organizations including churches, schools, after-school programs, and preschools were involved (Hallett, 2010; Hallett, 2012).

Recent endeavors have expanded IR horizons. Through a collaboration with the California League of Cities'/California Center for Public Health Advocacy's Healthy Eating/Active Living Cities Campaign (http://www.HEALcitiescampaign.org), 37 cities have adopted policies advocating activity breaks in meetings lasting an hour or longer, including Fremont, Fullerton, Pasadena, Redding, San Leandro, and Solano Beach. In addition, we have three youth empowerment projects (Usher's New Look Foundation, New Orlean's Rethinkers, and Detroit's Generation with Promise), a hit music video spin-off (Beyonce's "Move Your Body"), and several corporate initiatives (dissemination of one of the DVDs as a part of IBM's worksite wellness program, adoption by one of Kaiser Permanente's Los Angeles region medical centers,(Yancey, Herrmann, & Creighton, in Press) and a national corporate marketing campaign, KEEN's *Recess Is Back. Recess Is Back*, in partnership with IR, produced and distributed a worksite toolkit free for downloading from KEEN's website (http://recess.keenfootwear.com/recess-at-work/).

Fig. 19.6

Passive Diffusion

Media Coverage

The first evidence of the appeal of the IR concept to mass audiences was the uptake of an AP story covering Yancey's talk at a Cooper Institute for Aerobics Research annual meeting on PA dissemination (Simon, 2006). A total of 35 newspapers across 18 states and territories ran this story between December 2006 and

Fig. 19.7

February 2007 quoting her research on the benefits of activity breaks in the workplace, most adding local flavor with interviews of employers in their regions who'd adopted similar strategies.

A UCLA Magazine article served as a springboard for a subsequent article. LA-based NPR staff writer Patti Neighmond's segment aired in February 2009. The piece was followed by a web-based dialogue hosted by NPR health editor Joe Neel on the "micro-exercise" movement that attracted over 400 people and lasted 45 min. They surveyed the people who tuned in and 29% indicated that their employers already provide short exercise breaks—another 37% responded "I wish!" The story and blog are still on their website along with an insightful web-only synthesis of the lessons informing IR:

Exercising With a Crowd Is Easier

Yancey describes the mini-fitness sessions as a part of a "captive audience strategy." It can be tough to get some people to break their work routine even for 10 min to exercise, she says, though they'll have fun if they do. So sometimes, while addressing a conference, she will stop midway and tell the gathered crowd that they are going to stop for a little exercise. "People kind of frown, look around nervously, particularly those who are overweight or obese and not used to exercising in public," she says.

But once Yancey puts on the DVD and turns on the music, "they do it because everyone else is doing it." That's the key, she says. "We're social beings. The motivation is social." And, often, even short exercise breaks will entice people to adopt healthier lifestyles — better diets and exercise — over the long run.

Company Support Is Crucial

To make daily exercise a priority, top-down leadership is necessary for bottom-up support, Yancey says. Some companies have started pushing back from the conference table to institute "walking meetings" or even replaced the seats around the conference table with elliptical machines. As a start, she says, companies might institute a sort of "sitting" ban similar to smoking bans — at least during some meetings, for those who are able. The most successful intervention, she says, may require the CEO and other managers to join in a five- or 10-min recess break like the sessions she teaches: a brief, low-impact, simple and structured group physical activity, usually done to music and integrated into the organizational routine at work.

The People Who Need It Most Will Get the Most Out Of It

Critics sometimes complain that short breaks don't raise the heart rate enough to help folks who are already in good shape lose weight or increase their fitness. That may be true. But they'll be refreshed and have fun, and it's the best way to get to others who are true couch potatoes. Yancey's studies show that even a little exercise in the afternoon increases the likelihood that people will take the extra initiative and get more exercise in the evening or on the weekend.

What's Good for the Worker Is Good for the Company

Retailer L.L. Bean instituted daily, mini-exercise breaks 15 years ago throughout its assembly plant with great results, Yancey says. The breaks were five minutes each, three times a day. At the end of the shift, the company found a 30-min return on productivity for an investment of 15 min of physical activity. "The number of bags and shoes that they do not produce in those 15 min," she says, "they actually get back and then some." Yancey is now involved in a study looking at how employees fare at more than 70 work sites instituting similar programs across Los Angeles County. She expects findings within three years.

Generated primarily by the intentional workplace (vs. school/youth) focus of PR for the book *Instant Recess: Building a Fit Nation 10 Minutes at a Time*, coverage has followed in many major newspapers, magazines, TV and radio broadcast networks, and blogs. For example, Neighmond's subsequent 2011 story on the perils of prolonged sitting, in which Yancey and her executive assistant Danielle Osby were interviewed, put the book in the top 2500 sellers for one day on Amazon.com. This "bounce" was similar to that produced by Jane Brody's *New York Times* column on IR appearing on November 23, 2010 (Figure 19.9). Undoubtedly, interest in IR has

Fig. 19.9

been amplified by Yancey's appointment in April 2010 to the Board of Directors of the Partnership for a Healthier America, the nonprofit formed by prominent health foundations to support First Lady Michelle Obama's Let's Move campaign. A Reuter's article proclaimed "Routine Recess a Hit at White House Childhood Obesity Conference," with subheading "A doctor's endorsement of frequent recess breaks—and not just for kids—drew an appreciative response from experts meeting at a White House summit on childhood obesity on Friday and led to one newspaper tongue in cheek to portray formally dressed white collar workers sprinting down a running track under the caption: "Do adults need recess, too? (see Fig. 19.9)." The *Washington Post* subsequently dubbed Instant Recess the "calling card" of the National Physical Activity Plan at the time of its May 2010 release. IR was mentioned in articles in the *Los Angeles Times*, *New York Times*, and *Washington Post* during the spring through fall of 2011. The Washington Post even had an artist create a dozen illustrations of body movements that have been featured in Instant Recess DVDs, as illustrated in Fig. 19.10.

Spontaneous implementation of IR initiatives. We are now beginning to see organizations adopt IR on their own without any contact with the program's creators, marking its development into a self-sustaining movement. A number of projects have recently been initiated without advance contact with IR leadership. Google alerts and periodic web searches with "Instant Recess" and "Toni Yancey" as the keywords are used to monitor this diffusion via news stories and blog posts. Four sectors are represented among these groups, with examples provided below.

- Religious institutions—Cleveland, OH-based United Church of Christ, through its Health and Social Justice Ministry, utilized its website and outreach seminars to promote IR adoption by member congregations. The Youth Ministry then developed and led an IR break at the 2011 annual conference on the main convention floor with 3500+ delegates.
- School districts—The Midlands, TX school district adopted IR as a result of its physical education coordinator's internet exposure to the DVDs.

The New York Times

PERSONAL HEALTH

It's Time for Recess: Just Keep on Moving

By JANE E. BRODY

Published: November 22, 2010

Fig. 19.8

- Universities—University of Kentucky developed its "Recess @ Work" initiative based on IR, after exposure through word-of-mouth dissemination, likely resulting from school philanthropic outreach by Allen Rossum, the first professional athlete to embrace IR.
- Health care orgs—The executive director of Washington, DC-based safety net clinic La Clinica del Pueblo read and adapted the IR book in developing a Recess at Work program. The nonprofit Association of Clinicians for the Underserved produced a documentary about this effort.

Funding and Revenue Generation

The original funding for the *Lift Off!* (2000) and IR (2006) came from the California state health department's USDA-funded Nutrition Network promoting healthy eating and physical activity among Food Stamp recipients and eligible families. Subsequently, six foundation grants, three from The California Endowment and three from RWJF (two from the Active Living Research program), have supported IR implementation in schools in Los Angeles; schools and churches in Winston-Salem, NC; preschools in Springfield, MA; and professional sports venues in Los Angeles and San Diego (Whitt-Glover et al., 2011; Yancey et al., 2009).

The Washington Post

HEALTH&SCIENCE

TUESDAY, SEPTEMBER 6, 2011

ECO LOGIC
Big old energy guzzlers
Compare the environmental impact of aging desktop computers with sleek new tablets and smartphones. E4

HOW & WHY
Burning questions
How hot peppers and horseradish might lead to advances in pain management. E3

If office exercises don't inspire you, there are lots of other ways to get a move on — and good reasons to do so. Consumer Reports, E2

A workout at work?

WE ALL NEED TO GET UP AND MOVE, BUT WHAT CAN WE DO? In the spirit of public service (and because our boss made us), The Post's infographics department tested exercises in and around our cubicles twice a day for a week to see which ones real people could incorporate into a workday. The moves were suggested by experts whose jobs involve studying motion, preventing obesity and generally getting people off their duffs. We rejected a few immediately — jumping jacks? Not in this bra! — but chose these 12. Our observations aren't scientific, but they're definitely real.

BY BONNIE BERKOWITZ AND LAURA STANTON

Difficult?
Sweaty?
Humiliating?

RAISE THE ROOF (20 reps)
TRICEPS KICK (20 reps)
THE HULK (20 reps)
HAMSTRING CURL (20 reps)
KNEE LIFT (20 reps)
HALLELUJAH (20 reps)
PUNCHING (20 reps)
DESK PUSHUP (10 reps)
SIDE LUNGE (10 per side)
JUMP SQUATS (10)
CHAIR DIPS (10)
WALK (10 min)

Experts offer ideas for the deskbound

BY CHRISTIAN TORRES

Labor Day is over, as are summer vacations for most people, so it's time to head back to the daily grind. But work today doesn't usually mean breaking a sweat. More and more of us are spending our 9 to 5 at a desk — and we're less healthy as a result.

A study published in May by the online journal PLoS One estimates that Americans are burning more than 100 fewer calories per day in the workplace than they did just a few decades ago, when fewer jobs were confined to a desk.

"We've had massive changes in the [workplace] environment, and in this case, it's a loss of physically active jobs," said lead author Tim Church, an exercise researcher at Pennington Biomedical Research Center in Baton Rouge.

Church and his colleagues found that the number of people in jobs requiring moderate physical activity decreased from 48 percent in 1960 to 20 percent in 2008. The researchers also found a match between the drop in calories burned and increase in average weight during the past five decades.

A few creative types have come up with ideas to increase workplace activity. For example, endocrinologist James Levine of the Mayo Clinic has promoted the treadmill desk, which lets you walk slowly as you work at an attached desktop; factory-made models cost $2,000 and up. There are under-desk step machines such as the $195 Gamercize PC-Sport: if you stop pedaling, your mouse or keyboard stop working. To add upper-body exercises, there's the $569 GymyGym, an office chair equipped with built-in resistance bands.

But you don't have to spend that much money to get a workout. Fitness experts are also promoting low-cost — if occasionally funny-looking — options for improving your fitness during office hours. Some of our Washington Post colleagues tried them out, as you can see on this page.

EXERCISE CONTINUED ON E5

on washingtonpost.com

Epilogue: Together we raise the roof, but we walk alone

After the test week, more than half the participants wanted to continue — but only as a group. We felt more alert, we were warmer in our Arctic-climate office, and we were guaranteed a good chuckle twice a day. But solo? While some deemed chair dips, desk pushups and side lunges discreet enough, most preferred to just take a walk.

Fig. 19.10

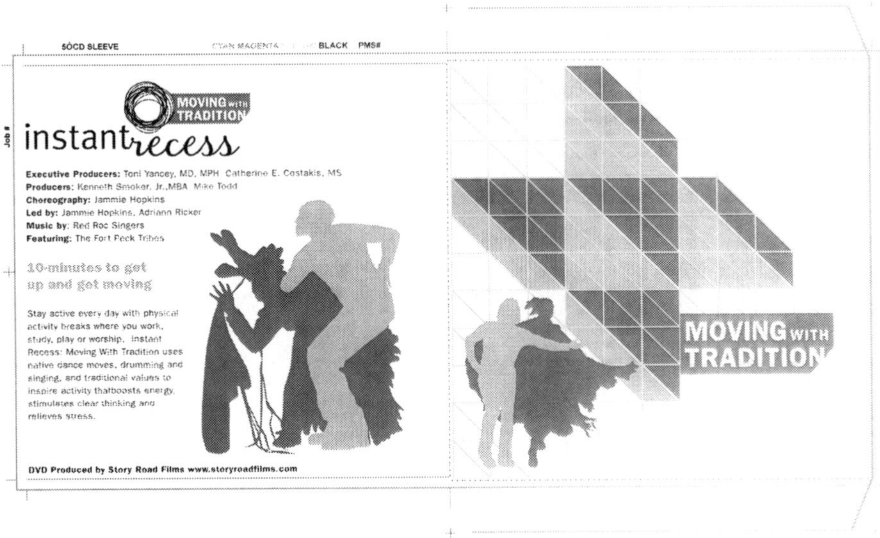

Fig. 19.11

UCLA has four current federal IR grants: a NIH-funded cluster randomized trial that tests the adoption, influence, and sustainability of "push" or "opt-out" organizational practice and policy changes that make the active choice the default, including IR breaks(Yancey, Bell-Lewis, et al., in preparation; Hopkins, Glenn, Cole, McCarthy, Yancey, 2012); a NIH-/CDC-funded CPCRN grant with IR and other "active by default" approaches as one of several featured intervention approaches; and a CDC-funded REACH US grant to disseminate these strategies (Maxwell et al., 2011) and a recent $20 million 5-year national dissemination effort funded by the CDC. Through the latter project, ethnic dance-based IR breaks have been co-choreographed with American Indians on Montana's Fort Peck Reservation (powwow dance-based *Moving with Tradition*) (StoryRoad Films, 2010) (see Fig. 19.11 for a picture of the Moving with Tradition DVD storage sleeve), Filipinos in Los Angeles, Vietnamese and Chinese Americans in Philadelphia (University of Pennsylvania), an Appalachian-serving free clinic in West Virginia, and the First Lady's *Let's Move* Faith Communities initiative.

One element of IR partnering arrangements that should be highlighted is the channeling of revenues produced by the sales of youth-focused IR materials into nonprofits. The primary beneficiary is the Public Health Institute, which serves as the main fiscal agent for the California Department of Public Health's USDA-funded obesity prevention efforts targeting Food Stamp recipients and eligible families. This serves to address the many licensing and revenue-sharing issues involved in the sometimes uneasy interface between public health and business—major league professional sports organizations and athletes, musicians, and other profit-making concerns.

Evaluation

IR has been evaluated in a variety of ways, including demonstration projects, (Yancey et al., 2006; Lara et al., 2008; Taylor et al., 2010) pilot trials, (Hopkins et al., 2012; Yancey, McCarthy, et al., in preparation) randomized controlled trials, (Whitt-Glover et al., 2011; Woods, McCarthy, Whitt-Glover, in preparation) and business case studies (Yancey, Herrmann et al., in Press; Yancey, 2010). Several of our collaborators have begun to adopt and adapt the recess break concept into their own research. For example, a University of Texas researcher has renamed them "booster breaks," securing an NINR small grant to evaluate their efficacy. Findings on IR and related interventions have been written up in two books (*Instant Recess: Building a Fit Nation 10 Minutes at a Time* and *Booster Breaks: Improving Employee Health One Break at a Time*), 20 journal articles, three journal editorials, and six book chapters. Table 19.2 provides a synopsis of the outcomes from these studies.

Conclusion

The essence of marketing, social or commercial, is understanding the consumer—feeling, listening to, and connecting with your audience. How you think and what you create is very much a product of your background and experiences, and there are no neutral observers. We all perceive the world through a cultural lens. If you don't understand the people you're trying to influence *in your bones*—if you don't get how they think or what they feel, on a live-it, breathe-it, sleep-it level, you will not get traction no matter how broad your reach or high your visibility, penetration, or exposure. If you want your product or service to sell, you have to go to the people you're trying to reach. Don't expect them to come to you. If you're not a cultural insider, you'll have to do a lot more showing up to gain acceptance. But being a cultural insider doesn't give you an automatic pass. A third generation college-educated Latino of Mexican heritage who learned Spanish in school is not necessarily going to be welcomed with open arms in a neighborhood of recent Mexican immigrants. And even if you grew up in that 'hood and moved away, you may still have a lot to learn about the current situation for people living there. You have to do some research. That's where focus groups, surveys, case studies and comparisons, and experiments come in. Do your homework on the competition so you can demonstrate the superiority of your offer. And when you get there, you damn straight better offer them something *they* want, not just something *you* think they need! And there have to be some sparks flying! Namely, forward thinkers in physical activity and public health research and practice who can convince the involved stakeholders and decision makers of the utility of this approach.

Acknowledgments This chapter was adapted from Chapter 4 of Yancey T. Instant Recess: Building a Fit Nation 10 Minutes at a Time. Berkeley, CA: University of California Press, 2010

Table 19.2 Instant Recess® Dissemination and Diffusion Timeline

Time Period	Sources of Support	Major Partners	CDs & DVDs Distributed; Web Page Views	Active/Passive Diffusion	Media Impressions (via Google search⁺)
1999–2001	USDA-funded CA DHS Nutrition Network LAC CHS	Community Health Councils	Not available	Active	0
2002–2006	The California Endowment (TCE), RWJF	California WIC, Community Health Councils	1338 direct sales/donations (Based on 2006 data only)	Primarily active, passive via word-of-mouth	30
2007–2009	NIH, CDC, TCE, RWJF, UCLA KP Center for Health Equity	LAC DPH, San Diego Padres, California WIC	3621 direct sales/donations*	Mixture of active and passive	41,850
2010- mid- 2012	NIH, CDC, UCLA KP Center for Health Equity	Los Angeles Sparks, San Diego Padres, WIC, LA's First AME Church, UCC, KEEN	5763 direct sales/donations* and 10,785 orders fulfilled by CA DPH**; 9917 page views	Primarily passive via Web 2.0 IT	135,974

*Does not include distribution by state & local health/education departments, **Includes 251 CDs shipped since May 2007 and 10, 534 DVDs shipped since May 2008, ⁺Keywords: Toni Yancey, Lift Off, Instant Recess

References

Abroms, L. C., & Maibach, E. W. (2008). The effectiveness of mass communication to change public behavior. *Annual Review of Public Health, 29*, 219–34.

Alexancer, R., Whitt-Glover, M., Ham, S., Sutton, N., Belnap, J., Yancey, A. (2012). Impact of physical activity breaks on Healthy Activity Children Policy (HSP-S-000) adherence in middle schools. In American College of Sports Medicine, San Francisco.

Belcher, B. R., Berrigan, D., Dodd, K. W., Emken, B. A., Chou, C. P., & Spruijt-Metz, D. (2010). Physical activity in US youth: Effect of race/ethnicity, age, gender, and weight status. *Medicine and Science in Sports and Exercise, 42*(12), 2211–21.

Bernhardt, J. M., Mays, D., & Kreuter, M. W. (2011). Dissemination 2.0: Closing the gap between knowledge and practice with new media and marketing. *Journal of Health Communication, 16*(Suppl 1), 32–44.

Brown, W. J., Bauman, A. E., & Owen, N. (2009). Stand up, sit down, keep moving: turning circles in physical activity research? *British Journal of Sports Medicine, 43*(2), 86–8.

Crawford, P. B., Gosliner, W., Strode, P., Samuels, S. E., Burnett, C., Craypo, L., et al. (2004). Walking the talk: Fit WIC wellness programs improve self-efficacy in pediatric obesity prevention counseling. *American Journal of Public Health, 94*(9), 1480–5.

Das, A. More Wii warriors are playing Hurt. New York Times. 2009 April 20; Sect. D5.

Foerster, S. B., Kizer, K. W., Disogra, L. K., Bal, D. G., Krieg, B. F., & Bunch, K. L. (1995). California's "5 a day–for better health!" campaign: an innovative population-based effort to effect large-scale dietary change. *American Journal of Preventive Medicine, 11*(2), 124–31.

Frazão, E. (1999). *America's eating habits: Changes & consequences*. Washington, DC: U.S. Dept. of Agriculture, Economic Research Service, Food and Rural Economics Division.

Grier, S., & Bryant, C. A. (2005). Social marketing in public health. *Annual Review of Public Health, 26*, 319–39.

Gu, B. Chinese workers unite – To exercise again. In http://worldblog.msnbc.msn.com: msnbc; 2010.

Hallett, V. Instant recess promotes health for adults by making exercise a group activity. The Washington Post. 2010 May 27.

Hallett, V. To get it, they take the stares at work. In; 2012. p. METRO; Pg. T11.

Ham, S. A., & Ainsworth, B. E. (2010). Disparities in data on Healthy People 2010 physical activity objectives collected by accelerometry and self-report. *American Journal of Public Health, 100*(Suppl 1), S263–8.

Hawkins, M. S., Storti, K. L., Richardson, C. R., King, W. C., Strath, S. J., Holleman, R. G., et al. (2009). Objectively measured physical activity of USA adults by sex, age, and racial/ethnic groups: a cross-sectional study. *International Journal of Behavioral Nutrition and Physical Activity, 6*, 31.

Hinnant, A., Oh, H. J., Caburnay, C. A., & Kreuter, M. W. (2011). What makes African American health disparities newsworthy? An experiment among journalists about story framing. *Health Education Research, 26*(6), 937–47.

Hopkins, J., Glenn, B., Cole, BL., McCarthy, WJ., Yancey, AK. (2012). Implementing organizational physical activity and healthy eating strategies on paid time: Process Evaluation of the UCLA WORKING pilot. *Health Education Research,* 27:385–98.

Hopkins, J. M., Guinyard, J. J., Yancey, A. K. (2011). Engaging organizations in sustainable physical activity interventions. In: International Society of Behavioral Nutrition and Physical Activity Annual Conference, Minneapolis, MN.

Huhman, M., Heitzler, C., & Wong, F. (2004). The VERB campaign logic model: a tool for planning and evaluation. *Preventing Chronic Disease, 1*(3), A11.

Institute of Medicine (U.S.) (2006). Committee on Food Marketing and the Diets of Children and Youth., McGinnis JM, Gootman JA, Kraak VI. *Food marketing to children and youth : threat or opportunity?* Washington, DC: National Academies Press.

Lara, A., Yancey, A. K., Tapia-Conye, R., Flores, Y., Kuri-Morales, P., Mistry, R., et al. (2008). Pausa para tu Salud: Reduction of weight and waistlines by integrating exercise breaks into workplace organizational routine. *Preventing Chronic Disease, 5*(1), A12.

Maxwell, A., Yancey, A., AuYoung, M., Guinyard, J., McCarthy, W., Bastani, R. (2011). Dissemination of organizational wellness practice and policy change: A mid-project process evaluation of the L. A. basin REACH US Center of Excellence in Elim. Preventing Chronic Disease, 8:A115.

Mitchell, J., Whitt-Glover, M., Richardson, I., Cole, B., Heil, D., Yancey, A. (2010). Evaluation of a community-wide initiative to promote physical activity breaks. In: RWJF Active Living Research Annual Conference, San Diego, CA.

Rumbach, D. Warming up to work: On-the-job stretching aimed at curbing injuries, reducing costs. South Bend Tribune, 2007 July 25.

Simon, E. Companies are promoting better lifestyles. Associated Press 2006 December 6.

Taveras, E. M., Rifas-Shiman, S. L., Field, A. E., Frazier, A. L., Colditz, G. A., & Gillman, M. W. (2004). The influence of wanting to look like media figures on adolescent physical activity. *The Journal of Adolescent Health, 35*(1), 41–50.

Taylor, W. C., Shegog, R., Chen, V., Rempel, D. M., Baun, M. P., Bush, C. L., et al. (2010). The Booster Break program: Description and feasibility test of a worksite physical activity daily practice. *Work, 37*(4), 433–43.

Troiano, R. P., Berrigan, D., Dodd, K. W., Masse, L. C., Tilert, T., & McDowell, M. (2008). Physical activity in the United States measured by accelerometer. *Medicine and Science in Sports and Exercise, 40*(1), 181–8.

Valente, T. W., Murphy, S., Huang, G., Gusek, J., Greene, J., & Beck, V. (2007). Evaluating a minor storyline on ER about teen obesity, hypertension, and 5 a day. *Journal of Health Communication, 12*(6), 551–66.

Whitt-Glover, M. C., Ham, S. A., & Yancey, A. K. (2011). Instant Recess®: A practical tool for increasing physical activity during the school day. *Progress in Community Health Partnerships, 5*(3), 289–97.

Whitt-Glover, M. C., Heil, D., Hornbuckle, L. M., Ham, S. A., Ainsworth, B. E., Yancey, A. K. (2010). A calibration method to improve criterion validity of self-reported physical activity. In American College of Sports Medicine, Baltimore, MD.

Woods, D. (2011). Implementation and evaluation of Instant Recess in elementary school children. Dissertation. In Los Angeles, CA: UCLA.

Woods, D., McCarthy, W., Whitt-Glover, M., Yancey, A. Evaluation of Instant Recess® exercise breaks as a means for implementing LAUSD physical activity policy in elementary schools. In preparation.

Wile, D. (1996). *Lost tĐai-chi classics from the late ChĐing dynasty*. Albany: State University of New York Press.

Yancey, A. K. (2009). The meta-volition model: Organizational leadership is the key ingredient in getting society moving, literally! *Preventive Medicine, 49*, 342–51.

Yancey, A. K. (2010). *Instant recess: Building a fit nation 10 minutes at a time*. Berkeley: University of California Press.

Yancey, A., Bell-Lewis, L., McCarthy, W., Glenn, B., Hopkins, J., Wong, W. Decreasing sitting, prompting physical activity and arresting waistline expansion: WORKING pilot study outcomes. In preparation.

Yancey, A., Herrmann, A., Creighton, T. (in press). Moving the needle on physical activity: Instant recess at Kaiser Permanente's South Bay Health Center. In R. Pate, C. Bryant, D. Buchner, M. Scrag M (Eds.), Implementing Physical Activity Strategies. Champaign, IL: Human Kinetics.

Yancey, A. K., Lewis, L. B., Guinyard, J. J., Sloane, D. C., Nascimento, L. M., Galloway-Gilliam, L., et al. (2006). Putting promotion into practice: The African Americans building a legacy of health organizational wellness program. *Health Promotion Practice, 7*(3 Suppl), 233S–46S.

Yancey, A., McCarthy, W., Glenn, B., Hopkins, J., Wong, W., Patel, M. Intervening in human services agencies to promote organizational wellness: WORKING pilot study design, development and baseline findings. In preparation.

Yancey, A. K., McCarthy, W. J., Taylor, W. C., Merlo, A., Gewa, C., Weber, M. D., et al. (2004). The Los Angeles Lift Off: A sociocultural environmental change intervention to integrate physical activity into the workplace. *Preventive Medicine, 38*(6), 848–56.

Yancey, A. K., Winfield, D., Larsen, J., Anderson, M., Jackson, P., Overton, J., et al. (2009). Live, learn and play: Building strategic alliances between professional sports and public health. *Preventive Medicine, 49*, 322–25.

Chapter 20
Communities Leveraging the Assets of a National Social Marketing Campaign: Experiences with VERB™. *It's What You Do*!

Marian Huhman and Carrie D. Patnode

Introduction

The VERB. *It's what you do!* social marketing campaign used mass media, school and community promotions, the Internet, and partnerships with national organizations and local communities to encourage children aged 9–13 years (tweens) to be physically active every day (Wong et al., 2004). In the authorizing legislation for VERB, the US Congress specified that the same communication methods used by the best kids' marketers should be adopted to communicate messages to help children develop healthy lifestyles. CDC chose to focus the campaign on physical activity because of the substantial evidence regarding the physical and psychological benefits to children of being physically active (Strong et al., 2005), including physical activity's role in maintaining a healthy weight (U.S. Department of Health and Human Services, 2008). (See Development and Release of the 2008 Physical Activity Guidelines for Americans: Children and Adolescents by Wargo, Fulton, & Lee, this volume, Chap. 21). The goal of the campaign was to help establish positive physical activity habits in the tween years in hopes that these habits would continue as the children became adolescents and young adults.

Successfully competing with the vast amount of marketing directed at and viewed daily by this segment of youth required hiring and partnering with a number of creative and media agencies, including those with substantial experience working on popular commercial youth brands and those with insight on ethnic-specific markets. For a full list of agencies that VERB contracted with for advertising, marketing,

M. Huhman, Ph.D. (✉)
University of Illinois Urbana Champaign, Urbana, IL, USA
e-mail: mhuhman@illinois.edu

C.D. Patnode, Ph.D., M.P.H.
Kaiser Permanente, Center for Health Research, Portland, OR, USA

J.D. Williams et al. (eds.), *Advances in Communication Research to Reduce Childhood Obesity*, DOI 10.1007/978-1-4614-5511-0_20,

public relations, please see Wong et al. (2008). As is true in commercial marketing, developing a media-driven national brand; maintaining an appealing message across geographic, economic, and racial/ethnic groups; and integrating traditional media with more nontraditional forms of marketing require considerable investment. With a cumulative congressional appropriation of $339 million, VERB was able to use the sophisticated techniques of commercial marketers. This included building the VERB brand (Asbury, Wong, Price, & Nolin, 2008), conducting extensive formative research (Berkowitz, Huhman, Heitzler, et al., 2008), using professional actors and celebrity athletes, and buying media and promotional opportunities to ensure reaching a substantial proportion of the target audience. A largely consistent level of marketing activities was maintained from June 2002 through September 2006, when funding for the campaign ended.

The national presence of VERB through paid advertising on multiple tween-centric media outlets (e.g., television channels such as MTV and Nickelodeon and magazines such as *Sports Illustrated for Kids*) facilitated the penetration of the campaign into communities where tweens could sample the product of physical activity through community and school promotions, community events, and partnerships with other national brands that were conducting their own community tours and promotions. Tweens learned to associate the VERB brand with having fun and trying new ways to be physically active. The VERB campaign, operating at the national level though these multiple communication and marketing activities, was aimed at creating a demand among tweens for physical activity at the community level. In addition, some communities responded by developing their *own* programs for physical activity and using the VERB brand. In using the VERB brand, local community activities could capitalize on the cachet and cool factor associated with the images the tweens were seeing in the national marketing campaign.

In this chapter, we describe strategies that were used in the VERB campaign that brought VERB to communities as part of the CDC-sponsored national campaign and we explain how some communities put their own resources into programs and events to facilitate the uptake of VERB by their local tweens. We also discuss a challenge faced by VERB and one that will be an emerging issue for public health campaigns: helping public health practitioners in local communities use, but not dilute, campaign assets (e.g., branded materials including advertisements) that were being maintained by commercial marketers at the national level. The evaluation methods and results are presented as well as lessons learned and considerations for future communication and marketing activities with both national and community foci.

Campaign Strategy

National paid advertising, mainly on cable channels popular with the tween segment, was the primary campaign component throughout the life of the campaign. In line with the principles of social marketing (Kotler & Lee, 2008), this advertising served as a vehicle to drive the consumer (tweens) to purchase the product (to engage in physical activity); thus, creating demand. The ads illustrated the positive benefits of physical activity and tried to motivate tweens to "find their Verb" and invite them to become part of the VERB movement.

While VERB continued to use traditional (national) advertising channels throughout the campaign, implementation of locally designed activities to provide tweens with opportunities to experience the brand (VERB) and sample of the product (physical activity) on an interactive basis became critically important once brand awareness was established. This product sampling approach is an example of the shift in contemporary advertising from strictly traditional forms of advertising which are designed to reach large audiences with small personal involvement (e.g., broadcast media like television, radio, and print) to forms of "experiential" marketing designed to reach smaller audiences and offer more personal involvement (Heitzler, Asbury, & Kusner, 2008). In this case, experiential marketing through local implementation and community involvement was designed to increase the supply of physical activity opportunities (targeting both the "place" and "price" of social marketing). This included highlighting existing community programs and facilities and increasing the quality and quantity of such opportunities. (Bretthauer-Mueller et al., 2008).

Strategies for engaging communities included both a "top-down" (or community-placed) approach and a "bottom-up" (or community-based") approach. Partners at the national and local level were essential in executing activities within both approaches. The *top-down* approach involved engaging community organizations and local outlets to disseminate marketing and promotional activities developed by the campaign. In this scenario, communities and local experts had very little input on the structure, format, and timing of the activities That is, materials were conceptualized and developed internally by the campaign creative staff and were sent to community groups and organizations to disseminate and implement through programs in their respective communities.

On the other hand, the *bottom-up* approach involved supporting communities to capitalize on the VERB brand assets to develop programs and events tailored according to the resources and needs of their community. In this situation, local experts and/or existing coalitions approached VERB directly (often times through personal and professional contacts) about initiating their own VERB-related promotions in their communities. VERB fully engaged communities as campaign partners by helping them assess their needs, build capacity, and customize VERB-related materials and activities to meet those needs. Selected examples of community involvement at both levels are described below.

Highlighted Community Examples

Top-down approach. Campaign planners used experiential marketing tactics as a chance for tweens to interact with VERB and experience what the VERB brand was all about: engaging in active play. The main goals of these community-placed activities were to: (1) reinforce VERB messages that were already reaching tweens through traditional media channels operating at the national level; (2) provide trial opportunities for tweens to engage in physical activity; (3) offer on-site incentives for participating in physical activity; and (4) raise awareness of local opportunities for children to be physically active (Heitzler et al., 2008). These activities took the form of mobile tours and guerrilla marketing, event sponsorships, and the distribution of promotional kits to schools and community organizations.

Mobile and guerilla marketing involved going directly to VERB's target audience—to interact with tweens face-to-face in usually a short-term encounter. Guerrilla marketing involves unconventional methods of promotional activities, for example through "street teams". VERB's street teams were composed of energetic, engaging young adults who were hired to catch the attention of tweens and interact with them at sporting events, malls, parks, or other recreational outlets. Typically the street team members had performance skills that would hold the interest of tweens such as juggling, walking on stilts, or break dancing.

Mobile tours, such as the VERB *Anytour,* featured six custom trucks that were wrapped with colorful figures and designs that traveled throughout the country spreading the VERB messages and engaging tweens along the way. The *Anytour* stopped at nearly 1,000 events across approximately 80 US communities, spanning about 9 months, and reaching an estimated 1,340,000 tweens. *Anytour* played off the national advertising platform at the time, "Anytime, Anywhere" that communicated the message that tweens can engage in physical activity anytime and anywhere. The young adults who were hired to execute the mobile and guerrilla marketing were ambassadors of the VERB message and became the face of the campaign. These ambassadors would reinforce physical activity the tweens were already doing and would encourage them to try new activities. The trucks stayed in a local area for about one week, setting up activity areas with equipment carried on the trucks—basketball hoops, set ups for street hockey and Dance Dance revolution, and jump rope areas—and invite tweens to play.

Event sponsorships were opportunities to further advance the young brand of VERB and its messages and to build affinity for the brand by associating with brands or celebrities that were well known among tweens. For example, VERB cosponsored with Nickelodeon to bring the Wild & Crazy Kids (WACK) show to over 14,000 tweens in nine cities. Other events sponsored or cosponsored by VERB were the Asian-oriented Harvest Moon Festival in Los Angeles and the Calle Ocho Street Festival in Miami.

VERB also developed and disseminated school and community programs, particularly in years 2 through 4. These promotions typically involved a turn-key kit containing the materials and instructions needed for a teacher or recreational leader to engage a classroom or group of tweens in an entertaining and physically active experience. One such example was VERB *Anytime Doubletime*. The *Anytime Doubletime* promotion involved encouraging tweens to make two games into one. National distributors (e.g., Scholastic) were hired by the campaign to disseminate the materials (at no cost) to schools within their portfolio. Schools and communities organizations could also request these materials directly by completing an online request form with the CDC. Typically, these promotions were used in the schools or community organizations for 2 to 6 weeks. Over the course of the campaign, VERB implemented four school-directed promotions, each reaching 2,000–3,000 elementary or middle schools. Additionally, the same promotions used for the schools plus two additional promotions were implemented with 20,000 ready-to-use kits delivered to youth-serving recreational centers (e.g., Boys and Girls Clubs), community- and faith-based organizations. We estimated that the school- and community-based organizations together reached more than 1 million children.

Another example was the partnership with the Girl Scouts of America. This partnership began with the co-branding of *Anytime Doubletime* kits for distribution to troops and councils. The campaign was invited to consult with the Girl Scout organization as they considered a healthy lifestyles initiative to be delivered across its membership. In addition to the opportunity to incorporate VERB messages into their already existing programs and to deliver physical activity in using VERB approaches, the invitation generated conversations about a VERB patch or badge program, and an opportunity to work with the Girl Scouts' new, hipper branch, Studio 2B, to conduct audience-research or implement street-marketing activities in the campaign's next phase. VERB was provided complimentary space at the national Girl Scouts conference held in Atlanta in 2005, and the national office encouraged all councils across the country to embrace VERB in the promotion of physical activity. CDC provided each council with additional resources to generate excitement and keep their interest high.

Besides these national programs that were delivered to hundreds of communities, in its first 2 years, VERB embarked on a somewhat different approach to engage targeted communities in a more concentrated fashion. Nine communities were initially selected to receive augmented marketing activities; six of these evolved into what VERB planners called "high-dose communities," receiving supplemental advertising and promotions and assessment of the outcomes (Berkowitz, Huhman, & Nolin, 2008). Advertising on traditional media channels (TV, radio, and print, out of home) was increased by 50% in these communities over the overall national media buy and relationships with existing community coalitions were sought to partner with them to copresent VERB promotions in their communities.

In selecting the set of high dose communities, VERB planners sought to balance factors of geography (seeking representation of broad areas of the country), population size (a range of large to small was desired), racial and ethnic diversity, and very importantly, the size and cost of the media market for the city. For example, New York City has a large population and media market and offered rich ethnic and racial diversity, but the cost of the New York City media market was much more expensive than Los Angeles, which is comparable in terms of population size and diversity Therefore, Los Angeles was selected.

The distinctive feature of this high-dose effort was the partnering of the community groups and coalitions with the creative agencies and affiliated media organizations that were developing the VERB brand and advertising. The CDC VERB team negotiated the needs of the creative agencies to maximize efficiency with putting on a major promotion such as the WACK show and the needs of the community groups who had preferences about logistics of the event such as dates, venue, and transportation methods.

Bottom-up approach. After the VERB brand was established and partners learned about the importance of brand protection (i.e., maintaining the personality and meaning of the brand), a strategy evolved that found communities using the VERB brand to develop materials for their community that featured the VERB logo, bringing VERB's cachet to the community's efforts. VERB also provided many of the previously mentioned activity toolkits for schools and organizations to use with tweens. CDC consulted with community partners to ensure consistent messages with the national campaign through a set of brand guidelines by helping them (1) reframe their physical activity programs as fun and exciting and avoid a *should do, good for you* message; (2) connect the VERB brand to the point of purchase; and (3) drive tweens to the opportunities, places, and programs where they could "purchase" the product of physical activity (Bretthauer-Mueller et al., 2008).

One of the most comprehensive and successful bottom up community programs was VERB Summer Scorecard, which Lexington, KY first implemented in the summer of 2004 and continued for several summers. A high-functioning coalition of more than 50 members from businesses, schools, health services, recreation centers, parents, coaches, and the transportation system decided to focus its efforts on youth physical activity. The centerpiece of VERB Summer Scorecard was the actual scorecard, a wallet-sized card with 24 squares on it; each square represented one hour of physical activity. Participating businesses and recreational outlets stamped the cards and gave tweens discounts on physical activities and events, such as free swimming at community pools and reduced admission prices to skating rinks and sports clinics.

The coalition used a planning and implementation approach called "community-based prevention marketing," developed by the Florida Prevention Research Center. With assistance from the Prevention Research Center, the coalition quickly developed a "marketing mind-set" and worked to develop the "places" for tweens to be active at the right "price," and even negotiated with the transportation system that a Scorecard could be used as bus fare—thus removing an important barrier for tweens getting to their preferred places to be active.

CDC's VERB team helped keep program development costs low for the coalition by providing the extensive audience research about tweens and parents that had been done by CDC to develop the VERB brand and messages. CDC's team supported the Lexington coalition's efforts through consultation on the brand guidelines and local marketing strategies. In addition, CDC provided guidance on the coalition's plans for evaluation. By the end of 2006, 17 other communities in several states (e.g., Indiana, Iowa, and Florida) had adapted the Lexington VERB Scorecard program for their community. VERB Summer Scorecard in Sarasota, FL closely modeled the Lexington, KY program and was also evaluated through a partnership with the Florida Prevention Research Center (McDermott et al., 2009). Some other US communities had programs planned for 2012, 6 years after VERB's national funding ended.

Evaluation Results

The VERB campaign was evaluated extensively. Process evaluation, which assesses whether a program is implemented as planned, included monitoring the reach and frequency of the advertising, conducting a national tracking survey to monitor the likeability of the VERB brand (Huhman, Price, & Potter, 2008), and assessing the number of promotions and events, attendance at events, and receptiveness of tweens to the promotional events.

VERB also conducted an annual outcome evaluation through nationally representative telephone surveys (Potter, Judkins, Nolin, & Huhman, 2008). The evaluation surveyed tweens and parents regarding their attitudes and behaviors related to physical activity. The survey tool, the Youth Media Campaign Longitudinal Survey (YMCLS), was developed specifically for VERB and included measures for the awareness and understanding of the VERB brand and messages, psychosocial measures known to influence physical activity, and measures of physical activity sessions in nonschool hours in the past 7 days and on the day prior to the survey. The YMCLS was found to be reliable and valid in measuring tweens physical activity (Welk et al., 2007).

The YMCLS included three scales that assessed psychosocial dimensions of physical activity: (1) outcome expectations—child's beliefs about the benefits of participating in physical activities; (2) self-efficacy—child's confidence to overcome barriers to engaging in physical activities; and (3) social influences—positive norms for physical activity held by peers. The physical activity measures were divided into organized sessions of physical activity (with a coach or leader) and free-time sessions (done in their free time, alone, or with friends). The outcome evaluation showed that after year one of the campaign 74% of US tweens were aware of VERB, and 90% of those who were aware, understood at least one of the key messages. Subgroups of tweens (e.g., girls, younger tweens) who were aware of the campaign did significantly more physical activity than tweens who were not aware (Huhman et al., 2005). After 2 years of the campaign, the psychosocial measure of outcome expectations and the physical activity measures of free-time sessions in the past 7 days and physical activity done on the day prior to the survey showed total population-level effects (meaning no signficant differences across gender, age, race, SES groups). After controlling for baseline levels of physical activity, tweens who were aware of VERB reported more physical activity sessions in their free time than tweens who were not aware of the campaign (Huhman et al., 2007). After 4 years of the campaign, the final outcome analysis showed continuing effects, and a dose–response analysis found that increasing amounts of VERB exposure resulted in stronger attitude and behavioral effects. Some positive VERB effects were sustained as tweens aged into their later teen years (Huhman et al., 2010).

The VERB Summer Scorecard in Lexington, KY was also assessed with process and outcome measures. In 2004, tweens redeemed more than 350 completed *VERB Scorecards* that reported more than 8,400 h of physical activity during the 13-week community campaign. They redeemed more than twice as many completed *VERB Scorecards* in 2005 and 2006. Scorecard participants were more likely to be physically active than tweens who did not participate. In addition to the individual-level variables, the efforts in Lexington led to changes in macro-level variables, strengthening the local health department's relationship with local media, making changes in public transportation, and building new relationships between public health and local businesses (Bryant et al., 2010). For example, the bus system agreed to accept the VERB Scorecards as bus tickets, giving children free transportation to sites where they could be physically active.

The Sarasota County program evaluators used a post only comparison group design to evaluate their 2005 Summer Scorecard program (Debate et al., 2009). They found that tweens who participated in the intervention were more likely to be physically active than tweens in the comparison group and more physically active than youth in the intervention community who did not participate in Scorecard. Sarasota evaluators also used their Scorecard experiences to study community capacity to implement and sustain health interventions and to form partnerships among the community, the school district, and the university. (Debate et al., 2009; McDermott et al., 2009). Across the Sarasota and Lexington initiatives, community capacity building included training adult and youth members of the coalition to conduct focus groups (Lexington), schooling coalition groups in both communities in how to "think like marketers" and apply a systematic process of prevention marketing to their work, and sponsoring team members to attend national conferences on social marketing.

Lessons Learned: Future Endeavors

As a public health effort, VERB planners at CDC were eager to involve communities in the campaign. We know that supporting communities to develop solutions that fit their unique needs increase the likelihood of success by giving ownership and responsibility to the entities that can sustain the efforts while building community capacity. Despite our commitment to these values, community engagement was one of the most challenging aspects of the VERB campaign. Both pathways—top down to communities from the national campaign and bottom up in helping communities that came to VERB to design their own campaign activities—posed challenges but also produced notable successes and offered many lessons learned.

The initial attempts to reach out to the campaign's designated "high-dose" communities included working with local coalition members and VERB champions to assemble the audience for the WACK show being staged by the national media agencies. Because the WACK event occurred during the school day, community coalition leaders or public health agency members chose which schools would participate, obtained parent consent for participation, and arranged transportation of the tweens to the event. CDC brought the tour to the community while the community partner identified and transported tweens to the VERB-sponsored events that were scheduled on specific days and time. Transporting hundreds of children to the VERB events was complicated, expensive, and resource-intensive for our community partners and was stressful for some of the coalition groups.

Hosting a professional, expensive, and highly rehearsed event like the WACK show fairly quickly exposed the divergent views between the private sector marketing entities and the community members. The community members were excited to host these celebrity-driven events and offered informed opinions on the venue, how to involve the schools, and transport the children to the event. However, the creative agencies were not used to accommodating community input on business decisions or tailoring campaign activities and schedules for individual communities. The values of the creative agencies and media partners from the private sector centered on cost-efficient and timely delivery of edgy, attention-getting concepts and products to as many tweens as possible. Communities did not understand initially that in-market activities such as WACK were owned by VERB's media organization partners who controlled the decisions that affected their own programs; CDC nor the creative agencies hired by CDC had control over these issues.

Thus, for the first 2 years, VERB planners and communities grappled with the best way to partner with each other. Communities were ready to partner, but VERB was cautious until the brand was firmly established and campaign products were developed that were appropriate for communities to use. Plus, the CDC creative team and the creative agencies were very concerned that all communications to the target audience were "on brand". That is, they worried that the introduction of materials and events that may not be seen as cool or relevant to tweens, even though well intentioned, could dilute the assets of the young VERB brand.

From this experience, CDC and the creative agencies learned that a better strategy was to implement the experiential marketing and promotional activities nationally as described above and across multiple communities instead of in-market events, such as the Nickelodeon Wild and Crazy Kids show. In the words of VERB director, Faye Wong, "The change in strategy brought *VERB to tweens* instead of *tweens to VERB*" (Wong, Greenwell, Gates, & Berkowitz, 2008, S181).

As VERB was developing strategies to engage tweens in multiple US communities through experiential marketing, communities continued to be interested in monetary and nonmonetary support from VERB for promotion of their own programs. However, direct monetary support was prohibited by the Congressional guidelines that specified that VERB could not directly fund community activities or programs. Nonmonetary assets were supplied, such as the turn key kits to schools and youth-oriented programs and written materials like tip sheets for parents on how to make physical activity a fun family event. We also could not give communities VERB TV ads to air on their local stations, as some communities had hoped, because of restrictions on using ads that had been developed and paid for by the media agencies. The gap between what VERB could support and provide in communities and what communities wanted proved frustrating for both CDC and communities.

The main nonmonetary asset that VERB could offer communities was the VERB brand. This was challenging because establishing a new brand requires maintaining control over all the messages and images associated with the brand to keep the brand clear and consistent in the minds of the target audience. Again, the creative agencies feared erosion of VERB brand affinity if locally produced events and programs were VERB branded but turned out to be off message, adult-centric, or in some other way unappealing to the tween audience. Thus, we were asking communities with little marketing experience to match the sophistication of professional marketers. Our solution was to provide communities with ready-to-use communication and marketing materials (e.g., press releases for events being hosted by the community) as well as campaign art work, and clear guidelines on how to use the brand. If a community coalition was not already working with a social marketing or community prevention marketing approach, CDC's partnership team worked with the coalition members to learn to "think like a marketer." Having a marketing mind-set (e.g., putting the tween's motivations and barriers at the center of the plan) was highly instrumental in facilitating communication between VERB planners and community partners. A shared understanding aided CDC's efforts to help communities stage events that would be appealing to tweens and most importantly be on message: that physical activity was fun, cool, and a way to be social with friends.

We learned from working with communities that presenting to community partners what they will gain from being a part of the partnership increases the chance they will come on board and make meaningful contributions. For example, the police department may be more likely to help if the offer is framed as a way for them to interact with disadvantaged youth in a nonthreatening manner. Local transit companies can be encouraged to offer free bus rides to youth participants as a way to initiate them to become more regular bus riders.

Another lesson is the importance of checking in with community partners throughout the campaign, allowing organizers to see what is going well and what needs to be adjusted. The best laid plans can be altered in ways that planners never anticipated, especially when multiple community partners are involved. For example, on regular site visits, the Lexington team found that some signage was not well placed or placed at all. Some staff members were giving misinformation to the public and confusion about transportation was keeping some youth from participating. Communicating regularly through site visits, phone calls, and email strengthens implementation and allows for mid-course adjustments, heading off problems at an early stage. Communities can also use low cost resources for monitoring the implementation of program events, such as sending graduate students or volunteers to activities to observe and write detailed field notes as feedback for organizers.

We feel that the communication strategy to establish a brand as a platform for the VERB messages was the right decision given the goal of implementing a national campaign and given the resources that VERB had. Establishing a national presence of the brand through the work of the commercial marketers while establishing relationships with communities can give time for the campaign to develop marketing and communication materials for the communities.

If targeting specific communities, we would suggest that communities be chosen based on their readiness to engage with the campaign rather than on our criteria for the high dose communities (e.g., geography, size, and diversity). Readiness to engage would include factors such as: (1) an existing coalition or community network that can facilitate access to the supply of physical activity opportunities in the community; (2) a champion within the network who can provide leadership and ensure follow through; (3) its own funding (including donated media time and space) to support community-wide campaigns or promotional events; (4) a willingness to adopt marketing mind-set.

As in all cases of a massive undertaking like the VERB campaign, attention to defining roles and responsibilities early on can reduce disagreement and tensions down the road. In VERB's case, we did not know how the intersections with communities would play out. We made decisions on roles and responsibilities as they evolved. The fast pace of a commercial marketing venture meant little time to help communities with their learning curves for framing physical activity from a marketing perspective for tweens in their communities.

We would suggest that future endeavors evaluate more rigorously the outcomes of community-based initiatives and compare these efforts to the outcomes that are being measured by national level evaluations. Although some of the members of the CDC team feared that community-based activities would dilute the VERB assets for the tweens in the communities implementing their own VERB events, we assessed, albeit anecdotally, that the VERB brand was not diminished in these communities. This information would be important to inform future campaigns.

A final suggestion for future planning would be to engage stakeholders in communities earlier and strategically to be champions for the national campaign. As a federal agency, CDC could not officially advocate for continuing the VERB campaign. Plus, our primary constituents, tweens, were not in a position to "lobby" for us. Thus, community partners could have been encouraged to voice their support for the campaign, especially since VERB was moving toward more integration with communities as part of sustaining VERB—by keeping VERB as an inspiration to tweens to be physically active in the places where they lived and played.

Conclusion

CDC was charged by Congress to use the sophisticated tactics of the best kid marketers to essentially "sell" physical activity to children. The outcome of that charge, VERB. *It's what you do!,* demonstrated that a combination of strong media, national promotions, and local, often experiential activities can help children to be more physically active, thus, addressing an important aspect of the problem of childhood obesity. We believe that communities played a vital role in the success of this marketing and communication approach. Whereas the advertising created buzz about the brand itself and conveyed empowering messages about adopting and maintaining active lifestyles, local implementation and community engagement gave tweens the opportunity to "sample the product" and be active in the "places" that they live—their own communities.

References

Asbury, L. D., Wong, F. L., Price, S. M., & Nolin, M. J. (2008). The VERB campaign: Applying a branding strategy in public health. *American Journal of Preventive Medicine, 34*, S183–S187.

Berkowitz, J. M., Huhman, M., Heitzler, C. D., Potter, L. D., Nolin, M. J., & Banspach, S. W. (2008). Overview of formative, process, and outcome evaluation methods used in the VERB campaign. *American Journal of Preventive Medicine, 34*, S222–S229.

Berkowitz, J. M., Huhman, M., & Nolin, M. J. (2008). Did augmenting the VERB campaign advertising in select communities have an effect on awareness, attitudes, and physical activity? *American Journal of Preventive Medicine, 34*, S257–S266.

Bretthauer-Mueller, R., Berkowitz, J. M., Thomas, M., McCarthy, S., Green, L. A., Melancon, H., et al. (2008). Catalyzing community action within a national campaign: VERB community and national partnerships. *American Journal of Preventive Medicine, 34*, S210–S221.

Bryant, C. A., Courtney, A. H., McDermott, R. J., Alfonso, M. L., Baldwin, J. A., Nickelson, J., et al. (2010). Promoting physical activity among youth through community-based prevention marketing. *The Journal of School Health, 80*, 214–224.

Debate, R. D., Baldwin, J. A., Thompson, A., Nickelson, J., Alfonso, M. L., Bryant, C. A., et al. (2009). *Amer J Com Psycho, 44*, 363–373.

Heitzler, C. D., Asbury, L. D., & Kusner, S. L. (2008). Bringing "play" to life: The use of experiential marketing in the VERB campaign. *American Journal of Preventive Medicine, 34*, S188–S193.

Huhman, M. E., Potter, L. D., Nolin, M. J., Piesse, A., Judkins, D. R., Banspach, S. W., et al. (2010). Evaluation of the VERB™ campaign's influence on children's physical activity, 2002–2006. *American Journal of Public Health, 100*(4), 638–645.

Huhman, M., Potter, L. D., Wong, F. L., Banspach, S. W., Duke, J. C., & Heitzler, C. D. (2005). Effects of a mass media campaign to increase physical activity among children: Year-1 results of the VERB campaign. *Pediatrics, 116*, e277–e284.

Huhman, M., Price, S. M., & Potter, L. D. (2008). Branding play for children. VERB(tm) It's what you do. In D. Evans & G. Hastings (Eds.), *Public health branding: Applying marketing for social change.* (pp. 109–126). Oxford: Oxford University Press.

Huhman, M. E., Potter, L. D., Duke, J. C., Judkins, D. R., Heitzler, C. D., & Wong, F. L. (2007). Evaluation of a national physical activity intervention for children: VERB campaign, 2002–2004. *American Journal of Preventive Medicine, 32*, 38–43.

Kotler, P., & Lee, N. (2008). *Social marketing: Influencing behaviors for good.* Thousand Oaks, CA: Sage.

McDermott, R. J., Nickelson, J., Baldwin, J. A., Bryant, C. A., Alfonso, M., Phillips, L. M., et al. (2009). A community-school district-university partnership for assessing physical activity of tweens. *Preventing Chronic Disease, 6*, A15.

Potter, L. D., Judkins, D. R., Nolin, M. J., & Huhman, M. (2008). Methodology of the outcome evaluation of the VERB™ campaign. *American Journal of Preventive Medicine, 34*, S230–S240.

Strong, W. B., Malina, R. M., Blimkie, C. J., Daniels, S. R., Dishman, R. K., Gutin, B., et al. (2005). Evidence based physical activity for school-age youth. *The Journal of Pediatrics, 146*, 732–737.

U.S. Department of Health and Human Services (2008). *Physical Activity Guidelines Advisory Committee Report* Accessed September 16, 2011.

Welk, G. J., Wickel, E., Peterson, M., Heitzler, C. D., Fulton, J. E., & Potter, L. D. (2007). Reliability and validity of questions on the youth media campaign longitudinal survey. *Medicine and Science in Sports and Exercise, 39*, 612–621.

Wong, F., Huhman, M., Heitzler, C., Asbury, L., Bretthauer-Mueller, R., McCarthy, S., et al. (2004). VERB – A social marketing campaign to increase physical activity among youth. *Preventing Chronic Disease, 1*, A10.

Wong, F. L., Greenwell, M., Gates, S., & Berkowitz, J. M. (2008). It's what you do! Reflections on the VERB campaign. *American Journal of Preventive Medicine, 34*, S175–S182.

Chapter 21
Development and Release of the 2008 Physical Activity Guidelines for Americans: Children and Adolescents

Jane D. Wargo, Janet E. Fulton, and Sarah M. Lee

List of Abbreviations

PAG	Physical Activity Guidelines
PAGAC	Physical Activity Guidelines Advisory Committee
HHS/USDHHS	U.S. Department of Health and Human Services
ODPHP	Office of Disease Prevention and Health Promotion
CDC	Centers for Disease Control and Prevention
IOM	Institute of Medicine
DASH	Division of Adolescent and School Health
CSEP	Canadian Society for Exercise Physiology
PE	Physical education
PEP	Physical Education for Progress
AAHPERD	American Alliance for Health, Physical Education, Recreation & Dance
NASPE	National Alliance for Sport and Physical Education

The findings and conclusions in this report are those of the authors and do not necessarily represent the official position of the USDHHS or the CDC.

J.D. Wargo (✉)
Presidential Youth Fitness Program
e-mail: jane@presidentialyouthfitnessprogram.org

J.E. Fulton
Division of Nutrition, Physical Activity and Obesity,
Centers for Disease Control and Prevention, 4770 Buford Highway NE, MS K-46, Atlanta, GA 30341-3717, U.S.

S.M. Lee
School Health Branch, Division of Population Health, Centers for Disease Control and Prevention, 4770 Buford Highway NE, Mail stop K12, Atlanta, GA, 30341, U.S.

J.D. Williams et al. (eds.), *Advances in Communication Research to Reduce Childhood Obesity*, DOI 10.1007/978-1-4614-5511-0_21,

Physical Activity Guidelines Development

The 2008 Physical Activity Guidelines for Americans (PAG) are the first, evidence-based, comprehensive guidelines for physical activity published by the federal government (USDHHS, 2008). Based on the 2008 Physical Activity Guidelines Federal Advisory Committee (PAGAC) Report, the PAG provide guidance for health professionals and policymakers on the amounts and types of physical activity that provide substantial health benefits for Americans aged six years and older (USDHHS).

The guidelines for youth address three key components for physical activity prescription: the amount, the type, and the intensity of physical activity. Physical activity amount is prescribed by the guideline to do at least one hour of physical activity daily. Type of physical activity is prescribed as aerobic, bone-strengthening and muscle-strengthening activities on at least 3 days per week. Intensity is prescribed as moderate or vigorous intensity and relates to aerobic activities. The guidelines also emphasize the need to provide a variety of age-appropriate activities for children and adolescents. A brief summary of the key guidelines for children and adolescents is presented below.

Physical Activity Guidelines for Children and Adolescents

- Children and adolescents should do 60 min (1 h) or more of physical activity daily.
  - *Aerobic*: Most of the 60 or more minutes a day should be either moderate- or vigorous-intensity aerobic physical activity, and should include vigorous-intensity physical activity at least 3 days a week.
  - *Muscle-strengthening*: As part of their 60 or more minutes of daily physical activity, children and adolescents should include muscle-strengthening physical activity on at least 3 days of the week.
  - *Bone-strengthening*: As part of their 60 or more minutes of daily physical activity, children and adolescents should include bone-strengthening physical activity on at least 3 days of the week.
- It is important to encourage young people to participate in physical activities that are appropriate for their age, that are enjoyable, and that offer variety (USDHHS, 2008, p 16).

Examples of physical activities that can help youth meet the guidelines for aerobic, muscle-strengthening, and bone-strengthening activities are provided (Table 21.1). A variety of physical activities can help youth meet the aforementioned prescriptions for intensity and type outlined in the guidelines. This reinforces the concept that youth benefit from participating in a variety of physical activities including lifetime activities, sports, free play, and active games. Given that physical activity

Table 21.1 Examples of moderate- and vigorous- intensity aerobic physical activities and muscle-strengthening and bone-strengthening activities for children and adolescents

Aerobic activity	
Moderate-intensity activities	Hiking, skateboarding, rollerblading Bicycle riding Brisk walking
Vigorous-intensity activities	Active games involving running and chasing (tag) Bicycling riding Jumping rope Martial arts (such as karate) Running Sports (soccer, ice or field hockey, tennis, swimming, basketball) Cross country skiing
Muscle-strengthening activity	Games such as tug-of-war Modified push-ups (with knees on the floor) Resistance exercises using body weight or resistance bands Rope or tree climbing Sit-ups (curl-ups or crunches) Swinging on playground equipment/bars
Bone-strengthening activity	Games such as hopscotch Hopping, skipping, jumping Jumping rope Running Sports such as gymnastics, basketball, volleyball, tennis

Source: U.S. Department of Health and Human Services. (2008). 2008 Physical activity guidelines for Americans. Washington, DC: U.S. Department of Health and Human Services

often declines as youth grow older (Caspersen, Pereira, & Curran, 2000), it is important for them to be exposed to a variety of activities through sports and recreational venues, and to develop the skills and knowledge necessary to be confident in their ability to be active throughout childhood and into adolescence and adulthood (Van Der Horst, Paw, Twisk, & Van Mechelen, 2007).

More than 80% of U.S. adolescents do not meet current physical activity guidelines for aerobic and muscle-strengthening physical activity (CDC, 2011). Not enough of the U.S. youth population, therefore, is participating in sufficient amounts of physical activity to lay the foundation for lifelong health and well-being.

The health benefits of participating in physical activity for school-age children and adolescents are numerous and are highlighted below. The findings are based on a comprehensive review of the scientific literature on the association between physical activity and a variety of risk factors for adult onset diseases such as osteoporosis and heart disease. Because youth do not often develop chronic diseases, the review focused on how participation in physical activity benefits the risk factors for chronic diseases. For example, elevated blood pressure is a known risk factor for adult onset heart disease and stroke. The findings from the PAGAC report noted that physically active youth have improved insulin sensitivity and better lipid profiles than their less active counterparts and therefore concluded there was strong evidence that participation in regular physical activity improved cardiovascular and metabolic health biomarkers (PAGAC, 2008).

Health Benefits Associated with Regular Physical Activity for Youth Ages 6–17 (USDHHS, 2008)

Strong Evidence

- Improved cardiorespiratory and muscular fitness
- Improved bone health
- Improved cardiovascular and metabolic health biomarkers
- Favorable body composition

Moderate evidence

- Reduced symptoms of depression

History of Youth Physical Activity Recommendations

Underscoring the importance of physical activity for health in recent decades is the inclusion of objectives addressing youth physical activity in Healthy People (USDHHS, 1991, 2000, 2010). Healthy People provides the 10-year health promotion and disease prevention objectives for improving the health of all Americans (USDHHS, 2010). Healthy People uses existing science to formulate objectives and guide recommendations for achieving those objectives. Other events and initiatives in the 15 years prior to the development of the PAG are described in this section and may facilitate a better understanding of the current guidelines.

In 1994, a consensus conference resulted in the release of the first physical activity guidelines specifically for adolescents (Sallis, Patrick, & Long, 1994). The 1994 guidelines called for 30 min of physical activity daily or nearly every day through games, sport, transportation, work, physical education (PE), recreation or planned exercise and for vigorous activities to be performed at least 3 days per week.

The 1996 *Surgeon General's Report on Physical Activity and Health* provided the first summary of research conducted over decades on physical activity behaviors, outcomes, benefits, and interventions among all age groups and sub-populations (USDHHS, 1996). The report outlined key findings on the characteristics that influence physical activity among youth, such as self-efficacy, enjoyment of physical activity, support from others, positive beliefs about the benefits of physical activity, and lack of perceived barriers to being active. For younger children, the report also concluded that interventions through PE class in elementary school can increase levels of physical activity. This conclusion serves as the foundation for recommendations in recent years to implement high-quality school-based PE (Guide to Community Preventive Services, 2011; Wechsler, McKenna, Lee, & Dietz, 2004) and/or physical activity initiatives (CDC, 2010a).

In 1998, the National Association for Sport and Physical Education published the first guidelines addressing the physical activity needs of children ages 5–12 years (NASPE, 1998). These guidelines recommended at least 60 min and up to several hours of physical activity each day attained through participation in a variety of activities requiring various levels of intensity. The 1998 guidelines also suggested that extended periods of inactivity are not part of a normal, healthy child's development.

Other influential factors include the 2005 Institute of Medicine (IOM) Report, *Preventing Childhood Obesity: Health in the Balance* (Koplan, Liverman, & Kraak, 2005). This report provided an action plan to prevent childhood obesity by implementing strategies that target media and marketing, communities, schools, and home environments and address the energy balance equation, which includes physical activity.

Finally, is the 2005 paper by Strong et al., which recommended that youth participate in 60 min of physical activity at least 5 days per week, and the 2006 IOM workshop addressing the adequacy of the evidence to support development of the PAG (Strong et al., 2005; IOM, 2007). The IOM workshop sessions addressing youth drew heavily from the Strong et al. paper (IOM, p 96) and suggested that regular physical activity can improve aerobic fitness and muscular strength (IOM, p 145). The strongest evidence showed moderate to high weight-bearing physical activities (such as jumping rope) improved measures of bone health (IOM, p 98). Areas needing further investigation identified by the IOM Committee centered around reducing participation in sedentary behaviors such as television viewing as it pertains to unhealthy weight gain, specifically (IOM, p 101). The issue of replacing sedentary behaviors with active pursuits such as playing games or sports or safely walking or riding a bicycle to a destination was suggested in the Guidelines as a potentially viable strategy to improve physical activity levels of U.S. youth (USDHHS, 2008, p 19).

Communications Activities Associated with the Release of the Guidelines

The PAG were developed with a communications budget to facilitate development of materials to target the adult population addressed in the Guidelines. Approximately, $500,000 was allotted to develop the materials that accompanied the release of the PAG (Harris, personal communication, July 1, 2011). These funds were used to conduct market research and to develop and test materials, all of which focused on adults and, specifically, adults with low health literacy. The items are available for download from the PAG website, http://www.health.gov/paguidelines.

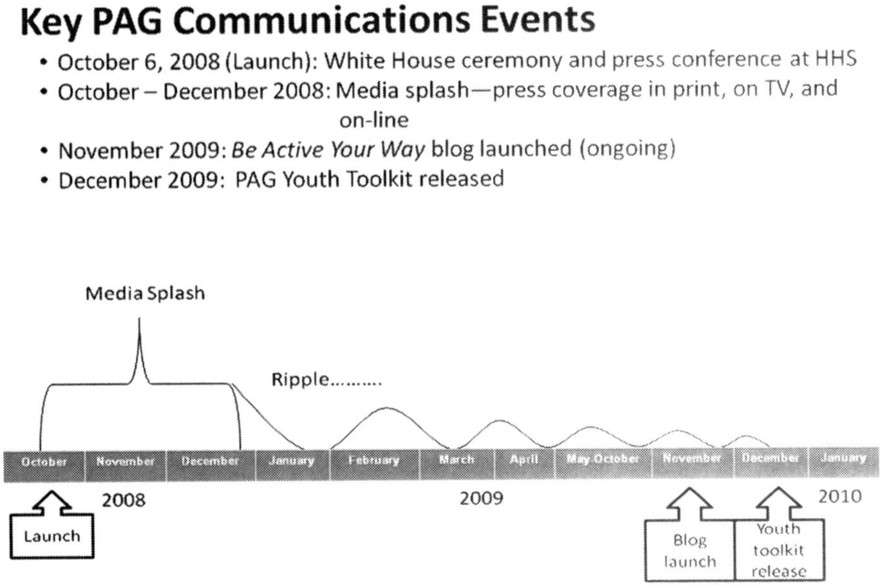

Modified figure used by permission, Melissa Cunningham, MS, MPH, RD

Fig. 21.1 Key PAG Communications Events

Three offices within the Department of Health and Human Services (HHS), the Office of Disease Prevention and Health Promotion (ODPHP), the Centers for Disease Control and Prevention, Division of Nutrition, Physical Activity and Obesity, and the President's Council on Fitness, Sports & Nutrition collaborated on communications' activities leading up to the launch of the PAG. The initial promotion of the PAG lasted approximately 3 months—from October through December 2008. The initial release period concentrated on disseminating information about the Guidelines as widely as possible to public health professionals and organizations with an interest in physical activity. As depicted in Fig. 21.1, Key PAG Communication Events, primary outlets for PAG message dissemination were print and regional television news services and various websites. Although news coverage dropped off, organizations that signed on as PAG Supporters and HHS offices and agencies continued to highlight the new guidelines via listservs, websites, and other information-sharing channels.

Message Dissemination

With limited resources to extensively promote the Guidelines, ODPHP strategically decided to rely on a website (http://www.health.gov, maintained by ODPHP) and partner organizations to help disseminate both the Guidelines themselves and messages from the PAG about the amount of physical activity Americans need to achieve health benefits.

Key partner organizations (e.g., American College of Sports Medicine, National Association of Sport and Physical Education, etc.) were invited to the launch of the Guidelines in October 2008 to speak about their organization's plans to promote the Guidelines. All partners were formally recognized as "Supporters" on the website and received the general PAG toolkit (http://www.health.gov/paguidelines/toolkit.aspx). Partners were encouraged to share ideas and strategies to promote physical activity through the adult-focused *Be Active Your Way* blog, the official blog of the PAG. To date, the blog highlights 22 categories addressing strategies to promote physical activity. Posts have focused on older adults, adults with disabilities, and workplace physical activity (USDHHS, 2011). Youth and schools are categories that have yet to be addressed.

The initial message development and dissemination activities were focused on adults. The CDC's Division of Adolescent and School Health (DASH) developed and released in 2009, a Youth Physical Activity Guidelines Toolkit (http://www.cdc.gov/Healthyyouth/physicalactivity/guidelines.htm#1). The youth toolkit consists of items to help public health and education professionals who work with youth ages six to seventeen understand the Guidelines for children and adolescents and to help them identify actions they can take to facilitate more physical activity among this age group. The resources in the toolkit included fact sheets on the role of schools, communities, and families in promoting youth physical activity as well as PowerPoint presentations, a promotional poster, and facilitator's guide, and a promotional video that public health professionals, school wellness coordinators, and others can use to promote these messages. Providing clear action steps that can be taken is a key difference between the toolkits targeting the adult population and the one developed for youth physical activity by CDC.

Over the course of 2010, slightly less than 4,000 toolkits were mailed (DeBastiani, Lee, Williams, Carroll, & Fulton, 2011—unpublished manuscript). The largest point of access for the toolkit was through a website (http://www.cdc.gov/healthyyouth/physicalactivity/guidelines.htm), which had approximately 16,300 section downloads. Representatives of schools, afterschool programs, YMCAs, and park and recreation departments made the most number of requests to receive a toolkit, whereas the toolkit publications targeting schools were downloaded most frequently.

Future Communication Efforts and Updates

At this time, there is no systematic process in place to update the PAG or further communications efforts associated with the PAG. Legislation introduced in Congress in 2008 (Physical Activity Guidelines for Americans Act, 2008) and again in 2009 (Physical Activity Guidelines for Americans Act, 2009) and 2011 (Healthy Lifestyles and Prevention America Act, 2011) calls for a standardized process to update the

PAG every 5 years. Passage of this legislation would keep the PAG on a similar time course as the Dietary Guidelines for Americans, which are required by law to be published at least every 5 years (CNPP, 2010). To date, however, the legislation has not been passed.

Conducting a review of the scientific evidence to update the PAG is a resource-intensive process—requiring both staff and financial commitments. At this time, it is uncertain if there will be sufficient justification and/or resources to update the PAG in the near future. However, organizations and professionals working in the area of physical activity and health are interested in the development of a more robust communication campaign to increase awareness of the 2008 Guidelines and measure the effectiveness of communication products and activities on knowledge of the amounts and types of physical activity needed to improve health.

In 2011, the Canadian Society for Exercise Physiology (CSEP) released the Canadian Physical Activity Guidelines and the Canadian Sedentary Behavior Guidelines for Children and Youth (CSEP, 2011). Recognizing that more needed to be done to facilitate dissemination of the Guidelines, CSEP hosted a workshop for stakeholders to discuss beneficial and disadvantageous Guidelines'-related communications activities. The workshop also served to identify collaborations that may prove helpful and the best use of collective resources. Participating organizations represented all age groups. Among the recommendations were establishing a Guidelines brand with a specific look and feel; developing a web presence housing all Guidelines-related materials; partnering with a corporate or third party entity to support initiatives; and developing a communications plan and an evaluation strategy (CSEP, p. 18).

Efforts in the U.S. may take a cue from recommendations outlined at the Canadian stakeholder's workshop, although there are some efforts underway that are consistent with those recommendations. For example, the Supporter Network described earlier in this chapter provides a network through which information can be shared. The PAG web presence at http://www.health.gov/paguidelines includes all Guidelines materials and all federal resources available to support the Guidelines, as well as access to the *Be Active Your Way* blog. However, the U.S. currently lacks a formal Guidelines communication plan or formal evaluation strategy to evaluate the effectiveness of Guidelines-related materials.

Improving Physical Activity Behavior in Children and Adolescents

Even though there is no ongoing large-scale communications campaign to promote the Guidelines, work continues in the area of physical activity promotion for youth. What follows is an overview of strategies, campaigns, and initiatives that may help move the needle on physical activity among youth in spite of the absence of a coordinated, national campaign to promote it. This is not a comprehensive list, but provides some examples of efforts happening nationally and some examples addressing policies, specifically. All of these examples address the school setting in some capacity.

Physical Education

Considering the amount of time children and adolescents spend in and around school and the value physical activity programming in schools has on student health, well-being, and academic success (CDC, 2010a), it is not surprising that a number of initiatives address the school environment. Enhanced school-based PE programs have proven effective in increasing the physical activity levels of school-aged youth (Kahn et al., 2002) by increasing the number of minutes students are engaged in moderate or vigorous intensity activity while in class. The reality, however, is that a number of barriers limit the ability of schools to implement PE at the recommended quality and quantity. For many schools, barriers to implementation may include pressure to show improvements in standardized test scores, limited time for PE curriculum implementation, and insufficient funding for PE resources including qualified personnel (Lounsbery, McKenzie, Trost, & Smith, 2011) and in upper grades, policies allowing exemptions from PE for participation in sports or school or community-based programs (CDC).

In 2006, 3.8% of elementary schools, 7.9% of middle schools, and just 2.1% of high schools provided daily PE or its equivalent (150 min per week in elementary school or 225 min per week in middle and high schools) for all the students in the school (CDC, 2007). In 2009, only one-third of students in grades nine to twelve reported attending PE class on a daily basis (CDC, 2009). There is, therefore, a need to improve the provision of PE for youth attending U.S. schools. Healthy People 2020, the 10-year agenda for improving the nation's health, includes goals for increasing daily PE in elementary, middle, and high schools, as well as student participation in daily PE (USDHHS, 2010). A change in district- and school-level policies requiring PE is necessary to see progress toward achieving the Healthy People goals.

Providing quality PE in schools is one way to increase physical activity behaviors among youth, but it is not the only way. With nearly 80% of American youth not achieving the minimum amount of aerobic activity each day (i.e., 60 min) (CDC, 2010b), efforts from a variety of physical activity interest groups may be required to achieve a measurable improvement. Interest groups (often termed "sectors") represent levels of the socio-ecological model (McLeroy, Bibeau, Steckler, & Glanz, 1988) to include the interpersonal (e.g., parents, friends, health care providers), organizational (e.g., schools, companies), community (e.g., media), and policy (e.g., legislators) levels. Multiple sectoral efforts working in cooperation at the national and local levels as well as in cooperation with partner organizations need to be engaged in the effort to improve youth physical activity.

National Physical Activity Plan

There is not one organization, government or otherwise, or corporate entity identified to take a lead role in furthering Guidelines dissemination or uptake as recommended in the Canadian workshop (CSEP, 2011), however, the U.S. National Physical

Activity Plan (http://www.physicalactivityplan.org/theplan.php), launched in May 2010 may help serve this purpose by pooling the resources and expertise of a variety of entities. A public–private collaboration, the National Plan is guided by the socio-ecological model of health behavior (National Physical Activity Plan, 2010a, b). It is organized into eight sectors targeting business and industry; education; health care; mass media; parks, recreation, fitness and sports; public health; transportation, land use, and community design; and volunteer and non-profit organizations. Within each sector are overarching strategies and specific tactics that target increasing physical activity among people of all ages and socio-demographic groups. The National Plan generally emphasizes strategies and tactics that will modify environments or enact policies to improve physical activity. Even though strategies address the population spectrum, there are strategies and tactics outlined, in particular, for the education sector that are designed to address youth physical activity (through PE and school-based physical activity offerings) specifically (http://www.physicalactivityplan.org/education.php, Accessed January 5, 2012). The National Plan has great potential to facilitate positive changes on a variety of levels and in a number of settings as long as professionals from the sectors take action based on the strategies and tactics provided. This could help ensure a more coordinated approach.

National Initiatives

First Lady Michelle Obama's *Let's Move!* (http://www.letsmove.gov) initiative also follows a multi-sector, multi-level approach to improve youth physical activity on a national scale. Through its partnerships and targeted outreach, *Let's Move!* addresses physical activity opportunities in schools, day care centers, and park and recreation venues and programming offered by youth-serving organizations. In addition to reaching out through public and private organizations, it targets Mayors, healthcare providers, and Native American tribal organizations (The White House, 2011).

The Alliance for a Healthier Generation (http://www.healthiergeneration.org), established in 2005 by the American Heart Association and the William J. Clinton Foundation, works with partners to address access to and consumption of healthy foods and awareness of the importance of physical activity and opportunities to be physically active within healthcare, schools, industry, and among youth themselves. Similarly, in 2002, in response to a call from then-Surgeon General Dr. David Satcher, Action for Healthy Kids (http://www.actionforhealthykids.org) was established to bring organizations together to work with schools to address the obesity epidemic. At the core of Action for Healthy Kids is a network of volunteers helping to improve the health of students by ensuring they have the knowledge to make healthy food choices and to be active every day (Action for Healthy Kids, 2011). All of these efforts address both physical activity and nutrition and rely on volunteers and partner organizations coming together to improve physical activity environments and/or behaviors.

Policies and Legislation

Policy and legislative actions have enhanced physical activity opportunities within the school setting. These include passage in 2000 of the Physical Education for Progress (PEP) Act. The act led to the development of the PEP grant (Physical Education for Progress Act, 2000). Local education agencies and community-based organizations are eligible to receive the grants to initiate, expand, or enhance PE programs, including after-school programs, for students in kindergarten through 12th grade. Grant recipients must implement programs that help students make progress toward meeting state standards. Funds can be used to provide equipment and support to enable students to participate actively in PE activities. Funds also may support staff and teacher training and education (Department of Education, 2011).

In 2005, Congress authorized federal funding of a national Safe Routes to School program (National Center for Safe Routes to School, 2008). Safe Routes to School programs promote the development of safe routes to and from school to facilitate bicycling and walking. Although grassroots efforts supporting the concept of Safe Routes to School-type programming were in existence prior to the 2005 bill, it was Federal funding of the program that lead to nationwide implementation. Federal funds helped establish programs in each state lead by a Safe Routes to School state coordinator.

School-Based Initiatives

Initiatives including the National Football League's *Play60* and *Fuel Up to Play60* (a joint effort between the National Football League and the National Dairy Council) supplement broader national initiatives (described above) by focusing on a specific population (school-aged youth) and on specific levels within the social ecological framework (parents and schools). *Let's Move in School*, an initiative of the American Alliance for Health, Physical Education, Recreation and Dance (AAHPERD) and the National Association for Sport and Physical Education (NASPE) targets teachers, principals, superintendents, school boards, and parents. The goal is to make sure every school has a comprehensive physical activity program with quality PE at its core (AAHPERD, 2011). The previously mentioned Safe Routes to School program addresses the entire socio-ecological framework by addressing policy changes for transportation to or from and around schools, social norms regarding bicycling and walking to or from school, school environments that can promote bicycling and walking, parental engagement and organizational support, and, finally, the interest of school-aged youth in walking and bicycling to school. Walk to School Day, the national awareness day led by the National Center for Safe Routes to School has influenced environmental and/or policy changes that address active transportation to and from school. In 2008, 75% of walk to school event organizers reported that the event led to changes that improve walking conditions for students including the addition of sidewalks (National Center for Safe Routes to School, 2008).

The Future

Improvements to physical activity policies and environments in multiple settings such as schools, communities, and health care may affect measurable change in physical activity levels among U.S. youth. Schools provide a captive audience of students to enact quality physical activity programs during PE, recess, and other opportunities throughout the school day, yet there are also other segments of society suitable for environmental- or policy-directed interventions. Some societal segments, for example, may consider implementing environmental changes or developing policies to affect community design, transportation and safety, health care, and park and recreation offerings for youth.

In the future, therefore, it will be important to disseminate and evaluate communication efforts for the Physical Activity Guidelines, but it is also becoming increasingly important to initiate resonant communication messages for key target audiences that provide information on environmental- and policy-directed strategies to improve youth physical activity.

References

Action for Healthy Kids. (2011). About us. Retrieved from http://www.actionforhealthykids.org/about-us/.

American Alliance for Health Physical Education Recreation and Dance. (2011). Let's move in school: About. Retrieved from http://www.aahperd.org/letsmoveinschool/about/index.cfm.

Canadian Society for Exercise Physiology. (2011, May 18). Canadian physical activity guidelines, Canadian sedentary behaviour guidelines for children and youth: Stakeholder focus group workshop summary report. Retrieved from http://www.csep.ca/CMFiles/Guidelines/GuidelinesStakeholderWorkshopReport18MAY2011_smfile.pdf.

Caspersen, C., Pereira, M., & Curran, K. (2000). Changes in physical activity patterns in the United States, by sex and cross-sectional age. *Medicine & Science in Sports & Exercise, 32*(9), 1601–1609.

Center for Nutrition Policy and Promotion. (2010). 2010 Dietary guidelines for Americans backgrounder: History and process. Retrieved from http://www.cnpp.usda.gov/Publications/DietaryGuidelines/2010/PolicyDoc/Backgrounder.pdf.

Centers for Disease Control and Prevention. (2010b). Youth Risk Behavior Surveillance--United States, 2009. Surveillance Summaries, [June 4, 2010]. MMWR.59(SS–5).

Centers for Disease Control and Prevention, Division of Adolescent and School Health. (2007). School health policies and programs study, 2006: Physical education. Retrieved from http://www.cdc.gov/healthyyouth/shpps/2006/factsheets/pdf/FS_PhysicalEducation_SHPPS2006.pdf.

Centers for Disease Control and Prevention, Division of Adolescent and School Health. (2009). Trends in the prevalence of physical activity: National YRBS: 1991–2009. Retrieved from http://www.cdc.gov/healthyyouth/yrbs/pdf/us_physical_trend_yrbs.pdf.

Centers for Disease Control and Prevention, Division of Adolescent and School Health. (2010). *The association between school based physical activity, including physical education, and academic performance.* Atlanta, GA: U.S. Department of Health and Human Services.

DeBastiani, S., Lee, S., Williams, K., Carroll, D., & Fulton, J. (2011). Evaluation of the Centers for Disease Control and Prevention's youth physical activity guidelines toolkit. Unpublished manuscript.

Guide to Community Preventive Services. (2011). Behavioral and social approaches to increase physical activity: Enhanced school-based physical education. Retrieved from www.thecommunityguide.org/pa/behavioral-social/schoolbased-pe.html.

Healthy lifestyles and prevention America act, S.174, 112th Congress. (2011).

Institute of Medicine. (2007). Adequacy of evidence for physical activity guidelines development: Workshop summary. Washington, DC: National Academies Press. Retrieved from http://www.nap.edu/catalog.php?record_id=11819#toc.

Kahn, E., Ramsey, L., Brownson, R., Heath, G., Howze, E., Powell, K., et al. (2002). The effectiveness of interventions to increase physical activity. A systematic review. *American Journal of Preventive Medicine, 22*(4S), 67–72.

Koplan, J., Liverman, C., & Kraak, V. (Eds). (2005). *Preventing childhood obesity: Health in the balance*. Washington, DC: National Academies Press. Retrieved from http://books.nap.edu/openbook.php?record_id=11015&page=R1.

Lounsbery, M., McKenzie, T., Trost, S., & Smith, N. (2011). Facilitators and barriers to adopting evidence-based physical education in elementary schools. *Journal of Physical Activity & Health, 8*(1S), S17–S25.

McLeroy, K., Bibeau, D., Steckler, A., & Glanz, K. (1988). An ecological perspective on health promotion programs. *Health Education Quarterly, 15*(4), 351–377.

National Association for Sport and Physical Education. (1998). *Physical Activity for Children: A statement of guidelines*. Reston, VA: NASPE Publications.

National Center for Safe Routes to School. (2008). Many steps one tomorrow: A report on the first three years of the national safe routes to school program. Retrieved from http://www.saferoutesinfo.org/sites/default/files/page/SRTS%203%20Year%20Report.pdf.

National Physical Activity Plan. (2010). The plan. Retrieved from http://www.physicalactivityplan.org/theplan.php.

National Physical Activity Plan. (2010). Education. Retrieved from http://www.physicalactivityplan.org/education.php.

Physical Activity Guidelines Advisory Committee. (2008). *Physical activity guidelines advisory committee report, 2008*. Washington, DC: U.S. Department of Health and Human Services.

Physical activity guidelines for Americans act of 2008, S.2748, 110th Congress. (2008).

Physical activity guidelines for Americans act of 2009, S.1810, 111th Congress. (2009).

Physical education for progress act, H.R. 4577, 106th Congress. (2000).

Sallis, J., Patrick, K., & Long, B. (1994). Overview of the international consensus conference on physical activity guidelines for adolescents. *Pediatric Exercise Science, 6*, 299–301.

Strong, W., Malina, R., Blimkie, C., Daniels, S., Dishman, R., Gutin, B., et al. (2005). Evidence based physical activity for school-aged youth. *Journal of Pediatrics, 146*(6), 732–737.

The White House. (2011). Let's move: Programs. Retrieved from http://www.letsmove.gov/programs.

U.S. Department of Education. (2011). Carol M. White physical education program: Purpose. Retrieved from http://www2.ed.gov/programs/whitephysed/index.html.

U.S. Department of Health and Human Services. (1991). *Healthy people 2000: National health promotion and disease prevention objectives*. Washington, DC: Public Health Service.

U.S. Department of Health and Human Services. (1996). *Physical activity and health: A report of the Surgeon General*. Atlanta, GA: U.S. Department of Health and Human Services, Centers for Disease Control and Prevention, National Center for Chronic Disease Prevention and Health Promotion. Retrieved from http://www.cdc.gov/nccdphp/sgr/pdf/sgrfull.pdf.

U.S. Department of Health and Human Services. (2000). *Healthy people 2010* (2nd ed.). Washington, DC: U.S. Government Printing Office.

U.S. Department of Health and Human Services. (2008). *2008 Physical activity guidelines for Americans*. Washington, DC: U.S. Department of Health and Human Services.

U.S. Department of Health and Human Services. (2011). Be active your way blog. Retrieved from http://www.health.gov/paguidelines/blog/.

U.S. Department of Health and Human Services, Office of Disease Prevention and Health Promotion. (2010). Healthy people 2020. Washington, DC. Available at http://www.healthypeople.gov/2020/topicsobjectives2020/objectiveslist.aspx?topicId=33.

Van Der Horst, K., Paw, M., Twisk, J., & Van Mechelen, W. (2007). A brief review on correlates of physical activity and sedentariness in youth. *Medicine & Science in Sports & Exercise, 39*(8), 1241–1250.

Wechsler, H., McKenna, M., Lee, S., & Dietz, W. (2004, December). The role of schools in preventing childhood obesity. *The State Education Standard, 5*(2), 4–12.

Part VII
Thinking Outside the Box: Finding Solutions to Reverse Childhood Obesity

Chapter 22
Voluntary Health Organizations and Nonprofit Advocacy Organizations Play Critical Roles in Making Community Norms More Supportive of Healthier Eating and Increased Physical Activity

William J. McCarthy, Harold Goldstein, Matthew Sharp, and Eric Batch

Recent food choice and physical activity-related policies adopted in California illustrate the important roles that voluntary health organizations and nonprofit advocacy organizations have been playing in efforts to influence policies, community attitudes, and behavioral norms with respect to healthy food choices and increased daily physical activity. Using the history of tobacco control as validation, we outline the major steps that voluntary health organizations and nonprofit advocacy organizations typically take to get nutrition and physical activity-related policies adopted. These steps include: making the problem meaningful, mobilizing local stakeholders, addressing opposition concerns, accumulating and publicizing evidence for community concern, negotiating a sustainable solution, and nurturing implementation of enacted policies. Broadcast and print media play critically important roles in putting pressure on elected officials, as well as potentially galvanizing community support at significant moments in the policy-adoption process, but it is ultimately an organic convergence of hard-working policymakers jockeying within the political system and committed grassroots activists calling and visiting legislative offices, hosting strategy sessions, and engaging public media of all kinds who persuade legislative bodies to adopt health-promotion policies. It is also vigilant stakeholders who ensure appropriate enforcement or strengthening of the policies long term. Mobilizing a critical mass of local advocacy efforts in disparate towns and cities

W.J. McCarthy (✉)
UCLA Division of Cancer Prevention and Control Research,
650 Charles Young Drive, Los Angeles, CA 90095-6900
e-mail: wmccarth@ucla.edu

H. Goldstein
California Center for Public Health Advocacy (CCPHA), Davis, CA 95617, USA

M. Sharp
California Food Policy Advocates (CFPA), Los Angeles, CA 90012

E. Batch
American Heart Association (AHA), 816 S. Figueroa St. Los Angeles, CA USA 90017-2400

J.D. Williams et al. (eds.), *Advances in Communication Research to Reduce Childhood Obesity*, DOI 10.1007/978-1-4614-5511-0_22,

is labor intensive but may be more effective in changing community norms statewide or nationwide than relying exclusively on broadcasting health-promotion media messages to effect sustainable community norm change. A detailed example of a vulnerable community combating the effects of junk food marketing with community mobilization and legal advocacy is well described in Kramer et al. (Chap. 18).

Introduction

While most of the examples discussed in this chapter are taken from policy-adoption efforts that took place in California, they could just as easily have taken place in other parts of the country. Most of these examples have, in fact, been replicated throughout the U.S. Prior to California's pioneering Senate Bill 19 Pupil Nutrition Act of 2001 (SB 19) (California Senate, 2001a), all state legislative activity involving nutrition had dealt with food safety, not nutritional quality, and was concerned to minimize risk of acute food-borne illnesses rather than minimize risk of obesity-related disease. The enactment of SB 19 and its successors, SB 677 (California Senate, 2003), SB12 (California Senate, 2005a), and SB 965 (California Senate, 2005b) was a game-changing event that bears close examination for how advocacy organizations such as the California Center for Public Health Advocacy (CCPHA) and California Food Policy Advocates (CFPA) and voluntary health organizations such as the American Cancer Society (ACS) and American Heart Association (AHA) were critical players in framing the debate, mobilizing constituents, and helping policymaker champions broker legislative solutions designed to promote healthier food choices. Before we review the steps that led to the passage of SB 19, it is instructive to review recent tobacco control history because tobacco control is the public health template for how voluntary health organizations and advocacy groups catalyzed the adoption of public health policies initially opposed by monied interests. The lessons from tobacco control illustrate the critical role that voluntary health organizations and advocacy groups such as Americans for Nonsmokers Rights had in choreographing the combination of grassroots mobilization and cultivated champion policymakers to effect adoption of consequential public health policies despite implacable opposition by well-financed opponents.

Lessons from the History of Tobacco Control

Historically, voluntary health organizations such as the ACS were reluctant to get involved in local or state policy making, even though it was partly the ACS' federal lobbying efforts that resulted in President Nixon endorsing a "war on cancer" in 1971 that increased federal investment in cancer-related research (National Cancer Institute (NCI), 2012). Part of this reticence to get involved in local or state policy making stemmed from fear of alienating well-heeled donors. The ACS was also responding to federal restrictions on lobbying for organizations wanting to maintain their 401(c)(3) nonprofit, tax-exempt status (Independent Sector, 2011).

The American Cancer Society-California Division did not have a full-time, on-staff lobbyist until 1982[1]. The first year that the ACS conferred its annual Capitol Dome award to honor volunteer contributions in the public policy arena was 1994[2]. By contrast, today the ACS says "Defeating cancer is as much a matter of public policy as scientific discovery (American Cancer Society, 2011)." What explained this turnaround? A big part of the reason for the 180 degree turn from avoidance to embrace of advocacy was the success that the ACS California Division (and coalition partners) had in passing California's Proposition 99 in 1988, which increased the state excise tax on cigarettes by 25 cents per pack and generated more than $100 million for tobacco control annually (Hill, 2001). Together with the American Lung Association, AHA and other, mostly medical organizations, it pooled about $1.6 million and thousands of volunteers to successfully beat back the tobacco industry's $21.4 million campaign to defeat Proposition 99 (Traynor & Glantz, 1996). What did the ACS achieve as a result of it's full-throated foray into state policy-making? It helped to generate $100 million funding per year for a comprehensive tobacco-control program that subsequently reduced state tobacco use 50% among adults from 24% in 1988 to 12% in 2010 (California Department of Public Health, 2011). Between 1989 and 2004 the new tobacco control resources made possible by Proposition 99 reduced heart disease and lung cancer deaths and reduced California health care costs by an estimated $86 billion (Lightwood, Dinno, & Glantz, 2008). The ACS applied the lessons learned from Proposition 99 and applied them to the rest of the nation, with the result that "70 percent of the U.S. population is now covered by a smoke-free law (American Cancer Society 2011a, b)." Until the passage of Proposition 99, the "war on cancer" initiated by President Nixon in 1969 was considered a failure because cancer deaths continued rising year after year (Sporn, 1996). In recent years, by contrast, the ACS has been able to trumpet measurable declines in cancer-related deaths among Americans, sparing the lives of 767,000 Americans who would have died had not progress been made in prevention, early detection, and treatment (Jemal, Ward, & Thun, 2010). But much of this decline was attributable to declines in lung cancer deaths, for which tobacco use is the proximal cause (Jemal et al.). The prevalence of tobacco use among U.S. adults over the age of 18 years dropped 50% from 1965 to 2006 (National Center for Health Statistics (NCHS), 2009), yet tobacco use still accounts for approximately 30% of all cancer deaths (Jemal et al.). If the ACS is "winning" the war against cancer, its success is largely attributable to its decision in the 1980s to embrace public policy advocacy for the purpose of advancing local and state tobacco-control policies.

Total tobacco use among youth and adults in Sweden (Furberg, Lichtenstein, Pedersen, Bulik, & Sullivan, 2006), Norway, and Finland is higher than total tobacco use among youth and adults in California, despite the fact that these three Scandinavian countries scored 9 or 10 out of a maximum of 10 points for legislated restrictions on tobacco product advertising (Laugesen & Meads, 1991) in 1991. Norway and Finland banned the advertising of all tobacco products in 1975 and

[1]The first full-time, on-staff lobbyist for the ACS California Division was Betsy Hite, who subsequently spearheaded the campaign for Proposition 99.

[2]The first California Division recipient was William J. McCarthy, Ph.D.

1978 (Rimpela, Aaro, & Rimpela, 1993), respectively, more than a decade before California voters created California's now-world renowned comprehensive tobacco-control program with the passage of Proposition 99 in 1988 (Bal, Kizer, Felten, Mozar, & Niemeyer, 1990). One reason that explains why California residents enjoy more tobacco-free living than residents of Sweden, Norway, and Finland is that tobacco-control policies have typically been adopted and implemented in a top-down fashion by federal authorities in Scandinavia, whereas tobacco-control policies in California have typically been initiated by cities and counties in response to grass-roots activists before state legislators felt compelled to have similar policies applied uniformly throughout California (Shipan & Volden, 2006). In brief, Scandinavians have governments that proactively have taken steps to protect citizens whether or not the citizens were prepared to accept such protections whereas California citizens typically get health policies adopted first at the local level, by mobilizing the local electorate to pressure their local representatives to adopt policies that would protect them. Only later, after a critical mass of similar local policies have been adopted, does the cumulative local support for policy adoption get converted to policy adoption at the state level. This difference in top-down policy making in Scandinavia versus the more bottom-up policy making in California means that tobacco-control policies adopted in California already have been vetted by citizen groups and local legislators by the time they get adopted statewide and hence are more readily accepted by those affected by such policies than might be the case for tobacco-control policies imposed by well-intentioned but locally unaware national legislators. One of the remarkable lessons learned during California's persistent accumulation of increasingly restrictive state tobacco-use policies is that these policies have been largely self-policing (Jacobson & Wasserman, 1999). A benefit of the multi-year, labor-intensive, incrementalist bottom-up approach to California tobacco-control policy making is that by the time that policy is adopted statewide it has immediate normative legitimacy at the local level. In California, violations of most state tobacco-control laws are seen by locals as violating their community norms, which will invite immediate criticism and possible ostracism of the violator if the transgression is not corrected. For example, implementation of California's workplace smoking ban required few resources for enforcement because most workers and most employers welcomed the law and took it upon themselves to promote adherence to the law, without requiring enforcement by police or health department authorities (Jacobson & Wasserman, 1999). Moreover, as government-imposed workplace smoking bans have proliferated across the U.S., the voluntary adoption of smoking bans in personal residences has also increased (Cheng, Glantz, & Lightwood, 2011), illustrating a widening community acceptance of the norm that spaces where people congregate for any purpose should be smoke free. Particularly for college-educated persons, government adoption of smoke-free policies appears to stimulate voluntary adoption of similar policies at home (Cheng et al., 2011).

Lessons learned during recent decades of progress in adopting increasingly stringent tobacco-control policies can be seen being applied to the crafting, passage, and implementation of state nutrition policies, notably SB 19 and its successors: SB 677, SB 12, and SB 965. These lessons include addressing six phased challenges common to most health policy campaigns: (1) make the problem meaningful, (2) mobilize local stakeholders, (3) accumulate and publicize evidence for community concern, (4) address opposition concerns, (5) negotiate a sustainable solution, and (6) enforce or strengthen the solution. Table 22.1 outlines the major phases in the development of a health policy from the first step of identifying an issue of concern

Table 22.1 Phases in the development of a health policy, ranging from identifying a health issue of concern to the community to nurturing the policy solution adopted to remedy the issue

Policy adoption phase	Strategies to grow the issue or its solution	Effect of growing the issue or its solution
1. Make the problem meaningful to local stakeholders	Invoke scientific evidence	Legitimize the issue locally
	Document local concern through surveys and interviews	Require local leaders to take a stand on the issue
	Identify practical solutions	Make the issue appear solvable
2. Mobilize local stakeholders	Recruit allies from community leaders	Community leaders can help recruit an army of volunteer advocates
	Recruit policymaker champion(s)	Let campaign strategy be guided by leaders with inside knowledge of the policy-making process
3. Accumulate evidence and conduct public education	Assemble experts to support the issue	Although health benefits alone won't usually be enough to get a policy adopted, this increases proponents' credibility
	Frame the issue proactively. Be nimble, reframing to maximize community concern about the issue	Anticipate how the opposition will frame the issue; be prepared to subordinate health goal to fit within greater ethical system that politicians and constituents will readily support
4. Address opposition concerns	Neutralize hardcore vested interests	Seize opportunities to contrast the expected community benefits if the policy is adopted versus the self-serving economic benefits of opponents if the policy is defeated
	Minimize collateral damage; make would-be opponents allies	Discuss modified solutions for would-be opponents who acknowledge the community benefits of the proposed policy
5. Negotiate sustainable solution	Have policymaker champion draft potential policy	Set the stage for negotiating a sustainable solution
	Deploy the volunteer advocates to solicit support for the new policy solution	Increase the political stakes for policymakers opposed to the proposed solution
	Provide policymaker champion continual feedback about community willingness to accept modified solution	Help the policymaker champion balance political expediency versus community benefit

(continued)

Table 22.1 (continued)

Policy adoption phase	Strategies to grow the issue or its solution	Effect of growing the issue or its solution
6. Nurture enforcement of the solution or strengthen the solution	Build in periodic evaluation	Document the community health benefits regularly
	Build in periodic enforcement	Regularly hold policy targets accountable for maintaining community health benefits
	Continue expanding the health benefits of the solution or be prepared to replace the solution; community health promotion is an ongoing process, not a destination	Solutions are dynamic and will continue to change over time; continued vigilance is needed to maintain community support for the solution or its successors

to the community to the last step of nurturing community support for the solution adopted to remedy the issue. Below we review the history of California's pioneering school nutrition laws to illustrate these phases. A common thread linking these lessons is the need to document local constituent concerns about the problem and local constituent support for proposed solutions. In this way the cumulative adoption and documented sustainability of policies at the local level help to incubate the eventual adoption of similar policies at the state and federal levels.

The History Behind California's Pioneering School Nutrition SB 19, Illustrates the 6 Phases of Policy Adoption.

The adoption process documented for several recent California food choice and physical activity policies illustrates the steps needed to move from (1) identifying a specific barrier to healthier food choices and adequate daily physical activity to (2) adopting a policy to overcome the barrier to (3) ensuring long-term support for the policy once adopted. Below we discuss our first example used to illustrate the six phases of the policy-adoption process. This example describes the process by which California's pioneering school nutrition policy, Senate Bill 19 (California Senate, 2001a), became law and, in particular, focuses on the role that the CCPHA played in shepherding the policy through each of the six phases.

Make the Problem Meaningful to Local Stakeholders

In the late 1990s, the Southern California chapter of the American Public Health Association (SCPHA) determined that something needed to be done about the growing epidemic of obesity. The well-documented trends showed a relentless increased prevalence of obesity affecting all age groups below age 65, affecting all ethnic groups and affecting all socioeconomic levels, although low-income groups suffered disproportionately (Kuczmarski, Flegal, Campbell, & Johnson, 1994) (Whitaker, Wright, Pepe, Seidel, & Dietz, 1997) (Troiano, Flegal, Kuczmarski, Campbell, & Johnson, 1995). The Executive Director of the SCPHA was Harold Goldstein, who had recently completed a stint as Director of Health Promotion Initiatives for the Los Angeles County Department of Health Services. Even before the Centers for Disease Control and researchers began characterizing these adverse trends as a social epidemic (Christakis & Fowler, 2007), Goldstein realized that it would take more than conventional health education to reverse the epidemic, it would take advocacy of new policies designed to make it easier for residents of California to make healthier food choices and to engage in physical activity at work, at school and in their own neighborhoods (Nestle & Jacobson, 2000).

- Document significant community concern for the problem in selected localities.

Goldstein founded the CCPHA in 1999, a nonpartisan, nonprofit organization established jointly by the Northern and Southern California public health associations to raise awareness about critical public health issues and mobilize communities to promote effective health policies (Goldstein, 2009). He was particularly interested in reducing the disproportionate burden of obesity in low-income communities and minority communities. He organized grassroots teams of diverse local residents in six low-income legislative districts in Los Angeles County (California Center for Public Health Advocacy (CCPHA), 2012b). These teams educated legislators and other community leaders about the importance of nutrition and fitness for children and adolescents. They identified community needs and concerns through eight Town Hall Meetings and a series of neighborhood surveys. They organized local projects and events to raise awareness among community residents, the media, and policymakers. They educated legislators by sharing information, research findings, and policy recommendations [California Center for Public Health Advocacy (CCPHA)]. The most common suggestion arising from these town hall meetings and surveys was to improve the quality of school food.

- Invoke convincing scientific evidence of a problem

Armed with this knowledge and financial support from the California Endowment, Goldstein then convened a National Consensus Panel on School Nutrition, comprised of state and federal experts in school nutrition (California Center for Public Health Advocacy (CCPHA), 2002). The ten-member panel issued a report calling for minimum nutrition standards for competitive foods, that is, foods that were sold in competition with school lunches and therefore did not have to adhere to USDA school nutrition guidelines. More specifically, the report called for eliminating the on-campus sale of all beverages except for milk, water, and beverages with at least

50% fruit juice. The report also recommended banning the on-campus sale of snack foods that either had more than 35% by weight sugar (except dried fruit) or contained more than 30% of calories from fat as well as selected snack foods that exceeded standard portion sizes. These were, in fact, the nutrition standards adopted by the state legislature and adopted into law in the form of SB 19 California Senate, 2001a. Senate Bill 19 (Pupil Nutrition Act) the Pupil Nutrition, Health and Achievement Act of 2001. SB 19 also included an increase in state reimbursement for the costs of school meals of 10 cents per meal, to be implemented starting in 2004. In the interim, it appropriated funds for planning grants. These first-ever state school nutrition standards eventually became the school nutrition standards for 20 other states that adopted versions of SB 19 to benefit their own students (Center for Science in the Public Interest, 2008).

- Identify practical solutions to the problem

From the start, Goldstein sought out leaders of constituencies, such as the California School Nutrition Association (California School Nutrition Association, 2012) (previously called the California School Food Service Association), for their input, to ensure that the proposed solution would be practical to implement. The resulting proposed nutrition standards for competitive foods were specific, were actionable, and had been vetted by experienced school food service professionals, ensuring their acceptability to the school food service professionals who would be directly affected by the proposed legislation.

Policy making usually entails compromises, at least in the short run, that fall short of the ideal but nonetheless represent significant progress relative to the status quo. The California School Food Service Association initially opposed SB 19 (California Senate, 2001b) until the legislation was amended to include an increase of 10 cents per meal in the state reimbursement for school meals whereupon they dropped their opposition (California Senate, 2001c). The anticipated $60 million cost of this amendment then made it politically impossible to get the legislature to implement SB 19 in the current session, so the implementation was made contingent on funds being appropriated in the Budget Act of 2003, when a new legislative session would be responsible for finding the money (California Senate, 2001a). In practice, everybody "knew" that SB 19 would never be implemented as written, because the state did not have the $60 million in annual funding needed to fund it. As a compromise to appease the proponents of SB 19, legislative leaders included $5.5 million to fund pilot studies ("planning grants") of 10 middle schools or high schools that voluntarily adopted SB 19 standards in 2002 and 2003. The decision to make the legislation apply only to elementary schools and middle schools but not to high schools was a political calculation that this policy effort to modify food-choice behavior would be more acceptable to legislators if only young children were impacted. Although the beverage association fought the proposed legislation to the end and lost with respect to schools being permitted to sell soda beverages to students, it nonetheless scored a victory in maintaining the schools' ability to sell sports drinks to students, despite the recommendation of the National Consensus Panel (California Center for Public Health Advocacy (CCPHA), 2002) to ban their sale.

The inclusion of planning grants to be administered during the interval between the passage of SB 19 in 2001 and its theoretical implementation date of January 2004 assuaged the concerns of some legislators who feared that school food service directors would be unprepared for the transition when it came, at least in terms of living without the supplemental income that had been derived from sales of these now-banned foods. By accepting the planning grants-only version of SB 19 for 2002 and 2003, the proponents of SB 19 took the gamble that the outcomes of the planning grants would be positive. Fortunately, the evaluation results of these planning grants demonstrated that the average school district adopting SB 19 nutrition standards for competitive foods reported significant increases in National School Lunch Program (NSLP) participation with the result that the increase in NSLP revenues offset the observed decreases in revenue from the now-restricted sale of a la carte foods (Center for Weight & Health, 2004).

The results of the planning grant evaluations, in conjunction with ever-increasing scientific evidence of the harm associated with child obesity, made it possible to drop the state school meal reimbursement provision that was supposed to kick in with full implementation of SB 19 in 2004 and still get SB 677 (California Senate, 2003) passed in 2003. SB 677 adopted the SB 19 restrictions on soda beverage sales on campus but it did not apply to high schools and did not include sports drinks, contrary to the recommendations of the National Consensus Panel on School Nutrition (California Center for Public Health Advocacy (CCPHA), 2002)). Further increases in public support, made it possible later to extend SB 19 nutrition standards to high schools and to drop sports drinks and still get SB 12 (California Senate, 2005a) and SB 965 (California Senate, 2005b) passed in 2005. SB 965 (Escutia, 2005) (California Senate, 2005b) improved on SB 677 by extending the ban to high schools and by including sports drinks with the sodas as beverages not to be sold on campus during the school day. A companion bill, SB 12 (Escutia, 2005), extended the ban on snack foods of minimal nutritional value to high schools. If one takes the long view, early compromises that fall well short of fully addressing public health concerns can pave the way for future legislation that conforms more strongly to the public health recommendations that prompted the legislation in the first place.

Once a community health issue has traction, as evidenced by local advocacy and media coverage, it is necessary to get local policymakers to take a stand. In other words, the community health issue needs to have sufficient legitimacy among the local electorate that their future electoral support for the policymaker is likely to be influenced by the policymaker's position on the issue. This politicization of the issue is a necessary step in the campaign to get the policy adopted, because policymaker support is critical to getting the policy adopted, even if the ultimate decision is by plebiscite instead of by elected representatives (Midwest Academy, 2000).

Mobilize Local Stakeholders

- Identify and recruit community champions and partnering organizations with access to community activists to support community mobilization efforts

Early on in the campaign to pass SB 19, the CCPHA joined forces with other organizations in order to increase their political clout. With only five full-time equivalent staff and access to a limited cadre of volunteers, CCPHA needed allies that had considerably greater staff and volunteer resources. In practice, even the largest health advocacy organizations need allies to get valued health policies adopted. Table 22.2 lists the resources of some of these partners. The list of SB 19 supporters eventually included a wide range of groups, including the AHA, the Western Growers Association, the California PTA, two teacher unions, Kaiser Permanente, the California Dietetic Association, the Strategic Alliance to Prevent Childhood Obesity, county health departments, hospitals, and various child health-promotion groups (California Senate, 2001c). These other groups, notably the Strategic Alliance and the AHA, were instrumental in soliciting their volunteers to make phone calls to their legislators and to write advocacy letters at key moments during the journey of Senator Escutia's school nutrition bills through the legislative process.

It is worth noting what advocacy resources the major partners featured, as outlined in Table 22.2. All of them included dedicated, full-time advocacy professionals, with at least one dedicated to lobbying and policy analysis and at least one dedicated to mobilizing community members. All of them featured regular advocacy activities for training volunteers in advocacy skills and registration for volunteer advocates to receive legislative alerts by email. The two advocacy organizations differed from the two voluntary health organizations in putting most of their resources into policy analysis, whereas the ACS and AHA invest considerable resources in policy analysis, lobbying, and recruiting and training volunteer grassroots activists. The California state advocacy staff at the ACS and AHA at times had less autonomy than their counterparts at CCPHA and the California Food Policy Advocates (CFPA) in negotiating legislative language with legislators. If the proposed language is not contained within their policy guidance documents, ACS and AHA staff have to get approval before agreeing to specific legislative language. On the other hand, CCPHA and CFPA have more leverage with legislators when partnering with the ACS or the AHA because the latter are highly trusted and can trigger hundreds of emails, phone calls, and letters from their large networks of volunteer advocates and thereby provide political cover to legislators otherwise wary of getting enmeshed in controversies that might alienate a segment of their constituents.

The ACS and AHA have similar national and state advocacy staff organizational structures, so the following description of AHA advocacy staff and activities would well describe those of the ACS as well. After this was written the ACS announced a reorganization that included shifting most of their advocacy staff to ACS-CAN, its nonpartisan advocacy affiliate. The advocacy activities facilitated by AHA staff dedicated to advocacy of legislative initiatives are consistent with the AHA mission to reduce cardiovascular disease through primary prevention (Lloyd-Jones et al., 2010), and to facilitate access to treatment resources for those who suffer from cardiovascular disease. The advocacy staff for each state typically include a director of government relations and a grassroots director. Large states typically include additional advocacy staff in addition to these two positions. They lobby legislators and send out email messages as needed, usually on the average of two a month.

Table 22.2 Advocacy resources as of 2012 for mobilizing community members to support new food choice and physical activity policies

	American Cancer Society (ACS), American Cancer Society Cancer Action Network (ACSCAN)	American Heart Association (AHA)	California Food Policy Advocates (CFPA)	California Center for Public Health Advocacy (CCPHA)
Total advocacy staff for the U.S., D.C., NYC, 50 states and Puerto Rico	1 national office 97 state-level or regional-level positions (American Cancer Society Cancer Action Network (ACS CAN), 2012)	1 National office in Dallas. Association is broken up into 7 Affiliates. 1 state-level position; 6 advocacy consultants (American Heart Association (AHA), 2012)	8 (Oakland) 4 (Los Angeles) (California Food Policy Advocates (CFPA), 2011)	10 (Davis) 3 (Oakland) 10 (Southern California) (California Center for Public Health Advocacy (CCPHA), 2012c)
Total California-based advocacy staff	8 (Sacramento) 6 (Regional) (American Cancer Society-California Division, 2011)	2 (Sacramento) 2 (Los Angeles) 1 (San Diego) 1 (Oakland) (American Heart Association (AHA), 2011a)	8 (Oakland) 4 (Los Angeles) (California Food Policy Advocates (CFPA), 2011)	10 (Davis) 3 (Oakland) 10 (Southern California) (California Center for Public Health Advocacy (CCPHA), 2012c)
Volunteer base	2–3 million volunteers nationally, 304,000 in California(American Cancer Society-California Division, 2011)	222,000 advocacy volunteers and 20.5 million volunteers and supporters nationally (American Heart Association (AHA), 2011c); 18,000 advocates in California	[Not applicable]	[Not applicable]
Office locations	900 community offices with at least one in every state; 40 ACS Discovery Shops; 44 offices in California(American Cancer Society-California Division, 2011)	150 offices, with at least one in every state except Wyoming; 12 in California (American Heart Association (AHA), 2011a)	2 offices in California (California Food Policy Advocates (CFPA), 2011)	3 offices in California (California Center for Public Health Advocacy (CCPHA), 2012c)

(continued)

Table 22.2 (continued)

	American Cancer Society (ACS), American Cancer Society Cancer Action Network (ACSCAN)	American Heart Association (AHA)	California Food Policy Advocates (CFPA)	California Center for Public Health Advocacy (CCPHA)
Regular advocacy activities	Quadrennial "Celebration on the Hill" annual Legislative Day in Sacramento for Legislative ambassador training & legislative advocacy	Annual California Lobby Day in Sacramento for advocacy training and legislative advocacy ; Regular legislative in-district meetings	CFPA sponsors five state legislative proposals annually, in addition to coordinating numerous other policy development and advocacy activities with many coalitions and partners, including Strategic Alliance, California Hunger Action Coalition, Child Care Food Program Roundtable, among others	CCPHA trains local residents in advocacy for healthier eating and improved physical activity environments and mobilizes community grassroots teams to educate policymakers
Internet site for volunteer advocates	http://www.acscan.org, *for both federal and state-specific actions; alerts are sent out as needed*	http://yourethecure.org/default.aspx, *for both federal and state-specific actions*; *You're the Cure Advocacy e-newsletter (monthly)*	http://cfpa.net/subscribe*;* *Nutrition Action Alert readers receive timely updates on food and nutrition policies affecting low-income Californians. CFPA sends out alerts as needed, usually three or four per month*	http://publichealthadvocacy.e-actionmax.com/signup.asp *CCPHA provides legislative updates to members of its* ***Statewide Advocacy Network****—a network of people interested in improving nutrition and physical activity environments in California*

They also organize meetings between their advocacy volunteers and legislators to discuss specific legislative bills of interest to the AHA. The AHA has national policy priorities and statements that guide the policy work in each state. New policies that the AHA might support can be suggested by volunteers, staff, or legislators. All policies are vetted by advocacy staff first, however, but it is ultimately AHA leadership that decides whether to accept advocacy staff recommendations to take a position on an issue. If AHA leadership agrees to support the advocacy staff recommendations, then advocacy staff disseminate the AHA support/oppose position to the legislature and the AHA's large network of advocacy volunteers, encouraging them to take actions such as visiting legislators' offices, making phone calls to legislators to express support or opposition, and writing letters to the editors of local broadcast stations and print media.

- Identify and recruit legislative/policy-making champions willing to craft and negotiate the legislative details

Martha Escutia was a first-term state senator when Goldstein first met her. Three events conspired to anoint her a legislative champion for healthier school meals. One was that she had been previously diagnosed with gestational diabetes, which sensitized her to the disease and made her aware that one's daily food choices can affect risk of type 2 diabetes. The second was a study documenting the high prevalence of junk foods sold to students by California public schools (Purcell, 2000). The third (in 2005) was evidence that her legislative district had a particularly high death rate from diabetes (more on this later) (California Center for Public Health Advocacy (CCPHA), 2005). Her first legislative effort to combat diabetes was SB 1320, which focused on ensuring high-quality diabetes care for school children with type 1 diabetes attending California public schools. SB 1320 was supported by the Diabetes Coalition of California and several individual letters. Although the bill was passed by both houses of the legislature, Governor Davis vetoed it, saying. School health staffing needs are determined at the local level based on local priorities and should remain so (Davis, 2000)." The governor's veto was motivated in part by a price tag of between \$13.8 million to \$25.7 million a year to implement this legislation, which he said were amounts not included in the state budget (Davis, 2000).

Goldstein helped convince Senator Escutia that the primary prevention of diabetes could be more impactful than helping children already diagnosed with diabetes to get access to required medications while at school. She became the legislative champion for banning the sale of sugar-sweetened beverages and high-fat, high-sugar snacks from the campuses of California schools (SB 19, Escutia, 2001 (California Senate, 2001a); SB 12, Escutia, 2005 (California Senate, 2005a); SB 965, Escutia, 2005 (California Senate, 2005b)). The opposition to this legislation, predictably, included beverage and confectionary companies, the Grocery Manufacturers of America, the California Chamber of Commerce, and the Dairy Institute (California Senate, 2001c). The CCPHA staff coordinated their community mobilization efforts with legislative staff from Escutia's office to bring pressure to bear on legislators prior to critical votes. Having a legislative champion to guide the nature and timing of advocacy efforts by the public health activists was critical to

CCPHA's success in getting California's pioneering school nutrition law through the twists and turns of the legislative approval process and signed by the governor.

Accumulate Evidence and Conduct Public Education

- Assemble experts who support the issue and can vouch for community concern

University researchers with findings that underscore the importance of a health issue can elicit significant media attention at relatively low cost, particularly when the findings are supported by voluntary health organizations that have high public credibility in health-related matters. Scientific support that validates a community concern is important in mobilizing selected stakeholders, as the CCPHA did at the start with its national panel of experts but it is equally important in broader attempts to engage the media and more directly influence community attitudes toward the issue. Although health benefits alone won't usually be enough to get a policy adopted, scientific evidence confirming such benefits increases the public's trust that proponents are motivated by concern for community well being.

- Engage in opportunistic marketing efforts to maximize pressure on undecided legislators/policy makers and to reinforce community education efforts

As previously noted, SB 677 prohibited elementary and middle schools from selling food soda beverages, but did not affect high schools. Legislative efforts to extend SB 19 standards to high schools beyond the 10 pilot study districts and into all California schools K-12 (SB 12) and to prohibit soda sales in high schools (SB 965) were as difficult as the passage of SB 19 had been. Even with the strong support of newly elected governor Schwarzenegger, neither of these bills had any assurance of passing. Just three weeks before the legislature was due for final votes on these proposals, CCPHA released the results of a study on the prevalence of child obesity by assembly district (Goldstein, 2009). The study showed that the prevalence of child obesity in California had risen from 26.5% to 28.1% in just 4 years (2001–2005) and that the obesity epidemic had worsened in 90% of state legislative districts during that time (Goldstein, 2009). The report couched these findings in the context of other literature showing the high cost of treating obesity and obesity-related medical conditions, and provided every legislator data on the prevalence of overweight children in his/her district (Goldstein, 2009). Local data like these are powerful because constituents hold their local legislators accountable for improving their community's health and because they provide fodder for stories in the local media. Because of the timing of their release, these data permitted the media to spell out concretely the locally relevant implications of these important pieces of state legislation (Goldstein, 2009).

The tobacco industry lost considerable political influence when public health activists succeeded in depicting the industry as engaged in predatory marketing aimed at children (Difranza et al., 1991) and at low-income and minority communities (Pucci, Joseph, & Siegel, 1998) (Gardiner, 2004). Conversely, tobacco industry members have invested enormous resources recently to rehabilitate their public image by reframing their business as the responsible marketing of acknowledgeably risky products to informed adults (McDaniel & Malone, 2005). The public relations framing of the debate over the adoption of a public health policy can be critical to public support for the policy. As the public relations debacle over tobacco company marketing of Uptown cigarettes illustrated (Balbach, Gasior, & Barbeau, 2003), however, it's not the side with the most marketing dollars that wins. It's the side with the most boots on the ground, the most stories in the news, the most visits to legislative offices, the greatest number of callers to talk shows, and the most persuasive story to tell. While the marketing of tobacco products and the marketing of food products entail necessarily different messages, there are nonetheless important lessons learned from the history of tobacco control that could prepare public health activists for the public relations battles that will be forthcoming from the food manufacturers and their marketing partners (Brownell & Warner, 2009) as public health activists push for more policies to reduce Americans' intake of foods of minimum nutritional value.

Address Opposition Concerns

- Identify implacably hostile opponents of the proposed solutions

A popular tool for use by community organizers in planning a policy adoption campaign is the Midwest Academy Strategy chart (Midwest Academy, 2000). One of the questions that must be answered in using this chart is, "Who are your opponents?" In the case of SB 19 and its successors, the industries that were consistently opposed to the proposed law were beverage companies and confectioners, because the proposed law(s) threatened to reduce the market for their products. The Grocery Manufacturers of America and the Dairy Institute also opposed the final version of the legislation (California Senate, 2001c). Early identification of opponents is important for preparing grassroots advocates to counter the arguments that the opponents would make when justifying their opposition.

- Frame messages to highlight the problem and the practicality of proposed solutions

In the scientific literature, the term most often used to refer to "junk food" is: "foods of minimum nutritional value (Drewnowski, 2005)." This jargony language does not appear in the legislative language of SB 19. Instead, the legislative language identifies problem foods as including the following: "fast foods, the most common of which are sodas, pizza, cookies, chips, and burritos." The legislation mentioned the results of a statewide nutrition survey conducted of a random sample of California school districts that showed that these problem foods were sold by 95% of school districts in California (Public Health Institute, 2000). The use of the specific, immediately recognizable term: "junk" foods and referencing credible evidence of nearly universal school district exploitation of children's preferences for "junk foods" communicated the problem graphically and convincingly. The challenge of convincing a low nutrition-literacy public about the likely practical effects of the recommended solution was also met by the CCPHA convening a National Consensus Panel of 10 experts recruited from around the nation who could authoritatively recommend consensus food standards for California schools.

Negotiate a Sustainable Solution

- Negotiate with potential opponents who acknowledge the benefits of the overall goal but disagree with the methods for achieving the goal.

In July 2001, the California School Food Service Association (CSFSA) was officially opposed to Senator Escutia's draft legislation (California Senate, 2001b) because many food service directors feared that a ban on the sale of foods of minimum nutritional value would deprive them of a significant revenue stream that many depended on in order to offset deficits incurred in administering the NSLP. On the other hand, many CSFSA members were registered dietitians who acknowledged the legitimacy of efforts to reduce student consumption of foods of minimum nutritional value. By September 2001, the California Food Service Association had dropped its opposition to SB 19 (California Senate, 2001c). The CCPHA helped to broker a deal whereby the legislation was amended to include an increase of 10 cents per meal in the state reimbursement for school meals. This significant increase in state support for reimbursable school lunches allayed the concerns of the leadership of the CSFSA that the bill would create a financial hardship for its members, even though privately they still expressed reservations about the bill. The downside to this deal was that Senator Escutia's bill now carried a $60 million annual price tag, which could dissuade lawmakers from supporting the bill on grounds that the state could not afford the cost.

Nurture Continued Community Support for the Solution

- Build in evaluation.

To ensure continued support for the policy it is generally a good idea to build into the solution evaluation resources that can help to document the benefits of the new policy, to illustrate periodically to constituents why the policy should not be repealed. The success of smoking bans in bars and restaurants in California became assured when evaluations of the impact of the bans showed (1) no adverse effect on revenues (Glantz, 2000), (2) large decreases in respiratory symptoms among bar employees (Hahn et al., 2006), and (3) overwhelming public support for the new smoking restrictions (Tang et al., 2003). For the two-year period between January 2002 and January 2004 the SB 19 legislative language appropriated $4 million in funding for a major pilot test of early implementation of SB 19 in representative school districts from all over the state. The evaluation results of this pilot study were important in demonstrating not only the administrative feasibility of SB 19 adoption but financial feasibility as well. The results showed that overall school district food service fiscal health remained stable, instead of worsening as had been feared (Center for Weight & Health, 2004).

- Build in periodic enforcement

The public health benefits of a new law will be smaller than expected if adherence to the policy is poor. It helps to build in resources to ensure enforcement of the policy. State policies requiring automobile drivers to wear seat belts were more successful when the policies included penalties for those drivers observed by the police to be driving without their seat belts on (Zambon et al., 2007). For these reasons, the authors of SB 19 incorporated stipulations that the California Superintendent of Instruction randomly select 10% of school districts statewide to assess compliance with the law and for the Superintendent to require any school district found to be in non-compliance to file a corrective plan.

- Build on the solution or change the solution

The history of tobacco control suggests that as long as there are profits to be made by importuning Americans to engage in unhealthy behaviors, industry will keep looking for ways to circumvent public health policies designed to reduce the prevalence of such behaviors (Yach & Bialous, 2001). As an industry, food manufacturers collectively spend many billions more than the tobacco industry ever did in marketing products of questionable value to one's health (Brownell & Warner, 2009). Moreover, some major food manufacturers (e.g., Kraft) were largely owned by companies (e.g., Altria/Phillip Morris) that sold tobacco products and had direct access, therefore, to legal and public relations experts knowledgeable about strategies proven to be effective in slowing progress in tobacco control (Brownell & Warner, 2009).

Not content with only the impact that it has had on school nutrition competitive food standards nationwide, the CCPHA has been building on its success by expanding the targets for its campaign to reduce population obesity risk. In 2006 CCPHA partnered with Governor Schwarzenegger to get first-ever dedicated funding for elementary school physical education ($40 million annually; $500 million one-time appropriation). In 2008 CCPHA joined with the ACS to pass the first-in-the-nation state legislation (SB 120) mandating that chain restaurants post calorie information on menus and menu boards. In the 2010 California legislative session, a CCPHA and CFPA-sponsored bill and AHA supported was enacted that would ensure the provision of only healthful beverages in childcare settings (AB 2084, Brownley) (California Center for Public Health Advocacy (CCPHA), 2012a). California Food Policy Advocates (CFPA) also sponsored successful legislation (SB 1413, Leno) requiring school districts to make free, fresh drinking water available in school food service areas by 2012, which CCPHA and the AHA supported (California Center for Public Health Advocacy (CCPHA), 2012a). CCPHA has also been promoting policies at the local level that would eliminate the sale and marketing of sugary drinks on city- or county-owned property, at city- or county-sponsored events, and at youth venues like parks, zoos, and childcare and afterschool settings (California Center for Public Health Advocacy (CCPHA), 2010). Simultaneously, the campaign has been promoting the availability of free, fresh drinking water in all public venues.

Below we discuss the second example used to reinforce lessons about the policy adoption process addressed above. This second example focuses on the role of CFPA in facilitating the adoption by the Los Angeles Unified School district of several significant school nutrition policies.

California Food Policy Advocates (CFPA)

California Food Policy Advocates (CFPA) is a statewide policy and advocacy organization dedicated to improving the health and well being of low-income Californians by increasing their access to nutritious and affordable food (California Food Policy Advocates (CFPA), 2011). CFPA has been the behind-the-scenes broker of several forward-looking nutrition- and physical activity-related policy changes adopted by the Los Angeles Unified School District in the last decade and has been particularly active in ensuring full implementation of the policies subsequent to their adoption. During this period Matt Sharp has been the senior advocate in the CFPA's Los Angeles office. Below we review several case examples that illustrate how the CFPA was able to cultivate inside champions (former L.A. Unified School District (LAUSD) Board Member Marlene Canter, LAUSD food services division deputy director David Binkle) and years of dogged advocacy for policies to improve nutrition quality for students into significant changes in local school district nutrition policies. "Accidental champions" emerged who helped close the deal with respect to LAUSD adoption of ambitious new policies, such as LAUSD Superintendent Roy Romer and L.A. County Board of Supervisors member Zev Yaroslavsky, both of whom recognized the value of prevention when each was diagnosed with type 2 diabetes. Examples of such policy changes include the LAUSD adopting several landmark policies: 1) banning soft drink sales on campus during the school day three years before state laws restricted soda sales at school, 2) adjusting breakfast and lunch menus to incorporate Institute of Medicine (IOM) recommendations for improving the nutrient quality of school meals before these recommendations became legally required and, 3) dropping chocolate milk from the school meal menu (California Food Policy Advocates (CFPA), 2012). In the case of banning soft drink sales, the presentations on the role of soda consumption in the childhood obesity epidemic by pediatrician Dr. Fran Kaufman to LAUSD's Board of Education and to the L.A. County Board of Supervisors resulted in surprisingly quick support from the leaders of both entities for eliminating a suspected contributor to type 2 diabetes from school campuses: sugar-sweetened beverages, also known as "soft drinks (Center for Food and Justice, 2002; Hayasaki, 2002)." In the case of #2 incorporating the 2005 Dietary Guidelines for Americans standards into food services practices, the district's improvements were facilitated by two important factors. First, the district and its external partners convened a committee of committed stakeholders dedicated to finding practical ways to improve nutrition while simultaneously expanding participation, thereby addressing administrators' key concern about fiscal solvency. Second, the district benefited from interest and attention from its local government partners. These partners included the City of Los Angeles (which formed a high-level Food Policy Council) and the County of Los Angeles Department of Public Health. This convergence of interests was facilitated by a grant to the LAUSD from the $16 million Communities Putting Prevention to Work (CPPW) "Project RENEW" initiative (Los Angeles County Department of Public Health, 2011). These local government partners provided resources and practical strategies to the LAUSD for realizing the high expectations of elected officials, community organizations, and parents, for cutting-edge improvements in cafeteria offerings in District schools. CFPA cultivation of administrative champions, particularly deputy director of Food Services David Binkle who was responsible for menu development, was critical to progress (Watanabe, 2011).

In the case of #3 dropping chocolate milk from the menu, CFPA served as an honest broker of information about the benefits and costs of such a decision. The public impetus to limit the choice of type of milk served in the LAUSD was sparked by a savvy media campaign led by Jamie Oliver, the London-based school food advocate, but the decision by LAUSD Superintendent John Deasy to change the menus and eliminate flavored milk was influenced by thoughtful advice to the Superintendent from a variety of external stakeholders and facilitated by CFPA (Blume, 2011). In all three cases, the instigating events were supported and amplified by grassroots efforts including students, concerned parents, and other activists but the ultimate drivers of the policy changes were various champions whose ability to communicate with each other was facilitated by CPFA staff, who were seen as independent of both industry ties and the LAUSD Food Services Division. Over the course of ten years, CFPA staff also provided the institutional memory and the social glue for convening and maintaining relationships between numerous partners, including key pressure groups, together in an effective coalition and used its influence with the media judiciously to move the advocacy campaigns forward at critical junctures (California Food Policy Advocates (CFPA), 2012).

The American Heart Association (AHA)

The AHA has mobilized thousands of volunteers to support federal and state initiatives to optimize the nutrition and physical activity health of students and the neighborhoods around public schools. For example, a cadre of AHA *You're the Cure* advocates sent 25,000 messages to Congress in support of the 2010 Healthy, Hunger-free Kids Act (U.S. Congress, 2010b). In 2011, *You're the Cure* advocates sent 30,000 messages to Congress in support of the USDA adoption of updated national nutrition school meal standards, which would ensure that school meals include more fruits, vegetables, and whole grain foods, and limit the sodium and saturated fat. The AHA has been actively supporting initiatives to promote healthier levels of physical activity as well. In this vein, the AHA has been actively supporting initiatives to expand community access to school site recreational facilities by strengthening joint-use agreements. In addition, the AHA has led the charge to fight back the proposed budget cuts of the state physical fitness test, the Fitnessgram, a mandate requiring local school boards to administer and report results to the California Department of Education, annual physical performance tests to pupils in grades 5, 7 and 9. For a number of years, it has been proposed to be eliminated but due to heavy lobbying by the AHA along with the California Association of Health, Parks, Physical Education, Recreation and Dance and CCPHA the funding has been maintained. Preservation of this program is important in a number of ways. It is used by schools to determine the fitness levels of students and provide direction for curricular plans. Students use the results to develop personal fitness programs for improvement and parents use the results to help their children plan fitness activities to improve their health. The Fitnessgram also provides extremely important data at both the local and state level. Results from the test are used to monitor changes in the physical fitness of California students which is important to researchers studying childhood obesity. Furthermore, these data help policy-makers make informed decisions related to physical fitness and childhood obesity.

Reliance on legislation to change community food-choice practices and physical activity levels is problematic inasmuch as special interests have ways of blunting the intent of public health legislation. A recent case in point was Congressional interference with USDA's, seven-year, science-based process to align school breakfast and lunch nutrient standards and meal patterns with the Dietary Guidelines for Americans. Among other things, the proposed regulations sought to boost students' fruit and vegetable intake, to increase their consumption of whole grains and to limit their consumption of starchy vegetables. The Institute of Medicine, which had provided USDA a detailed plan for translating the Dietary Guidelines for Americans into specific, practical changes to school breakfast and lunch menus, said that implementation would help reduce children's risk of consuming excessive calories (Stallings, Suitor, Taylor, & Editors, 2010). Had these rules been fully implemented, students could expect to eat fewer French fries and fewer pizzas. Before the regulations were enacted in January 2012, Congress attached amendments to USDA's annual budget forbidding the USDA from limiting starchy vegetables and requiring the USDA to continue allowing a one-eighth cup of tomato paste (typically the amount found on a slice of pizza) to receive credit for providing students with a standard one-serving half cup of tomato solids. The tomato paste requirement was pushed by a Senator from Minnesota, where Schwan's Food Service Inc. is headquartered. Schwan's Food Service, Inc. is a Marshall, Minn.-based company that supplies frozen pizzas to 75% of U.S. schools (Adams, 2011). The potato requirement was pushed by legislators from Maine and Colorado, two big potato-producing states (Adams). These amendments passed with bipartisan support triggering subsequent widespread media derision of Congress as endorsing the notion that a slice of pizza was equivalent to a full serving of vegetables (Daily Mail Reporter, 2011). A spokesperson for Mission Readiness, an organization of retired generals concerned with maximizing national security readiness called the vote "a national disgrace" because obesity is the leading cause of medical disqualification for would-be recruits into the nation's armed forces. (Daily Mail Reporter)

Increased consumption of energy dense and nutrient-poor foods such as French fries and pizzas is believed to increase children's obesity risk (Harris, Pomeranz, Lobstein, & Brownell, 2009) and documentably increases adults' obesity risk (Mozaffarian, Hao, Rimm, Willett, & Hu, 2011). Conversely, increased consumption of calorie-poor, nutrient-rich foods such as non-starchy vegetables and fresh fruit is commonly associated with increased probability of maintaining a healthy weight (Mozaffarian et al.; Vernarelli, Mitchell, Hartman, & Rolls, 2011).

The arguments in favor of the amendments that undermined USDA efforts to encourage children to eat more non-starchy vegetables and less pizza did not refute the basis for the proposed new rules but instead asserted that the USDA was overreaching its responsibility and depriving parents of a say in what foods their children should eat at school (Daily Mail Reporter, 2011). School food services administrators (in concert with industry) waged an aggressive campaign to undermine the proposed regulations by arguing that the nutrition changes were too costly. Congress appropriated over $3 billion/year to assist schools in purchasing more expensive food ingredients and made other policy changes designed to save school food service budgets $6 billion/year through improved accounting procedures and controls (U.S. Department of Agriculture (USDA), 2011). But because school food services had sought $35 billion/year in additional federal reimbursement at the beginning of the legislative process (School Nutrition Association, 2011), the steps Congress took to minimize the impact of the new nutritional requirements were perceived as insufficient (School Nutrition Association).

Another persuasive argument was the assertion that providing more fresh fruits and minimally processed non-starchy vegetables was simply too expensive at a time when schools nationwide had seen major budget cuts because of government cost-cutting (Daily Mail Reporter, 2011). The AHA mobilized thousands of its advocacy volunteers to remind legislators of the long-term health and academic benefits that would accrue to the nation's children by fully implementing the new USDA school meal rules but these advocacy messages failed to overcome the lobbying efforts of pizza purveyors and potato growers (American Heart Association, 2011b). President Obama felt he had no choice but to sign these amendments to the annual USDA appropriations bill into law, because the appropriations bill was embedded in a must-pass $182 billion omnibus bill authorizing continued funding of several major government departments, including the departments of Agriculture, Commerce, Justice, Transportation and Housing and Urban Development (Ryan, 2011).

Federal or state laws preempting local policy changes squelch the grassroots activism and local experimentation needed to build support for state and federal action. State or federal preemption of local decision-making authority has been one of the tobacco industry's most successful strategies for squelching changes (Siegel et al., 1997) in community norms at the local level because it deprives local activists of the galvanizing benefit of potential local policy change. In the nutrition area, state preemption of restaurant menu board nutrition labeling was the price that state-level advocates were willing to pay, with potentially negative consequences for future efforts to change local community norms by building on the statewide bill to provide a stronger law with respect to sodium intake, for example, by making the nutrition information more accessible to consumers. California's pioneering SB 1420 menu labeling law (California Senate, 2008) mandated calorie information be placed on menu boards in all large chain restaurants operating in California. This was a result of a two year campaign led by CCPHA, AHA and ACS. After numerous concessions were made to address the opposition's and other legislator's concerns, preemption was added to the bill. At that point the AHA withdrew its support for the proposed legislation. The American Cancer Society California Division Government Relations Office grappled with whether to support SB 1420 after the preemption clause was included. It decided to continue to support it, as did the CCPHA, despite the inclusion of the preemption clause, because they felt that having the state of California adopt any kind of restaurant labeling bill would accelerate national efforts with similar goals. Indeed, the Patient Protection and Affordable Care Act (U.S. Congress, 2010a) passed by Congress subsequently superseded California's SB 1420 by mandating menu board calorie information in chain restaurants nationwide. The federal act was supported by the National Restaurant Association because it provided uniformity with respect to the requirement to provide calorie information on menu boards but the law also preempted localities from requiring restaurants to provide additional menu board information. Federal preemption made good sense for nationally uniform food facts labels as mandated by the Nutrition Labeling and Education Act of 1990 (U.S. Congress, 1990). If public health activists want to require local chain restaurants to post information about the sodium content of menu items, the new federal law preempts their right to get a local ordinance passed to force local restaurants to post sodium levels. Their only recourse now is to convince Congress to pass such a requirement. Without a history of successful local implementation of such a requirement it will be more challenging to get Congress to support such a change. Despite complaints by the National Restaurant Association that this new requirement was onerous for its members and therefore limited the coverage of the menu-labeling policy to chains with at least 20 restaurants, it nonetheless insisted on including a voluntary option for food retail establishments that were not covered by the legislation. Why would food retailers voluntarily adopt this "onerous" federal menu-labeling requirement? The answer lies in guidance prepared for the industry by the U.S. Food and Drug Administration (FDA), which is responsible for crafting the rules that will guide implementation of the new menu-labeling requirements (U.S. Food and Drug Administration (FDA), 2011). The FDA noted that food retailers not covered by the federal legislation could still be regulated under State and local nutrition-labeling laws UNLESS they elected to participate in the federal program by voluntarily registering every other year with the FDA (U.S. Food and Drug Administration (FDA), 2011). The federal menu-labeling legislation thereby protects all local food retailers from being subject to localities or states requiring more menu board nutrition information than the calorie information now required of chain restaurants. However, the law also imposed no restrictions on state or local menu or menu board requirements for establishments not subject to the law, such as restaurant chains with fewer than twenty establishments. Recognizing that the state and localities could go further than federal law for those restaurants not already covered, the fact that there was preemption in California's state law made it unclear whether or not localities could could go further, Hence the introduction and passage of SB 20 (2011) by Senator Padilla which repealed SB 1420 and instead references federal law and rules. Preemption therefore can be a powerful tool used by industry to squelch public health activism at the local level and to prevent the kinds of local policy-adoption experiments that typically help build momentum and capacity to adopt similar policies at the state and federal levels. In this case, however, because this first-in-the-nation state law established the precedent that state authority could be used to regulate health information in the restaurant setting, there was disagreement among public health advocates as to whether the costs of preemption outweighed the benefits of establishing a precedent that could stimulate similar policy-making federally (and subsequently did just that!). This example nonetheless illustrates how a preemption clause can turn a law originally designed to promote public health into a federal law that makes more comprehensive policy adoption in the future more difficult.

Summary

In sum, the steps typically needed to move a health issue of hypothetical community concern through the policy-adoption process is an organic process, requiring a critical mass of local activists converging with hard-working legislative champions to mobilize community stakeholders, gain the attention of the media and politicize the issue to the point where legislators have more to lose than gain by opposing the adoption of the new policy. Mobilizing local policy advocacy efforts in disparate towns and cities is labor intensive but may be more effective in changing community norms statewide or nationwide than relying exclusively on state or national media health-promotion campaigns to effect sustainable community norm change. At the same time, once there is sufficient momentum at the local level for policy change, strong state laws become politically feasible. Similarly, when the accumulation of similar state policies reaches a critical threshold, then strong federal policies become possible. Of course, in reality, it's not a black/white choice between bottom-up local grassroots organizing versus top-down media messages. Community advocates readily acknowledge the importance of strategically timed press releases to get free media coverage of their message to influence community norms. Contrariwise, ostensibly media-driven efforts such as the VERB campaign (Wong et al., 2004) try to amplify their message through on-the-ground community mobilization efforts. The most successful campaigns use a combination of bottom-up grassroots mobilization of constituents and top-down strategic marketing to achieve maximum effect. Efforts to change community food-choice norms and physical activity practices will benefit from the combined efforts of voluntary health organizations, nutrition alliances and physical activity coalitions coupled with strategic marketing messages from public health experts and legislative champions. This combination yielded solutions to tobacco-use prevention (Traynor & Glantz, 1996), to drunk driving (McCarthy

& Wolfson, 1996) and to addressing the lack of effective treatment for AIDS (Carpenter Center for the Visual Arts, 2009). This combination can work, too, in efforts to find community-level solutions to the obesity epidemic.

References

Adams, J. U. (2011). 'Pizza vegetable' controversy is hot potato. *Los Angeles Times*, 4. Retrieved from http://articles.latimes.com/2011/nov/28/health/la-he-school-lunch-nutrition-20111128.

American Cancer Society. (2011). How we fight back. (p. 1). Available from http://www.cancer.org/AboutUs/HowWeHelpYou/advocacy-public-policy.

American Cancer Society. (2011). Facts about ACS. Available from http://www.cancer.org/AboutUs/WhoWeAre/acs-fact-sheet.

American Cancer Society Cancer Action Network (ACS CAN). (2012). American Cancer Society Cancer Action Network (ACS CAN). Retrieved January 16, 2012, from http://www.acscan.org/.

American Cancer Society-California Division. (2011). *FY11 California Division, Inc. Board of Directors Handbook.* American Cancer Society-California Division.

American Heart Association (AHA). (2011a). American Heart Association advocacy contacts. Available from http://www.heart.org/HEARTORG/General/AHA-Media-Advocacy-Contacts_UCM_311304_Article.jsp#.Tw_jBWGyHng.

American Heart Association (AHA). (2011b). Fight for healthier school meals continues. *Advocacy Pulse, 14*(8), 1–3.

American Heart Association (AHA). (2011c). Membership. Available from http://my.americanheart.org/professional/Membership/Membership_UCM_316891_SubHomePage.jsp.

American Heart Association (AHA). (2012). All advocacy contacts. Available from http://www.heart.org/HEARTORG/General/AHA-Media-Advocacy-Contacts_UCM_311304_Article.jsp#.Tw3tDIFsfZc.

Bal, D. G., Kizer, K. W., Felten, P. G., Mozar, H. N., & Niemeyer, D. (1990). Reducing tobacco consumption in California – Development of a statewide anti-tobacco use campaign. [Article]. *JAMA-Journal of the American Medical Association, 264*(12), 1570–1574.

Balbach, E. D., Gasior, R. J., & Barbeau, E. M. (2003). R.J. Reynolds' targeting of African Americans: 1988–2000. [Article]. *American Journal of Public Health, 93*(5), 822–827.

Blume, H. (2011). LAUSD to remove chocolate, strawberry milk from schools, superintendent says. Available from http://articles.latimes.com/print/2011/apr/28/local/la-me-lausd-milk-20110428.

Brownell, K. D., & Warner, K. E. (2009). The perils of ignoring history: Big tobacco played dirty and millions died. How similar is big food? [Article]. *Milbank Quarterly, 87*(1), 259–294.

California Center for Public Health Advocacy (CCPHA). (2002). National Consensus Panel on School Nutrition: Recommendations for competitive food standards in California Schools. Available from http://www.publichealthadvocacy.org/PDFs/school_food_stan_pdfs/Nutrition_Standards_Report_-_Final.pdf.

California Center for Public Health Advocacy (CCPHA). (2005). The growing epidemic: Child overweight rates on the rise in California Assembly Districts. Available from http://www.publichealthadvocacy.org/_PDFs/research_pdfs/fullpolicyreport.pdf.

California Center for Public Health Advocacy (CCPHA). (2010). 2010 Annual Report. Available from http://www.publichealthadvocacy.org/_PDFs/financials_AR/CCPHA2010AnnualReport.pdf.

California Center for Public Health Advocacy (CCPHA). (2012a). 2010 Legislation. Retrieved January 16, 2012, from http://www.publichealthadvocacy.org/legislation10.html.

California Center for Public Health Advocacy (CCPHA). (2012b). Los Angeles County Grassroots Teams Score Successes on School Nutrition. Retrieved January 16, 2012, from http://www.publichealthadvocacy.org/teams.html.

California Center for Public Health Advocacy (CCPHA). (2012c). Staff. Retrieved January 16, 2012, from http://www.publichealthadvocacy.org/staff.html.

California Department of Public Health. (2011). Smoking prevalence among California and U.S. minus California adults, 1984–2010. Available from http://www.cdph.ca.gov/programs/tobacco/Documents/Media/2010%20adult%20and%20youth%20prevalence%20memo_figures%20%287%29v2.pdf.

California Food Policy Advocates (CFPA). (2011). About Us. Available from http://cfpa.net/about-us.

California Food Policy Advocates (CFPA). (2012). CFPA milestones. Available from http://cfpa.net/our-history.

California School Nutrition Association. (2012). California School Nutrition Association. Retrieved January 16, 2012, from http://www.calsna.org/.

California Senate. (2001a). Senate Bill 19 (Pupil Nutrition Act). Available from http://leginfo.ca.gov/pub/01-02/bill/sen/sb_0001-0050/sb_19_bill_20011014_chaptered.pdf.

California Senate. (2001b). Senate Health and Human Services Committee 6/6/2001 Analysis. Available from http://leginfo.ca.gov/pub/01-02/bill/sen/sb_0001-0050/sb_19_cfa_20010319_151120_sen_comm.html.

California Senate. (2001c). Senate Health and Human Services Committee 9/10/2001 Analysis. Available from http://leginfo.ca.gov/pub/01-02/bill/sen/sb_0001-0050/sb_19_cfa_20020116_134859_sen_floor.html.

California Senate. (2003). Senate Bill 677 (Elementary and middle school beverage ban). Available from http://leginfo.ca.gov/pub/03-04/bill/sen/sb_0651-0700/sb_677_bill_20030917_chaptered.pdf.

California Senate. (2005a). Senate Bill 12 (Junk food ban for all schools). Available from http://leginfo.ca.gov/pub/05-06/bill/sen/sb_0001-0050/sb_12_bill_20050915_chaptered.pdf.

California Senate. (2005b). Senate Bill 965 (Modified beverage ban at all schools). Available from http://leginfo.ca.gov/pub/05-06/bill/sen/sb_0951-1000/sb_965_bill_20050915_chaptered.pdf.

California Senate. (2008). Senate Bill 1420 (Menu labeling) Available from http://info.sen.ca.gov/pub/07-08/bill/sen/sb_1401-1450/sb_1420_bill_20080930_chaptered.pdf.

California Senate. (2011). SB 20 (Repeal of state menu labeling law; replace with language mandating adherence to federal menu labeling law) Available from http://leginfo.ca.gov/pub/11-12/bill/sen/sb_0001-0050/sb_20_bill_20111002_chaptered.pdf.

Carpenter Center for the Visual Arts. (2009). An exhibition: ACT-UP New York: Activism, Art, and the AIDS Crisis, 1987–1993. Retrieved from http://www.ves.fas.harvard.edu/ACTUP.html.

Center for Food and Justice. (2002). CHALLENGING THE SODA COMPANIES: The Los Angeles Unified School District Soda Ban. Available from http://departments.oxy.edu/uepi/cfj/publications/Challenging_the_Soda_Companies.pdf.

Center for Science in the Public Interest. (2008). State School Foods Report Card-2007. Available from http://www.cspinet.org/2007schoolreport.pdf.

Center for Weight & Health. (2004). Dollars and sense: The financial impact of selling healthier school foods. Available from http://www.cspinet.org/nutritionpolicy/Dollarssense_07.pdf.

Cheng, K. W., Glantz, S. A., & Lightwood, J. M. (2011). Association between smokefree laws and voluntary smokefree-home rules. [Article]. *American Journal of Preventive Medicine, 41*(6), 566–572.

Christakis, N. A., & Fowler, J. H. (2007). The spread of obesity in a large social network over 32 years. [Article]. *New England Journal of Medicine, 357*(4), 370–379.

Daily Mail Reporter. (2011). The land where pizza is one of your five-a-day… because it is covered in tomato paste. Retrieved from http://www.dailymail.co.uk/news/article-2062056/Pizza-vegetable--covered-tomato-paste.html

Davis, G. (2000). Veto message for SB 1320. Available from http://leginfo.ca.gov/pub/99-00/bill/sen/sb_1301-1350/sb_1320_vt_20000928.html.

Difranza, J. R., Richards, J. W., Paulman, P. M., Wolfgillespie, N., Fletcher, C., Jaffe, R. D., et al. (1991). RJR Nabisco's cartoon camel promotes camel cigarettes to children. [Article]. *JAMA-Journal of the American Medical Association, 266*(22), 3149–3153.

Drewnowski, A. (2005). Concept of a nutritious food: toward a nutrient density score. [Review]. *American Journal of Clinical Nutrition, 82*(4), 721–732.

Furberg, H., Lichtenstein, P., Pedersen, N. L., Bulik, C., & Sullivan, P. F. (2006). Cigarettes and oral snuff use in Sweden: Prevalence and transitions. [Article]. *Addiction, 101*(10), 1509–1515.

Gardiner, P. S. (2004). The African Americanization of menthol cigarette use in the United States. [Article; Proceedings Paper]. *Nicotine & Tobacco Research, 6*, S55–S65.

Glantz, S. A. (2000). Effect of smokefree bar law on bar revenues in California. [Letter]. *Tobacco Control, 9*(1), 111–112.

Goldstein, H. (2009). Translating research into public policy. [Editorial Material]. *Journal of Public Health Policy, 30*, S16–S20.

Hahn, E. J., Rayens, M. K., York, N., Okoli, C. T. C., Zhang, M., Dignan, M., et al. (2006). Effects of a smoke-free law on hair nicotine and respiratory symptoms of restaurant and bar workers. [Article]. *Journal of Occupational and Environmental Medicine, 48*(9), 906–913.

Harris, J. L., Pomeranz, J. L., Lobstein, T., & Brownell, K. D. (2009). A crisis in the marketplace: How food marketing contributes to childhood obesity and what can be done. *Annual Review Of Public Health, 30*, 211–225.

Hayasaki, E. (2002). L.A. Unified: The soft drinks won't be allowed on campuses starting in 2004. They may be replaced by more healthful beverages. Available from http://articles.latimes.com/print/2002/aug/28/local/me-soda28.

Hill, E. (2001). Legislative analyst report on implementation of Proposition 99-An overview. Available from http://www.lao.ca.gov/1991/reports/346_0591_implementation_of_prop_99.pdf.

Independent Sector. (2011). Lobbying guidelines for public charities (p. 1). Available from http://www.independentsector.org/lobbying_guidelines_public_charities.

Jacobson, P. D., & Wasserman, J. (1999). The implementation and enforcement of tobacco control laws: Policy implications for activists and the industry. [Article]. *Journal of Health Politics Policy and Law, 24*(3), 567–598.

Jemal, A., Ward, E., & Thun, M. (2010). Declining death rates reflect progress against cancer. [Article]. *Plos One, 5*(3).

Kuczmarski, R. J., Flegal, K. M., Campbell, S. M., & Johnson, C. L. (1994). Increasing prevalence of overweight among U.S. adults – The National Health and Nutrition Examination Surveys, 1960 to 1991. [Article]. *JAMA-Journal of the American Medical Association, 272*(3), 205–211.

Laugesen, M., & Meads, C. (1991). Tobacco advertising restrictions, price, income, and tobacco consumption in OECD countries, 1960–1986. [Article]. *British Journal of Addiction, 86*(10), 1343–1354.

Lightwood, J. M., Dinno, A., & Glantz, S. A. (2008). Effect of the California Tobacco Control Program on personal health care expenditures. [Article]. *Plos Medicine, 5*(8), 1214–1222.

Lloyd-Jones, D. M., Hong, Y. L., Labarthe, D., Mozaffarian, D., Appel, L. J., Van Horn, L., et al. (2010). Defining and setting national goals for cardiovascular health promotion and disease reduction. The American Heart Association's strategic impact goal through 2020 and beyond. [Review]. *Circulation, 121*(4), 586–613.

Los Angeles County Department of Public Health. (2011). RENEW Community Action Plan objectives. Available from http://lahealthaction.org/library/RENEW_L.A._County_Information_Handout.pdf.

McCarthy, J. D., & Wolfson, M. (1996). Resource mobilization by local social movement organizations: Agency, strategy, and organization in the movement against drinking and driving. [Article]. *American Sociological Review, 61*(6), 1070–1088.

McDaniel, P. A., & Malone, R. E. (2005). Understanding Philip Morris's pursuit of US government regulation of tobacco. [Review]. *Tobacco Control, 14*(3), 193–200.

Midwest Academy. (2000). Midwest Academy Strategy Chart. Available from http://www.tcsg.org/sfelp/toolkit/MidwestAcademy_01.pdf.

Mozaffarian, D., Hao, T., Rimm, E. B., Willett, W. C., & Hu, F. B. (2011). Changes in diet and lifestyle and long-term weight gain in women and men. [Article]. *New England Journal of Medicine, 364*(25), 2392–2404.

National Cancer Institute (NCI). (2012). National Cancer Act of 1971. Retrieved January 16, 2012, from http://dtp.nci.nih.gov/timeline/noflash/milestones/M4_Nixon.htm.

National Center for Health Statistics (NCHS). (2009). Health United States, 2008. Available from http://www.cdc.gov/nchs/data/hus/hus08.pdf.

Nestle, M., & Jacobson, M. F. (2000). Halting the obesity epidemic: A public health policy approach. [Article]. *Public Health Reports, 115*(1), 12–24.

Nutrition Labeling and Education Act of 1990 (1990).

Public Health Institute. (2000). 2000 California High School fast food survey. Available from http://www.phi.org/pdf-library/fastfoodsurvey2000.pdf.

Public law 111–148. The Patient Protection and Affordable Care Act, 124 STAT. 119 C.F.R. (2010a).

Pucci, L. G., Joseph, H. M., & Siegel, M. (1998). Outdoor tobacco advertising in six Boston neighborhoods – Evaluating youth exposure. [Article]. *American Journal of Preventive Medicine, 15*(2), 155–159.

Purcell, A. (2000). 2000 California High School fast food survey: Findings and recommendations. Available from http://www.phi.org/pdf-library/fastfoodsurvey2000.pdf.

Rimpela, M. K., Aaro, L. E., & Rimpela, A. H. (1993). The effects of tobacco sales promotion on initiation of smoking – Experiences from Finland and Norway. *Scandinavian Journal of Social Medicine. Supplementum, 49*, 5–23.

Ryan, J. (2011). Congress approves minibus spending bill, sends to Obama. Available from http://thehill.com/blogs/floor-action/senate/194453-senate-approves-minibus-continuing-resolution-sends-to-the-president.

School Nutrition Association. (2011). SNA Submits Comments on Proposed School Meal Standards. Available from http://schoolnutrition.org/Blog.aspx?id=15197&blogid=564.

Shipan, C. R., & Volden, C. (2006). Bottom-up federalism: The diffusion of antismoking policies from US cities to states. [Article]. *American Journal of Political Science, 50*(4), 825–843.

Siegel, M., Carol, J., Jordan, J., Hobart, R., Schoenmarklin, S., DuMelle, F., et al. (1997). Preemption in tobacco control – Review of an emerging public health problem. [Article]. *JAMA-Journal of the American Medical Association, 278*(10), 858–863.

Sporn, M. B. (1996). The war on cancer. [Review]. *Lancet, 347*(9012), 1377–1381.

Stallings, V. A., Suitor, C. W., Taylor, E. D. (Eds.). (2010). *School meals: Building blocks for healthy children*. Available from http://www.nap.edu/catalog/12751.html.

Tang, H., Cowling, D. W., Lloyd, J. C., Rogers, T., Koumjian, K. L., Stevens, C. M., et al. (2003). Changes of attitudes and patronage behaviors in response to a smoke-free bar law. [Article]. *American Journal of Public Health, 93*(4), 611–617.

Traynor, M. P., & Glantz, S. A. (1996). California's tobacco tax initiative: The development and passage of Proposition 99. [Review]. *Journal of Health Politics Policy and Law, 21*(3), 543–585.

Troiano, R. P., Flegal, K. M., Kuczmarski, R. J., Campbell, S. M., & Johnson, C. L. (1995). Overweight prevalence and trends for children and adolescents – The National Health and Nutrition Examination Surveys, 1963 to 1991. [Article]. *Archives of Pediatrics & Adolescent Medicine, 149*(10), 1085–1091.

U.S. Congress. (1990). Nutrition Labeling and Education Act of 1990 Public Law No: 101-535. Available from http://thomas.loc.gov/cgi-bin/bdquery/z?d101:HR03562:@@@L&summ2=m&|TOM:/bss/d101query.html|.

U.S. Congress. (2010b). Public Law 111–296. Healthy, Hunger- Free Kids Act. Available from http://www.gpo.gov/fdsys/pkg/PLAW-111publ296/pdf/PLAW-111publ296.pdf.

U.S. Department of Agriculture (USDA). (2011). Healthy Hunger-Free Kids Act of 2010. Available from http://www.fns.usda.gov/cnd/Governance/Legislation/CNR_2010.htm.

U.S. Food and Drug Administration (FDA). (2011). Guidance for Industry: Questions and Answers Regarding the Effect of Section 4205 of the Patient Protection and Affordable Care Act of 2010 on State and Local Menu and Vending Machine Labeling Laws. Available from http://www.fda.gov/food/guidancecomplianceregulatoryinformation/guidancedocuments/foodlabelingnutrition/ucm223408.htm.

Vernarelli, J. A., Mitchell, D. C., Hartman, T. J., & Rolls, B. J. (2011). Dietary energy density is associated with body weight status and vegetable intake in US children. [Article]. *Journal of Nutrition, 141*(12), 2204–2210.

Watanabe, T. (2011). L.A. schools' healthful lunch menu panned by students. Available from http://articles.latimes.com/print/2011/dec/17/local/la-me-food-lausd-20111218.

Whitaker, R. C., Wright, J. A., Pepe, M. S., Seidel, K. D., & Dietz, W. H. (1997). Predicting obesity in young adulthood from childhood and parental obesity. [Article; Proceedings Paper]. *New England Journal of Medicine, 337*(13), 869–873.

Wong, F., Huhman, M., Heitzler, C., Asbury, L., Bretthauer-Mueller, R., McCarthy, S., et al. (2004). VERB – A social marketing campaign to increase physical activity among youth. *Preventing Chronic Disease, 1*(3), A10.

Yach, D., & Bialous, S. A. (2001). Junking science to promote tobacco. [Article]. *American Journal of Public Health, 91*(11), 1745–1748.

Zambon, F., Fedeli, U., Visentin, C., Marchesan, M., Avossa, F., Brocco, S., et al. (2007). Evidence-based policy on road safety: The effect of the demerit points system on seat belt use and health outcomes. [Article]. *Journal of Epidemiology and Community Health, 61*(10).

Chapter 23
Childhood Obesity and Exergames: Assessments and Experiences from Singapore

May O. Lwin, Benjamin J. Li, and Jerome D. Williams

Like many globalized countries, Singapore faces increasing rates of obesity. Asia as a whole too is seeing a phenomenal rise in weight gain. For instance, it has been estimated that six to ten million people become obese each year in China (MacLeod, 2008). The prevalence of obesity among adolescent children aged 14–17 years old in India had risen to 29% and 11.3% in private and government-funded schools, respectively (Bhardwaj, Misra, Khurana, Gulati, Shah, Vikram, 2008). In Singapore itself, the 2010 National Health Survey revealed that over a span of 6 years, the obesity prevalence among the general population increased from 6.9% to 10.8%, signifying a 0.7% annual increase (Health Promotion Board, 2010). Coming on the back of climbing obesity rates since 1992, the increase is the largest seen so far (see Fig. 23.1). Together with an overweight prevalence of 25.6% (Ministry of Health, 2005), over 36% of the population are ascertained as either overweight or obese. About 9.5% of those aged 7–16 are classified as obese (Soon, Yang, Wong, & Lam, 2008). Sensing the increasing severity of the problem, health institutions have in

M.O. Lwin (✉)
Division of Public and Promotional Communication,
WKW School of Communication and Information,
Nanyang Technological University, #04-42, 31 Nanyang Link,
637718, Singapore
e-mail: tmaylwin@ntu.edu.sg

B.J. Li
Division of Communication Research, WKW School of Communication and Information,
Nanyang Technological University, #05-18, 31 Nanyang Link, 637718, Singapore
e-mail: jbli1@ntu.edu.sg

J.D. Williams
Management and Global Business, Rutgers Business School, Rutgers University,
1 Washington Park Building WP 1040, Newark, NJ 07102, USA
e-mail: jeromew@business.rutgers.edu

J.D. Williams et al. (eds.), *Advances in Communication Research to Reduce Childhood Obesity*, DOI 10.1007/978-1-4614-5511-0_23,

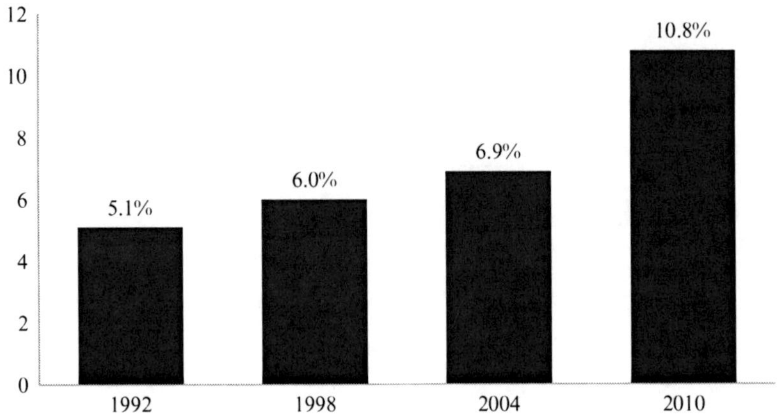

Fig. 23.1 Prevalence of obesity in Singapore from 1992 to 2010 measured in percentage of population

recent years set up weight management programs to help overweight and obese Singapore children manage the problem (Singapore Heart Foundation, 2008).

To combat the prevalence of obesity among children, the Singapore government has introduced several school-based interventions over the past two decades through the education and health ministries. Among the interventions is the noteworthy Trim and Fit (TAF) program. Introduced in 1992 by the Ministry of Education to all primary and secondary schools, the TAF program aimed to reduce the prevalence of overweight students through a two-prong approach of healthy nutrition and regular physical activity (Soon et al., 2008). Schools were equipped with fitness stations, sports facilities, and health-and-fitness rooms. Overweight students were required to engage in additional physical exercise every day, and healthier food options were made available through the installation of fruit and juice machines in school canteens.

While these intervention programs resulted in a system for overweight students to be more physically active in school, the increasing concern among educators and health practitioners is that these activities do not translate into a healthy lifestyle outside of the schooling environment. As a testament to the lack of an active lifestyle, more than 50% of Singaporeans do not participate in any form of sports and exercise (Health Promotion Board, 2010). In particular, children are spending long hours on screen-based activities, such as watching television, using computers, and playing video games. A recent survey revealed that Singapore youth spend on average 9 h a day on the Internet and watching television, compared to the regional average of 6.8 h (Synovate, 2009). There is substantial evidence associating longer time spent on sedentary screen-based activities with lower exercise and higher obesity levels among children (Kautiainen, Koivusilta, Lintonen, Virtanen, & Rimpelä, 2005; Scragg, Quigley, & Taylor, 2006).

One way to bridge the gap between the lack of healthy behaviors and the popularity of screen-based activities is through the use of health-themed video games.

These interventions can be classified into two broad categories. First, games with health messages educate players with health knowledge. The ultimate goal here is to equip players with the resource to make informed choices in diet and exercise. Research on these games revealed that these interventions have been effective in increasing knowledge regarding healthier food choices and behaviors. For instance, games that draw players emotionally into the story create an immersive environment that can contribute to intrinsic motivation (Baranowski et al., 2008). In a meta-analysis by Vogel et al. (2006), the use of interactive simulations or games were reported to produce higher cognitive gains and better attitudes toward learning compared to those using traditional teaching methods. In affirmation of the meta-analysis by Vogel et al. (2006), a computer game designed in a study by (Peng, 2009) to include key interactive features such as tailoring and role-playing was found to be an effective channel in teaching nutrition, increasing self-efficacy, and perceived benefits of healthy eating.

Second, there has been a rising interest in video games that use a *physically* immersive experience aim to encourage physical activity and exercise. These games are known popularly as *exergames*. As children are spending more time with sedentary screen-based activities, exergames offer the possibility of making physical exercise a lifestyle habit among overweight children by allowing players to engage with the game through body movements and activity. Research in this area has been gaining momentum, and various research studies have been undertaken in Singapore to gain a deeper understanding into the following questions: What are the changing media usage habits of Singaporean children? Are video games, in particular, exergames, an integral part of daily lives? Can exergames serve as an effective platform for exercise promotion among Singapore children? If so, are there elements within exergames that can enhance the gaming experience to promote better attitudes and motivations toward physical activity?

Exergame Research

Research in exergames has examined two key areas: technology and game intervention effectiveness. These are reviewed in the following sections.

Technology of Exergames

The technology of exergames can be split into three categories—controllers, software, and systems.

Controllers. Traditional game controllers allow players to only use their fingers to control the game through the use of a gamepad. The first exergames make use of dance pads to track lower limb movements. Games such as *Dance Dance*

Revolution require players to step on the correct symbols, while staying in beat with the music. Transferring game operation from fingers to feet opened up the possibility of using digital games to exercise and this has garnered interest from health researchers.

Later innovations such as the Sony EyeToy and the Microsoft Kinect picked up player movements using a camera mounted on top of the television set. Players are able to control their characters in-game using both upper body and lower body gestures, and usually see themselves on screen the form of their mirror image or silhouette.

The Sony Playstation Move and Nintendo Wii, on the other hand, use accelerometers and infrared sensors in the controllers to sense player movement. Players wield these baton-shaped controllers in their hands and control the game by moving the controllers in various directions. Games that require the use of lower limb movements (such as running or jumping) usually come with fabric straps that players can wear on their thighs. The game controllers can then be inserted into the straps to sense the movement of the lower limbs.

Software. Dance games constitute the most popular form of exergames at the moment (Thin & Poole, 2010), with titles such as *Dance Dance Revolution* and *Dance Central* requiring players to move their bodies to control their characters. Players score points based on how accurately they replicate the dance moves shown on screen. Other than having an intense body workout to some high-tempo songs, advanced players are known to memorize dance sequences that they can replicate or challenge others outside of the gaming environment (Hoysniemi, 2006).

Sports games such as the *Mario & Sonic at the Olympic Games* and *Kinect Sports* offer an array of sporting activities, such as tennis, soccer, boxing, track and field, and beach volleyball. Players move their bodies during game activity, and the movements are picked up by various game controllers. Virtual sports games form an interesting avenue for research with regard to individual characteristics such as competition (player versus player) and collaboration (players versus computer opponents) (Song, Kim, Tenzek, & Lee, 2010).

Workout and fitness games on video game consoles were almost unheard of a decade ago, but due to technology advancement in recent years has resulted in this new genre gaining popularity. Titles such as *Wii Fit* and *Gold's Gym Cardio Workout* allow players to engage in various workouts such as kickboxing, aerobics, and muscle toning with the aid of a virtual trainer. The presence of positive encouragement through the trainer and other health messages opens up research possibilities in the area of health communication and motivation.

Systems. Among video game consoles, the most popular exergames are those that are based on the platforms designed by Microsoft *(Xbox 360)*, Nintendo *(Wii)*, and Sony *(Playstation 3)*. Recent exergame research has centered on the *Nintendo Wii*, in part due to its early popularity among audiences, family-friendly game titles, simple control system, and gentle learning curve. However, the hands-free control system of the Microsoft *Kinect* shows promise in incorporating a full-body workout for players.

An area which shows signs of promise is mobile phone gaming. Mobile phones are beginning to have faster processing speed and better graphics, while the popularity of smartphones like the *Apple iPhone* and phones running on the *Google Android* platform has seen developers introducing exergames on mobile phones. For instance, *SpecTrek*, which makes use of the Global Positioning System and camera functions on smartphones, requires players to track down "ghosts" on their mobile phones. The augmented reality (AR) ghost hunting game tasks the player to locate ghosts using the local map and then the phone camera to scan and catch ghosts. Other applications in development include *Zombies, Run!*, where players are required to run around in the real world to collect supplies in a zombie apocalypse. These AR exergames appear to provide a real-world extension of the exergames that are typically based in the living room, as players are not bound by space constraints and can be engaged with the real-life environment.

Effectiveness of Exergames

Physiological benefits. Studies that examined the effects of exergames often looked at their contribution to the energy output of players. Energy expenditure is measured through heart rate monitoring, via the use of a chest strap and an accompanying monitoring device, and oxygen consumption through the use of a facemask and analyzer unit. Studies on the effectiveness of *Dance Dance Revolution* found players' heart rates averaging between 137 and 147 beats per minute, as compared to the resting heart rate of 60–80 beats per minute (Tan, Aziz, Chua, & Teh, 2002; Yang & Graham, 2005). Work by Lanningham-Foster et al. (2006) and Smith (2005) also found supporting evidence that heart rates of exergame players are comparable to those engaged in traditional aerobic exercises. Individuals playing Nintendo Wii games burned significantly more energy than those playing normal screen-based sedentary games (Graves, Stratton, Ridgers, & Cable, 2007), while overweight children were found to burn more calories than their normal weight counterparts (Unnithan, Houser, & Fernhall, 2006).

Other Benefits. Aside from increasing energy expenditure, exergames have been found to reap benefits in other areas. When introduced in third- and fourth-grade classrooms, students found themselves attending school more often, had better social skills and reported being more enthusiastic about physical activity and sports (Chamberlin & Gallagher, 2008). Overweight and obese children who played exergames over time had increased self-esteem and self-efficacy scores (Brubaker, 2006; Staiano et al., 2011). Children who were allowed to play exergames were more likely to spend less total time playing computer and video games, and spent a greater proportion of that time on games that encourage the use of physical activity (Ni Mhurchu et al., 2008).

Exergame Research in Singapore

We embarked on a research program on exergames in Singapore in 2005. Supported by the Singapore Ministry of Health, in particular, the Health Promotion Board, and the Singapore Heart Foundation, our agenda includes the following:

(a) An assessment of the health profiles, changing lifestyles, and exercise patterns of young Singaporeans.
(b) The potential use of digital games for health promotion and health education.
(c) The potential use of digital games for educating overweight and obese children (alongside clinical weight management programs).

Prior to our recent studies, there had been few documented explorations into the field of exergaming in Singapore. Tan et al. (2002) conducted a study with 40 teenagers to assess the intensity and aerobic demands of a dance-themed exergame. Results showed that energy output during the game met the minimum requirements from the American College of Sports Medicine (ACSM) for cardiorespiratory daily requirements, and the authors recommended that exergames be placed in homes so as to provide more regular workout sessions. The dearth of research on exergames prompted us to take an in-depth look into its effectiveness in promoting physical exercise among overweight children in Singapore.

Research has shown that an improvement in attitudes toward a health behavior can encourage individuals to engage in it (Armitage & Conner, 2001; Godin & Kok, 1996). In particular, people who have more positive attitudes to exercise were found to exercise more (Blue, 1995). Here, we are interested to examine the extent to which exergames can provide an improvement in the exercise motivations among Singapore children. Among our studies we examined research in these key areas: the health profile, media, and exercise habits of Singapore children and youth, the effectiveness of exergames in improving attitudes and motivations toward exercise, and in-game and external factors that influence the effectiveness of exergames. These are summarized next:

Health Profile, Media, and Exercise Habits of Singapore Children and Youth

We undertook a paper and pen survey with high school and elementary students in 2010. The respondents' height and weight were measured by the Physical Education teachers in each school. Body mass index (BMI) was then computed using the formula BMI = kg/m^2. Subsequently, respondents were classified into underweight (BMI < 5%), normal weight (5% < BMI < 85%), overweight (85% < BMI <95%), and obese (BMI > 95%) based on the BMI-for-age percentile chart developed by the Centers for Disease Control and Prevention (CDC) in the USA. However, we also present the breakdown based on local BMI criteria.

Table 23.1 Weight Profile of School Students in Singapore

(*N*=1,273)	Count	Percent
Based on CDC chart		
Underweight (UW) (<5%)	113	8.8
Normal weight (NW) (5%–85%)	710	55.6
Overweight (OW) (85%–95%)	216	16.9
Obese (OB) (≥95%)	234	18.3
Based on HPB chart		
Severely Underweight (<3%)	53	4.2
Underweight (3%–5%)	39	3.1
Normal (5%–90%)	906	70.9
Overweight (90%–97%)	195	15.3
Severely overweight (>97%)	80	6.3

Elementary and high school students (41.5% and 58.5%, respectively), aged between 10 and 15 years old (mean age of 11.4 years old) from nine Singaporean schools participated in this study (male = 55.1%; female = 44.9%). The proportion of the ethnic group—61.7% Chinese, 25.5% Malay, 7.7% Indian, and 5% of other races—is roughly representative of the resident population in Singapore.

Based on CDC's BMI-for-age percentile, out of the 1,278 respondents, 55.8% were found to have a normal weight, 8.9% are underweight, 17% are overweight, and 18.4% are obese. A classification based on the BMI-for-age percentile chart from Health Promotion Board (HPB) resulted in 4.2% respondents who are severely underweight, 3.1% are underweight, 70.9% have a normal weight, 15.3% are overweight, and 6.3% are severely overweight. The BMI-for-age percentile breakdowns from both CDC and HPB charts can be found in Table 23.1.

In terms of exercise profile, we found that elementary school children undertake strenuous exercises more than their older counterparts in high school (see Table 23.2). This trend is likely to be linked to children's increased use of online media as they grow. This is explored in our follow-up study discussed next.

In another current project, which is supported by the Singapore Ministry of Health, a large-scale survey is being undertaken in elementary and high schools in Singapore to assess how prevalent exergames are within the new media context (Lwin, 2011). The emergence of new media, however, has changed the media consumption pattern of children and youth. Similar to children in other countries our findings are in agreement that Internet use has displaced television consumption (Lee & Kuo, 2002). Our preliminary findings suggest not just a generation of children who are highly exposed to the online and mobile phone environments but a growing penetration of exergames within Singapore households. Our initial results show that over 5% of children (and families) whether overweight or of normal weight play such games during leisure time and often as a family activity that involves more than one generation. Some families own more than one type of exergame, and exergames are played both with friends and family members of varying ages.

Table 23.2 Exercise habit and type of exercise (by educational level)

Exercise Habit (Times per week)	Elementary (n=530)		High School (n=748)	
	Mean	SD	Mean	SD
Strenuous Exercise (Heart Beats Rapidly) (e.g., running, jogging, hockey, football, soccer, squash, basketball, cross country skiing, judo, roller skating, vigorous swimming, vigorous long-distance bicycling)	2.84	2.03	2.20	1.87
Moderate Exercise (Not Exhausting) (e.g., fast walking, baseball, tennis, easy bicycling, volleyball, badminton, easy swimming, popular and folk dancing)	2.36	1.91	2.03	1.77
Mild Exercise (Minimal Effort) (e.g., yoga, archery, fishing, bowling, golf, easy walking)	2.38	2.50	1.91	2.21
	Elementary (n=530)		High school (n=748)	
Type of exercise	Count	%	Count	%
Skipping	132	24.9	146	19.5
Running	275	51.9	264	35.3
Swimming	337	63.6	303	40.5
Tennis/badminton	284	53.6	370	49.5
Cycling	322	60.8	408	54.5
Combatives	87	16.4	65	8.7
Push up/sit up	79	14.9	85	11.4
Basketball	194	36.6	261	34.9
Volleyball	93	17.5	122	16.3
Soccer	157	29.6	206	27.5
Active games	199	37.5	162	21.7
Others	1	0.2	0	0.0

Improving Exercise Attitudes with Exergames (Obese and Overweight Children)

We conducted a study with overweight children to assess the effectiveness of exergames to improve their attitudes toward exercise (Li, Lwin, & Jung, 2011). We worked with the Singapore authorities to determine the qualified (overweight) children and identified suitable participants out of an entire cohort of 800 students who were currently enrolled in the school's obesity management program and identified by the school as those needing help in reducing their weight. Participants of the obesity management program are required to engage in additional exercise sessions every week, and are given advice on how to maintain a healthier diet. In addition, the shortlisted students were further screened by a check on their BMI, which is one of the most widely accepted ways to distinguish individuals of different weight categories (Cole, Bellizzi, Flegal, & Dietz, 2000; Dietz & Robinson, 1998). Children are generally described as being overweight if their BMI is at the 95th percentile or higher (Kuczmarski et al., 2002; Mei et al., 2002; Ogden et al., 2006). For Asian populations, individuals with a BMI of 23 and above are considered overweight (Choo, 2002). The average BMI of participants in this study was 25.9 (SD=3.63). After the two-step selection process was complete, a total of 140 students made the final cut and participated in the experiment.

The program included each participant using *the Nintendo Wii* to participate in an exergame titled *Active: Personal Trainer*. Students were asked to fill out a pre-test questionnaire that asked about their attitude and motivation to exercise, and to engage with a pre-selected workout game. After the workout, participants were asked to fill up a post-test questionnaire with the aforementioned measures. We found that participants reported higher levels of exercise attitude, exercise motivation, and motivation to use digital gaming interventions for exercise. These results suggest that the exergames show promise in promoting exercise attitudes among overweight children.

Improving Exercise Attitudes with Exergames (Normal Weight Children)

We conducted another study, this time with normal weight children to assess the effectiveness of exergames to improve their attitudes toward exercise when coupled with health education messages (Lwin & Malik, 2012). We deployed an intervention program utilizing Wii games play during physical education classes coupled with health messaging among elementary school children in Singapore. The results indicate that when children who were exposed to threat-framed messages, which communicated risks of not exercising such as growing obese, played Wii active exergames during PE lessons, they reported more positive physical activity attitude, self-efficacy, perceived behavioral control, and group norm than those who underwent regular PE lessons and exposed to the same messages.

Influence of In-Game Cues and Other Factors

While the previous studies add support to a growing interest of research into the effectiveness of exergames on improving exercise attitudes and behavior among overweight and obese children, less is known about how various aspects of the game can influence its effectiveness. We conducted a study to answer whether graphical representations in exergames, in the form of the player's in-game avatar, can influence overweight children's attitudes and behaviors in the game. We sought to examine how overweight children respond to visual cues within an exergame in the form of avatars (Li, Lwin, Wong, & Chong, 2011). A between-subjects factorial design study was conducted where we created avatars of various body sizes were created within the *Active: Personal Trainer* game. They were further remodeled to include both male and female versions of the normal and overweight avatars.

Our findings showed that participants who were assigned to avatars of overweight body size have poorer exercise attitude, exercise motivation, motivation to use the exergames to exercise and game performance than those assigned to avatars of normal body size.

With the increasing popularity of the Nintendo Wii and other upcoming video game consoles that allow for consumers to work out in the comfort of their homes, more exercise-themed games are being released that set the appearance of user avatars based on their weight. The Wii Fit, for example, allows for the creation of avatars of varying body sizes based on the height and weight values that users input into the system (Loguidice & Loguidice, 2010). Our findings suggest that designing avatars that are slim and toned may provide more motivation and yield more positive attitudinal and behavioral changes in children who play the game.

Other Research Areas

Another area that is currently being explored is the use of exergames by overweight and obese children who are seeking medical attention. More than just having a higher than normal BMI, these children are already suffering from health problems as a result of obesity, or have been diagnosed by doctors as being more susceptible to health problems than other overweight children. Studies are being carried out now with the partnership of hospitals and health institutions in Singapore. At the weight management centers where these children are attending weekly workout sessions to reduce their body weight, exergames are incorporated into the program in an effort to improve their exercise attitudes and habits as they have fun. This study aims to examine how exergames can improve overweight Singapore children's exercise attitudes over a 12-week period.

With regard to game elements, game genre is an area that is being actively explored in exergame research. Exergames come in various attractive themes, such as dance, sports, fitness/workout, and adventure. While the appeal of these genres to different age groups and genders have been well documented in conventional computer and video games (Quaiser-Pohl, Geiser, & Lehmann, 2006; Sherry & Lucas, 2003), their attractiveness and subsequent motivational pull to exercise within an exergame has been relatively unexplored. How does the genre of exergames influence their effectiveness? Do overweight children's exercise attitudes differ between being assigned a particular genre or if they are allowed to choose a genre of exergame? These questions are being explored in an ongoing study with overweight and obese Singapore children.

With the rising rate of obesity among Singapore children, it is encouraging to see that exergames are reasonably effective in improving exercise attitudes and motivations among overweight children. A more focused exploration into the use of exergames by target groups and the effects of various in-game elements will allow health practitioners and educators to better utilize these digital gaming interventions in the near future.

Conclusion

Research has found that children and youth today are faced with many digital devices and new media offerings that can impede physical activity. However, the exergame offers potential to reduce the amount of sedentary activities undertaken by this generation while still allowing the use of digital devices and media typically considered as increasing sedentary time. With the right type of games and gaming concepts, exergames can influence not just the level of physical activity but also influence attitudes and perceptions toward exercise. In addition, exergames can offer a platform for imparting health messages. Taken as a whole, our research findings present a number of key considerations for policymakers and educators. Educators can consider using exergames not as a replacement to physical activities in school but as a supplement to motivate and encourage this digital generation to be more active. Adding on to the repertoire of aerobic workouts and sports introductory lessons currently available in Singapore schools, exergames will be a refreshing and appealing health intervention for schoolchildren.

Efforts should also be focused on raising the profile of exergames among game developers and publishers, as popularity of game genres is often the driving force behind game quality and innovation. As the Singapore government is increasingly promoting itself as a hub for video game design (Nutt, 2010), authorities can consider incentivising the development of exergames by local game developers. Such incentives can come in the form of grants for developers working on exergames that appeal to the local audience or infrastructural support for budding game designers and entrepreneurs. The end product of an appealing and quality exergame may increase the motivational factor of the exergame as a health intervention tool.

Looking forward, we plan to execute a number of exciting research projects to further knowledge in this field which will include hospital and clinical-based intervention programs as well as expanding our study to include adults. Much work remains to be done as technology evolves and video games become increasingly sophisticated.

Acknowledgement The authors gratefully acknowledge the Ministry of Health Centre for Health Service Research, the Health Promotion Board, the Ministry of Education, and the Singapore Heart Foundation for their support in the research described in this chapter.

References

Armitage, C. J., & Conner, M. (2001). Efficacy of the theory of planned behaviour: A meta-analytic review. *The British Journal of Social Psychology, 40*(4), 471–499.

Baranowski, T., Buday, R., Thompson, D. I., & Baranowski, J. (2008). Playing for Real: Video Games and Stories for Health-Related Behavior Change. *American Journal of Preventive Medicine, 34*(1), 74–82.e10.

Bhardwaj, S., Misra, A., Khurana, L., Gulati, S., Shah, P., & Vikram, N. K. (2008). Childhood obesity in Asian Indians: a burgeoning cause of insulin resistance, diabetes, and sub-clinical inflammation. *Asia Pacific Journal of Clinical Nutrition, 17*(S1), 172–175.

Blue, C. L. (1995). The predictive capacity of the theory of reasoned action and the theory of planned behavior in exercise research: an integrated literature review. *Research in Nursing and Health, 18*(2), 105–121.

Brubaker, B. (2006). Teachers join the Dance Dance Revolution: Educators begin training to use the exercise video game. *The Dominion Post*. Retrieved from http://www.redorbit.com/news/scifi-gaming/424434/teachers_join_the__dance_dance_revolution/index.html.

Chamberlin, B., & Gallagher, R. (2008). *Exergames using video games to promote physical activity*. Paper presented at the Children, Youth and Families At Risk Conference, San Antonio, TX.

Choo, V. (2002). WHO reassesses appropriate body-mass index for Asian populations. *The Lancet, 360*(9328), 235.

Cole, T. J., Bellizzi, M. C., Flegal, K. M., & Dietz, W. H. (2000). Establishing a standard definition for child overweight and obesity worldwide: International survey. *British Medical Journal, 320*(7244), 1240–1243.

Dietz, W. H., & Robinson, T. N. (1998). Use of the body mass index (BMI) as a measure of overweight in children and adolescents. *The Journal of Pediatrics, 132*(2), 191–193.

Godin, G., & Kok, G. (1996). The theory of planned behavior: A review of its applications to health-related behaviors. *American Journal of Health Promotion, 11*(2), 87–98.

Graves, L., Stratton, G., Ridgers, N. D., & Cable, N. T. (2007). Comparison of energy expenditure in adolescents when playing new generation and sedentary computer games: Cross sectional study. *British Medical Journal, 335*(1), 1282–1284.

Health Promotion Board. (2010). Life's better and brighter when we get healthy together! Retrieved September 2, 2011, from http://www.hpb.gov.sg/news/article.aspx?id=9008.

Hoysniemi, J. (2006). International survey on the Dance Dance Revolution game. *Computers in Entertainment, 4*(2), 8.

Kautiainen, S., Koivusilta, L., Lintonen, T., Virtanen, S. M., & Rimpelä, A. (2005). Use of information and communication technology and prevalence of overweight and obesity among adolescents. *International Journal of Obesity, 29*(1), 925–933.

Kuczmarski, R. J., Ogden, C. L., Guo, S. S., Grummer-Strawn, L. M., Flegal, K. M., & Mei, Z. (2002). 2000 CDC growth charts for the United States: Methods and development. *Vital & Health Statistics – Series 11 L Data From the National Health Survey, 246*, 1–190.

Lanningham-Foster, L., Jensen, T. B., Foster, R. C., Redmond, A. B., Walker, B. A., Heinz, D., et al. (2006). Energy expenditure of sedentary screen time compared with active screen time for children. *Pediatrics, 118*(6), e1831–e1835.

Lee, W. & Kuo, E.C.Y. (2002). Internet and displacement effect: Children's media use and activities in Singapore. *Journal of Computer-Mediated Communication, 9*(2). Retrieved March 4, 2010, from http://jcmc.indiana.edu/vol7/issue2/singapore.html.

Li, B., Lwin, M., & Jung, Y. (2011). *Impact of visual and social cues on exercise attitudes and behavior of overweight children playing an exergame*. Paper presented at the 61st Annual International Communication Association Conference, Boston, MA.

Li, B., Lwin, M., Wong, M. L., & Chong, S. M. (2011). *Gender differences and the influence of in-game factors on the effectiveness of exergames on overweight children*. Paper presented at the 2011 American Marketing Association Marketing & Public Policy Conference, Washington, DC.

Loguidice, C. T., & Loguidice, B. (2010). *Wii fitness for dummies*. Hoboken, NJ: Wiley.

Lwin, M. O. (2011). *Children and adolescents' media and digital exposure in Singapore*. Working Paper.

Lwin, M. O., & Malik, S. (2012). The efficacy of exergames incorporated physical education lessons in influencing drivers of physical activity: A comparison of children and pre-adolescents. *Psychology of Sport and Exercise, 13*(6), 756–760.

MacLeod, C. (2008). China wrestles with growing obesity. *USA Today*. . http://www.usatoday.com/news/world/2008-12-18-chinaweight_N.htm. Accessed 22 Jan 2009.

Mei, Z., Grummer-Strawn, L. M., Pietrobelli, A., Goulding, A., Goran, M. I., & Dietz, W. H. (2002). Validity of body mass index compared with other body-composition screening indexes for the assessment of body fatness in children and adolescents. *The American Journal of Clinical Nutrition, 75*, 978–985.

Ministry of Health. (2005). National Health Survey 2004. Retrieved September 2, 2011, from http://www.moh.gov.sg/mohcorp/publicationsreports.aspx?id=2984.

Ni Mhurchu, C., Maddison, R., Jiang, Y., Jull, A., Prapavessis, H., & Rodgers, A. (2008). Couch potatoes to jumping beans: A pilot study of the effect of active video games on physical activity in children. *International Journal of Behavioral Nutrition and Physical Activity, 5*(1), 8.

Nutt, C. (2010). Q&A: Singapore's Government On encouraging game industry growth. Retrieved October 22, 2011, from http://www.gamasutra.com/view/news/28815/QA_Singapores_Government_On_Encouraging_Game_Industry_Growth.php.

Ogden, C. L., Carroll, M. D., Curtin, L. R., McDowell, M. A., Tabak, C. J., & Flegal, K. M. (2006). Prevalence of overweight and obesity in the United States, 1999–2004. *Journal of the American Medical Association, 295*, 1549–1555.

Peng, W. (2009). Design and Evaluation of a Computer Game to Promote a Healthy Diet for Young Adults. *Health Communication, 24*(2), 115–127.

Quaiser-Pohl, C., Geiser, C., & Lehmann, W. (2006). The relationship between computer-game preference, gender, and mental-rotation ability. *Personality and Individual Differences, 40*, 609–619.

Scragg, R., Quigley, R., & Taylor, R. (2006). Does watching TV contribute to increased body weight and obesity in children? Scientific Committee of the Agencies for Nutrition Action.

Sherry, J., & Lucas, K. (2003). *Video game uses and gratifications as predictors of use and game preference*. Paper presented at the International Communication Association Annual Convention, San Diego, CA.

Singapore Heart Foundation. (2008). Weight management. Retrieved September 3, 2011, from http://www.myheart.org.sg/a-heart-healthy-lifestyle/weight-management/.

Smith, B. K. (2005). Physical fitness in virtual worlds. *IEEE Computer, 38*(10), 101–103.

Song, H., Kim, J., Tenzek, K., & Lee, K. (2010). *Intrinsic motivation in exergames: Competition, competitiveness, and the conditional indirect effect of presence*. Paper presented at the annual meeting of the International Communication Association, Suntec Singapore International Convention & Exhibition Centre, Suntec City, Singapore.

Soon, G., Yang, H. K., Wong, M. L., & Lam, P. W. (2008). *Obesity prevention and control efforts in Singapore*. Seattle, WA: The National Bureau of Asian Research.

Staiano, A. E., Terry, A., Watson, K., Scanlon, P., Abraham, A., & Calvert, S. L. (2011). *Physical activity intervention for weight loss in overweight and obese adolescents*. Paper presented at the biennial meeting of the Society for Research in Child Development, Montreal, Canada.

Synovate. (2009). Synovate survey shows that young Asians are driven by media and music Retrieved September 2, 2011, from http://www.synovate.com/news/article/2009/03/synovate-survey-shows-that-young-asians-are-driven-by-media-and-music.html.

Tan, B., Aziz, A. R., Chua, K., & Teh, K. C. (2002). Aerobic demands of the dance simulation game. *International Journal of Sports Medicine, 23*(2), 125–129.

Thin, A., & Poole, N. (2010). Dance-based ExerGaming: User experience design implications for maximizing health benefits based on exercise intensity and perceived enjoyment. In Z. Pan, A. Cheok, W. Müller, X. Zhang, & K. Wong (Eds.), *Transactions on edutainment IV* (Vol. 6250, pp. 189–199).

Unnithan, V. B., Houser, W., & Fernhall, B. (2006). Evaluation of the energy cost of playing a dance simulation video game in overweight and non-overweight children and adolescents. *International Journal of Sports Medicine, 27*(10), 804–809.

Vogel, J. J., Vogel, D. S., Cannon-Bowers, J., Bowers, C. A., Muse, K., & Wright, M. (2006). Computer gaming and interactive simulations for learning: A meta-analysis. *Journal of Educational Computing Research, 34*(3), 229–243.

Yang, S. P., & Graham, G. M. (2005). Project GAME (Gaming activities for more exercise). *Research Quarterly for Exercise and Sport, 76*(1 (Supplement)), A-96.

Chapter 24
Leveraging Industry Efforts to Fight Childhood Obesity: A Multi-Sectored Approach to Communications

Anthony C. Signorelli and George Perlov

Introduction

The issue of childhood obesity in the USA came to the forefront in 2004 following the TIME/ABC News Summit on Obesity, the *Time Magazine* special issue on child obesity (Lemonick, 2004), and the release of the Institute of Medicine's (IOM) groundbreaking report on the topic (McGinnis, Gootman, & Kraak, 2006). The report found that obesity rates had doubled among children aged 2–5 and tripled among children aged 6–11 over the past three decades; over nine million children were reported to be overweight or obese.

With a long history of shining a light on the most important issues facing the country, the Ad Council recognized the urgency of this burgeoning crisis and began planning a program that would bring more resources and reach to its traditional public service communications campaigns. The guiding idea behind the collaborative program was to supply a series of consistent, research-based messages that corporations, nonprofits and government agencies could use in their own marketing and communications materials to promote healthy lifestyle habits. Through these collective efforts the program aimed to make parents and their children aware of the importance of leading a healthy lifestyle and to begin to shift entrenched attitudes and behaviors about eating and exercise habits.

By the fall of 2004, the Ad Council had reached out to the companies served by its Board of Directors, the nonprofit and government agencies that sponsor its public service campaigns, the members of its Advisory Committee as well as to

A.C. Signorelli, M.B.A. (✉)
Vice President, Campaign Director at the Ad Council
e-mail: asignorelli@adcouncil.org

G. Perlov, M.P.A.
Marketing and Communications Consultant based in New York City

J.D. Williams et al. (eds.), *Advances in Communication Research to Reduce Childhood Obesity*, DOI 10.1007/978-1-4614-5511-0_24,

the volunteer ad agencies which create the public service campaigns to begin to build a steering committee that could begin to shape this new initiative.

Within months, the Coalition for Healthy Children (CHC) was formed, a literature review was underway and underwriting funds were committed by The Robert Wood Johnson Foundation to begin to build the infrastructure.

Objectives and Guidelines

The first activity of the CHC was to define the audiences and communications objectives for the initiative. The Coalition team spoke with experts in the health and wellness arena, met with academics and researchers and eventually conducted a literature review to understand the most effective measures individuals could take to prevent childhood obesity. The recommendation coming out of these meetings was that it was equally important to address messages to parents (the gatekeepers) and kids (the consumers) in order to achieve maximum impact.

The group also made the distinction between this communications effort and other tactics designed to address childhood obesity (i.e., access to healthy food, poor environments for play and exercise, school lunch, etc.). The CHC would focus its energy on educational messages that would help individuals, as this would be the greatest contribution the Ad Council and its Coalition members could make.

Another critical piece in the development of the program was making sure that guidelines for using the messages with food products and beverage offerings would be adhered to by Coalition members. In keeping with the overall focus of the program, it was decided that Coalition members in these industries could only use the messages on products that met specific nutrition criteria. The guidelines were based on those created by the Alliance for a Healthier Generation, a joint venture between the Clinton Foundation and the American Heart Association, as well as the 2005 U.S. Dietary Guidelines for Americans (HHS & USDA, 2005), which were developed by the U.S. Department of Health and Human Services (HHS) and the U.S. Department of Agriculture (USDA). To join the Coalition, members were asked to sign an agreement that they would help spread the word about the Coalition and its messages within their organizations, that they would report back to the Ad Council the use of Coalition messages and visual assets in their marketing materials, and that they would not use their membership status in the Coalition to deflect any criticism of their products, policies or marketing efforts.

The Ad Council formally launched the Coalition for Healthy Children at a summit meeting with all members in July 2005. At the time, 30 member organizations were in attendance—the Coalition grew to over 50 members in 2009, which included organizations such as the American Heart Association, Boys & Girls Clubs of America, Cartoon Network, Coca Cola Company, DreamWorks Animation, General Mills, Kraft Foods, McDonald's, National Basketball Association, National Football League, Sears Holding Company, Sesame Workshop, and Univision Communications (see Table 24.1 for a complete list of members).

Table 24.1 Coalition Member Organizations (as of September 2009)

Albemarle State Policy Center
Action for Healthy Kids
The Advertising Council
Alloy Media + Marketing
American Association of Advertising Agencies
The American College of Sports Medicine
American Council for Fitness and Nutrition
American Diabetes Association
American Dietetic Association Foundation
American Heart Association
b.little + Company
Big Green Company
Boys & Girls Clubs of America
BYU Adlab
Cartoon Network
Center for Advancing Nutrition & Activity Penn State University
Coca Cola Company
Creative Consumer Concepts (C3)
Del Monte Foods
DreamWorks Animation SKG
Fundacion Azteca America
General Mills
Girl Scouts of the USA
GSD&M Idea City
Healthy Directions
The Hershey Company
International Food Information Council Foundation (IFIC)
Iowa Department of Public Health
JMH Education
Kellogg Company
Kids Health/The Nemours Foundation Center for Children's Health Media
Kraft Foods
Ladies Professional Golf Association
Magazine Publishers of America
McCann Erickson
McDonald's Corporation
Michigan Nutrition Network
National Basketball Association
National Confectioners Association
National Fatherhood Initiative
National Football League
National Recreation and Park Association
Pennsylvania Department of Health

(continued)

Table 24.1 (continued)

PepsiCo, Inc.
School Nutrition Association
Sears Holding Co.
Sesame Workshop
Shaping America's Health - Association for Weight Management & Obesity Prevention
Strottman International, Inc.
SUBWAY (FAFT)
TIME Magazine
Univision Communications, Inc.
YMCA of the USA

Formative Research and Message Development

Given the wealth of information available on preventing obesity in children, the first step the Coalition team took to begin developing the communications effort was to organize a literature review in order to identify those preventive behaviors that parents and children could easily adopt on their own. We were looking for individual actions that could lead to behavior change. Hundreds of published reports, articles, and existing programs were amassed, and our research team pored through them to find logical groupings that could be developed into message areas. Ultimately, three key areas were identified as the focus of the program:

- Kids getting an hour of exercise each day.
- Knowing the basics of energy balance—calories in/calories out.
- Exerting control when it comes to portion size.

In addition, the importance of parents modeling positive behaviors for their kids, regarding eating and exercise and making better food choices, was also identified as an important factor for consideration.

The Coalition team partnered with Strottman International, a leading kid and family marketing agency to create and test messages in support of these three areas. Strottman was charged with developing a few messages in support of each of these categories, which would then be tested among kids and parents. Four focus groups utilizing proprietary Strottman techniques among parents and four among kids (aged 6–9 and 10–13) were held in early 2005 in Atlanta and Chicago to explore proposed messages for clarity of meaning, relevance, and potential for action. Teachers were included in the parent groups as their influence was also seen as critical in this effort.

This research uncovered a host of insights including:

- Kids feel they already know about and how to make healthy lifestyle choices but choose not to.
- Messages need to be direct and reference food, activity, or exercise to be comprehended.

- Messages that are perceived to be accusatory or guilt-causing are rejected by moms.
- Messages that sound "catchy" are preferred, but still need to deliver on comprehension and content.
- Participants feel that messages about healthy lifestyle don't belong on unhealthy food and beverage packaging.
- Context, clarity and directness are most important in getting the message across.

The implications from the research also pointed to recommendations for those messages that did not test well:

- Consider taking a positive, partner-like attitude and tone.
- Consider putting messages into the context of the family's world and use their vernacular.
- Consider messages that create a positive mental image.
- Consider messages that are solution- or action-oriented and attainable without sounding preachy.

Using these guidelines, Strottman and ad agency McCann Erickson reworked and revised the messaging, and then put these revised message concepts through quantitative testing. Over 1,000 demographically representative parents of children aged 6–12 and kids aged 8–12 were exposed to these messages in an online survey and queried on the key measures of message comprehension, newness of message, intent to act, and importance or meaningfulness. While some messages tested well, others did not. See Fig. 24.1 for the complete list of parent- and child-directed messages that were ultimately deemed most effective.

At this point, the messages and the research were shared with Coalition members and experts in the field of childhood obesity prevention. After a lengthy discussion and feedback period, it was decided that some of the messages needed to be simplified and further refined. Having member input at this point was critical to ensuring that the messages would be fully utilized by member organizations. Based on a request from Coalition members to place messages on collateral materials or product packaging, visual identities for each of the concepts were also created with help from ad agency GSD&M Idea City and students from Brigham Young University's AdLab.

The Ad Council worked with LightSpeed Research to conduct an online quantitative test of the revised messages and the new visual assets among over 1,100 demographically representative parents and kids during the summer of 2007. Metrics utilized were the same as those in the previous quantitative tests and the results were strong. In this study, half of respondents were shown visual assets without any accompanying message and half of respondents were shown the assets with the accompanying message. Findings indicated that the Energy Balance and Physical Activity messages clearly communicated their intended messages and were motivating and likable among kids and parents. The portion control message fell just short in communicating its message and motivating kids and therefore was subsequently

Coalition for Healthy Children Messages

Parent-Directed Messages

Encourage Your Kids to Be a Player: Get up and Play an Hour a Day.

What's good about getting up to play with your children? The fresh air, the quality time together, and – just as important – the exercise you all are getting. Being physically active is easy to incorporate into the time you spend as a family. The best part is, the more fun you and your kids have together, the healthier you all will be.

Tell your Kids: Eat Well. Play Hard. Make it Balance.

Teach your kids all about balance. Show them that to be their best they have to balance how much they eat with how much they get up and play each day. It's like the classic PB&J sandwich. Too much jelly or not enough peanut butter can make all the difference. It's the balance of the two that makes the sandwich so great.

The Amount Counts: Keep Portions Under Control.

Healthy eating isn't only about what your kids eat; it's about how much they eat. Help your kids understand that portion size matters. Encourage them to stop eating when they've had an appropriate amount, not necessarily when they've finished the whole bag or entire bottle. The right amount is just as important as the right diet.

Kid-Directed Messages

Be a Player: Get up and Play an Hour a Day.

Computer games may be fun, but the real test of strength is if you're tough enough to ride your bike, jump rope, swim or play team sports with your friends. The more you get up and play, the healthier you'll be.

Eat Well. Play Hard. Make it Balance.

Eating healthy and being active fit together like peanut butter and jelly. Too much jelly or not enough peanut butter can make all the difference in a great sandwich. To be your best, it's important to balance how much you eat with how much you get up and play each day. Make eating well and playing hard balance, like two halves of the perfect sandwich.

The Amount Counts: Keep Portions Under Control.

Bigger isn't always better. Healthy eating isn't only about what you eat, it's about how much you eat. Start with a small portion size - a handful, a scoop, a few. You don't need to finish the whole bag or entire bottle.

Fig. 24.1 Coalition messages and visuals for parents and children

revised before proceeding to the dissemination phase. In all cases, comprehension increased when respondents were shown both stimuli. This suggested that Coalition members would have more success when utilizing both the written and visual elements for each message area.

With this kind of data supporting the saliency of these messages, the Coalition team felt confident that the combined efforts of Coalition members to disseminate these messages would lead to significant impact.

Message Dissemination

The simplicity, clarity, and relevance to their own marketing messages made it easy for members to support the Coalition's messages. As soon as the messages and visual assets were ready to use.

Coalition members began to incorporate them in their marketing and communications campaigns with guidance and support from the Ad Council team. From packaging and online promotions, to advertising and content development, to fully integrating marketing programs, members brought creativity, innovation, and social purpose to these efforts.

The Ad Council team met with the advertising and marketing departments of member organizations to better understand their needs and to help strategize how to best incorporate the messages. In some cases, the messages enhanced member organizations' pre-existing efforts. In other situations, the messages were co-branded with members' branded efforts, and in a few situations, new, fully integrated health and wellness programs were created based on the Coalition messages. The Ad Council team reviewed all proposed uses of the messages and made sure that they followed the suggested guidelines regarding product usage. They also provided support for member organizations when and where appropriate.

During the initial years of the Coalition, member organizations focused primarily on communications promoting the benefits of physical activity and put their resources behind the "Be a Player" message. Over time, a few programs were developed around energy balance and portion control, although not to the extent of the physical activity messages.

The Ad Council also worked with existing public service campaign sponsors like the U.S. Department of Health and Human Services' (HHS) Obesity Prevention campaign and the U.S. Department of Agriculture's (USDA) Nutrition Education campaign to create partnerships with other member organizations to jointly promote the messages. Distributed via the Ad Council's extensive media distribution network, these ads reached over 33,000 media companies across the country.

Meetings with child health advocates, academics, and other experts also built greater awareness for the Coalition's work among these important constituents. Ad Council Coalition staff have participated as keynote speakers at many national conferences, including the FCC Task Force on Childhood Obesity and the FTC/HHS "Weighing In" workshop. Staff was also asked to speak with the IOM (Institute of Medicine) committee responsible for child obesity prevention and brief the CDC (Centers for Disease Control and Prevention) on Coalition activities. The Coalition team worked closely with CARU (Children's Advertising Review Unit) to support their Children's Food and Beverage Advertising Initiative. The effort is designed to shift the mix of advertising messaging to children to encourage healthier dietary choices and healthy lifestyles. As part of this collaboration, the CHC provided messages and visual assets to the marketers participating in the effort, so they could be incorporated into their communications efforts and evaluated accordingly. The Coalition team also developed active relationships with industry groups such as the Grocery Manufacturers of America (GMA), International Food Information Council (IFIC), and the Association of National Advertisers (ANA).

A highpoint of the Coalition's visibility-building came when Corporate CEO members were invited to a White House Roundtable with former President Bush to talk about their various obesity prevention programs, followed by former HHS Secretary Leavitt's launch of new HHS sponsored Childhood Obesity Prevention PSAs featuring DreamWorks Animation's *Shrek* characters. The press coverage from that campaign launch was done extensively in local and national news.

The following are just a few examples of the ways member organizations utilized the program messages in their marketing and communications programs:

Kraft Foods: Online Games and Cartoon Network Partnership

Kraft Foods teamed up with Cartoon Network to develop a 30-s PSA featuring Cartoon Network characters that reminded kids to be physically active and incorporated the Coalition's "Be a Player" message and visual asset. Kraft Foods also created a 10-s online game preload targeted toward kids. This mini web cartoon about the importance of being active streamed before visitors played a video game on Kraft Foods' child-directed websites.

National Football League: NFL PLAY 60—The NFL Movement for an Active Generation

The NFL created its PLAY 60 youth fitness campaign in concert with the Coalition's physical activity focused communications. The "get up and play an hour a day" message can be seen throughout the Play 60 campaign, which features partnerships with the United Way, American Heart Association, National Dairy Council, U.S. Department of Health and Human Services, and many other corporations, nonprofits, and government agencies. In 2007, the NFL launched PLAY 60, a national youth health and fitness campaign focused on increasing the health and wellness of young fans by encouraging them to be active for at least 60 min a day. In addition to national reach through PSAs and online programs, PLAY 60 is also implemented at the grassroots level by all 32 NFL Clubs through NFL's in-school, after-school, and team-based programs. The Ad Council/NFL multimedia campaign that was launched in 2007 featured NFL star players Reggie Bush, Antonio Gates, and Jason Witten. More information on NFL PLAY 60 can be found on NFLRUSH.com, which features fitness tips, player recipes, NFL player fitness blogs and videos, and many other activities. Young people visiting the site can pledge their commitment and learn from the pros how to stay healthy and active.

Walt Disney Studios Home Entertainment: Energy Balance Communications from Jungle Book and Pinocchio Characters

Walt Disney Studios Home Entertainment partnered with the Ad Council's ongoing campaign with USDA to promote healthy lifestyle habits by supporting the energy balance message for kids and families.

TV, radio, and interactive and billboard PSAs featured characters from Disney's *Jungle Book* and *Pinocchio* modeling positive behaviors. In addition, messages promoting energy balance and MyPyramid.gov were featured in Disney parks, on key chains and magnet give-aways, and throughout Radio Disney's national mobile tours.

Kmart: Retail and Online Promotion

Kmart's "New Day Kids Way" promotion supported the Coalition's physical activity message throughout the mega-marketer's retail environment and online networks. It featured in-store signage, placement in Kmart circulars, online integration, and distribution of brochures at Kmart locations nationwide. Through an online promotion kids were invited to upload photos or videos of themselves enjoying an active lifestyle and the have their family and friends vote for them online.

Ladies Professional Golf Association: PSA's Featuring Star Golfers

With support from the UPS Foundation, Ladies Professional Golf Association (LPGA) created TV, print, and internet PSAs featuring championship players Lorena Ochoa, Karrie Webb, and Natalie Gulbis, who urged families to "get up and play an hour a day." The association extended the reach of the physical activity message through partnerships with ESPN and Wegman's supermarket chains.

McDonald's: Packaging and Online Message Promotion

McDonald's promoted the Coalition's physical activity message by placing the "Be a Player" visual on American Idol and *Shrek the Third* promotional Happy Meal boxes, along with ideas for kids to get moving. The Coalition's energy balance message was featured on Happy Meal bags, which encouraged kids and families to take steps to be healthy. McDonald's also promoted this message on their http://www.HappyMeal.com web site and linked to the U.S. Department of Health and Human Services health and wellness website, http://www.HealthierUS.gov.

PepsiCo: Advertising, a Wellness Program, and In-Store Displays

PepsiCo's national promotion featured the Coalition's "Be a Player" physical activity message in conjunction with their Smart Spot™ line of products. The campaign encouraged families to get more active through America on the Move, a free wellness program. Working with Wal Mart, PepsiCo set up retail point-of-service displays in Wal Mart Super Centers and Discount Stores and sent a http://www.Walmart.com email blast. The company also created a customized "Be a Player" ad for *All You* magazine.

qubo: PSA Featuring Animated Characters and Olympic Athletes

qubo, the children's television network, lent their animated characters to star in a new set of public service announcements. Characters from the popular programs, *Veggie Tales*, *Jane and the Dragon* and *3-2-1 Penguins*! were seen promoting physical activity, energy balance, and portion control messages alongside U.S. 2008 Olympic gold medalists, Shawn Johnson, Sanya Richards, Misty May-Treanor, and Kerri Walsh. qubo Channel is a 24/7 children's television network currently available on cable, Satellite, Telcos, and over-the-air. qubo programming blocks can also be seen on NBC, ION Television and, Telemundo.

DreamWorks Animation SKG: Shrek Promoting Physical Activity

DreamWorks Animation, SKG brought their popular Shrek property to the issue of childhood obesity to coincide with the launch of the *Shrek the Third* movie. PSAs featuring Shrek characters were developed to promote physical activity among parents and children across television, outdoor, and Internet media. The Outdoor Advertising Association of America (OAAA) engaged its members, which include CBS Outdoor, Clear Channel Outdoor, and the Lamar Advertising Company, to post the "Be a Player" billboards on all available sites. Nickelodeon also supported the television PSAs in heavy rotation. Inserts featuring the "Be a Player" message were included by DreamWorks Animation in DVD cases for the release of *Shrek the Third*.

Subway : In-School and Take Home Materials for Kids

SUBWAY® developed in-school materials featuring the Coalition's physical activity message in an effort to reach kids and parents with important healthy lifestyle information. Free kits for the classroom were created to encourage teachers and parents to show their kids how staying healthy and active can be FUN. Materials included letters to parents, a teacher's guide, stickers, classroom posters, and a calendar/planner.

YMCA: Healthy Family Home

Healthy Family Home is a resource to help families make their home environment a place where healthy living is practiced every day. Developed by the YMCA of the USA and made possible by a contribution from the Eli Lilly Company, Healthy Family Home helps families make healthier decisions in three key areas: Play Every Day, Healthy Eating, and Family Time. Healthy Family Home includes a Starter Kit and web resources with ideas and activities to help families maintain healthy lifestyles. YMCAs across the country are incorporating Healthy Family Home into their youth and family programming. More information can be found at http://www.ymca.net or http://www.healthyfamilyhome.org.

Program Results and Evaluation

In just a few years, the Coalition for Healthy Children has provided dozens of organizations with research and strategies to help reduce child obesity via communications. The net impact of this collaborative work is more consistent messages that address the issue of child obesity in American society, and the beginnings of attitude and behavior change among target audiences that are leading to positive health outcomes.

To help understand the entire CHC program in a graphic, easy-to-comprehend model, the Ad Council Coalition team developed and shared with members the Logic Model diagram below (see Fig. 24.2). It visually depicts all program inputs (activities), outputs, and expected outcomes, and it provides a framework for evaluating the overall program impact at each stage of the effort.

Building membership in the Coalition was critical to the program's success, and outreach by the Ad Council team began even before the research was conducted and the messages developed. By the time the program launched in 2005, 30 organizations had signed on and that number has grown to over 54 in 2009. Coalition members have been able to develop new partnerships and collaborative projects with other members, as well as with the Ad Council's U.S. government campaign sponsors

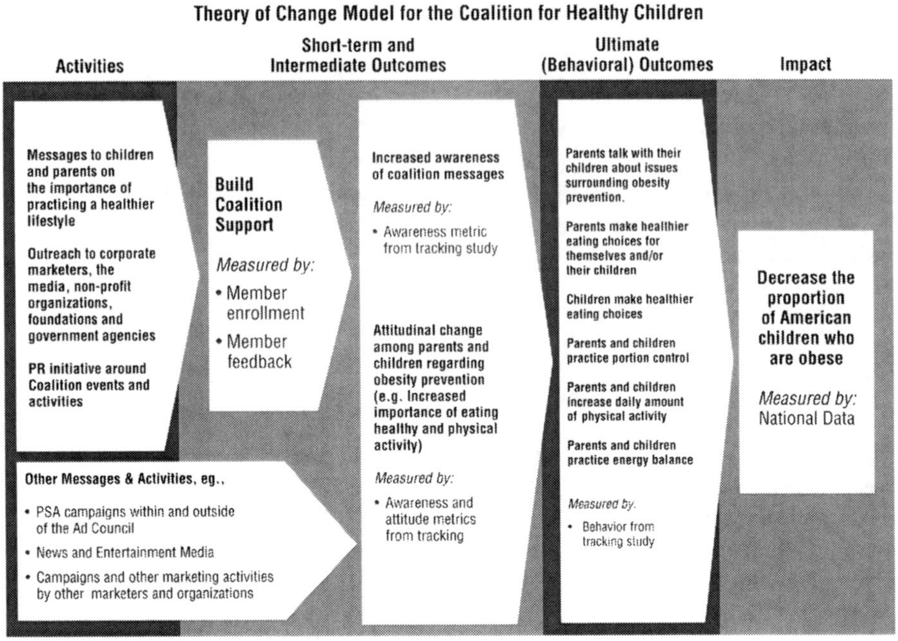

Fig. 24.2 Theory of change model for coalition activities

working in this area. They also provided much useful feedback and counsel to the Ad Council Coalition team as the messages were developed, tested, and refined. According to an externally conducted program evaluation report from Asibey Consulting, Coalition members cited the opportunities for networking and for access to the research-based messages as a key benefit for them, and they also recognize and respect the important non-partisan, non-political role the Ad Council has played in pulling these sometime competing organizations resources together.

The combined marketing efforts of all Coalition partners have reached millions of Americans in multiple retail, educational, and media environments. All of these efforts could not be captured or included here; however, below is a partial accounting of significant member-generated programs:

- *Kmart* estimates that the circulars it distributed garnered approximately 40 million impressions, in-store materials received approximately 15 million impressions, and email marketing reached 1.4 million subscribers during the promotional period in 2007.
- *Kraft Food*'s PSA on physical activity ran in heavy rotation on the Cartoon Network in second and third quarter 2007.
- The *LPGA* "Get Up and Play" PSAs received over $8.6 million in estimated donated media and public relations support, as well as more than 268 million household impressions.
- *Walt Disney*'s *Pinocchio* and *Jungle Book* PSA effort in support of the USDA Nutrition Education campaign garnered an estimated $47 million in donated media placements and over 600 million household impressions.

- The *NFL* Play 60 campaign appeared extensively in children's television programming on NBC, during nationally televised NFL games on FOX and CBS, in *Sports Illustrated* magazine, and was widely featured during Thanksgiving weekend NFL activities. Initial estimates put the media support for this effort at $54.7 million, with over 645 million household impressions.
- *PepsiCo*'s Walmart promotion was seen by shoppers in 6,793 stores that receive approximately 140 million customer visits per week. Its email blast reached 20 million households, and the circulation for its ad in "All You" magazine is 700,000. PepsiCo estimates these media garnered an estimated 158 million consumer impressions during the promotion period in 2007.
- *qubo's* characters were widely seen in PSAs during NBC's Saturday morning cartoons. They have generated approximately $3.9 million of donated airtime and public relations, as well as 143 million household impressions.
- *DreamWorks Animation*'s campaign materials featuring Shrek have received over $16.9 million in estimated donated media, including the value of public relations impressions, and over 792 million household impressions. News coverage highlights included high-profile national segments on *The Today Show*, CNN, and AP Radio, as well as more than 200 local TV news stories.

In order to measure overall program impact, a quantitative tracking study of parents and their kids was initiated prior to program launch in 2005. The research was conducted by the Futures Company (formerly Yankelovich). Successive research waves were fielded in 2007 and 2009 to measure reported changes in awareness, attitudes, and behaviors regarding physical activity, energy balance, and portion control, as well as a number of related measures. The most recent wave consisted of 1,514 interviews with children aged 6–12 and the same number of interviews with the children's parents. Oversamples of African-American and Hispanic American participants were taken to ensure accurate representation, including a subset of interviews conducted in Spanish. Interviews were conducted in demographically representative malls across the country where participants took a computer-based survey (self-administered where possible).

One caveat that needs to be stated at this point is that because the research was not conducted using an experimental design with test and control cells, it is impossible to gather whether any shifts in awareness, attitudes, or behaviors were directly caused by the CHC program messages. In addition, this communications effort took place amid other healthy lifestyle marketing and communications programs and concurrently with marketing and advertising campaigns for a host of food, fast food, and less healthy lifestyle products and services. A more detailed content analysis of these external efforts might shed some additional light on the results.

The data present a mixed bag of results. Some measures saw improvement while others declined. What appears to be driving the results is the fact that the physical activity message was the one most heavily promoted by the Ad Council and the one most utilized by member organizations during the 3-year period being measured, especially in kid-targeted media and marketing environments. The good news here is that there have been some significant positive shifts in kids' attitudes and behaviors regarding the physical activity message and overall healthy

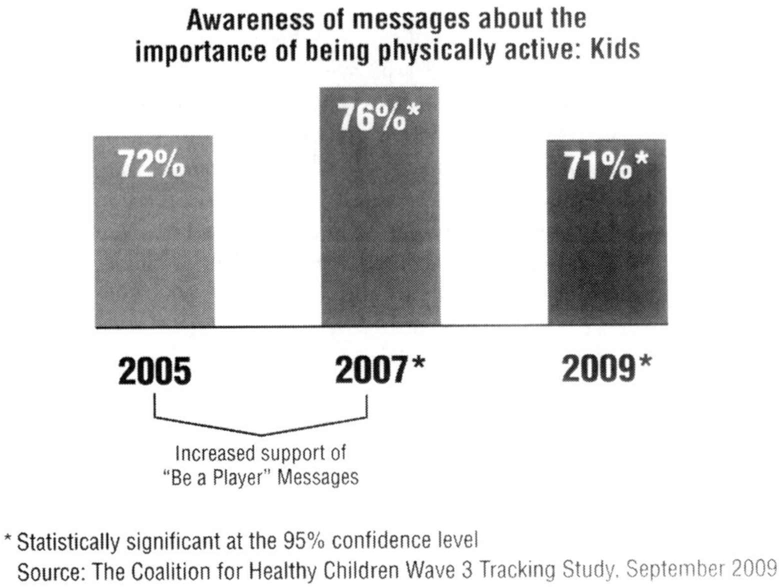

Fig. 24.3 Physical activity messages increased in 2007, but returned to baseline in 2009

lifestyles. Little to no change in other measures is not a surprise to the Ad Council coalition team given the lack of emphasis and adoption of other message areas by member organizations.

One critical finding in both successive waves of the research was disparity between Hispanic respondents and others. On virtually all measures of awareness, attitudes, and behavior, Hispanics lagged significantly behind other groups. Language and cultural differences regarding healthy eating habits appear to be one of the major reasons for these differences, as well as a lack of emphasis by marketers to address this particular population with healthy lifestyle communications at the time. What follows are a few highlighted findings and data points that exemplify the overall learnings.

Awareness of Concepts and Messages

Results from the tracking study suggest that since 2005, awareness of most Coalition message concepts has remained relatively constant among kids and parents; however, there was a significant increase in concept awareness among kids about the importance of being physically active from 2005 to 2007. It was during this time period that many Coalition members were promoting the "Be a Player" message. Consequently, when marketing support declined after 2007, awareness of these messages dropped back down to benchmark levels in 2009 (see Fig. 24.3).

Awareness of Visual Assets

	BE A PLAYER	EAT WELL PLAY HARD make it balance	THE AMOUNT COUNTS KEEP PORTIONS UNDER CONTROL
Total Kids	38%	35%	24%
White	39%	35%	24%
African-American	44%	45%	29%
Hispanic	25%	25%	21%
Total Parents	32%	31%	19%
White	32%	30%	18%
African-American	39%	37%	27%
Hispanic	27%	28%	17%

Source: The Coalition for Healthy Children Wave 3 Tracking Study, September 2009

Fig. 24.4 Awareness of coalition message visuals among key audiences

Awareness of the three visual assets was not measured in 2005 or 2007; however, in 2009 recognition among kids and parents was fairly strong (see Fig. 24.4). More than 1 out of every 3 children reported that they recognized the "Be a Player" physical activity and "Eat Well, Play Hard" energy balance messages. Significantly fewer kids said they recognized "The Amount Counts" portion control message, which is not surprising because this message has not yet been heavily promoted by Coalition members. Parents were less likely than their children to recognize all three visual assets, but still had a moderate level of awareness. And Hispanic children and their parents were significantly less likely than other parents to say they had seen the visual assets. This discrepancy among Hispanic respondents was to be expected given that most of these messages were not marketed in Spanish. Finally, African American kids had the greatest levels of awareness, with 44 % and 45 % reporting having seen the "Be a Player" and "Eat Well, Play Hard" visuals.

Attitudes and Behavior Regarding Healthy Lifestyles

Since the Coalition began, kids' attitudes toward healthy eating and exercise have improved (see Fig. 24.5). In 2009, significantly more kids report caring a lot about being healthy, eating healthy, and getting enough physical activity than they did in 2005.

Further, kids increasingly understand the amount of time they need to run around and play everyday to be healthy (see Fig. 24.6). In 2009, 68 % of children reported that they should run around and play at least an hour a day (vs. 62 % in 2007).

Activities you do most often when not in school:

Total Kids	2005		2009
Do something active outside	71%	→	78%*
Do something active inside	57%	→	64%*
Play on a sports team such as basketball, hockey, soccer	46%	→	49%

* Statistically significant at the 95% confidence level
Source: The Coalition for Healthy Children Wave 3 Tracking Study, September 2009

Fig. 24.5 Children were more active indoors and outdoors in 2009

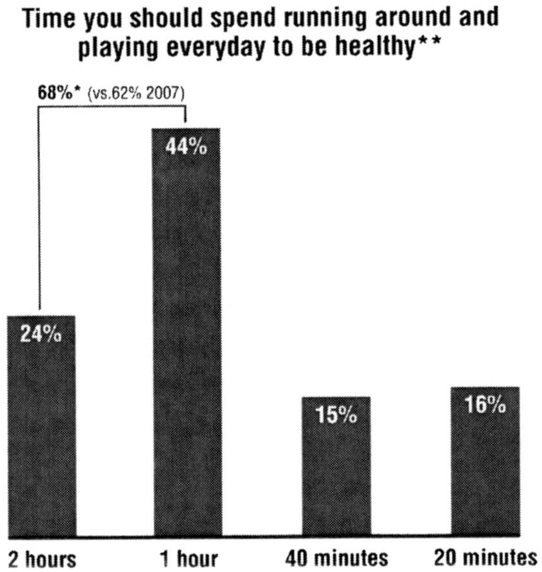

* Statistically significant at the 95% confidence level
** Strongly/somewhat agree
Note: This question was not asked in the 2005 benchmark survey.
Source: The Coalition for Healthy Children Wave 3 Tracking Study, September 2009

Fig. 24.6 Significantly more kids understood the need to be active for over 1-hour each day in 2009

Since 2005, kids better understand that physical activities like playing a game of tag, basketball, or soccer are good for their health. And more kids in 2009 report that they do something active inside and outside than when first measured in 2005 (see Fig. 24.7).

Unfortunately these positive shifts in kid's attitudes and behaviors regarding physical activity were not replicated in other areas necessary for children to attain a healthy lifestyle. Most kids understand the importance of eating healthy foods, energy balance, and portion control; however, despite this understanding there are

Kids Care A Lot About:

Total Kids	2005		2009
Being healthy	71%	→	78%*
Eating healthy	62%	→	67%*
Getting enough physical activity	55%	→	68%*

* Statistically significant at the 95% confidence level
Source: The Coalition for Healthy Children Wave 3 Tracking Study, September 2009

Fig. 24.7 Data showing kid's attitudes toward healthy habits improved over time

Kids Gap Analysis – 2009

	Very Important	Describes Me Very Well	Difference Gap
Healthy Food Choices			
Eating healthy foods	72%	55%	17%
Balance			
Eating foods that help me do my best	67%	53%	14%
Balancing how much I run and play with how much I eat	54%	41%	13%
Portion Control			
Watching how much I eat	54%	36%	18%
Physical Activity			
Being physically active on a regular basis	68%	66%	2%

Source: The Coalition for Healthy Children Wave 3 Tracking Study, September 2009

Fig. 24.8 Illustrates the gap between children's beliefs and actual behavior

significant gaps in their behavior related to these concepts (see Fig. 24.8). This suggests much room for growth, particularly in the areas of portion control and energy balance.

In regard to parents' attitudes about their kids' healthy lifestyles, the tracking research suggests that they increasingly recognize the importance of eating healthy and being physically active (see Fig. 24.9). In 2009, approximately 3 out of 4 parents reported that it is "very important" that their child has healthy eating habits and/or is physically active on a regular basis; these percentages have significantly increased since the benchmark survey in 2005.

Further, the vast majority of parents in 2009 continued to recognize the role they play in what their child eats or drinks; nearly 9 out of 10 reported that the food and beverages their child consumes reflects on them as parents (see Fig. 24.10). Also, while parents are becoming less confused about what foods are healthy for their families, many continue to feel guilty about their child's eating habits.

Overall, the data collected among parents illustrates a similar story to their children. Most parents understand the importance of their children living a healthy

Importance to parents that their kids lead healthy lifestyles

Very Important	2005	2007	2009
Is physically fit	67%	67%	71%
Has healthy eating habits	67%	71%	72%*
Is physically active on a regular basis	67%	71%	75%*
Balances what they eat or drink with how active they are	59%	60%	59%
Doesn't eat too much	46%	49%	51%
Doesn't eat too little	53%	50%	50%

* Statistically significant at the 95% confidence level
Source: The Coalition for Healthy Children Wave 3 Tracking Study, September 2009

Fig. 24.9 Importance to parents that their kids lead healthy lifestyles

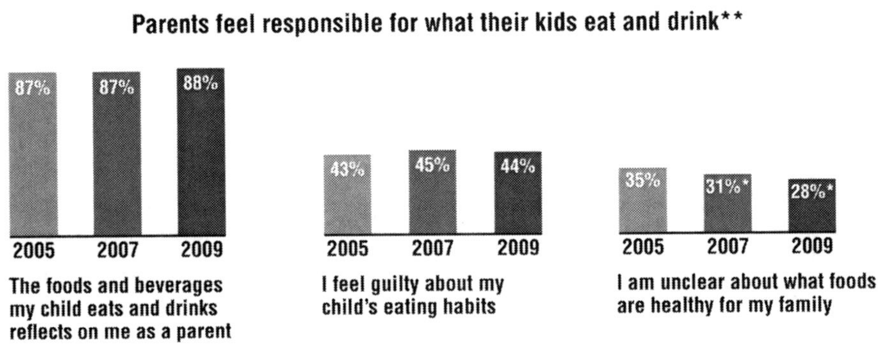

* Statistically significant at the 95%confidence level
** Strongly/somewhat agree
Source: The Coalition for Healthy Children Wave 3 Tracking Study, September 2009

Fig. 24.10 Parents feel responsible for what their kids eat and drink

lifestyle—through healthy food choices, energy balance, physical activity, and portion control—yet there remains a large gap between these attitudes and their child's behavior (see Fig. 24.11).

Moving Forward

The Ad Council is proud of the work it has accomplished with the support of Coalition member organizations to begin to change attitudes and behaviors that will ultimately help stem the growing tide of childhood obesity in this country. However, like most major health initiatives, more communications efforts need to be developed and sustained if we are to see continued success. The tracking research, member feedback, and the external evaluation of the program effort have

Parents Gap Analysis – 2009

	Very Important	Describes Child Completely	Difference Gap
Healthy Food Choices			
Has healthy eating habits	72%	38%	34%
Portion Control			
Doesn't eat too much	51%	41%	10%
Encouraging Physical Activity			
Is physically fit	71%	52%	19%
Is physically active on a regular basis	75%	59%	16%
Balance			
Balances what they eat or drink with how active they are	59%	39%	20%

Source: The Coalition for Healthy Children Wave 3 Tracking Study, September 2009

Fig. 24.11 Illustrates the gap between parent's attitudes and children's behaviors in 2009

identified opportunities to improve the group's overall efforts and improve our chances of achieving further success in the years ahead.

Many members utilized Coalition messages to develop mass-audience campaigns that reached millions of Americans and many are continuing their own healthy lifestyle programs. However, some member efforts were short-lived and not incorporated into ongoing marketing programs. The dips seen in tracking data from 2007 to 2009 on key awareness metrics attest to the fact that in order to be successful in changing attitudes and behaviors over time, members need to bang a steady drumbeat on obesity prevention messages. The public still needs constant reminders to take action and to gain new consciousness around energy balance and portion control messages.

In addition, the continued gap between general audience and Latino respondents in the tracking study identified a critical need to better engage this audience in the initiative. In the fall of 2008, the Ad Council hosted an expert panel to understand healthy lifestyle issues-facing Hispanics and determine the most appropriate communications strategies for reaching this audience. The panel included representatives from the American Diabetes Association, American Dietetic Association, Alliance for Healthier Generation, President's Council on Fitness and Sports, Office of the U.S. Surgeon General, HHS Office of Disease Prevention & Health Promotion, and National Heart, Lung, and Blood Institute. Based on panel input, volunteer ad agency Casanova Pendrill developed a series of messages that were tested through focus groups and other qualitative methods with Hispanic mothers and children. Messages were refined throughout the research process and measures were taken to ensure cultural relevance for the Spanish-speaking population. In addition, Casanova Pendrill developed a series of visual assets to accompany and support the overall messages based on feedback from consumers (see Fig. 24.12). The new Spanish language materials were then quantitatively tested and shared with Coalition members to promote in their own communications channels, ensuring that relevant communications are made available to the underserved Hispanic community.

Fig. 24.12 Hispanic-targeted messages & visuals

The Coalition model has proven that united efforts behind a common program can make a significant difference when sustained over time. With research-based messages as a cornerstone of the Coalition for Healthy Children and sophisticated methods for tracking impact, we have begun to see some shifts in individual beliefs and behaviors among our target audiences. Efforts on the legislative level, school-based initiatives, community interventions, and the combined programs of many corporations, advocacy organizations, and social service agencies are also needed to make headway in reducing child obesity rates. With continued commitment from all the Coalition member organizations, as well as these other environmental activities, there is hope that we are making progress in the fight against this epidemic and are getting one step closer to achieving healthier outcomes for all of our children.

Acknowledgments The Ad Council would like to thank the following people for their contributions to the Coalition for Healthy Children initiative over the years:

- Arthur Greenwald for the inspiration to develop the program
- David Morse, Kathryn Thomas, and Dwayne Proctor at the Robert Wood Johnson Foundation for their support and funding of the program
- Joan Chiaramonte for conducting the initial literature review
- Brady Darvin and the team at Strottman International for their research and insights

- Nat Puccio and the Strategic Planning department at McCann Erickson for their creative framing of the program
- John Page and Jane Thurston at The Futures Group for developing and reporting on the tracking study
- Jeff Sheets and his talented students at the Brigham Young University AdLab and David Rockwood and the Creative team at GSD&M Idea City for designing the visual assets
- Elizabeth Johnson, Ernesto Lopez, JJ Valera, and the Creative team at Casanova Pendrill for their research and development of Spanish language materials
- Benjamin Bobkoff and George Perlov for writing and designing the Ad Council's "Report to the Nation," which served as the basis for this chapter
- Heidi Arthur, Gina Ermilio, Sheri Klein, Mary Lyons, and Anthony Signorelli at the Ad Council for all their hard work in launching and managing the Coalition for Healthy Children

References

Lemonick, M. (2004). *Why we grew so big*. Special Issue. *TIME*, June 7

McGinnis, J. M., Gootman, J., & Kraak, V. I. (2006). *Food marketing to children and youth: threat or opportunity?* Washington, DC: The National Academies Press, Institute of Medicine.

U.S. Department of Health and Human Services & U.S. Department of Agriculture. (2005). *Dietary guidelines for Americans 2005* (HHS Publication number: HHS-ODPHP-2005-01-DGA-A). Washington, DC: Author. Retrieved from http://www.health.gov/dietaryguidelines/dga2005/document/pdf/DGA2005.pdf.

Index

J.D. Williams et al. (eds.), *Advances in Communication Research to Reduce Childhood Obesity*, DOI 10.1007/978-1-4614-5511-0,

CPSIA information can be obtained at www.ICGtesting.com
Printed in the USA
LVOW13*1921181213
365921LV00014B/730/P